THE POEMS OF
JOHN DRYDEN

THE POEMS OF
JOHN DRYDEN

EDITED BY

JAMES KINSLEY

VOLUME II

OXFORD
AT THE CLARENDON PRESS
1958

Oxford University Press, Amen House, London E.C.4

GLASGOW NEW YORK TORONTO MELBOURNE WELLINGTON
BOMBAY CALCUTTA MADRAS KARACHI KUALA LUMPUR
CAPE TOWN IBADAN NAIROBI ACCRA

PRINTED IN GREAT BRITAIN

CONTENTS

Contents

THE HIND
AND THE PANTHER

A POEM, In Three Parts

—Antiquam exquirite matrem. }
Et vera, incessu, patuit Dea.— } VIRG.

TO THE READER

*T*HE *Nation is in too high a Ferment, for me to expect either fair War, or
even so much as fair Quarter from a Reader of the opposite Party. All Men
are engag'd either on this side or that: and tho' Conscience is the common Word,
which is given by both, yet if a Writer fall among Enemies, and cannot give the
Marks of* Their *Conscience, he is knock'd down before the Reasons of his own are* 5
heard. A Preface, *therefore, which is but a bespeaking of Favour, is altogether
useless. What I desire the* Reader *should know concerning me, he will find in the
Body of the Poem; if he have but the patience to peruse it. Only this Advertise-
ment let him take before hand, which relates to the Merits of the Cause. No
general Characters of Parties, (call 'em either Sects or Churches) can be so fully* 10
*and exactly drawn, as to Comprehend all the several Members of 'em; at least all
such as are receiv'd under that Denomination. For example; there are some of the
Church by Law Establish'd, who envy not Liberty of Conscience to Dissenters;
as being well satisfied that, according to their own Principles, they ought not to
persecute them. Yet these, by reason of their fewness, I could not distinguish from* 15
*the Numbers of the rest with whom they are Embodied in one common Name: On
the other side there are many of our Sects, and more indeed then I could reasonably
have hop'd, who have withdrawn themselves from the Communion of the* Panther;
*and embrac'd this Gracious Indulgence of His Majesty in point of Toleration. But
neither to the one nor the other of these is this Satyr any way intended: 'tis* 20
*aim'd only at the refractory and disobedient on either side. For those who are come
over to the Royal Party are consequently suppos'd to be out of Gunshot. Our
Physicians have observ'd, that in Process of Time, some Diseases have abated of
their Virulence, and have in a manner worn out their Malignity, so as to be no
longer Mortal: and why may not I suppose the same concerning some of those who* 25
have formerly been Enemies to Kingly Government, As well as Catholick Religion?

The Hind and the Panther. Text from the first edition, 1687 (*A*), collated with the second (*B*)
and third (*C*) editions, 1687, and the Edinburgh (*E*) and Dublin (*D*) editions, 1687
  To the Reader. 7 find] know E

I hope they have now another Notion of both, as having found, by Comfort-able Experience, that the Doctrine of Persecution is far from being an Article of our Faith.

'Tis not for any Private Man to Censure the Proceedings of a Foreign Prince: 30 *but, without suspicion of Flattery, I may praise our own, who has taken contrary Measures, and those more suitable to the Spirit of Christianity. Some of the Dis-senters in their Addresses to His Majesty have said* That he has restor'd God to his Empire over Conscience: *I Confess I dare not stretch the Figure to so great a boldness: but I may safely say, that Conscience is the Royalty and Pre-* 35 *rogative of every Private man. He is absolute in his own Breast, and accountable to no Earthly Power, for that which passes only betwixt God and Him. Those who are driven into the Fold are, generally speaking, rather made Hypocrites then Converts.*

This Indulgence being granted to all the Sects, it ought in reason to be expected, 40 *that they should both receive it, and receive it thankfully. For at this time of day to refuse the Benefit, and adhere to those whom they have esteem'd their Persecu-tors, what is it else, but publickly to own that they suffer'd not before for Con-science sake; but only out of Pride and Obstinacy to separate from a Church for those Impositions, which they now judge may be lawfully obey'd? After they* 45 *have so long contended for their Classical Ordination, (not to speak of Rites and Ceremonies) will they at length submit to an Episcopal? If they can go so far out of Complaisance to their old Enemies, methinks a little reason should perswade 'em to take another step, and see whether that wou'd lead 'em.*

Of the receiving this Toleration thankfully, I shall say no more, than that 50 *they ought, and I doubt not they will consider from what hands they receiv'd it. 'Tis not from a Cyrus, a Heathen Prince, and a Foreigner, but from a Christian King, their Native Sovereign: who expects a Return in Specie from them; that the Kindness which He has Graciously shown them, may be retaliated on those of his own perswasion.* 55

As for the Poem in general, I will only thus far satisfie the Reader: That it was neither impos'd on me, nor so much as the Subject given me by any man. It was written during the last Winter and the beginning of this Spring; though with long interruptions of ill health, and other hindrances. About a Fortnight before I had finish'd it, His Majesties Declaration for Liberty of Conscience came 60 *abroad: which, if I had so soon expected, I might have spar'd my self the labour of writing many things which are contain'd in the third part of it. But I was always in some hope, that the Church of England might have been perswaded to have taken off the Penal Lawes and the Test, which was one Design of the Poem when I propos'd to my self the writing of it.* 65

'*Tis evident that some part of it was only occasional, and not first intended. I mean that defence of my self, to which every honest man is bound, when he is injuriously attacqu'd in Print: and I refer my self to the judgment of those who have read the* Answer to the Defence of the late Kings Papers, *and that of the* Dutchess, (*in which last I was concerned*) *how charitably I have been* 70 *represented there. I am now inform'd both of the Author and Supervisers of his Pamphlet: and will reply when I think he can affront me: for I am of* Socrates's *Opinion that all Creatures cannot. In the mean time let him consider, whether he deserv'd not a more severe reprehension then I gave him formerly; for using so little respect to the Memory of those whom he pretended to answer: and, at his* 75 *leisure look out for some Original Treatise of Humility, written by any Protestant in English, (I believe I may say in any other Tongue:) for the magnified Piece of* Duncomb *on that Subject, which either he must mean or none, and with which another of his Fellows has upbraided me, was Translated from the Spanish of* Rodriguez: *tho' with the Omission of the* 17th, *the* 24th, *the* 25th, *and the* 80 *last Chapter, which will be found in comparing of the Books.*

He would have insinuated to the World that Her late Highness died not a Roman Catholick: He declares himself to be now satisfied to the contrary; in which he has giv'n up the Cause: for matter of Fact was the Principal Debate betwixt us. In the mean time he would dispute the Motives of her 85 *Change: how prepostrously let all men judge, when he seem'd to deny the Subject of the Controversy, the Change it self. And because I would not take up this ridiculous Challenge, he tells the World I cannot argue: but he may as well infer that a Catholick cannot fast, because he will not take up the Cudgels against Mrs.* James, *to confute the Protestant Religion.* 90

I have but one word more to say concerning the Poem as such, and abstracting from the Matters either Religious or Civil which are handled in it. The first part, *consisting most in general Characters and Narration, I have endeavour'd to raise, and give it the Majestick Turn of Heroick Poesie. The* second, *being Matter of Dispute, and chiefly concerning Church Authority, I was oblig'd to* 95 *make as plain and perspicuous as possibly I cou'd: yet not wholly neglecting the Numbers, though I had not frequent occasions for the Magnificence of Verse. The* third, *which has more of the Nature of Domestick Conversation, is, or ought to be more free and familiar than the two former.*

There are in it two Episodes, *or Fables, which are interwoven with the main* 100 *Design; so that they are properly parts of it, though they are also distinct Stories of themselves. In both of these I have made use of the Common Places of* Satyr, *whether true or false, which are urg'd by the Members of the one Church against the other. At which I hope no* Reader *of either Party will be scandaliz'd;*

94 *raise, and*] om. E

because they are not of my Invention: but as old, to my knowledge, as the Times 105
of Boccace *and* Chawcer *on the one side, and as those of the* Reformation *on the
other.*

THE HIND AND THE PANTHER

THE FIRST PART

A MILK white *Hind*, immortal and unchang'd,
   Fed on the lawns, and in the forest rang'd;
Without unspotted, innocent within,
She fear'd no danger, for she knew no sin.
Yet had she oft been chas'd with horns and hounds,   5
And Scythian shafts; and many winged wounds
Aim'd at Her heart; was often forc'd to fly,
And doom'd to death, though fated not to dy.
   Not so her young, for their unequal line
Was Heroe's make, half humane, half divine.   10
Their earthly mold obnoxious was to fate,
Th' immortal part assum'd immortal state.
Of these a slaughtered army lay in bloud,
Extended o'er the *Caledonian* wood,
Their native walk; whose vocal bloud arose,   15
And cry'd for pardon on their perjur'd foes;
Their fate was fruitfull, and the sanguin seed
Endu'd with souls, encreas'd the sacred breed.
So Captive *Israel* multiply'd in chains
A numerous Exile, and enjoy'd her pains.   20
With grief and gladness mixt, their mother view'd
Her martyr'd offspring, and their race renew'd;
Their corps to perish, but their kind to last,
So much the deathless plant the dying fruit surpass'd.
   Panting and pensive now she rang'd alone,   25
And wander'd in the kingdoms, once Her own.
The common Hunt, though from their rage restrain'd
By sov'reign pow'r, her company disdain'd:
Grin'd as They pass'd, and with a glaring eye

Gave gloomy signs of secret enmity.   30
'Tis true, she bounded by, and trip'd so light
They had not time to take a steady sight.
For truth has such a face and such a meen
As to be lov'd needs onely to be seen.

   The bloudy *Bear* an *Independent* beast,   35
Unlick'd to form, in groans her hate express'd.
Among the timorous kind the *Quaking Hare*
Profess'd neutrality, but would not swear.
Next her the *Buffoon Ape*, as Atheists use,
Mimick'd all Sects, and had his own to chuse: 40
Still when the Lyon look'd, his knees he bent,
And pay'd at Church a Courtier's Complement.

   The bristl'd *Baptist Boar*, impure as He,
(But whitn'd with the foam of sanctity)
With fat pollutions fill'd the sacred place,   45
And mountains levell'd in his furious race,
So first rebellion founded was in grace.
But since the mighty ravage which he made
In *German* Forests, had his guilt betrayd,
With broken tusks, and with a borrow'd name   50
He shun'd the vengeance, and conceal'd the shame;
So lurk'd in Sects unseen. With greater guile
False *Reynard* fed on consecrated spoil:
The graceless beast by *Athanasius* first
Was chas'd from *Nice* . . . . nurs'd   55
His impious race the . . . .
And natures King through natu . . . . cks view'd.
Revers'd they view'd him lessen'd to their eye,
Nor in an Infant could a God descry:
New swarming Sects to this obliquely tend,   60
Hence they began, and here they all will end.

   What weight of antient witness can prevail
If private reason hold the publick scale?
But, gratious God, how well dost thou provide
For erring judgments an unerring Guide?   65
Thy throne is darkness in th' abyss of light,
A blaze of glory that forbids the sight;
O teach me to believe Thee thus conceal'd,
And search no farther than thy self reveal'd;

But her alone for my Directour take   70
Whom thou hast promis'd never to forsake!
My thoughtless youth was wing'd with vain desires,
My manhood, long misled by wandring fires,
Follow'd false lights; and when their glimps was gone,
My pride struck out new sparkles of her own.   75
Such was I, such by nature still I am,
Be thine the glory, and be mine the shame.
Good life be now my task: my doubts are done,
(What more could fright my faith, than Three in One?)
Can I believe eternal God could lye   )   80
Disguis'd in mortal mold and infancy?   )
That the great maker of the world could dye?   )
And after that, trust my imperfect sense
Which calls in question his omnipotence?
Can I my reason to my faith compell,   85
And shall my sight, and touch, and taste rebell?
Superiour faculties are set aside,
Shall their subservient organs be my guide?
Then let the moon usurp the rule of day,
And winking tapers shew the sun his way;   90
For what my senses can themselves perceive
I need no revelation to believe.
Can they who say the Host should be descry'd
By sense, define a body glorify'd?
Impassible, and penetrating parts?   95
Let them declare by what mysterious arts
He shot that body through th' opposing might   )
Of bolts and barrs impervious to the light,   )
And stood before his train confess'd in open sight.   )
    For since thus wondrously he pass'd, 'tis plain   100
One single place two bodies did contain,
And sure the same omnipotence as well
Can make one body in more places dwell.
Let reason then at Her own quarry fly,
But how can finite grasp infinity?   105
    'Tis urg'd again that faith did first commence
By miracles, which are appeals to sense,
And thence concluded that our sense must be

77 shame] sham D

The motive still of credibility.
For latter ages must on former wait,   110
And what began belief, must propagate.
 But winnow well this thought, and you shall find,
'Tis light as chaff that flies before the wind.
Were all those wonders wrought by pow'r divine
As means or ends of some more deep design?   115
Most sure as means, whose end was this alone,
To prove the god-head of th' eternal Son.
God thus asserted: man is to believe
Beyond what sense and reason can conceive.
And for mysterious things of faith rely   120
On the Proponent, heav'ns authority.
If then our faith we for our guide admit,
Vain is the farther search of humane wit,
As when the building gains a surer stay,
We take th' unusefull scaffolding away: 125
Reason by sense no more can understand,
The game is play'd into another hand.
Why chuse we then like *Bilanders* to creep
Along the coast, and land in view to keep,
When safely we may launch into the deep?   130
In the same vessel which our Saviour bore
Himself the Pilot, let us leave the shoar,
And with a better guide a better world explore.
Could He his god-head veil with flesh and bloud
And not veil these again to be our food?   135
His grace in both is equal in extent,
The first affords us life, the second nourishment.
And if he can, why all this frantick pain
To construe what his clearest words contain,
And make a riddle what He made so plain?   140
To take up half on trust, and half to try,
Name it not faith, but bungling biggottry.
Both knave and fool the Merchant we may call
To pay great summs, and to compound the small.
For who wou'd break with heav'n, and wou'd not break for all?   145
Rest then, my soul, from endless anguish freed;
Nor sciences thy guide, nor sense thy creed.
Faith is the best ensurer of thy bliss;

The Bank above must fail before the venture miss.
But heav'n and heav'n-born faith are far from Thee   150
Thou first Apostate to Divinity.
Unkennel'd range in thy *Polonian* Plains;
A fiercer foe th' insatiate *Wolfe* remains.
   Too boastfull *Britain* please thy self no more,
That beasts of prey are banish'd from thy shoar: 155
The *Bear*, the *Boar*, and every salvage name,
Wild in effect, though in appearance tame,
Lay waste thy woods, destroy thy blissfull bow'r,
And muzl'd though they seem, the mutes devour.
More haughty than the rest the *wolfish* race,   160
Appear with belly Gaunt, and famish'd face:
Never was so deform'd a beast of Grace.
His ragged tail betwixt his leggs he wears
Close clap'd for shame, but his rough crest he rears,
And pricks up his predestinating ears.   165
His wild disorder'd walk, his hagger'd eyes,
Did all the bestial citizens surprize.
Though fear'd and hated, yet he ruled awhile
As Captain or Companion of the spoil.
Full many a year his hatefull head had been   170
For tribute paid, nor since in *Cambria* seen:
The last of all the litter scap'd by chance,
And from *Geneva* first infested *France*.
Some authours thus his pedigree will trace,
But others write him of an upstart race: 175
Because of *Wickliff*'s brood no mark he brings
But his innate antipathy to kings.
These last deduce him from th' *Helvetian* kind
Who near the *Leman lake* his Consort lin'd.
That fi'ry *Zuynglius* first th' affection bred,   180
And meagre *Calvin* blest the nuptial bed.
In *Israel* some believe him whelp'd long since
When the proud *Sanhedrim* oppress'd the Prince.
Or, since he will be *Jew*, derive him high'r
When *Corah* with his brethren did conspire,   185
From *Moyses* hand the Sov'reign sway to wrest,
And *Aaron* of his Ephod to devest:

Vid. Pref.
to Heyl.
Hist. of
Presb.

       179 *Leman*] *Lemnian* D

Till opening Earth made way for all to pass,
And cou'd not bear the burd'n of a *class*.
The *Fox* and he came shuffl'd in the dark,   190
If ever they were stow'd in *Noah*'s ark:
Perhaps not made; for all their barking train
The Dog (a common species) will contain.
And some wild currs, who from their masters ran
Abhorring the supremacy of man,   195
In woods and caves the rebel-race began.
 O happy pair, how well have you increas'd,
What ills in Church and State have you redress'd!
With teeth untry'd, and rudiments of claws
Your first essay was on your native laws: 200
Those having torn with ease, and trampl'd down
Your Fangs you fastn'd on the miter'd crown,
And freed from God and monarchy your town.
What though your native kennel still be small
Bounded betwixt a puddle and a wall,   205
Yet your victorious colonies are sent
Where the north ocean girds the continent.
Quickn'd with fire below your monsters breed,
In Fenny *Holland* and in fruitfull *Tweed*.
And like the first the last affects to be   210
Drawn to the dreggs of a Democracy.
As where in fields the fairy rounds are seen,
A rank sow'r herbage rises on the green,
So, springing where these mid-night Elves advance,
Rebellion prints the foot-steps of the Dance.   215
Such are their doctrines, such contempt they show
To heav'n above, and to their Prince below,
As none but Traytours and Blasphemers know.
God, like the Tyrant of the skyes is plac'd,
And kings like slaves beneath the crowd debas'd.   220
So fulsome is their food, that flocks refuse
To bite, and onely dogs for physick use.
As where the lightning runs along the ground,
No husbandry can heal the blasting wound,
Nor bladed grass, nor bearded corn succeeds,   225
But scales of scurf, and putrefaction breeds:

224 wound, *B C*: wound *A*

Such warrs, such waste, such fiery tracks of dearth
Their zeal has left, and such a teemless earth.
But as the Poisons of the deadliest kind
Are to their own unhappy coasts confin'd,   230
As onely *Indian* shades of sight deprive,
And magick plants will but in *Colchos* thrive;
So Presbyt'ry and pestilential zeal
Can onely flourish in a common-weal.

    From *Celtique* woods is chas'd the *wolfish* crew;   235
But ah! some pity e'en to brutes is due:
Their native walks, methinks, they might enjoy
Curb'd of their native malice to destroy.
Of all the tyrannies on humane kind
The worst is that which persecutes the mind.   240
Let us but weigh at what offence we strike,
'Tis but because we cannot think alike.
In punishing of this, we overthrow
The laws of nations and of nature too.
Beasts are the subjects of tyrannick sway,   245
Where still the stronger on the weaker prey.
Man onely of a softer mold is made;
Not for his fellows ruine, but their aid.
Created kind, beneficent and free,
The noble image of the Deity.   250
    One portion of informing fire was giv'n
To Brutes, th' inferiour family of heav'n:
The Smith divine, as with a careless beat,
Struck out the mute creation at a heat:
But, when arriv'd at last to humane race,   255
The god-head took a deep consid'ring space:
And, to distinguish man from all the rest,
Unlock'd the sacred treasures of his breast:
And mercy mix'd with reason did impart;
One to his head, the other to his heart: 260
Reason to rule, but mercy to forgive:
The first is law, the last prerogative.
And like his mind his outward form appear'd;
When issuing naked, to the wondring herd,
He charm'd their eyes, and for they lov'd, they fear'd.   265

    232 thrive; *B C*: thrive, *A*   264 herd, *B C*: herd *A*

Not arm'd with horns of arbitrary might,
Or claws to seize their furry spoils in fight,
Or with increase of feet t' o'ertake 'em in their flight.
Of easie shape, and pliant ev'ry way;
Confessing still the softness of his clay,   270
And kind as kings upon their coronation day:
With open hands, and with extended space
Of arms, to satisfie a large embrace.
Thus kneaded up with milk, the new made man
His kingdom o'er his kindred world began: 275
Till knowledge misapply'd, misunderstood,
And pride of Empire sour'd his balmy bloud.
Then, first rebelling, his own stamp he coins;
The murth'rer *Cain* was latent in his loins,
And bloud began its first and loudest cry   280
For diff'ring worship of the Deity.
Thus persecution rose, and farther space
Produc'd the mighty hunter of his race.
Not so the blessed *Pan* his flock encreas'd,
Content to fold 'em from the famish'd beast: 285
Mild were his laws; the Sheep and harmless Hind
Were never of the persecuting kind.
Such pity now the pious Pastor shows,
Such mercy from the *British* Lyon flows,
That both provide protection for their foes.   290
   Oh happy Regions, *Italy* and *Spain*,
Which never did those monsters entertain!
The *Wolfe*, the *Bear*, the *Boar*, can there advance
No native claim of just inheritance.
And self-preserving laws, severe in show,   295
May guard their fences from th' invading foe.
Where birth has plac'd 'em let 'em safely share
The common benefit of vital air.
Themselves unharmfull, let them live unharm'd;
Their jaws disabl'd, and their claws disarm'd: 300
Here, onely in nocturnal howlings bold,
They dare not seize the Hind nor leap the fold.
More pow'rfull, and as vigilant as they,
The *Lyon* awfully forbids the prey.

Their rage repress'd, though pinch'd with famine sore,   ) 305
They stand aloof, and tremble at his roar;   }
Much is their hunger, but their fear is more.   )

   These are the chief; to number o'er the rest,
And stand, like *Adam*, naming ev'ry beast,
Were weary work; nor will the Muse describe   310
A slimy-born and sun-begotten Tribe:
Who, far from steeples and their sacred sound,
In fields their sullen conventicles found:
These gross, half-animated lumps I leave;
Nor can I think what thoughts they can conceive.   315
But if they think at all, 'tis sure no high'r
Than matter, put in motion, may aspire.
Souls that can scarce ferment their mass of clay;   )
So drossy, so divisible are They,   }
As wou'd but serve pure bodies for allay:) 320
Such souls as *Shards* produce, such beetle things
As onely buz to heav'n with ev'ning wings;
Strike in the dark, offending but by chance,
Such are the blind-fold blows of ignorance.
They know not beings, and but hate a name,   325
To them the *Hind* and *Panther* are the same.

   The *Panther* sure the noblest, next the *Hind*,
And fairest creature of the spotted kind;
Oh, could her in-born stains be wash'd away,
She were too good to be a beast of Prey!   330
How can I praise, or blame, and not offend,
Or how divide the frailty from the friend!
Her faults and vertues lye so mix'd, that she
Nor wholly stands condemn'd, nor wholly free.
Then, like her injur'd *Lyon*, let me speak,   335
He can not bend her, and he would not break.
Unkind already, and estrang'd in part,
The *Wolfe* begins to share her wandring heart.
Though unpolluted yet with actual ill,
She half commits, who sins but in Her will.   340
If, as our dreaming *Platonists* report,
There could be spirits of a middle sort,
Too black for heav'n, and yet too white for hell,

308 *Editor's paragraph*

Who just dropt half way down, nor lower fell;
So pois'd, so gently she descends from high,   345
It seems a soft dismission from the sky.
Her house not ancient, whatsoe'er pretence
Her clergy Heraulds make in her defence.
A second century not half-way run
Since the new honours of her bloud begun.   350
A *Lyon* old, obscene, and furious made
By lust, compress'd her mother in a shade.
Then, by a left-hand marr'age weds the Dame,
Cov'ring adult'ry with a specious name:
So schism begot; and sacrilege and she,   355
A well-match'd pair, got graceless heresie.
God's and kings rebels have the same good cause,
To trample down divine and humane laws:
Both would be call'd Reformers, and their hate,
Alike destructive both to church and state: 360
The fruit proclaims the plant; a lawless Prince
By luxury reform'd incontinence,
By ruins, charity; by riots, abstinence.
Confessions, fasts and penance set aside;
Oh with what ease we follow such a guide!   365
Where souls are starv'd, and senses gratify'd.
Where marr'age pleasures, midnight pray'r supply,
And mattin bells (a melancholy cry)
Are tun'd to merrier notes, *encrease* and *multiply.*
Religion shows a Rosie colour'd face;   370
Not hatter'd out with drudging works of grace;
A down-hill Reformation rolls apace.
What flesh and bloud wou'd croud the narrow gate,
Or, till they waste their pamper'd paunches, wait?
All wou'd be happy at the cheapest rate.   375
　　Though our lean faith these rigid laws has giv'n,
The full fed *Musulman* goes fat to heav'n;
For his *Arabian* Prophet with delights
Of sense, allur'd his eastern Proselytes.
The jolly *Luther*, reading him, began   380
T' interpret Scriptures by his *Alcoran;*
To grub the thorns beneath our tender feet,

344 down] done *B C*   371 grace; *B C:* grace, *A*

And make the paths of *Paradise* more sweet:
Bethought him of a wife e'er half way gone,
(For 'twas uneasy travailing alone;)   385
And in this masquerade of mirth and love,
Mistook the bliss of heav'n for *Bacchanals* above.
Sure he presum'd of praise, who came to stock
Th' etherial pastures with so fair a flock,
Burnish'd, and bat'ning on their food, to show   390
The diligence of carefull herds below.
    Our *Panther* though like these she chang'd her head,
Yet, as the mistress of a monarch's bed,
Her front erect with majesty she bore,
The Crozier weilded, and the Miter wore.   395
Her upper part of decent discipline
Shew'd affectation of an ancient line:
And fathers, councils, church and churches head,
Were on her reverend *Phylacteries* read.
But what disgrac'd and disavow'd the rest,   400
Was *Calvin's* brand, that stigmatiz'd the beast.
Thus, like a creature of a double kind,
In her own labyrinth she lives confin'd.
To foreign lands no sound of Her is come,
Humbly content to be despis'd at home.   405
Such is her faith, where good cannot be had,
At least she leaves the refuse of the bad.
Nice in her choice of ill, though not of best,
And least deform'd, because reform'd the least.
In doubtfull points betwixt her diff'ring friends,   410
Where one for substance, one for sign contends,
Their contradicting terms she strives to join,
Sign shall be substance, substance shall be sign.
A real presence all her sons allow,
And yet 'tis flat Idolatry to bow,   415
Because the god-head's there they know not how.
Her Novices are taught that bread and wine
Are but the visible and outward sign
Receiv'd by those who in communion join.
But th' inward grace, or the thing signify'd,   420
His bloud and body, who to save us dy'd;

The faithfull this thing signify'd receive.
What is't those faithfull then partake or leave?
For what is signify'd and understood,
Is, by her own confession, flesh and blood.   425
Then, by the same acknowledgement, we know
They take the sign, and take the substance too.
The lit'ral sense is hard to flesh and blood,
But nonsense never can be understood.

  Her wild belief on ev'ry wave is tost,   430
But sure no church can better morals boast.
True to her king her principles are found;
Oh that her practice were but half so sound!
Stedfast in various turns of state she stood,
And seal'd her vow'd affection with her bloud;   435
Nor will I meanly tax her constancy,
That int'rest or obligement made the tye,
(Bound to the fate of murdr'd Monarchy:)
(Before the sounding Ax so falls the Vine,
Whose tender branches round the Poplar twine.)   440
She chose her ruin, and resign'd her life,
In death undaunted as an *Indian* wife:
A rare example: but some souls we see
Grow hard, and stiffen with adversity:
Yet these by fortunes favours are undone,   445
Resolv'd into a baser form they run,
And bore the wind, but cannot bear the sun.
Let this be natures frailty or her fate,
Or *Isgrim's counsel, her new chosen mate;   * *The Wolfe.*
Still she's the fairest of the fallen crew,   450
No mother more indulgent but the true.

  Fierce to her foes, yet fears her force to try,
Because she wants innate auctority;
For how can she constrain them to obey
Who has herself cast off the lawfull sway?   455
Rebellion equals all, and those who toil
In common theft, will share the common spoil.
Let her produce the title and the right
Against her old superiours first to fight;
If she reform by Text, ev'n that's as plain   460
For her own Rebels to reform again.

As long as words a diff'rent sense will bear,
And each may be his own Interpreter,
Our ai'ry faith will no foundation find:
The word's a weathercock for ev'ry wind: 465
The *Bear*, the *Fox*, the *Wolfe*, by turns prevail,
The most in pow'r supplies the present gale.
The wretched *Panther* crys aloud for aid
To church and councils, whom she first betray'd;
No help from Fathers or traditions train,   470
Those ancient guides she taught us to disdain.
And by that scripture which she once abus'd
To Reformation, stands herself accus'd.
What bills for breach of laws can she prefer,
Expounding which she owns herself may err?   475
And, after all her winding ways are try'd,
If doubts arise she slips herself aside,
And leaves the private conscience for the guide.
If then that conscience set th' offender free,
It barrs her claim to church auctority.   480
How can she censure, or what crime pretend,
But Scripture may be constru'd to defend?
Ev'n those whom for rebellion she transmits
To civil pow'r, her doctrine first acquits;
Because no disobedience can ensue,   485
Where no submission to a Judge is due.
Each judging for himself, by her consent,
Whom thus absolv'd she sends to punishment.
Suppose the Magistrate revenge her cause,
'Tis onely for transgressing humane laws.   490
How answ'ring to its end a church is made,
Whose pow'r is but to counsell and persuade?
O solid rock, on which secure she stands!
Eternal house, not built with mortal hands!
Oh sure defence against th' infernal gate,   495
A patent during pleasure of the state!
    Thus is the *Panther* neither lov'd nor fear'd,
A mere mock Queen of a divided Herd;
Whom soon by lawfull pow'r she might controll,
Her self a part submitted to the whole.   500
Then, as the Moon who first receives the light

By which she makes our nether regions bright,
So might she shine, reflecting from afar
The rays she borrow'd from a better star:
Big with the beams which from her mother flow   505
And reigning o'er the rising tides below:
Now, mixing with a salvage croud, she goes
And meanly flatters her invet'rate foes.
Rul'd while she rules, and losing ev'ry hour
Her wretched remnants of precarious pow'r.   510
    One evening while the cooler shade she sought,
Revolving many a melancholy thought,
Alone she walk'd, and look'd around in vain,
With rufull visage for her vanish'd train:
None of her sylvan subjects made their court;   515
Levées and couchées pass'd without resort.
So hardly can Usurpers manage well
Those, whom they first instructed to rebell:
More liberty begets desire of more,
The hunger still encreases with the store.   520
Without respect they brush'd along the wood
Each in his clan, and fill'd with loathsome food
Ask'd no permission to the neighb'ring flood.
The *Panther* full of inward discontent
Since they wou'd goe, before 'em wisely went: 525
Supplying want of pow'r by drinking first,
As if she gave 'em leave to quench their thirst.
Among the rest, the *Hind,* with fearfull face
Beheld from far the common wat'ring place,
Nor durst approach; till with an awfull roar   530
The sovereign *Lyon* bad her fear no more.
Encourag'd thus she brought her younglings nigh,
Watching the motions of her Patron's eye,
And drank a sober draught; the rest amaz'd
Stood mutely still, and on the stranger gaz'd: 535
Survey'd her part by part, and sought to find
The ten-horn'd monster in the harmless *Hind,*
Such as the *Wolfe* and *Panther* had design'd.
They thought at first they dream'd, for 'twas offence
With them, to question certitude of sense,   540

Their guide in faith; but nearer when they drew,
And had the faultless object full in view,
Lord, how they all admir'd her heav'nly hiew!
Some, who before her fellowship disdain'd,
Scarce, and but scarce, from in-born rage restrain'd,   545
Now frisk'd about her, and old kindred feign'd.
Whether for love or int'rest, ev'ry sect
Of all the salvage nation shew'd respect:
The Vice-roy *Panther* could not awe the herd,
The more the company the less they fear'd.   550
The surly *Wolfe* with secret envy burst,
Yet cou'd not howl, the *Hind* had seen him first:
But what he durst not speak, the *Panther* durst.

  For when the herd suffis'd did late repair
To ferny heaths, and to their forest lare,   555
She made a mannerly excuse to stay,
Proff'ring the *Hind* to wait her half the way:
That since the Sky was clear, an hour of talk,
Might help her to beguile the tedious walk.
With much good-will the motion was embrac'd,   560
To chat awhile on their adventures pass'd:
Nor had the gratefull *Hind* so soon forgot
Her friend and fellow-suff'rer in the plot.
Yet wondring how of late she grew estrang'd,
Her forehead cloudy, and her count'nance chang'd,   565
She thought this hour th' occasion would present
To learn her secret cause of discontent,
Which, well she hop'd, might be with ease redress'd,
Consid'ring Her a well-bred civil beast,
And more a Gentlewoman than the rest.   570
After some common talk what rumours ran,
The Lady of the spotted-muff began.

THE HIND AND THE PANTHER

THE SECOND PART

DAME, said the *Panther*, times are mended well
Since late among the *Philistines* you fell,
The toils were pitch'd, a spacious tract of ground
With expert hunts-men was encompass'd round;
Th' Enclosure narrow'd; the sagacious pow'r   5
Of hounds, and death drew nearer ev'ry hour.
'Tis true, the younger *Lyon* scap'd the snare,
But all your priestly calves lay strugling there;
As sacrifices on their Altars laid;
While you their carefull mother wisely fled   10
Not trusting destiny to save your head.
For, what e'er promises you have apply'd
To your unfailing church, the surer side
Is four fair leggs in danger to provide.
And what e'er tales of *Peter*'s chair you tell,   15
Yet, saving reverence of the miracle,
The better luck was yours to 'scape so well.
   As I remember, said the sober *Hind*,
Those toils were for your own dear self design'd,
As well as me; and, with the self same throw,   20
To catch the quarry, and the vermin too,
(Forgive the sland'rous tongues that call'd you so.)
How e'er you take it now, the common cry
Then ran you down for your rank loyalty;
Besides, in Popery they thought you nurst,   25
(As evil tongues will ever speak the worst,)
Because some forms, and ceremonies some
You kept, and stood in the main question dumb.
Dumb you were born indeed, but thinking long
The *Test* it seems at last has loos'd your tongue.   30
And, to explain what your forefathers meant,
By real presence in the sacrament,

The Second Part. 6 hounds, and death *B C*: hounds and death, *A*

(After long fencing push'd, against a wall,)
Your *salvo* comes, that he's not there at all:
There chang'd your faith, and what may change may fall.　　35
Who can believe what varies every day,
Nor ever was, nor will be at a stay?
　　Tortures may force the tongue untruths to tell,
And I ne'er own'd my self infallible,
Reply'd the *Panther*; grant such Presence were,　　　　40
Yet in your sense I never own'd it there.
A real *vertue* we by faith receive,
And that we in the sacrament believe.
　　Then said the *Hind*, as you the matter state
Not onely *Jesuits* can equivocate;　　　　　　　45
For *real*, as you now the word expound,
From solid substance dwindles to a sound.
Methinks an *Æsop*'s fable you repeat,
You know who took the shadow for the meat:
Your churches substance thus you change at will,　　50
And yet retain your former figure still.
I freely grant you spoke to save your life,
For then you lay beneath the butcher's knife.
Long time you fought, redoubl'd batt'ry bore,
But, after all, against your self you swore;　　　　55
Your former self, for ev'ry hour your form
Is chop'd and chang'd, like winds before a storm.
Thus fear and int'rest will prevail with some,
For all have not the gift of martyrdome.
　　The *Panther* grin'd at this, and thus reply'd;　　60
That men may err was never yet deny'd.
But, if that common principle be true,
The Cannon, Dame, is level'd full at you.
But, shunning long disputes, I fain wou'd see
That wond'rous wight infallibility.　　　　　　65
Is he from heav'n this mighty champion come,
Or lodg'd below in subterranean *Rome*?
First, seat him somewhere, and derive his race,
Or else conclude that nothing has no place.
　　Suppose (though I disown it) said the *Hind*,　　70
The certain mansion were not yet assign'd,
The doubtfull residence no proof can bring

Against the plain existence of the thing.
Because *Philosophers* may disagree,
If sight b' emission or reception be,   } 75
Shall it be thence inferr'd, I do not see?
But you require an answer positive,
Which yet, when I demand, you dare not give,
For fallacies in Universals live.
I then affirm that this unfailing guide   80
In Pope and gen'ral councils must reside;
Both lawfull, both combin'd, what one decrees
By numerous votes, the other ratifies:
On this undoubted sense the church relies.
'Tis true, some Doctours in a scantier space,   85
I mean in each apart, contract the place.
Some, who to greater length extend the line,
The churches after acceptation join.
This last circumference appears too wide,
The church diffus'd is by the council ty'd;   90
As members by their representatives
Oblig'd to laws which Prince and Senate gives:
Thus some contract, and some enlarge the space;
In Pope and council who denies the place,
Assisted from above with God's unfailing grace?   } 95
Those Canons all the needfull points contain;
Their sense so obvious, and their words so plain,
That no disputes about the doubtfull Text
Have, hitherto, the lab'ring world perplex'd:
If any shou'd in after times appear,   100
New Councils must be call'd, to make the meaning clear.
Because in them the pow'r supreme resides;
And all the promises are to the guides.
This may be taught with sound and safe defence:
But mark how sandy is your own pretence,   105
Who setting Councils, Pope, and Church aside,
Are ev'ry man his own presuming guide.
The sacred books, you say, are full and plain,
And ev'ry needfull point of truth contain:
All who can read, Interpreters may be: 110
Thus though your sev'ral churches disagree,

86 apart,] apart *A B C*

Yet ev'ry Saint has to himself alone
The secret of this Philosophick stone.
These principles your jarring sects unite,
When diff'ring Doctours and disciples fight.   115
Though *Luther*, *Zuinglius*, *Calvin*, holy chiefs
Have made a battel Royal of beliefs;
Or like wild horses sev'ral ways have whirl'd
The tortur'd Text about the Christian World;
Each *Jehu* lashing on with furious force,   120
That *Turk* or *Jew* cou'd not have us'd it worse.
No matter what dissention leaders make
Where ev'ry private man may save a stake,
Rul'd by the Scripture and his own advice
Each has a blind by-path to Paradise;   125
Where driving in a circle slow or fast,
Opposing sects are sure to meet at last.
A wondrous charity you have in store
For all reform'd to pass the narrow door:
So much, that *Mahomet* had scarcely more.   130
For he, kind Prophet, was for damning none,
But *Christ* and *Moyses* were to save their own:
Himself was to secure his chosen race,
Though reason good for *Turks* to take the place,
And he allow'd to be the better man   135
In virtue of his holier *Alcoran*.

  True, said the *Panther*, I shall ne'er deny
My breth'ren may be sav'd as well as I:
Though *Huguenots* contemn our ordination,
Succession, ministerial vocation,   140
And *Luther*, more mistaking what he read,
Misjoins the sacred Body with the Bread;
Yet, *Lady*, still remember I maintain,
The Word in needfull points is onely plain.

  Needless or needfull I not now contend,   145
For still you have a loop-hole for a friend,
(Rejoyn'd the Matron) but the rule you lay
Has led whole flocks, and leads them still astray
In weighty points, and full damnation's way.
For did not *Arius* first, *Socinus* now,   150

113 this] his *C*   114 your] you *B C*

The Son's eternal god-head disavow,
And did not these by Gospel Texts alone
Condemn our doctrine, and maintain their own?
Have not all hereticks the same pretence
To plead the Scriptures in their own defence?   155
How did the *Nicene* council then decide
That strong debate, was it by Scripture try'd?
No, sure to those the Rebel would not yield,
Squadrons of Texts he marshal'd in the field;
That was but civil war, an equal set,   160
Where Piles with piles, and eagles Eagles met.
With Texts point-blank and plain he fac'd the Foe:
And did not *Sathan* tempt our Saviour so?
The good old Bishops took a simpler way,
Each ask'd but what he heard his Father say,   165
Or how he was instructed in his youth,
And by traditions force upheld the truth.
    The *Panther* smil'd at this, and when, said she,
Were those first Councils disallow'd by me?
Or where did I at sure tradition strike,   170
Provided still it were Apostolick?
    Friend, said the *Hind*, you quit your former ground,
Where all your Faith you did on Scripture found;
Now 'tis tradition join'd with holy writ,
But thus your memory betrays your wit.   175
    No, said the *Panther*, for in that I view,
When your tradition's forg'd, and when 'tis true.
I set 'em by the rule, and as they square
Or deviate from undoubted doctrine there
This Oral fiction, that old Faith declare.   180
    (*Hind.*) The Council steer'd it seems a diff'rent course,
They try'd the Scripture by tradition's force;
But you tradition by the Scripture try;
Pursu'd, by Sects, from this to that you fly,
Nor dare on one foundation to rely.   185
The word is then depos'd, and in this view,
You rule the Scripture, not the Scripture you.
Thus said the *Dame*, and, smiling, thus pursu'd,
I see tradition then is disallow'd,
When not evinc'd by Scripture to be true,   190

And Scripture, as interpreted by you.
But here you tread upon unfaithfull ground;
Unless you cou'd infallibly expound.
Which you reject as odious Popery,
And throw that doctrine back with scorn on me.   195
Suppose we on things traditive divide,
And both appeal to Scripture to decide;
By various texts we both uphold our claim,
Nay, often ground our titles on the same:
After long labour lost, and times expence,   200
Both grant the words, and quarrel for the sense.
Thus all disputes for ever must depend;
For no dumb rule can controversies end.
Thus when you said tradition must be try'd
By Sacred Writ, whose sense your selves decide,   205
You said no more, but that your selves must be
The judges of the Scripture sense, not we.
Against our church tradition you declare
And yet your Clerks wou'd sit in *Moyses* chair:
At least 'tis prov'd against your argument,   210
The rule is far from plain, where all dissent.
     If not by Scriptures how can we be sure
(Reply'd the *Panther*) what tradition's pure?
For you may palm upon us new for old,
All, as they say, that glitters is not gold.   215
     How but by following her, reply'd the Dame,
To whom deriv'd from sire to son they came;
Where ev'ry age do's on another move,
And trusts no farther than the next above;
Where all the rounds like *Jacob*'s ladder rise,   220
The lowest hid in earth, the topmost in the skyes.
     Sternly the salvage did her answer mark,
Her glowing eye-balls glitt'ring in the dark,
And said but this, since lucre was your trade,
Succeeding times such dreadfull gaps have made   225
'Tis dangerous climbing: to your sons and you
I leave the ladder, and its omen too.
     (*Hind.*) The *Panther*'s breath was ever fam'd for sweet,
But from the *Wolfe* such wishes oft I meet:

223 eye-balls *B C*: eye'balls *A*

You learn'd this language from the blatant beast,   230
Or rather did not speak, but were possess'd.
As for your answer 'tis but barely urg'd;
You must evince tradition to be forg'd;
Produce plain proofs; unblemish'd authours use
As ancient as those ages they accuse;   235
Till when 'tis not sufficient to defame:
An old possession stands, till Elder quitts the claim.
Then for our int'rest which is nam'd alone
To load with envy, we retort your own.
For when traditions in your faces fly,   240
Resolving not to yield, you must decry:
As when the cause goes hard, the guilty man
Excepts, and thins his jury all he can;
So when you stand of other aid bereft,
You to the twelve Apostles would be left.   245
Your friend the *Wolfe* did with more craft provide
To set those toys traditions quite aside:
And *Fathers* too, unless when reason spent
He cites 'em but sometimes for ornament.
But, Madam *Panther*, you, though more sincere,   250
Are not so wise as your Adulterer:
The private spirit is a better blind
Than all the dodging tricks your authours find.
For they, who left the Scripture to the crowd,
Each for his own peculiar judge allow'd;   255
The way to please 'em was to make 'em proud.
Thus, with full sails, they ran upon the shelf;
Who cou'd suspect a couzenage from himself?
On his own reason safer 'tis to stand,
Than be deceiv'd and damn'd at second hand.   260
But you who *Fathers* and traditions take,
And garble some, and some you quite forsake,
Pretending church auctority to fix,
And yet some grains of private spirit mix,
Are like a *Mule* made up of diff'ring seed,   265
And that's the reason why you never breed;
At least not propagate your kind abroad,
For home-dissenters are by statutes aw'd.

257 Thus, *B C*: Thus: *A*   shelf; *B C*: shelf, *A*

And yet they grow upon you ev'ry day,
While you (to speak the best) are at a stay,
For sects that are extremes, abhor a middle way.　　　270
Like tricks of state, to stop a raging flood,
Or mollify a mad-brain'd Senate's mood:
Of all expedients never one was good.
Well may they argue, (nor can you deny)　　　275
If we must fix on church auctority,
Best on the best, the fountain, not the flood,
That must be better still, if this be good.
Shall she command, who has herself rebell'd?
Is *Antichrist* by *Antichrist* expell'd?　　　280
Did we a lawfull tyranny displace,
To set aloft a bastard of the race?
Why all these wars to win the Book, if we
Must not interpret for our selves, but she?
Either be wholly slaves or wholly free.　　　285
For *purging* fires traditions must not fight;
But they must prove Episcopacy's right:
Thus those led horses are from service freed;
You never mount 'em but in time of need.
Like mercenary's, hir'd for home defence,　　　290
They will not serve against their native Prince.
Against domestick foes of *Hierarchy*
These are drawn forth, to make fanaticks fly,
But, when they see their countrey-men at hand,
Marching against 'em under church-command,　　　295
Straight they forsake their colours, and disband.
　Thus she, nor cou'd the *Panther* well enlarge
With weak defence against so strong a charge;
But said, for what did *Christ* his Word provide,
If still his church must want a living guide?　　　300
And if all saving doctrines are not there,
Or sacred Pen-men cou'd not make 'em clear,
From after ages we should hope in vain
For truths, which men inspir'd, cou'd not explain.
　Before the Word was written, said the *Hind*:　　　305
Our Saviour preach'd his Faith to humane kind;
From his Apostles the first age receiv'd

306 kind; *B C*: kind, *A*

Eternal truth, and what they taught, believ'd.
Thus by tradition faith was planted first,
Succeeding flocks succeeding Pastours nurs'd. 310
This was the way our wise Redeemer chose,
(Who sure could all things for the best dispose,)
To fence his fold from their encroaching foes.
He cou'd have writ himself, but well foresaw
Th' event would be like that of *Moyses* law; 315
Some difference wou'd arise, some doubts remain,
Like those, which yet the jarring *Jews* maintain.
No written laws can be so plain, so pure,
But wit may gloss, and malice may obscure,
Not those indited by his first command, 320
A Prophet grav'd the text, an Angel held his hand.
Thus faith was e'er the written word appear'd,
And men believ'd, not what they read, but heard.
But since th' Apostles cou'd not be confin'd,
To these, or those, but severally design'd 325
Their large commission round the world to blow;
To spread their faith they spread their labours too.
Yet still their absent flock their pains did share,
They hearken'd still, for love produces care.
And as mistakes arose, or discords fell, 330
Or bold seducers taught 'em to rebell,
As charity grew cold, or faction hot,
Or long neglect, their lessons had forgot,
For all their wants they wisely did provide,
And preaching by Epistles was supply'd: 335
So great Physicians cannot all attend,
But some they visit, and to some they send.
Yet all those letters were not writ to all;
Nor first intended, but occasional,
Their absent sermons; nor if they contain 340
All needfull doctrines, are those doctrines plain.
Clearness by frequent preaching must be wrought,
They writ but seldome, but they daily taught.
And what one Saint has said of holy *Paul*,
He darkly writ, is true apply'd to all. 345

For this obscurity could heav'n provide
More prudently than by a living guide,
As doubts arose, the difference to decide?
A guide was therefore needfull, therefore made,
And, if appointed, sure to be obey'd.   350
Thus, with due rev'rence, to th' Apostles writ,
By which my sons are taught, to which, submit;
I think, those truths their sacred works contain,
The church alone can certainly explain,
That following ages, leaning on the past,   355
May rest upon the Primitive at last.
Nor wou'd I thence the word no rule infer,
But none without the church interpreter.
Because, as I have urg'd before, 'tis mute,
And is it self the subject of dispute.   360
But what th' Apostles their successours taught,
They to the next, from them to us is brought,
Th' undoubted sense which is in scripture sought.
From hence the church is arm'd, when errours rise,
To stop their entrance, and prevent surprise;   365
And safe entrench'd within, her foes without defies.
By these all festring sores her councils heal,
Which time or has disclos'd, or shall reveal,
For discord cannot end without a last appeal.
Nor can a council national decide   370
But with subordination to her Guide:
(I wish the cause were on that issue try'd.)
Much less the scripture; for suppose debate
Betwixt pretenders to a fair estate,
Bequeath'd by some Legator's last intent;   375
(Such is our dying Saviour's Testament:)
The will is prov'd, is open'd, and is read;
The doubtfull heirs their diff'ring titles plead:
All vouch the words their int'rest to maintain,
And each pretends by those his cause is plain.   380
Shall then the testament award the right?
No, that's the *Hungary* for which they fight;
The field of battel, subject of debate;
The thing contended for, the fair estate.

367 councils] counsels *B C*   383 debate; *B C*: debate, *A*

The sense is intricate, 'tis onely clear   385
What vowels and what consonants are there.
Therefore 'tis plain, its meaning must be try'd
Before some judge appointed to decide.
    Suppose, (the fair Apostate said,) I grant,
The faithfull flock some living guide should want,   390
Your arguments an endless chase persue:
Produce this vaunted Leader to our view,
This mighty *Moyses* of the chosen crew.
    The Dame, who saw her fainting foe retir'd,
With force renew'd, to victory aspir'd;   395
(And looking upward to her kindred sky,
As once our Saviour own'd his Deity,
Pronounc'd his words—*she whom ye seek am I.*)
Nor less amaz'd this voice the *Panther* heard,
Than were those *Jews* to hear a god declar'd.   400
Then thus the matron modestly renew'd;
Let all your prophets and their sects be view'd,
And see to which of 'em your selves think fit
The conduct of your conscience to submit:
Each Proselyte wou'd vote his Doctor best,   405
With absolute exclusion to the rest:
Thus wou'd your *Polish* Diet disagree,
And end as it began in Anarchy:
Your self the fairest for election stand,
Because you seem crown-gen'ral of the land;   410
But soon against your superstitious lawn
Some Presbyterian Sabre wou'd be drawn:
In your establish'd laws of sov'raignty
The rest some fundamental flaw wou'd see,
And call Rebellion gospel-liberty.   415
To church-decrees your articles require
Submission modify'd, if not entire;
Homage deny'd, to censures you proceed;
But when *Curtana* will not doe the deed,
You lay that pointless clergy-weapon by,   420
And to the laws, your sword of justice, fly.
Now this your sects the more unkindly take
(Those prying varlets hit the blots you make)

401 modestly renew'd; *B C*: modesty renew'd, *A*   410 land; *B C*: land, *A*

Because some ancient friends of yours declare,
Your onely rule of faith the Scriptures are,   425
Interpreted by men of judgment sound,
Which ev'ry sect will for themselves expound:
Nor think less rev'rence to their doctours due
For sound interpretation, than to you.
If then, by able heads, are understood   430
Your brother prophets, who reform'd abroad,
Those able heads expound a wiser way,
That their own sheep their shepherd shou'd obey.
But if you mean your selves are onely sound,
That doctrine turns the reformation round,   435
And all the rest are false reformers found.
Because in sundry points you stand alone,
Not in communion join'd with any one;
And therefore must be all the church, or none.
Then, till you have agreed whose judge is best,   440
Against this forc'd submission they protest:
While *sound* and *sound* a diff'rent sense explains
Both play at hard-head till they break their brains:
And from their chairs each others force defy,
While unregarded thunders vainly fly.   445
I pass the rest, because your church alone
Of all usurpers best cou'd fill the throne.
But neither you, nor any sect beside
For this high office can be qualify'd,
With necessary gifts requir'd in such a guide.   450
For that which must direct the whole, must be
Bound in one bond of faith and unity:
But all your sev'ral churches disagree.
The *Consubstantiating* church and Priest
Refuse communion to the *Calvinist*;   455
The *French* reform'd, from preaching you restrain,
Because you judge their ordination vain;
And so they judge of yours, but Donors must ordain.
In short, in doctrine, or in discipline
Not one reform'd, can with another join: 460
But all from each, as from damnation fly;
No union, they pretend, but in *Non-Popery*.

Nor shou'd their members in a synod meet,
Cou'd any church presume to mount the seat
Above the rest, their discords to decide; 465
None wou'd obey, but each wou'd be the guide:
And face to face dissentions wou'd encrease;
For onely distance now preserves the peace.
All in their turns accusers, and accus'd:
Babel was never half so much confus'd. 470
What one can plead, the rest can plead as well;
For amongst equals lies no last appeal,
And all confess themselves are fallible.
Now since you grant some necessary guide,
All who can err are justly laid aside: 475
Because a trust so sacred to confer
Shows want of such a sure interpreter:
And how can he be needfull who can err?
Then, granting that unerring guide we want,
That such there is you stand oblig'd to grant: 480
Our Saviour else were wanting to supply
Our needs, and obviate that necessity.
It then remains that church can onely be
The guide, which owns unfailing certainty;
Or else you slip your hold, and change your side, 485
Relapsing from a necessary guide.
But this annex'd condition of the crown,
Immunity from errours, you disown,
Here then you shrink, and lay your weak pretensions down.
For petty royalties you raise debate; 490
But this unfailing universal state
You shun; nor dare succeed to such a glorious weight.
And for that cause those promises detest
With which our Saviour did his Church invest:
But strive t' evade, and fear to find 'em true, 495
As conscious they were never meant to you:
All which the mother church asserts her own,
And with unrivall'd claim ascends the throne.
So when of old th' Almighty father sate
In Council, to redeem our ruin'd state, 500

463 meet, *B C*: meet; *A*   488 disown, *B C*: disown. *A*   495 t' evade]
t' invade *D*

Millions of millions at a distance round,
Silent the sacred Consistory crown'd,
To hear what mercy mixt with justice cou'd propound.
All prompt with eager pity, to fulfill
The full extent of their Creatour's will: 505
But when the stern conditions were declar'd,
A mournfull whisper through the host was heard,
And the whole hierarchy with heads hung down
Submissively declin'd the pondrous proffer'd crown.
Then, not till then, th' eternal Son from high   510
Rose in the strength of all the Deity;
Stood forth t' accept the terms, and underwent
A weight which all the frame of heav'n had bent,
Nor he Himself cou'd bear, but as omnipotent.
Now, to remove the least remaining doubt,   515
That ev'n the blear-ey'd sects may find her out,
Behold what heav'nly rays adorn her brows,
What from his Wardrobe her belov'd allows
To deck the wedding-day of his unspotted spouse.
Behold what marks of majesty she brings;   520
Richer than ancient heirs of Eastern kings:
Her right hand holds the sceptre and the keys,
To shew whom she commands, and who obeys:
With these to bind, or set the sinner free,
With that t' assert spiritual Royalty.   525

Marks of
the Catho-
lick Church   One in herself not rent by schism, but sound,
from the   Entire, one solid shining Diamond,
Nicene   Not sparkles shatter'd into sects like you,
Creed.   One is the church, and must be to be true:
One central principle of unity.   530
As undivided, so from errours free,
As one in faith, so one in sanctity.
Thus she, and none but she, th' insulting rage
Of Hereticks oppos'd from age to age:
Still when the Gyant-brood invades her throne   535
She stoops from heav'n, and meets 'em half way down,
And with paternal thunder vindicates her crown.

524 free, *B C:* free *A*   531 *indented in A B C*

But like *Ægyptian* Sorcerers you stand,
And vainly lift aloft your magick wand,
To sweep away the swarms of vermin from the land: ⎤ 540
You cou'd like them, with like infernal force
Produce the plague, but not arrest the course.
But when the boils and botches, with disgrace
And publick scandal sat upon the face,
Themselves attack'd, the *Magi* strove no more, ⎤ 545
They saw God's finger, and their fate deplore;
Themselves they cou'd not cure of the dishonest sore. ⎦

 Thus one, thus pure, behold her largely spread
Like the fair ocean from her mother bed;
From East to West triumphantly she rides, 550
All shoars are water'd by her wealthy Tides.

 The Gospel-sound diffus'd from Pole to Pole,
Where winds can carry, and where waves can roll.
The self same doctrine of the Sacred page
Convey'd to ev'ry clime in ev'ry age. 555

 Here let my sorrow give my satyr place,
To raise new blushes on my *British* race;
Our sayling ships like common shoars we use, ⎤
And through our distant colonies diffuse
The draughts of Dungeons, and the stench of stews. ⎦ 560
Whom, when their home-bred honesty is lost,
We disembogue on some far *Indian* coast:
Thieves, Pandars, Palliards, sins of ev'ry sort,
Those are the manufactures we export;
And these the Missionaires our zeal has made: ⎤ 565
For, with my countrey's pardon be it said,
Religion is the least of all our trade. ⎦

 Yet some improve their traffick more than we, ⎤
For they on gain, their onely God, rely:
And set a publick price on piety. ⎦ 570
Industrious of the needle and the chart
They run full sail to their *Japponian* Mart:
Prevention fear, and prodigal of fame ⎤
Sell all of Christian to the very name;
Nor leave enough of that, to hide their naked shame. ⎦ 575

---

552 Gospel-sound *B C*: Golspel's-sound *A*   561 their] the *C*   565 Missionaires *A E: Missioners B C*: Missionaries *D*

Thus, of three marks which in the Creed we view,
Not one of all can be apply'd to you:
Much less the fourth; in vain alas you seek
Th' ambitious title of Apostolick:
God-like descent! 'tis well your bloud can be   580
Prov'd noble, in the third or fourth degree:
For all of ancient that you had before
(I mean what is not borrow'd from our store)
Was Errour fulminated o'er and o'er.
Old Heresies condemn'd in ages past,   585
By care and time recover'd from the blast.
    'Tis said with ease, but never can be prov'd,
The church her old foundations has remov'd,
And built new doctrines on unstable sands:
Judge that ye winds and rains; you prov'd her, yet she stands. 590
Those ancient doctrines charg'd on her for new,
Shew when, and how, and from what hands they grew.
We claim no pow'r when Heresies grow bold
To coin new faith, but still declare the old.
How else cou'd that obscene disease be purg'd   595
When controverted texts are vainly urg'd?
To prove tradition new, there's somewhat more
Requir'd, than saying, 'twas not us'd before.
Those monumental arms are never stirr'd
Till Schism or Heresie call down *Goliah*'s sword.   600
    Thus, what you call corruptions, are in truth,
The first plantations of the gospel's youth,
Old standard faith: but cast your eyes again
And view those errours which new sects maintain
Or which of old disturb'd the churches peacefull reign,   605
And we can point each period of the time,
When they began, and who begot the crime;
Can calculate how long th' eclipse endur'd,
Who interpos'd, what digits were obscur'd:
Of all which are already pass'd away,   610
We know the rise, the progress and decay.
    Despair at our foundations then to strike
Till you can prove your faith Apostolick;
A limpid stream drawn from the native source;
Succession lawfull in a lineal course.   615

Prove any church oppos'd to this our head,
So one, so pure, so unconfin'dly spread,
Under one chief of the spiritual state,
The members all combin'd, and all subordinate.
Shew such a seamless coat, from schism so free,　　　　　620
In no communion join'd with heresie:
If such a one you find, let truth prevail:
Till when your weights will in the balance fail:
A church unprincipl'd kicks up the scale.

But if you cannot think, (nor sure you can　　　　　625
Suppose in God what were unjust in man,)
That he, the fountain of eternal grace,
Should suffer falshood for so long a space
To banish truth, and to usurp her place:
That seav'n successive ages should be lost　　　　　630
And preach damnation at their proper cost;
That all your erring ancestours should dye,
Drown'd in th' Abyss of deep Idolatry;
If piety forbid such thoughts to rise,
Awake and open your unwilling eyes:　　　　　635
God has left nothing for each age undone
From this to that wherein he sent his Son:
Then think but well of him, and half your work is done.

See how his church adorn'd with ev'ry grace
With open arms, a kind forgiving face,　　　　　640
Stands ready to prevent her long lost sons embrace.
Not more did *Joseph* o'er his brethren weep,
Nor less himself cou'd from discovery keep,
When in the croud of suppliants they were seen,
And in their crew his best beloved *Benjamin*.　　　　　645
That pious *Joseph* in the church behold,
To feed your famine, and refuse your gold;
The *Joseph* you exil'd, the *Joseph* whom you sold.
Thus, while with heav'nly charity she spoke,
A streaming blaze the silent shadows broke:　　　　　650
Shot from the skyes a chearfull azure light;
The birds obscene to forests wing'd their flight,
And gaping graves receiv'd the wandring guilty spright.

*The re-
nunciation
of the Bene-
dictines to
the Abby
Lands.*

625–6 can . . . man,) *B C:* can) . . . man, *A D E*　　　630 seav'n *B C:* nine *A D E.*
See Commentary　　　650 broke:] broke; *B C*　　　651 skyes] skyes: *B C*

Such were the pleasing triumphs of the sky
For *James* his late nocturnal victory;   655
The pledge of his Almighty patron's love,
The fire-works which his angel made above.

I saw my self the lambent easie light
Guild the brown horrour and dispell the night;
The messenger with speed the tidings bore,   660
News which three lab'ring nations did restore,
But heav'ns own *Nuncius* was arriv'd before.

By this, the *Hind* had reach'd her lonely cell;
And vapours rose, and dews unwholsome fell.
When she, by frequent observation wise,   665
As one who long on heav'n had fix'd her eyes,
Discern'd a change of weather in the skyes.
The Western borders were with crimson spread,
The moon descending look'd all flaming red,
She thought good manners bound her to invite   670
The stranger Dame to be her guest that night.
'Tis true, course dyet and a short repast,
(She said) were weak inducements to the tast
Of one so nicely bred, and so unus'd to fast.
But what plain fare her cottage cou'd afford,   675
A hearty welcome at a homely board
Was freely hers; and, to supply the rest,
An honest meaning and an open breast.
Last, with content of mind, the poor man's Wealth;
A grace-cup to their common Patron's health.   680
This she desir'd her to accept and stay,
For fear she might be wilder'd in her way,
Because she wanted an unerring guide;
And then the dew-drops on her silken hide
Her tender constitution did declare,   685
Too Lady-like a long fatigue to bear,
And rough inclemencies of raw nocturnal air.
But most she fear'd that travelling so late,
Some evil minded beasts might lye in wait;
And without witness wreak their hidden hate.   690
The *Panther*, though she lent a list'ning ear,
Had more of *Lyon* in her than to fear:

660 bore,] bore; *A B C*   676 A] An *D*

Yet wisely weighing, since she had to deal
With many foes, their numbers might prevail,
Return'd her all the thanks she cou'd afford; 695
And took her friendly hostess at her word.
Who ent'ring first her lowly roof, (a shed
With hoary moss and winding Ivy spread,
Honest enough to hide an humble Hermit's head,)
Thus graciously bespoke her welcome guest: 700
So might these walls, with your fair presence blest
Become your dwelling-place of everlasting rest,
Not for a night, or quick revolving year,
Welcome an owner, not a sojourner.
This peacefull Seat my poverty secures, 705
War seldom enters but where wealth allures;
Nor yet despise it, for this poor aboad
Has oft receiv'd, and yet receives a god;
A god victorious of the Stygian race
Here laid his sacred limbs, and sanctified the place. 710
This mean retreat did mighty *Pan* contain;
Be emulous of him, and pomp disdain,
And dare not to debase your soul to gain.
    The silent stranger stood amaz'd to see
Contempt of wealth, and wilfull poverty: 715
And, though ill habits are not soon controll'd,
A while suspended her desire of gold.
But civily drew in her sharpn'd paws,
Not violating hospitable laws,
And pacify'd her tail, and lick'd her frothy jaws. 720
    The *Hind* did first her country Cates provide;
Then couch'd her self securely by her side.

THE HIND AND THE PANTHER

THE THIRD PART

MUCH malice mingl'd with a little wit
Perhaps may censure this mysterious writ,
Because the Muse has peopl'd *Caledon*
With *Panthers*, *Bears*, and *Wolves*, and Beasts unknown,
As if we were not stock'd with monsters of our own. 5

Let *Æsop* answer, who has set to view,
Such kinds as *Greece* and *Phrygia* never knew;
And mother *Hubbard* in her homely dress
Has sharply blam'd a *British Lioness*,
That *Queen*, whose feast the factious rabble keep,   10
Expos'd obscenely naked and a-sleep.
Led by those great examples, may not I
The wanted organs of their words supply?
If men transact like brutes 'tis equal then
For brutes to claim the privilege of men.   15
   Others our *Hind* of folly will endite,
To entertain a dang'rous guest by night.
Let those remember that she cannot dye
Till rolling time is lost in round eternity;
Nor need she fear the *Panther*, though untam'd,   20
Because the *Lyon*'s peace was now proclam'd;
The wary salvage would not give offence,
To forfeit the protection of her *Prince*;
But watch'd the time her vengeance to compleat,
When all her furry sons in frequent Senate met.   25
Mean while she quench'd her fury at the floud,
And with a Lenten sallad cool'd her bloud.
Their commons, though but course, were nothing scant,
Nor did their minds an equal banquet want.
   For now the *Hind*, whose noble nature strove   30
T' express her plain simplicity of love,
Did all the honours of her house so well,
No sharp debates disturb'd the friendly meal.
She turn'd the talk, avoiding that extreme,
To common dangers past, a sadly pleasing theam;   35
Remembring ev'ry storm which toss'd the state,
When both were objects of the publick hate,
And drop'd a tear betwixt for her own childrens fate.
   Nor fail'd she then a full review to make
Of what the *Panther* suffer'd for her sake.   40
Her lost esteem, her truth, her loyal care,
Her faith unshaken to an exil'd Heir,
Her strength t' endure, her courage to defy;
Her choice of honourable infamy.
On these prolixly thankfull, she enlarg'd,   45

Then with acknowledgments herself she charg'd:
For friendship of it self, an holy tye,
Is made more sacred by adversity.
Now should they part, malicious tongues wou'd say,
They met like chance companions on the way,   50
Whom mutual fear of robbers had possess'd;
While danger lasted, kindness was profess'd;
But that once o'er, the short-liv'd union ends:
The road divides, and there divide the friends.
    The *Panther* nodded when her speech was done,   55
And thank'd her coldly in a hollow tone.
But said her gratitude had gone too far
For common offices of Christian care.
If to the lawfull Heir she had been true,
She paid but *Cæsar* what was *Cæsar*'s due.   60
I might, she added, with like praise describe
Your suff'ring sons, and so return your bribe;
But incense from my hands is poorly priz'd,
For gifts are scorn'd where givers are despis'd.
I serv'd a turn, and then was cast away;   } 65
You, like the gawdy fly, your wings display,
And sip the sweets, and bask in your Great *Patron*'s day.
    This heard, the *Matron* was not slow to find
What sort of malady had seiz'd her mind;
Disdain, with gnawing envy, fell despight,   70
And canker'd malice stood in open sight.
Ambition, int'rest, pride without controul,
And jealousie, the jaundice of the soul;
Revenge, the bloudy minister of ill,
With all the lean tormenters of the will.   75
'Twas easie now to guess from whence arose
Her new made union with her ancient foes,
Her forc'd civilities, her faint embrace,
Affected kindness with an alter'd face:
Yet durst she not too deeply probe the wound,   80
As hoping still the nobler parts were sound;
But strove with Anodynes t' asswage the smart,
And mildly thus her med'cine did impart.
    Complaints of Lovers help to ease their pain,

The Third Part. 77 foes,] foes. B C

It shows a Rest of kindness to complain,   85
A friendship loth to quit its former hold,
And conscious merit may be justly bold.
But much more just your jealousie would show,
If others good were injury to you:
Witness ye heav'ns how I rejoice to see   90
Rewarded worth, and rising loyalty.
Your Warrier Offspring that upheld the crown,
The scarlet honours of your peacefull gown,
Are the most pleasing objects I can find,
Charms to my sight, and cordials to my mind: 95
When vertue spoomes before a prosp'rous gale
My heaving wishes help to fill the sail,
And if my pray'rs for all the brave were heard,
Cæsar should still have such, and such should still reward.

    The labour'd earth your pains have sow'd and till'd: 100
'Tis just you reap the product of the field.
Yours be the harvest, 'tis the beggars gain
To glean the fallings of the loaded wain.
Such scatter'd ears as are not worth your care,
Your charity for alms may safely spare,   } 105
And alms are but the vehicles of pray'r.
My daily bread is litt'rally implor'd,
I have no barns nor granaries to hoard;
If *Cæsar* to his own his hand extends,
Say which of yours his charity offends: } 110
You know he largely gives to more than are his friends.
Are you defrauded when he feeds the poor?
Our mite decreases nothing of your store;
I am but few, and by your fare you see
My crying sins are not of luxury.   115
Some juster motive sure your mind withdraws,
And makes you break our friendships holy laws,   }
For barefac'd envy is too base a cause.
    Show more occasion for your discontent,
Your love, the *Wolf*, wou'd help you to invent,   120
Some *German* quarrel, or, as times go now,
Some *French*, where force is uppermost, will doe.
When at the fountains head, as merit ought

109 hand] hands *D*   112 poor? *B C*: poor, *A*

To claim the place, you take a swilling draught,
How easie 'tis an envious eye to throw,   125
And tax the sheep for troubling streams below,
Or call her, (when no farther cause you find,)
An enemy profess'd of all your kind.
But then, perhaps, the wicked World wou'd think,
The *Wolf* design'd to eat as well as drink.   130
   This last allusion gaul'd the *Panther* more,
Because indeed it rubb'd upon the sore.
Yet seem'd she not to winch, though shrewdly pain'd:
But thus her Passive character maintain'd.
   I never grudg'd, whate're my foes report,   135
Your flaunting fortune in the *Lyon*'s court.
You have your day, or you are much bely'd,
But I am always on the suff'ring side:
You know my doctrine, and I need not say
I will not, but I cannot disobey.   140
On this firm principle I ever stood:
He of my sons who fails to make it good,
By one rebellious act renounces to my bloud.
   Ah, said the *Hind*, how many sons have you
Who call you mother, whom you never knew!   145
But most of them who that relation plead
Are such ungratious youths as wish you dead.
They gape at rich revenues which you hold,
And fain would nible at your grandame gold;
Enquire into your years, and laugh to find   150
Your crazy temper shews you much declin'd.
Were you not dim, and doted, you might see
A pack of cheats that claim a pedigree,
No more of kin to you, than you to me.
Do you not know, that for a little coin,   155
Heralds can foist a name into the line;
They ask you blessing but for what you have,
But once possess'd of what with care you save,
The wanton boyes wou'd piss upon your grave.
   Your sons of Latitude that court your grace,   160
Though most resembling you in form and face,
Are far the worst of your pretended race.
And, but I blush your honesty to blot,

Pray god you prove 'em lawfully begot:
For, in some *Popish* libells I have read,   165
The *Wolf* has been too busie in your bed.
At least their hinder parts, the belly piece,
The paunch, and all that *Scorpio* claims are his.
Their malice too a sore suspicion brings;
For though they dare not bark, they snarl at kings: 170
Nor blame 'em for intruding in your line,
Fat Bishopricks are still of right divine.
　　Think you your new *French* Proselytes are come
To starve abroad, because they starv'd at home?
Your benefices twinckl'd from afar,   175
They found the new *Messiah* by the star:
Those *Swisses* fight on any side for pay,
And 'tis the living that conforms, not they.
Mark with what management their tribes divide, ⎫
Some stick to you, and some to t'other side, ⎬ 180
That many churches may for many mouths provide. ⎭
More vacant pulpits wou'd more converts make,
All wou'd have latitude enough to take;
The rest unbenefic'd, your sects maintain: ⎫
For ordinations without cures are vain, ⎬ 185
And chamber practice is a silent gain. ⎭
Your sons of breadth at home, are much like these,
Their soft and yielding metals run with ease,
They melt, and take the figure of the mould:
But harden, and preserve it best in gold.   190
　　Your *Delphick* Sword, the *Panther* then reply'd,
Is double edg'd, and cuts on either side.
Some sons of mine who bear upon their shield,
Three steeples Argent in a sable field,
Have sharply tax'd your converts, who unfed   195
Have follow'd you for miracles of bread;
Such who themselves of no religion are,
Allur'd with gain, for any will declare.
Bare lyes with bold assertions they can face,
But dint of argument is out of place.   200
The grim Logician puts 'em in a fright,

---

184 maintain: *B*: maintain *A*: maintain; *C*   188 yielding] easie *A* (*text*) *D E*:
yielding *A* (*errata*) *B C*

'Tis easier far to flourish than to fight.
Thus our eighth *Henry*'s marriage they defame;
They say the schism of beds began the game,
Devorcing from the *Church* to wed the Dame: ⎱ 205
Though largely prov'd, and by himself profess'd
That conscience, conscience wou'd not let him rest,
I mean, not till possess'd of her he lov'd,
And old, uncharming *Catherine* was remov'd.
For sundry years before did he complain, 210
And told his ghostly Confessour his pain.
With the same impudence, without a ground,
They say, that look the reformation round,
No *Treatise of Humility* is found.
But if none were, the Gospel does not want, 215
Our *Saviour* preach'd it, and I hope you grant,
The Sermon in the mount was *Protestant*:
   No doubt, reply'd the *Hind*, as sure as all
The writings of Saint *Peter* and Saint *Paul*.
On that decision let it stand or fall. 220
Now for my converts, who you say unfed
Have follow'd me for miracles of bread,
Iudge not by hear-say, but observe at least,
If since their change, their loaves have been increast.
The *Lyon* buyes no Converts, if he did, 225
Beasts wou'd be sold as fast as he cou'd bid.
Tax those of int'rest who conform for gain,
Or stay the market of another reign.
Your broad-way sons wou'd never be too nice
To close with *Calvin*, if he paid their price; 230
But rais'd three steeples high'r, wou'd change their note,
And quit the Cassock for the Canting-coat.
Now, if you damn this censure, as too bold,
Judge by your selves, and think not others sold.
   Mean-time my sons accus'd, by fames report 235
Pay small attendance at the *Lyon*'s court,
Nor rise with early crowds, nor flatter late,
(For silently they beg who daily wait.)
Preferment is bestow'd that comes unsought,

204 say] saw *D*   205 Dame:] Dame. *A B C*   208 mean, *B*: mean *A C*

Attendance is a bribe, and then 'tis bought.   240
How they shou'd speed, their fortune is untry'd,
For not to ask, is not to be deny'd.
For what they have, their *God* and *King* they bless,
And hope they shou'd not murmur, had they less.
But, if reduc'd subsistence to implore,   245
In common prudence they wou'd pass your door;
Unpitty'd *Hudibrass*, your Champion friend,
Has shown how far your charities extend.
This lasting verse shall on his tomb be read,
He sham'd you living, and upbraids you dead.   250
    With odious *Atheist* names you load your foes,
Your lib'ral *Clergy* why did I expose?
It never fails in charities like those.
In climes where true religion is profess'd,
That imputation were no laughing jest.   255
But *Imprimatur*, with a Chaplain's name,
Is here sufficient licence to defame.
What wonder is't that black detraction thrives,
The Homicide of names is less than lives;
And yet the perjur'd murtherer survives.   260
    This said, she paus'd a little, and suppress'd
The boiling indignation of her breast;
She knew the vertue of her blade, nor wou'd
Pollute her satyr with ignoble bloud:
Her panting foes she saw before her lye,   265
And back she drew the shining weapon dry:
So when the gen'rous *Lyon* has in sight
His equal match, he rouses for the fight;
But when his foe lyes prostrate on the plain,
He sheaths his paws, uncurls his angry mane;   270
And, pleas'd with bloudless honours of the day,
Walks over, and disdains th' inglorious Prey.
So *JAMES*, if great with less we may compare,
Arrests his rowling thunder-bolts in air;
And grants ungratefull friends a lengthn'd space,   275
T' implore the remnants of long suff'ring grace.
    This breathing-time the *Matron* took; and then,
Resum'd the thrid of her discourse agen.
Be vengeance wholly left to pow'rs divine,

And let heav'n judge betwixt your sons and mine: 280
If joyes hereafter must be purchas'd here
With loss of all that mortals hold so dear,
Then welcome infamy and publick shame,
And, last, a long farwell to worldly fame.
'Tis said with ease, but oh, how hardly try'd 285
By haughty souls to humane honour ty'd!
O sharp convulsive pangs of agonizing pride!
Down then thou rebell, never more to rise,
And what thou didst, and do'st so dearly prize,
That fame, that darling fame, make that thy sacrifice. 290
'Tis nothing thou hast giv'n, then add thy tears
For a long race of unrepenting years:
'Tis nothing yet; yet all thou hast to give,
Then add those *may-be* years thou hast to live.
Yet nothing still: then poor, and naked come, 295
Thy father will receive his unthrift home,
And thy blest Saviour's bloud discharge the mighty sum.
   Thus (she pursu'd) I discipline a son
Whose uncheck'd fury to revenge wou'd run:
He champs the bit, impatient of his loss, 300
And starts a-side, and flounders at the cross.
Instruct him better, gracious God, to know,
As thine is vengeance, so forgiveness too.
That suff'ring from ill tongues he bears no more
Than what his Sovereign bears, and what his Saviour bore. 305
   It now remains for you to school your child,
And ask why *God*'s anointed he revil'd;
A *King* and *Princess* dead! did *Shimei* worse?
The curser's punishment should fright the curse:
Your son was warn'd, and wisely gave it o're, 310
But he who councell'd him, has paid the score:
The heavy malice cou'd no higher tend,
But wo to him on whom the weights descend:
So to permitted ills the *Dæmon* flyes:
His rage is aim'd at him who rules the skyes; 315
Constrain'd to quit his cause, no succour found,
The foe discharges ev'ry Tyre around,
In clouds of smoke abandoning the fight,
But his own thundring peals proclaim his flight.

In *Henry's* change his charge as ill succeeds,   320
To that long story little answer needs,
Confront but *Henry's* words with *Henry's* deeds.
Were space allow'd, with ease it might be prov'd,
What springs his blessed reformation mov'd.
The dire effects appear'd in open sight,   325
Which from the cause, he calls a distant flight,
And yet no larger leap than from the sun to light.
   Now last your sons a double *Pæan* sound,
A Treatise of Humility is found.
'Tis found, but better had it ne'er been sought   330
Than thus in Protestant procession brought.
The fam'd original through *Spain* is known,
Rodriguez work, my celebrated son,
Which yours, by ill-translating made his own,
Conceal'd its authour, and usurp'd the name,   335
The basest and ignoblest theft of fame.
My Altars kindl'd first that living coal,
Restore, or practice better what you stole:
That vertue could this humble verse inspire,
'Tis all the restitution I require.   340
   Glad was the *Panther* that the charge was clos'd,
And none of all her fav'rite sons expos'd.
For laws of arms permit each injur'd man,
To make himself a saver where he can.
Perhaps the plunder'd merchant cannot tell   345
The names of Pirates in whose hands he fell:
But at the den of thieves he justly flies,
And ev'ry *Algerine* is lawfull prize.
No private person in the foes estate
Can plead exemption from the publick fate.   350
Yet Christian laws allow not such redress;
Then let the greater supersede the less.
But let th' Abbettors of the *Panther's* crime
Learn to make fairer wars another time.
Some characters may sure be found to write   355
Among her sons, for 'tis no common sight
A spotted Dam, and all her offspring white.
   The *Salvage*, though she saw her plea controll'd,
Yet wou'd not wholly seem to quit her hold,

But offer'd fairly to compound the strife; 360
And judge conversion by the convert's life.
'Tis true, she said, I think it somewhat strange
So few shou'd follow profitable change:
For present joys are more to flesh and bloud,
Than a dull prospect of a distant good. 365
'Twas well alluded by a son of mine,
(I hope to quote him is not to purloin.)
Two magnets, heav'n and earth, allure to bliss,
The larger loadstone that, the nearer this:
The weak attraction of the greater fails, 370
We nodd a-while, but neighbourhood prevails:
But when the greater proves the nearer too,
I wonder more your converts come so slow.
Methinks in those who firm with me remain,
It shows a nobler principle than gain. 375
 Your inf'rence wou'd be strong (the *Hind* reply'd)
If yours were in effect the suff'ring side:
Your clergy sons their own in peace possess,
Nor are their prospects in reversion less.
My Proselytes are struck with awfull dread, 380
Your bloudy Comet-laws hang blazing o're their head.
The respite they enjoy but onely lent,
The best they have to hope, protracted punishment.
Be judge your self, if int'rest may prevail,
Which motives, yours or mine, will turn the scale. 385
While pride and pomp allure, and plenteous ease,
That is, till man's predominant passions cease,
Admire no longer at my slow encrease.
 By education most have been misled,
So they believe, because they so were bred. 390
The *Priest* continues what the nurse began,
And thus the child imposes on the man.
The rest I nam'd before, nor need repeat:
But int'rest is the most prevailing cheat,
The sly seducer both of age and youth; 395
They study that, and think they study truth:
When int'rest fortifies an argument
Weak reason serves to gain the wills assent;
For souls already warp'd receive an easie bent.

Add long prescription of establish'd laws,   400
And picque of honour to maintain a cause,
And shame of change, and fear of future ill,
And Zeal, the blind conductor of the will;
And chief among the still mistaking crowd,
The fame of teachers obstinate and proud,   405
And more than all, the private Judge allow'd.
Disdain of Fathers which the daunce began,
And last, uncertain who's the narrower span,
The clown unread, and half-read gentleman.
    To this the *Panther*, with a scornfull smile: 410
Yet still you travail with unwearied toil,
And range around the realm without controll
Among my sons, for Proselytes to prole,
And here and there you snap some silly soul.
You hinted fears of future change in state,   415
Pray heav'n you did not prophesie your fate;
Perhaps you think your time of triumph near,
But may mistake the season of the year;
The *Swallows* fortune gives you cause to fear.
    For charity (reply'd the *Matron*) tell   420
What sad mischance those pretty birds befell.
    Nay, no mischance, (the salvage Dame reply'd)
But want of wit in their unerring guide,
And eager haste, and gaudy hopes, and giddy pride.
Yet, wishing timely warning may prevail,   425
Make you the moral, and I'll tell the tale.
    The *Swallow*, privileg'd above the rest
Of all the birds, as man's familiar Guest,
Pursues the Sun in summer brisk and bold,
But wisely shuns the persecuting cold: 430
Is well to chancels and to chimneys known,
Though 'tis not thought she feeds on smoak alone.
From hence she has been held of heav'nly line,
Endu'd with particles of soul divine.
This merry Chorister had long possess'd   435
Her summer seat, and feather'd well her nest:
Till frowning skys began to change their chear
And time turn'd up the wrong side of the year;

403 will; *B C*: will, *A*

The shedding trees began the ground to strow
With yellow leaves, and bitter blasts to blow. 440
Sad auguries of winter thence she drew,
Which by instinct, or Prophecy, she knew:
When prudence warn'd her to remove betimes
And seek a better heav'n, and warmer clymes.

    Her sons were summon'd on a steeples height, 445
And, call'd in common council, vote a flight;
The day was nam'd, the next that shou'd be fair,
All to the gen'ral rendezvouz repair,
They try their flutt'ring wings and trust themselves in air.
But whether upward to the moon they go, 450
Or dream the winter out in caves below,
Or hawk at flies elsewhere, concerns us not to know.

    Southwards, you may be sure, they bent their flight,
And harbour'd in a hollow rock at night:
Next morn they rose and set up ev'ry sail, 455
The wind was fair, but blew a *mackrel* gale:
The sickly young sat shivring on the shoar,
Abhorr'd salt-water never seen before,
And pray'd their tender mothers to delay
The passage, and expect a fairer day. 460

    With these the *Martyn* readily concurr'd,
A church-begot, and church-believing bird;
Of little body, but of lofty mind,
Round belly'd, for a dignity design'd,
And much a dunce, as *Martyns* are by kind. 465
Yet often quoted Cannon-laws, and *Code*,
And Fathers which he never understood,
But little learning needs in noble bloud.
For, sooth to say, the *Swallow* brought him in,
Her houshold Chaplain, and her next of kin. 470
In Superstition silly to excess,
And casting Schemes, by planetary guess:
In fine, shortwing'd, unfit himself to fly,
His fear foretold foul weather in the sky.

    Besides, a *Raven* from a wither'd Oak, 475
Left of their lodging, was observ'd to croke.

That omen lik'd him not, so his advice
Was present safety, bought at any price:
(A seeming pious care, that cover'd cowardise.)
To strengthen this, he told a boding dream,   480
Of rising waters, and a troubl'd stream,
Sure signs of anguish, dangers and distress,
With something more not lawfull to express:
By which he slyly seem'd to intimate
Some secret revelation of their fate.   485
For he concluded, once upon a time,
He found a leaf inscrib'd with sacred rime,
Whose antique characters did well denote
The *Sibyl's* hand of the *Cumæan* Grott:
The mad Divineress had plainly writ,   490
A time shou'd come (but many ages yet,)
In which, sinister destinies ordain,
A *Dame* shou'd drown with all her feather'd train,
And seas from thence be call'd the *Chelidonian* main.
At this, some shook for fear, the more devout   495
Arose, and bless'd themselves from head to foot.
   'Tis true, some stagers of the wiser sort
Made all these idle wonderments their sport:
They said, their onely danger was delay,
And he who heard what ev'ry fool cou'd say,   500
Wou'd never fix his thoughts, but trim his time away.
The passage yet was good, the wind, 'tis true,
Was somewhat high, but that was nothing new,
Nor more than usual *Equinoxes* blew.
The Sun (already from the scales declin'd)   505
Gave little hopes of better days behind,
But change from bad to worse of weather and of wind.
Nor need they fear the dampness of the Sky
Should flag their wings, and hinder them to fly,
'Twas onely water thrown on sails too dry.   510
But, least of all *Philosophy* presumes
Of truth in dreams, from melancholy fumes:
Perhaps the *Martyn*, hous'd in holy ground,
Might think of Ghosts that walk their midnight round,
Till grosser atoms tumbling in the stream   515

478 price: *B C*: price. *A*   482 signs *B C*: sign *A*

Of fancy, madly met and clubb'd into a dream.
As little weight his vain presages bear,
Of ill effect to such alone who fear.
Most prophecies are of a piece with these,
Each *Nostradamus* can foretell with ease: 520
Not naming persons, and confounding times,
One casual truth supports a thousand lying rimes.
   Th' advice was true, but fear had seiz'd the most,
And all good counsel is on cowards lost.
The question crudely put, to shun delay,   525
'Twas carry'd by the *major* part to stay.
   His point thus gain'd, Sir *Martyn* dated thence
His pow'r, and from a Priest became a Prince.
He order'd all things with a busie care,
And cells, and refectories did prepare,   530
And large provisions lay'd of winter fare.
But now and then let fall a word or two
Of hope, that heav'n some miracle might show,
And, for their sakes, the sun shou'd backward go;
Against the laws of nature upward climb,   535
And, mounted on the *Ram*, renew the prime:
For which two proofs in Sacred story lay,
Of *Ahaz* dial, and of *Joshuah*'s day.
In expectation of such times as these
A chapell hous'd 'em, truly call'd of ease: 540
For *Martyn* much devotion did not ask,
They pray'd sometimes, and that was all their task.
   It happen'd (as beyond the reach of wit
Blind prophecies may have a lucky hit)
That, this accomplish'd, or at least in part,   545
Gave great repute to their new *Merlin*'s art.
Some *Swifts, the Gyants of the *Swallow* kind,   * *Other-*
Large limb'd, stout-hearted, but of stupid mind,   *wise call'd*
(For *Swisses*, or for *Gibeonites* design'd,)   *Martlets.*
These Lubbers, peeping through a broken pane,   550
To suck fresh air, survey'd the neighbouring plain,
And saw (but scarcely cou'd believe their eyes)
New blossoms fiourish, and new flow'rs arise;
As God had been abroad, and walking there,
Had left his foot-steps, and reform'd the year: 555

The sunny hills from far were seen to glow
With glittering beams, and in the meads below
The burnish'd brooks appear'd with liquid gold to flow.
At last they heard the foolish *Cuckow* sing,
Whose note proclaim'd the holy day of spring.   560
   No longer doubting, all prepare to fly,
And repossess their patrimonial sky.
The *Priest* before 'em did his wings display;
And, that good omens might attend their way,
As luck wou'd have it, 'twas St. *Martyn*'s day.   565
   Who but the *Swallow* now triumphs alone,
The Canopy of heaven is all her own,
Her youthfull offspring to their haunts repair;
And glide along in glades, and skim in air,
And dip for insects in the purling springs,   570
And stoop on rivers to refresh their wings.
Their mothers think a fair provision made,
That ev'ry son can live upon his trade,
And now the carefull charge is off their hands,
Look out for husbands, and new nuptial bands: 575
The youthfull widow longs to be supply'd;
But first the lover is by Lawyers ty'd
To settle jointure-chimneys on the bride.
So thick they couple, in so short a space,
That *Martyns* marr'age offrings rise apace;   580
Their ancient houses, running to decay,
Are furbish'd up, and cemented with clay;
They teem already; store of eggs are laid,
And brooding mothers call *Lucina*'s aid.
Fame spreads the news, and foreign fowls appear   585
In flocks to greet the new returning year,
To bless the founder, and partake the cheer.
   And now 'twas time (so fast their numbers rise)
To plant abroad, and people colonies;
The youth drawn forth, as *Martyn* had desir'd,   590
(For so their cruel destiny requir'd)
Were sent far off on an ill fated day;
The rest wou'd need conduct 'em on their way,
And *Martyn* went, because he fear'd alone to stay.

580 offrings *A (errata) B C:* offsprings *A (text) D E*   593 need] needs *C*

So long they flew with inconsiderate haste 595
That now their afternoon began to waste;
And, what was ominous, that very morn
The Sun was entr'd into *Capricorn*;
Which, by their bad Astronomers account,
That week the virgin balance shou'd remount; 600
An infant moon eclips'd him in his way,
And hid the small remainders of his day:
The crowd amaz'd, pursu'd no certain mark;
But birds met birds, and justled in the dark;
Few mind the publick in a Panick fright; 605
And fear increas'd the horrour of the night.
Night came, but unattended with repose,
Alone she came, no sleep their eyes to close,
Alone, and black she came, no friendly stars arose.
   What shou'd they doe, beset with dangers round, 610
No neighb'ring Dorp, no lodging to be found,
But bleaky plains, and bare unhospitable ground.
The latter brood, who just began to fly
Sick-feather'd, and unpractis'd in the sky,
For succour to their helpless mother call, 615
She spread her wings; some few beneath 'em craul,
She spread 'em wider yet, but cou'd not cover all.
T' augment their woes, the winds began to move
Debate in air, for empty fields above,
Till *Boreas* got the skyes, and powr'd amain 620
His ratling hail-stones mix'd with snow and rain.
   The joyless morning late arose, and found
A dreadfull desolation reign a-round,
Some buried in the Snow, some frozen to the ground:
The rest were strugling still with death, and lay 625
The *Crows* and *Ravens* rights, an undefended prey;
Excepting *Martyn*'s race, for they and he
Had gain'd the shelter of a hollow tree,
But soon discover'd by a sturdy clown,
He headed all the rabble of a town, 630
And finish'd 'em with bats, or poll'd 'em down.

612 bleaky] bleakly D   628 a] an D

Martyn himself was caught a-live, and try'd
For treas'nous crimes, because the laws provide
No *Martyn* there in winter shall abide.
High on an Oak which never leaf shall bear,   635
He breath'd his last, expos'd to open air,
And there his corps, unbless'd, are hanging still,
To show the change of winds with his prophetick bill.
   The patience of the *Hind* did almost fail,
For well she mark'd the malice of the tale: 640
Which Ribbald art their church to *Luther* owes,
In malice it began, by malice grows,
He sow'd the *Serpent*'s teeth, an iron-harvest rose.
But most in *Martyn*'s character and fate,
She saw her slander'd sons, the *Panther*'s hate,   645
The people's rage, the persecuting state:
Then said, I take th' advice in friendly part,
You clear your conscience, or at least your heart:
Perhaps you fail'd in your fore-seeing skill,
For *Swallows* are unlucky birds to kill: 650
As for my sons, the family is bless'd,
Whose ev'ry child is equal to the rest:
No church reform'd can boast a blameless line;
Such *Martyns* build in yours, and more than mine:
Or else an old fanatick Authour lyes   655
Who summ'd their Scandals up by Centuries.
But, through your parable I plainly see
The bloudy laws, the crowds barbarity:
The sun-shine that offends the purblind sight,
Had some their wishes, it wou'd soon be night.   660
Mistake me not, the charge concerns not you,
Your sons are male-contents, but yet are true,
As far as non-resistance makes 'em so,
But that's a word of neutral sense you know,
A passive term which no relief will bring,   665
But trims betwixt a rebell and a king.
   Rest well assur'd the *Pardelis* reply'd,
My sons wou'd all support the regal side,
Though heav'n forbid the cause by battel shou'd be try'd.
   The Matron answer'd with a loud Amen,   670
And thus pursu'd her argument agen.

If as you say, and as I hope no less,
Your sons will practise what your self profess,
What angry pow'r prevents our present peace?
The *Lyon*, studious of our common good,   675
Desires, (and Kings desires are ill withstood,)
To join our Nations in a lasting love;
The barrs betwixt are easie to remove,
For sanguinary laws were never made above.
If you condemn that Prince of Tyranny   680
Whose mandate forc'd your *Gallick* friends to fly,
Make not a worse example of your own,
Or cease to rail at causeless rigour shown,
And let the guiltless person throw the stone.
His blunted sword, your suff'ring brotherhood   685
Have seldom felt, he stops it short of bloud:
But you have ground the persecuting knife,
And set it to a razor edge on life.
Curs'd be the wit which cruelty refines,
Or to his father's rod the *Scorpion* joins;   690
Your finger is more gross than the great Monarch's loins.
But you perhaps remove that bloudy note,
And stick it on the first Reformers coat.
Oh let their crime in long oblivion sleep,
'Twas theirs indeed to make, 'tis yours to keep.   695
Unjust, or just, is all the question now,
'Tis plain, that not repealing you allow.
    To name the Test wou'd put you in a rage,
You charge not that on any former age,
But smile to think how innocent you stand   700
Arm'd by a weapon put into your hand.
Yet still remember that you weild a sword
Forg'd by your foes against your Sovereign Lord.
Design'd to hew th' imperial Cedar down,
Defraud Succession, and dis-heir the Crown.   705
T' abhor the makers, and their laws approve,
Is to hate Traytors, and the treason love.
What means it else, which now your children say,
We made it not, nor will we take away.

706 the] their C

Suppose some great Oppressour had by slight   710
Of law, disseis'd your brother of his right,
Your common sire surrendring in a fright;
Would you to that unrighteous title stand,
Left by the villain's will to heir the land?
More just was *Judas*, who his Saviour sold;   715
The sacrilegious bribe he cou'd not hold,
Nor hang in peace, before he rendr'd back the gold.
What more could you have done, than now you doe,
Had *Oates* and *Bedlow*, and their Plot been true?
Some specious reasons for those wrongs were found;   720
The dire Magicians threw their mists around,
And wise men walk'd as on inchanted ground.
But now when time has made th' imposture plain,
(Late though he follow'd truth, and limping held her train,)
What new delusion charms your cheated eyes again?   725
The painted Harlot might awhile bewitch,
But why the Hag uncas'd, and all obscene with itch?

The first Reformers were a modest race,
Our Peers possess'd in peace their native place:
And when rebellious arms o'return'd the state,   730
They suffer'd onely in the common fate;
But now the Sov'reign mounts the regal chair
And mitr'd seats are full, yet *David*'s bench is bare:
Your answer is, they were not dispossess'd,
They need but rub their mettle on the Test   735
To prove their ore: 'twere well if gold alone
Were touch'd and try'd on your discerning stone;
But that unfaithfull Test, unfound will pass
The dross of Atheists, and sectarian brass:
As if th' experiment were made to hold   740
For base productions, and reject the gold:
Thus men ungodded may to places rise,
And sects may be preferr'd without disguise:
No danger to the church or state from these,
The Papist onely has his Writ of ease.   745
No gainfull office gives him the pretence
To grind the Subject or defraud the Prince.
Wrong conscience, or no conscience may deserve

744 to *A* (*errata*) *B C*: from *A* (*text*) *D E*

To thrive, but ours alone is privileg'd to sterve.
   Still thank your selves you cry, your noble race   750
We banish not, but they forsake the place.
Our doors are open: true, but e'er they come,
You toss your censing Test, and fume the room;
As if 'twere *Toby*'s rival to expell,
And fright the fiend who could not bear the smell.   755
   To this the *Panther* sharply had reply'd,
But, having gain'd a Verdict on her side,
She wisely gave the loser leave to chide;
Well satisfy'd to have the But and peace,
And for the Plaintiff's cause she car'd the less,   760
Because she su'd *in formâ Pauperis*;
Yet thought it decent something shou'd be said,
For secret guilt by silence is betray'd:
So neither granted all, nor much deny'd,
But answer'd with a yawning kind of pride.   765
   Methinks such terms of proferr'd peace you bring
As once *Æneas* to th' *Italian* King:
By long possession all the land is mine,
You strangers come with your intruding line,
To share my sceptre, which you call to join.   770
You plead like him an ancient Pedigree,
And claim a peacefull seat by fates decree.
In ready pomp your Sacrificer stands,
T' unite the *Trojan* and the *Latin* bands,
And that the League more firmly may be ty'd,   775
Demand the fair *Lavinia* for your bride.
Thus plausibly you veil th' intended wrong,
But still you bring your exil'd gods along;
And will endeavour in succeeding space,
Those houshold Poppits on our hearths to place.   780
Perhaps some barb'rous laws have been preferr'd,
I spake against the *Test*, but was not heard;
These to rescind, and Peerage to restore,
My gracious Sov'reign wou'd my vote implore:
I owe him much, but owe my conscience more.   785
   Conscience is then your Plea, reply'd the Dame,
Which well-inform'd will ever be the same.
But yours is much of the *Camelion* hew,

To change the dye with ev'ry diff'rent view.

When first the *Lyon* sat with awfull sway   790
Your conscience taught you duty to obey:
He might have had your Statutes and your Test,
No conscience but of subjects was profess'd.
He found your temper, and no farther try'd,
But on that broken reed your church rely'd.   795
In vain the sects assay'd their utmost art
With offer'd treasure to espouse their part,
Their treasures were a bribe too mean to move his heart.
But when by long experience you had proov'd,
How far he cou'd forgive, how well he lov'd;   800
A goodness that excell'd his godlike race,
And onely short of heav'ns unbounded grace:
A floud of mercy that o'erflowed our Isle,
Calm in the rise, and fruitfull as the *Nile*:
Forgetting whence your *Ægypt* was supply'd,   805
You thought your Sov'reign bound to send the tide:
Nor upward look'd on that immortal spring,
But vainly deem'd, he durst not be a king:
Then conscience, unrestrain'd by fear, began
To stretch her limits, and extend the span,   810
Did his indulgence as her gift dispose,
And made a wise Alliance with her foes.
Can conscience own th' associating name,
And raise no blushes to conceal her shame?
For sure she has been thought a bashfull Dame.   815
But if the cause by battel shou'd be try'd,
You grant she must espouse the regal side:
O *Proteus* Conscience, never to be ty'd!
What *Phœbus* from the *Tripod* shall disclose,
Which are in last resort, your friends or foes?   820
Homer, who learn'd the language of the sky,
The seeming *Gordian* knot wou'd soon unty;
Immortal pow'rs the term of conscience know,
But int'rest is her name with men below.

Conscience or int'rest be't, or both in one;   825
(The *Panther* answer'd in a surly tone,)
The first commands me to maintain the Crown,

804 *Nile*:] *Nile*, *A B C*

The last forbids to throw my barriers down.
Our penal laws no sons of yours admit,
Our *Test* excludes your Tribe from benefit. 830
These are my banks your ocean to withstand,
Which proudly rising overlooks the land:
And once let in, with unresisted sway
Wou'd sweep the Pastors and their flocks away.
Think not my judgment leads me to comply 835
With laws unjust, but hard necessity:
Imperious need which cannot be withstood
Makes ill authentick, for a greater good.
Possess your soul with patience, and attend:
A more auspicious Planet may ascend; 840
Good fortune may present some happier time,
With means to cancell my unwilling crime;
(Unwilling, witness all ye Pow'rs above)
To mend my errours and redeem your love:
That little space you safely may allow, 845
Your all-dispensing pow'r protects you now.
    Hold, said the *Hind*, 'tis needless to explain;
You wou'd *postpone* me to another reign:
Till when you are content to be unjust,
Your part is to possess, and mine to trust. 850
A fair exchange propos'd of future chance,
For present profit and inheritance:
Few words will serve to finish our dispute,
Who will not now repeal wou'd persecute;
To ripen green revenge your hopes attend, 855
Wishing that happier Planet wou'd ascend:
For shame let Conscience be your Plea no more,
To will hereafter, proves she might before;
But she's a Bawd to gain, and holds the Door.
    Your care about your Banks, infers a fear 860
Of threatning Floods, and Inundations near;
If so, a just Reprise would only be
Of what the Land usurp'd upon the Sea;
And all your Jealousies but serve to show
Your Ground is, like your Neighbour-Nation, low. 865
T' intrench in what you grant unrighteous Laws,
Is to distrust the justice of your Cause;

And argues that the true Religion lyes
In those weak Adversaries you despise.
   Tyrannick force is that which least you fear,   870
The sound is frightfull in a Christian's ear;
Avert it, Heav'n; nor let that Plague be sent
To us from the dispeopled Continent.
   But Piety commands me to refrain;
Those Pray'rs are needless in this Monarch's Reign.   875
Behold! how he protects your Friends opprest,
Receives the Banish'd, succours the Distress'd:
Behold, for you may read an honest open Breast.
He stands in Day-light, and disdains to hide
An Act to which, by Honour he is ty'd,   880
A generous, laudable, and Kingly Pride.
Your Test he would repeal, his Peers restore,
This when he says he means, he means no more.
   Well, said the *Panther*, I believe him just,
And yet—
         And yet, 'Tis but because you must,   885
You would be trusted, but you would not trust.
The *Hind* thus briefly, and disdain'd t' inlarge
On Pow'r of *Kings*, and their Superiour charge,
As Heav'ns Trustees before the Peoples choice:
Tho' sure the *Panther* did not much rejoyce   890
To hear those *Echo's* giv'n of her once Loyal voice.
   The *Matron* woo'd her Kindness to the last,
But cou'd not win; her hour of Grace was past.
Whom thus persisting when she could not bring
To leave the *Woolf*, and to believe her King,   895
She gave Her up, and fairly wish'd her Joy
Of her late Treaty with her new Ally:
Which well she hop'd wou'd more successfull prove,
Than was the *Pigeons*, and the *Buzzards* love.
The *Panther* ask'd, what concord there cou'd be   900
Betwixt two kinds whose Natures disagree?
The *Dame* reply'd, 'Tis sung in ev'ry Street,
The common chat of Gossips when they meet:
But, since unheard by you, 'tis worth your while
To take a wholesome Tale, tho' told in homely stile.   905
   A Plain good Man, whose Name is understood,

(So few deserve the name of Plain and Good)
Of three fair lineal Lordships stood possess'd,
And liv'd, as reason was, upon the best;
Inur'd to hardships from his early Youth,   910
Much had he done, and suffer'd for his truth:
At Land, and Sea, in many a doubtfull Fight,
Was never known a more advent'rous Knight,
Who oftner drew his Sword, and always for the right.

   As Fortune wou'd (his fortune came tho' late)   915
He took Possession of his just Estate:
Nor rack'd his Tenants with increase of Rent,
Nor liv'd too sparing, nor too largely spent;
But overlook'd his Hinds, their Pay was just,
And ready, for he scorn'd to go on trust: 920
Slow to resolve, but in performance quick;
So true, that he was awkard at a trick.
For little Souls on little shifts rely,
And coward Arts of mean Expedients try:
The noble Mind will dare do anything but lye.   925
False Friends, (his deadliest foes,) could find no way
But shows of honest bluntness to betray;
That unsuspected plainness he believ'd,
He look'd into Himself, and was deceiv'd.
Some lucky Planet sure attends his Birth,   930
Or Heav'n wou'd make a Miracle on Earth;
For prosp'rous Honesty is seldom seen:
To bear so dead a weight, and yet to win.
It looks as Fate with Nature's Law would strive,
To shew Plain dealing once an age may thrive: 935
And, when so tough a frame she could not bend,
Exceeded her Commission to befriend.
   This gratefull man, as Heav'n encreas'd his Store,
Gave *God* again, and daily fed his Poor;
His House with all convenience was purvey'd,   940
The rest he found, but rais'd the Fabrick where he pray'd;
And in that Sacred Place, his beauteous Wife
Employ'd Her happiest hours of Holy Life.
   Nor did their Alms extend to those alone
Whom common Faith more strictly made their own;   945

919 Hinds] *Hinds A B C*   924 coward] cowards *C*   945 own; *B C:* own, *A*

A sort of *Doves* were hous'd too near their Hall,
Who cross the Proverb, and abound with Gall.
Tho' some 'tis true, are passively inclin'd,
The greater Part degenerate from their kind;
Voracious Birds, that hotly Bill and breed,   950
And largely drink, because on Salt they feed.
Small Gain from them their Bounteous Owner draws,
Yet, bound by Promise, he supports their Cause,
As Corporations priviledg'd by Laws.
   That House which harbour to their kind affords   955
Was built, long since, God knows, for better Birds;
But flutt'ring there they nestle near the Throne,
And lodge in Habitations not their own,
By their high Crops, and Corny Gizzards known.
Like *Harpy's* they could scent a plenteous board,   960
Then to be sure they never fail'd their Lord.
The rest was form, and bare Attendance paid,
They drunk, and eat, and grudgingly obey'd.
The more they fed, they raven'd still for more,
They drain'd from *Dan*, and left *Beersheba* poor;   965
All this they had by Law, and none repin'd,
The pref'rence was but due to *Levi's* Kind,
But when some Lay-preferment fell by chance
The Gourmands made it their Inheritance.
When once possess'd, they never quit their Claim,   970
For then 'tis sanctify'd to Heav'ns high Name;
And Hallow'd thus they cannot give Consent,
The Gift should be prophan'd by Worldly management.
   Their Flesh was never to the Table serv'd,
Tho' 'tis not thence inferr'd the Birds were starv'd;   975
But that their Master did not like the Food,
As rank, and breeding Melancholy Blood.
Nor did it with His Gracious Nature suite,
Ev'n tho' they were not Doves, to persecute:
Yet He refus'd, (nor could they take Offence)   980
Their Glutton Kind should teach him abstinence.
Nor Consecrated Grain their Wheat he thought,
Which new from treading in their Bills they brought:
But left his Hinds each in his Private Pow'r,

971 Heav'ns] Hea'vens *A B C*

That those who like the Bran might leave the Flow'r. 985
He for himself, and not for others chose,
Nor would He be impos'd on, nor impose;
But in their Faces His Devotion paid,
And Sacrifice with Solemn Rites was made,
And Sacred Incense on His Altars laid. 990
   Besides these jolly Birds whose Crops impure,
Repay'd their Commons with their Salt Manure;
Another Farm he had behind his House,
Not overstock't, but barely for his use;
Wherein his poor Domestick Poultry fed, 995
And from His Pious Hands receiv'd their Bread.
Our pamper'd Pigeons with malignant Eyes,
Beheld these Inmates, and their Nurseries:
Tho' hard their fare, at Ev'ning, and at Morn
A Cruise of Water and an Ear of Corn; 1000
Yet still they grudg'd that Modicum, and thought
A Sheaf in ev'ry single Grain was brought;
Fain would they filch that little Food away,
While unrestrain'd those happy Gluttons prey.
And much they griev'd to see so nigh their Hall, 1005
The Bird that warn'd St. *Peter* of his Fall;
That he should raise his miter'd Crest on high,
And clap his Wings, and call his Family
To Sacred Rites; and vex th' Etherial Pow'rs
With midnight Mattins, at uncivil Hours: 1010
Nay more, his quiet Neighbours should molest,
Just in the sweetness of their Morning rest.
   Beast of a Bird, supinely when he might
Lye snugg and sleep, to rise before the light:
What if his dull Forefathers us'd that cry, 1015
Cou'd he not let a Bad Example dye?
The World was fall'n into an easier way,
This Age knew better, than to Fast and Pray.
Good Sense in Sacred Worship would appear
So to begin, as they might end the year. 1020
Such feats in former times had wrought the falls
Of crowing Chanticleers in Cloyster'd Walls.

1001 Modicum *A (errata) B–E:* Modi'um *A (text)*

Expell'd for this, and for their Lands they fled;
And Sister Partlet with her hooded head
Was hooted hence, because she would not pray a Bed.					1025
The way to win the restiff World to God,
Was to lay by the Disciplining Rod,
Unnatural Fasts, and Foreign Forms of Pray'r;
Religion frights us with a meen severe.
'Tis Prudence to reform her into Ease,					1030
And put Her in undress to make Her pleas:
A lively Faith will bear aloft the Mind,
And leave the Luggage of Good Works behind.
   Such Doctrines in the Pigeon-house were taught,
You need not ask how wondrously they wrought;					1035
But sure the common Cry was all for these
Whose Life, and Precept both encourag'd Ease.
Yet fearing those alluring Baits might fail,
And Holy Deeds o're all their Arts prevail:
(For Vice, tho' frontless, and of harden'd Face					1040
Is daunted at the sight of awfull Grace)
An hideous Figure of their Foes they drew,
Nor Lines, nor Looks, nor Shades, nor Colours true;
And this Grotesque design, expos'd to Publick view.
One would have thought it some *Ægyptian* Piece,					1045
With Garden-Gods, and barking Deities,
More thick than *Ptolemy* has stuck the Skies.
All so perverse a Draught, so far unlike,
It was no Libell where it meant to strike:
Yet still the daubing pleas'd, and Great and Small					1050
To view the Monster crowded Pigeon-hall.
There Chanticleer was drawn upon his knees
Adoring Shrines, and Stocks of Sainted Trees,
And by him, a mishapen, ugly Race;
The Curse of God was seen on ev'ry Face:					1055
No *Holland* Emblem could that Malice mend,
But still the worse the look the fitter for a Fiend.
   The Master of the Farm displeas'd to find
So much of Rancour in so mild a kind,
Enquir'd into the Cause, and came to know,					1060

1023 fled; *B C*: fled, *A*			1026 restiff *A (errata) B–E*: restless *A (text)*
1031 undress *A (errata) B–E*: undrest *A (text)*			1045 some *B C*: an *A D E*

The Passive Church had struck the foremost blow:
With groundless Fears, and Jealousies possest,
As if this troublesome intruding Guest
Would drive the Birds of *Venus*, from their Nest.
A Deed his inborn Equity abhorr'd,   1065
But Int'rest will not trust, tho God should plight his Word.

   A Law, the Source of many Future harms,
Had banish'd all the Poultry from the Farms;
With loss of Life, if any should be found
To crow or peck on this forbidden Ground.   1070
That Bloody Statute chiefly was design'd
For *Chanticleer* the white, of Clergy kind;
But after-malice did not long forget
The Lay that wore the Robe, and Coronet;
For them, for their Inferiours and Allyes,   1075
Their Foes a deadly *Shibboleth* devise:
By which unrighteously it was decreed,
That none to Trust, or Profit should succeed,
Who would not swallow first a poysonous wicked Weed:
Or that, to which old *Socrates* was curs't,   1080
Or Henbane-Juice to swell 'em till they burst.
The Patron (as in reason) thought it hard
To see this Inquisition in his Yard,
By which the Soveraign was of Subjects use debarr'd.
   All gentle means he try'd, which might withdraw   1085
Th' Effects of so unnatural a Law:
But still the Dove-house obstinately stood
Deaf to their own, and to their Neighbours good:
And which was worse, (if any worse could be)
Repented of their boasted Loyalty: 1090
Now made the Champions of a cruel Cause,
And drunk with Fumes of Popular Applause;
For those whom God to ruine has design'd,
He fits for Fate, and first destroys their Mind.
   New Doubts indeed they daily strove to raise,   1095
Suggested Dangers, interpos'd Delays,
And Emissary Pigeons had in store,
Such as the *Meccan* Prophet us'd of yore,
To whisper Counsels in their Patrons Ear,

1079 Weed: *B*: Weed, *A*: Weed. *C*

And veil'd their false Advice with Zealous Fear.   1100
The Master smiled to see 'em work in vain,
To wear him out, and make an idle reign:
He saw, but suffer'd their Protractive Arts,
And strove by mildness to reduce their Hearts;
But they abus'd that Grace to make Allyes,   1105
And fondly clos'd with former Enemies;
For Fools are double Fools endeav'ring to be wise.
   After a grave Consult what course were best,
One more mature in Folly than the rest,
Stood up, and told 'em, with his head aside,   1110
That desp'rate Cures must be to desp'rate Ills apply'd:
And therefore since their main impending fear
Was from th' encreasing race of *Chanticleer*:
Some Potent Bird of Prey they ought to find,
A Foe profess'd to him, and all his kind: 1115
Some haggar'd *Hawk*, who had her eyry nigh,
Well pounc'd to fasten, and well wing'd to fly;
One they might trust, their common wrongs to wreak:
The *Musquet*, and the *Coystrel* were too weak,
Too fierce the *Falcon*, but above the rest,   1120
The noble *Buzzard* ever pleas'd me best;
Of small Renown, 'tis true, for not to lye,
We call him but a *Hawk* by courtesie.
I know he haunts the *Pigeon*-House and Farm,
And more, in time of War, has done us harm;   1125
But all his hate on trivial Points depends,
Give up our Forms, and we shall soon be friends.
For *Pigeons* flesh he seems not much to care,
Cram'd *Chickens* are a more delicious fare;
On this high Potentate, without delay,   1130
I wish you would conferr the Sovereign sway:
Petition him t' accept the Government,
And let a splendid Embassy be sent.
   This pithy speech prevail'd, and all agreed,
Old Enmity's forgot, the *Buzzard* should succeed.   1135
   Their welcom Suit was granted soon as heard,
His Lodgings furnish'd, and a Train prepar'd,
With *B's* upon their Breast, appointed for his Guard.
He came, and Crown'd with great Solemnity,

God save King *Buzzard*, was the gen'rall cry.   1140
   A Portly Prince, and goodly to the sight,
He seem'd a Son of *Anach* for his height:
Like those whom stature did to Crowns prefer;
Black-brow'd, and bluff, like *Homer's Jupiter*:
Broad-back'd, and Brawny built for Loves delight,   1145
A Prophet form'd, to make a female Proselyte.
A Theologue more by need than genial bent,
By Breeding sharp, by Nature confident.
Int'rest in all his Actions was discern'd;
More learn'd than Honest, more a Wit than learn'd.   1150
Or forc'd by Fear, or by his Profit led,
Or both conjoyn'd, his Native clime he fled:
But brought the Vertues of his Heav'n along;
A fair Behaviour, and a fluent Tongue.
And yet with all his Arts he could not thrive;   1155
The most unlucky Parasite alive.
Loud Praises to prepare his Paths he sent,
And then himself pursu'd his Compliment:
But, by reverse of Fortune chac'd away,
His Gifts no longer than their Author stay: 1160
He shakes the Dust against th' ungrateful race,
And leaves the stench of Ordures in the place.
Oft has he flatter'd, and blasphem'd the same,
For in his Rage, he spares no Sov'rains name:
The Hero, and the Tyrant change their style   1165
By the same measure that they frown or smile;
When well receiv'd by hospitable Foes,
The kindness he returns, is to expose:
For Courtesies, tho' undeserv'd and great,
No gratitude in Fellon-minds beget,   } 1170
As tribute to his Wit, the churl receives the treat.
His praise of Foes is venemously Nice,
So touch'd, it turns a Vertue to a Vice: }
A Greek, *and bountiful forewarns us twice.*
Sev'n Sacraments he wisely do's disown,   1175

1147 genial *A (some copies) B C*: nat'ral *A (some*
copies) B C: Nation *A (some copies) D E*   1149 was] were *C*   1151 his Profit
A (some copies) B C D E: Ambition *A (some copies)*   1152 both conjoyn'd, his
Native *A (some copies) B C*: both, his own unhappy *A (some copies) D E*   1154
fluent *A (some copies) B C*: flatt'ring *A (some copies) D E*

Because he knows Confession stands for one;
Where Sins to sacred silence are convey'd,
And not for Fear, or Love, to be betray'd:
But he, uncall'd, his Patron to controul,
Divulg'd the secret whispers of his Soul: 1180
Stood forth th' accusing *Sathan* of his Crimes,
And offer'd to the *Moloch* of the Times.
Prompt to assayle, and careless of defence,
Invulnerable in his Impudence;
He dares the World, and eager of a name, 1185
He thrusts about, and justles into fame.
Frontless, and Satyr-proof he scow'rs the streets,
And runs an *Indian* muck at all he meets.
So fond of loud Report, that not to miss
Of being known (his last and utmost bliss) } 1190
He rather would be known, for what he is.

   Such was, and is the Captain of the test,
Tho' half his Vertues are not here express't; }
The modesty of Fame conceals the rest.
The spleenful *Pigeons* never could create 1195
A Prince more proper to revenge their hate:
Indeed, more proper to revenge, than save;
A King, whom in his wrath, th' Almighty gave:
For all the Grace the Landlord had allow'd,
But made the *Buzzard* and the *Pigeons* proud; } 1200
Gave time to fix their Friends, and to seduce the crowd.
They long their Fellow-Subjects to inthrall,
Their Patrons promise into question call, }
And vainly think he meant to make 'em Lords of all.

   False Fears their Leaders fail'd not to suggest, 1205
As if the *Doves* were to be dispossess't;
Nor Sighs, nor Groans, nor gogling Eyes did want;
For now the *Pigeons* too had learn'd to Cant.
The House of Pray'r is stock'd with large encrease;
Nor Doors, nor Windows can contain the Press: 1210
For Birds of ev'ry feather fill th' abode;
Ev'n Atheists out of envy own a God:
And reeking from the Stews, Adult'rers come,
Like *Goths* and *Vandals* to demolish *Rome.*
That Conscience which to all their Crimes was mute, 1215

Now calls aloud, and cryes to Persecute.
No rigour of the Laws to be releas'd,
And much the less, because it was their Lords request:
They thought it great their Sov'rain to controul,
And nam'd their Pride, Nobility of Soul.   1220
    'Tis true, the *Pigeons*, and their Prince Elect
Were short of Pow'r their purpose to effect:
But with their Quills, did all the hurt they cou'd,
And cuff'd the tender *Chickens* from their food:
And much the *Buzzard* in their Cause did stir,   1225
Tho' naming not the Patron, to infer
With all respect, He was a gross Idolater.
    But when th' Imperial owner did espy
That thus they turn'd his Grace to villany,
Not suff'ring wrath to discompose his mind,   1230
He strove a temper for th' extreams to find,
So to be just, as he might still be kind.
Then, all Maturely weigh'd, pronounc'd a Doom
Of Sacred Strength for ev'ry Age to come.
By this the Doves their Wealth and State possess,   1235
No Rights infring'd, but Licence to oppress:
Such Pow'r have they as Factious Lawyers long
To Crowns ascrib'd, that Kings can do no wrong.
But, since His own Domestick Birds have try'd
The dire Effects of their destructive Pride,   1240
He deems that Proof a Measure to the rest,
Concluding well within his Kingly Breast,
His Fowl of Nature too unjustly were opprest.
He therefore makes all Birds of ev'ry Sect
Free of his Farm, with promise to respect   1245
Their sev'ral Kinds alike, and equally protect.
His Gracious Edict the same Franchise yields
To all the wild Encrease of Woods and Fields,
And who in Rocks aloof, and who in Steeples builds.
To *Crows* the like Impartial Grace affords,   1250
And *Choughs* and *Daws*, and such Republick Birds:
Secur'd with ample Priviledge to feed,
Each has his District, and his Bounds decreed:
Combin'd in common Int'rest with his own,

But not to pass the Pigeons *Rubicon*.   1255
  Here ends the Reign of this pretended Dove;
All Prophecies accomplish'd from above,
For *Shiloh* comes the Scepter to Remove.
Reduc'd from Her Imperial High Abode,
Like *Dyonysius* to a private Rod: 1260
The Passive Church, that with pretended Grace
Did Her distinctive Mark in Duty place,
Now Touch'd, Reviles Her Maker to his Face.
  What after happen'd is not hard to guess;
The small Beginnings had a large Encrease,   1265
And Arts and Wealth succeed (the secret spoils of Peace.)
'Tis said the Doves repented, tho' too late,
Become the Smiths of their own Foolish Fate:
Nor did their Owner hasten their ill hour:
But, sunk in Credit, they decreas'd in Pow'r: 1270
Like Snows in warmth that mildly pass away,
Dissolving in the Silence of Decay.
  The *Buzzard* not content with equal place,
Invites the feather'd *Nimrods* of his Race,
To hide the thinness of their Flock from Sight,   1275
And all together make a seeming, goodly Flight:
But each have sep'rate Int'rests of their own,
Two *Czars*, are one too many for a Throne.
Nor can th' Usurper long abstain from Food,
Already he has tasted Pigeons Blood: 1280
And may be tempted to his former fare,
When this Indulgent Lord shall late to Heav'n repair.
Bare benting times, and moulting Months may come,
When lagging late, they cannot reach their home:
Or Rent in Schism, (for so their Fate decrees,)   1285
Like the Tumultuous Colledge of the Bees;
They fight their Quarrel, by themselves opprest,
The Tyrant smiles below, and waits the falling feast.
  Thus did the gentle *Hind* her fable end,
Nor would the *Panther* blame it, nor commend;   1290
But, with affected Yawnings at the close,
Seem'd to require her natural repose.
For now the streaky light began to peep;

1275 their] the *D*

And setting stars admonish'd both to sleep.
The Dame withdrew, and, wishing to her Guest   1295
The peace of Heav'n, betook her self to rest.
Ten thousand Angels on her slumbers waite
With glorious Visions of her future state.

A Song for St CECILIA's Day, 1687

I

FROM Harmony, from heav'nly Harmony
This universal Frame began.
When Nature underneath a heap
Of jarring Atomes lay,
And cou'd not heave her Head,   5
The tuneful Voice was heard from high,
Arise ye more than dead.
Then cold, and hot, and moist, and dry,
In order to their stations leap,
And MUSICK'S pow'r obey.   10
From Harmony, from heav'nly Harmony
This universal Frame began:
From Harmony to Harmony
Through all the compass of the Notes it ran,
The Diapason closing full in Man.   15

II

What Passion cannot MUSICK raise and quell!
When *Jubal* struck the corded Shell,
His list'ning Brethren stood around
And wond'ring, on their Faces fell
To worship that Celestial Sound.   20
Less than a God they thought there cou'd not dwell
Within the hollow of that Shell
That spoke so sweetly and so well.
What Passion cannot MUSICK raise and quell!

III

The TRUMPETS loud Clangor   25
Excites us to Arms
With shrill Notes of Anger
And mortal Alarms.
The double double double beat
Of the thundring DRUM   30
Cryes, hark the Foes come;
Charge, Charge, 'tis too late to retreat.

A Song. Text from the first edition, 1687. Reprinted in Examen Poeticum, *1693*

IV

The soft complaining FLUTE
In dying Notes discovers
The Woes of hopeless Lovers,   35
Whose Dirge is whisper'd by the warbling LUTE.

V

Sharp VIOLINS proclaim
Their jealous Pangs, and Desperation,
Fury, frantick Indignation,
Depth of Pains, and height of Passion,   40
For the fair, disdainful Dame.

VI

But oh! what Art can teach
What human Voice can reach
The sacred ORGANS praise?
Notes inspiring holy Love,   45
Notes that wing their heav'nly ways
To mend the Choires above.

VII

Orpheus cou'd lead the savage race;
And Trees unrooted left their place;
Sequacious of the Lyre: 50
But bright *CECILIA* rais'd the wonder high'r;
When to her ORGAN, vocal Breath was giv'n
An Angel heard, and straight appear'd
Mistaking Earth for Heaven.

Grand CHORUS

As from the pow'r of sacred Lays   55
   The Spheres began to move,
And sung the great Creator's praise
   To all the bless'd above;
So when the last and dreadful hour
This crumbling Pageant shall devour,   60
The TRUMPET *shall be heard on high,*
The Dead shall live, the Living die,
And MUSICK *shall untune the Sky.*

[*Lines on* Milton]

THREE *Poets*, in three distant *Ages* born,
  Greece, *Italy*, and *England* did adorn.
The *First* in loftiness of thought Surpass'd;
The *Next* in Majesty; in both the *Last*.
The force of *Nature* cou'd no farther goe: 5
To make a *Third* she joynd the former two.

Lines on Milton. *Text from* Paradise Lost. A Poem in Twelve Books. . . . The Fourth
Edition, *1688*

BRITANNIA REDIVIVA

A POEM ON THE
BIRTH OF THE PRINCE

Dii Patrii Indigetes, & Romule, Vestaque Mater,
Quæ Tuscum Tiberim, & Romana Palatia servas,
Hunc saltem everso Puerum *succurrere sæclo*
Ne prohibete: satis jampridem sanguine nostro
Laomedonteæ luimus Perjuria *Trojæ.*
                                      VIRG. Georg. I.

BRITANNIA REDIVIVA

A POEM ON THE PRINCE
Born on the 10*th* of *June,* 1688

O UR Vows are heard betimes! and Heaven takes care
    To grant, before we can conclude the Pray'r:
Preventing Angels met it half the way,
And sent us back to Praise, who came to Pray.

  Just on the Day, when the high mounted Sun   5
Did farthest in his Northern Progress run,
He bended forward and ev'n stretch'd the Sphere
Beyond the limits of the lengthen'd year;
To view a Brighter Sun in *Britaine* Born;
That was the Bus'ness of his longest Morn,   10
The Glorious Object seen t'was time to turn.

  Departing Spring cou'd only stay to shed
Her bloomy beauties on the Genial Bed,
But left the manly Summer in her sted,
With timely Fruit the longing Land to chear,   15
And to fulfill the promise of the year.
Betwixt two Seasons comes th' Auspicious Heir,
This Age to blossom, and the next to bear.

  (*a*) Last solemn Sabbath saw the Church attend;
The Paraclete in fiery Pomp descend;   20
But when his Wondrous (*b*) Octave rowl'd again,
He brought a Royal Infant in his Train.

        (*a*) *Whit-Sunday.*   (*b*) *Trinity-Sunday.*

Britannia Rediviva. Text from the first edition, 1688, collated with the edition of c. 1691

So great a Blessing to so good a King
None but th' Eternal Comforter cou'd bring.
    Or did the Mighty Trinity conspire, 25
As once, in Council to Create our Sire?
It seems as if they sent the New-Born Guest
To wait on the Procession of their Feast;
And on their Sacred Anniverse decree'd
To stamp their Image on the promis'd Seed. 30
Three Realms united, and on One bestow'd,
An Emblem of their Mystick Union show'd:
The Mighty Trine the Triple Empire shar'd,
As every Person wou'd have One to guard.
    Hail Son of Pray'rs! by holy Violence 35
Drawn down from Heav'n; but long be banish'd thence,
And late to thy Paternal Skyes retire:
To mend our Crimes whole Ages wou'd require:
To change th' inveterate habit of our Sins,
And finish what thy Godlike Sire begins. 40
Kind Heav'n, to make us *English-Men* again,
No less can give us than a Patriarchs Reign.
    The Sacred Cradle to your Charge receive
Ye Seraphs, and by turns the Guard relieve;
Thy Father's Angel and Thy Father joyn 45
To keep Possession, and secure the Line,
But long defer the Honours of thy Fate,
Great may they be like his, like his be late.
That *James* this running Century may view,
And give his Son an Auspice to the New. 50
    Our wants exact at least that moderate stay:
For see the (*c*) Dragon winged on his way,
To watch the (*d*) Travail, and devour the Prey.
Or, if Allusions may not rise so high,
Thus, when *Alcides* rais'd his Infant Cry, 55
The Snakes besieg'd his Young Divinity:
But vainly with their forked Tongues they threat;
For Opposition makes a Heroe Great.
To needful Succour all the Good will run;
And *Jove* assert the Godhead of his Son. 60

(*c*) *Alluding only to the Common-wealth Party, here and in other places of the Poem.*
(*d*) Rev. 12. v. 4.

O still repining at your present state,
Grudging your selves the Benefits of Fate,
Look up, and read in Characters of Light
A Blessing sent you in your own Despight.
The Manna falls, yet that Cœlestial Bread   65
Like *Jews* you munch, and murmure while you feed.
May not your Fortune be like theirs, Exil'd,
Yet forty Years to wander in the Wild:
Or if it be, may *Moses* live at least
To lead you to the Verge of promis'd Rest.   70
   Tho' Poets are not Prophets, to foreknow
What Plants will take the Blite, and what will grow,
By tracing Heav'n his Footsteps may be found:
Behold! how awfully He walks the round!
God is abroad, and wondrous in his ways,   75
The Rise of Empires, and their Fall surveys;
More (might I say) than with an usual Eye,
He sees his bleeding Church in Ruine lye,
And hears the Souls of Saints beneath his Altar cry.
Already has he lifted high, the (*e*) Sign   80
Which Crown'd the Conquering Arms of *Constantine*:
The (*f*) Moon grows pale at that presaging sight,
And half her Train of Stars have lost their Light.
   Behold another (*g*) *Sylvester*, to bless
The Sacred Standard and secure Success;   85
Large of his Treasures, of a Soul so great,
As fills and crowds his Universal Seat.
   Now view at home a (*h*) second *Constantine*;
(The former too, was of the *Brittish* Line)
Has not his healing Balm your Breaches clos'd,   90
Whose Exile many sought, and few oppos'd?
Or, did not Heav'n by its Eternal Doom
Permit those Evils, that this Good might come?
So manifest, that ev'n the Moon-ey'd Sects
See *Whom* and *What* this Providence protects.   95
Methinks, had we within our Minds no more
Than that One Shipwrack on the Fatal (*i*) Ore,

(*e*) *The Cross.*   (*f*) *The Crescent, which the* Turks *bear for their Arms.*   (*g*) *The Pope in the time of* Constantine *the Great, alluding to the present Pope.*   (*h*) K. James *the Second.*   (*i*) *The Lemmon Ore.*

That only thought may make us think again,
What Wonders God reserves for such a Reign.
To dream that Chance his Preservation wrought,   100
Were to think *Noah* was preserv'd for nought;
Or the Surviving Eight were not design'd
To people Earth, and to restore their Kind.
   When humbly on the Royal Babe we gaze,
The Manly Lines of a Majestick face   105
Give awful joy: 'Tis Paradise to look
On the fair Frontispiece of Nature's Book;
If the first opening Page so charms the sight,
Think how th' unfolded Volume will delight!
   See how the Venerable Infant lyes   110
In early Pomp; how through the Mother's Eyes
The Father's Soul, with an undaunted view
Looks out, and takes our Homage as his due.
See on his future Subjects how He smiles,
Nor meanly flatters, nor with craft beguiles;   115
But with an open face, as on his Throne,
Assures our Birthrights, and assumes his own.
   Born in broad Day-light, that th' ungrateful Rout
May find no room for a remaining doubt:
Truth, which it self is light, does darkness shun,   120
And the true Eaglet safely dares the Sun.
   (*k*) Fain wou'd the Fiends have made a dubious birth,
Loth to confess the Godhead cloath'd in Earth.
But sickned after all their baffled lyes,
To find an Heir apparent of the Skyes: 125
Abandon'd to despair, still may they grudge,
And owning not the Saviour, prove the Judge.
   Not Great (*l*) *Æneas* stood in plainer Day,
When, the dark mantling Mist dissolv'd away,
He to the *Tyrians* shew'd his sudden face,   130
Shining with all his Goddess Mother's Grace:
For She her self had made his Count'nance bright,
Breath'd honour on his eyes, and her own Purple Light.

(*k*) *Alluding to the Temptations in the Wilderness.*   (*l*) Virg. *Æneid.* **I.**

---

100 wrought,] wrought; *88* [*91*]

If our Victorious (*m*) *Edward*, as they say,
Gave *Wales* a Prince on that Propitious Day,   135
Why may not Years revolving with his Fate
Produce his Like, but with a longer Date?
One who may carry to a distant shore
The Terrour that his Fam'd Forefather bore.
But why shou'd *James* or his Young Hero stay   140
For slight Presages of a Name or Day?
We need no *Edward*'s Fortune to adorn
That happy moment when our Prince was born:
Our Prince adorns his Day, and Ages hence
Shall wish his Birth-day for some future Prince.   145
　(*n*) Great *Michael*, Prince of all th' Ætherial Hosts,
And what e're In-born Saints our *Britain* boasts;
And thou, th' (*o*) adopted Patron of our Isle,
With chearful Aspects on this Infant smile:
The Pledge of Heav'n, which dropping from above,   150
Secures our Bliss, and reconciles his Love.
　Enough of Ills our dire Rebellion wrought,
When, to the Dregs, we drank the bitter draught;
Then airy Atoms did in Plagues conspire,
Nor did th' avenging Angel yet retire,   155
But purg'd our still encreasing Crimes with Fire.
Then perjur'd Plots, the still impending Test,
And worse; but Charity conceals the Rest:
Here stop the Current of the sanguine flood,
Require not, Gracious God, thy Martyrs Blood;   160
But let their dying pangs, their living toyl,
Spread a Rich Harvest through their Native Soil:
A Harvest ripening for another Reign,
Of which this Royal Babe may reap the Grain.
　Enough of Early Saints one Womb has giv'n;   165
Enough encreas'd the Family of Heav'n:
Let them for his, and our Attonement go;
And Reigning blest above, leave him to Rule below.
　Enough already has the Year foreslow'd
His wonted Course, the Seas have overflow'd,   170
The Meads were floated with a weeping Spring,

(*m*) Edw. *the black Prince, Born on Trinity-Sunday.*   (*n*) *The Motto of the Poem*
explain'd.   (*o*) *St.* George.

And frighten'd birds in Woods forgot to sing;
The Strong-limb'd Steed beneath his harness faints,
And the same shiv'ring sweat his Lord attaints.
When will the Minister of Wrath give o're?   175
Behold him; at (*p*) *Araunah*'s threshing-floor.
He stops, and seems to sheath his flaming brand;
Pleas'd with burnt Incense, from our *David*'s hand.
David has bought the *Jebusites* abode,
And rais'd an Altar to the Living God.   180
   Heav'n, to reward him, make his Joys sincere;
No future Ills, nor Accidents appear
To sully and pollute the Sacred Infant's Year.
Five Months to Discord and Debate were giv'n:
He sanctifies the yet remaining Sev'n.   185
Sabbath of Months! henceforth in Him be blest,
And prelude to the Realms perpetual Rest!
   Let his Baptismal Drops for us attone;
Lustrations for (*q*) Offences not his own.
Let Conscience, which is Int'rest ill disguis'd,   190
In the same Font be cleans'd, and all the Land Baptiz'd.
   (*r*) Un-nam'd as yet; at least unknown to Fame:
Is there a strife in Heav'n about his Name?
Where every Famous Predecessour vies,
And makes a Faction for it in the Skies?   195
Or must it be reserv'd to thought alone?
Such was the Sacred (*s*) *Tetragrammaton*.
Things worthy silence must not be reveal'd:
Thus the true Name of (*t*) *Rome* was kept conceal'd,
To shun the Spells, and Sorceries of those   200
Who durst her Infant Majesty oppose.
But when his tender strength in time shall rise
To dare ill Tongues, and fascinating Eyes;
This Isle, which hides the little Thund'rer's Fame,
Shall be too narrow to contain his Name: 205
Th' Artillery of Heav'n shall make him known;
(*u*) *Crete* cou'd not hold the God, when *Jove* was grown.

(*p*) *Alluding to the passage in the* I. *Book of Kings, Ch.* 24. v. 20th.   (*q*) *Original Sin.*   (*r*) *The Prince Christen'd, but not nam'd.*   (*s*) Jehovah, *or the name of God unlawful to be pronounc'd by the* Jews.   (*t*) *Some Authors say, That the true name of* Rome *was kept a secret;* ne hostes incantamentis Deos elicerent.   (*u*) Candie *where* Jupiter *was born and bred secretly.*

As *Joves* (*x*) Increase, who from his Brain was born,
Whom Arms and Arts did equally adorn,
Free of the Breast was bred, whose milky taste   210
Minerva's Name to *Venus* had debas'd;
So this Imperial Babe rejects the Food
That mixes Monarchs with *Plebeian* blood:
Food that his inborn Courage might controul,
Extinguish all the Father in his Soul,   215
And, for his *Estian* Race, and *Saxon* Strain,
Might re-produce some second *Richard*'s Reign.
Mildness he shares from both his Parents blood,
But Kings too tame are despicably good:
Be this the Mixture of this Regal Child,   220
By Nature Manly, but by Virtue Mild.

   Thus far the Furious Transport of the News,
Had to Prophetick Madness fir'd the Muse;
Madness ungovernable, uninspir'd,
Swift to foretel whatever she desir'd;   225
Was it for me the dark Abyss to tread,
And read the Book which Angels cannot read?
How was I punish'd when the (*y*) sudden blast,
The Face of Heav'n, and our young Sun o'recast!
Fame, the swift Ill, encreasing as she rowl'd,   230
Disease, Despair, and Death, at three reprises told:
At three insulting strides she stalk'd the Town,
And, like Contagion, struck the Loyal down.
Down fell the winnow'd Wheat; but mounted high,
The Whirl-wind bore the Chaff, and hid the Sky.   235
Here black Rebellion shooting from below
(As Earth's (*z*) Gigantick brood by moments grow)
And here the Sons of God are petrify'd with Woe:
An *Appoplex* of Grief! so low were driv'n
The Saints, as hardly to defend their Heav'n.   240

   As, when pent Vapours run their hollow round,
Earth-quakes, which are Convulsions of the ground,
Break bellowing forth, and no Confinement brook,
Till the Third settles, what the Former shook;

(*x*) Pallas, *or* Minerva; *said by the Poets, to have been bred up by Hand.* (*y*) *The sudden false Report of the Prince's Death.* (*z*) *Those Gyants are feign'd to have grown 15 Ells every day.*

Such heavings had our Souls; till slow and late,   245
Our life with his return'd, and Faith prevail'd on Fate.
By Prayers the mighty *Blessing* was implor'd,
To Pray'rs was granted, and by Pray'rs restor'd.
    So e're the (a) *Shunamite* a Son conceiv'd,
The Prophet promis'd, and the Wife believ'd,   250
A Son was sent, the Son so much desir'd,
But soon upon the Mother's Knees expir'd.
The troubled Seer approach'd the mournful Door,
Ran, pray'd, and sent his Past'ral-Staff before,
Then stretch'd his Limbs upon the Child, and mourn'd,   255
Till Warmth, and breath, and a new Soul return'd.
    Thus Mercy stretches out her hand, and saves
Desponding *Peter* sinking in the Waves.
    As when a sudden Storm of Hail and Rain
Beats to the ground the yet unbearded Grain,   260
Think not the hopes of Harvest are destroy'd
On the flat Field, and on the naked void;
The light, unloaded stem, from tempest free'd,
Will raise the youthful honours of his head;
And, soon restor'd by native vigour, bear   265
The timely product of the bounteous Year.
    Nor yet conclude all fiery *Trials* past,
For Heav'n will exercise us to the last;
Sometimes will check us in our full carreer,
With doubtful blessings, and with mingled fear;   270
That, still depending on his daily Grace,
His every mercy for an alms may pass.
With sparing hands will Dyet us to good;
Preventing Surfeits of our pamper'd blood.
So feeds the Mother-bird her craving young,   275
With little Morsels, and delays 'em long.
    True, this last blessing was a Royal Feast,
But, where's the Wedding Garment on the Guest?
Our Manners, as Religion were a Dream,
Are such as teach the Nations to *Blaspheme*.   280
In Lusts we wallow, and with Pride we swell,
And Injuries, with Injuries repell;
Prompt to Revenge, not daring to forgive,

        (a) *In the second Book of* Kings, *Chap.* 4*th.*

Our Lives unteach the Doctrine we believe;
Thus *Israel* Sin'd, impenitently hard,   285
And vainly thought the (*b*) present Ark their Guard;
But when the haughty *Philistims* appear,
They fled abandon'd, to their Foes, and fear;
Their God was absent, though his Ark was there.
Ah! lest our Crimes shou'd snatch this Pledge away,   290
And make our Joys the blessing of a day!
For we have sin'd him hence, and that he lives,
God to his promise, not our practice gives.
Our Crimes wou'd soon weigh down the guilty Scale,
But *James*, and *Mary*, and the Church prevail.   295
Nor (*c*) *Amaleck* can rout the *Chosen Bands*,
While *Hur* and *Aaron* hold up *Moses* hands.
    By living well, let us secure his days,
Mod'rate in hopes, and humble in our ways.
No force the Free-born Spirit can constrain,   300
But Charity, and great Examples gain.
Forgiveness is our thanks, for such a day;
'Tis Godlike, God in his own Coyn to pay.
    But you, Propitious Queen, translated here,
From your mild Heav'n, to rule our rugged Sphere,   305
Beyond the Sunny walks, and circling Year:
You, who your Native Clymate have bereft
Of all the Virtues, and the Vices left;
Whom Piety, and Beauty make their boast,
Though Beautiful is well in Pious lost;   310
So lost, as Star-light is dissolv'd away,
And melts into the brightness of the day;
Or Gold about the Regal Diadem,
Lost to improve the lustre of the Gem:
What can we add to your Triumphant Day?   315
Let the Great Gift the beauteous Giver pay.
For shou'd our thanks awake the rising Sun,
And lengthen, as his latest shaddows run,
That, tho' the longest day, wou'd soon, too soon be done.

(*b*) Sam. 4*th.* v. 10*th.*   (*c*) Exod. 17. v. 8*th.*

---

306 Year:] Year. *88* [*91*]   314 Gem:] Gem. *88* [*91*]

Let Angels voices, with their harps conspire,   320
But keep th' auspicious Infant from the Quire;
Late let him sing above, and let us know
No sweeter Musick, than his Cryes below.

    Nor can I wish to you, Great Monarch, more
Than such an annual Income to your store;   325
The Day, which gave this *Unit*, did not shine
For a less Omen, than to fill the *Trine*.
After a *Prince*, an *Admiral* beget,
The *Royal Sov'raign* wants an Anchor yet.
Our Isle has younger Titles still in store,   330
And when th' exhausted Land can yield no more,
Your Line can force them from a Foreign shore.

    The Name of Great, your Martial mind will sute,
But Justice, is your Darling Attribute:
Of all the *Greeks*, 'twas but (*d*)one *Hero's* due,   335
And, in him, *Plutarch* Prophecy'd of you.
A Prince's favours but on few can fall,
But Justice is a Virtue shar'd by all.

    Some Kings the name of Conq'rours have assum'd,
Some to be Great, some to be Gods presum'd;   340
But boundless pow'r, and arbitrary Lust
Made Tyrants still abhor the Name of Just;
They shun'd the praise this Godlike Virtue gives,
And fear'd a Title, that reproach'd their Lives.

    The Pow'r from which all Kings derive their state,   345
Whom they pretend, at least, to imitate,
Is equal both to punish and reward;
For few wou'd love their God, unless they fear'd.

    Resistless Force and Immortality
Make but a Lame, Imperfect Deity: 350
Tempests have force unbounded to destroy,
And Deathless Being ev'n the Damn'd enjoy,
And yet Heav'ns Attributes, both last and first,
One without life, and one with life accurst;
But Justice is Heav'ns self, so strictly He,   355
That cou'd it fail, the God-head cou'd not be.

      (*d*)   Aristides, *see his Life in* Plutarch.

---

324 Monarch,] Monarch *88* [*91*]

This Virtue is your own; but Life and State
Are One to Fortune subject, One to Fate:
Equal to all, you justly frown or smile,
Nor Hopes, nor Fears your steady Hand beguile;   } 360
Your self our Ballance hold, the Worlds, our Isle.

THE PROLOGUE and EPILOGUE
to the *HISTORY OF BACON IN VIRGINIA*

PROLOGUE

Spoken by a Woman

PLAYS you will have; and to supply your Store,
  Our Poets trade to ev'ry Foreign Shore:
This is the Product of *Virginian* Ground,
And to the Port of *Covent-Garden* bound.
Our Cargo is, or should at least, be Wit: 5
Bless us from you damn'd Pyrates of the Pit:
And Vizard-Masks, those dreadful Apparitions;
She-Privateers, of Venomous Conditions,   }
That clap us oft aboard with *French* Commissions.
You Sparks, we hope, will wish us happy Trading;   10
For you have Ventures in our Vessel's Lading;
And tho you touch at this or t'other Nation;
Yet sure *Virginia* is your dear Plantation.
Expect no polish'd Scenes of Love shou'd rise
From the rude Growth of *Indian* Colonies.   15
Instead of Courtship, and a tedious pother,
They only tip the Wink at one another;   }
Nay often the whole Nation, pig together.
You Civil *Beaus*, when you pursue the Game,
With manners mince the meaning of—that same: } 20
But ev'ry part has there its proper Name.   }

The Prologue and Epilogue. Text from the separate edition of 1689. See Commentary

Good Heav'ns defend me, who am yet unbroken
From living there, where such Bug-words are spoken:
Yet surely, Sirs, it does good Stomachs show,
To talk so savour'ly of what they do.   25
But were I Bound to that broad speaking land,
What e're they said, I would not understand,
But innocently, with a Ladies Grace,
Wou'd learn to whisk my Fan about my Face.
However, to secure you, let me swear,   30
That no such base *Mundungus* Stuff is here.
We bring you of the best the Soyl affords:
Buy it for once, and take it on our Words.
You wou'd not think a Countrey-Girl the worse,
If clean and wholsome, tho her Linnen's course.   35
Such are our Scenes; and I dare boldly say,
You may laugh less at a far better Play.
The Story's true; the Fact not long a-go;
The *Hero* of our Stage was *English* too:
And bate him one small frailty of Rebelling,   40
As brave as e're was born at *Iniskelling*.

EPILOGUE

Spoken by a Woman

By this time you have lik'd, or damn'd our Plot;
Which tho I know, my Epilogue knows not:
For if it cou'd foretel, I shou'd not fail,
In decent wise, to thank you, or to rail.
But he who sent me here, is positive,   5
This Farce of Government is sure to thrive;
Farce is a Food as proper for your lips,
As for *Green-Sickness*, crumpt Tobacco-pipes.
Besides, the Author's dead, and here you sit,
Like the Infernal Judges of the Pit: 10
Be merciful; for 'tis in you this day,
To save or damn her Soul; and that's her Play.
She who so well cou'd Love's kind Passion paint,
We piously believe, must be a Saint:

Men are but Bunglers, when they wou'd express   15
The sweets of Love, the dying tenderness;
But Women, by their own abundance, measure,
And when they write, have deeper sense of Pleasure.
Yet tho her Pen did to the Mark arrive,
'Twas common Praise, to please you, when alive;   20
But of no other Woman, you have read,
Except this one, to please you, now she's dead.
'Tis like the Fate of Bees, whose golden pains,
Themselves extinguish'd, in their Hive remains.
Or in plain terms to speak, before we go,   25
What you young Gallants, by experience, know,
This is an Orphan Child; a bouncing Boy,
'Tis late to lay him out, or to destroy.
Leave your Dog-tricks, to lie and to forswear,
Pay *you* for Nursing, and we'll keep him here.   30

PROLOGUE and EPILOGUE
to *DON SEBASTIAN*

PROLOGUE
To DON SEBASTIAN King of *Portugal*

Spoken by a Woman

THE Judge remov'd, tho he's no more My Lord,
    May plead at Bar, or at the Council-Board:
So may cast Poets write; there's no Pretension,
To argue loss of Wit from loss of Pension.
Your looks are cheerful; and in all this place   5
I see not one, that wears a damning face.
The *British* Nation, is too brave to show,
Ignoble vengeance, on a vanquish'd foe.
At least be civil to the Wretch imploring;
And lay your Paws upon him, without roaring: 10

Prologue and Epilogue. Text from Don Sebastian, King of Portugal: A Tragedy, *1690*,
collated with the edition of 1692
  Prologue. 8 foe.] foe, *90 92*

Suppose our Poet was your foe before;
Yet now, the bus'ness of the Field is o'er;
'Tis time to let your Civil Wars alone,
When Troops are into Winter-quarters gone.
Jove was alike to *Latian* and to *Phrygian*;   15
And you well know, a Play's of no Religion.
Take good advice, and please your selves this day;
No matter from what hands you have the Play.
Among good Fellows ev'ry health will pass,
That serves to carry round another glass: 20
When, with full bowls of *Burgundy* you dine, ⎫
Tho at the Mighty Monarch you repine,   ⎬
You grant him still most Christian, in his Wine. ⎭

    Thus far the Poet, but his brains grow Addle;
And all the rest is purely from this Noddle.   25
You've seen young Ladies at the Senate door,
Prefer Petitions, and your grace implore;
How ever grave the Legislators were,
Their Cause went ne'er the worse for being fair.
Reasons as weak as theirs, perhaps I bring;   30
But I cou'd bribe you, with as good a thing.
I heard him make advances of good Nature;
That he for once, wou'd sheath his cutting Satyr:
Sign but his Peace, he vows he'll ne'er again
The sacred Names of Fops and Beau's profane.   35
Strike up the Bargain quickly; for I swear,
As Times go now, he offers very fair.
Be not too hard on him, with Statutes neither, ⎫
Be kind; and do not set your Teeth together,   ⎬
To stretch the Laws, as Coblers do their Leather. ⎭   40
Horses, by Papists are not to be ridden;
But sure the Muses Horse was ne'er forbidden.
For in no Rate-Book, it was ever found
That *Pegasus* was valued at Five-pound:
Fine him to daily Drudging and Inditing;   45
And let him pay his Taxes out, in Writing.

    28 were,] were. *90 92*   29 fair.] fair, *90 92*

EPILOGUE
To Don Sebastian, King of Portugall

Spoken betwixt Antonio *and* Morayma

Mor. I QUAK'D at heart for fear the Royal Fashion
  Shou'd have seduc'd Us two to Separation:
  To be drawn in, against our own desire,
  Poor I to be a Nun, poor You a Fryar.

Ant. I trembled when the Old Mans hand was in,   5
  He would have prov'd we were too near of kin:
  Discovering old Intrigues of Love, like t'other,
  Betwixt my Father and thy sinfull Mother;
  To make Us Sister Turk and Christian Brother.

Mor. Excuse me there; that League shou'd have been rather 10
  Betwixt your Mother and my *Mufti*-Father;
  'Tis for my own and my Relations Credit
  Your Friends shou'd bear the Bastard, mine shou'd get it.

Ant. Suppose us two *Almeyda* and *Sebastian*
  With Incest prov'd upon us:—

Mor.   Without question 15
  Their Conscience was too queazy of digestion.

Ant. Thou woud'st have kept the Councell of thy Brother
  And sinn'd till we repented of each other.

Mor. Beast as you are on Natures Laws to trample;
  'Twere fitter that we follow'd their Example 20
  And since all Marriage in Repentance ends,
  'Tis good for us to part while we are Friends.
  To save a Maids remorses and Confusions
  E'en leave me now before We try Conclusions.

Ant. To copy their Example first make certain 25
  Of one good hour like theirs before our parting;
  Make a debauch o're Night of Love and Madness;
  And marry when we wake in sober sadness.

Mor. I'le follow no new Sects of your inventing,
  One Night might cost me nine long months repenting: 30
  First wed, and if you find that life a fetter,
  Dye when you please, the sooner Sir the better:
  My wealth wou'd get me love e're I cou'd ask it:
  Oh there's a strange Temptation in the Casket:

All these Young Sharpers wou'd my grace importune,   35
And make me thundring Votes of lives and fortune.

PROLOGUE TO *THE PROPHETESS*

Spoken by Mr. BETTERTON

WHAT *Nostradame*, with all his Art can guess
      The Fate of our approaching *Prophetess*?
A Play which like a Prospective set right,
Presents our vast Expences close to sight;
But turn the Tube, and there we sadly view   5
Our distant gains; and those uncertain too.
A sweeping Tax, which on our selves we raise;
And all like you, in hopes of better days.
When will our Losses warn us to be wise!
Our Wealth decreases, and our Charges rise: 10
Money the sweet Allurer of our hopes,
Ebbs out in Oceans, and comes in by Drops.
We raise new Objects to provoke delight;
But you grow sated e're the second sight.
False Men, even so, you serve your Mistresses;   15
They rise three Storys, in their towring dress;
And after all, you love not long enough,
To pay the Rigging, e're you leave 'em off.
Never content, with what you had before;
But true to Change, and *English* Men all ore.   20
New Honour calls you hence; and all your Care
Is to provide the horrid pomp of War:
In Plume and Scarf, Jack-boots and Bilbo Blade
Your Silver goes, that should support our Trade,
[But we shall flourish, sure, when you are paid.]   25
Go unkind Hero's, leave our Stage to mourn,
Till rich from vanquish'd Rebels you return;

Prologue. Text from The Prophetess: or, The History of Dioclesian, *1690, collated with*
Poems on Affairs of State. Part III, *1698, and* The Annual Miscellany: For the Year
1694, 1708. See Commentary
      Spoken by Mr. BETTERTON. *om. 98*   3 which] that *98*   5 there] then *98*
6 gains] Gain *98*   8 hopes] hope *98*   12 in Oceans, and] by Oceans, but *98*
14 grow] are *98*   15 serve] use *98*   18 leave] turn *98*   21 New]
Now *98 08*   22 the horrid] for the fierce *98*   24 Your] The *98*   that]
which *98*   Trade, *98:* Trade. *90 08*   25 But . . . paid. *added in 98*

And the fat Spoyls of *Teague* in Tryumph draw,
His Firkin-Butter, and his Usquebaugh.
Go Conquerors of your Male and Female Foes;   30
Men without Hearts, and Women without Hose.
Each bring his Love, a *Bogland* Captive home,
Such proper Pages, will long Trayns become:
With Copper-Collars, and with brawny Backs,
Quite to put down the Fashion of our Blacks.   35
Then shall the pious Muses pay their Vows,
And furnish all their Lawrels for your brows;
Their tuneful Voice shall rise for your delights;
We want not Poets fit to sing your fights.
But you bright Beauties, for whose only sake,   40
These doughty Knights such dangers undertake,
When they with happy Gales are gone away,
With your propitious Presence grace our Play;
And with a sigh, their empty seats survey.
Then think on that bare Bench my Servant sate;   45
I see him Ogle still, and hear him Chat:
Selling facetious Bargains, and propounding
That witty Recreation, call'd Dum-founding.
Their Loss with patience, we will try to bear;
And wou'd do more to see you often here.   50
That our Dead Stage, Reviv'd by your fair eyes,
Under a Female Regency may rise.

32 *Bogland* 98 08: Bogland 90   34 Copper-Collars] Copper Culters 98   39
sing] Write 98   fights] Flights 08   40 bright] brisk 98   49 try]
strive 98   51 fair] bright 98

PROLOGUE, EPILOGUE and SONGS
from *AMPHITRYON*

PROLOGUE

To *Amphitryon*; or, *The Two Sosia's*

Spoken by Mrs. *Bracegirdle*

THE lab'ring Bee, when his sharp Sting is gone,
   Forgets his Golden Work, and turns a Drone:
Such is a Satyr, when you take away
That Rage, in which his Noble Vigour lay.
What gain you, by not suffering him to teize ye? 5
He neither can offend you, now, nor please ye.
The Honey-bag, and Venome, lay so near,
That both, together, you resolv'd to tear;
And lost your Pleasure, to secure your Fear.
How can he show his Manhood, if you bind him 10
To box, like Boys, with one Hand ty'd behind him?
This is plain levelling of Wit; in which
The Poor has all th' advantage, not the Rich.
The Blockhead stands excus'd, for wanting Sense;
And Wits turn Blockheads in their own defence. 15
Yet, though the Stages Traffick is undone,
Still *Julian's* interloping Trade goes on:
Though Satyr on the Theatre you smother,
Yet in Lampoons, you Libel one another.
The first produces still, a second Jig; 20
You whip 'em out, like School-boys, till they gig:
And, with the same success, we Readers guess;
For, ev'ry one, still dwindles to a less.
And much good Malice, is so meanly drest,
That we wou'd laugh, but cannot find the Jest. 25
If no advice your Rhiming Rage can stay,
Let not the Ladies suffer in the Fray.
Their tender Sex, is priviledg'd from War;
'Tis not like Knights, to draw upon the Fair.

Prologue, Epilogue and Songs. Text from Amphitryon; or, The Two Sosia's. A Comedy, *1690, collated with the edition of 1694*

What Fame expect you from so mean a Prize?   30
We wear no murd'ring Weapons, but our Eyes.
Our Sex, you know, was after yours design'd;   ⎫
The last Perfection of the Makers mind: ⎬
Heav'n drew out all the Gold for us, and left your Dross behind. ⎭
Beauty, for Valours best Reward, He chose;   35
Peace, after War; and after Toil, Repose.
Hence ye Prophane; excluded from our sights;   ⎫
And charm'd by Day, with Honour's vain delights, ⎬
Go, make your best of solitary Nights.   ⎭
Recant betimes, 'tis prudence to submit: 40
Our Sex, is still your Overmatch, in Wit:
We never fail, with new, successful Arts,
To make fine Fools of you; and all your Parts.

EPILOGUE

Spoken by *Phædra*. Mrs. *Mountfort*

I'M thinking, (and it almost makes me mad,)
How sweet a time, those Heathen Ladies had.
Idolatry, was ev'n their Gods own trade;
They Worshipt the fine Creatures they had made.
Cupid, was chief of all the Deities;   5
And Love was all the fashion, in the Skies.
When the sweet Nymph, held up the Lilly hand,
Jove, was her humble Servant, at Command.
The Treasury of Heav'n was ne're so bare,
But still there was a Pension for the Fair.   10
In all his Reign, Adultry was no Sin;
For *Jove*, the good Example did begin.
Mark, too, when he usurp'd the Husband's name,
How civilly he sav'd the Ladies fame.
The secret Joys of Love, he wisely hid;   15
But you, Sirs, boast of more, than e'er you did.
You teize your Cuckolds; to their face torment 'em;
But *Jove* gave his, new Honours to content 'em.
And, in the kind remembrance of the Fair,
On each exalted Son, bestow'd a Star.   20

For those good deeds, as by the date appears,
His Godship, flourish'd full Two thousand Years.
At last, when He and all his Priests grew old,
The Ladies grew in their devotion cold;
And, that false Worship wou'd no longer hold.   ⎫ 25
   Severity of Life did next begin;
(And always does, when we no more can Sin.)
That Doctrine, too, so hard, in Practice, lyes,
That, the next Age may see another rise.
Then, Pagan Gods, may, once again, succeed;   ⎫ 30
And *Jove*, or *Mars*, be ready, at our need,
To get young Godlings; and, so, mend our breed.   ⎭

SONGS

I

SONG

I

CELIA, that I once was blest
Is now the Torment of my Brest;
   Since to curse me, you bereave me
   Of the Pleasures I possest:
Cruel Creature, to deceive me!   5
   First to love, and then to leave me!

II

Had you the Bliss refus'd to grant,
   Then I had never known the want:
   But possessing once the Blessing,
   Is the Cause of my Complaint: 10
   Once possessing is but tasting;
   'Tis no Bliss that is not lasting.

III

Celia now is mine no more;
   But I am hers; and must adore:

Song. 4 Pleasures] Pleasure *Songs in Amphitryon, with the Musick* (S)   8 Then I] I
then S

Nor to leave her will endeavour;   15
Charms, that captiv'd me before,
No unkindness can dissever;
Love that's true, is Love for ever.

II

Mercury's SONG to *Phædra*

I

FAIR *Iris* I love, and hourly I dye,
    But not for a Lip, nor a languishing Eye:
She's fickle and false, and there we agree;
For I am as false, and as fickle as she:
We neither believe what either can say;   5
And, neither believing, we neither betray.

II

'Tis civil to swear, and say things of course;
We mean not the taking for better for worse.
When present, we love; when absent, agree:
I think not of *Iris*, nor *Iris* of me: 10
The Legend of Love no Couple can find
So easie to part, or so equally join'd.

III

A Pastoral Dialogue betwixt Thyrsis *and* Iris

I

Thyrsis. FAIR *Iris* and her Swain
        Were in a shady Bow'r;
    Where *Thyrsis* long in vain
        Had sought the Shepherd's hour:
At length his Hand advancing upon her snowy Breast; 5
    He said, O kiss me longer,
    And longer yet and longer,
        If you will make me Blest.

Mercury's Song. 1 Fair . . . love] For . . . sigh *S*   4 For . . . she] O these are the
Virtues that Captivate me *S*   12 equally] easily *S*
A Pastoral Dialogue. 4 Shepherd's] happy *S*

II

Iris.	An easie yielding Maid,	
	By trusting is undone;	10
	Our Sex is oft betray'd,	
	By granting Love too soon.	
	If you desire to gain me, your Suff'rings to redress;	
	Prepare to love me longer,	
	And longer yet, and longer,	15
	Before you shall possess.	

III

Thyrsis. The little Care you show,
  Of all my Sorrows past;
Makes Death appear too slow,
  And Life too long to last.   20
Fair *Iris* kiss me kindly, in pity of my Fate;
  And kindly still, and kindly,
   Before it be too late.

IV

Iris. You fondly Court your Bliss,
  And no Advances make;   25
'Tis not for Maids to kiss,
  But 'tis for Men to take.
So you may Kiss me kindly, and I will not rebell;
  And kindly still, and kindly,
   But Kiss me not and tell.   30

V

A RONDEAU

Chorus. Thus at the height we love and live,
  And fear not to be poor:
We give, and give, and give, and give,
  Till we can give no more:
But what to day will take away,   35
  To morrow will restore.
Thus at the heighth we love and live,
  And fear not to be poor.

26 kiss] give *S* 30 Kiss me not] doe not kiss *S*

PROLOGUE to *THE MISTAKES*

Enter Mr. *Bright.*

GENTLEMEN, *we must beg your pardon; here's no Prologue to be had to
day; Our New Play is like to come on, without a Frontispiece; as bald as
one of you young Beaux, without your Perriwig. I left our young Poet, sniveling
and sobbing behind the Scenes, and cursing some body that has deceiv'd him.*

Enter Mr. *Bowen.*

Hold your prating to the Audience: Here's honest Mr. Williams, *just come
in, half mellow, from the* Rose-Tavern. *He swears he is inspir'd with Claret,
and will come on, and that* Extempore *too, either with a Prologue of his own
or something like one: O here he comes to his Tryal, at all Adventures; for my
part I wish him a good Deliverance.*

Exeunt Mr. *Bright,* and Mr. *Bowen.*

Enter Mr. Williams.

Save ye Sirs, save ye! I am in a hopefull way.   ⎫
I shou'd speak something, in Rhyme, now, for the Play: ⎬
But the duce take me, if I know what to say.   ⎭
I'le stick to my Friend the Authour, that I can tell ye,
To the last drop of Claret, in my belly.   5
So far I'me sure 'tis Rhyme—that needs no granting:
And, if my verses feet stumble—you see my own are wanting.
Our young Poet, has brought a piece of work,   ⎫
In which, though much of Art there does not lurk,   ⎬
It may hold out three days—And that's as long as *Cork.*   ⎭ 10
But, for this Play—(which till I have done, we show not,)
What may be its fortune—By the Lord—I know not.
This I dare swear, no malice here is writ:
'Tis Innocent of all things—ev'n of wit.
He's no high Flyer—he makes no sky Rockets,   15
His Squibbs are only levell'd at your Pockets.
And if his Crackers light among your pelf
You are blown-up: if not, then he's blown-up himself.
By this time, I'me something recover'd of my fluster'd madness:
And, now, a word or two in sober sadness.   20

Prologue. Text from Harris's The Mistakes, or, The False Report: A Tragicomedy,
1691

Ours is a Common Play: and you pay down
A Common Harlots price—just half a Crown.
You'le say, I play the Pimp, on my Friends score;
But since 'tis for a Friend your gibes give o're:
For many a Mother has done that before.　　　　　25
How's this, you cry? an Actor write?—we know it;
But *Shakspear* was an Actor, and a Poet.
Has not Great *Johnsons* learning, often fail'd?
But *Shakspear*'s greater Genius, still prevail'd.
Have not some writing Actors, in this Age　　　　30
Deserv'd and found Success upon the Stage?
To tell the truth, when our old Wits are tir'd,
Not one of us, but means to be inspir'd.
Let your kind presence grace our homely cheer;
Peace and the Butt, is all our bus'ness here:　　　35
So much for that;—and the Devil take small beer.

PROLOGUE, EPILOGUE and SONGS
from *KING ARTHUR*

Prologue to the OPERA

Spoken by Mr. *Betterton*

SURE there's a Dearth of Wit in this dull Town,
When silly Plays so savoury go down:
As when Clipp'd Money passes, 'tis a sign
A Nation is not over-stock'd with Coin.
Happy is he, who, in his own Defence,　　　　　5
Can Write just level to your humble Sence;
Who higher than your Pitch can never go;
And doubtless, he must creep, who Writes below.
So have I seen in Hall of Knight, or Lord,
A weak Arm, throw on a long Shovel-Board,　　　10
He barely lays his Piece, bar Rubs and Knocks,
Secur'd by Weakness not to reach the Box.

Prologue, Epilogue and Songs. Text from King Arthur: or, The British Worthy. A Dramatick Opera, *1691, collated with the edition of 1695. See Commentary*

A Feeble Poet will his Bus'ness do;
Who straining all he can, comes up to you:
For if you like your Selves, you like him too.   } 15
An Ape his own Dear Image will embrace;
An ugly *Beau* adores a Hatchet Face:
So some of you, on pure instinct of Nature,
Are led, by Kind, t' admire your fellow Creature.
In fear of which, our House has sent this Day,   20
T' insure our New-Built-Vessel, call'd a Play.
No sooner Nam'd, than one crys out, These Stagers
Come in good time, to make more Work for Wagers.
The Town divides, if it will take, or no;
The Courtiers Bet, the Cits, the Merchants too;   } 25
A sign they have but little else to do.
Betts, at the first, were Fool-Traps; where the Wise
Like Spiders, lay in Ambush for the Flies:
But now they're grown a common Trade for all,
And Actions, by the News-Book, Rise and Fall.   } 30
Wits, Cheats, and Fops, are free of Wager-Hall.
One Policy, as far as *Lyons* carries;
Another, nearer home sets up for *Paris*.
Our Betts, at last, wou'd ev'n to *Rome* extend,
But that the Pope has prov'd our Trusty Friend.   35
Indeed, it were a Bargain, worth our Money,
Cou'd we insure another *Ottobuoni*.
Among the rest, there are a sharping Sett,
That Pray for us, and yet against us Bett:
Sure Heav'n it self, is at a loss to know,   40
If these wou'd have their Pray'rs be heard, or no:
For in great Stakes, we piously suppose,
Men Pray but very faintly they may lose.
Leave off these Wagers; for in Conscience Speaking,
The City needs not your new Tricks for Breaking: 45
And if you Gallants lose, to all appearing
You'll want an Equipage for Volunteering;
While thus, no Spark of Honour left within ye,
When you shou'd draw the Sword, you draw the Guinea.

The *EPILOGUE*

Spoken by Mrs. BRACEGIRDLE

I'VE had to Day a Dozen *Billet-Doux*
From *Fops*, and *Wits*, and *Cits*, and *Bowstreet-Beaux*;
Some from *Whitehal*, but from the *Temple* more;
A *Covent-Garden* Porter brought me four.
I have not yet read all: But, without feigning,   5
We *Maids* can make shrewd Ghesses at your Meaning.
What if, to shew your Styles, I read 'em here?
Me thinks I hear one cry, *Oh Lord, forbear:*
No, Madam, no; by Heav'n, that's too severe.
Well then, be safe—   10
But swear henceforwards to renounce all Writing,
And take this Solemn Oath of my Inditing,
As you love Ease, and hate Campagnes and Fighting.
Yet, 'Faith, 'tis just to make some few Examples:
What if I shew'd you one or two for Samples?   15
Pulls one out. Here's one desires my Ladiship to meet
At the kind Couch above in *Bridges-Street.*
Oh Sharping Knave! That wou'd have you know what,
For a Poor Sneaking Treat of *Chocolat.*
Pulls out another. Now, in the Name of Luck, I'll break this open,   20
Because I Dreamt last Night I had a Token;
The Superscription is exceeding pretty,
To the Desire of all the Town and City.
Now, *Gallants*, you must know, this pretious *Fop*,
Is Foreman of a Haberdashers-Shop: 25
One who devoutly Cheats; demure in Carriage;
And Courts me to the Holy Bands of Marriage.
But with a *Civil Inuendo* too,
My Overplus of Love shall be for you.
Reads.—*Madam, I swear your Looks are so Divine,*   30
When I set up, your Face shall be my Sign:
Tho Times are hard; to shew how I Adore you,
Here's my whole Heart, and half a Guinea for you.
But have a care of Beaux; They're false, my Honey;
And which is worse, have not one Rag of Money.   35
See how Maliciously the Rogue would wrong ye;

But I know better Things of some among ye.
My wisest way will be to keep the Stage,
And trust to the Good Nature of the Age;
And he that likes the *Musick* and the *Play*,   40
Shall be my Favourite Gallant to Day.

SONGS

I

*W*ODEN, first to thee,
  A Milk white Steed, in Battle won,
We have Sacrific'd.
Chor.   We have Sacrific'd.
Vers. Let our next Oblation be,   5
 To *Thor*, thy thundring Son,
 Of such another.
Chor.   We have Sacrific'd.
Vers. A third; (of *Friezeland* breed was he,)
 To *Woden*'s Wife, and to *Thor*'s Mother: 10
 And now we have atton'd all three:
 We have Sacrific'd.
Chor.   We have Sacrific'd.
2 *Voc.* The White Horse Neigh'd aloud.
 To *Woden* thanks we render.   15
 To *Woden*, we have vow'd.
Chor. To *Woden*, our Defender.
      [*The four last Lines in* CHORUS.
Vers. The Lot is Cast, and *Tanfan* pleas'd:
Chor. Of Mortal Cares you shall be eas'd,
 Brave Souls to be renown'd in Story.   20
 Honour prizing,
 Death despising,
 Fame acquiring
 By Expiring,
 Dye, and reap the fruit of Glory.   25
 Brave Souls to be renown'd in Story.

Vers. I call ye all,
    To *Woden*'s Hall;
    Your Temples round
    With Ivy bound,   30
    In Goblets Crown'd,
And plenteous Bowls of burnish'd Gold;
    Where you shall Laugh,
    And dance and quaff,
The Juice, that makes the *Britons* bold.   35

II

A Battle supposed to be given behind the Scenes, with Drums, Trumpets, and Military Shouts and Excursions: After which, the Britons, *expressing their Joy for the Victory, sing this Song of Triumph.*

COME if you dare, our Trumpets sound;
Come if you dare, the Foes rebound:
We come, we come, we come, we come,
Says the double, double, double Beat of the Thundring Drum.

    Now they charge on amain,   5
    Now they rally again:
The Gods from above the Mad Labour behold,
And pity Mankind that will perish for Gold.

The Fainting *Saxons* quit their Ground,
Their Trumpets Languish in the Sound;   10
They fly, they fly, they fly, they fly;
Victoria, Victoria, the Bold *Britons* cry.

    Now the Victory's won,
    To the Plunder we run:
We return to our Lasses like Fortunate Traders,   15
Triumphant with Spoils of the Vanquish'd Invaders.

III

Phil. \
sings. / HITHER this way, this way bend,
    Trust not that Malicious Fiend:
    Those are false deluding Lights,
    Wafted far and near by Sprights.
    Trust 'em not, for they'll deceive ye;   5
    And in Bogs and Marshes leave ye.

Chor. of Phil. Spirits.   Hither this way, this way bend.
Chor. of Grimb. Spirits. This way, this way bend.
Phil.⎱ If you step, no Danger thinking,
sings.⎰ Down you fall, a Furlong sinking: 10
      'Tis a Fiend who has annoy'd ye;
      Name but Heav'n, and he'll avoid ye.
Chor. of Phil. Spirits.   Hither this way, this way bend.
Chor. of Grimb. Spirits. This way, this way bend.
Philidels Spirits.   Trust not that Malicious Fiend.   15
Grimbalds Spirits.   Trust me, I am no Malicious Fiend.
Philidels Spirits.   Hither this way, *&c.*

.   .   .   .

[Grimbald] sings. Let not a Moon-born Elf mislead ye,
      From your Prey, and from your Glory.
      Too far, Alas, he has betray'd ye: 20
      Follow the Flames, that wave before ye:
      Sometimes sev'n, and sometimes one;
      Hurry, hurry, hurry, hurry on.

2

      See, see, the Footsteps plain appearing,
      That way *Oswald* chose for flying: 25
      Firm is the Turff, and fit for bearing,
      Where yonder Pearly Dews are lying.
      Far he cannot hence be gone;
      Hurry, hurry, hurry, hurry on.

.   .   .   .

Philidel sings.   Hither this way . . .   30

IV

Enter Shepherds and Shepherdesses.

1 Shepherd⎱ How blest are Shepherds, how happy their Lasses,
sings.⎰ While Drums and Trumpets are sounding Alarms!
      Over our Lowly Sheds all the Storm passes;
      And when we die, 'tis in each others Arms.
      All the Day on our Herds, and Flocks employing;   5
      All the Night on our Flutes, and in enjoying.
Chor. All the Day, *&c.*

2

Bright Nymphs of *Britain*, with Graces attended,
Let not your Days without Pleasure expire;
Honour's but empty, and when Youth is ended,   10
All Men will praise you, but none will desire.
Let not Youth fly away without Contenting;
Age will come time enough, for your Repenting.
Chor. Let not Youth, *&c.*
Here the Men offer their Flutes to the Women, which they refuse.

2 Shepherdess. Shepherd, Shepherd, leave Decoying,   15
    Pipes are sweet, a Summers Day;
    But a little after Toying,
      Women have the Shot to Pay.

Here are Marriage-Vows for signing,
    Set their Marks that cannot write: 20
After that, without Repining,
    Play and Welcom, Day and Night.
Here the Women give the Men Contracts, which they accept.

Chor.⎫ Come, Shepherds, lead up, a lively Measure;
of all.⎰ The Cares of Wedlock, are Cares of Pleasure:
But whether Marriage bring Joy, or Sorrow,   25
Make sure of this Day, and hang to Morrow.

V

Phil. WE must work, we must haste;
Noon-Tyde Hour, is almost past:
Sprights, that glimmer in the Sun,
Into Shades already run.
Osmond will be here, anon.   5

  .   .   .   .

Philidel approaches Emmeline, *sprinkling some of the Water over her Eyes,
out of the Vial.*
    Phil.   Thus, thus I infuse
        These Soveraign Dews.

IV. 23 up,] up *95*

Fly back, ye Films, that Cloud her sight,
And you, ye Chrystal Humours bright,
Your Noxious Vapours purg'd away,   10
Recover, and admit the Day.
Now cast your Eyes abroad, and see
   All but me.

VI

Airy Spirits appear in the Shapes of Men and Women.

Man sings.   OH Sight, the Mother of Desires,
     What Charming Objects dost thou yield!
      'Tis sweet, when tedious Night expires,
     To see the Rosie Morning guild
      The Mountain-Tops, and paint the Field!   5
     But, when *Clorinda* comes in sight,
     She makes the Summers Day more bright;
     And when she goes away, 'tis Night.
Chor.   When Fair *Clorinda* comes in sight, *&c.*

Wom. sings.   'Tis sweet the Blushing Morn to view;   10
     And Plains adorn'd with Pearly Dew:
     But such cheap Delights to see,
      Heaven and Nature,
      Give each Creature;
     They have Eyes, as well as we.   15
      This is the Joy, all Joys above,
       To see, to see,
       That only she,
      That only she we love!
Chor.   This is the Joy, all Joys above, *&c.*   20

Man sings.   And, if we may discover,
     What Charms both Nymph and Lover,
      'Tis, when the Fair at Mercy lies,
     With Kind and Amorous Anguish,
     To Sigh, to Look, to Languish,   25
      On each others Eyes!
Chor. of all   And if we may discover, *&c.*
Men & Wom.

VII

Osmond *strikes the Ground with his Wand: The Scene changes to a Prospect of Winter in Frozen Countries.*

Cupid *Descends.*

Cup. sings.　WHAT ho, thou *Genius* of the Clime, what ho!
　　　　　Ly'st thou asleep beneath those Hills of Snow?
　　　　　Stretch out thy Lazy Limbs; Awake, awake,
　　　　　And Winter from thy Furry Mantle shake.

Genius *Arises.*

Genius.　　What Power art thou, who from below,　　　　　5
　　　　　Hast made me Rise, unwillingly, and slow,
　　　　　From Beds of Everlasting Snow!
　　　　　See'st thou not how stiff, and wondrous old,
　　　　　Far unfit to bear the bitter Cold,
　　　　　I can scarcely move, or draw my Breath;　　　　10
　　　　　Let me, let me, Freeze again to Death.

Cupid.　　Thou Doting Fool, forbear, forbear;
　　　　　What, Dost thou Dream of Freezing here?
　　　　　At Loves appearing, all the Skie clearing,
　　　　　　The Stormy Winds their Fury spare:　　　　15
　　　　　Winter subduing, and Spring renewing,
　　　　　　My Beams create a more Glorious Year.
　　　　　Thou Doting Fool, forbear, forbear;
　　　　　What, Dost thou Dream of Freezing here?

Genius.　　Great Love, I know thee now;　　　　　　20
　　　　　Eldest of the Gods art Thou:
　　　　　Heav'n and Earth, by Thee were made.
　　　　　　Humane Nature,
　　　　　　Is thy Creature,
　　　　　Every where Thou art obey'd.　　　　　　25

Cupid.　　No part of my Dominion shall be waste,
　　　　　　To spread my Sway, and sing my Praise,
　　　　　　Ev'n here I will a People raise,
　　　　　Of kind embracing Lovers, and embrac'd.

Cupid *waves his Wand, upon which the Scene opens, and discovers a Prospect of Ice and Snow to the end of the Stage.*

Singers and Dancers, Men and Women, appear.

Man. See, see, we assemble,   30
   Thy Revels to hold:
   Though quiv'ring with Cold,
  We Chatter and Tremble.

Cupid. 'Tis I, 'tis I, 'tis I, that have warm'd ye;
   In spight of Cold Weather,   35
   I've brought ye together:
  'Tis I, 'tis I, 'tis I, that have arm'd ye.

Chor. 'Tis Love, 'tis Love, 'tis Love that has warm'd us;
   In spight of Cold Weather,
   He brought us together: 40
  'Tis Love, 'tis Love, 'tis Love that has arm'd us.

Cupid. Sound a Parley, ye Fair, and surrender;
  Set your selves, and your Lovers at ease;
   He's a Grateful Offender
   Who Pleasure dare seize: 45
  But the Whining Pretender
   Is sure to displease.

     2

  Since the Fruit of Desire is possessing,
   'Tis Unmanly to Sigh and Complain;
  When we Kneel for Redressing,   50
   We move your Disdain:
  Love was made for a Blessing,
   And not for a Pain.

  A Dance; after which the Singers and Dancers depart.

     VIII

As [Arthur] *is going to the Bridge, two Syrens arise from the Water; They
shew themselves to the Waste, and Sing.*

  1 Syren. O PASS not on, but stay,
     And waste the Joyous Day
     With us in gentle Play:
    Unbend to Love, unbend thee:
     O lay thy Sword aside,   5
     And other Arms provide;

    For other Wars attend thee,
     And sweeter to be try'd.
Chor. For other Wars, *&c.*
Both sing. Two Daughters of this Aged Stream are we;   10
    And both our Sea-green Locks have comb'd for thee;
    Come Bathe with us an Hour or two,
    Come Naked in, for we are so;
    What Danger from a Naked Foe?
    Come Bathe with us, come Bathe, and share,   15
    What Pleasures in the Floods appear;
    We'll beat the Waters till they bound,
    And Circle round, around, around,
    And Circle round, around.

IX

. . . Nymphs *and* Sylvans *come out from behind the Trees. Base and two* *Trebles sing the following Song to a* Minuet.
  Dance with the Song, all with Branches in their Hands.

   Song. HOW happy the Lover,
     How easie his Chain,
     How pleasing his Pain?
    How sweet to discover!
     He sighs not in vain.   5
    For Love every Creature
    Is form'd by his Nature;
    No Joys are above
    The Pleasures of Love.

  The Dance continues with the same Measure play'd alone.

2

    In vain are our Graces,   10
     In vain are your Eyes,
     If Love you despise;
    When Age furrows Faces,
     'Tis time to be wise.
    Then use the short Blessing,   15
    That Flies in Possessing:
    No Joys are above
    The Pleasures of Love.

X

Merlin waves his Wand; the Scene changes, and discovers the British Ocean in a Storm. Æolus in a Cloud above: Four Winds hanging, &c.

Æolus ⎫ YE Blust'ring Brethren of the Skies,
singing. ⎰ Whose Breath has ruffl'd all the Watry Plain,
    Retire, and let *Britannia* Rise,
  In Triumph o'er the Main.
      Serene and Calm, and void of fear,   5
      The Queen of Islands must appear:
      Serene and Calm, as when the Spring
      The New-Created World began,
      And Birds on Boughs did softly sing,
      Their Peaceful Homage paid to Man,   10
      While *Eurus* did his Blasts forbear,
      In favour of the Tender Year.
    Retreat, Rude Winds, Retreat,
    To Hollow Rocks, your Stormy Seat;
    There swell your Lungs, and vainly, vainly threat.   15

Æolus ascends, and the four Winds fly off. The Scene opens, and discovers a calm Sea, to the end of the House. An Island arises, to a soft Tune; Britannia seated in the Island, with Fishermen at her Feet, &c. The Tune changes; the Fishermen come ashore, and Dance a while; After which, Pan and a Nereide come on the Stage, and sing.

Pan *and* Nereide *Sing.*

  Round thy Coasts, Fair Nymph of *Britain*,
    For thy Guard our Waters flow:
Proteus all his Herd admitting,
    On thy Greens to Graze below.
  Foreign Lands thy Fishes Tasting,   20
  Learn from thee Luxurious Fasting.

Song of three Parts.

  For Folded Flocks, on Fruitful Plains,
  The Shepherds and the Farmers Gains,
    Fair *Britain* all the World outvyes;
  And *Pan,* as in *Arcadia* Reigns,   25
    Where Pleasure mixt with Profit lyes.

2

Though *Jasons* Office was Fam'd of old,
The *British* Wool is growing Gold;
   No Mines can more of Wealth supply:
It keeps the Peasant from the Cold,   30
   And takes for Kings the *Tyrian* Dye.

The last Stanza *sung over again betwixt* Pan *and the* Nereide. *After which
the former Dance is varied, and goes on.*

Enter Comus *with three Peasants, who sing the following Song in Parts.*

Com.	YOUR Hay it is Mow'd, and your Corn is Reap'd;
	Your Barns will be full, and your Hovels heap'd:
	Come, my Boys, come;
	Come, my Boys, come; 35
	And merrily Roar out Harvest Home;
	Harvest Home,
	Harvest Home;
	And merrily Roar out Harvest Home.
Chorus.	Come, my Boys, come, *&c.* 40
1 Man.	We ha' cheated the Parson, we'll cheat him agen;
	For why shou'd a Blockhead ha' One in Ten?
	One in Ten,
	One in Ten,
	For why shou'd a Blockhead ha' One in Ten? 45
Chorus.	One in Ten,
	One in Ten;
	For why shou'd a Blockhead ha' One in Ten?
2 [Man].	For Prating so long like a Book-learn'd Sot,
	Till Pudding and Dumplin burn to Pot; 50
	Burn to Pot,
	Burn to Pot;
	Till Pudding and Dumplin burn to Pot.
Chorus.	Burn to Pot, *&c.*
3 [Man].	We'll toss off our Ale till we canno' stand, 55
	And Hoigh for the Honour of Old *England*:
	Old *England*,
	Old *England*;
	And Hoigh for the Honour of Old *England*.
Chorus.	Old *England*, *&c.* 60

The Dance vary'd into a round Country-Dance.

Enter Venus.

Venus. Fairest Isle, all Isles Excelling,
    Seat of Pleasures, and of Loves;
  Venus here, will chuse her Dwelling,
    And forsake her *Cyprian* Groves.

2

Cupid, from his Fav'rite Nation,   65
    Care and Envy will Remove;
Jealousie, that poysons Passion,
    And Despair that dies for Love.

3

Gentle Murmurs, sweet Complaining,
    Sighs that blow the Fire of Love;   70
Soft Repulses, kind Disdaining,
    Shall be all the Pains you prove.

4

Every Swain shall pay his Duty,
    Grateful every Nymph shall prove;
And as these Excel in Beauty,   75
    Those shall be Renown'd for Love.

XI

The Scene opens above, and discovers the Order of the Garter.

(*Honour sings.*)

I

Hon. ST. *GEORGE,* the Patron of our Isle,
    A Soldier, and a Saint,
On that Auspicious Order smile,
    Which Love and Arms will plant.

2

Our Natives not alone appear   5
    To Court this Martiall Prize;
But Foreign Kings, Adopted here,
    Their Crowns at Home despise.

3

Our Soveraign High, in Aweful State,
His Honours shall bestow;   10
And see his Sceptr'd Subjects wait
On his Commands below.

A full Chorus of the whole Song: After which the Grand Dance.

TO SIR GEORGE ETHEREGE

Mr. D.—— Answer

To you who live in chill Degree,
(As Map informs) of Fifty three;
And do not much for Cold attone
By bringing thither Fifty one:
(Methinks) all Climes shou'd be alike,   5
From Tropick, e'en to Pole Artick;
Since you have such a Constitution,
As cannot suffer Diminution;
You can be old in grave Debate,
And young in Loves Affairs of State,   10
And both to Wives and Husbands show
The vigour of a Plenipo——
Like mighty Missioner you come,
Ad partes infidelium;
A work of wondrous Merit sure,   15
So far to go, so much endure,
And all to preach to German Dame,
Where sound of *Cupid* never came.
Less had you done, had you been sent,
As far as *Drake*, or *Pinto* went,   20
For Cloves and Nutmegs to the Line-a,
Or even for Oranges to *China*;
That had indeed been Charity
Where Love-sick Ladies helpless lye
Chop'd, and for want of Liquor dry;   25

To Sir George Etherege. Text from The History of Adolphus . . . With a Collection of Songs and Love-Verses. By several Hands, *1691 (HA), collated with* Sylvæ, *1702 (S).*
Mr. D.—— Answer] A Letter From Mr. *Dryden* to Sir *George Etheridge S*
    8 cannot suffer] no where suffers *S*   10 Loves Affairs] Love-affairs *S*   11
Husbands *S*: Husband *HA*   16 endure] t'endure *S*   21 and] or *S*   25
Chop'd] Chapt *S*

But you have made your Zeal appear,
Within the Circle of the Bear;
What Region of the World so dull,
That is not of your Labours full.
Triptolemus, (so Sing the Nine)   30
Strew'd plenty from his Cart Divine;
But (spight of all those Fable-makers)
He never sow'd on Almaine Acres;
No, that was left by fates Decree,
To be perform'd and sung by thee.   35
Thou break'st thro' Forms, with as much Ease
As the French King thro' Articles;
In grand Affairs thy days are spent
In waging weighty Complement,
With such as Monarchs represent;   40
They whom such vast Fatigues attend,
Want some soft minutes to unbend,
To shew the World, that now and then
Great Ministers are mortal Men.
Then Rhenish Rummers walk the Round,   45
In Bumpers every King is Crown'd;
Besides Three holy Miter'd Hectors,
And the whole Colledge of Electors;
No health of Potentate is sunk,
That pays to make his Envoy Drunk.   50
These Dutch delights I mention'd last
Suit not, I know, your English Tast,
For Wine, to leave a Whore, or Play,
Was ne'er your Excellencies way;
Nor need the Title give offence,   55
For here you were his Excellence;
For Gaming, Writing, Speaking, Keeping,
His Excellence for all but sleeping.
Now if you tope in Form, and Treat,
'Tis the sour Sawce, to the sweet Meat,   60
The Fine you pay for being Great.
Nay, there's a harder Imposition,

28 World] Earth's *S*   30 Sing] sung *S*   32 those] these *S*   41 whom]
who *S*   49 sunk] drunk *S*   55 the] this *S*   56 his] your *S*   62
there's] here's *S*

917.19. II   I

Which is (indeed) the Court Petition,
That setting Worldly Pomp aside,
(Which Poet has at Font defi'd.)   65
You wou'd be pleas'd in humble way,
To write a trifle call'd a Play:
This truly is, a Degradation,
But wou'd oblige the Crown and Nation,
Next to your Wise Negotiation: 70
If you pretend, as well you may,
Your high Degree, your Friends will say,
The Duke St. *Aignan* made a Play;
If Gallick Peer affect you scarce,
His Grace of B.⸺ has made a Farce,   75
And you whose comick Wit is Terseal,
Can hardly fall below Rehearsal.
Then finish what you once began,
But scrible faster if you can;
For yet no George, to our discerning,   80
E'er Writ without a Ten years warning.

TO Mr. Southern; ON HIS COMEDY,
called the WIVES EXCUSE

SURE there's a Fate in Plays; and 'tis in vain
To write, while these malignant Planets Reign:
Some very foolish Influence rules the Pit,
Not always kind to Sence, or just to Wit.
And whilst it lasts, let Buffoonry succeed,   5
To make us laugh; for never was more need.
Farce, in it self, is of a nasty scent;
But the gain smells not of the Excrement.
The *Spanish* Nymph, a Wit and Beauty too,
With all her Charms bore but a single show: 10
But, let a Monster *Muscovite* appear,
He draws a crowded Audience round the Year.

63 Court] Court's *S*   65 defi'd] deny'd *S*   74 Peer affect] Wit convince *S*
75 B.⸺] *Bucks S*   78 once] have *S*   81 E'er] Has *S*
To Mr. Southern. Text from The Wives Excuse: or, Cuckolds make Themselves.
A Comedy, *1692*

May be thou hast not pleas'd the Box and Pit,
Yet those who blame thy Tale, commend thy Wit;
So *Terence* Plotted; but so *Terence* Writ.   15
Like his thy Thoughts are true, thy Language clean,
Ev'n Lewdness is made Moral, in thy Scene.
The Hearers may for want of *Nokes* repine,
But rest secure, the Readers will be thine.
Nor was thy Labour'd *Drama*, damn'd or hiss'd,   20
But with a kind Civility, dismiss'd:
With such good manners as the *Wife did use,   *The Wife
Who, not accepting, did but just refuse.   *in the*
There was a glance at parting; such a look   *Play,* Mrs.
                                                Friendall.
As bids thee not give o're, for one rebuke.   25
But if thou wou'dst be seen, as well as read;
Copy one living Author, and one dead;
The Standard of thy Style, let *Etherege* be:
For Wit, th' Immortal Spring of *Wycherly*.
Learn after both, to draw some just Design,   30
And the next Age will learn to Copy thine.

ELEONORA:

A PANEGYRICAL POEM
Dedicated to the MEMORY of the Late
COUNTESS OF ABINGDON

—Superas evadere ad auras,
Hoc opus, hic labor est. Pauci, quos æquus amavit
Juppiter, aut ardens evexit ad æthera virtus;
Diis geniti potuere.   Virgil Æneid. l. 6.

TO THE RIGHT HONOURABLE
THE Earl of *Abingdon &c.*

MY LORD,

*T*HE *Commands, with which You honour'd me some Months ago, are now perform'd: They had been sooner; but betwixt ill health, some business, and many troubles, I was forc'd to deferr them till this time. Ovid, going to his Banishment, and Writing from on Shipbord to his Friends, excus'd the Faults of his Poetry by his Misfortunes; and told them, that good Verses never flow, but* 5 *from a serene and compos'd Spirit. Wit, which is a kind of* Mercury, *with Wings fasten'd to his Head and Heels, can flye but slowly, in a damp air. I therefore chose rather to Obey You late, than ill: if at least I am capable of writing any thing, at any time, which is worthy Your Perusal and Your Patronage. I cannot say that I have escap'd from a Shipwreck; but have only gain'd a Rock* 10 *by hard swimming; where I may pant a while and gather breath: For the Doctors give me a sad assurance, that my Disease never took its leave of any man, but with a purpose to return. However, my Lord, I have laid hold on the Interval, and menag'd the small Stock which Age has left me, to the best advantage, in performing this inconsiderable service to my Ladies Memory. We, who are* 15 *Priests of* Apollo, *have not the Inspiration when we please; but must wait till the God comes rushing on us, and invades us with a fury, which we are not able to resist: which gives us double strength while the Fit continues, and leaves us languishing and spent, at its departure. Let me not seem to boast, my Lord; for I have really felt it on this Occasion; and prophecy'd beyond my natural power.* 20 *Let me add, and hope to be believ'd, that the Excellency of the Subject contributed much to the Happiness of the Execution: And that the weight of thirty Years was taken off me, while I was writing. I swom with the Tyde, and the Water under me was buoyant. The Reader will easily observe, that I was transported, by the*

Eleonora. Text from the first edition, 1692

multitude and variety of my Similitudes; which are generally the product of a 25
luxuriant Fancy; and the wantonness of Wit. Had I call'd in my Judgment to
my assistance, I had certainly retrench'd many of them. But I defend them not;
let them pass for beautiful faults amongst the better sort of Critiques: For the
whole Poem, though written in that which they call Heroique Verse, is of the
Pindarique nature, as well in the Thought as the Expression; and as such, 30
requires the same grains of allowance for it. It was intended, as Your Lordship
sees in the Title, not for an Elegie; but a Panegyrique. A kind of Apotheosis,
indeed; if a Heathen Word may be applyed to a Christian use. And on all Occa-
sions of Praise, if we take the Ancients for our Patterns, we are bound by
Prescription to employ the magnificence of Words, and the force of Figures, to 35
adorn the sublimity of Thoughts. Isocrates *amongst the* Grecian *Orators; and*
Cicero, *and the younger* Pliny, *amongst the* Romans, *have left us their Pre-*
cedents for our security: For I think I need not mention the inimitable Pindar,
who stretches on these Pinnions out of sight, and is carried upward, as it were,
into another World. 40

    This at least, my Lord, I may justly plead, that if I have not perform'd so
well as I think I have, yet I have us'd my best endeavours to excel my self. One
Disadvantage I have had, which is, never to have known, or seen my Lady: And
to draw the Lineaments of her Mind, from the Description which I have receiv'd
from others, is for a Painter to set himself at work without the living Original 45
before him. Which the more beautiful it is, will be so much the more difficult for
him to conceive; when he has only a relation given him, of such and such Features
by an Acquaintance or a Friend; without the Nice Touches which give the best
Resemblance, and make the Graces of the Picture. Every Artist is apt enough to
flatter himself, (and I amongst the rest) that their own ocular Observations, 50
would have discover'd more perfections, at least others, than have been deliver'd
to them: Though I have receiv'd mine from the best hands, that is, from Persons
who neither want a just Understanding of my Lady's Worth, nor a due Venera-
tion for her Memory.

    Doctor Donn *the greatest Wit, though not the best Poet of our Nation,* 55
acknowledges, that he had never seen Mrs. Drury, *whom he has made immortal*
in his admirable Anniversaries; I have had the same fortune; though I have not
succeeded to the same Genius. However, I have follow'd his footsteps in the Design
of his Panegyrick, which was to raise an Emulation in the living, to Copy out the
Example of the dead. And therefore it was, that I once intended to have call'd 60
this Poem, the Pattern: And though on a second consideration, I chang'd the
Title into the Name of that Illustrious Person, yet the Design continues, and
Eleonora *is still the Pattern of Charity, Devotion, and Humility; of the best*
Wife, the best Mother, and the best of Friends.

And now, my Lord, though I have endeavour'd to answer Your Commands, yet 65
I cou'd not answer it to the World, nor to my Conscience, if I gave not Your
Lordship my Testimony of being the best Husband now living: I say my Testi-
mony only: For the praise of it, is given You by Your self. They who despise the
Rules of Virtue both in their Practice and their Morals, will think this a very
trivial Commendation. But I think it the peculiar happiness of the Countess of 70
Abingdon, to have been so truly lov'd by you, while she was living, and so grate-
fully honour'd, after she was dead. Few there are who have either had, or cou'd
have such a loss; and yet fewer who carried their Love and Constancy beyond the
Grave. The exteriours of Mourning, a decent Funeral, and black Habits, are the
usual stints of Common Husbands: and perhaps their Wives deserve no better than 75
to be mourn'd with Hypocrisie, and forgot with ease. But You have distinguish'd
Your self from ordinary Lovers, by a real, and lasting grief for the Deceas'd.
And by endeavouring to raise for her, the most durable Monument, which is
that of Verse. And so it wou'd have prov'd if the Workman had been equal to
the Work; and Your Choice of the Artificer, as happy as Your Design. Yet, as 80
Phidias when he had made the Statue of Minerva, *cou'd not forbear to ingrave*
his own Name, as Author of the Piece; so give me leave to hope, that by sub-
scribing mine to this Poem, I may live by the Goddess, and transmit my Name to
Posterity by the memory of Hers. 'Tis no flattery, to assure Your Lordship, that
she is remember'd in the present Age, by all who have had the Honour of her 85
Conversation and Acquaintance. And that I have never been in any Company
since the news of her death was first brought me, where they have not extoll'd her
Virtues; and even spoken the same things of her in Prose, which I have done in
Verse.

I therefore think my self oblig'd to thank Your Lordship for the Commission 90
which You have given me: How I have acquitted my self of it, must be left to the
Opinion of the World, in spight of any Protestation, which I can enter against
the present Age, as Incompetent, or Corrupt Judges. For my Comfort they are
but Englishmen, *and as such, if they Think Ill of me to Day, they are inconstant*
enough, to Think Well of me to Morrow. And, after all, I have not much to 95
thank my Fortune that I was born amongst them. The Good of both Sexes are so
few, in England, *that they stand like Exceptions against General Rules: And*
though one of them has deserv'd a greater Commendation, than I cou'd give her,
they have taken care, that I shou'd not tire my Pen, with frequent exercise on the
like Subjects; that Praises, like Taxes, shou'd be appropriated; and left almost as 100
Individual as the Person. They say my Talent is Satyre; if it be so, 'tis a Fruitful
Age; and there is an extraordinary Crop to gather. But a single hand is in-
sufficient for such a Harvest: They have sown the Dragons Teeth themselves; and
'tis but just they shou'd reap each other in Lampoons. You, my Lord, who have

the Character of Honour, though 'tis not my Happiness to know You, may stand 105
aside, with the small Remainders of the English Nobility, truly such, and unhurt
your selves, behold the mad Combat. If I have pleas'd You, and some few others,
I have obtain'd my end. You see, I have disabled my self, like an Elected Speaker
of the House; yet like him I have undertaken the Charge; and find the Burden
sufficiently recompenc'd by the Honour. Be pleas'd to accept of these my Unworthy 110
Labours; this Paper Monument; and let her Pious Memory, which I am sure
is Sacred to You, not only plead the Pardon of my many Faults, but gain me
Your Protection, which is ambitiously sought by,

MY LORD,
Your Lordship's
Most Obedient Servant,
John Dryden.

ELEONORA:

A PANEGYRICAL POEM
Dedicated to the MEMORY OF THE
Late Countess of *ABINGDON*

As, when some Great and Gracious Monarch dies,   *The Intro-*
  Soft whispers, first, and mournful Murmurs rise   *duction.*
Among the sad Attendants; then, the sound
Soon gathers voice, and spreads the news around,
Through Town and Country, till the dreadful blast   5
Is blown to distant Colonies at last;
Who, then perhaps, were off'ring Vows in vain,
For his long life, and for his happy Reign:
So slowly, by degrees, unwilling Fame
Did Matchless *Eleonora*'s fate proclaim,   10
Till publick as the loss, the news became.
   The Nation felt it, in th' extremest parts;
With eyes o'reflowing, and with bleeding hearts: *Of her*
But most the Poor, whom daily she supply'd;   *Charity.*
Beginning to be such, but when she dy'd.   15
For, while she liv'd, they slept in peace, by night;

Secure of bread, as of returning light;
And, with such firm dependence on the Day,
That need grew pamper'd; and forgot to pray:
So sure the Dole, so ready at their call,   20
They stood prepar'd to see the Manna fall.

    Such Multitudes she fed, she cloath'd, she nurst,
That she, her self, might fear her wanting first.
Of her Five Talents, other five she made;
Heav'n, that had largely giv'n, was largely pay'd: 25
And, in few lives, in wondrous few, we find
A Fortune, better fitted to the Mind.
Nor did her Alms from Ostentation fall,
Or proud desire of Praise; the Soul gave all:
Unbrib'd it gave; or, if a bribe appear,   30
No less than Heav'n; to heap huge treasures, there.

    Want pass'd for Merit, at her open door,
Heav'n saw, he safely might increase his Poor.
And trust their Sustenance with her so well,
As not to be at charge of Miracle.   35
None cou'd be needy, whom she saw, or knew;
All, in the Compass of her Sphear, she drew:
He who cou'd touch her Garment, was as sure,
As the first Christians of th' Apostles cure.
The distant heard, by Fame, her pious deeds;   40
And laid her up, for their extremest needs;
A future Cordial, for a fainting Mind;
For, what was ne're refus'd, all hop'd to find;
Each in his turn: The Rich might freely come,
As to a Friend; but to the Poor, 'twas Home.   45
As to some Holy House th' Afflicted came;
The Hunger-starv'd, the Naked, and the Lame;
Want and Diseases fled before her Name.
For zeal like hers, her Servants were too slow;
She was the first where need requir'd, to go;   50
Her self the Foundress, and Attendant too.

    Sure she had Guests sometimes to entertain,
Guests in disguise, of her Great Master's Train:
Her Lord himself might come, for ought we know;
Since in a Servant's form he liv'd below: 55
Beneath her Roof, he might be pleas'd to stay:

Or some benighted Angel, in his way
Might ease his Wings; and seeing Heav'n appear
In its best work of Mercy, think it there,
Where all the deeds of Charity and Love   60
Were in as constant Method, as above:
All carry'd on; all of a piece with theirs;
As free her Alms, as diligent her cares;
As loud her Praises, and as warm her Pray'rs.   64

*Of her pru-
dent Man-
agement.*

   Yet was she not profuse; but fear'd to wast,
And wisely manag'd, that the stock might last;
That all might be supply'd; and she not grieve
When Crouds appear'd, she had not to relieve.
Which to prevent, she still increas'd her store;
Laid up, and spar'd, that she might give the more: 70
So *Pharaoh*, or some Greater King than he,
Provided for the sev'nth Necessity:
Taught from above, his Magazines to frame;
That Famine was prevented e're it came.
Thus Heav'n, though All-sufficient, shows a thrift   75
In his Oeconomy, and bounds his gift:
Creating for our Day, one single Light;
And his Reflection too supplies the Night:
Perhaps a thousand other Worlds, that lye
Remote from us, and latent in the Sky,   80
Are lighten'd by his Beams, and kindly nurst;
Of which our Earthly Dunghil is the worst.

   Now, as all Vertues keep the middle line,
Yet somewhat more to one extreme incline,
Such was her Soul; abhorring Avarice,   85
Bounteous, but, almost bounteous to a Vice:
Had she giv'n more, it had Profusion been,
And turn'd th' excess of Goodness, into Sin.

*Of her
Humility.*

   These Vertues rais'd her Fabrick to the Sky;
For that which is next Heav'n, is Charity.   90
But, as high Turrets, for their Ay'ry steep
Require Foundations, in proportion deep:
And lofty Cedars, as far, upward shoot,
As to the neather Heav'ns they drive the root;
So low did her secure Foundation lye,   95
She was not Humble, but Humility.

Scarcely she knew that she was great, or fair,
Or wise, beyond what other Women are,
Or, which is better, knew; but never durst compare.
For to be consc'ious of what all admire,   100
And not be vain, advances Vertue high'r:
But still she found, or rather thought she found,
Her own worth wanting, others to abound:
Ascrib'd above their due to ev'ry one,
Unjust and scanty to her self alone.   105

*Of her
Piety.*

 Such her Devotion was, as might give rules
Of Speculation, to disputing Schools;
And teach us equally the Scales to hold
Betwixt the two Extremes of hot and cold;
That pious heat may mod'rately prevail,   110
And we be warm'd, but not be scorch'd with zeal.
Business might shorten, not disturb her Pray'r;
Heav'n had the best, if not the greater share.
An Active life, long Oraisons forbids;
Yet still she pray'd, for still she pray'd by deeds.   115
 Her ev'ry day was Sabbath: Only free
From hours of Pray'r, for hours of Charity.
Such as the *Jews* from servile toil releast;
Where works of Mercy were a part of rest:
Such as blest Angels exercise above,   120
Vary'd with Sacred Hymns, and Acts of Love;
Such Sabbaths as that one she now enjoys;
Ev'n that perpetual one, which she employs,
(For such vicissitudes in Heav'n there are)
In Praise alternate, and alternate Pray'r.   125
All this she practis'd here; that when she sprung
Amidst the Quires, at the first sight she sung.
Sung, and was sung her self, in Angels Lays;
For praising her, they did her Maker praise.
All Offices of Heav'n so well she knew,   130
Before she came, that nothing there was new.
And she was so familiarly receiv'd,
As one returning, not as one arriv'd.

*Of her
various
Vertues.*

 Muse, down again precipitate thy flight;
For how can Mortal Eyes sustain Immortal Light!   135
But as the Sun in Water we can bear,

Yet not the Sun, but his Reflection there,
So let us view her here, in what she was;
And take her Image, in this watry Glass:
Yet look not ev'ry Lineament to see;   140
Some will be cast in shades; and some will be
So lamely drawn, you scarcely know, 'tis she.
For where such various Vertues we recite,
'Tis like the Milky-Way, all over bright,
But sown so thick with Stars, 'tis undistinguish'd Light.   145

   Her Vertue, not her Vertues let us call,
For one Heroick comprehends 'em all:
One, as a Constellation is but one;
Though 'tis a Train of Stars, that, rolling on,
Rise in their turn, and in the Zodiack run.   150
Ever in Motion; now 'tis Faith ascends,
Now Hope, now Charity, that upward tends,
And downwards with diffusive Good, descends.

   As in Perfumes compos'd with Art and Cost,
'Tis hard to say what Scent is uppermost;   155
Nor this part Musk or Civet can we call,
Or Amber, but a rich Result of all;
So, she was all a Sweet; whose ev'ry part,
In due proportion mix'd, proclaim'd the Maker's Art.
No single Virtue we cou'd most commend;   160
Whether the Wife, the Mother, or the Friend;
For she was all, in that supreme degree,
That, as no one prevail'd, so all was she.
The sev'ral parts lay hidden in the Piece;
Th' Occasion but exerted that, or this.   165

   A Wife as tender, and as true withall,   *Of her Con-*
As the first Woman was, before her fall: *jugal Vir-*
Made for the Man, of whom she was a part;   *tues.*
Made, to attract his Eyes, and keep his Heart.
A second *Eve*, but by no Crime accurst;   170
As beauteous, not as brittle as the first.
Had she been first, still Paradise had bin,
And Death had found no entrance by her sin.
So she not only had preserv'd from ill
Her Sex and ours, but liv'd their Pattern still.   175

   Love and Obedience to her Lord she bore,

She much obey'd him, but she lov'd him more.
Not aw'd to Duty by superior sway;
But taught by his Indulgence to obey.
Thus we love God as Author of our good;   180
So Subjects love just Kings, or so they shou'd.
Nor was it with Ingratitude return'd;
In equal Fires the blissful Couple burn'd:
One Joy possess'd 'em both, and in one Grief they mourn'd.
His Passion still improv'd: he lov'd so fast   185
As if he fear'd each day wou'd be her last.
Too true a Prophet to foresee the Fate
That shou'd so soon divide their happy State:
When he to Heav'n entirely must restore
That Love, that Heart, where he went halves before.   190
Yet as the Soul is all in ev'ry part,
So God and He, might each have all her Heart.

Of her love to her Children.   So had her Children too; for Charity
Was not more fruitful, or more kind than she:
Each under other by degrees they grew;   195
A goodly Perspective of distant view:
Anchises look'd not with so pleas'd a Face
In numb'ring o'er his future *Roman* Race,
And Marshalling the Heroes of his name
As, in their Order, next to light they came;   200
Nor *Cybele* with half so kind an Eye,
Survey'd her Sons and Daughters of the Skie.
Proud, shall I say, of her immortal Fruit,
As far as Pride with Heav'nly Minds may suit.

Her care of their Education.   Her pious love excell'd to all she bore;   205
New Objects only multiply'd it more.
And as the Chosen found the perly Grain
As much as ev'ry Vessel cou'd contain;
As in the Blissfull Vision each shall share,
As much of Glory, as his Soul can bear;   210
So did she love, and so dispence her Care.
Her eldest thus, by consequence, was best;
As longer cultivated than the rest:
The Babe had all that Infant care beguiles,
And early knew his Mother in her smiles: 215
But when dilated Organs let in day

To the young Soul, and gave it room to play,
At his first aptness, the Maternal Love
Those Rudiments of Reason did improve:
The tender Age was pliant to command;   220
Like Wax it yielded to the forming hand:
True to th' Artificer, the labour'd Mind
With ease was pious, generous, just and kind;
Soft for Impression from the first, prepar'd,
Till Vertue, with long exercise, grew hard;   225
With ev'ry Act confirm'd; and made, at last
So durable, as not to be effac'd,
It turn'd to Habit; and, from Vices free,
Goodness resolv'd into Necessity.

    Thus fix'd she Virtue's Image, that's her own,   230
Till the whole Mother in the Children shone;
For that was their Perfection: she was such,
They never cou'd express her Mind too much.
So unexhausted her Perfections were,
That, for more Children, she had more to spare: 235
For Souls unborn, whom her untimely death
Depriv'd of Bodies, and of mortal breath:
And (cou'd they take th' Impressions of her Mind)
Enough still left to sanctifie her Kind.   239

Of her Friendship.

    Then wonder not to see this Soul extend
The bounds, and seek some other self, a Friend:
As swelling Seas to gentle Rivers glide,
To seek repose, and empty out the Tyde;
So this full Soul, in narrow limits pent,
Unable to contain her, sought a vent,   245
To issue out, and in some friendly breast
Discharge her Treasures, and securely rest.
T' unbosom all the secrets of her Heart,
Take good advice, but better to impart.
For 'tis the bliss of Friendship's holy state   250
To mix their Minds, and to communicate;
Though Bodies cannot, Souls can penetrate.
Fixt to her choice; inviolably true;
And wisely chusing, for she chose but few.
Some she must have; but in no one cou'd find   255
A Tally fitted for so large a Mind.

The Souls of Friends, like Kings in Progress are;
Still in their own, though from the Pallace far:
Thus her Friend's Heart her Country Dwelling was,
A sweet Retirement to a courser place: 260
Where Pomp and Ceremonies enter'd not;
Where Greatness was shut out, and Buis'ness well forgot.
 This is th' imperfect draught; but short as far
As the true height and bigness of a Star
Exceeds the Measures of th' Astronomer.   265
She shines above we know, but in what place,
How near the Throne, and Heav'ns Imperial Face,
By our weak Opticks is but vainly ghest;
Distance and Altitude conceal the rest.

*Reflections
on the
shortness of
her life.*

 Tho all these rare Endowments of the Mind   270
Were in a narrow space of life confin'd;
The Figure was with full Perfection crown'd;
Though not so large an Orb, as truly round.
 As when in glory, through the publick place,
The Spoils of conquer'd Nations were to pass,   275
And but one Day for Triumph was allow'd,
The Consul was constrain'd his Pomp to crowd;
And so the swift Procession hurry'd on,
That all, though not distinctly, might be shown;
So, in the straiten'd bounds of life confin'd,   280
She gave but glimpses of her glorious Mind:
And multitudes of Vertues pass'd along;
Each pressing foremost in the mighty throng;
Ambitious to be seen, and then make room,
For greater Multitudes that were to come.   285
 Yet unemploy'd no Minute slipt away;
Moments were precious in so short a stay.
The haste of Heav'n to have her was so great,
That some were single Acts, though each compleat;
But ev'ry Act stood ready to repeat.   290
 Her fellow Saints with busie care, will look
For her blest Name, in Fate's eternal Book;
And, pleas'd to be outdone, with joy will see
Numberless Vertues, endless Charity;
But more will wonder at so short an Age;   295
To find a Blank beyond the thirti'th Page;

And with a pious fear begin to doubt
The Piece imperfect, and the rest torn out.
But 'twas her Saviour's time; and, cou'd there be
A Copy near th' Original, 'twas she.

She dy'd in her thirty third year.
300

    As precious Gums are not for lasting fire,
They but perfume the Temple, and expire,
So was she soon exhal'd; and vanish'd hence;
A short sweet Odour, of a vast expence.

She vanish'd, we can scarcely say she dy'd;
For but a Now, did Heav'n and Earth divide:
She pass'd serenely with a single breath,
This Moment perfect health, the next was death.

305

One sigh, did her eternal Bliss assure;
So little Penance needs, when Souls are almost pure.

The manner of her death.
310

As gentle Dreams our waking Thoughts pursue;
Or, one Dream pass'd, we slide into a new;
(So close they follow, such wild Order keep,
We think our selves awake, and are asleep:)
So softly death succeeded life, in her;
She did but dream of Heav'n, and she was there.

315

    No Pains she suffer'd, nor expir'd with Noise;
Her Soul was whisper'd out, with God's still Voice:
As an old Friend is beckon'd to a Feast,
And treated like a long familiar Guest;
He took her as he found; but found her so,
As one in hourly readiness to go.

320

Ev'n on that day, in all her Trim prepar'd;
As early notice she from Heav'n had heard,
And some descending Courtier, from above
Had giv'n her timely warning to remove:
Or counsell'd her to dress the nuptial Room;
For on that Night the Bridegroom was to come.

Her preparedness to dye.

325

He kept his hour, and found her where she lay
Cloath'd all in white, the Liv'ry of the Day:
Scarce had she sinn'd, in thought, or word, or act;
Unless Omissions were to pass for fact:
That hardly Death a Consequence cou'd draw,
To make her liable to Nature's Law.

329
She dy'd on Whitsunday night.

And that she dy'd, we only have to show,
The mortal part of her she left below:

335

The rest (so smooth, so suddenly she went)
Look'd like Translation, through the Firmament;
Or like the fiery Carr, on the third Errand sent.

*Apostrophe
to her Soul.*

    O happy Soul! If thou canst view from high,   340
Where thou art all Intelligence, all Eye,
If looking up to God, or down to us,
Thou find'st, that any way be pervious,
Survey the ruines of thy House, and see
Thy widow'd, and thy Orphan Family;   345
Look on thy tender Pledges left behind:
And, if thou canst a vacant Minute find
From Heav'nly Joys, that Interval afford
To thy sad Children, and thy mourning Lord.
See how they grieve, mistaken in their love,   350
And shed a beam of Comfort from above;
Give 'em, as much as mortal Eyes can bear,
A transient view of thy full glories there;
That they with mod'rate sorrow may sustain
And mollifie their Losses, in thy Gain.   355
Or else divide the grief, for such thou wert,
That shou'd not all Relations bear a part,
It were enough to break a single heart.

*Epipho-
nema: or
close of the
Poem.*

    Let this suffice: Nor thou, great Saint, refuse
This humble Tribute of no vulgar Muse: 360
Who, not by Cares, or Wants, or Age deprest,
Stems a wild Deluge with a dauntless brest:
And dares to sing thy Praises, in a Clime
Where Vice triumphs, and Vertue is a Crime:
Where ev'n to draw the Picture of thy Mind,   365
Is Satyr on the most of Humane Kind:
Take it, while yet 'tis Praise; before my rage
Unsafely just, break loose on this bad Age;
So bad, that thou thy self had'st no defence,
From Vice, but barely by departing hence.   370

    Be what, and where thou art; To wish thy place,
Were in the best, Presumption, more than grace.
Thy Reliques (such thy Works of Mercy are)
Have, in this Poem, been my holy care.

As Earth thy Body keeps, thy Soul the Sky, 375
So shall this Verse preserve thy Memory;
For thou shalt make it live, because it sings of thee.

PROLOGUE, EPILOGUE and SONG
from *CLEOMENES*

PROLOGUE

Spoke by Mr. MOUNTFORT

I THINK or hope, at least, the Coast is clear,
That none but Men of Wit and Sence are here:
That our Bear-Garden Friends are all away,
Who bounce with Hands and Feet, and cry Play, Play.
Who to save Coach-hire, trudge along the Street, 5
Then print our Matted Seats with dirty Feet;
Who, while we speak, make Love to Orange-Wenches,
And between Acts stand strutting on the Benches:
Where got a Cock-horse, making vile Grimaces,
They to the Boxes show their Booby Faces. 10
A Merry-Andrew, such a Mob will serve,
And treat 'em with such Wit as they deserve:
Let 'em go People *Ireland*, where there's need
Of such new Planters to repair the Breed;
Or to *Virginia* or *Jamaica* Steer, 15
But have a care of some *French* Privateer;
For if they should become the Prize of Battle,
They'll take 'em Black and White for *Irish* Cattle.
Arise true Judges in your own Defence,
Controul those Foplings, and declare for Sence: 20
For should the Fools prevail, they stop not there,
But make their next Descent upon the Fair.
Then rise ye Fair; for it concerns you most,
That Fools no longer should your Favours boast;
'Tis time you should renounce 'em, for we find 25

Prologue, Epilogue and Song. Text from Cleomenes, the Spartan Heroe. A Tragedy, *1692*

They plead a senseless Claim to Woman kind:
Such Squires are only fit for Country Towns,
To stink of Ale; and dust a Stand with Clownes:
Who, to be chosen for the Lands Protectors,
Tope and get Drunk before their Wise Electors.   30
Let not Farce Lovers your weak Choice upbraid,
But turn 'em over to the Chamber-maid.
Or if they come to see our Tragick Scenes,
Instruct them what a *Spartan* Hero means:
Teach 'em how manly Passions ought to move,   35
For such as cannot Think can never Love:
And since they needs will judge the Poets Art,
Point 'em with Fescu's to each shining Part.
Our Author hopes in you, but still in pain,
He fears your Charms will be employ'd in vain;   40
You can make Fools of Wits, we find each Hour,
But to make Wits of Fools, is past your Power.

EPILOGUE

Spoke by Mrs. BRACEGIRDLE

THIS Day, the Poet bloodily inclin'd,
   Has made me die, full sore against my Mind!
Some of you naughty Men, I fear, will cry,
Poor Rogue! would I might teach thee how to die!
Thanks for your Love; but I sincerely say,   5
I never mean to die, your wicked way.
Well, since it is Decreed all Flesh must go,
(And I am Flesh, at least for ought you know;)
I first declare, I die with pious Mind,
In perfect Charity with all Mankind.   10
Next for my Will:—— I have, in my dispose,
Some certain Moveables would please you Beaux;
As, first, my Youth; for as I have been told,
Some of you, modish Sparks, are dev'lish old.
My Chastity I need not leave among yee: 15
For to suspect old Fops, were much to wrong ye.
You swear y'are Sinners; but for all your haste,
Your Misses shake their Heads, and find you chaste.

I give my Courage to those bold Commanders
That stay with us, and dare not go for *Flanders*.   20
I leave my Truth, (to make his Plot more clear,)
To Mr. *Fuller*, when he next shall swear.
I give my Judgment, craving all your Mercyes,
To those that leave good Plays, for damn'd dull Farces.
My small Devotion let the Gallants share   25
That come to ogle us at Evening Pray'r.
I give my Person—let me well consider,
Faith e'en to him that is the fairest Bidder.
To some rich Hunks, if any be so bold
To say those dreadful Words, *To have and hold.*   30
But stay—to give, and be bequeathing still,
When I'm so poor, is just like *Wickham*'s Will:
Like that notorious Cheat, vast Sums I give,
Only that you may keep me while I live.
Buy a good Bargain, Gallants, while you may,   35
I'll cost you but your Half-a-Crown a day.

SONG

NO no, poor suff'ring Heart no Change endeavour,
  Choose to sustain the smart, rather than leave her;
My ravish'd Eyes behold such Charms about her,
I can dye with her, but not live without her.
One tender Sigh of hers to see me Languish,   5
Will more than pay the price of my past Anguish:
Beware O cruel Fair, how you smile on me,
'Twas a kind Look of yours that has undone me.

2

Love has in store for me one happy Minute,
And She will end my pain who did begin it;   10
Then no day void of Bliss, or Pleasure leaving,
Ages shall slide away without perceiving:
Cupid shall guard the Door the more to please us,
And keep out Time and Death when they would seize us:
Time and Death shall depart, and say in flying,   15
Love has found out a way to Live by Dying.

EPILOGUE to *HENRY THE SECOND*

Spoke by Mrs. *Bracegirdle*

THUS you the sad Catastrophe have seen,
   Occasion'd by a Mistress and a Queen.
Queen *Eleanor* the Proud was *French*, they say;
But *English* Manufacture got the Day:
Jane Clifford was her Name, as Books aver,   5
Fair Rosamond was but her *Nom de Guerre*.
Now tell me, Gallants, wou'd you lead your Life
With such a Mistress, or with such a Wife?
If One must be your Choice, which d'ye approve,
The Curtain-Lecture, or the Curtain-Love?   10
Wou'd ye be Godly with perpetual Strife,
Still drudging on with homely *Joan* your Wife;
Or take your Pleasure in a wicked way,
Like honest Whoring *Harry* in the Play?
I guess your minds: The Mistress wou'd be taking,   15
And nauseous Matrimony sent a packing.
The Devil's in ye all; Mankind's a Rogue,
You love the Bride, but you detest the Clog:
After a Year, poor Spouse is left i'th' lurch;
And you, like *Haynes*, return to Mother-Church.   20
Or, if the name of Church comes cross your mind,
Chappels of Ease behind our Scenes you find:
The Play-house is a kind of Market-place;
One chaffers for a Voice, another for a Face.
Nay, some of you, I dare not say how many,   25
Would buy of me a Pen'worth for your Peny.
Ev'n this poor Face (which with my Fan I hide)
Would make a shift my Portion to provide,
With some small Perquisites I have beside.
Though for your Love, perhaps, I should not care,   30
I could not hate a Man that bids me fair.
What might ensue, 'tis hard for me to tell;
But I was drench'd to day for loving well,
And fear the Poyson that would make me swell.

Epilogue. Text from Henry the Second, King of England; with the Death of Rosamond.
A Tragedy, *1693*

THE SATIRES

of Decimus Junius Juvenalis.

Translated into English Verse.

By Mr. DRYDEN,

and Several other Eminent Hands.

Together with the

SATIRES

of Aulus Persius Flaccus.

Made English by Mr. DRYDEN.

To which is Prefix'd a Discourse concerning
the Original and Progress of SATIRE.

Quicquid agunt homines, votum, timor, Ira, voluptas,
Gaudia, discursus, nostri est farrago libelli.

The Satires of . . . Juvenalis. Text from the first edition,
1693, collated with the second edition, 1697

TO THE Right Honourable CHARLES,
Earl of *Dorset* and *Middlesex*,
Lord Chamberlain of Their Majesties Household:
Knight of the Most Noble Order of the GARTER, *&c.*

My Lord,

THE Wishes and Desires of all good Men, which have attended your Lordship from your First appearance in the World, are at length accomplish'd in your obtaining those Honours and Dignities, which you have so long deserv'd. There are no Factions, tho irreconcilable to one another, that are not united in their Affection to you, and the 5 Respect they pay you. They are equally pleas'd in your Prosperity, and wou'd be equally concern'd in your Afflictions. *Titus Vespasian* was not more the Delight of Human-kind. The Universal Empire made him only more known, and more Powerful, but cou'd not make him more belov'd. He had greater Ability of doing Good, but your Inclination 10 to it, is not less; And tho' you could not extend your Beneficence to so many Persons, yet you have lost as few days as that Excellent Emperour; and never had his Complaint to make when you went to Bed, that the Sun had shone upon you in vain, when you had the Opportunity of relieving some unhappy man. This, My Lord, has justly 15 acquir'd you as many Friends, as there are Persons who have the Honour to be known to you: Meer Acquaintance you have none: You have drawn them all into a nearer Line: And they who have Convers'd with you, are for ever after inviolably yours. This is a Truth so generally acknowledg'd, that it needs no Proof: 'Tis of the Nature of a 20 first Principle, which is receiv'd as soon as it is propos'd; and needs not the Reformation which *Descartes* us'd to his: For we doubt not, neither can we properly say, we think we admire and love you, above all other men: There is a certainty in the Proposition, and we know it. With the same Assurance I can say, you neither have Enemies, nor can scarce 25 have any; for they who have never heard of you, can neither Love or Hate you: And they who have, can have no other notion of you, than that which they receive from the Publick, that you are the best of Men. After this, my Testimony can be of no farther use, than to declare it to be Day-light at High-Noon: And all who have the benefit of sight, 30 can look up, as well, and see the Sun.

Address. Their Majesties Household:] His Majesty's Houshold, *97*

'Tis true, I have one Priviledge which is almost particular to my self, that I saw you in the *East* at your first arising above the Hemisphere: I was as soon Sensible as any Man of that Light, when it was but just shoot- 35 ing out, and beginning to Travel upwards to the Meridian. I made my early Addresses to your Lordship, in my Essay of Dramatick Poetry; and therein bespoke you to the World: Wherein, I have the right of a First Discoverer. When I was my self, in the Rudiments of my Poetry, without Name, or Reputation in the World, having rather the Ambi- 40 tion of a Writer, than the skill; when I was Drawing the Out-Lines of an Art without any Living Master to Instruct me in it; an Art which had been better Prais'd than Study'd here in *England*, wherein *Shakespear* who Created the Stage among us, had rather Written happily, than knowingly and justly; and *Johnson*, who by studying *Horace*, had been 45 acquainted with the Rules, yet seem'd to envy to Posterity that Know- ledge, and like an Inventer of some useful Art, to make a Monopoly of his Learning: When thus, as I may say, before the use of the Load- stone, or knowledge of the Compass, I was sailing in a vast Ocean, without other help, than the Pole-Star of the Ancients, and the Rules of the *French* Stage amongst the Moderns, which are extreamly different 50 from ours, by reason of their opposite taste; yet even then, I had the presumption to Dedicate to your Lordship: A very unfinish'd Piece, I must Confess, and which only can be excus'd, by the little Experience of the Author, and the Modesty of the Title, *An Essay*. Yet I was stronger in Prophecy than I was in Criticism: I was Inspir'd to foretell 55 you to Mankind, as the Restorer of Poetry, the greatest Genius, the truest Judge, and the best Patron.

Good Sence and good Nature, are never separated, tho' the Ignorant World has thought otherwise. Good Nature, by which I mean Bene- ficence and Candor, is the Product of right Reason: Which of necessity 60 will give Allowance to the Failings of others, by considering that there is nothing perfect in Mankind; and by distinguishing that which comes nearest to Excellency, tho not absolutely free from Faults, will certainly produce a Candor in the Judge. 'Tis incident to an Elevated Under- standing, like your Lordships, to find out the Errors of other men: But 65 'tis your Prerogative to pardon them; to look with Pleasure on those things, which are somewhat Congenial, and of a remote Kindred to your own Conceptions: And to forgive the many Failings of those, who with their wretched Art, cannot arrive to those Heights that you possess, from a happy, abundant, and Native Genius. Which are as 70 inborn to you, as they were to *Shakespear*; and for ought I know to

Homer; in either of whom we find all Arts and Sciences, all Moral and Natural Philosophy, without knowing that they ever Study'd them.

There is not an *English* Writer this day living, who is not perfectly convinc'd, that your Lordship excels all others, in all the several parts 75 of Poetry which you have undertaken to adorn. The most Vain, and the most Ambitious of our Age have not dar'd to assume so much, as the Competitours of *Themistocles*: They have yielded the first place, without dispute; and have been arrogantly content, to be esteem'd as second to your Lordship; and even that also, with a *Longo, sed proximi* 80 *Intervallo*. If there have been, or are any, who go farther in their Self-conceipt, they must be very singular in their Opinion: They must be like the *Officer*, in a Play, who was call'd Captain, Lieutenant, and Company. The World will easily conclude, whether such unattended Generals can ever be capable of making a Revolution in *Parnassus*. 85

I will not attempt in this place, to say any thing particular of your *Lyrick Poems*, though they are the Delight and Wonder of this Age, and will be the Envy of the next. The Subject of this Book confines me to Satire: And in that, an Author of your own Quality, (whose Ashes I will not disturb,) has given you all the Commendation, which his self 90 sufficiency cou'd afford to any Man: *The best Good Man, with the worst-Natur'd Muse*. In that Character, methinks I am reading *Johnson*'s Verses to the Memory of *Shakespear*: An Insolent, Sparing, and Invidious Panegyrick: Where good Nature, the most God-like Commendation of a Man, is only attributed to your Person, and deny'd to your Writings: 95 for they are every where so full of Candour, that like *Horace*, you only expose the Follies of Men, without Arraigning their Vices; and in this excel him, That You add that pointedness of Thought, which is visibly wanting in our Great *Roman*. There is more of Salt in all your Verses, than I have seen in any of the Moderns, or even of the Ancients: But 100 you have been sparing of the Gaul; by which means you have pleas'd all Readers, and offended none. *Donn* alone, of all our Countrymen, had your Talent; but was not happy enough to arrive at your Versification. And were he Translated into Numbers, and *English*, he wou'd yet be wanting in the Dignity of Expression. That which is the prime Vertue, 105 and chief Ornament of *Virgil*, which distinguishes him from the rest of Writers, is so conspicuous in your Verses, that it casts a shadow on all your Contemporaries; we cannot be seen, or but obscurely, while you are present. You equal *Donn*, in the Variety, Multiplicity, and Choice of Thoughts; you excel him in the Manner, and the Words. 110 I Read you both, with the same Admiration, but not with the same

Delight. He affects the Metaphysicks, not only in his Satires, but in his Amorous Verses, where Nature only shou'd reign; and perplexes the Minds of the Fair Sex with nice Speculations of Philosophy, when he shou'd ingage their hearts, and entertain them with the softnesses of 115 Love. In this (if I may be pardon'd for so bold a truth) Mr. *Cowley* has Copy'd him to a fault; so great a one, in my Opinion, that it throws his *Mistress* infinitely below his Pindariques, and his latter Compositions; which are undoubtedly the best of his Poems, and the most Correct. For my own part, I must avow it freely to the World, that I never 120 attempted any thing in Satire, wherein I have not study'd your Writings as the most perfect Model. I have continually laid them before me; and the greatest Commendation, which my own partiality can give to my Productions, is that they are Copies, and no farther to be allow'd, than as they have something more or less of the Original. Some few 125 Touches of your Lordship, some secret Graces which I have endeavour'd to express after your manner, have made whole Poems of mine to pass with approbation: But take your Verses altogether, and they are inimitable. If therefore I have not written better, 'tis because you have not written more. You have not set me sufficient Copy to 130 Transcribe; and I cannot add one Letter of my own invention, of which I have not the Example there.

'Tis a general Complaint against your Lordship, and I must have leave to upbraid you with it, that, because you need not write, you will not. Mankind that wishes you so well, in all things that relate 135 to your prosperity, have their intervals of wishing for themselves, and are within a little of grudging you the fulness of your Fortune: They wou'd be more malicious if you us'd it not so well, and with so much generosity.

Fame is in it self a real good, if we may believe *Cicero*, who was per- 140 haps too fond of it. But even Fame, as *Virgil* tells us, acquires strength by going forward. Let *Epicurus* give Indolency as an Attribute to his Gods, and place in it the happiness of the blest: The Divinity which we Worship, has given us not only a Precept against it, but his own Example to the contrary. The World, my Lord, wou'd be content to 145 allow you a Seventh Day for rest; or if you thought that hard upon you, we wou'd not refuse you half your time: If you came out, like some Great Monarch, to take a Town but once a year, as it were for your diversion, though you had no need to extend your Territories: In short, if you were a bad, or which is worse, an indifferent Poet, we 150 wou'd thank you for our own quiet, and not expose you to the want of yours. But when you are so great, and so successful, and when we have that necessity of your Writing, that we cannot subsist in Poetry without it; any more, (I may almost say,) than the World without the daily Course of ordinary Providence, methinks this Argument might 155 prevail with you, my Lord, to foregoe a little of your Repose for the Publick Benefit. 'Tis not that you are under any force of working daily Miracles, to prove your Being; but now and then somewhat of extraordinary, that is any thing of your production, is requisite to refresh your Character. 160

This, I think, my Lord, is a sufficient Reproach to you; and shou'd I carry it as far as Mankind wou'd Authorise me, wou'd be little less than Satire. And, indeed, a provocation is almost necessary, in behalf of the World, that you might be induc'd sometimes to write; and in relation to a multitude of Scriblers, who daily pester the World with their 165 insufferable Stuff, that they might be discourag'd from Writing any more. I complain not of their Lampoons and Libels, though I have been the Publick Mark for many years. I am vindictive enough to have repell'd force by force, if I cou'd imagine that any of them had ever reach'd me; but they either shot at Rovers, and therefore miss'd, or 170 their Powder was so weak, that I might safely stand them, at the nearest distance. I answer'd not the *Rehearsall*, because I knew the Author sate to himself when he drew the Picture, and was the very *Bays* of his own Farce. Because also I knew, that my Betters were more concern'd than I was in that Satire: And lastly, because Mr. *Smith*, and Mr. *Johnson*, 175 the main Pillars of it, were two such Languishing Gentlemen in their Conversation, that I cou'd liken them to nothing but to their own Relations, those Noble Characters of Men of Wit and Pleasure about the Town. The like Considerations have hinder'd me from dealing with the lamentable Companions of their Prose and Doggrel. I am so far from 180 defending my Poetry against them, that I will not so much as expose theirs. And for my Morals, if they are not proof against their attacks, let me be thought by Posterity, what those Authors wou'd be thought, if any Memory of them, or of their Writings cou'd endure so long, as to another Age. But these dull Makers of Lampoons, as harmless as 185 they have been to me, are yet of dangerous Example to the Publick: Some Witty Men may perhaps succeed to their Designs, and mixing Sence with Malice, blast the Reputation of the most Innocent amongst Men, and the most Virtuous amongst Women.

Heaven be prais'd, our common Libellers are as free from the imputa- 190 tion of Wit, as of Morality; and therefore what ever Mischief they have design'd, they have perform'd but little of it. Yet these ill Writers, in all justice ought themselves to be expos'd: As *Persius* has given us a fair Example in his First Satire; which is level'd particularly at them: And none is so fit to Correct their Faults, as he who is not only clear 195 from any in his own Writings, but is also so just, that he will never defame the good; and is arm'd with the power of Verse, to Punish and make Examples of the bad. But of this, I shall have occasion to speak further, when I come to give the Definition and Character of true Satires.

In the mean time, as a Councellour bred up in the knowledge of the 200 Municipal and Statute Laws, may honestly inform a just Prince how far his Prerogative extends; so I may be allow'd to tell your Lordship, who by an undisputed Title, are the King of Poets, what an extent of Power you have, and how lawfully you may exercise it, over the petulant Scriblers of this Age. As Lord Chamberlain, I know, you are absolute 205 by your Office, in all that belongs to the Decency and Good Manners of the Stage. You can banish from thence Scurrility and Profaneness, and restrain the licentious insolence of Poets and their Actors, in all things that shock the Publick Quiet, or the Reputation of Private Persons, under the notion of *Humour*. But I mean not the Authority, 210 which is annex'd to your Office: I speak of that only which is inborn and inherent to your Person. What is produc'd in you by an Excellent Wit, a Masterly and Commanding Genius over all Writers: Whereby you are impower'd, when you please, to give the final decision of Wit; to put your Stamp on all that ought to pass for current; and set a 215 Brand of Reprobation on Clipt Poetry, and false Coyn. A Shilling dipt in the *Bath* may go for Gold amongst the Ignorant, but the Scepters on the Guinies shew the difference. That your Lordship is form'd by Nature for this Supremacy, I cou'd easily prove, (were it not already granted by the World) from the distinguishing Character of your 220 Writing. Which is so visible to me, that I never cou'd be impos'd on to receive for yours, what was written by any others; or to mistake your Genuine Poetry, for their Spurious Productions. I can farther add with truth (though not without some Vanity in saying it) that in the same Paper, written by divers Hands, whereof your Lordship's was 225 only part, I cou'd separate your Gold from their Copper: And tho I cou'd not give back to every Author his own Brass, (for there is not the same Rule for distinguishing betwixt bad and bad, as betwixt ill and excellently good) yet I never fail'd of knowing what was yours, and what was not: And was absolutely certain, that this, or the other Part 230 was positively yours, and cou'd not possibly be Written by any other.

True it is, that some bad Poems, though not all, carry their Owners Marks about 'em. There is some peculiar aukardness, false Grammar, imperfect Sense, or at the least Obscurity; some Brand or other on this Buttock, or that Ear, that 'tis notorious who are the Owners of the 235 Cattel, though they shou'd not Sign it with their Names. But your Lordship, on the contrary, is distinguish'd, not only by the Excellency of your Thoughts, but by your Stile, and Manner of expressing them. A Painter judging of some Admirable Piece, may affirm with certainty, that it was of *Holben*, or *Vandyke*: But Vulgar Designs, and Common 240 Draughts, are easily mistaken, and misapply'd. Thus, by my long Study of your Lordship, I am arriv'd at the knowledge of your particular manner. In the Good Poems of other Men, like those Artists, I can only say, this is like the Draught of such a one, or like the Colouring of another. In short, I can only be sure, that 'tis the Hand of a good 245 Master: But in your Performances 'tis scarcely possible for me to be deceiv'd. If you write in your strength, you stand reveal'd at the first view; and shou'd you write under it, you cannot avoid some Peculiar Graces, which only cost me a second Consideration to discover you: For I may say it, with all the severity of Truth, that every Line of 250 yours is precious. Your Lordship's only fault is, that you have not written more: Unless I cou'd add another, and that yet greater, but I fear for the Publick, the Accusation wou'd not be true, that you have written, and out of a vicious Modesty will not Publish.

Virgil has confin'd his Works within the compass of Eighteen Thou- 255 sand Lines, and has not treated many Subjects; yet he ever had, and ever will have the Reputation of the best Poet. *Martial* says of him, that he cou'd have excell'd *Varius* in Tragedy, and *Horace* in Lyrick Poetry, but out of deference to his Friends he attempted neither.

The same prevalence of Genius is in your Lordship, but the World 260 cannot pardon your concealing it on the same consideration; because we have neither a Living *Varius*, nor a *Horace*, in whose Excellencies both of *Poems*, *Odes* and *Satires*, you had equall'd them, if our Language had not yielded to the *Roman* Majesty, and length of time had not added a Reverence to the Works of *Horace*. For good Sense is the same in all 265 or most Ages; and course of Time rather improves Nature, than impairs her. What has been, may be again: Another *Homer*, and another *Virgil* may possibly arise from those very Causes which produc'd the first: Though it wou'd be impudence to affirm that any such have yet appear'd. 270

'Tis manifest, that some particular Ages have been more happy than others in the production of Great Men, in all sorts of Arts and Sciences: As that of *Eurypides, Sophocles, Aristophanes,* and the rest for Stage-Poetry amongst the *Greeks*: That of *Augustus,* for Heroick, Lyrick, Dramatick, Elegiaque, and indeed all sorts of Poetry; in the Persons of *Virgil,* 275 *Horace, Varius, Ovid,* and many others; especially if we take into that Century the latter end of the Commonwealth; wherein we find *Varro, Lucretius,* and *Catullus*: And at the same time liv'd *Cicero,* and *Salust,* and *Cæsar.* A Famous Age in Modern Times, for Learning in every kind, was that of *Lorenzo de Medici,* and his Son *Leo* the Tenth. Wherein 280 Painting was reviv'd, and Poetry flourish'd, and the *Greek* Language was restor'd.

Examples in all these are obvious: But what I wou'd infer, is this; That in such an Age 'tis possible some Great Genius may arise, to equal any of the Antients; abating only for the Language. For great Contem- 285 poraries whet and cultivate each other: And mutual Borrowing, and Commerce, makes the Common Riches of Learning, as it does of the Civil Government.

But suppose that *Homer* and *Virgil* were the only of their Species, and that Nature was so much worn out in producing them, that she is never 290 able to bear the like again; yet the Example only holds in Heroick Poetry: In Tragedy and Satire I offer my self to maintain against some of our Modern Criticks, that this Age and the last, particularly in *England,* have excell'd the Ancients in both those kinds; and I wou'd instance in *Shakespear* of the former, in your Lordship of the latter sort. 295

Thus I might safely confine my self to my Native Country: But if I wou'd only cross the Seas, I might find in *France* a living *Horace* and a *Juvenal,* in the Person of the admirable *Boileau*: Whose Numbers are Excellent, whose Expressions are Noble, whose Thoughts are Just, whose Language is Pure, whose Satire is pointed, and whose Sense is 300 close; What he borrows from the Ancients, he repays with Usury of his own: in Coin as good, and almost as Universally valuable: For setting prejudice and Partiality apart, though he is our Enemy, the Stamp of a *Louis,* the Patron of all Arts, is not much inferiour to the Medal of an *Augustus Cæsar.* Let this be said without entring into 305 the interests of Factions and Parties; and relating only to the Bounty of that King to Men of Learning and Merit: A Praise so just, that even we who are his Enemies, cannot refuse it to him.

Now if it may be permitted me to go back again, to the Considera- tion of *Epique* Poetry, I have confess'd, that no Man hitherto has 310

278 *Cicero,* 97: *Cicero* 93   295 in your Lordship of] of your Lordship in *93* 97

reach'd, or so much as approach'd to the Excellencies of *Homer* or of
Virgil; I must farther add, that *Statius*, the best Versificator next to
Virgil, knew not how to Design after him, though he had the Model
in his Eye; that *Lucan* is wanting both in Design and Subject, and is
besides too full of Heat, and Affectation; that amongst the Moderns, 315
Ariosto neither Design'd Justly, nor observ'd any Unity of Action, or
Compass of Time, or Moderation in the Vastness of his Draught; his
Style is Luxurious, without Majesty, or Decency; and his Adventures,
without the compass of Nature and Possibility: *Tasso*, whose Design
was Regular, and who observ'd the Rules of Unity in Time and Place, 320
more closely than *Virgil*, yet was not so happy in his Action; he confesses himself to have been too Lyrical, that is, to have written beneath
the Dignity of Heroick Verse, in his *Episodes* of *Sophronia*, *Erminia*, and
Armida; his Story is not so pleasing as *Ariosto*'s; he is too flatulent sometimes, and sometimes too dry; many times unequal, and almost always 325
forc'd; and besides, is full of Conceipts, points of Epigram and Witti-
cisms; all which are not only below the Dignity of *Heroick* Verse, but
contrary to its Nature: *Virgil* and *Homer* have not one of them. And
those who are guilty of so boyish an Ambition in so grave a Subject,
are so far from being consider'd as Heroique Poets, that they ought to 330
be turn'd down from *Homer* to the *Anthologia*, from *Virgil* to *Martial*
and *Owen*'s Epigrams, and from *Spencer* to *Fleckno*; that is, from the top
to the bottom of all Poetry. But to return to *Tasso*, he borrows from the
Invention of *Boyardo*, and in his Alteration of his Poem, which is
infinitely for the worse, imitates *Homer* so very servilely, that (for 335
Example) he gives the King of *Jerusalem* Fifty Sons, only because *Homer*
had bestow'd the like number on King *Priam*; he kills the youngest in
the same manner, and has provided his Hero with a *Patroclus*, under
another Name, only to bring him back to the Wars, when his Friend
was kill'd. The *French* have perform'd nothing in this kind, which is 340
not far below those two *Italians*, and subject to a thousand more Reflections, without examining their Saint *Lewis*, their *Pucelle*, or their
Alarique: The *English* have only to boast of *Spencer* and *Milton*, who
neither of them wanted either Genius, or Learning, to have been perfect
Poets; and yet both of them are liable to many Censures. For there is 345
no Uniformity in the Design of *Spencer*: He aims at the Accomplishment
of no one Action: He raises up a Hero for every one of his Adventures;
and endows each of them with some particular Moral Virtue, which
renders them all equal, without Subordination or Preference. Every one
is most Valiant in his own Legend; only we must do him that Justice 350

to observe, that Magnanimity, which is the Character of Prince *Arthur*, shines throughout the whole Poem; and Succours the rest, when they are in Distress. The Original of every Knight, was then living in the Court of Queen *Elizabeth*: And he attributed to each of them that Virtue, which he thought was most conspicuous in them: An Ingenious 355 piece of Flattery, tho' it turn'd not much to his Account. Had he liv'd to finish his Poem, in the six remaining Legends, it had certainly been more of a piece; but cou'd not have been perfect, because the Model was not true. But Prince *Arthur*, or his chief Patron, Sir *Philip Sidney*, whom he intended to make happy, by the Marriage of his *Gloriana*, 360 dying before him, depriv'd the Poet, both of Means and Spirit, to accomplish his Design: For the rest, his Obsolete Language, and the ill choice of his Stanza, are faults but of the Second Magnitude: For notwithstanding the first he is still Intelligible, at least, after a little practice; and for the last, he is the more to be admir'd; that labour- 365 ing under such a difficulty, his Verses are so Numerous, so Various, and so Harmonious, that only *Virgil*, whom he profestly imitated, has surpass'd him, among the *Romans*; and only Mr. *Waller* among the *English*.

As for Mr. *Milton*, whom we all admire with so much Justice, his 370 Subject is not that of an Heroique Poem; properly so call'd: His Design is the Losing of our Happiness; his Event is not prosperous, like that of all other *Epique* Works: His Heavenly Machines are many, and his Humane Persons are but two. But I will not take Mr. *Rymer*'s Work out of his Hands. He has promis'd the World a Critique on that Author; 375 wherein, tho' he will not allow his Poem for Heroick, I hope he will grant us, that his Thoughts are elevated, his Words Sounding, and that no Man has so happily Copy'd the Manner of *Homer*; or so copiously translated his *Grecisms*, and the *Latin* Elegancies of *Virgil*. 'Tis true, he runs into a flat of Thought, sometimes for a Hundred Lines together, 380 but 'tis when he is got into a Track of Scripture: His Antiquated words were his Choice, not his Necessity; for therein he imitated *Spencer*, as *Spencer* did *Chawcer*. And tho', perhaps, the love of their Masters, may have transported both too far, in the frequent use of them; yet in my Opinion, Obsolete Words may then be laudably reviv'd, when either 385 they are more Sounding, or more Significant than those in practice: And when their Obscurity is taken away, by joining other Words to them which clear the Sense; according to the Rule of *Horace*, for the admission of new Words. But in both cases, a Moderation is to be observ'd, in the use of them: For unnecessary Coynage, as well as 390 unnecessary Revival, runs into Affectation; a fault to be avoided on either hand. Neither will I Justifie *Milton* for his Blank Verse, tho' I may excuse him, by the Example of *Hannibal Caro*, and other *Italians*, who have us'd it: For whatever Causes he alledges for the abolishing of Rhyme (which I have not now the leisure to examine) his own particu- 395 lar Reason is plainly this, that Rhyme was not his Talent; he had neither the Ease of doing it, nor the Graces of it; which is manifest in his *Juvenilia*, or Verses written in his Youth: Where his Rhyme is always constrain'd and forc'd, and comes hardly from him at an Age when the Soul is most pliant; and the Passion of Love, makes almost 400 every Man a Rhymer, tho' not a Poet.

By this time, My Lord, I doubt not but that you wonder, why I have run off from my Biass so long together, and made so tedious a Digres- sion from Satire to Heroique Poetry. But if You will not excuse it, by the tattling Quality of Age, which, as Sir *William Davenant* says, is 405 always Narrative; yet I hope the usefulness of what I have to say on this Subject, will qualifie the remoteness of it; and this is the last time I will commit the Crime of Prefaces; or trouble the World with my Notions of any thing that relates to Verse. I have then, as You see, observ'd the Failings of many great Wits amongst the Moderns, who 410 have attempted to write an *Epique* Poem: Besides these, or the like Animadversions of them by other Men, there is yet a farther Reason given, why they cannot possibly succeed, so well as the Ancients, even tho' we cou'd allow them not to be Inferiour, either in Genius or Learning, or the Tongue in which they write; or all those other wonder- 415 ful Qualifications which are necessary to the forming of a true Accom- plish'd Heroique Poet. The fault is laid on our Religion: They say that Christianity is not capable of those Embellishments which are afforded in the Belief of those Ancient Heathens.

And 'tis true, that in the severe notions of our Faith, the Fortitude 420 of a Christian consists in Patience, and Suffering for the Love of God, what ever hardships can befall him in the World; not in any great Attempt; or in performance of those Enterprises which the Poets call Heroique; and which are commonly the Effects of Interest, Ostentation, Pride and Worldly Honour. That Humility and Resignation are our 425 prime Vertues; and that these include no Action, but that of the Soul: When as, on the Contrary, an Heroique Poem requires, to its necessary Design, and as its last Perfection, some great Action of War, the Ac- complishment of some Extraordinary Undertaking; which requires the

420 Faith, *97*: Faith; *93*   422 him *om. 97*

Strength and Vigour of the Body, the Duty of a Souldier, the Capacity 430
and Prudence of a General; and, in short, as much, or more of the
Active Virtue, than the Suffering. But to this, the Answer is very
Obvious. God has plac'd us in our several Stations; the Virtues of a
private Christian are Patience, Obedience, Submission, and the like;
but those of a Magistrate, or General, or a King, are Prudence, Counsel, 435
active Fortitude, coercive Power, awful Command, and the Exercise of
Magnanimity, as well as Justice. So that this Objection hinders not,
but that an Epique Poem, or the Heroique Action of some Great Commander, Enterpris'd for the Common Good, and Honour of the
Christian Cause, and Executed happily, may be as well Written now, 440
as it was of old by the Heathens; provided the Poet be endu'd with the
same Talents; and the Language, though not of equal Dignity, yet as
near approaching to it, as our Modern Barbarism will allow, which is
all that can be expected from our own or any other now extant, though
more Refin'd, and therefore we are to rest contented with that only 445
Inferiority, which is not possibly to be Remedy'd.

I wish, I cou'd as easily remove that other difficulty which yet
remains. 'Tis Objected by a great *French* Critique, as well as an
Admirable Poet, yet living, and whom I have mention'd with that
Honour, which his Merit exacts from me, I mean *Boileau*, that the 450
Machines of our Christian Religion in Heroique Poetry, are much more
feeble to Support that weight than those of *Heathenism*. Their Doctrine,
grounded as it was on Ridiculous Fables, was yet the Belief of the Two
Victorious Monarchies, the *Grecian*, and *Roman*. Their Gods did not
only interest themselves in the Event of Wars (which is the Effect of a 455
Superiour Providence) but also espous'd the several Parties, in a Visible
Corporeal Descent, mannag'd their Intrigues, and Fought their Battels
sometimes in Opposition to each other: Tho' *Virgil* (more discreet than
Homer in that last Particular) has contented himself with the Partiality
of his Deities, their Favours, their Counsels or Commands, to those 460
whose Cause they had espous'd, without bringing them to the Out-
rageousness of Blows. Now, our Religion (says he) is depriv'd of the
greatest part of those Machines; at least the most Shining in Epique
Poetry. Tho' St. *Michael* in *Ariosto* seeks out *Discord*, to send her
amongst the *Pagans*, and finds her in a Convent of Friars, where Peace 465
should Reign, which indeed is fine Satire; and *Satan*, in *Tasso*, excites
Solyman, to an Attempt by Night on the Christian Camp, and brings
an Host of Devils to his Assistance; yet the Arch-Angel, in the former
Example, when *Discord* was restive, and would not be drawn from her

belov'd Monastery with fair Words, has the Whip-hand of her, Drags 470
her out with many stripes, sets her, on Gods-name, about her business;
and makes her know the difference of Strength betwixt a Nuncio of
Heaven, and a Minister of Hell: The same Angel, in the latter Instance
from *Tasso* (as if God had never another Messenger, belonging to the
Court, but was confin'd like *Jupiter* to *Mercury*, and *Juno* to *Iris*,) when 475
he sees his time, that is, when half of the *Christians* are already kill'd,
and all the rest are in a fair way to be Routed, stickles betwixt the Remainders of God's Host, and the Race of Fiends; Pulls the Devils backward by their Tails, and drives them from their quarry; or otherwise
the whole business had miscarri'd, and *Jerusalem* remain'd untaken. 480
This, says *Boileau*, is a very unequal Match for the Poor Devils; who are
sure to come by the worst of it in the Combat; for nothing is more
easie, than for an Almighty Power to bring his old Rebels to Reason,
when he Pleases. Consequently, what pleasure, what Entertainment
can be rais'd from so pitiful a Machine? Where we see the Success of the 485
Battel, from the very beginning of it? Unless that, as we are *Christians*,
we are glad that we have gotten God on our side, to maul our Enemies,
when we cannot do the work our selves. For if the Poet had given the
Faithful more Courage, which had cost him nothing, or at least have
made them exceed the *Turks* in Number, he might have gain'd the 490
Victory for us *Christians*, without interessing Heaven in the quarrel;
and that with as much ease, and as little Credit to the Conqueror, as
when a Party of a Hundred Souldiers defeats another which consists
only of Fifty.

This, my Lord, I confess is such an Argument against our Modern 495
Poetry, as cannot be answer'd by those Mediums, which have been
us'd. We cannot hitherto boast, that our Religion has furnish'd us with
any such Machines, as have made the Strength and Beauty of the
Ancient Buildings.

But, what if I venture to advance an Invention of my own, to supply 500
the manifest defect of our new Writers: I am sufficiently sensible of my
weakness, and 'tis not very probable, that I shou'd succeed in such a
Project, whereof I have not had the least hint from any of my Predecessors, the Poets, or any of their Seconds, and Coadjutors, the
Critiques. Yet we see the Art of War is improv'd in Sieges, and new 505
Instruments of Death are invented daily. Something new in Philosophy
and the Mechanicks is discover'd almost every Year: And the Science
of Former Ages is improv'd by the Succeeding. I will not detain you

479 their Tails] the Tails 97

with a long Preamble to that, which better Judges will, perhaps, conclude to be little worth.   510

'Tis this, in short, That *Christian* Poets have not hitherto been acquainted with their own Strength. If they had search'd the Old Testament as they ought, they might there have found the Machines which are proper for their Work; and those more certain in their effect, than it may be the New-Testament is, in the Rules sufficient for 515 Salvation. The perusing of one Chapter in the Prophecy of *Daniel*, and Accommodating what there they find, with the Principles of *Platonique* Philosophy, as it is now Christianis'd, wou'd have made the Ministry of Angels as strong an Engine, for the Working up Heroique Poetry, in our Religion, as that of the Ancients has been to raise theirs by all the 520 Fables of their Gods, which were only receiv'd for Truths by the most ignorant, and weakest of the People.

'Tis a Doctrine almost Universally receiv'd by Christians, as well Protestants as Catholicks, that there are Guardian Angels appointed by God Almighty, as his Vicegerents, for the Protection and Government 525 of Cities, Provinces, Kingdoms, and Monarchies; and those as well of Heathens, as of true Believers. All this is so plainly prov'd from those Texts of *Daniel*, that it admits of no farther Controversie. The Prince of the *Persians*, and that other of the *Grecians*, are granted to be the Guardians and Protecting Ministers of those Empires. It cannot be 530 deny'd, that they were opposite, and resisted one another. St. *Michael* is mention'd by his Name, as the Patron of the *Jews*, and is now taken by the Christians, as the Protector General of our Religion. These Tutelar *Genij*, who presided over the several People and Regions committed to their Charge, were watchful over them for good, as far as 535 their Commissions cou'd possibly extend. The General Purpose, and Design of all, was certainly the Service of their Great Creatour. But 'tis an undoubted Truth, that for Ends best known to the Almighty Majesty of Heaven, his Providential Designs for the benefit of his Creatures, for the Debasing and Punishing of some Nations, and the 540 Exaltation and Temporal Reward of others, were not wholly known to these his Ministers; else why those Factious Quarrels, Controversies, and Battels amongst themselves, when they were all United in the same Design, the Service and Honour of their common Master? But being instructed only in the General, and zealous of the main Design; and as 545 Finite Beings, not admitted into the Secrets of Government, the last resorts of Providence, or capable of discovering the final Purposes of God, who can work Good out of Evil, as he pleases; and irresistably sways all manner of Events on Earth, directing them finally for the best, to his Creation in General, and to the Ultimate End of his own Glory in Particular: They must of necessity be sometimes ignorant of the Means conducing to those Ends, in which alone they can jarr, and oppose each other. One Angel, as we may suppose the Prince of *Persia*, as he is call'd, judging, that it would be more for God's Honour, and the Benefit of his People, that the *Median* and *Persian* Monarchy, which deliver'd them from the *Babylonish* Captivity, shou'd still be uppermost: And the Patron of the *Grecians*, to whom the Will of God might be more particularly Reveal'd, contending on the other side, for the Rise of *Alexander* and his Successors, who were appointed to punish the Backsliding *Jews*, and thereby to put them in mind of their Offences, that they might Repent, and become more Virtuous, and more Observant of the Law Reveal'd. But how far these Controversies and appearing Enmities of those glorious Creatures may be carri'd; how these Oppositions may best be manag'd, and by what Means conducted, is not my business to shew or determine: These things must be left to the Invention and Judgment of the Poet: If any of so happy a Genius be now living, or any future Age can produce a Man, who being Conversant in the Philosophy of *Plato*, as it is now accommodated to Christian use; for (as *Virgil* gives us to understand by his Example) that is the only proper of all others for an *Epique* Poem; who to his Natural Endowments, of a large Invention, a ripe Judgment, and a strong Memory, has join'd the knowledge of the Liberal Arts and Sciences, and particularly, Moral Philosophy, the Mathematicks, Geography and History, and with all these Qualifications is born a Poet; knows, and can practice the variety of Numbers, and is Master of the Language in which he Writes; if such a Man, I say, be now arisen, or shall arise, I am vain enough to think, that I have propos'd a Model to him, by which he may build a Nobler, a more Beautiful and more Perfect Poem, than any yet extant since the Ancients.

There is another part of these Machines yet wanting; but by what I have said, it wou'd have been easily supply'd by a Judicious Writer. He cou'd not have fail'd, to add the opposition of ill Spirits to the good; they have also their Design, ever opposite to that of Heaven; and this alone, has hitherto been the practice of the Moderns: But this imperfect System, if I may call it such, which I have given, will infinitely advance and carry farther that Hypothesis of the Evil Spirits contending with the Good. For being so much weaker since their Fall, than those blessed

Beings, they are yet suppos'd to have a permitted Power from God, of acting ill, as from their own deprav'd Nature they have always the Will of designing it. A great Testimony of which we find in Holy Writ, 590 when God Almighty suffer'd *Satan* to appear in the Holy Synod of the Angels, (a thing not hitherto drawn into Example by any of the Poets,) and also gave him Power over all things belonging to his Servant *Job*, excepting only Life.

Now what these Wicked Spirits cannot compass, by the vast dis- 595 proportion of their Forces, to those of the Superiour Beings: They may by their Fraud and Cunning carry farther, in a seeming League, Confederacy or Subserviency to the Designs of some good Angel, as far as consists with his purity, to suffer such an aid, the end of which may possibly be disguis'd, and conceal'd from his finite Knowledge. This is 600 indeed to suppose a great Errour in such a Being: Yet since a Devil can appear like an Angel of Light; since Craft and Malice may sometimes blind for a while a more perfect Understanding; and lastly, since *Milton* has given us an Example of the like nature, when *Satan* appearing like a Cherub, to *Uriel*, the Intelligence of the Sun, Circumvented him even 605 in his own Province, and pass'd only for a Curious Traveller through those new Created Regions, that he might observe therein the Workmanship of God, and praise him in his Works: I know not why, upon the same supposition, or some other, a Fiend may not deceive a Creature of more Excellency than himself, but yet a Creature; at least 610 by the connivance, or tacit permission of the Omniscient Being.

Thus, my Lord, I have as briefly as I cou'd, given your Lordship, and by you the World, a rude draught of what I have been long labouring in my Imagination. And what I had intended to have put in practice, (though far unable for the attempt of such a Poem) and to have left the 615 Stage, to which my Genius never much inclin'd me, for a Work which wou'd have taken up my Life in the performance of it. This too, I had intended chiefly for the Honour of my Native Country, to which a Poet is particularly oblig'd: Of two Subjects, both relating to it, I was doubtful, whether I shou'd chuse that of King *Arthur*, Conquering the 620 *Saxons*; which being farther distant in Time, gives the greater Scope to my Invention: Or that of *Edward* the Black Prince in subduing *Spain*, and Restoring it to the Lawful Prince, though a Great Tyrant, *Don Pedro* the Cruel: Which for the compass of Time, including only the Expedition of one Year: For the greatness of the Action, and its 625

608 Works: I] Works. I *beginning new paragraph 93 97*   613 World, 97: World *93*

answerable Event; for the Magnanimity of the *English* Hero, oppos'd
to the Ingratitude of the person whom he restor'd; and for the many
Beautiful Episodes, which I had interwoven with the principal Design,
together with the Characters of the chiefest *English* Persons; wherein,
after *Virgil* and *Spencer*, I wou'd have taken occasion to represent my 630
living Friends and Patrons of the Noblest Families, and also shadow'd
the Events of future Ages, in the Succession of our Imperial Line. With
these helps, and those of the Machines, which I have mention'd; I might
perhaps have done as well as some of my Predecessors; or at least
chalk'd out a way, for others to amend my Errors in a like Design. But 635
being encourag'd only with fair Words, by King *Charles* II, my little
Sallary ill paid, and no prospect of a future Subsistance, I was then Discourag'd in the beginning of my Attempt; and now Age has overtaken
me; and Want, a more insufferable Evil, through the Change of the
Times, has wholly disenabl'd me. Tho' I must ever acknowledge, to 640
the Honour of your Lordship, and the Eternal Memory of your Charity,
that since this Revolution, wherein I have patiently suffer'd the Ruin
of my small Fortune, and the loss of that poor Subsistance which I had
from two Kings, whom I had serv'd more Faithfully than Profitably to
my self; then your Lordship was pleas'd, out of no other Motive, but 645
your own Nobleness, without any Desert of mine, or the least Sollicita-
tion from me, to make me a most bountiful Present, which at that time,
when I was most in want of it, came most seasonably and unexpectedly
to my Relief. That Favour, my Lord, is of it self sufficient to bind any
Grateful Man, to a perpetual Acknowledgment, and to all the future 650
Service, which one of my mean Condition, can be ever able to perform.
May the Almighty God return it for me, both in Blessing you here,
and Rewarding you hereafter. I must not presume to defend the Cause
for which I now suffer, because your Lordship is engag'd against it:
But the more you are so, the greater is my Obligation to you: For your 655
laying aside all the Considerations of Factions and Parties, to do an
Action of pure disinteress'd Charity. This is one amongst many of your
shining Qualities, which distinguish you from others of your Rank:
But let me add a farther Truth, That without these Ties of Gratitude,
and abstracting from them all, I have a most particular Inclination to 660
Honour you; and if it were not too bold an Expression, to say, I Love
you. 'Tis no shame to be a Poet, tho' 'tis to be a bad one. *Augustus
Cæsar* of old, and Cardinal *Richlieu* of late, wou'd willingly have been
such; and *David* and *Solomon* were such. You, who without Flattery,

626 answerable 97: answearable 93

are the best of the present Age in *England*, and wou'd have been so, 665
had you been born in any other Country, will receive more Honour in
future Ages, by that one Excellency, than by all those Honours to
which your Birth has intitl'd you, or your Merits have acquir'd you.

Ne, forte, pudori,
Sit tibi Musa Lyræ solers, & Cantor Apollo.   670

I have formerly said in this Epistle, that I cou'd distinguish your
Writings from those of any others: 'Tis now time to clear my self from
any imputation of Self-conceit on that Subject. I assume not to my
self any particular lights in this Discovery; they are such only as are
obvious to every Man of Sense and Judgment, who loves Poetry, and 675
understands it. Your Thoughts are always so remote from the common
way of thinking, that they are, as I may say, of another Species, than
the Conceptions of other Poets; yet you go not out of Nature for any
of them: Gold is never bred upon the Surface of the Ground; but lies
so hidden, and so deep, that the Mines of it are seldom found; but the 680
force of Waters casts it out from the Bowels of Mountains, and exposes
it amongst the Sands of Rivers; giving us of her Bounty, what we cou'd
not hope for by our search. This Success attends your Lordship's
Thoughts, which wou'd look like Chance, if it were not perpetual, and
always of the same tenour. If I grant that there is Care in it, 'tis such 685
a Care as wou'd be ineffectual, and fruitless in other Men. 'Tis the
Curiosa felicitas which *Petronius* ascribes to *Horace* in his *Odes*. We have
not wherewithal to imagine so strongly, so justly, and so pleasantly:
In short, if we have the same Knowledge, we cannot draw out of it the
same Quintessence; we cannot give it such a Turn, such a Propriety, 690
and such a Beauty. Something is deficient in the Manner, or the Words,
but more in the Nobleness of our Conception. Yet when you have
finish'd all, and it appears in its full Lustre, when the Diamond is not
only found, but the Roughness smooth'd, when it is cut into a Form,
and set in Gold, then we cannot but acknowledge, that it is the Perfect 695
Work of Art and Nature: And every one will be so vain, to think he
himself cou'd have perform'd the like, till he attempts it. 'Tis just the
Description that *Horace* makes of such a Finish'd Piece: It appears so
easie, *Ut sibi quivis speret idem, sudet multum, frustraque laboret, ausus idem.*
And besides all this, 'tis Your Lordships particular Talent to lay your 700
Thoughts so close together, that were they closer, they wou'd be
crouded, and even a due connexion wou'd be wanting. We are not kept

690 Turn] Term *97*

in expectation of two good lines, which are to come after a long Parenthesis of twenty bad; which is the *April* Poetry of other Writers, a mixture of Rain and Sun-shine by fits: You are always bright, even 705 almost to a fault, by reason of the excess. There is continual abundance, a Magazine of Thought, and yet a perpetual Variety of Entertainment; which creates such an Appetite in your Reader, that he is not cloy'd with any thing, but satisfy'd with all. 'Tis that which the *Romans* call *Cœna dubia*; where there is such plenty, yet withall so much Diversity, 710 and so good Order, that the choice is difficult betwixt one Excellency and another; and yet the Conclusion, by a due Climax, is evermore the best; that is, as a Conclusion ought to be, ever the most proper for its place. See, my Lord, whether I have not studi'd Your Lordship with some Application: And since You are so Modest, that You will not be 715 Judge and Party, I appeal to the whole World, if I have not drawn Your Picture to a great degree of likeness, tho' 'tis but in Meniature: And that some of the best Features are yet wanting. Yet what I have done is enough to distinguish You from any other, which is the Proposition that I took upon me to demonstrate. 720

And now, my Lord, to apply what I have said, to my present Business; the Satires of *Juvenal* and *Persius*, appearing in this New *English* Dress, cannot so properly be Inscrib'd to any Man as to Your Lordship, who are the First of the Age in that way of Writing. Your Lordship, amongst many other Favours, has given me Your Permission for this 725 Address; and You have particularly Encourag'd me by Your Perusal and Approbation of the *Sixth* and *Tenth Satires* of *Juvenal*, as I have Translated them. My fellow Labourers, have likewise Commission'd me, to perform in their behalf this Office of a Dedication to you; and will acknowledge with all possible Respect and Gratitude, your Accep- 730 tance of their Work. Some of them have the Honour to be known to your Lordship already; and they who have not yet that happiness, desire it now. Be pleas'd to receive our common Endeavours with your wonted Candor, without Intitleing you to the Protection of our common Failings, in so difficult an Undertakeing. And allow me your 735 Patience, if it be not already tir'd with this long Epistle, to give you from the Best Authors, the Origine, the Antiquity, the Growth, the Change, and the Compleatment of Satire among the *Romans*. To Describe, if not Define, the Nature of that Poem, with it's several Qualifications and Virtues, together with the several sorts of it. To 740 compare the Excellencies of *Horace*, *Persius* and *Juvenal*, and shew the

717 in Meniature] in a Meniature 97

particular Manners of their Satires. And lastly, to give an Account of this New Way of Version which is attempted in our Performance. All which, according to the weakness of my Ability, and the best Lights which I can get from others, shall be the Subject of my following 745 Discourse.

The most Perfect Work of Poetry, says our Master *Aristotle*, is Tragedy. His Reason is, because it is the most United; being more severely confin'd within the Rules of Action, Time and Place. The Action is entire of a Piece, and one, without Episodes: The Time 750 limited to a Natural Day: And the Place Circumscrib'd at least within the Compass of one Town, or City. Being exactly Proportion'd thus, and Uniform in all it's Parts, The Mind is more Capable of Comprehending the whole Beauty of it without distraction.

But after all these Advantages, an Heroique Poem is certainly the 755 greatest Work of Human Nature. The Beauties and Perfections of the other are but Mechanical; those of the Epique are more Noble. Tho' *Homer* has limited his Place to *Troy*, and the Fields about it; his Actions to Forty Eight Natural Days, whereof Twelve are Holy-days, or Cessation from business, during the Funerals of *Patroclus*. To proceed, the 760 Action of the Epique is greater: The Extention of Time enlarges the Pleasure of the Reader, and the Episodes give it more Ornament, and more Variety. The Instruction is equal; but the first is only Instructive, the latter Forms a Hero, and a Prince.

If it signifies any thing which of them is of the more Ancient Family, 765 the best and most absolute Heroique Poem was written by *Homer*, long before Tragedy was Invented: But, if we consider the Natural Endowments, and acquir'd Parts which are necessary to make an accomplish'd Writer in either Kind, Tragedy requires a less and more confin'd Knowledge: moderate Learning, and Observation of the Rules is sufficient, 770 if a Genius be not wanting. But in an Epique Poet, one who is worthy of that Name, besides an Universal Genius, is requir'd Universal Learning, together with all those Qualities and Acquisitions which I have nam'd above, and as many more as I have through haste or negligence omitted. And after all, he must have exactly Study'd *Homer* and *Virgil*, 775 as his Patterns, *Aristotle* and *Horace* as his Guides, and *Vida* and *Bossu*, as their Commentators, with many others both *Italian* and *French* Critiques, which I want leisure here to Recommend.

In a Word, what I have to say, in Relation to This Subject, which does not Particularly concern Satire, is, That the greatness of an 780 Heroique Poem, beyond that of a Tragedy, may easily be discover'd by observing, how few have attempted that Work, in comparison of those who have Written Drama's; and of those few, how small a number have Succeeded. But leaving the Critiques on either side to contend about the preference due to this or that sort of Poetry; I will hasten to 785 my present business, which is the Antiquity and Origine of Satire, according to those Informations which I have receiv'd from the Learned *Casaubon, Heinsius, Rigaltius, Dacier* and the *Dauphin's Juvenal*; to which I shall add some Observations of my own.

There has been a long Dispute amongst the Modern Critiques, 790 whether the *Romans* deriv'd their Satire from the *Grecians*, or first Invented it themselves. *Julius Scaliger* and *Heinsius*, are of the first Opinion; *Casaubon, Rigaltius, Dacier*, and the Publisher of the *Dauphin's Juvenal* maintain the Latter. If we take Satire in the general significa-tion of the Word, as it is us'd in all Modern Languages, for an Invective, 795 'tis certain that it is almost as old as Verse; and tho' Hymns, which are praises of God, may be allow'd to have been before it, yet the defama-tion of others was not long after it. After God had Curs'd *Adam* and *Eve* in Paradise, the Husband and Wife excus'd themselves, by laying the blame on one another; and gave a beginning to those Conjugal 800 Dialogues in Prose; which the Poets have perfected in Verse. The Third Chapter of *Job* is one of the first Instances of this Poem in Holy Scrip-ture: Unless we will take it higher, from the latter end of the second; where his Wife advises him to curse his Maker.

This Original, I confess, is not much to the Honour of Satire; but 805 here it was Nature, and that deprav'd: When it became an Art, it bore better Fruit. Only we have learnt thus much already, that Scoffs and Revilings are of the growth of all Nations; and consequently that neither the *Greek* Poets borrow'd from other People their Art of Railing, neither needed the *Romans* to take it from them. But considering Satire 810 as a Species of Poetry; here the War begins amongst the Criticks. *Scaliger* the Father will have it descend from *Greece* to *Rome*; and derives the word Satyre, from *Satyrus*, that mixt kind of Animal, or, as the Ancients thought him, Rural God, made up betwixt a Man and a Goat; with a Humane Head, Hook'd Nose, Powting Lips, a Bunch, or Struma 815 under the Chin, prick'd Ears, and upright Horns; the Body shagg'd with hair, especially from the waste, and ending in a Goat, with the legs and feet of that Creature. But *Casaubon*, and his Followers, with Reason, condemn this derivation; and prove that from *Satyrus*, the word *Satira*, as it signifies a Poem, cannot possibly descend. For *Satira* 820 is not properly a Substantive, but an Adjective; to which, the word *Lanx*, in *English* a Charger, or large Platter, is understood: So that the *Greek* Poem made according to the Manners of a Satyr, and expressing his Qualities, must properly be call'd Satyrical, and not Satire: And thus far 'tis allow'd, that the *Grecians* had such Poems; but that they 825 were wholly different in Specie, from that to which the *Romans* gave the Name of Satire.

    Aristotle divides all Poetry, in relation to the Progress of it, into Nature without Art: Art begun, and Art Compleated. Mankind, even the most Barbarous, have the Seeds of Poetry implanted in them. The 830 first Specimen of it was certainly shewn in the Praises of the Deity, and Prayers to him: And as they are of Natural Obligation, so they are likewise of Divine Institution. Which *Milton* observing, introduces *Adam* and *Eve*, every Morning adoring God in Hymns and Prayers. The first Poetry was thus begun, in the wild Notes of Nature, before the inven- 835 tion of Feet, and Measures. The *Grecians* and *Romans* had no other Original of their Poetry. Festivals and Holydays soon succeeded **to** Private Worship, and we need not doubt but they were enjoyn'd by the true God to his own People; as they were afterwards imitated by the *Heathens*; who by the light of Reason knew they were to invoke 840 some Superiour Being in their Necessities, and to thank him for his Benefits. Thus the *Grecian* Holydays were Celebrated with Offerings to *Bacchus* and *Ceres*, and other Deities, to whose Bounty they suppos'd they were owing for their Corn and Wine, and other helps of Life. And the Ancient *Romans*, as *Horace* tells us, paid their thanks to Mother 845 Earth, or *Vesta*, to *Silvanus*, and their *Genius*, in the same manner. But as all Festivals have a double Reason of their Institution; the first of Religion, the other of Recreation, for the unbending of our Minds: So both the *Grecians* and *Romans* agreed, after their Sacrifices were perform'd, to spend the remainder of the day in Sports and Merriments; 850 amongst which, Songs and Dances, and that which they call'd Wit, (for want of knowing better,) were the chiefest Entertainments. The *Grecians* had a notion of Satyres, whom I have already describ'd; and taking them, and the *Sileni*, that is the young Satyrs and the old, for the Tutors, Attendants, and Humble Companions of their *Bacchus*, 855 habited themselves like those Rural Deities, and imitated them in their Rustick Dances, to which they join'd Songs, with some sort of rude Harmony, but without certain Numbers; and to these they added a kind of Chorus.

830 Barbarous, *97*: Barbarous *93*   835 Nature] Natural Poetry *97*

The *Romans* also (as Nature is the same in all places) though they 860
knew nothing of those *Grecian* Demi-Gods, nor had any Communication with *Greece*, yet had certain Young Men, who at their Festivals,
Danc'd and Sung after their uncouth manner, to a certain kind of Verse,
which they call'd *Saturnian*; what it was, we have no very certain light
from Antiquity to discover; but we may conclude, that, like the 865
Grecian, it was void of Art, or at least with very feeble beginnings of it.
Those Ancient *Romans*, at these Holydays, which were a mixture of
Devotion and Debauchery, had a Custom of reproaching each other
with their Faults, in a sort of *Extempore* Poetry, or rather of tunable
hobling Verse; and they answer'd in the same kind of gross Raillery; 870
their Wit and their Musick being of a piece. The *Grecians*, says *Casaubon*,
had formerly done the same, in the Persons of their petulant Satyrs:
But I am afraid he mistakes the matter, and confounds the Singing and
Dancing of the Satyrs, with the Rustical Entertainments of the first
Romans. The Reason of my Opinion is this; that *Casaubon* finding little 875
light from Antiquity, of these beginnings of Poetry, amongst the
Grecians, but only these Representations of *Satyrs*, who carry'd *Canisters*
and *Cornucopias* full of several Fruits in their hands, and danc'd with
them at their Publick Feasts: And afterwards reading *Horace*, who
makes mention of his homely *Romans*, jesting at one another in the same 880
kind of Solemnities, might suppose those wanton *Satyrs* did the same.
And especially because *Horace* possibly might seem to him, to have
shewn the Original of all Poetry in general, including the *Grecians*, as
well as *Romans*: Though 'tis plainly otherwise, that he only describ'd
the beginning, and first Rudiments of Poetry in his own Country. The 885
Verses are these, which he cites from the First Epistle of the Second
Book, which was Written to *Augustus*.

> *Agricolæ prisci, fortes, parvoq; beati,*
> *Condita post frumenta, levantes tempore festo*
> *Corpus & ipsum animum spe finis dura ferentem,*   890
> *Cum sociis operum, & pueris, & conjuge fidâ,*
> *Tellurem Porco, Silvanum lacte piabant;*
> *Floribus & vino Genium memorem brevis ævi:*
> *Fescennina per hunc inventa licentia morem*
> *Versibus alternis, opprobria rustica fudit.*   895

> *Our Brawny Clowns of Old, who turn'd the soyl,*
> *Content with little, and inur'd to toyl,*
> *At Harvest home, with Mirth and Country Cheer*

Restor'd their Bodies for another year:
Refresh'd their Spirits, and renew'd their Hope,   900
Of such a future Feast, and future Crop.
Then with their Fellow-joggers of the Ploughs,
Their little Children, and their faithful Spouse;
A Sow they slew to Vesta's *Deity;*
And kindly Milk, Silvanus, *pour'd to thee.*   905
With Flow'rs, and Wine, their Genius they ador'd;
A short Life, and a merry, was the word.
From flowing Cups defaming Rhymes ensue,
And at each other homely Taunts they threw.

Yet since it is a hard Conjecture, that so Great a Man as *Casaubon* 910
shou'd misapply what *Horace* writ concerning Ancient *Rome*, to the
Ceremonies and Manners of Ancient *Greece*, I will not insist on this
Opinion, but rather judge in general, that since all Poetry had its
Original from Religion, that of the *Grecians* and *Rome* had the same
beginning: Both were invented at Festivals of Thanksgiving: And both 915
were prosecuted with Mirth and Raillery, and Rudiments of Verses:
Amongst the *Greeks*, by those who Represented *Satyrs*; and amongst the
Romans by real Clowns.

For, Indeed, when I am Reading *Casaubon*, on these two Subjects,
methinks I hear the same Story told twice over with very little altera- 920
tion. Of which *Dacier* takeing notice, in his Interpretation of the *Latine*
Verses which I have Translated, says plainly, that the beginning of
Poetry was the same, with a small variety in both Countries: And that
the Mother of it in all Nations, was Devotion. But what is yet more
wonderful, that most Learned Critique takes notice also, in his Illustra- 925
tions on the First Epistle of the Second Book, that as the Poetry of the
Romans, and that of the *Grecians*, had the same beginning at Feasts of
Thanksgiving, as it has been Observ'd; and the old Comedy of the
Greeks which was Invective, and the Satire of the *Romans* which was of
the same Nature, were begun on the very same Occasion, so the 930
Fortune of both in process of time was just the same; the old Comedy
of the *Grecians* was forbidden, for its too much License in exposing of
particular Persons, and the Rude Satire of the *Romans* was also Punish'd
by a Law of the *Decemviri*, as *Horace* tells us, in these Words,

Libertasque recurrentes accepta per Annos   935
Lusit amabiliter, donec jam sævus apertam
In rabiem verti cœpit jocus; & per honestas

Ire domos impune minax: Doluere cruento
Dente lacessiti; fuit intactis quoque cura
Conditione super communi: Quinetiam Lex,   940
Pœnaq; lata, malo quæ nollet carmine quemquam
Describi, vertere modum formidine fustis;
Ad benedicendum delectandumq; redacti.

The Law of the *Decemviri*, was this. *Siquis Occentassit malum Carmen,* *sive Condidisit, quod Infamiam faxit, Flagitiumve alteri, Capital esto.* A strange 945 likeness, and barely possible: But the Critiques being all of the same Opinion, it becomes me to be silent, and submit to better Judgments than my own.

But to return to the *Grecians,* from whose Satyrick Drama's, the Elder *Scaliger* and *Heinsius,* will have the *Roman* Satire to proceed, I am 950 to take a View of them first, and see if there be any such Descent from them as those Authors have pretended.

Thespis, or whosoever he were that Invented Tragedy, (for Authors differ) mingl'd with them a Chorus and Dances of *Satyres,* which had before been us'd, in the Celebration of their Festivals; and there they 955 were ever afterwards retain'd. The Character of them was also kept, which was Mirth and Wantonness: And this was given, I suppose, to the folly of the Common Audience, who soon grow weary of good Sense; and as we daily see, in our own Age and Country, are apt to forsake Poetry, and still ready to return, to Buffoonry and Farce. From 960 hence it came, that in the *Olympique-Games,* where the Poets contended for Four Prizes, the Satyrique Tragedy was the last of them: for in the rest, the *Satyrs* were excluded from the Chorus. Amongst the Plays of *Eurypides,* which are yet remaining, there is one of these Satyriques, which is call'd the *Cyclops*; in which we may see the nature of those 965 Poems; and from thence conclude, what likeness they have to the *Roman* Satire.

The Story of this *Cyclops,* whose Name was *Polyphemus,* so famous in the *Grecian* Fables, was, That *Ulysses,* who with his Company was driven on that Coast of *Sicily,* where those *Cyclops* Inhabited, coming to 970 ask Relief from *Silenus,* and the *Satyres,* who were Herdsmen to that One-ey'd Gyant, was kindly receiv'd by them, and entertain'd; till being perceiv'd by *Polyphemus,* they were made Prisoners, against the Rites of Hospitality, for which *Ulysses* Eloquently pleaded, were afterwards put down into the Den, and some of them devour'd: After 975 which, *Ulysses* having made him Drunk, when he was asleep, thrust a great Firebrand into his Eye, and so Revenging his Dead Followers, escap'd with the remaining Party of the Living: And *Silenus* and the *Satyrs*, were freed from their Servitude under *Polyphemus*, and remitted to their first Liberty, of attending and accompanying their Patron 980 *Bacchus*.

This was the Subject of the Tragedy, which being one of those that end with a happy Event, is therefore by *Aristotle* judg'd below the other sort, whose Success is unfortunate. Notwithstanding which, the *Satyrs*, who were part of the *Dramatis Personæ*, as well as the whole 985 *Chorus*, were properly introduc'd into the Nature of the Poem, which is mix'd of Farce and Tragedy. The Adventure of *Ulysses* was to entertain the Judging part of the Audience, and the uncouth Persons of *Silenus*, and the Satyrs, to divert the Common People, with their gross Railleries. 990

Your Lordship has perceiv'd, by this time, that this Satyrique Tragedy, and the *Roman* Satire have little Resemblance in any of their Features. The very Kinds are different: For what has a Pastoral Tragedy to do with a Paper of Verses Satirically written? The Character and Raillery of the Satyres is the only thing that cou'd pretend to a 995 likeness: Were *Scaliger* and *Heinsius* alive to maintain their Opinion. And the first Farces of the *Romans*, which were the Rudiments of their Poetry, were written before they had any Communication with the *Greeks*; or, indeed, any Knowledge of that People.

And here it will be proper to give the Definition of the *Greek* Satyrique 1000 Poem from *Casaubon*, before I leave this Subject. The Satyrique, says he, is a Dramatick Poem, annex'd to a Tragedy; having a Chorus, which consists of Satyrs: The Persons Represented in it, are Illustrious Men: The Action of it is great; the Stile is partly Serious, and partly Jocular; and the Event of the Action most commonly is Happy. 1005

The *Grecians*, besides these Satyrique Tragedies, had another kind of Poem, which they call'd *Silli*; which were more of kin to the *Roman* Satire: Those *Silli* were indeed Invective Poems, but of a different Species from the *Roman* Poems of *Ennius*, *Pacuvius*, *Lucilius*, *Horace*, and the rest of their Successors. They were so call'd, says *Casaubon* in one 1010 place, from *Silenus*, the Foster-Father of *Bacchus*; but in another place, bethinking himself better, he derives their Name ἀπὸ τοῦ σιλλαίνειν, from their Scoffing and Petulancy. From some Fragments of the *Silli*, written by *Timon*, we may find, that they were Satyrique Poems, full of *Parodies*; that is, of Verses patch'd up from great Poets, and turn'd 1015

983 *Aristotle 97: Aristotle, 93*   992 Resemblance] resemblances 97   of their] other 97

into another Sence than their Author intended them. Such amongst the
Romans is the Famous *Cento* of *Ausonius*; where the words are *Virgil*'s:
But by applying them to another Sense, they are made a Relation of a
Wedding-Night; and the Act of Consummation fulsomly describ'd in
the very words of the most Modest amongst all Poets. Of the same 1020
manner are our Songs, which are turn'd into Burlesque; and the serious
words of the Author perverted into a ridiculous meaning. Thus in
Timon's *Silli* the words are generally those of *Homer*, and the Tragick
Poets; but he applies them Satyrically, to some Customs and Kinds of
Philosophy, which he arraigns. But the *Romans* not using any of these 1025
Parodies in their Satyres; sometimes, indeed, repeating Verses of other
Men, as *Persius* cites some of *Nero*'s; but not turning them into another
meaning, the *Silli* cannot be suppos'd to be the Original of *Roman*
Satire. To these *Silli* consisting of *Parodies*, we may properly add, the
Satires which were written against particular Persons; such as were the 1030
Iambiques of *Archilocus* against *Lycambes*, which *Horace* undoubtedly
imitated in some of his *Odes* and *Epodes*, whose Titles bear sufficient
witness of it: I might also name the Invective of *Ovid* against *Ibis*; and
many others: But these are the Under-wood of Satire, rather than the
Timber-Trees: They are not of General Extension, as reaching only to 1035
some Individual Person. And *Horace* seems to have purg'd himself from
those Splenetick Reflections in those *Odes* and *Epodes*, before he under-
took the Noble Work of Satires; which were properly so call'd.

Thus, my Lord, I have at length disengag'd my self from those
Antiquities of *Greece*; and have prov'd, I hope, from the best Critiques, 1040
that the *Roman* Satire was not borrow'd from thence, but of their own
Manufacture: I am now almost gotten into my depth; at least by the
help of *Dacier*, I am swimming towards it. Not that I will promise
always to follow him, any more than he follows *Casaubon*; but to keep
him in my Eye, as my best and truest Guide; and where I think he may 1045
possibly mislead me, there to have recourse to my own lights, as I
expect that others should do by me.

Quintilian says, in plain words, *Satira quidem tota, nostra est:* And
Horace had said the same thing before him, speaking of his Predecessor
in that sort of Poetry, *Et Græcis intacti Carminis Auctor*. Nothing can be 1050
clearer than the Opinion of the Poet, and the Orator, both the best
Criticks of the two best Ages of the *Roman* Empire, that Satire was
wholly of *Latin* growth, and not transplanted from *Athens* to Rome. Yet,

1032 bear sufficient] bear a sufficient 97   1050 *Auctor*] *Author* 93 97
1052 Empire, that] Empire, than that 93 97   1053 from *Athens* to Rome 97: to
Rome from *Athens* 93

as I have said, *Scaliger*, the Father, according to his Custom, that is, insolently enough, contradicts them both; and gives no better Reason, 10 than the derivation of *Satyrus* from σάθυ *Salacitas*; and so from the Lechery of those Fauns, thinks he has sufficiently prov'd, that Satyre is deriv'd from them. As if Wantonness and lubricity, were Essential to that sort of Poem, which ought to be avoided in it. His other Allegation, which I have already mention'd, is as pitiful: That the *Satyres* carried Platters and Canisters full of Fruit, in their Hands. If they had enter'd empty-handed, had they been ever the less *Satyres*? Or were the Fruits and Flowers, which they offer'd, any thing of kin to Satyre? Or any Argument that this Poem was Originally *Grecian*? *Casaubon* judg'd better, and his Opinion is grounded on sure Authority; that *Satyre* was deriv'd from *Satura*, a *Roman* word, which signifies Full, and Abundant; and full also of Variety, in which nothing is wanting to its due Perfection. 'Tis thus, says *Dacier*, that we lay a full Colour, when the Wool has taken the whole Tincture, and drunk in as much of the Dye as it can receive. According to this Derivation, from *Satur* comes *Satura*, or *Satira*: According to the new spelling; as *optumus* and *maxumus* are now spell'd *optimus* and *maximus*. *Satura*, as I have formerly noted, is an Adjective, and relates to the word *Lanx*, which is understood. And this *Lanx*, in *English* a Charger, or large Platter, was yearly fill'd with all sorts of Fruits, which were offer'd to the Gods at their Festivals, as the *Premices*, or First Gatherings. These Offerings of several sorts thus mingl'd, 'tis true, were not unknown to the *Grecians*, who call'd them παγκαρπὸν θυσίαν, a Sacrifice of all sorts of Fruits; and πανσπερμίαν, when they offer'd all kinds of Grain. *Virgil* has mention'd these Sacrifices in his *Georgiques*, *Lancibus & pandis, fumantia reddimus Exta:* And in another place, *Lancesq; & liba feremus.* That is, we offer the smoking Entrails in great Platters; and we will offer the Chargers, and the Cakes.

This word *Satura* has been afterward apply'd to many other sorts of Mixtures; as *Festus* calls it a kind of *Olla*, or hotch-potch, made of several sorts of Meats. Laws were also call'd *Leges Saturæ*; when they were of several Heads and Titles; like our tack'd Bills of Parliament. And *per Saturam legem ferre*, in the *Roman* Senate, was to carry a Law without telling the Senatours, or counting Voices, when they were in haste. *Salust* uses the word *per Saturam Sententias exquirere;* when the Majority was visibly on one side. From hence it might probably be conjectur'd, that the Discourses or Satyres of *Ennius*, *Lucilius*, and

Horace, as we now call them, took their Name; because they are full of various Matters, and are also Written on various Subjects, as *Porphyrius* says. But *Dacier* affirms, that it is not immediately from thence that these Satyres are so call'd: For that Name had been us'd formerly 1095 for other things, which bore a nearer resemblance to those Discourses of *Horace*. In explaining of which, (continues *Dacier*) a Method is to be pursu'd, of which *Casaubon* himself has never thought, and which will put all things into so clear a light, that no farther room will be left for the least Dispute. 1100

During the space of almost four hundred years, since the Building of their City, the *Romans* had never known any Entertainments of the Stage: Chance and Jollity first found out those Verses which they call'd *Saturnian*, and *Fescennine*: Or rather Humane Nature, which is inclin'd to Poetry, first produc'd them, rude and barbarous, and unpolish'd, as 1105 all other Operations of the Soul are in their beginnings, before they are Cultivated with Art and Study. However, in occasions of Merriment they were first practis'd; and this rough-cast unhewn Poetry, was instead of Stage-Plays for the space of an hundred and twenty years together. They were made *extempore*, and were, as the *French* call them, 1110 *Impromptus*: For which the *Tarsians* of Old were much Renown'd; and we see the daily Examples of them in the *Italian* Farces of *Harlequin*, and *Scaramucha*. Such was the Poetry of that Salvage People, before it was tun'd into Numbers, and the Harmony of Verse. Little of the *Saturnian* Verses is now remaining; we only know from Authors, that they were 1115 nearer Prose than Poetry, without feet, or measure. They were ἔνρυθμοι, but not ἔμμετροι: Perhaps they might be us'd in the solemn part of their Ceremonies, and the *Fescennine*, which were invented after them, in their Afternoons Debauchery, because they were scoffing, and obscene.

The *Fescennine* and *Saturnian* were the same; for as they were call'd 1120 *Saturnian* from their Ancientness, when *Saturn* Reign'd in *Italy*; they were also call'd *Fescennine*, from *Fescennia*, a Town in the same Country, where they were first practis'd. The Actors with a Gross and Rustick kind of raillery, reproach'd each other with their Failings; and at the same time were nothing sparing of it to their Audience. Somewhat of 1125 this Custom was afterwards retain'd in their *Saturnalia*, or Feasts of *Saturn*, Celebrated in *December*; at least all kind of freedom in Speech was then allow'd to Slaves, even against their Masters; and we are not without some imitation of it in our *Christmas Gambols*. Souldiers also us'd

1103 Stage] State 97
1122 *Fescennia*] *Fescenina* 93 97

those *Fescennine* Verses, after Measure and Numbers had been added to 113 them, at the Triumph of their Generals: Of which we have an Example, in the Triumph of *Julius Cæsar* over *Gaul*, in these Expressions: *Cæsar Gallias subegit, Nicomedes Cæsarem: Ecce Cæsar nunc triumphat, qui subegit Gallias; Nicomedes non triumphat, qui subegit Cæsarem.* The vapours of Wine made those first Satyrical Poets amongst the *Romans*; which, says 113 *Dacier*, we cannot better represent, than by imagining a Company of Clowns on a Holyday, dancing Lubberly, and upbraiding one another in *Extempore* Doggrel, with their Defects and Vices, and the Stories that were told of them in Bake-houses, and Barbers Shops.

When they began to be somewhat better bred, and were entring, as 114 I may say, into the first Rudiments of Civil Conversation, they left these Hedge Notes, for another sort of Poem, somewhat polish'd, which was also full of pleasant Raillery, but without any mixture of obscenity. This sort of Poetry appear'd under the name of Satire, because of its variety: And this Satire was adorn'd with Compositions of Musick, and 114 with Dances: but Lascivious Postures were banish'd from it. In the *Tuscan* Language, says *Livy*, the word *Hister* signifies a Player: And therefore those Actors, which were first brought from *Etruria* to *Rome*, on occasion of a Pestilence; when the *Romans* were admonish'd to avert the Anger of the Gods by Plays, in the Year *ab Urbe Condita*, CCCXC. 115 Those Actors, I say, were therefore call'd *Histriones*: And that Name has since remain'd, not only to Actors *Roman* born, but to all others of every Nation. They Play'd not the former *extempore* stuff of *Fescennine* Verses, or Clownish Jests; but what they Acted, was a kind of civil cleanly Farce, with Musick and Dances, and Motions that were proper 115 to the Subject.

In this Condition *Livius Andronicus* found the Stage, when he attempted first, instead of Farces, to supply it with a Nobler Entertainment of Tragedies and Comedies. This Man was a *Grecian* born, and being made a Slave by *Livius Salinator*, and brought to *Rome*, had the 116 Education of his Patron's Children committed to him. Which trust he discharg'd, so much to the satisfaction of his Master, that he gave him his Liberty.

Andronicus thus become a Freeman of *Rome*, added to his own Name that of *Livius* his Master; and, as I observ'd, was the first Author of a 116 Regular Play in that Commonwealth. Being already instructed in his Native Country, in the Manners and Decencies of the *Athenian* Theater, and Conversant in the *Archæa Comœdia*, or old Comedy of *Aristophanes*,

1132 Expressions: 97: Expressions. 93   1135 those] the 97

and the rest of the *Grecian* Poets; he took from that Model his own designing of Plays for the *Roman* Stage. The first of which was repre- 1170 sented in the Year 514. since the building of *Rome*, as *Tully*, from the Commentaries of *Atticus*, has assur'd us; it was after the end of the first *Punick* War, the year before *Ennius* was born. *Dacier* has not carry'd the matter altogether thus far; he only says, that one *Livius Andronicus* was the first Stage-Poet at *Rome*: But I will adventure on this hint, to 1175 advance another Proposition, which I hope the Learned will approve. And though we have not any thing of *Andronicus* remaining to justifie my Conjecture, yet 'tis exceeding probable, that having read the Works of those *Grecian* Wits, his Countrymen, he imitated not only the ground-work, but also the manner of their Writing. And how grave soever 1180 his Tragedies might be, yet in his Comedies he express'd the way of *Aristophanes*, *Eupolis*, and the rest, which was to call some Persons by their own Names, and to expose their Defects to the laughter of the People. The Examples of which we have in the foremention'd *Aristo-phanes*, who turn'd the wise *Socrates* into Ridicule; and is also very free 1185 with the management of *Cleon*, *Alcibiades*, and other Ministers of the *Athenian* Government. Now if this be granted, we may easily suppose, that the first hint of Satirical Plays on the *Roman* Stage, was given by the *Greeks*. Not from their *Satyrica*, for that has been reasonably ex-ploded in the former part of this Discourse: But from their old Comedy, 1190 which was imitated first by *Livius Andronicus*. And then *Quintilian* and *Horace* must be cautiously Interpreted, where they affirm, that Satire is wholly *Roman*; and a sort of Verse, which was not touch'd on by the *Grecians*. The reconcilement of my Opinion to the Standard of their Judgment, is not however very difficult, since they spoke of Satire, not 1195 as in its first Elements, but as it was form'd into a separate Work; begun by *Ennius*, pursu'd by *Lucilius*, and compleated afterwards by *Horace*. The Proof depends only on this *Postulatum*, that the Comedies of *Andronicus*, which were imitations of the *Greek*, were also imitations of their Railleries, and Reflections on particular Persons. For if this be 1200 granted me, which is a most probable Supposition, 'tis easie to infer, that the first light which was given to the *Roman Theatrical* Satire, was from the Plays of *Livius Andronicus*. Which will be more manifestly dis-cover'd, when I come to speak of *Ennius*: In the mean time I will return to *Dacier*. 1205

The People, says he, ran in Crowds to these New Entertainments of *Andronicus*, as to Pieces which were more Noble in their kind, and more

perfect than their former Satires, which for some time they neglected
and abandon'd. But not long after, they took them up again, and then
they joyn'd them to their Comedies: Playing them at the end of every   121
Drama; as the *French* continue at this Day to Act their Farces; in the
nature of a separate Entertainment, from their Tragedies. But more
particularly they were joyn'd to the *Atellane* Fables, says *Casaubon*;
which were Plays invented by the *Osci*. Those Fables, says *Valerius
Maximus*, out of *Livy*, were temper'd with the *Italian* severity, and free   121
from any note of Infamy, or Obsceneness; and as an old Commentator
on *Juvenal* affirms, the *Exodiarii*, which were Singers and Dancers,
enter'd to entertain the People with light Songs, and Mimical Gestures,
that they might not go away oppress'd with Melancholly, from those
serious Pieces of the Theater. So that the Ancient Satire of the *Romans*   122
was in Extemporary Reproaches: The next was Farce, which was
brought from *Tuscany*: To that Succeeded the Plays of *Andronicus*, from
the old Comedy of the *Grecians*: And out of all these, sprung two several
Branches of new *Roman* Satire; like different Cyens from the same
Root. Which I shall prove with as much Brevity as the Subject will   122
allow.

A Year after *Andronicus* had open'd the *Roman* Stage, with his new
Drama's, *Ennius* was Born: who, when he was grown to Mans Estate,
haveing seriously consider'd the Genius of the People, and how eagerly
they follow'd the first Satires, thought it wou'd be worth his Pains, to   123
refine upon the Project, and to write Satires not to be Acted on the
Theater, but Read. He preserv'd the Ground-work of their Pleasantry,
their Venom, and their Raillery on particular Persons, and general
Vices: And by this means, avoiding the danger of any ill Success, in a
Publick Representation, he hop'd to be as well receiv'd in the Cabinet,   123
as *Andronicus* had been upon the Stage. The Event was answerable to
his Expectation. He made Discourses in several sorts of Verse, vari'd
often in the same Paper; Retaining still in the Title, their Original
Name of Satire. Both in relation to the Subjects and the variety of
Matters contain'd in them, the Satires of *Horace* are entirely like them;   124
only *Ennius*, as I said, confines not himself to one sort of Verse, as
Horace does; but takeing Example from the *Greeks*, and even from
Homer himself, in his *Margites*, which is a kind of Satire, as *Scaliger*
observes, gives himself the License, when one sort of Numbers comes
not easily, to run into another, as his Fancy Dictates. For he makes no   124
difficulty, to mingle Hexameters with Iambique Trimeters; or with
Trochaique Tetrameters; as appears by those Fragments which are yet

remaining of him: *Horace* has thought him worthy to be Copy'd; inserting many things of his into his own Satires, as *Virgil* has done into his *Æneids*.   1250

Here we have *Dacier* making out that *Ennius* was the first Satyrist in that way of Writing, which was of his Invention; that is, Satire abstracted from the Stage, and new modell'd into Papers of Verses, on several Subjects. But he will have *Ennius* take the Ground-work of Satire from the first Farces of the *Romans*; rather than from the form'd 1255 Plays of *Livius Andronicus*, which were Copy'd from the *Grecian* Comedies. It may possibly be so; but *Dacier* knows no more of it than I do. And it seems to me the more probable Opinion, that he rather imitated the fine Railleries of the *Greeks*, which he saw in the Pieces of *Andronicus*, than the Coursness of his old Country-men, in their 1260 Clownish Extemporary way of jeering.

But besides this, 'tis Universally Granted, that *Ennius* though an *Italian*, was excellently Learn'd in the *Greek* Language. His Verses were stuff'd with Fragments of it, even to a fault: And he himself believ'd, according to the *Pithagorean* Opinion, that the Soul of *Homer* was trans- 1265 fus'd into him: Which *Persius* observes, in his *Sixth Satire: Postquam desertuit esse Mæonides*. But this being only the private Opinion of so inconsiderable a Man as I am, I leave it to the farther Disquisition of the Critiques, if they think it worth their notice. Most evident it is, that whether he imitated the *Roman* Farce, or the *Greek* Comedies, he is to 1270 be acknowledg'd for the first Author of *Roman Satire*; as it is properly so call'd; and distinguish'd from any sort of Stage-Play.

Of *Pacuvius*, who succeeded him, there is little to be said, because there is so little remaining of him: Only that he is taken to be the Nephew of *Ennius*, his Sisters Son; that in probability he was instructed 1275 by his Uncle, in his way of Satire, which we are told he has Copy'd; but what Advances he made we know not.

Lucilius came into the World, when *Pacuvius* flourish'd most; he also made Satires after the manner of *Ennius*, but he gave them a more graceful turn; and endeavour'd to imitate more closely the *vetus* 1280 *Comœdia* of the *Greeks*: Of the which the old Original *Roman* Satire had no Idea, till the time of *Livius Andronicus*. And though *Horace* seems to have made *Lucilius* the first Author of Satire in Verse, amongst the *Romans*; in these Words, *Quid cum est* Lucilius *ausus Primus in hunc operis componere carmina morem:* He is only thus to be understood, That 1285 *Lucilius* had given a more graceful turn to the Satire of *Ennius* and *Pacuvius*; not that he invented a new Satire of his own: And *Quintilian* seems to Explain this Passage of *Horace* in these words; *Satira quidem tota nostra est, in qua primus insignem laudem adeptus est* Lucilius.

Thus, both *Horace* and *Quintilian*, give a kind of Primacy of Honour 129 to *Lucilius*, amongst the Latin Satirists. For as the *Roman* Language grew more Refin'd, so much more capable it was of receiving the *Grecian* Beauties in his time: *Horace* and *Quintilian* cou'd mean no more, than that *Lucilius* writ better than *Ennius* and *Pacuvius*: And on the same account we prefer *Horace* to *Lucilius*: Both of them imitated 129 the old *Greek* Comedy; and so did *Ennius* and *Pacuvius* before them. The polishing of the Latin Tongue, in the Succession of Times, made the only difference. And *Horace* himself, in two of his Satires, written purposely on this Subject, thinks the *Romans* of his Age, were too Partial in their Commendations of *Lucilius*; who writ not only loosely, and 130 muddily, with little Art, and much less Care, but also in a time when the Latin Tongue was not yet sufficiently purg'd from the Dregs of Barbarism; and many significant and sounding Words, which the *Romans* wanted, were not admitted even in the times of *Lucretius* and *Cicero*; of which both complain.   130

But to proceed, *Dacier* justly taxes *Casaubon*, for saying, That the Satires of *Lucilius* were wholly different in *Specie*, from those of *Ennius* and *Pacuvius*. *Casaubon* was led into that mistake, by *Diomedes* the Grammarian, who in effect says this. Satire amongst the *Romans*, but not amongst the *Greeks*, was a biteing invective Poem, made after the 131 Model of the Ancient Comedy; for the Reprehension of Vices: Such as were the Poems of *Lucilius*, of *Horace*, and of *Persius*. But in former times, the Name of Satire was given to Poems, which were compos'd of several sorts of Verses; such as were made by *Ennius*, and *Pacuvius*; more fully expressing the Etymology of the word Satire, from *Satura*, which we 131 have observ'd. Here 'tis manifest, that *Diomedes* makes a Specifical Distinction betwixt the Satires of *Ennius*, and those of *Lucilius*. But this, as we say in *English*, is only a Distinction without a Difference; for the Reason of it, is ridiculous, and absolutely false. This was that which cozen'd honest *Casaubon*, who relying on *Diomedes*, had not sufficiently 132 examin'd the Origine and Nature of those two Satires; which were entirely the same, both in the Matter and the Form. For all that *Lucilius* perform'd beyond his Predecessors, *Ennius* and *Pacuvius*, was only the adding of more Politeness, and more Salt; without any change in the Substance of the Poem: And tho' *Lucilius* put not together in 132 the same Satire several sorts of Verses, as *Ennius* did; yet he compos'd several Satires, of several sorts of Verses; and mingl'd them with Greek

Verses: One Poem consisted only of Hexameters; and another was entirely of Iambiques; a third of Trochaiques; as is visible by the Fragments yet remaining of his Works. In short, if the Satires of *Lucilius* 1330 are therefore said to be wholly different from those of *Ennius*, because he added much more of Beauty and Polishing to his own Poems, than are to be found in those before him; it will follow from hence, that the Satires of *Horace* are wholly different from those of *Lucilius*, because *Horace* has not less surpass'd *Lucilius* in the Elegancy of his Writing, 1335 than *Lucilius* surpass'd *Ennius* in the turn and Ornament of his. This Passage of *Diomedes* has also drawn *Dousa*, the Son, into the same Error of *Casaubon*, which, I say, not to expose the little Failings of those Judicious Men, but only to make it appear, with how much Diffidence and Caution we are to Read their Works; when they treat 1340 a Subject of so much Obscurity, and so very ancient, as is this of Satire.

Having thus brought down the History of Satire from its Original, to the times of *Horace*, and shewn the several changes of it, I shou'd here discover some of those Graces which *Horace* added to it, but that 1345 I think it will be more proper to defer that Undertaking, till I make the Comparison betwixt him and *Juvenal*. In the mean while, following the Order of Time, it will be necessary to say somewhat of another kind of Satire, which also was descended from the Ancients: 'Tis that which we call the *Varronian* Satire, but which *Varro* himself calls the *Menip-* 1350 *pean*; because *Varro*, the most Learn'd of the *Romans*, was the first Author of it, who imitated, in his Works, the Manners of *Menippus* the *Gadarenian*, who profess'd the Philosophy of the *Cyniques*.

This sort of Satire was not only compos'd of several sorts of Verse, like those of *Ennius*, but was also mix'd with Prose; and Greek was 1355 sprinkl'd amongst the Latin. *Quintilian*, after he had spoken of the Satire of *Lucilius*, adds what follows. *There is another and former kind of Satire, Compos'd by* Terentius Varro, *the most Learn'd of the* Romans: *In which he was not satisfy'd alone, with mingling in it several sorts of Verse.* The only difficulty of this Passage, is, that *Quintilian* tells us, that this Satire 1360 of *Varro* was of a former kind. For how can we possibly imagine this to be, since *Varro*, who was contemporary to *Cicero*, must consequently be after *Lucilius*? But *Quintilian* meant not, that the Satire of *Varro* was in order of Time before *Lucilius*; he wou'd only give us to understand, that the *Varronian* Satire, with mixture of several sorts of Verses, was 1365 more after the manner of *Ennius* and *Pacuvius*, than that of *Lucilius*, who was more severe, and more correct; and gave himself less liberty in the mixture of his Verses, in the same Poem.

We have nothing remaining of those *Varronian* Satires, excepting some inconsiderable Fragments; and those for the most part much 1370 corrupted. The Titles of many of them are indeed preserv'd, and they are generally double: From whence, at least, we may understand, how many various Subjects were treated by that Author. *Tully*, in his Academicks, introduces *Varro* himself giving us some light concerning the Scope and Design of those Works. Wherein, after he had shewn his 1375 Reasons why he did not *ex professo* write of Philosophy, he adds what follows. Notwithstanding, *says he*, that those Pieces of mine, wherein I have imitated *Menippus*, though I have not Translated him, are sprinkled with a kind of mirth, and gayety: Yet many things are there inserted, which are drawn from the very intrails of Philosophy, and 1380 many things severely argu'd: Which I have mingl'd with Pleasantries on purpose, that they may more easily go down with the Common sort of Unlearn'd Readers. The rest of the Sentence is so lame, that we can only make thus much out of it; that in the Composition of his Satires, he so temper'd Philology with Philosophy, that his Work was a mixture 1385 of them both. And *Tully* himself confirms us in this Opinion; when a little after he addresses himself to *Varro* in these words. *And you your self have compos'd a most Elegant and Compleat Poem; you have begun Philosophy in many Places: Sufficient to incite us, though too little to Instruct us.* Thus it appears, that *Varro* was one of those Writers whom they call'd 1390 σπουδογελοῖοι, studious of laughter; and that, as Learned as he was, his business was more to divert his Reader, than to teach him. And he Entitled his own Satires *Menippean*: Not that *Menippus* had written any Satires, (for his were either Dialogues or Epistles) but that *Varro* imitated his Style, his Manner, and his Facetiousness. All that we 1395 know farther of *Menippus*, and his Writings, which are wholly lost; is, that by some he is esteem'd, as, amongst the rest, by *Varro*: By others he is noted of Cynical Impudence, and Obscenity: That he was much given to those *Parodies*, which I have already mention'd; that is, he often quoted the Verses of *Homer* and the Tragick Poets, and turn'd 1400 their serious meaning into something that was Ridiculous; whereas *Varro's* Satires are by *Tully* call'd Absolute, and most Elegant, and Various Poems. *Lucian*, who was emulous of this *Menippus*, seems to have imitated both his Manners and his Style in many of his Dialogues; where *Menippus* himself is often introduc'd as a Speaker in them, and 1405

1375 those 97: these 93

as a perpetual Buffoon: Particularly his Character is express'd in the beginning of that Dialogue which is call'd Νεκυομαντεία. But *Varro*, in imitating him, avoids his impudence and filthiness, and only expresses his witty Pleasantry.

This we may believe for certain, That as his Subjects were various, 1410 so most of them were Tales or Stories of his own invention. Which is also manifest from Antiquity, by those Authors who are acknowledg'd to have written *Varronian* Satires, in imitation of his: Of whom the Chief is *Petronius Arbiter*, whose Satire, they say, is now Printing in *Holland*, wholly recover'd, and made compleat: When 'tis made publick, 1415 it will easily be seen by any one Sentence, whether it be supposititious, or genuine. Many of *Lucian*'s Dialogues may also properly be call'd *Varronian* Satires; particularly his *True History*: And consequently the *Golden Ass* of *Apuleius*, which is taken from him. Of the same stamp is the Mock Deification of *Claudius*, by *Seneca*: And the *Symposium* or *Cæsars* 1420 of *Julian* the Emperour. Amongst the Moderns we may reckon the *Encomium Moriæ* of *Erasmus*, *Barclay*'s *Euphormio*, and a Volume of *German* Authors, which my ingenious Friend Mr. *Charles Killigrew* once lent me. In the English I remember none, which are mix'd with Prose, as *Varro*'s were: But of the same kind is Mother *Hubbard*'s Tale in 1425 *Spencer*; and (if it be not too vain, to mention any thing of my own) the Poems of *Absalom*, and *Mac Fleckno*.

This is what I have to say in General of Satire: Only as *Dacier* has observ'd before me, we may take notice, That the word Satire is of a more general signification in Latin, than in French, or English. For 1430 amongst the *Romans* it was not only us'd for those Discourses which decry'd Vice, or expos'd Folly; but for others also, where Virtue was recommended. But in our Modern Languages we apply it only to invective Poems, where the very Name of Satire is formidable to those Persons, who wou'd appear to the World, what they are not in them- 1435 selves. For in English, to say Satire, is to mean Reflection, as we use that word in the worst Sense; or as the *French* call it, more properly, *Medisance*. In the Criticism of Spelling, it ought to be with *i* and not with *y*; to distinguish its true derivation from *Satura*, not from *Satyrus*. And if this be so, then 'tis false spell'd throughout this Book: For here 1440 'tis written Satyr. Which having not consider'd at the first, I thought it not worth Correcting afterwards. But the *French* are more nice, and never spell it any other ways than Satire.

I am now arriv'd at the most difficult part of my Undertaking, which

1407 Νεκυομαντεία] Νεκυομαντία 93 97   1443 ways] way 97

is, to compare *Horace* with *Juvenal* and *Persius*: 'Tis observ'd by 1445
Rigaltius, in his Preface before *Juvenal*, written to *Thuanus*, that these
three Poets have all their particular *Partisans*, and Favourers: Every
Commentator, as he has taken pains with any of them, thinks himself
oblig'd to prefer his Author to the other two: To find out their Failings,
and decry them, that he may make room for his own Darling. Such is 1450
the partiality of Mankind, to set up that Interest which they have once
espous'd, though it be to the prejudice of Truth, Morality, and common Justice. And especially in the productions of the Brain. As Authors
generally think themselves the best Poets, because they cannot go out
of themselves, to judge sincerely of their Betters: So it is with Critiques, 1455
who, having first taken a liking to one of these Poets, proceed to
Comment on him, and to Illustrate him; after which they fall in love
with their own Labours, to that degree of blind fondness, that at length
they defend and exalt their Author, not so much for his sake as for their
own. 'Tis a folly of the same Nature, with that of the *Romans* them- 1460
selves, in their Games of the *Circus*; the Spectators were divided in their
Factions, betwixt the *Veneti* and the *Prasini*: Some were for the Charioteer
in Blue, and some for him in Green. The Colours themselves were but
a Fancy; but when once a Man had taken pains to set out those of his
Party, and had been at the trouble of procuring Voices for them, the 1465
Case was alter'd: He was concern'd for his own Labour: And that so
earnestly, that Disputes and Quarrels, Animosities, Commotions, and
Bloodshed, often happen'd: And in the Declension of the *Grecian*
Empire, the very Soveraigns themselves ingag'd in it, even when the
Barbarians were at their doors; and stickled for the preference of 1470
Colours, when the safety of their People was in question. I am now, my
self, on the brink of the same Precipice; I have spent some time on the
Translation of *Juvenal*, and *Persius*: And it behoves me to be wary, lest,
for that Reason, I shou'd be partial to them, or take a prejudice against
Horace. Yet, on the other side, I wou'd not be like some of our Judges, 1475
who wou'd give the Cause for a Poor Man, right or wrong: For though
that be an Errour on the better hand, yet it is still a partiality: And a
Rich Man, unhear'd, cannot be concluded an Oppressor. I remember
a saying of K. *Charles* the Second, on Sir *Matthew Hales*, (who was
doubtless an Uncorrupt and Upright Man) That his Servants were sure 1480
to be Cast on any Trial, which was heard before him: Not that he
thought the Judge was possibly to be brib'd; but that his Integrity
might be too scrupulous: And that the Causes of the Crown were
always suspicious, when the Priviledges of Subjects were concern'd.

It had been much fairer, if the Modern Critiques, who have imbark'd 1485
in the Quarrels of their favourite Authors, had rather given to each his
proper due; without taking from another's heap, to raise their own.
There is Praise enough for each of them in particular, without encroaching on his Fellows, and detracting from them, or Enriching themselves
with the Spoils of others. But to come to particulars: *Heinsius* and 1490
Dacier, are the most principal of those, who raise *Horace* above *Juvenal*
and *Persius*. *Scaliger* the Father, *Rigaltius*, and many others, debase
Horace, that they may set up *Juvenal*: And *Casaubon*, who is almost
single, throws Dirt on *Juvenal* and *Horace*, that he may exalt *Persius*,
whom he understood particularly well, and better than any of his 1495
former Commentators; even *Stelluti* who succeeded him. I will begin
with him, who in my Opinion defends the weakest Cause, which is
that of *Persius*; and labouring, as *Tacitus* professes of his own Writing,
to divest my self of partiality, or prejudice, consider *Persius*, not as a
Poet, whom I have wholly Translated, and who has cost me more 1500
labour and time, than *Juvenal*; but according to what I judge to be his
own Merit; which I think not equal in the main, to that of *Juvenal* or
Horace; and yet in some things to be preferr'd to both of them.

First, then, for the Verse, neither *Casaubon* himself, nor any for him,
can defend either his Numbers, or the Purity of his *Latin*. *Casaubon* gives 1505
this point for lost; and pretends not to justifie either the Measures, or
the Words of *Persius*: He is evidently beneath *Horace* and *Juvenal*, in
both.

Then, as his Verse is scabrous, and hobbling, and his Words not
every where well chosen, the purity of *Latin* being more corrupted, 1510
than in the time of *Juvenal*, and consequently of *Horace*, who writ when
the Language was in the heighth of its perfection; so his diction is hard;
his Figures are generally too bold and daring; and his Tropes, particularly his Metaphors, insufferably strain'd.

In the third place, notwithstanding all the diligence of *Casaubon*, 1515
Stelluti, and a *Scotch* Gentleman (whom I have hear'd extreamly commended for his Illustrations of him:) yet he is still obscure: Whether he
affected not to be understood, but with difficulty; or whether the fear
of his safety under *Nero*, compell'd him to this darkness in some places;
or that it was occasion'd by his close way of thinking, and the brevity 1520
of his Style, and crowding of his Figures; or lastly, whether after so
long a time, many of his Words have been corrupted, and many
Customs, and Stories relating to them, lost to us; whether some of
these Reasons, or all, concurr'd to render him so cloudy; we may be

bold to affirm, that the best of Commentators can but guess at his 152:
Meaning, in many passages: And none can be certain that he has
divin'd rightly.

After all, he was a Young Man, like his Friend and Contemporary
Lucan: Both of them Men of extraordinary Parts, and great acquir'd
Knowledge, considering their Youth. But neither of them had arriv'd 153c
to that Maturity of Judgment, which is necessary to the accomplishing
of a form'd Poet. And this Consideration, as on the one hand it lays
some Imperfections to their charge, so on the other side 'tis a candid
excuse for those Failings, which are incident to Youth and Inexperience;
and we have more Reason to wonder, how they, who Dyed before the 153:
Thirtieth Year of their Age, cou'd write so well, and think so strongly;
than to accuse them of those Faults, from which Humane Nature, and
more especially in Youth, can never possibly be exempted.

To consider *Persius* yet more closely: He rather insulted over Vice
and Folly, than expos'd them, like *Juvenal* and *Horace*. And as Chaste, 154c
and Modest as he is esteem'd, it cannot be deny'd, but that in some
places, he is broad and fulsom, as the latter Verses of the Fourth Satire,
and of the Sixth, sufficiently witness. And 'tis to be believ'd, that he
who commits the same Crime often, and without Necessity, cannot
but do it with some kind of Pleasure.   154:

To come to a conclusion, He is manifestly below *Horace*; because he
borrows most of his greatest Beauties from him: And *Casaubon* is so far
from denying this, that he has written a Treatise purposely concerning
it; wherein he shews a multitude of his Translations from *Horace*, and
his imitations of him, for the Credit of his Author; which he calls 155c
Imitatio Horatiana.

To these defects, which I casually observ'd, while I was Translating
this Author, *Scaliger* has added others: He calls him, in plain terms, a
silly Writer, and a trifler; full of Ostentation of his Learning; and after
all, unworthy to come into Competition with *Juvenal* and *Horace*.   155:

After such terrible Accusations, 'tis time to hear what his Patron
Casaubon can alledge in his Defence. Instead of answering, he excuses
for the most part; and when he cannot, accuses others of the same
Crimes. He deals with *Scaliger*, as a Modest Scholar with a Master. He
Compliments him with so much Reverence, that one wou'd swear he 156:
Fear'd him as much at least as he Respected him. *Scaliger* will not allow
Persius to have any Wit: *Casaubon* Interprets this in the mildest Sense;
and confesses his Author was not good at turning things into a pleasant

1548 this, *97*: this; *93*

Ridicule; or in other words, that he was not a laughable Writer. That he was *ineptus*, indeed, but that was, *non aptissimus ad jocandum*. But that he was Ostentatious of his Learning, that, by *Scaliger*'s good Favour, he denies. *Persius* shew'd his Learning, but was no Boaster of it; he did *ostendere*, but not *ostentare*; and so, he says, did *Scaliger*: Where, me-thinks, *Casaubon* turns it handsomly, upon that supercilious Critick, and silently insinuates, that he himself was sufficiently vain-glorious; and a boaster of his own Knowledge. All the Writings of this Venerable *Censor*, continues *Casaubon*, which are χρυσοῦ χρυσότερα, more golden, than Gold it self, are every where smelling of that Thyme, which, like a Bee, he has gather'd from Ancient Authors: But far be Ostentation and Vain-Glory from a Gentleman, so well Born, and so Nobly Edu-cated as *Scaliger*: But, says *Scaliger*, he is so obscure, that he has got himself the Name of *Scotinus*, a dark Writer. Now, says *Casaubon*, 'tis a wonder to me, that any thing cou'd be obscure to the Divine Wit of *Scaliger*; from which nothing cou'd be hidden. This is indeed a strong Compliment, but no Defence. And *Casaubon*, who cou'd not but be sensible of his Author's blind side, thinks it time to abandon a Post that was untenable. He acknowledges that *Persius* is obscure in some places; but so is *Plato*, so is *Thucydides*; so are *Pindar*, *Theocritus*, and *Aristophanes* amongst the *Greek* Poets; and even *Horace* and *Juvenal*, he might have added, amongst the *Romans*. The Truth is, *Persius* is not sometimes, but generally obscure: And therefore *Casaubon*, at last, is forc'd to excuse him, by alledging that it was *se defendendo*, for fear of *Nero*; and that he was commanded to Write so cloudily by *Cornutus*, in virtue of Holy Obedience to his Master. I cannot help my own Opinion; I think *Cornutus* needed not to have Read many Lectures to him on that Sub-ject. *Persius* was an apt Scholar; and when he was bidden to be obscure, in some places, where his Life and Safety were in question, took the same Counsel for all his Book; and never afterwards Wrote ten Lines together clearly. *Casaubon*, being upon this Chapter, has not fail'd, we may be sure, of making a Compliment to his own dear Comment. If *Persius*, says he, be in himself obscure, yet my Interpretation has made him intelligible. There is no question, but he deserves that Praise, which he has given to himself: But the Nature of the thing, as *Lucretius* says, will not admit of a perfect Explanation. Besides many Examples which I cou'd urge; the very last Verse of his last Satire, upon which he particularly values himself in his Preface, is not yet sufficiently expli-cated. 'Tis true, *Holiday* has endeavour'd to justifie his Construction; but *Stelluti* is against it: And, for my part, I can have but a very dark

Notion of it. As for the Chastity of his Thoughts, *Casaubon* denies not, but that one particular passage, in the Fourth Satire, *At, si unctus cesses,* 1605 &c. is not only the most obscure, but the most obscene of all his Works: I understood it; but for that Reason turn'd it over. In defence of his boistrous Metaphors, he quotes *Longinus,* who accounts them as instruments of the Sublime: Fit to move and stir up the Affections, particularly in Narration. To which it may be reply'd, That where the Trope 1610 is far fetch'd, and hard, 'tis fit for nothing but to puzzle the Understanding: And may be reckon'd amongst those things of *Demosthenes,* which *Æschines,* call'd θαύματα not ῥήματα; that is Prodigies, not Words. It must be granted to *Casaubon,* that the Knowledge of many things is lost in our Modern Ages, which were of familiar notice to the Ancients: 1615 And that Satire is a Poem of a difficult Nature in it self, and is not written to Vulgar Readers. And through the Relation which it has to Comedy, the frequent change of Persons, makes the Sense perplex'd; when we can but Divine, who it is that speaks: Whether *Persius* himself, or his Friend and Monitor; or, in some places, a third Person. But 1620 *Casaubon* comes back always to himself, and concludes, that if *Persius* had not been obscure, there had been no need of him for an Interpreter. Yet when he had once enjoyn'd himself so hard a Task, he then consider'd the *Greek* Proverb, that he must χελώνης φαγεῖν ἢ μὴ φαγεῖν; either eat the whole Snail, or let it quite alone; and so, he went through 1625 with his laborious Task, as I have done with my difficult Translation.

Thus far, my Lord, you see it has gone very hard with *Persius*: I think he cannot be allow'd to stand in competition, either with *Juvenal* or *Horace.* Yet, for once, I will venture to be so vain, as to affirm, That none of his hard Metaphors, or forc'd Expressions, are in my Transla- 1630 tion: But more of this in its proper place, where I shall say somewhat in particular, of our general performance, in making these two Authors *English.* In the mean time I think my self oblig'd, to give *Persius* his undoubted due; and to acquaint the World, with *Casaubon,* in what he has equall'd, and in what excell'd his two Competitors.   1635

A Man who is resolv'd to praise an Author, with any appearance of Justice, must be sure to take him on the strongest side; and where he is least liable to Exceptions. He is therefore oblig'd to chuse his Mediums accordingly: *Casaubon,* who saw that *Persius* cou'd not laugh with a becomeing Grace, that he was not made for jeasting, and that a 1640 merry Conceit was not his Talent, turn'd his Feather, like an *Indian,* to another light, that he might give it the better Gloss. Moral Doctrine, says he, and Urbanity, or well-manner'd Wit, are the two things which constitute the *Roman* Satire. But of the two, that which is most Essential to this Poem, and is as it were the very Soul which animates it, is the 1645 scourging of Vice, and Exhortation to Virtue. Thus Wit, for a good Reason, is already almost out of Doors: And allow'd only for an Instrument, a kind of Tool, or a Weapon, as he calls it, of which the Satyrist makes use, in the compassing of his Design. The End and Aim of our three Rivals, is consequently the same. But by what Methods they 1650 have prosecuted their intention, is farther to be consider'd. Satire is of the nature of Moral Philosophy; as being instructive: He therefore, who instructs most Usefully, will carry the Palm from his two Antagonists. The Philosophy in which *Persius* was Educated, and which he professes through his whole Book, is the Stoick: The most noble, 1655 most generous, most beneficial to Humane Kind, amongst all the Sects, who have given us the Rules of Ethiques, thereby to form a severe Virtue in the Soul; to raise in us an undaunted Courage, against the assaults of Fortune; to esteem as nothing the things that are without us, because they are not in our Power; not to value Riches, Beauty, 1660 Honours, Fame, or Health, any farther than as conveniences, and so many helps to living as we ought, and doing good in our Generation. In short, to be always Happy, while we possess our Minds, with a good Conscience, are free from the slavery of Vices, and conform our Actions and Conversation to the Rules of right Reason. See here, my Lord, an 1665 Epitome of *Epictetus*; the Doctrine of *Zeno*, and the Education of our *Persius*. And this he express'd, not only in all his Satires, but in the manner of his Life. I will not lessen this Commendation of the Stoick Philosophy, by giving you an account of some Absurdities in their Doctrine, and some perhaps Impieties, if we consider them by the 1670 Standard of Christian Faith: *Persius* has faln into none of them: And therefore is free from those imputations. What he teaches, might be taught from Pulpits, with more profit to the Audience, than all the nice Speculations of Divinity, and Controversies concerning Faith; which are more for the Profit of the Shepherd, than for the Edification of the 1675 Flock. Passion, Interest, Ambition, and all their Bloody Consequences of Discord and of War, are banish'd from this Doctrine. Here is nothing propos'd but the quiet and tranquility of the Mind; Virtue lodg'd at home, and afterwards diffus'd in her general Effects, to the improvement, and good of Humane Kind. And therefore I wonder not, that the 1680 present Bishop of *Salisbury*, has recommended this our Author, and the Tenth Satyr of *Juvenal*, in his Pastoral Letter, to the serious perusal and

1678 of the Mind 97: of Mind 93

Practice of the Divines in his Diocese, as the best Common Places for their Sermons, as the Store-Houses and Magazines of Moral Virtues, from whence they may draw out, as they have occasion, all manner of 168 Assistance, for the accomplishment of a Virtuous Life, which the Stoicks have assign'd for the great End and Perfection of Mankind. Herein, then it is, that *Persius* has excell'd both *Juvenal* and *Horace*. He sticks to his one Philosophy: He shifts not sides, like *Horace*, who is sometimes an *Epicuræan*, sometimes a Stoick, sometimes an Eclectick; 169 as his present Humour leads him: Nor declaims like *Juvenal* against Vices, more like an Orator, than a Philosopher. *Persius* is every where the same: True to the Dogma's of his Master: What he has learnt, he teaches vehemently; and what he teaches, that he Practices himself. There is a Spirit of sincerity in all he says: You may easily discern that 169 he is in earnest, and is perswaded of that Truth which he inculcates. In this I am of opinion, that he excels *Horace*, who is commonly in jeast, and laughs while he instructs: And is equal to *Juvenal*, who was as honest and serious as *Persius*, and more he cou'd not be.

　　Hitherto I have follow'd *Casaubon*, and enlarg'd upon him; because 170 I am satisfi'd that he says no more than Truth; the rest is almost all frivolous. For he says that *Horace* being the Son of a Tax-gatherer, or a Collector, as we call it, smells every where of the meanness of his Birth, and Education: His conceipts are vulgar, like the Subjects of his Satires; that he does *Plebeium sapere*; and Writes not with that Elevation, 170 which becomes a Satyrist: That *Persius* being nobly born, and of an opulent Family, had likewise the advantage of a better Master; *Cornutus* being the most Learned of his time, a Man of a most Holy Life; the chief of the Stoick Sect at *Rome*; and not only a great Philosopher, but a Poet himself; and in probability a Coadjutor of *Persius*. That, as for 171 *Juvenal*, he was long a Declaimer, came late to Poetry; and had not been much conversant in Philosophy.

　　'Tis granted that the Father of *Horace* was *Libertinus*, that is one degree remov'd from his Grandfather, who had been once a Slave: But *Horace*, speaking of him, gives him the best Character of a Father, 171 which I ever read in History: And I wish a witty Friend of mine now living had such another. He bred him in the best School, and with the best Company of young Noblemen. And *Horace*, by his gratitude to his Memory, gives a certain Testimony that his Education was ingenuous. After this, he form'd himself abroad, by the Conversation of Great Men. 172 *Brutus* found him at *Athens*, and was so pleas'd with him, that he took

him thence into the Army, and made him *Tribunus Militum,* a Colonel
in a Legion, which was the Preferment of an Old Souldier. All this was
before his Acquaintance with *Mecenas,* and his introduction into the
Court of *Augustus,* and the familiarity of that great Emperour: Which, 1725
had he not been well-bred before, had been enough to civilise his Conversation, and render him accomplish'd, and knowing in all the Arts
of Complacency and good behaviour; and, in short, an agreeable Companion for the retir'd hours and privacies of a Favourite, who was first
Minister. So that, upon the whole matter, *Persius* may be acknowledg'd 1730
to be equal with him, in those respects, tho' better born, and *Juvenal*
inferiour to both. If the Advantage be any where, 'tis on the side of
Horace; as much as the Court of *Augustus Cæsar,* was superiour to that
of *Nero.* As for the Subjects which they treated, it will appear hereafter,
that *Horace* writ not vulgarly on vulgar Subjects: Nor always chose 1735
them. His Stile is constantly accommodated to his Subject, either high
or low: If his fault be too much lowness, that of *Persius* is the fault of the
hardness of his Metaphors, and obscurity: And so they are equal in the
failings of their Stile; where *Juvenal* manifestly Triumphs over both of
them.   1740

    The Comparison betwixt *Horace* and *Juvenal* is more difficult; because
their Forces were more equal: A Dispute has always been, and ever will
continue, betwixt the Favourers of the two Poets. *Non nostrum est tantas
componere lites.* I shall only venture to give my own Opinion, and leave
it for better Judges to determine. If it be only argu'd in general, which 1745
of them was the better Poet; the Victory is already gain'd on the side
of *Horace. Virgil* himself must yield to him in the delicacy of his Turns,
his choice of Words, and perhaps the Purity of his Latin. He who says
that *Pindar* is inimitable, is himself inimitable in his *Odes.* But the Contention betwixt these two great Masters, is for the Prize of Satire. In 1750
which Controversie, all the *Odes,* and *Epodes* of *Horace* are to stand
excluded. I say this, because *Horace* has written many of them Satirically, against his private Enemies: Yet these, if justly consider'd, are
somewhat of the Nature of the *Greek Silli,* which were Invectives against
particular Sects and Persons. But *Horace* had purg'd himself of this 1755
Choler, before he enter'd on those Discourses, which are more properly
call'd the *Roman* Satire: He has not now to do with a *Lyce,* a *Canidia,*
a *Cassius Severus,* or a *Menas*; but is to correct the Vices and the Follies
of his Time, and to give the Rules of a Happy and Virtuous Life. In
a word, that former sort of Satire, which is known in *England* by the 1760
Name of Lampoon, is a dangerous sort of Weapon, and for the most part

Unlawful. We have no Moral right on the Reputation of other Men. 'Tis taking from them, what we cannot restore to them. There are only two Reasons, for which we may be permitted to write Lampoons; and I will not promise that they can always justifie us: The first is Revenge, 176 when we have been affronted in the same Nature, or have been any ways notoriously abus'd, and can make our selves no other Reparation. And yet we know, that, in Christian Charity, all Offences are to be forgiven; as we expect the like Pardon for those which we daily commit against Almighty God. And this Consideration has often made me 177 tremble when I was saying our Saviour's Prayer; for the plain Condition of the forgiveness which we beg, is the pardoning of others the Offences which they have done to us: For which Reason I have many times avoided the Commission of that Fault; ev'n when I have been notoriously provok'd. Let not this, my Lord, pass for Vanity in me: 177 For 'tis truth. More Libels have been written against me, than almost any Man now living: And I had Reason on my side, to have defended my own Innocence: I speak not of my Poetry, which I have wholly given up to the Criticks; let them use it, as they please; Posterity, perhaps, may be more favourable to me: For Interest and Passion, will lye 178 bury'd in another Age: And Partiality and Prejudice be forgotten. I speak of my Morals, which have been sufficiently aspers'd: That only sort of Reputation ought to be dear to every honest Man, and is to me. But let the World witness for me, that I have been often wanting to my self in that particular; I have seldom answer'd any scurrilous Lampoon: 178 When it was in my power to have expos'd my Enemies: And being naturally vindicative, have suffer'd in silence; and possess'd my Soul in quiet.

Any thing, tho' never so little, which a Man speaks of himself, in my Opinion, is still too much, and therefore I will wave this Subject; 179 and proceed to give the second Reason, which may justifie a Poet, when he writes against a particular Person; and that is, when he is become a Publick Nuisance. All those, whom *Horace* in his Satires, and *Persius* and *Juvenal* have mention'd in theirs, with a Brand of infamy, are wholly such. 'Tis an Action of Virtue to make Examples of vicious 179 Men. They may and ought to be upbraided with their Crimes and Follies: Both for their own amendment, if they are not yet incorrigible; and for the Terrour of others, to hinder them from falling into those Enormities, which they see are so severely punish'd, in the Persons of others: The first Reason was only an Excuse for Revenge: But 180 this second is absolutely of a Poet's Office to perform: But how few

Lampooners are there now living, who are capable of this Duty! When they come in my way, 'tis impossible sometimes to avoid reading them. But, good God, how remote they are in common Justice, from the choice of such Persons as are the proper Subject of Satire! And how 1805 little Wit they bring, for the support of their injustice! The weaker Sex is their most ordinary Theme: And the best and fairest are sure to be the most severely handled. Amongst Men, those who are prosperously unjust, are Intitled to a Panegyrick. But afflicted Virtue is insolently stabb'd with all manner of Reproaches. No Decency is consider'd, no 1810 fulsomness omitted; no Venom is wanting, as far as dullness can supply it. For there is a perpetual Dearth of Wit; a Barrenness of good Sense, and Entertainment. The neglect of the Readers, will soon put an end to this sort of scribling. There can be no pleasantry where there is no Wit: No Impression can be made, where there is no Truth for the 1815 Foundation. To conclude, they are like the Fruits of the Earth in this unnatural Season: The Corn which held up its Head, is spoil'd with rankness: But the greater part of the Harvest is laid along; and little of good Income, and wholesom Nourishment is receiv'd into the Barns. This is almost a digression, I confess to your Lordship; but a just 1820 indignation forc'd it from me. Now I have remov'd this Rubbish, I will return to the Comparison of *Juvenal* and *Horace*.

I wou'd willingly divide the Palm betwixt them; upon the two Heads of Profit and Delight, which are the two Ends of Poetry in general. It must be granted by the Favourers of *Juvenal*, that *Horace* is the more 1825 Copious, and Profitable in his Instructions of Humane Life. But in my particular Opinion, which I set not up for a Standard to better Judgments, *Juvenal* is the more delightful Author. I am profited by both, I am pleas'd with both; but I owe more to *Horace* for my Instruction; and more to *Juvenal*, for my Pleasure. This, as I said, is my particular Taste 1830 of these two Authors: They who will have either of them to excel the other in both qualities, can scarce give better Reasons for their Opinion, than I for mine: But all unbiass'd Readers, will conclude, that my Moderation is not to be Condemn'd: To such Impartial Men I must appeal: For they who have already form'd their Judgment, may justly 1835 stand suspected of prejudice; and tho all who are my Readers, will set up to be my Judges, I enter my *Caveat* against them, that they ought not so much as to be of my Jury. Or, if they be admitted, 'tis but Reason, that they shou'd first hear, what I have to urge in the Defence of my Opinion. 1840

1818 along;] along, *93 97*

That *Horace* is somewhat the better Instructor of the two, is prov'd from hence, that his Instructions are more general: *Juvenal*'s more limited. So that granting, that the Counsels which they give, are equally good for Moral Use; *Horace*, who gives the most various Advice, and most applicable to all Occasions, which can occurr to us, in the 1845 course of our Lives; as including in his Discourses, not only all the Rules of Morality, but also of Civil Conversation; is, undoubtedly, to be preferr'd to him, who is more circumscrib'd in his Instructions, makes them to fewer People, and on fewer Occasions, than the other. I may be pardon'd for using an Old Saying, since 'tis true, and to the 1850 purpose, *Bonum quo communius, eo melius*. *Juvenal*, excepting only his first Satire, is in all the rest confin'd, to the exposing of some particular Vice; that he lashes, and there he sticks. His Sentences are truly shining and instructive: But they are sprinkl'd here and there. *Horace* is teaching us in every Line, and is perpetually Moral; he had found out the 1855 Skill of *Virgil*, to hide his Sentences: To give you the Virtue of them, without shewing them in their full extent: Which is the Ostentation of a Poet, and not his Art: And this *Petronius* charges on the Authors of his Time, as a Vice of Writing, which was then growing on the Age. *Ne Sententiæ extra Corpus Orationis emineant:* He wou'd have them weav'd 1860 into the Body of the Work, and not appear emboss'd upon it, and striking directly on the Reader's view. Folly was the proper Quarry of *Horace*, and not Vice: And, as there are but few Notoriously Wicked Men, in comparison with a Shoal of Fools, and Fops; so 'tis a harder thing to make a Man Wise, than to make him Honest: For the Will is 1865 only to be reclaim'd in the one; but the Understanding is to be inform'd in the other. There are Blind-sides and Follies, even in the Professors of Moral Philosophy; and there is not any one Sect of them that *Horace* has not expos'd. Which, as it was not the Design of *Juvenal*, who was wholly employ'd in lashing Vices, some of them the most 1870 enormous that can be imagin'd; so perhaps, it was not so much his Talent. *Omne vafer vitium ridenti Flaccus amico, tangit, & admissus circum præcordia ludit*. This was the Commendation which *Persius* gave him: Where by *Vitium*, he means those little Vices, which we call Follies, the defects of Humane Understanding, or at most the Peccadillos of Life, 1875 rather than the Tragical Vices, to which Men are hurri'd by their unruly Passions and exorbitant Desires. But in the word *omne*, which is universal, he concludes, with me, that the Divine Wit of *Horace*, left nothing untouch'd; that he enter'd into the inmost Recesses of Nature; found out the Imperfections even of the most Wise and Grave, as well 1880 as of the Common People: Discovering, even in the great *Trebatius*, to whom he addresses the first Satire, his hunting after Business, and following the Court, as well as in the Persecutor *Crispinus*, his impertinence and importunity. 'Tis true, he exposes *Crispinus* openly, as a common Nuisance: But he rallies the other, as a Friend, more finely. The Ex- 1885 hortations of *Persius* are confin'd to Noblemen: And the Stoick Philosophy, is that alone, which he recommends to them: *Juvenal* Exhorts to particular Virtues, as they are oppos'd to those Vices against which he declaims: But *Horace* laughs to shame, all Follies, and insinuates Virtue, rather by familiar Examples, than by the severity of Precepts. 1890

This last Consideration seems to incline the Ballance on the side of *Horace*, and to give him the preference to *Juvenal*, not only in Profit, but in Pleasure. But, after all, I must confess, that the Delight which *Horace* gives me, is but languishing. Be pleas'd still to understand, that I speak of my own Taste only: He may Ravish other Men; but I am too 1895 stupid and insensible, to be tickl'd. Where he barely grins himself, and, as *Scaliger* says, only shews his white Teeth, he cannot provoke me to any Laughter. His Urbanity, that is, his Good Manners, are to be commended, but his Wit is faint; and his Salt, if I may dare to say so, almost insipid. *Juvenal* is of a more vigorous and Masculine Wit, he gives me 1900 as much Pleasure as I can bear: He fully satisfies my Expectation, he Treats his Subject home: His Spleen is rais'd, and he raises mine: I have the Pleasure of Concernment in all he says; He drives his Reader along with him; and when he is at the end of his way, I willingly stop with him: If he went another Stage, it wou'd be too far, it wou'd make a 1905 Journey of a Progress, and turn Delight into Fatigue. When he gives over, 'tis a sign the Subject is exhausted; and the Wit of Man can carry it no farther. If a Fault can be justly found in him; 'tis that he is sometimes too luxuriant, too redundant; says more than he needs, like my Friend the *Plain Dealer*, but never more than pleases. Add to this, that 1910 his Thoughts are as just as those of *Horace*, and much more Elevated. His Expressions are Sonorous and more Noble; his Verse more numerous, and his Words are suitable to his Thoughts, sublime and lofty. All these contribute to the Pleasure of the Reader, and the greater the Soul of him who Reads, his Transports are the greater. 1915 *Horace* is always on the Amble, *Juvenal* on the Gallop: But his way is perpetually on Carpet Ground. He goes with more impetuosity than *Horace*; but as securely; and the swiftness adds a more lively agitation to the Spirits. The low Style of *Horace*, is according to his Subject; that

1913 Thoughts, *97*: Thoughts; *93*

is generally groveling. I question not but he cou'd have rais'd it. For 1920
the First Epistle of the Second Book, which he writes to *Augustus*, (a
most instructive Satire concerning Poetry,) is of so much Dignity in
the Words, and of so much Elegancy in the Numbers, that the Author
plainly shews, the *Sermo Pedestris*, in his other Satires, was rather his
Choice than his Necessity. He was a Rival to *Lucilius* his Predecessor; 1925
and was resolv'd to surpass him in his own Manner. *Lucilius*, as we see
by his remaining Fragments, minded neither his Style nor his Numbers, nor his purity of words, nor his run of Verse. *Horace* therefore
copes with him in that humble way of Satire. Writes under his own
force, and carries a dead Weight, that he may match his Competitor 1930
in the Race. This I imagine was the chief Reason, why he minded only
the clearness of his Satire, and the cleanness of Expression, without
ascending to those heights, to which his own vigour might have carri'd
him. But limiting his desires only to the Conquest of *Lucilius*, he had
his Ends of his Rival, who liv'd before him; but made way for a new 1935
Conquest over himself, by *Juvenal* his Successor. He cou'd not give an
equal pleasure to his Reader, because he us'd not equal Instruments.
The fault was in the Tools, and not in the Workman. But Versification,
and Numbers, are the greatest Pleasures of Poetry: *Virgil* knew it, and
practis'd both so happily; that for ought I know, his greatest Excellency 1940
is in his Diction. In all other parts of Poetry, he is faultless; but in this
he plac'd his chief perfection. And give me leave, my Lord, since I have
here an apt occasion, to say, that *Virgil*, cou'd have written sharper
Satires, than either *Horace* or *Juvenal*, if he wou'd have employ'd his
Talent, that way. I will produce a Verse and half of his, in one of his 1945
Eclogues, to justifie my Opinion: And with *Comma's* after every Word,
to shew, that he has given almost as many lashes, as he has written
Syllables. 'Tis against a bad Poet; whose ill Verses he describes. *Non tu,
in triviis, indocte, solebas, stridenti, miserum, stipula, disperdere carmen?* But
to return to my purpose, when there is any thing deficient in Numbers, 1950
and Sound, the Reader is uneasie, and unsatisfi'd; he wants something
of his Complement, desires somewhat which he finds not: And this
being the manifest defect of *Horace*, 'tis no wonder, that finding it
supply'd in *Juvenal*, we are more Delighted with him. And besides this,
the Sauce of *Juvenal* is more poignant, to create in us an Appetite of 1955
Reading him. The Meat of *Horace* is more nourishing; but the Cookery
of *Juvenal* more exquisite; so that, granting *Horace* to be the more
general Philosopher; we cannot deny, that *Juvenal* was the greater
Poet, I mean in Satire. His Thoughts are sharper, his Indignation

against Vice is more vehement; his Spirit has more of the Common- 1960
wealth Genius; he treats Tyranny, and all the Vices attending it, as
they deserve, with the utmost rigour: And consequently, a Noble Soul
is better pleas'd with a Zealous Vindicator of *Roman* Liberty; than with
a Temporizing Poet, a well Manner'd Court Slave, and a Man who is
often afraid of Laughing in the right place: Who is ever decent, because 1965
he is naturally servile. After all, *Horace* had the disadvantage of the
Times in which he liv'd; they were better for the Man, but worse for
the Satirist. 'Tis generally said, that those Enormous Vices, which
were practis'd under the Reign of *Domitian*, were unknown in the Time
of *Augustus Cæsar*. That therefore *Juvenal* had a larger Field, than 1970
Horace. Little Follies were out of doors, when Oppression was to be
scourg'd instead of Avarice: It was no longer time to turn into Ridicule,
the false Opinions of Philosophers; when the *Roman* Liberty was to be
asserted. There was more need of a *Brutus* in *Domitian*'s Days, to redeem
or mend, than of a *Horace*, if he had then been Living, to Laugh at a Fly- 1975
Catcher. This Reflection at the same time excuses *Horace*, but exalts
Juvenal. I have ended, before I was aware, the Comparison of *Horace*
and *Juvenal*, upon the Topiques of Instruction and Delight; and indeed
I may safely here conclude that common-place: For if we make *Horace*
our Minister of State in Satire, and *Juvenal* of our private Pleasures: I 1980
think the latter has no ill bargain of it. Let Profit have the preheminence
of Honour, in the End of Poetry. Pleasure, though but the second in
degree, is the first in favour. And who wou'd not chuse to be lov'd
better, rather than to be more esteem'd? But I am enter'd already upon
another Topique; which concerns the particular Merits of these two 1985
Satirists. However, I will pursue my business where I left it: And carry
it farther than that common observation of the several Ages, in which
these Authors Flourish'd. When *Horace* writ his Satires, the Monarchy
of his *Cæsar* was in its newness; and the Government but just made easie
to the Conquer'd People. They cou'd not possibly have forgotten the 1990
Usurpation of that Prince upon their Freedom, nor the violent Methods
which he had us'd, in the compassing of that vast Design: They yet
remember'd his Proscriptions, and the Slaughter of so many Noble
Romans, their Defendors. Amongst the rest, that horrible Action of his,
when he forc'd *Livia* from the Arms of her Husband, who was con- 1995
strain'd to see her Marry'd, as *Dion* relates the Story; and, big with
Child as she was, convey'd to the Bed of his insulting Rival. The same
Dion Cassius gives us another instance of the Crime before mention'd:
That *Cornelius Sisenna*, being reproach'd in full Senate, with the Licentious

Conduct of his Wife, return'd this Answer; That he had Marry'd her 2000
by the Counsel of *Augustus*: Intimating, says my Author, that *Augustus*
had oblig'd him to that Marriage, that he might, under that covert,
have the more free access to her. His Adulteries were still before their
Eyes, but they must be patient, where they had not power. In other
things that Emperor was Moderate enough: Propriety was generally 200
secur'd; and the People entertain'd with publick Shows, and Donatives,
to make them more easily digest their lost Liberty. But *Augustus*, who
was conscious to himself, of so many Crimes which he had committed,
thought in the first place to provide for his own Reputation, by making
an Edict against Lampoons and Satires, and the Authors of those de- 2010
famatory Writings, which my Author *Tacitus*, from the Law-Term,
calls *famosos libellos*.

In the first Book of his *Annals*, he gives the following Account of it,
in these Words. *Primus Augustus cognitionem de famosis libellis specie legis
ejus, tractavit; commotus Cassii Severi libidine, quâ viros fœminasq; inlustres,* 201*
procacibus scriptis diffamaverat. Thus in *English. Augustus* was the first,
who under the colour of that Law took Cognisance of Lampoons; being
provok'd to it, by the petulancy of *Cassius Severus*, who had defam'd
many Illustrious Persons of both Sexes, in his Writings. The Law to
which *Tacitus* refers, was *Lex læsæ Majestatis*; commonly call'd, for the 2020
sake of brevity, *Majestas*; or as we say, High Treason: He means not
that this Law had not been Enacted formerly: For it had been made by
the *Decemviri*, and was inscrib'd amongst the rest in the Twelve Tables:
To prevent the aspersion of the *Roman* Majesty; either of the People
themselves, or their Religion, or their Magistrates: And the infringe- 202*
ment of it was Capital: That is, the Offender was Whipt to Death, with
the *Fasces*, which were born before their Chief Officers of *Rome*. But
Augustus was the first, who restor'd that intermitted Law. By the
words, *under colour of that Law*, He insinuates that *Augustus* caus'd it
to be Executed, on pretence of those Libels, which were written by 203c
Cassius Severus, against the Nobility: But in Truth, to save himself, from
such defamatory Verses. *Suetonius* likewise makes mention of it thus.
*Sparsos de se in Curiâ famosos libellos, nec expavit, & magna curâ redarguit:
Ac ne requisitis quidem Auctoribus, id modo censuit, cognoscendum post hac,
de iis qui libellos aut carmina ad infamiam cujuspiam sub alieno nomine edant.* 203*
Augustus was not afraid of Libels, says that Author: Yet he took all care
imaginable to have them answer'd; and then decreed that for the time
to come, the Authors of them shou'd be punish'd. But *Aurelius* makes

2021 brevity, 97: brevity 93

it yet more clear, according to my Sense, that this Emperor for his own sake durst not permit them. *Fecit id Augustus in speciem; & quasi grati-* 2040 *ficaretur Populo Romano, & Primoribus urbis; sed revera ut sibi consuleret: Nam habuit in animo, comprimere nimiam quorundam procacitatem in loquendo, à quâ nec ipse exemptus fuit. Nam suo nomine compescere erat invidiosum, sub alieno facile & utile. Ergò specie legis tractavit, quasi Populi Romani Majestas infamaretur.* This, I think is a sufficient Comment on that Passage of 2045 *Tacitus.* I will add only by the way, that the whole Family of the *Cæsars*, and all their Relations were included in the Law; because the Majesty of the *Romans* in the time of the Empire was wholly in that House: *Omnia Cæsar erat:* They were all accounted sacred, who belong'd to him. As for *Cassius Severus*, he was contemporary with *Horace*; and 2050 was the same Poet against whom he Writes in his *Epods*, under this Title, *In Cassium Severum Maledicum Poetam:* Perhaps intending to kill two Crows, according to our Proverb, with one Stone; and Revenge both himself and his Emperor together.

From hence I may reasonably conclude, That *Augustus*, who was not 2055 altogether so Good as he was Wise, had some By-respect, in the Enact-ing of this Law: For to do any thing for nothing, was not his Maxim. *Horace*, as he was a Courtier, comply'd with the Interest of his Master, and avoiding the Lashing of greater Crimes, confin'd himself to the ridiculing of Petty Vices, and common Follies: Excepting only some 2060 reserv'd Cases, in his *Odes* and *Epods*, of his own particular Quarrels; which either with permission of the Magistrate or without it, every Man will Revenge, tho' I say not that he shou'd; for *prior læsit*, is a good excuse in the Civil Law, if Christianity had not taught us to for-give. However, he was not the proper Man to arraign great Vices, at 2065 least if the Stories which we hear of him are true, that he Practis'd some, which I will not here mention, out of honour to him. It was not for a *Clodius* to accuse Adulterers, especially when *Augustus* was of that number: So that though his Age was not exempted from the worst of Villanies, there was no freedom left to reprehend them, by reason of the 2070 Edict. And our Poet was not fit to represent them in an odious Charac-ter, because himself was dipt in the same Actions. Upon this account, without farther insisting on the different tempers of *Juvenal* and *Horace*, I conclude, that the Subjects which *Horace* chose for Satire, are of a lower nature than those of which *Juvenal* has written.   2075

Thus I have treated in a new Method, the Comparison betwixt *Horace*, *Juvenal*, and *Persius*; somewhat of their particular manner

belonging to all of them is yet remaining to be consider'd. *Persius* was
Grave, and particularly oppos'd his Gravity to Lewdness, which was
the Predominant Vice in *Nero*'s Court, at the time when he publish'd 2080
his Satires, which was before that Emperour fell into the excess of
Cruelty. *Horace* was a Mild Admonisher, a Court Satirist, fit for the
gentle Times of *Augustus*, and more fit, for the Reasons which I have
already given. *Juvenal* was as proper for his Times, as they for theirs.
His was an Age that deserv'd a more severe Chastisement. Vices were 2085
more gross and open, more flagitious, more encourag'd by the Example
of a Tyrant; and more protected by his Authority. Therefore, wheresoever *Juvenal* mentions *Nero*, he means *Domitian*, whom he dares not
attack in his own Person, but Scourges him by Proxy. *Heinsius* urges in
praise of *Horace*, that according to the Ancient Art and Law of Satire, 2090
it shou'd be nearer to Comedy, than to Tragedy; Not declaiming
against Vice, but only laughing at it. Neither *Persius*, nor *Juvenal* were
ignorant of this, for they had both study'd *Horace*. And the thing it self
is plainly true. But as they had read *Horace*, they had likewise read
Lucilius, of whom *Persius* says *secuit Urbem; & genuinum fregit in illis;* 2095
meaning *Mutius* and *Lupus*: And *Juvenal* also mentions him in these
words, *Ense velut stricto, quoties Lucilius ardens Infremuit,* &c. So that they
thought the imitation of *Lucilius* was more proper to their purpose
than that of *Horace*. They chang'd Satire, says *Holiday*; but they chang'd
it for the better: For the business being to Reform great Vices, 2100
Chastisement goes farther than Admonition; whereas a perpetual
Grinn, like that of *Horace*, does rather anger than amend a Man.

Thus far that Learned Critick, *Barten Holiday*, whose Interpretation,
and Illustrations of *Juvenal* are as Excellent, as the Verse of his Translation and his *English* are lame and pitiful. For 'tis not enough to give us 2105
the meaning of a Poet, which I acknowledge him to have perform'd
most faithfully; but he must also imitate his Genius, and his Numbers;
as far as the *English* will come up to the Elegance of the Original. In few
words, 'tis only for a Poet to Translate a Poet. *Holiday* and *Stapylton*
had not enough consider'd this, when they attempted *Juvenal*: But I 2110
forbear Reflections; only I beg leave to take notice of this Sentence,
where *Holiday* says, *A perpetual Grinn, like that of* Horace, *rather angers
than amends a Man.* I cannot give him up the Manner of *Horace* in low
Satire so easily: Let the Chastisements of *Juvenal* be never so necessary
for his new kind of Satire; let him declaim as wittily and sharply as he 2115
pleases, yet still the nicest and most delicate touches of Satire consist
in fine Raillery. This, my Lord, is your particular Talent, to which even

Juvenal could not arrive. 'Tis not Reading, 'tis not imitation of an Author, which can produce this fineness: It must be inborn, it must proceed from a Genius, and particular way of thinking, which is not 2120 to be taught; and therefore not to be imitated by him who has it not from Nature: How easie it is to call Rogue and Villain, and that wittily! But how hard to make a Man appear a Fool, a Blockhead, or a Knave, without using any of those opprobrious terms! To spare the grossness of the Names, and to do the thing yet more severely, is to draw a full 2125 Face, and to make the Nose and Cheeks stand out, and yet not to employ any depth of Shadowing. This is the Mystery of that Noble Trade; which yet no Master can teach to his Apprentice: He may give the Rules, but the Scholar is never the nearer in his practice. Neither is it true, that this fineness of Raillery is offensive. A witty Man is 2130 tickl'd while he is hurt in this manner; and a Fool feels it not. The occasion of an Offence may possibly be given, but he cannot take it. If it be granted that in effect this way does more Mischief; that a Man is secretly wounded, and though he be not sensible himself, yet the malicious World will find it for him: Yet there is still a vast difference 2135 betwixt the slovenly Butchering of a Man, and the fineness of a stroak that separates the Head from the Body, and leaves it standing in its place. A man may be capable, as *Jack Ketche*'s Wife said of his Servant, of a plain piece of Work, a bare Hanging; but to make a Malefactor die sweetly, was only belonging to her Husband. I wish I cou'd apply it 2140 to my self, if the Reader wou'd be kind enough to think it belongs to me. The Character of *Zimri* in my *Absalom*, is, in my Opinion, worth the whole Poem: 'Tis not bloody, but 'tis ridiculous enough. And he for whom it was intended, was too witty to resent it as an injury. If I had rail'd, I might have suffer'd for it justly: But I manag'd my own Work 2145 more happily, perhaps more dextrously. I avoided the mention of great Crimes, and apply'd my self to the representing of Blind-sides, and little Extravagancies: To which, the wittier a Man is, he is generally the more obnoxious. It succeeded as I wish'd; the Jest went round, and he was laught at in his turn who began the Frolick. 2150

And thus, My Lord, you see I have preferr'd the Manner of *Horace*, and of your Lordship, in this kind of Satire, to that of *Juvenal*; and I think, reasonably. *Holiday* ought not to have Arraign'd so Great an Author, for that which was his Excellency and his Merit: Or if he did, on such a palpable mistake, he might expect, that some one might 2155 possibly arise, either in his own Time, or after him, to rectifie his Error,

2122 wittily! *97*: wittily? *93*   2124 terms! *97*: terms? *93*

and restore to *Horace*, that Commendation, of which he has so unjustly robb'd him. And let the Manes of *Juvenal* forgive me, if I say, that this way of *Horace* was the best, for amending Manners, as it is the most difficult. His was, an *Ense rescindendum*; but that of *Horace* was a Pleasant 2160 Cure, with all the Limbs preserv'd entire: And as our *Mountebanks* tell us in their Bills, without keeping the Patient within Doors for a Day. What they promise only, *Horace* has effectually Perform'd: Yet I contradict not the Proposition which I formerly advanc'd: *Juvenal*'s Times requir'd a more painful kind of Operation: But if he had liv'd in the 2165 Age of *Horace*, I must needs affirm, that he had it not about him. He took the Method which was prescrib'd him by his own Genius; which was sharp and eager; he cou'd not Rally, but he cou'd Declame: And as his provocations were great, he has reveng'd them Tragically. This notwithstanding, I am to say another Word, which, as true as it is, will 2170 yet displease the partial Admirers of our *Horace*. I have hinted it before; but tis time for me now to speak more plainly.

  This Manner of *Horace* is indeed the best; but *Horace* has not executed it, altogether so happily, at least not often. The Manner of *Juvenal* is confess'd to be Inferior to the former; but *Juvenal*, has excell'd him in 2175 his Performance. *Juvenal* has rail'd more wittily than *Horace* has rally'd. *Horace* means to make his Reader Laugh; but he is not sure of his Experiment. *Juvenal* always intends to move your Indignation; and he always brings about his purpose. *Horace*, for ought I know, might have tickl'd the People of his Age; but amongst the Moderns he is not so 2180 Successfull. They who say he Entertains so Pleasantly, may perhaps value themselves on the quickness of their own Understandings, that they can see a Jest farther off than other men. They may find occasion of Laughter, in the Wit-battel of the Two Buffoons, *Sarmentus* and *Cicerrus*: And hold their sides for fear of bursting, when *Rupilius* and 2185 *Persius* are Scolding. For my own part, I can only like the Characters of all Four, which are judiciously given: But for my heart I cannot so much as smile at their Insipid Raillery. I see not why *Persius* shou'd call upon *Brutus*, to revenge him on his Adversary: And that because he had kill'd *Julius Cesar*, for endeavouring to be a King, therefore he shou'd 2190 be desir'd to Murther *Rupilius*, only because his Name was Mr. *King*. A miserable Clench, in my Opinion, for *Horace* to Record: I have heard honest Mr. *Swan* make many a better, and yet have had the Grace to hold my Countenance. But it may be Puns were then in Fashion, as they were Wit in the Sermons of the last Age, and in the Court of 2195 King *Charles* the Second. I am sorry to say it, for the sake of *Horace*;

but certain it is, he has no fine Palate who can feed so heartily on Garbidge.

But I have already wearied my self, and doubt not but I have tir'd your Lordships Patience, with this long rambling, and I fear, trivial 2200 Discourse. Upon the one half of the Merits, that is, Pleasure, I cannot but conclude that *Juvenal* was the better Satirist: They who will descend into his particular Praises, may find them at large, in the Dissertation of the Learned *Rigaltius* to *Thuanus*. As for *Persius*, I have given the Reasons, why I think him Inferior to both of them. Yet I have one 2205 thing to add on that Subject.

Barten Holiday, who Translated both *Juvenal* and *Persius*, has made this distinction betwixt them, which is no less true than Witty; that, in *Persius* the difficulty is to find a Meaning; in *Juvenal*, to chuse a Meaning: So Crabbed is *Persius*, and so Copious is *Juvenal*: So much the 2210 Understanding is employ'd in one; and so much the Judgment in the other. So difficult it is, to find any Sense in the former, and the best Sense of the latter.

If, on the other side, any one suppose I have commended *Horace* below his Merit, when I have allow'd him but the Second Place, I desire 2215 him to consider, if *Juvenal*, a Man of Excellent Natural Endowments, besides the advantages of Diligence and Study, and coming after him, and Building upon his Foundations, might not probably, with all these helps, surpass him? And whether it be any dishonour to *Horace*, to be thus surpass'd; since no Art, or Science, is at once begun and perfected, 2220 but that it must pass first through many hands, and even through several Ages? If *Lucilius* cou'd add to *Ennius*, and *Horace* to *Lucilius*, why, without any diminution to the Fame of *Horace*, might not *Juvenal* give the last perfection to that Work? Or rather, what disreputation is it to *Horace*, that *Juvenal* Excels in the Tragical Satyre, as *Horace* does 2225 in the Comical? I have read over attentively, both *Heinsius* and *Dacier*, in their Commendations of *Horace*: But I can find no more in either of them, for the preference of him to *Juvenal*, than the Instructive Part; the Part of Wisdom, and not that of Pleasure; which therefore is here allow'd him, notwithstanding what *Scaliger* and *Rigaltius* have pleaded 2230 to the contrary for *Juvenal*. And to shew I am Impartial, I will here Translate what *Dacier* has said on that Subject.

I cannot give a more just Idea of the Two Books of Satires, made by *Horace*, than by compairing them to the Statues of the *Sileni*, to which *Alcibiades* compares *Socrates*, in the *Symposium*. They were Figures, 2235 which had nothing of agreeable, nothing of Beauty on their out-side: But when any one took the Pains to open them, and search into them, he there found the Figures of all the Deities. So, in the Shape that *Horace* Presents himself to us, in his Satires, we see nothing at the first View, which deserves our Attention. It seems that he is rather an Amusement for Children, than for the serious consideration of Men. But when we take away his Crust, and that which hides him from our sight; when we discover him to the bottom, then we find all the Divinities in a full Assembly: That is to say, all the Virtues, which ought to be the continual exercise of those, who seriously endeavour to Correct their Vices.

'Tis easy to Observe, that *Dacier*, in this Noble Similitude, has confin'd the Praise of his Author, wholly to the Instructive Part: The commendation turns on this, and so does that which follows.

In these Two Books of Satire, 'tis the business of *Horace* to instruct us how to combat our Vices, to regulate our Passions, to follow Nature, to give Bounds to our desires, to Distinguish betwixt Truth and Falshood, and betwixt our Conceptions of Things, and Things themselves. To come back from our prejudicate Opinions, to understand exactly the Principles and Motives of all our Actions; and to avoid the Ridicule, into which all men necessarily fall, who are Intoxicated with those Notions, which they have received from their Masters; and which they obstinately retain, without examining whether or no they are founded on right Reason.

In a Word, he labours to render us happy in relation to our selves, agreeable and faithful to our Friends, and discreet, serviceable, and well bred in relation to those with whom we are oblig'd to live, and to converse. To make his Figures Intelligible, to conduct his Readers through the Labyrinth of some perplex'd Sentence, or obscure Parenthesis, is no great matter. And as *Epictetus* says, there is nothing of Beauty in all this, or what is worthy of a Prudent Man. The Principal business, and which is of most Importance to us, is to shew the Use, the Reason, and the Proof of his Precepts.

They who endeavour not to correct themselves, according to so exact a Model; are just like the Patients, who have open before them a Book of Admirable Receipts, for their Diseases, and please themselves with reading it, without Comprehending the Nature of the Remedies; or how to apply them to their Cure.

Let *Horace* go off with these Encomiums, which he has so well deserv'd.

To conclude the contention betwixt our Three Poets, I will use the 2275
Words of *Virgil*, in his *Fifth Æneid* where *Æneas* proposes the Rewards
of the Foot-Race, to the Three first, who shou'd reach the Goal. *Tres
præmia primi, accipient; flavaque Caput nectentur Olivâ:* Let these Three
Ancients be preferr'd to all the Moderns; as first arriving at the Goal:
Let them all be Crown'd as Victours; with the Wreath that properly 2280
belongs to Satire. But, after that, with this distinction amongst them-
selves, *Primus equum phaleris insignem, Victor habeto.* Let *Juvenal* Ride first
in Triumph. *Alter Amazoniam pharetram; plenamque Sagittis Threiciis, lato
quam circumplectitur auro Balteus, & tereti subnectit Fibula gemmâ.* Let
Horace who is the Second, and but just the Second, carry off the 2285
Quivers, and the Arrows, as the Badges of his Satire; and the Golden
Belt and the Diamond Button. *Tertius, Argolico hoc Clypeo contentus abito.*
And let *Persius*, the last of the first Three Worthies, be contented with
this *Grecian* Shield, and with Victory not only over all the *Grecians*, who
were Ignorant of the *Roman* Satire, but over all the Moderns in Suc- 2290
ceeding Ages; excepting *Boileau* and your Lordship.

And thus, I have given the History of Satire, and deriv'd it as far as
from *Ennius*, to your Lordship; that is, from its first Rudiments of
Barbarity, to its last Polishing and Perfection: Which is, with *Virgil*,
in his Address to *Augustus*; 2295

> —*nomen famâ tot ferre per annos,*
> *Tithoni primâ quot abest ab origine Cæsar.*

I said only from *Ennius*; but I may safely carry it higher, as far as *Livius
Andronicus*; who, as I have said formerly, taught the first Play at *Rome*
in the Year *ab urbe conditâ*, 514. I have since desir'd my Learn'd Friend, 2300
Mr. *Maidwell*, to compute the difference of Times, betwixt *Aristophanes*,
and *Livius Andronicus*; and he assures me, from the best Chronologers,
that *Plutus*, the last of *Aristophanes* his Plays, was Represented at
Athens, in the Year of the 97th Olympiad; which agrees with the Year
Urbis Conditæ 364: So that the difference of Years betwixt *Aristophanes* 2305
and *Andronicus* is 150; from whence I have probably deduc'd, that
Livius Andronicus, who was a *Grecian*, had read the Plays of the Old
Comedy, which were Satyrical, and also of the New; for *Menander* was
fifty Years before him, which must needs be a great light to him, in his
own Plays; that were of the Satirical Nature. That the *Romans* had 2310
Farces before this, 'tis true; but then they had no Communication with

---

2283 *Amazoniam* 97: *Amazoniam,* 93   2286 Arrows, 97: Arrows; 93   Satire;
97: Satire, 93   2303 *Aristophanes* his] *Aristophanes*'s his 93: *Aristophanes*'s 97

Greece: So that *Andronicus* was the first, who wrote after the manner of the Old Comedy, in his Plays; he was imitated by *Ennius*, about Thirty Years afterwards. Though the former writ Fables; the latter, speaking properly, began the *Roman* Satire. According to that Description, which 231 *Juvenal* gives of it in his First; *Quicquid agunt homines, votum, timor, ira, voluptas, gaudia, discursus, nostri est farrago libelli*. This is that in which I have made bold to differ from *Casaubon, Rigaltius, Dacier*, and indeed, from all the Modern Critiques, that not *Ennius*, but *Andronicus* was the First; who by the *Archæa Comedia* of the *Greeks*, added many Beauties 232 to the first Rude and Barbarous *Roman* Satire: Which sort of Poem, tho' we had not deriv'd from *Rome*, yet Nature teaches it Mankind, in all Ages, and in every Country.

'Tis but necessary, that after so much has been said of Satire, some Definition of it should be given. *Heinsius*, in his Dissertations on *Horace*, 232 makes it for me, in these words; *Satire is a kind of Poetry, without a Series of Action, invented for the purging of our Minds; in which Humane Vices, Ignorance, and Errors, and all things besides, which are produc'd from them, in every Man, are severely Reprehended; partly Dramatically, partly Simply, and sometimes in both kinds of speaking; but for the most part Figuratively, and* 233 *Occultly; consisting in a low familiar way, chiefly in a sharp and pungent manner of Speech; but partly, also, in a Facetious and Civil way of Jesting; by which, either Hatred, or Laughter, or Indignation is mov'd.*—Where I cannot but observe, that this obscure and perplex'd Definition, or rather Description of Satire, is wholly accommodated to the *Horatian* way; and 233 excluding the Works of *Juvenal* and *Persius*, as foreign from that kind of Poem: The Clause in the beginning of it (*without a Series of Action*) distinguishes Satire properly from Stage-Plays, which are all of one Action, and one continu'd Series of Action. The End or Scope of Satire is to purge the Passions; so far it is common to the Satires of *Juvenal* 234 and *Persius*: The rest which follows, is also generally belonging to all three; till he comes upon us, with the Excluding Clause (*consisting in a low familiar way of Speech*) which is the proper Character of *Horace*; and from which, the other two, for their Honour be it spoken, are far distant. But how come Lowness of Style, and the Familiarity of Words 234 to be so much the Propriety of Satire, that without them, a Poet can be no more a Satirist, than without Risibility he can be a Man? Is the fault of *Horace* to be made the Virtue, and Standing Rule of this Poem? Is the *Grande Sophos* of *Persius*, and the Sublimity of *Juvenal* to be circumscrib'd, with the meanness of Words and vulgarity of Expression? If 235

2316 *homines*, 97: *homines* 93   2337 *without ... Action*] Editor's italics

Horace refus'd the pains of Numbers, and the loftiness of Figures, are they bound to follow so ill a Precedent? Let him walk a Foot with his Pad in his Hand, for his own pleasure; but let not them be accounted no Poets, who choose to mount, and shew their Horsmanship. *Holiday* is not afraid to say, that there was never such a fall, as from his Odes to his Satires, and that he, injuriously to himself, untun'd his Harp. The Majestique way of *Persius* and *Juvenal* was new when they began it; but 'tis old to us; and what Poems have not, with Time, receiv'd an Alteration in their Fashion? Which Alteration, says *Holiday*, is to after-times, as good a Warrant as the first. Has not *Virgil* chang'd the Manners of *Homer's* Hero's in his *Æneis*? certainly he has, and for the better. For *Virgil's* Age was more Civiliz'd, and better Bred; and he writ according to the Politeness of *Rome*, under the Reign of *Augustus Cæsar*; not to the Rudeness of *Agamemnon's* Age, or the Times of *Homer*. Why shou'd we offer to confine free Spirits to one Form, when we cannot so much as confine our Bodies to one Fashion of Apparel? Wou'd not *Donn's* Satires, which abound with so much Wit, appear more Charming, if he had taken care of his Words, and of his Numbers? But he follow'd *Horace* so very close, that of necessity he must fall with him: And I may safely say it of this present Age, That if we are not so great Wits as *Donn*, yet, certainly, we are better Poets.

But I have said enough, and it may be, too much on this Subject. Will your Lordship be pleas'd to prolong my Audience, only so far, till I tell you my own trivial Thoughts, how a Modern Satire shou'd be made. I will not deviate in the least from the Precepts and Examples of the Ancients, who were always our best Masters. I will only illustrate them, and discover some of the hidden Beauties in their Designs, that we thereby may form our own in imitation of them. Will you please but to observe, that *Persius*, the least in Dignity of all the Three, has, notwithstanding, been the first, who has discover'd to us this important Secret, in the designing of a perfect Satire; that it ought only to treat of one Subject; to be confin'd to one particular Theme; or, at least, to one principally. If other Vices occur in the management of the Chief, they shou'd only be transiently lash'd, and not be insisted on, so as to make the Design double. As in a Play of the *English* Fashion, which we call a *Tragecomedy*, there is to be but one main Design: And tho' there be an Under-plot, or Second Walk of Comical Characters and Adventures, yet they are subservient to the Chief Fable, carry'd along under it, and helping to it; so that the *Drama* may not seem a Monster

2355

2360

2365

2370

2375

2380

2385

2354 Horsmanship.] Horsmanship, *93 97*

with two Heads. Thus the *Copernican* Systeme of the Planets makes the 2390
Moon to be mov'd by the motion of the Earth, and carry'd about her
Orb, as a Dependant of hers: *Mascardi* in his Discourse of the *Doppia
favola*, or Double-tale in Plays, gives an Instance of it, in the famous
Pastoral of *Guarini*, call'd *Il Pastor Fido*; where *Corsica* and the Satyre are
the Under-parts: Yet we may observe, that *Corsica* is brought into the 2395
Body of the Plot, and made subservient to it. 'Tis certain, that the
Divine Wit of *Horace*, was not ignorant of this Rule, that a Play,
though it consists of many parts, must yet be one in the Action, and
must drive on the Accomplishment of one Design; for he gives this very
Precept, *Sit quodvis simplex duntaxat & unum;* yet he seems not much to 2400
mind it in his Satires, many of them consisting of more Arguments
than one; and the second without dependance on the first. *Casaubon* has
observ'd this before me, in his Preference of *Persius* to *Horace*: And will
have his own belov'd Author to be the first, who found out, and introduc'd this Method of confining himself to one Subject. I know it may 2405
be urg'd in defence of *Horace*, that this Unity is not necessary; because
the very word *Satura* signifies a Dish plentifully stor'd with all variety
of Fruits and Grains. Yet *Juvenal*, who calls his Poems a *Farrago*, which
is a word of the same signification with *Satura*; has chosen to follow the
same Method of *Persius*, and not of *Horace*. And *Boileau*, whose Example 2410
alone is a sufficient Authority, has wholly confin'd himself, in all his
Satires, to this Unity of Design. That variety which is not to be found
in any one Satire, is, at least, in many, written on several occasions.
And if Variety be of absolute necessity in every one of them, according
to the Etymology of the word; yet it may arise naturally from one 2415
Subject, as it is diversly treated, in the several Subordinate Branches
of it; all relating to the Chief. It may be illustrated accordingly with
variety of Examples in the Subdivisions of it; and with as many Precepts as there are Members of it; which altogether may compleat that
Olla, or Hotchpotch, which is properly a Satire.   2420

Under this Unity of Theme, or Subject, is comprehended another
Rule for perfecting the Design of true Satire. The Poet is bound, and
that *ex Officio*, to give his Reader some one Precept of Moral Virtue; and
to caution him against some one particular Vice or Folly. Other Virtues,
subordinate to the first, may be recommended, under that Chief Head; 2425
and other Vices or Follies may be scourg'd, besides that which he
principally intends. But he is chiefly to inculcate one Virtue, and insist
on that. Thus *Juvenal* in every Satire, excepting the first, tyes himself
to one principal Instructive Point, or to the shunning of Moral Evil.

Even in the Sixth, which seems only an Arraignment of the whole Sex 2430 of Womankind; there is a latent Admonition to avoid Ill Women, by shewing how very few, who are Virtuous and Good, are to be found amongst them. But this, tho' the Wittiest of all his Satires, has yet the least of Truth or Instruction in it. He has run himself into his old declamatory way, and almost forgotten, that he was now setting up for 2435 a Moral Poet.

Persius is never wanting to us in some profitable Doctrine, and in exposing the opposite Vices to it. His kind of Philosophy is one, which is the Stoique; and every Satire is a Comment on one particular *Dogma* of that Sect; unless we will except the first, which is against bad 2440 Writers; and yet ev'n there he forgets not the Precepts of the *Porch*. In general, all Virtues are every where to be prais'd, and recommended to Practice; and all Vices to be reprehended, and made either Odious or Ridiculous; or else there is a Fundamental Error in the whole Design. 2445

I have already declar'd, who are the only Persons that are the Adequate Object of Private Satire, and who they are that may properly be expos'd by Name for publick Examples of Vices and Follies; and therefore I will trouble your Lordship no farther with them. Of the best and finest manner of Satire, I have said enough in the Comparison betwixt 2450 *Juvenal* and *Horace*: 'Tis that sharp, well-manner'd way, of laughing a Folly out of Countenance, of which your Lordship is the best Master in this Age. I will proceed to the Versification, which is most proper for it, and add somewhat to what I have said already on that Subject. The sort of Verse which is call'd *Burlesque*, consisting of Eight Syllables, 2455 or Four Feet, is that which our Excellent *Hudibras* has chosen. I ought to have mention'd him before, when I spoke of *Donn*; but by a slip of an Old Man's Memory he was forgotten. The Worth of his Poem is too well known to need my Commendation, and he is above my Censure: His Satire is of the *Varronian* kind, though unmix'd with Prose. The 2460 choice of his Numbers is suitable enough to his Design, as he has manag'd it. But in any other Hand, the shortness of his Verse, and the quick returns of Rhyme, had debas'd the Dignity of Style. And besides, the double Rhyme, (a necessary Companion of Burlesque Writing) is not so proper for Manly Satire, for it turns Earnest too much to Jest, 2465 and gives us a Boyish kind of Pleasure. It tickles aukwardly with a kind of pain, to the best sort of Readers; we are pleas'd ungratefully, and, if I may say so, against our liking. We thank him not for giving us that

2457 spoke] spake *97*

unseasonable Delight, when we know he cou'd have given us a better, and more solid. He might have left that Task to others, who not being 247c able to put in Thought, can only make us grin with the Excrescence of a Word of two or three Syllables in the Close. 'Tis, indeed, below so great a Master to make use of such a little Instrument. But his good Sense is perpetually shining through all he writes; it affords us not the time of finding Faults: We pass through the Levity of his Rhyme, and 247; are immediately carri'd into some admirable useful Thought. After all, he has chosen this kind of Verse; and has written the best in it: And had he taken another, he wou'd always have excell'd. As we say of a Court-Favourite, that whatsoever his Office be, he still makes it uppermost, and most beneficial to himself. 248c

   The quickness of your Imagination, my Lord, has already prevented me; and you know before-hand, that I wou'd prefer the Verse of ten Syllables, which we call the *English* Heroique, to that of Eight. This is truly my Opinion. For this sort of Number is more Roomy. The Thought can turn it self with greater ease, in a larger compass. When 248; the Rhyme comes too thick upon us; it streightens the Expression; we are thinking of the Close, when we shou'd be employ'd in adorning the Thought. It makes a Poet giddy with turning in a Space too narrow for his Imagination. He loses many Beauties without gaining one Advantage. For a Burlesque Rhyme, I have already concluded to be none; or 249(if it were, 'tis more easily purchas'd in Ten Syllables than in Eight: In both occasions 'tis as in a Tennis-Court, when the Strokes of greater force, are given, when we strike out, and play at length. *Tassone* and *Boileau* have left us the best Examples of this way, in the *Secchia Rapita*, and the *Lutrin*. And next them *Merlin Coccajus* in his *Baldus*. I will speak 249. only of the two former, because the last is written in *Latin* Verse. The *Secchia Rapita*, is an *Italian* Poem; a Satire of the *Varronian* kind. 'Tis written in the Stanza of Eight, which is their Measure for Heroique Verse. The Words are stately, the Numbers smooth, the Turn both of Thoughts and Words is happy. The first six lines of the Stanza seem 250(Majestical and Severe: but the two last turn them all, into a pleasant Ridicule. *Boileau*, if I am not much deceiv'd, has model'd from hence, his famous *Lutrin*. He had read the Burlesque Poetry of *Scarron*, with some kind of Indignation, as witty as it was, and found nothing in *France* that was worthy of his Imitation. But he Copy'd the *Italian* so well, that his 250 own may pass for an Original. He writes it in the *French* Heroique Verse, and calls it an Heroique Poem: His Subject is Trivial, but his Verse is Noble. I doubt not but he had *Virgil* in his Eye, for we find

many admirable Imitations of him, and some *Parodies;* as particularly
this Passage in the Fourth of the *Eneids.* 2510

> *Nec tibi Diva Parens; generis nec Dardanus Auctor,*
> *Perfide; sed duris genuit te cautibus horrens*
> *Caucasus; Hyrcanæque admôrunt ubera tigres.*

Which he thus Translates, keeping to the Words, but altering the
Sense. 2515

> *Non, ton Pere a Paris, ne fut point Boulanger:*
> *Et tu n'es point du sang de Gervais Horloger:*
> *Ta Mere ne fut point la Maitresse d'un Coche;*
> *Caucase dans ses flancs, te forma d'une Roche:*
> *Une Tigresse affreuse, en quelque Antre écarté* 2520
> *Te fit, avec son laict, succer sa Cruauté.*

And, as *Virgil* in his Fourth *Georgique* of the Bees, perpetually raises the
Lowness of his Subject by the Loftiness of his Words; and ennobles it
by Comparisons drawn from Empires, and from Monarchs;

> *Admiranda tibi levium spectacula rerum,* 2525
> *Magnanimosq; Duces, totiusq; ordine gentis*
> *Mores & studia, & populos, & prælia dicam.*

And again,

> *Sed Genus immortale manet; multosque per annos*
> *Stat fortuna domûs, & avi numerantur avorum.* 2530

We see *Boileau* pursuing him in the same flights; and scarcely yielding
to his Master. This, I think, my Lord, to be the most Beautiful, and
most Noble kind of Satire. Here is the Majesty of the Heroique, finely
mix'd with the Venom of the other; and raising the Delight which
otherwise wou'd be flat and vulgar, by the Sublimity of the Expression. 2535
I cou'd say somewhat more of the Delicacy of this and some other of
his Satires; but it might turn to his Prejudice, if 'twere carry'd back to
France.

I have given Your Lordship, but this bare hint, in what Verse, and in
what manner this sort of Satire may best be manag'd. Had I time, I 2540
cou'd enlarge on the Beautiful Turns of Words and Thoughts; which
are as requisite in this, as in Heroique Poetry it self; of which this
Satire is undoubtedly a Species. With these Beautiful Turns I confess
my self to have been unacquainted, till about Twenty Years ago, in a

Conversation which I had with that Noble Wit of *Scotland*, Sir *George* 254:
Mackenzy: He asked me why I did not imitate in my Verses, the turns
of Mr. *Waller*, and Sir *John Denham*; of which, he repeated many to me:
I had often read with pleasure, and with some profit, those two Fathers
of our *English* Poetry; but had not seriously enough consider'd those
Beauties which give the last perfection to their Works. Some sprink- 255
lings of this kind, I had also formerly in my Plays, but they were casual,
and not design'd. But this hint, thus seasonably given me, first made
me sensible of my own wants, and brought me afterwards to seek for
the supply of them in other *English* Authors. I look'd over the Darling
of my youth, the Famous *Cowley*; there I found instead of them, the 255
Points of Wit, and Quirks of Epigram, even in the *Davideis*, a Heroick
Poem, which is of an opposite nature to those *Puerilities*; but no Elegant
turns, either on the word, or on the thought. Then I consulted a
Greater Genius, (without offence to the Manes of that Noble Author)
I mean *Milton*. But as he endeavours every where to express *Homer*, 256
whose Age had not arriv'd to that fineness, I found in him a true
sublimity, lofty thoughts, which were cloath'd with admirable *Grecisms*,
and ancient words, which he had been digging from the Mines of
Chaucer, and of *Spencer*, and which, with all their rusticity, had somewhat of Venerable in them. But I found not there neither that for which 256
I look'd. At last I had recourse to his Master, *Spencer*, the Author of that
immortal Poem, call'd the *Fairy-Queen*; and there I met with that which
I had been looking for so long in vain. *Spencer* had studi'd *Virgil* to as
much advantage as *Milton* had done *Homer*. And amongst the rest of his
Excellencies had Copy'd that. Looking farther into the *Italian*, I found 257
Tasso had done the same; nay more, that all the Sonnets in that Language are on the turn of the first thought; which Mr. *Walsh*, in his late
ingenious Preface to his Poems has observ'd. In short, *Virgil*, and *Ovid*
are the two Principal Fountains of them in *Latine* Poetry. And the
French at this day are so fond of them, that they judge them to be the 257
first Beauties. *Delicate*, *& bien tourné*, are the highest Commendations,
which they bestow, on somewhat which they think a Master-Piece.

   An Example of the turn on Words amongst a thousand others, is that,
in the last Book of *Ovid*'s *Metamorphoses*.

> *Heu quantum scelus est, in viscera, viscera condi!* 258
> *Congestoq; avidum pinguescere corpore corpus;*
> *Alteriusq; Animantem, Animantis vivere leto.*

An Example of the turn both on Thoughts and Words, is to be found in *Catullus*; in the Complaint of *Ariadne*, when she was left by *Theseus*.

> *Tum jam nulla viro juranti fœmina credat;* 2585
> *Nulla viri speret Sermones esse fideles:*
> *Qui dum aliquid cupiens animus prægestit apisci,*
> *Nil metuunt jurare; nihil promittere parcunt.*
> *Sed simul ac cupidæ mentis satiata libido est,*
> *Dicta nihil metuere; nihil perjuria curant.* 2590

An extraordinary turn upon the words, is that in *Ovid*'s *Epistolæ Heroidum*, of *Sappho* to *Phaon*.

> *Si nisi quæ formâ poterit te digna videri,*
> *Nulla futura tua est; nulla futura tua est.*

Lastly, a turn which I cannot say is absolutely on Words, for the 2595 Thought turns with them, is in the Fourth *Georgick* of *Virgil*; where *Orpheus* is to receive his Wife from Hell, on express Condition not to look on her 'till she was come on Earth.

> *Cùm subita incautum dementia cepit Amantem;*
> *Ignoscenda quidem, scirent si ignoscere Manes.* 2600

I will not burthen your Lordship with more of them; for I write to a Master, who understands them better than my self. But I may safely conclude them to be great Beauties. I might descend also to the Mechanick Beauties of Heroick Verse; but we have yet no English *Prosodia*, not so much as a tolerable Dictionary, or a Grammar; so that 2605 our Language is in a manner Barbarous; and what Government will encourage any one, or more, who are capable of Refining it, I know not. But nothing under a Publick Expence can go through with it. And I rather fear a declination of the Language, than hope an advancement of it in the present Age. 2610

I am still speaking to you, my Lord; though in all probability, you are already out of hearing. Nothing which my meanness can produce, is worthy of this long attention. But I am come to the last Petition of *Abraham*; If there be ten Righteous Lines, in this vast Preface, spare it for their sake; and also spare the next City, because it is but a little one. 2615

I wou'd excuse the performance of this Translation, if it were all my own; but the better, tho' not the greater part being the Work of some Gentlemen who have succeeded very happily in their Undertaking; let their Excellencies attone for my Imperfections, and those of my Sons.

2583 Example of . . . on] Example on . . . of *93 97*   2603 Beauties.] Beauties: *93 97*

I have perus'd some of the Satires, which are done by other Hands: 2620
And they seem to me as perfect in their kind, as any thing I have seen
in *English* Verse. The common way which we have taken, is not a
Literal Translation, but a kind of Paraphrase; or somewhat which is
yet more loose, betwixt a Paraphrase and Imitation. It was not possible
for us, or any Men, to have made it pleasant, any other way. If rendring 2625
the exact Sense of these Authors, almost line for line, had been our
business, *Barten Holiday* had done it already to our hands: And, by the
help of his Learned Notes and Illustrations, not only of *Juvenal*, and
Persius, but what yet is more obscure, his own Verses might be understood.   2630

But he wrote for Fame, and wrote to Scholars: We write only for the
Pleasure and Entertainment, of those Gentlemen and Ladies, who tho
they are not Scholars, are not Ignorant: Persons of Understanding and
good Sense; who not having been conversant in the Original, or at
least not having made *Latine* Verse so much their business, as to be 2635
Critiques in it, wou'd be glad to find, if the Wit of our Two great
Authors, be answerable to their Fame, and Reputation in the World.
We have therefore endeavour'd to give the Publick all the Satisfaction
we are able in this kind.

And if we are not altogether so faithful to our Author, as our Prede- 2640
cessours *Holiday* and *Stapylton*, yet we may Challenge to our selves this
praise, that we shall be far more pleasing to our Readers. We have follow'd our Authors, at greater distance; tho' not Step by Step, as they
have done. For oftentimes they have gone so close, that they have trod
on the Heels of *Juvenal* and *Persius*; and hurt them by their too near 2645
approach. A Noble Authour wou'd not be persu'd too close by a
Translator. We lose his Spirit, when we think to take his Body. The
grosser Part remains with us, but the Soul is flown away, in some
Noble Expression or some delicate turn of Words, or Thought. Thus
Holiday, who made this way his choice, seiz'd the meaning of *Juvenal*; 2650
but the Poetry has always scap'd him.

They who will not grant me, that Pleasure is one of the Ends of
Poetry, but that it is only a means of compassing the only end, which
is Instruction; must yet allow that without the means of Pleasure, the
Instruction is but a bare and dry Philosophy. A crude preparation of 2655
Morals, which we may have from *Aristotle* and *Epictetus*, with more
profit than from any Poet. Neither *Holiday* nor *Stapylton*, have imitated
Juvenal, in the Poetical part of him, his Diction and his Elocution. Nor

had they been Poets, as neither of them were; yet in the way they took, it was impossible for them to have Succeeded in the Poetique part. 2660

The *English* Verse, which we call Heroique, consists of no more than Ten Syllables; the *Latine* Hexameter sometimes rises to Seventeen; as for example, this Verse in *Virgil*,

Pulverulenta putrem sonitu quatit ungula Campum.

Here is the difference, of no less than Seven Syllables in a line, betwixt 2665 the *English* and the *Latine*. Now the Medium of these, is about Fourteen Syllables; because the Dactyle is a more frequent foot in Hexameters than the Spondee.

But *Holiday*, without considering that he Writ with the disadvantage of Four Syllables less in every Verse, endeavours to make one of his 2670 Lines, to comprehend the Sense of one of *Juvenal*'s. According to the falsity of the Proposition, was the Success. He was forc'd to crowd his Verse with ill sounding Monosyllables, of which our Barbarous Language affords him a wild plenty: And by that means he arriv'd at his Pedantick end, which was to make a literal Translation: His Verses 2675 have nothing of Verse in them, but only the worst part of it, the Rhyme: And that, into the bargain, is far from good. But which is more Intollerable, by cramming his ill chosen, and worse sounding Monosyllables so close together; the very Sense which he endeavours to explain, is become more obscure, than that of his Author. So that *Holiday* himself 2680 cannot be understood, without as large a Commentary, as that which he makes on his Two Authours. For my own part, I can make a shift to find the meaning of *Juvenal* without his Notes: but his Translation is more difficult than his Authour. And I find Beauties in the *Latine* to recompence my Pains; but in *Holiday* and *Stapylton*, my Ears, in the 2685 First Place, are mortally offended; and then their Sense is so perplex'd, that I return to the Original, as the more pleasing task, as well as the more easy.

This must be said for our Translation, that if we give not the whole Sense of *Juvenal*, yet we give the most considerable Part of it: We give 2690 it, in General, so clearly, that few Notes are sufficient to make us Intelligible: We make our Authour at least appear in a Poetique Dress. We have actually made him more Sounding, and more Elegant, than he was before in *English*: And have endeavour'd to make him speak that kind of *English*, which he wou'd have spoken had he liv'd in *England*, and had 2695 Written to this Age. If sometimes any of us (and 'tis but seldome) make him express the Customs and Manners of our Native Country, rather than of *Rome*; 'tis, either when there was some kind of Analogy, betwixt their Customes and ours; or when, to make him more easy to Vulgar Understandings, we gave him those Manners which are familiar to 270 us. But I defend not this Innovation, 'tis enough if I can excuse it. For to speak sincerely, the Manners of Nations and Ages, are not to be confounded: We shou'd either make them *English*, or leave them *Roman*. If this can neither be defended, nor excus'd, let it be pardon'd, at least, because it is acknowledg'd; and so much the more easily, as being a 270 fault which is never committed without some Pleasure to the Reader.

Thus, my Lord, having troubl'd You with a tedious Visit, the best Manners will be shewn in the least Ceremony. I will slip away while Your Back is turn'd, and while You are otherwise employ'd: with great Confusion, for having entertain'd You so long with this Discourse; and 271 for having no other Recompence to make You, than the Worthy Labours of my Fellow-Undertakers in this Work; and the Thankful Acknowledgments, Prayers, and perpetual good Wishes of,

My Lord,

Your Lordships,   271

Most Obliged, Most Humble,

Aug. 18. 1692   *and Most Obedient Servant,*

JOHN DRYDEN.

THE FIRST SATYR OF JUVENAL

ARGUMENT OF THE FIRST SATYR

THE Poet gives us first a kind of humorous Reason for his Writing: That being provok'd by hearing so many ill Poets rehearse their Works, he does himself Justice on them, by giving them as bad as they bring. But since no man will rank himself with ill Writers, 'tis easie to conclude, that if such Wretches cou'd draw an Audience, he thought it no hard matter to excel them, and gain 5 a greater esteem with the Publick. Next he informs us more openly, why he rather addicts himself to Satyr, than any other kind of Poetry. And here he discovers that it is not so much his indignation to ill Poets, as to ill Men, which has prompted him to write. He therefore gives us a summary and general view of the Vices and Follies reigning in his time. So that this first Satyr is the natural 10 Ground-work of all the rest. Herein he confines himself to no one Subject, but strikes indifferently at all Men in his way: In every following Satyr he has chosen some particular Moral which he wou'd inculcate; and lashes some particular

2717 Servant, 97: Servant. 93

Vice or Folly, (*An Art with which our Lampooners are not much acquainted.*)
But our Poet being desirous to reform his own Age, and not daring to attempt 15
it by an Overt act of naming living Persons, inveighs onely against those who
were infamous in the times immediately preceding his, whereby he not only
gives a fair warning to Great Men, that their Memory lies at the mercy of
future Poets and Historians, but also with a finer stroke of his Pen, brands
ev'n the living, and personates them under dead mens Names. 20
I *have avoided as much as I cou'd possibly the borrow'd Learning of Marginal*
Notes and Illustrations, and for that Reason have Translated this Satyr some-
what largely. And freely own (if it be a fault) that I have likewise omitted
most of the Proper Names, because I thought they wou'd not much edifie the
Reader. To conclude, if in two or three places I have deserted all the Com- 25
mentators, 'tis because I thought they first deserted my Author, or at least
have left him in so much obscurity, that too much room is left for guessing.

THE FIRST SATYR

STILL shall I hear, and never quit the Score,
  Stun'd with hoarse [1]*Codrus Theseid,* o're and o're?
Shall this Man's Elegies and t'others Play
Unpunish'd Murther a long Summer's day?
Huge [2]*Telephus,* a formidable page,   5
Cries Vengeance; and [3]*Orestes* bulky rage
Unsatisfy'd with Margins closely writ,
Foams o're the Covers, and not finish'd yet.
No Man can take a more familiar note
Of his own Home, than I of *Vulcan*'s Grott,   10
Or [4]*Mars his Grove,* or hollow winds that blow
From *Ætna*'s top, or tortur'd Ghosts below.
I know by rote the Fam'd Exploits of *Greece;*
The Centaurs fury, and the Golden Fleece;
Through the thick shades th' Eternal Scribler bauls;   15
And shakes the Statues on their Pedestals.
The[5] best and worst on the same Theme employs
His Muse, and plagues us with an equal noise.
    Provok'd by these Incorrigible Fools,
I left declaiming in pedantick Schools;   20
Where, with Men-boys, I strove to get Renown,
Advising[6] *Sylla* to a private Gown.

The First Satyr. 6 *Orestes*] *Orestes*'s 93 97

But, since the World with Writing is possest,
I'll versifie in spite; and do my best
To make as much waste Paper as the rest.   } 25
     But why I lift aloft the Satyrs[7] Rod,
And tread the Path which fam'd *Lucilius* trod,
Attend the Causes which my Muse have led:
When Sapless Eunuchs mount the Marriage-bed,
When [8]Mannish *Mevia* that two handed Whore,   30
Astride on Horse-back hunts the *Tuscan* Boar,
When all our Lords are by his Wealth outvy'd,
Whose[9] Razour on my callow-beard was try'd:
When I behold the Spawn of conquer'd *Nile*
Crispinus[10], both in Birth and Manners vile,   35
Pacing in pomp, with Cloak of *Tyrian* dye
Chang'd oft a day for needless Luxury;
And finding oft occasion to be fan'd,
Ambitious to produce his Lady-hand;
Charg'd[11] with light Summer-rings his fingers sweat,   40
Unable to support a Gem of weight:
Such fulsom Objects meeting every where,
'Tis hard to write, but harder to forbear.
     To view so lewd a Town, and to refrain,
What Hoops of Iron cou'd my Spleen contain!   45
When [12]pleading *Matho*, born abroad for Air,
With his Fat Paunch fills his new fashion'd Chair,
And after him the Wretch in Pomp convey'd,
Whose Evidence his Lord and Friend betray'd,
And but the wish'd Occasion does attend   } 50
From the poor Nobles the last Spoils to rend;
Whom ev'n Spies dread as their Superiour Fiend,
And bribe with Presents, or, when Presents fail,
They send their prostituted Wives for bail:
When Night-performance holds the place of Merit,   55
And Brawn and Back the next of Kin disherit;
For such good Parts are in Preferment's way,
The Rich Old Madam never fails to pay
Her Legacies by Nature's Standard giv'n,
One gains an Ounce, another gains Eleven: 60
A dear-bought Bargain, all things duly weigh'd,

51 rend;] rend, *93 97*   58 pay] pay, *93 97*

For which their thrice Concocted Blood is paid.
With looks as wan, as he who in the Brake
At unawares has trod upon a Snake.
Or play'd ¹³at *Lions* a declaiming Prize,   65
For which the Vanquish'd *Rhetorician* Dyes.

What Indignation boils within my Veins,
When perjur'd Guardians, proud with Impious Gains,
Choak up the Streets, too narrow for their Trains!
Whose Wards by want betray'd, to Crimes are led   70
Too foul to Name, too fulsom to be read!
When he who pill'd his Province scapes the Laws,
And keeps his Money though he lost his Cause:
His Fine begg'd off, contemns his Infamy,
Can rise at twelve, and get him Drunk e're three: 75
Enjoys his Exile, and, Condemn'd in vain,
Leaves thee, ¹⁴prevailing Province, to complain?

Such Villanies rous'd ¹⁵*Horace* into Wrath;
And 'tis more Noble to pursue his Path,
Than an Old Tale of *Diomede* to repeat,   80
Or lab'ring after *Hercules* to sweat,
Or wandring in the winding Maze of *Creet*.
Or with the winged Smith aloft to fly,
Or flutt'ring Perish with his foolish Boy.

With what Impatience must the Muse behold   85
The Wife by her procuring Husband sold?
For though the Law makes Null th' Adulterer's Deed
Of Lands to her, the Cuckold may succeed.
Who his taught Eyes up to the Cieling throws,
And sleeps all over but his wakeful Nose.   90
When he dares hope a Colonel's Command,
Whose Coursers kept, ran out his Father's Land;
Who yet a Stripling *Nero*'s Chariot drove,
Whirl'd o're the Streets, while his vain Master strove
With boasted Art to please his¹⁶ Eunuch-Love.   95
Wou'd it not make a modest Author dare
To draw his Table-Book within the Square,
And fill with Notes, when lolling at his ease
Mecenas-like¹⁷, the happy Rogue he sees
Born by Six weary'd Slaves in open View,   100

75 rise] raise 97   80 *Diomede*] Diomeda 97

Who Cancell'd an old Will, and forg'd a New:
Made wealthy at the small expence of Signing
With a wet Seal, and a fresh Interlining.
   The Lady, next, requires a lashing Line,
Who squeez'd a Toad into her Husband's Wine: 105
So well the fashionable Med'cine thrives,
That now 'tis Practis'd ev'n by Country Wives:
Poys'ning without regard of Fame or Fear:
And spotted Corps are frequent on the Bier.
Wou'dst thou to Honours and Preferments climb,   110
Be bold in Mischief, dare some mighty Crime,
Which Dungeons, Death, or Banishment deserves:
For Virtue is but dryly Prais'd, and Sterves.
Great Men, to great Crimes, owe their Plate Embost,
Fair Palaces, and Furniture of Cost;   115
And high Commands: A Sneaking Sin is lost.
Who can behold that rank Old Letcher keep
His Son's Corrupted Wife, [18]and hope to sleep?
Or that Male-Harlot, or that unfledg'd Boy,
Eager to Sin, before he can enjoy?   120
If Nature cou'd not, Anger would indite
Such woeful stuff as I or *S——ll* write.
   Count from the time, since Old [19]*Deucalion*'s Boat,
Rais'd by the Flood, did on *Parnassus* Float;
And scarcely Mooring on the Cliff, implor'd   125
An Oracle how Man might be restor'd;
When soften'd Stones and Vital Breath ensu'd,
And Virgins Naked were by Lovers View'd;
What ever since that Golden Age was done,
What Humane Kind desires, and what they shun,   130
Rage, Passions, Pleasures, Impotence of Will,
Shall this Satyrical Collection fill.
   What age so large a Crop of Vices bore,
Or when was Avarice extended more?
When were the Dice with more Profusion thrown?   135
The well fill'd Fob, not empty'd now alone,
But Gamesters for whole Patrimonies play;
The Steward brings the Deeds which must convey
The lost Estate: What more than Madness reigns,
When one short sitting many Hundreds Drains,   140

And not enough is left him to supply
Board-Wages, or a Footman's Livery?
   What Age so many Summer-Seats did see?
Or which, of our Forefathers far'd so well
As on seven Dishes at a private Meal?   145
Clients of Old were Feasted; now a poor
Divided Dole is dealt at th' outward Door;
Which by the Hungry Rout is soon dispatch'd:
The Paltry Largess, too, severely watch'd
E're given; and every Face observ'd with Care,   150
That no intruding Guest Usurp a share.
Known, you Receive: The Cryer calls aloud
Our Old Nobility of *Trojan* Blood,
Who gape among the Croud for their precarious Food.
The Prætors, and the Tribunes Voice is heard;   155
The Freedman justles and will be preferr'd;
First come, first serv'd, he Cries; and I, in spight
Of your Great Lordships, will Maintain my Right.
Tho born a Slave, tho[20] my torn Ears are bor'd,
'Tis not the Birth, 'tis Mony makes the Lord.   160
The Rents of Five fair Houses I receive;
What greater Honours can the Purple give?
The[21] Poor *Patrician* is reduc'd to keep
In Melancholly Walks a Grazier's Sheep:
Not [22]*Pallas* nor *Licinius* had my Treasure;   165
Then let the Sacred Tribunes wait my leasure.
Once a Poor Rogue, 'tis true, I trod the Street,
And trudg'd to *Rome* upon my Naked Feet:
Gold is the greatest God; though yet we see
No Temples rais'd to Mony's Majesty,   170
No Altars fuming to her Pow'r Divine,
Such as to Valour, Peace, and Virtue Shine,
And Faith, and Concord: [23]where the Stork on high
Seems to Salute her Infant Progeny:
Presaging Pious Love with her Auspicious Cry.   175
   But since our Knights and Senators account
To what their sordid begging Vails amount,
Judge what a wretched share the Poor attends,
Whose whole Subsistence on those Alms depends!
Their Houshold-Fire, their Rayment, and their Food,   180

Prevented[24] by those Harpies; when a wood
Of Litters thick besiege the Donor's Gate,
And begging Lords, and teeming Ladies wait
The promis'd Dole: Nay some have learn'd the trick
To beg for absent persons; feign them sick,   185
Close mew'd in their Sedans, for fear of air:
And for their Wives produce an empty Chair.
This is my Spouse: Dispatch her with her share.
'Tis[25] *Galla*: Let her Ladyship but peep:
No, Sir, 'tis pity to disturb her sleep.   190
   Such fine Employments our whole days divide:
The Salutations of the Morning-tide
Call up the Sun; those ended, to the Hall
We wait the Patron, hear the Lawyers baul,
Then[26] to the Statues; where amidst the Race   195
Of Conqu'ring *Rome*, some *Arab* shews his Face
Inscrib'd with Titles, and profanes the place.
Fit to be piss'd against, and somewhat more.
The Great Man, home conducted, shuts his door;
Old Clients, weary'd out with fruitless care,   200
Dismiss their hopes of eating, and despair.
Though much against the grain, forc'd to retire,
Buy Roots for Supper, and provide a Fire.
   Mean time his Lordship lolls within at ease,
Pamp'ring his Paunch with Foreign Rarities: 205
Both Sea and Land are ransack'd for the Feast,
And his own Gut the sole invited Guest.
Such Plate, such Tables, Dishes dress'd so well,
That whole Estates are swallow'd at a Meal.
Ev'n Parasites are banish'd from his Board: 210
(At once a sordid and luxurious Lord:)
Prodigious Throat, for which whole Boars are drest;
(A Creature form'd to furnish out a Feast.)
But present Punishment pursues his Maw,
When surfeited and swell'd, the Peacock raw   215
He bears into the Bath; whence want of Breath,
Repletions, Apoplex, intestate Death.
His Fate makes Table-talk, divulg'd with scorn,
And he, a Jeast, into his Grave is born.
   No Age can go beyond us: Future Times   220

Can add no farther to the present Crimes.
Our Sons but the same things can wish and do;
Vice is at stand, and at the highest flow.
Then Satyr spread thy Sails; take all the winds can blow.
Some may, perhaps, demand what Muse can yield   225
Sufficient strength for such a spacious Field?
From whence can be deriv'd so large a Vein,
Bold Truths to speak, and spoken to maintain;
When God-like Freedom is so far bereft
The Noble Mind, that scarce the Name is left?   230
E're *Scandalum Magnatum* was begot,
No matter if the Great forgave or not:
But if that honest licence now you take,
If, into Rogues Omnipotent, you rake,
Death is your Doom, impail'd upon a Stake: 235
Smear'd o're with Wax, and set on fire, to light
The Streets, and make a dreadful blaze by night.
    Shall They who drench'd three Uncles in a draught
Of poys'nous Juice, be then in Triumph brought,
Make Lanes among the People where they go,   240
And, mounted high on downy Chariots, throw
Disdainful glances on the Crowd below?
Be silent, and beware if such you see;
'Tis Defamation but to say, That's He!
    Against[27] bold *Turnus* the Great *Trojan* Arm,   245
Amidst their strokes the Poet gets no harm:
Achilles may in Epique Verse be slain,
And none of all his Myrmidons complain:
Hylas may drop his Pitcher, none will cry;
Not if he drown himself for company: 250
But when *Lucilius* brandishes his Pen,
And flashes in the face of Guilty Men,
A cold Sweat stands in drops on ev'ry part;
And Rage succeeds to Tears, Revenge to Smart.
Muse be advis'd; 'tis past consid'ring time,   255
When enter'd once the dangerous Lists of Rhime:
Since none the Living-Villains dare implead,
Arraign them in the Persons of the Dead.

EXPLANATORY NOTES

1 *COdrus*, or it may be *Cordus*, a bad Poet who wrote the Life and Actions of *Theseus*.   2 *Telephus*, the Name of a Tragedy.   3 *Orestes*, another Tragedy.   4 *Mars his Grove*. Some Commentators take this Grove to be a Place where Poets were us'd to repeat their Works to the People, but more probably, both this and *Vulcan*'s Grott, or Cave, and the rest of the Places and Names here mention'd, are only meant for the Common Places of *Homer*, in his *Iliads* and *Odysses*.   5 *The best and worst*; that is, the best and the worst Poets.   6 *Advising Sylla*, &c. This was one of the Themes given in the Schools of Rhetoricians, in the deliberative kind; Whether *Sylla* should lay down the Supreme Power of Dictatorship, or still keep it. 7 *Lucilius*, the first Satyrist of the *Romans*, who wrote long before *Horace*. 8 *Mevia*, a Name put for any Impudent or Mannish Woman.   9 *Whose Razour*, &c. *Juvenal*'s Barber now grown Wealthy.   10 *Crispinus*, an *Egyptian* Slave; now by his Riches transform'd into a Nobleman. 11 *Charg'd with light Summer Rings*, &c. The *Romans* were grown so Effeminate in *Juvenal*'s time, that they wore light Rings in the Summer, and heavier in the Winter.   12 *Matho*, a Famous Lawyer, mention'd in other Places by *Juvenal* and *Martial*.   13 *At Lyons*; a City in *France*, where Annual Sacrifices and Games were made in Honour of *Augustus Cæsar*. 14 *Prevailing Province*, &c. Here the Poet complains that the Governours of Provinces being accus'd for their unjust Exactions, though they were condemned at their Tryals, yet got off by Bribery.   15 *Horace*, who wrote Satyrs: 'Tis more Noble, says our Author, to imitate him in that way, than to write the Labours of *Hercules*, the Sufferings of *Diomedes* and his Followers, or the Flight of *Dedalus* who made the Labyrinth, and the Death of his Son *Icarus*.   16 *His Eunuch-Love*. *Nero* Marry'd *Sporus* an Eunuch; though it may be the Poet meant *Nero*'s Mistress in Mans Apparel.   17 *Mecenas-like*: *Mecenas* is often Tax'd by *Seneca* and others, for his Effeminacy.   18 *And hope to sleep*: The meaning is, that the very consideration of such a Crime, will hinder a Virtuous Man from taking his Repose.   19 *Deucalion* and *Pyrrha*, when the World was drown'd, escap'd to the top of Mount *Parnassus*; and were commanded to restore Mankind by throwing Stones over their Heads: The Stones he threw became Men, and those she threw became Women.   20 *Though my torn Ears are bor'd*: The Ears of all Slaves were bor'd as a Mark of their Servitude; which Custom is still usual in the *East-Indies*, and in other Parts, even for whole Nations; who bore Prodigious holes in their Ears, and wear vast Weights at them.   21 *The poor Patrician*; the poor Nobleman.   22 *Pallas*, or *Licinius*. *Pallas*, a Slave freed by *Claudius Cæsar*, and rais'd by his Favour to great Riches. *Licinius* was another Wealthy Freedman, belonging to *Augustus*.   23 *Where the Stork on*

high, &c. Perhaps the Storks were us'd to build on the top of the Temple dedicated to *Concord.* 24 *Prevented by those Harpies:* He calls the *Roman* Knights, *&c.* Harpies, or Devourers: In those Days the Rich made Doles intended for the Poor: But the Great were either so Covetous, or so Needy, 45 that they came in their Litters to demand their shares of the Largess; and thereby prevented, and consequently starv'd the Poor. 25 *'Tis Galla,* &c. The meaning is, that Noblemen wou'd cause empty Litters to be carried to the Giver's Door, pretending their Wives were within them: *'Tis Galla,* that is, my Wife: the next words *Let her Ladyship but peep,* are of 50 the Servant who distributes the Dole; Let me see her, that I may be sure she is within the Litter. The Husband answers, she is asleep, and to open the Litter would disturb her Rest. 26 *Next to the Statues,* &c. The Poet here tells you how the Idle pass'd their time; in going first to the Levees of the Great, then to the Hall, that is, to the Temple of *Apollo,* to 55 hear the Lawyers Plead, then to the Market-place of *Augustus,* where the Statues of the Famous *Romans* were set in Ranks on Pedestals: Amongst which Statues were seen those of Foreigners, such as *Arabs,* &c. who for no desert, but only on the Account of their Wealth, or Favour, were plac'd amongst the Noblest. 27 *Against bold* Turnus, *&c.* A Poet may safely 60 write an Heroick Poem, such as that of *Virgil,* who describes the Duel of *Turnus* and *Æneas;* or of *Homer,* who Writes of *Achilles* and *Hector;* or the death of *Hylas* the *Catamite* of *Hercules;* who stooping for Water, dropt his Pitcher, and fell into the Well after it. But 'tis dangerous to write Satyr like *Lucilius.* 65

THE THIRD SATYR OF JUVENAL

ARGUMENT OF THE THIRD SATYR

The Story of this Satyr speaks it self. Umbritius, *the suppos'd Friend of* Juvenal, *and himself a Poet, is leaving* Rome; *and retiring to* Cumæ. *Our Author accompanies him out of Town. Before they take leave of each other,* Umbritius *tells his Friend the Reasons which oblige him to lead a private life, in an obscure place. He complains that an honest man cannot get his bread at* Rome. *That* 5 *none but Flatterers make their Fortunes there: That* Grecians *and other Foreigners, raise themselves by those sordid Arts which he describes, and against which he bitterly inveighs. He reckons up the several Inconveniencies which arise from a City life; and the many Dangers which attend it. Upbraids the Noblemen with Covetousness, for not Rewarding good Poets; and arraigns the* 10 *Government for starving them. The great Art of this Satyr is particularly shown, in Common Places; and drawing in as many Vices, as cou'd naturally fall into the compass of it.*

THE THIRD SATYR

GRIEV'D tho I am, an Ancient Friend to lose,
 I like the Solitary Seat he chose:
In quiet ¹*Cumæ* fixing his Repose:
Where, far from Noisy *Rome* secure he Lives,
And one more Citizen to *Sybil* gives: 5
The Road to ²*Bajæ*, and that soft Recess
Which all the Gods with all their Bounty bless.
Tho I in ³*Prochyta* with greater ease
Cou'd live, than in a Street of Palaces.
What Scene so Desart, or so full of Fright,   10
As tow'ring Houses tumbling in the Night,
And *Rome* on Fire beheld by its own Blazing Light?
But worse than all the clatt'ring Tiles; and worse
Than thousand Padders, is the Poet's Curse.
Rogues that ⁴in Dog-days cannot Rhime forbear; 15
But without Mercy read, and make you hear.
 Now while my Friend just ready to depart,
Was packing all his Goods in one poor Cart;
He stopp'd a little at the Conduit-Gate,
Where ⁵*Numa* modell'd once the *Roman* State,   20
In Mighty Councels with his ⁶Nymph retir'd:
Though now the Sacred Shades and Founts are hir'd
By Banish'd Jews, who their whole Wealth can lay
In a small Basket, on a Wisp of Hay;
Yet such our Avarice is, that every Tree   25
Pays for his Head; not Sleep it self is free:
Nor Place, nor Persons now are Sacred held,
From their own Grove the Muses are expell'd.
Into this lonely Vale our Steps we bend,
I and my sullen discontented Friend: 30
The Marble Caves, and Aquæducts we view;
But how Adult'rate now, and different from the true!
How much more Beauteous had the Fountain been

The Third Satyr. 5 gives:] gives. *93 97* 13 all *97*: all, *93* 21 Nymph]
Nymphs *93 97. See Dryden's note*

Embellish't with her first Created Green,
Where Crystal Streams through living Turf had run,   35
Contented with an Urn of Native Stone!
  Then thus *Umbricius*, (with an Angry Frown,
And looking back on this degen'rate Town,)
Since Noble Arts in *Rome* have no support,
And ragged Virtue not a Friend at Court,   40
No Profit rises from th' ungrateful Stage,
My Poverty encreasing with my Age;
'Tis time to give my just Disdain a vent,
And, Cursing, leave so base a Government.
Where[7] *Dedalus* his borrow'd Wings laid by,   45
To that obscure Retreat I chuse to fly:
While yet few furrows on my Face are seen,
While I walk upright, and Old Age is green,
And [8]*Lachesis* has somewhat left to spin.
Now, now 'tis time to quit this cursed place;   50
And hide from Villains my too honest Face:
Here let [9]*Arturius* live, and such as he;
Such Manners will with such a Town agree.
Knaves who in full Assemblies have the knack
Of turning Truth to Lies, and White to Black: 55
Can hire large Houses, and oppress the Poor
By farm'd Excise; can cleanse the Common-shoare;
Can rent the Fishery; can bear the dead;
And teach their Eyes dissembled Tears to shed:
All this for Gain; for Gain they sell their very Head.   60
These Fellows (see what Fortune's pow'r can do)
Were once the Minstrels of a Country Show:
Follow'd the Prizes through each paltry Town,
By Trumpet-Cheeks, and Bloated Faces known.
But now, grown rich, on drunken Holy-days,   65
At their own Costs exhibit Publick Plays;
Where influenc'd by the Rabble's bloody will,
With[10] Thumbs bent back, they popularly kill.
From thence return'd, their sordid Avarice rakes
In Excrements again, and hires the Jakes.   70
Why hire they not the Town, not ev'ry thing,
Since such as they have Fortune in a String?

Who, for her pleasure, can her Fools advance;
And toss 'em topmost on the Wheel of Chance.
What's *Rome* to me, what bus'ness have I there,   75
I who can neither Lye nor falsly Swear?
Nor Praise my Patron's undeserving Rhimes,
Nor yet comply with him, nor with his Times;
Unskill'd in Schemes by Planets to foreshow
Like Canting Rascals, how the Wars will go: 80
I neither will, nor can Prognosticate
To the young gaping Heir, his Father's Fate:
Nor in the Entrails of a Toad have pry'd,
Nor carry'd Bawdy Presents to a Bride:
For want of these Town Virtues, thus, alone,   85
I go conducted on my way by none:
Like a dead Member from the Body rent;
Maim'd and unuseful to the Government.
   Who now is lov'd, but he who loves the Times,
Conscious of close Intrigues, and dipt in Crimes: 90
Lab'ring with Secrets which his Bosom burn,
Yet never must to publick light return;
They get Reward alone who can Betray:
For keeping honest Counsels none will pay.
He who can [11]*Verres*, when he will, accuse,   95
The Purse of *Verres* may at Pleasure use:
But let not all the Gold which [12]*Tagus* hides,
And pays the Sea in Tributary Tides,
Be Bribe sufficient to corrupt thy Breast;
Or violate with Dreams thy peaceful rest.   100
Great Men with jealous Eyes the Friend behold,
Whose secrecy they purchase with their Gold.
   I haste to tell thee, nor shall Shame oppose,
What Confidents our Wealthy *Romans* chose:
And whom I most abhor: To speak my Mind,   105
I hate, in *Rome*, a *Grecian* Town to find:
To see the Scum of *Greece* transplanted here,
Receiv'd like Gods, is what I cannot bear.
Nor *Greeks* alone, but *Syrians* here abound,
Obscene [13]*Orontes* diving under Ground,   110
Conveys[14] his Wealth to *Tyber*'s hungry Shoars,

73 Fools] Fool *97*

And fattens *Italy* with Foreign Whores:
Hether their crooked Harps and Customs come;
All find Receipt in Hospitable *Rome*.
The Barbarous Harlots croud the Publick Place: 115
Go Fools, and purchase an unclean Embrace;
The painted Mitre court, and the more painted Face.
Old [15]*Romulus*, and Father *Mars* look down,
Your Herdsman Primitive, your homely Clown
Is turn'd a *Beau* in a loose tawdry Gown.   120
His once unkem'd, and horrid Locks, behold
Stilling sweet Oyl; his Neck inchain'd with Gold:
Aping the Foreigners, in ev'ry Dress;
Which, bought at greater cost, becomes him less.
Mean time they wisely leave their Native Land,   125
From *Sycion*, *Samos*, and from *Alaband*,
And *Amydon*, to *Rome* they Swarm in Shoals:
So Sweet and Easie is the Gain from Fools.
Poor Refugies at first, they purchase here:
And, soon as Denizen'd, they dominere.   130
Grow to the Great, a flatt'ring Servile Rout:
Work themselves inward, and their Patrons out.
Quick Witted, Brazen-fac'd, with fluent Tongues,
Patient of Labours, and dissembling Wrongs.
Riddle me this, and guess him if you can,   135
Who bears a Nation in a single Man?
A Cook, a Conjurer, a Rhetorician,
A Painter, Pedant, a Geometrician,
A Dancer on the Ropes, and a Physician.
All things the hungry *Greek* exactly knows: 140
And bid him go to Heav'n, to Heav'n he goes.
In short, no *Scythian*, *Moor*, or *Thracian* Born,
But[16] in that Town which Arms and Arts adorn.
Shall he be plac'd above me at the Board,
In Purple Cloath'd, and lolling like a Lord?   145
Shall he before me sign, whom t'other Day
A small-craft Vessel hither did convey;
Where, stow'd with Prunes, and rotten Figs, he lay?
How little is the Priviledge become
Of being born a Citizen of *Rome*!   150
The *Greeks* get all by fulsom Flatteries;

A most peculiar Stroke they have at Lies.
They make a Wit of their Insipid Friend;
His blobber-Lips and beetle-Brows commend:
His long Crane Neck, and narrow Shoulders Praise;   155
You'd think they were describing *Hercules*.
A creaking Voice for a clear Trebble goes;
Tho harsher than a Cock that Treads and Crows.
We can as grosly Praise; but, to our Grief,
No Flatt'ry but from *Grecians* gains Belief.   160
Besides these Qualities, we must agree
They Mimick better on the Stage than we:
The Wife, the Whore, the Shepherdess they Play,
In such a Free, and such a Graceful way,
That we believe a very Woman shown;   165
And fancy something underneath the Gown.
But not [17]*Antiochus*, nor *Stratocles*,
Our Ears and Ravish'd Eyes can only please:
The Nation is compos'd of such as these.
All *Greece* is one Commedian: Laugh, and they   170
Return it louder than an Ass can bray:
Grieve, and they Grieve; if you Weep silently,
There seems a silent Eccho in their Eye:
They cannot *Mourn* like you; but they can Cry.
Call for a Fire, their Winter Cloaths they take: 175
Begin but you to shiver, and they shake:
In Frost and Snow, if you complain of Heat,
They rub th' unsweating Brow, and Swear they Sweat.
We live not on the Square with such as these:
Such are our Betters who can better please: 180
Who Day and Night are like a Looking-Glass;
Still ready to reflect their Patron's Face.
The Panegyrick Hand, and lifted Eye,
Prepar'd for some new Piece of Flattery.
Ev'n Nastiness, Occasions will afford: 185
They praise a belching, or well-pissing Lord.
Besides there's nothing Sacred, nothing free
From bold Attempts of their rank Leachery.
Through the whole Family their labours run;
The Daughter is debauch'd, the Wife is won;   190
Nor scapes the Bridegroom, or the blooming Son.

If none they find for their lewd purpose fit,
They with the Walls and very Floors commit.
They search the Secrets of the House, and so
Are worshipp'd there, and fear'd for what they know.   195
    And, now we talk of *Grecians*, cast a view
On what, in Schools, their Men of Morals do:
A rigid[18] Stoick his own Pupil slew.
A Friend, against a Friend, of his own Cloath,
Turn'd Evidence, and murther'd on his Oath.   200
What room is left for *Romans*, in a Town
Where *Grecians* Rule, and Cloaks control the Gown?
Some [19]*Diphilus*, or some *Protogenes*,
Look sharply out, our Senators to seize:
Engross 'em wholly, by their Native Art,   205
And fear no Rivals in their Bubbles heart:
One drop of Poison in my Patron's Ear,
One slight suggestion of a senseless fear,
Infus'd with cunning, serves to ruine me:
Disgrac'd and banish'd from the Family.   210
In vain forgotten Services I boast;
My long dependance in an hour is lost:
Look round the World, what Country will appear,
Where Friends are left with greater ease than here?
At *Rome* (nor think me partial to the Poor)   215
All Offices of ours are out of Door:
In vain we rise, and to their Levees run;
My Lord himself is up, before, and gone:
The Prætor bids his Lictors mend their pace;
Lest his Collegue outstrip him in the Race: 220
The childless Matrons are, long since, awake;
And, for Affronts, the tardy Visits take.
    'Tis frequent, here, to see a free-born Son
On the left-hand of a Rich Hireling run:
Because the wealthy Rogue can throw away,   225
For half a Brace of Bouts, a Tribune's pay:
But you, poor Sinner, tho you love the Vice,
And like the Whore, demurr upon the Price:
And, frighted with the wicked Sum, forbear
To lend a hand, and help her from the Chair.   230

Produce a Witness of unblemish'd life,
Holy as *Numa*, or as *Numa*'s Wife,
Or[20] him who bid th' unhallow'd Flames retire;
And snatch'd the trembling Goddess from the Fire:
The Question is not put how far extends   235
His Piety, but what he yearly spends:
Quick, to the Bus'ness; how he Lives and Eats;
How largely Gives, how splendidly he Treats:
How many thousand Acres feed his Sheep,
What are his Rents, what Servants does he keep?   240
Th' Account is soon cast up; the Judges rate
Our Credit in the Court, by our Estate.
Swear by our Gods, or those the *Greeks* adore,
Thou art as sure Forsworn, as thou art Poor:
The Poor must gain their Bread by Perjury: 245
And even the Gods, that other Means deny,
In Conscience must absolve 'em, when they lye.
     Add, that the Rich have still a Gibe in store:
And will be monstrous witty on the Poor:
For the torn Surtout and the tatter'd Vest,   250
The Wretch and all his Wardrobe are a Jest:
The greasie Gown, sully'd with often turning,
Gives a good hint, to say The Man's in Mourning:
Or if the Shoo be ript, or patches put,
He's wounded! see the Plaister on his Foot.   255
Want is the Scorn of ev'ry Wealthy Fool:
And Wit in Rags is turn'd to Ridicule.
     Pack hence, and from the Cover'd Benches rise,
(The Master of the Ceremonies cries)
This is no place for you, whose small Estate   260
Is not the Value of the settled Rate:
The Sons of happy Punks, the Pandars Heir,
Are priviledg'd to sit in triumph there;
To clap the first, and rule the Theatre.
Up to the Galleries, for shame, retreat: 265
For, by the[21] *Roscian* Law, the Poor can claim no Seat.
Who ever brought to his rich Daughter's Bed
The Man that poll'd but Twelve-pence for his Head?
Who ever nam'd a poor Man for his Heir,
Or call'd him to assist the Judging Chair?   270

The Poor were wise, who by the Rich oppress'd,
Withdrew, and sought a Sacred Place of Rest.
Once they did well, to free themselves from Scorn;
But had done better never to return.
Rarely they rise by Virtues aid, who lie   275
Plung'd in the depth of helpless Poverty.
   At *Rome* 'tis worse: where House-rent by the Year,
And Servants Bellies cost so Dev'llish dear;
And Tavern Bills run high for hungry Chear.
To drink or eat in Earthen Ware we scorn,   280
Which cheaply Country Cupboards does adorn:
And coarse blew Hoods on Holydays are worn.
Some distant parts of *Italy* are known,
Where²² none, but only dead Men, wear a Gown:
On Theatres of Turf, in homely State,   285
Old Plays they act, old Feasts they Celebrate:
The same rude Song returns upon the Crowd;
And, by Tradition, is for Wit allow'd.
The Mimick Yearly gives the same Delights:
And in the Mother's Arms the Clownish Infant frights.   290
Their Habits (undistinguish'd, by degree)
Are plain, alike; the same Simplicity,
Both on the Stage, and in the Pit, you see.
In his white Cloak the Magistrate appears;
The Country Bumpkin the same Liv'ry wears.   295
But here, Attir'd beyond our Purse we go,
For useless Ornament and flaunting Show:
We take on trust, in Purple Robes to shine;
And Poor, are yet Ambitious to be fine.
This is a common Vice; tho all things here   300
Are sold, and sold unconscionably dear.
What will you give that ²³*Cossus* may but view
Your Face, and in the Crowd distinguish you;
May take your Incense like a gracious God;
And answer only with a Civil Nod?   305
To please our Patrons, in this vicious Age,
We make our Entrance by the Fav'rite Page:
Shave his first down, and when he Polls his Hair,
The Consecrated Locks to Temples bear:
Pay Tributary Cracknels, which he sells;   310

And, with our Offerings, help to raise his Vails.
    Who fears, in Country Towns, a House's fall,
Or to be caught betwixt a riven Wall?
But we Inhabit a weak City, here;
Which Buttresses and Props but scarcely bear: 315
And 'tis the Village Masons daily Calling,
To keep the World's Metropolis from falling.
To cleanse the Gutters, and the Chinks to close;
And, for one Night, secure his Lord's Repose.
At *Cumæ* we can sleep, quite round the Year: 320
Nor Falls, nor Fires, nor Nightly Dangers fear;
While rolling Flames from *Roman* Turrets fly,
And the pale Citizens for Buckets cry.
Thy Neighbour has remov'd his Wretched Store
(Few Hands will rid the Lumber of the Poor)   325
Thy own third Story smoaks; while thou, supine,
Art drench'd in Fumes of undigested Wine.
For if the lowest Floors already burn,
Cock-lofts and Garrets soon will take the Turn.
Where[24] thy tame Pidgeons next the Tiles were bred,   330
Which in their Nests unsafe, are timely fled.
[25]*Codrus* had but one Bed, so short to boot,
That his short Wife's short Legs hung dangling out:
His Cup-board's Head, six Earthen Pitchers grac'd,
Beneath 'em was his Trusty Tankard plac'd: 335
And, to support this Noble Plate, there lay
A bending *Chiron* cast from honest Clay:
His few *Greek* Books a rotten Chest contain'd;
Whose Covers much of mouldiness complain'd:
Where Mice and Rats devour'd Poetick Bread;   340
And with Heroick Verse luxuriously were fed.
'Tis true, poor *Codrus* nothing had to boast,
And yet poor *Codrus* all that Nothing lost.
Beg'd naked through the Streets of wealthy *Rome*;
And found not one to feed, or take him home.   345
    But if the Palace of *Arturius* burn,
The Nobles change their Cloaths, the Matrons mourn;

337 *Chiron*] Chiron 93 97

The City Prætor will no Pleadings hear;
The very Name of Fire we hate and fear:
And look agast, as if the *Gauls* were here.   350
While yet it burns, th' officious Nation flies,
Some to condole, and some to bring supplies:
One sends him Marble to rebuild; and one
White naked Statues of the *Parian* Stone;
The Work of *Polyclete*, that seem to live: 355
While others, Images for Altars give:
One Books and Skreens, and *Pallas* to the Brest;
Another Bags of Gold; and he gives best.
Childless *Arturius*, vastly rich before,
Thus by his Losses multiplies his Store: 360
Suspected for Accomplice to the Fire,
That burnt his Palace but to build it higher.
    But, cou'd you be content to bid adieu
To the dear Play-house, and the Players too,
Sweet Country Seats are purchas'd ev'ry where,   365
With Lands and Gardens, at less price, than here
You hire a darksom Doghole by the year.
A small Convenience, decently prepar'd,
A shallow Well, that rises in your yard,
That spreads his easie Crystal Streams around;   370
And waters all the pretty spot of Ground.
There, love the Fork; thy Garden cultivate;
And give thy frugal Friends [26]a *Pythagorean* Treat.
'Tis somewhat to be Lord of some small Ground;
In which a Lizard may, at least, turn round.   375
    'Tis frequent, here, for want of sleep to dye;
Which Fumes of undigested Feasts deny;
And, with imperfect heat, in languid Stomachs fry.
What House secure from noise the poor can keep,
When ev'n the Rich can scarce afford to sleep?   380
So dear it costs to purchase Rest in *Rome*;
And hence the sources of Diseases come.
The Drover who his Fellow-drover meets,
In narrow passages of winding Streets;
The Waggoners, that curse their standing Teams,   385
Wou'd wake ev'n drousie *Drusus* from his Dreams.

354 Stone;] Stone: *93 97*   355 live:] live; *93*: live, *97*   374 be] the *97*

And yet the Wealthy will not brook delay;
But sweep above our Heads, and make their way;
In lofty Litters born, and read, and write,
Or sleep at ease: The Shutters make it Night.   39|
Yet still he reaches, first, the Publick Place:
The prease before him stops the Client's pace.
The Crowd that follows, crush his panting sides:
And trip his heels; he walks not, but he rides.
One Elbows him, one justles in the Shole: 39|
A Rafter breaks his Head, or Chairman's Pole:
Stockin'd with loads of fat Town-dirt he goes;
And some Rogue-Souldier, with his Hob-nail'd Shoos,
Indents his Legs behind in bloody rows.
  See with what Smoke our Doles we celebrate: 40|
A hundred Ghests, invited, walk in state:
A hundred hungry Slaves, with their *Dutch* Kitchins wait.
Huge Pans the Wretches on their heads must bear;
Which scarce [27]Gygantick *Corbulo* cou'd rear:
Yet they must walk upright beneath the load;   40|
Nay run, and running, blow the sparkling flames abroad.
Their Coats, from botching newly brought, are torn:
Unweildy Timber-trees, in Waggons born,
Stretch'd at their length, beyond their Carriage lye;
That nod, and threaten ruin from on high.   41
For, shou'd their Axel break, its overthrow
Wou'd crush, and pound to dust, the Crowd below:
Nor Friends their Friends, nor Sires their Sons cou'd know:
Nor Limbs, nor Bones, nor Carcass wou'd remain;
But a mash'd heap, a Hotchpotch of the Slain.   41
One vast destruction; not the Soul alone,
But Bodies, like the Soul, invisible are flown.
Mean time, unknowing of their Fellows Fate,
The Servants wash the Platter, scour the Plate,
Then blow the Fire, with puffing Cheeks, and lay   42|
The Rubbers, and the Bathing-sheets display;
And oyl them first; and each is handy in his way.
But he, for whom this busie care they take,
Poor Ghost, is wandring by the Stygian Lake:
Affrighted with [28]the Ferryman's grim Face;   42

New to the Horrours of that uncouth place:
His passage begs with unreguarded Pray'r:
And wants two Farthings to discharge his Fare.

    Return we to the Dangers of the Night;
And, first, behold our Houses dreadful height: 430
From whence come broken Potsherds tumbling down;   ⎫
And leaky Ware, from Garret Windows thrown: ⎬
Well may they break our Heads, that mark the flinty Stone. ⎭
'Tis want of Sence to sup abroad too late;
Unless thou first hast settled thy Estate.   435
As many Fates attend, thy Steps to meet,
As there are waking Windows in the Street.
Bless the good Gods, and think thy chance is rare
To have a Piss-pot only for thy share.

    The scouring Drunkard, if he does not fight   440
Before his Bed-time, takes no rest that Night.
Passing the tedious Hours in greater pain
Than [29]stern *Achilles*, when his Friend was slain:
'Tis so ridic'lous, but so true withall,
A Bully cannot sleep without a Braul.   445
Yet tho his youthful Blood be fir'd with Wine,
He wants not Wit, the Danger to decline:
Is cautious to avoid the Coach and Six,
And on the Lacquies will no Quarrel fix.
His Train of Flambeaus, and Embroider'd Coat   450
May Priviledge my Lord to walk secure on Foot.
But me, who must by Moon-light homeward bend,
Or lighted only with a Candle's end,
Poor me he fights, if that be fighting, where
He only Cudgels, and I only bear.   455
He stands, and bids me stand: I must abide;
For he's the stronger, and is Drunk beside.

    Where did you whet your Knife to Night, he cries,
And shred the Leeks that in your Stomach rise?
Whose windy Beans have stuff't your Guts, and where 460
Have your black Thumbs been dipt in Vinegar?
With what Companion Cobler have you fed,
On old Ox-cheeks, or He-Goats tougher Head?
What, are you Dumb? Quick with your Answer, quick;

---

444 ridic'lous *97*: ridiculous *93*

Before my Foot Salutes you with a Kick. 465
Say, in what nasty Cellar, under Ground,
Or what Church-Porch your Rogueship may be found?
Answer, or Answer not, 'tis all the same:
He lays me on, and makes me bear the blame.
Before the Bar, for beating him, you come; 470
This is a Poor Man's Liberty in *Rome*.
You beg his Pardon; happy to retreat
With some remaining Teeth, to chew your Meat.
    Nor is this all: for, when Retir'd, you think
To sleep securely; when the Candles wink, 475
When every Door with Iron Chains is barr'd,
And roaring Taverns are no longer heard;
The Ruffian Robbers, by no Justice aw'd,
And unpaid cut-Throat Soldiers are abroad.
Those Venal Souls, who harden'd in each ill 480
To save Complaints and Prosecution, kill.
Chas'd from their Woods and Bogs the Padders come ⎞
To this vast City, as their Native Home: ⎟
To live at ease, and safely sculk in *Rome*.   ⎠
    The Forge in Fetters only is employ'd; 485
Our Iron Mines exhausted and destroy'd
In Shackles; for these Villains scarce allow
Goads for the Teams, and Plough-shares for the Plough.
Oh happy Ages of our Ancestours,
Beneath[30] the Kings and Tribunitial Pow'rs! 490
One Jayl did all their Criminals restrain;
Which, now, the Walls of *Rome* can scarce contain.
    More I cou'd say; more Causes I cou'd show
For my departure; but the Sun is low:
The Waggoner grows weary of my stay; 495
And whips his Horses forwards on their way.
    Farewell; and when, like me, o'rewhelm'd with care, ⎞
You to your own [31]*Aquinum* shall repair,   ⎟
To take a mouthful of sweet Country air,   ⎠
Be mindful of your Friend; and send me word, 500
What Joys your Fountains and cool Shades afford:
Then, to assist your Satyrs, I will come:
And add new Venom, when you write of *Rome*.

EXPLANATORY NOTES

1 *CUmæ*, a small City in *Campania*, near *Puteoli*, or *Puzzolo* as it is call'd. The Habitation of the *Cumæan Sybil*.   2 *Bajæ*; Another little Town in *Campania*, near the Sea: A pleasant Place.   3 *Prochyta*: A small Barren Island belonging to the Kingdom of *Naples*.   4 *In Dog-days*. The Poets in *Juvenal*'s time, us'd to rehearse their Poetry in *August*.   5 *Numa*. The second King of *Rome*; who made their Laws, and instituted their Religion.   6 *Nymph. Ægeria*, a Nymph, or Goddess; with whom *Numa* feign'd to converse by Night; and to be instructed by her, in modeling his Superstitions.   7 *Where* Dædalus, *&c*. Meaning at *Cumæ*. 8 *Lachesis*; one of the three Destinies, whose Office was to spin the Life of every Man: as it was of *Clotho* to hold the Distaff, and *Atropos* to cut the Thread.   9 *Arturius*. Any debauch'd wicked Fellow who gains by the times.   10 *With Thumbs bent backward*. In a Prize of Sword-Players, when one of the Fencers had the other at his Mercy, the Vanquish'd Party implor'd the Clemency of the Spectators. If they thought he deserv'd it not, they held up their Thumbs and bent them backwards, in sign of Death.   11 *Verres*, Prætor in *Sicily*, Contemporary with *Cicero*; by whom accus'd of oppressing the Province, he was Condemn'd: His Name is us'd here for any Rich Vicious Man.   12 *Tagus*, a Famous River in *Spain*, which discharges it self into the Ocean near *Lisbone* in *Portugal*. It was held of old, to be full of Golden Sands.   13 *Orontes*, the greatest River of *Syria*: The Poet here puts the River for the Inhabitants of *Syria*. 14 *Tyber*; the River which runs by *Rome*.   15 *Romulus*; First King of *Rome*; Son of *Mars*, as the Poets feign; the first *Romans* were Originally Herdsmen.   16 *But in that Town*, &c. He means *Athens*; of which, *Pallas* the Goddess of Arms and Arts was Patroness.   17 *Antiochus and Stratocles*, two Famous *Grecian* Mimicks, or Actors in the Poet's time. 18 *A Rigid Stoick*, &c. *Publius Egnatius* a Stoick, falsly accus'd *Bareas Soranus*; as *Tacitus* tells us.   19 *Diphilus*, and *Protogenes*, &c. Were *Grecians* living in *Rome*.   20 *Or him who had*, &c. *Lucius Metellus* the High Priest; who when the Temple of *Vesta* was on Fire, sav'd the *Palladium*.   21 *For by the* Roscian *Law*, &c. *Roscius* a Tribune, who order'd the distinction of Places in Publick Shows, betwixt the Noblemen of *Rome* and the *Plebeians*. 22 *Where none but only dead Men*, &c. The meaning is, that Men in some parts of *Italy* never wore a Gown (the usual Habit of the *Romans*) till they were bury'd in one.   23 *Cossus* is here taken for any great Man. 24 *Where the tame Pidgeons*, &c. The *Romans* us'd to breed their tame Pidgeons in their Garrets.   25 *Codrus*, a Learned Man, very poor: by his Books suppos'd to be a Poet. For, in all probability, the Heroick Verses here mention'd, which Rats and Mice devour'd, wĦr *Homer*'s Works.

26 *A Pythagorean Treat*: He means Herbs, Roots, Fruits, and Sallads.
27 *Gygantick Corbulo. Corbulo* was a Famous General in *Nero*'s time, who
Conquer'd *Armenia*; and was afterwards put to Death by that Tyrant,
when he was in *Greece*, in reward of his great Services. His Stature was
not only tall, above the ordinary Size; but he was also proportionably 45
strong.   28 *The Ferry-Man's*, &c. *Charon* the Ferry-Man of Hell;
whose Fare was a Half-penny for every Soul.   29 *Stern* Achilles.
The Friend of *Achilles*, was *Patroclus* who was slain by *Hector*.   30 *Beneath
the Kings*, &c. *Rome* was Originally Rul'd by Kings; till for the Rape
of *Lucretia*, *Tarquin* the proud was expell'd. After which it was Govern'd 50
by two Consuls, Yearly chosen: but they oppressing the People, the
Commoners Mutiny'd; and procur'd Tribunes to be Created; who
defended their Priviledges, and often oppos'd the Consular Authority,
and the Senate.   31 *Aquinum*, was the Birth-place of *Juvenal*.

THE SIXTH SATYR OF JUVENAL

ARGUMENT OF THE SIXTH SATYR

*This Satyr, of almost double length to any of the rest, is a bitter invective against
the fair Sex. Tis, indeed, a Common-place, from whence all the Moderns have
notoriously stollen their sharpest Raileries. In his other Satyrs the Poet has only
glanc'd on some particular Women, and generally scourg'd the Men. But this
he reserv'd wholly for the Ladies. How they had offended him I know not: But 5
upon the whole matter he is not to be excus'd for imputing to all, the Vices of
some few amongst them. Neither was it generously done of him, to attack the
weakest as well as the fairest part of the Creation: Neither do I know what
Moral he cou'd reasonably draw from it. It could not be to avoid the whole
Sex, if all had been true which he alledges against them: for that had been to 10
put an end to Humane Kind. And to bid us beware of their Artifices, is a kind
of silent acknowledgment, that they have more wit than Men: which turns the
Satyr upon us, and particularly upon the Poet; who thereby makes a Complement, where he meant a Libel. If he intended only to exercise his Wit, he has
forfeited his Judgment, by making the one half of his Readers his mortal 15
Enemies: And amongst the Men, all the happy Lovers, by their own Experience, will disprove his Accusations. The whole World must allow this to be the
wittiest of his Satyrs; and truly he had need of all his parts, to maintain with
so much violence, so unjust a Charge. I am satisfied he will bring but few over
to his Opinion: And on that Consideration chiefly I ventur'd to translate him. 20*

*Though there wanted not another Reason, which was, that no one else would
undertake it: At least, Sir C. S., who cou'd have done more right to the
Author, after a long delay, at length absolutely refus'd so ungrateful an
employment: And every one will grant, that the Work must have been imperfect and lame, if it had appear'd without one of the Principal Members* 25
*belonging to it. Let the Poet therefore bear the blame of his own Invention;
and let me satisfie the World, that I am not of his Opinion. Whatever his*
Roman *Ladies were, the* English *are free from all his Imputations. They will
read with Wonder and Abhorrence, the Vices of an Age, which was the most
Infamous of any on Record. They will bless themselves when they behold those* 30
Examples related of Domitian's *time: They will give back to Antiquity those
Monsters it produc'd: And believe with reason, that the Species of those
Women is extinguish'd; or at least, that they were never here propagated. I may
safely therefore proceed to the Argument of a Satyr, which is no way relat-
ing to them: And first observe, that my Author makes their Lust the most* 35
*Heroick of their Vices: The rest are in a manner but digression. He skims them
over; but he dwells on this; when he seems to have taken his last leave of it, on
the sudden he returns to it: 'Tis one Branch of it in* Hippia, *another in*
Messalina, *but Lust is the main Body of the Tree. He begins with this Text
in the first line, and takes it up with Intermissions to the end of the Chapter.* 40
*Every Vice is a Loader; but that's a Ten. The Fillers, or intermediate Parts,
are their Revenge; their Contrivances of secret Crimes; their Arts to hide them;
their Wit to excuse them; and their Impudence to own them, when they can no
longer be kept secret. Then the Persons to whom they are most addicted; and
on whom they commonly bestow the last Favours. As Stage-Players, Fidlers,* 45
*Singing-Boys, and Fencers. Those who pass for Chast amongst them, are not
really so; but only for their vast Dowries, are rather suffer'd, than lov'd by
their own Husbands. That they are Imperious, Domineering, Scolding Wives:
Set up for Learning and Criticism in Poetry; but are false Judges. Love to
speak* Greek *(which was then the Fashionable Tongue, as* French *is now with* 50
*us.) That they plead Causes at the Bar, and play Prizes at the Bear-Garden.
That they are Gossips and News-Mongers: Wrangle with their Neighbours
abroad, and beat their Servants at home. That they lie in for new Faces once
a Month: are sluttish with their Husbands in private; and Paint and Dress in
Publick for their Lovers. That they deal with* Jews, *Diviners, and Fortune-* 55
*tellers: Learn the Arts of Miscarrying, and Barrenness. Buy Children, and
produce them for their own. Murther their Husbands Sons, if they stand in
their way to his Estate: and make their Adulterers his Heirs. From hence the
Poet proceeds to shew the Occasions of all these Vices; their Original, and how*

Argument. 22 Sir C. S.,] *Sir,* C. S. 93: *Sir* C. S. 97

Adult'rers next invade the Nuptial State,
And Marriage-Beds creak'd with a Foreign Weight;
All other Ills did Iron times adorn;
But Whores and Silver in one Age were Born.   35
   Yet thou, they say, for Marriage do'st provide:
Is this an Age to Buckle with a Bride?
They say thy Hair the Curling Art is taught,
The Wedding-Ring perhaps already bought:
A Sober Man like thee to change his Life!   40
What Fury wou'd possess thee with a Wife?
Art thou of ev'ry other Death bereft,
No Knife, no Ratsbane, no kind Halter left?
(For every Noose compar'd to Hers is cheap)
Is there no City Bridge from whence to leap?   45
Would'st thou become her Drudge who dost enjoy,
A better sort of Bedfellow, thy Boy?
He keeps thee not awake with nightly Brawls,
Nor with a beg'd Reward, thy Pleasure palls:
Nor with insatiate heavings calls for more,   50
When all thy Spirits were drain'd out before.
But still *Ursidius* Courts the Marriage-Bait,
Longs for a Son, to settle his Estate,
And takes no Gifts, tho ev'ry gapeing Heir
Wou'd gladly Grease the Rich Old Batchelour.   55
What Revolution can appear so strange,
As such a Leacher, such a Life to change?
A rank, notorious Whoremaster, to choose
To thrust his Neck into the Marriage Noose!
He who so often in a dreadful fright   60
Had in a Coffer scap'd the jealous Cuckold's sight,
That he to Wedlock, dotingly betrayd,
Should hope, in this lewd Town, to find a Maid!
The Man's grown Mad: To ease his Frantick Pain,
Run for the Surgeon; breathe the middle Vein: 65
But let a Heyfer with Gilt Horns be led
To *Juno*, Regent of the Marriage-Bed,
And let him every Deity adore,   ⎫
If his new Bride prove not an arrant Whore,   ⎬
In Head and Tail, and every other Pore.   ⎭   70
On 5 *Ceres* feast, restrain'd from their delight,

Few Matrons, there, but Curse the tedious Night:
Few whom their Fathers dare Salute, such Lust
Their Kisses have, and come with such a Gust.
With Ivy now Adorn thy Doors, and Wed;   75
Such is thy Bride, and such thy Genial Bed.
Think'st thou one Man, is for one Woman meant?
She, sooner, with one Eye wou'd be content.
   And yet, 'tis nois'd, a Maid did once appear
In some small Village, tho Fame says not where;   80
'Tis possible; but sure no Man she found;
'Twas desart, all, about her Father's Ground:
And yet some Lustful God might there make bold:
Are [6]*Jove* and *Mars* grown impotent and old?
Many a fair Nymph has in a Cave been spread,   85
And much good Love, without a Feather-Bed.
Whither wou'dst thou to chuse a Wife resort,
The Park, the Mall, the Play-house, or the Court?
Which way soever thy Adventures fall
Secure alike of Chastity in all.   90
   One sees a Dancing-Master Capring high,
And Raves, and Pisses, with pure Extasie:
Another does, with all his Motions, move,
And Gapes, and Grins, as in the feat of Love:
A third is Charm'd with the new Opera Notes,   95
Admires the Song, but on the Singer Doats:
The Country Lady, in the Box appears,
Softly She Warbles over, all she hears;
And sucks in Passion, both at Eyes, and Ears.
   The rest, (when now the long Vacation's come,   100
The noisie Hall and Theatres grown dumb)
Their Memories to refresh, and chear their hearts,
In borrow'd Breaches act the Players parts.
The Poor, that scarce have wherewithal to eat,
Will pinch, to make the Singing-Boy a Treat.   105
The Rich, to buy him, will refuse no price:
And stretch his Quail-pipe till they crack his Voice.
Tragedians, acting Love, for Lust are sought:
(Tho but the Parrots of a Poet's Thought.)
The Pleading Lawyer, tho for Counsel us'd,   110

In Chamber-practice often is refus'd.
Still thou wilt have a Wife, and father Heirs;
(The product of concurring Theatres.)
Perhaps a Fencer did thy Brows adorn,
And a young Sword-man to thy Lands is born.   115
   Thus *Hippia* loath'd her old Patrician Lord,
And left him for a Brother of the Sword:
To wondring[7] *Pharos* with her Love she fled,
To shew one Monster more than *Africk* bred:
Forgetting House and Husband, left behind,   120
Ev'n Children too; she sails before the wind;
False to 'em all, but constant to her Kind.
But, stranger yet, and harder to conceive,
She cou'd the Play-house, and the Players leave.
Born of rich Parentage, and nicely bred,   125
She lodg'd on Down, and in a Damask Bed;
Yet, daring now the Dangers of the Deep,
On a hard Mattress is content to sleep.
E're this, 'tis true, she did her Fame expose:
But that, great Ladies with great Ease can lose.   130
The tender Nymph cou'd the rude Ocean bear:
So much her Lust was stronger than her Fear.
But, had some honest Cause her Passage prest,
The smallest hardship had disturb'd her brest:
Each Inconvenience makes their Virtue cold: 135
But Womankind, in Ills, is ever bold.
Were she to follow her own Lord to Sea,
What doubts and scruples wou'd she raise to stay?
Her Stomach sick, and her head giddy grows;
The Tar and Pitch are nauseous to her Nose.   140
But in Love's Voyage nothing can offend;
Women are never Sea-sick with a Friend.
Amidst the Crew, she walks upon the boord;
She eats, she drinks, she handles every Cord:
And, if she spew, 'tis thinking of her Lord.   145
Now ask, for whom her Friends and Fame she lost?
What Youth, what Beauty, cou'd th' Adult'rer boast?
What was the Face, for which she cou'd sustain
To be call'd Mistress to so base a Man?

145 spew 97: spews 93

The Gallant, of his days had known the best: ⎫ 150
Deep Scars were seen indented on his breast;   ⎬
And all his batter'd Limbs requir'd their needful rest.   ⎭
A Promontory Wen, with griesly grace,
Stood high, upon the Handle of his Face:
His blear Eyes ran in gutters to his Chin;   155
His Beard was Stubble, and his Cheeks were thin.
But 'twas his Fencing did her Fancy move;
'Tis Arms and Blood and Cruelty they love.
But shou'd he quit his Trade, and sheath his Sword,
Her Lover wou'd begin to be her Lord.   160
    This was a private Crime; but you shall hear
What Fruits the Sacred Brows of Monarchs bear:
The[8] good old Sluggard but began to snore,
When from his side up rose th' Imperial Whore:
She who preferr'd the Pleasures of the Night   165
To Pomps, that are but impotent delight,
Strode from the Palace, with an eager pace,
To cope with a more Masculine Embrace:
Muffl'd she march'd, like *Juno* in a Clowd,
Of all her Train but one poor Wench allow'd,   170
One whom in Secret Service she cou'd trust;
The Rival and Companion of her Lust.
To the known Brothel-house she takes her way;   ⎫
And for a nasty Room gives double pay;   ⎬
That Room in which the rankest Harlot lay.   ⎭ 175
Prepar'd for fight, expectingly she lies,
With heaving Breasts, and with desiring Eyes:
Still as one drops, another takes his place,
And baffled still succeeds to like disgrace.
At length, when friendly darkness is expir'd,   180
And every Strumpet from her Cell retir'd,
She lags behind, and lingring at the Gate,
With a repining Sigh, submits to Fate:
All Filth without and all a Fire within,
Tir'd with the Toyl, unsated with the Sin.   185
Old *Cæsar's* Bed the modest Matron seeks;
The steam of Lamps still hanging on her Cheeks
In Ropy Smut; thus foul, and thus bedight,

187 Cheeks 97: Cheeks: *93*

She brings him back the Product of the Night.

   Now should I sing what Poisons they provide;   190
With all their Trumpery of Charms beside:
And all their Arts of Death, it would be known
Lust is the smallest Sin the Sex can own.
Cæsinia, still, they say, is guiltless found
Of every Vice, by her own Lord Renown'd: } 195
And well she may, she brought ten thousand Pound.
She brought him wherewithal to be call'd chaste;
His Tongue is ty'd in Golden Fetters fast:
He Sighs, Adores, and Courts her every Hour;
Who wou'd not do as much for such a Dower?   200
She writes Love-Letters to the Youth in Grace;
Nay, tips the wink before the Cuckold's Face;
And might do more: Her Portion makes it good:
Wealth[9] has the Priviledge of Widow-hood.

   These Truths with his Example you disprove,   205
Who with his Wife is monstrously in Love:
But know him better; for I heard him Swear
'Tis not that She's his Wife, but that She's Fair.
Let her but have three Wrinkles in her Face,
Let her Eyes Lessen, and her Skin unbrace,   210
Soon you will hear the Saucy Steward say,
Pack up with all your Trinkets, and away:
You grow Offensive both at Bed and Board,
Your Betters must be had to please my Lord.

   Mean time She's absolute upon the Throne;   215
And knowing time is Precious, loses none:
She must have Flocks of Sheep, with Wool more Fine
Than Silk, and Vinyards of the Noblest Wine:
Whole Droves of Pages for her Train she Craves;
And sweeps the Prisons for attending Slaves.   220
In short, whatever in her Eyes can come,
Or others have abroad; she wants at home.
When Winter shuts the Seas, and fleecy Snows
Make Houses white, she to the Merchant goes:
Rich Crystals of the Rock She takes up there,   225
Huge *Agat* Vases, and old *China* Ware:
Then [10]*Berenice*'s Ring her Finger proves,

202 Nay, *97*: Nay *93*

More Precious made by her incestuous Loves:
And infamously Dear: A Brother's Bribe,
Ev'n Gods Annointed, and of *Judah*'s Tribe: 230
Where barefoot they approach the Sacred Shrine,
And think it only Sin, to Feed on Swine.

   But is none worthy to be made a Wife
In all this Town? Suppose her free from strife,
Rich, Fair, and Fruitful: of Unblemish'd Life: 235
Chast as the *Sabines*, whose prevailing Charms
Dismiss'd their Husbands, and their Brothers Arms.
Grant her, besides, of Noble Blood, that ran
In Ancient Veins, e're Heraldry began:
Suppose all these, and take a Poet's word,   240
A Black Swan is not half so Rare a Bird.
A Wife, so hung with Virtues, such a freight;
What Mortal Shoulders cou'd support the weight!
Some Country Girl, scarce to a Curtsey bred,
Wou'd I much rather than [11]*Cornelia* Wed: 245
If Supercilious, Haughty, Proud, and Vain,
She brought her Father's Triumphs, in her Train.
Away with all your *Carthaginian* State,
Let vanquish'd *Hannibal* without Doors wait,
Too burly and too big, to pass my narrow Gate.   250

   Oh[12] *Pæan*, cries *Amphion*, bend thy Bow
Against my Wife, and let my Children go:
But sullen *Pæan* shoots, at Sons and Mothers too.
His *Niobe* and all his Boys he lost;
Ev'n her, who did her num'rous Offspring boast,   255
As Fair and Fruitful as the Sow that carry'd
The[13] Thirty Pigs at one large Litter Farrow'd.

   What Beauty or what Chastity can bear
So great a Price, if stately and severe
She still insults, and you must still adore;   260
Grant that the Hony's much, the Gall is more.
Upbraided with the Virtues she displays,
Sev'n Hours in Twelve, you loath the Wife you Praise
Some Faults, tho small, intolerable grow:
For what so Nauseous and Affected too,   265
As those that think they due Perfection want,
Who have not learnt to Lisp the[14] *Grecian* Cant?

In *Greece*, their whole Accomplishments they seek:
Their Fashion, Breeding, Language, must be *Greek*:
But Raw, in all that does to *Rome* belong,   270
They scorn to cultivate their Mother Tongue.
In *Greek* they flatter, all their Fears they speak,
Tell all their Secrets, nay, they Scold in *Greek*:
Ev'n in the Feat of Love, they use that Tongue.
Such Affectations may become the Young: 275
But thou, Old Hag of Threescore Years and Three,
Is shewing of thy Parts in *Greek*, for thee?
Ζωὴ καί ψυχή! All those tender words
The Momentary trembling Bliss affords,
The kind soft Murmurs of the private Sheets,   280
Are Bawdy, while thou speak'st in publick Streets.
Those words have Fingers; and their force is such,
They raise the Dead, and mount him with a touch.
But all Provocatives from thee are vain;
No blandishment the slacken'd Nerve can strain.   285
    If then thy Lawful Spouse thou canst not love,
What reason shou'd thy Mind to Marriage move?
Why all the Charges of the Nuptial Feast,
Wine and Deserts, and Sweet-meats to digest;
Th' indoweing Gold that buys the dear Delight;   290
Giv'n for thy first and only happy Night?
If thou art thus Uxoriously inclin'd,
To bear thy Bondage with a willing mind,
Prepare thy Neck, and put it in the Yoke:
But for no mercy from thy Woman look.   295
For tho, perhaps, she loves with equal Fires,
To Absolute Dominion she aspires;
Joys in the Spoils, and Triumphs o'er thy Purse;
The better Husband makes the Wife the worse.
Nothing is thine to give, or sell, or buy,   ⎞ 300
All Offices of Ancient Friendship dye;   ⎟
Nor hast thou leave to make a Legacy.   ⎠
By[15] thy Imperious Wife thou art bereft
A Priviledge, to Pimps and Panders left;

---

269 *Greek*: 97: *Greek*. *93*   274 Tongue. 97: Tongue, *93*   278 ψυχή 97:
ψυχή *93*

Thy Testament's her Will: Where she prefers   305
Her Ruffians, Drudges and Adulterers,
Adopting all thy Rivals for thy Heirs.

    Go[16] drag that Slave to Death; [17]your Reason, why
Shou'd the poor Innocent be doom'd to Dye?
What proofs? for, when Man's Life is in debate,   310
The Judge can ne're too long deliberate.
Call'st[18] thou that Slave a Man? the Wife replies:
Prov'd, or unprov'd, the Crime, the Villain Dies.
I have the Soveraign Pow'r to save or kill;
And give no other Reason but my Will.   315

    Thus the She-Tyrant Reigns, till pleas'd with change,
Her wild Affections to New Empires Range:
Another Subject-Husband she desires;
Divorc'd from him, she to the first retires,
While the last Wedding-Feast is scarcely o're;   320
And Garlands hang yet green upon the Door.
So still the Reck'ning rises; and appears
In total Sum, Eight Husbands in Five Years.
The Title for a Tomb-Stone might be fit;
But that it wou'd too commonly be writ.   325

    Her Mother Living, hope no quiet Day;
She sharpens her, instructs her how to Flea
Her Husband bare, and then divides the Prey.
She takes Love-Letters, with a Crafty smile,
And, in her Daughter's Answer, mends the stile.   330
In vain the Husband sets his watchful Spies;
She Cheats their cunning, or she bribes their Eyes.
The Doctor's call'd; the Daughter, taught the Trick,
Pretends to Faint; and in full Health is Sick.
The Panting Stallion at the Closet-Door   335
Hears the Consult, and wishes it were o're.
Can'st thou, in Reason, hope, a Bawd so known
Shou'd teach her other Manners than her own?
Her Int'rest is in all th' Advice she gives:
'Tis on the Daughter's Rents the Mother lives.   340
    No Cause is try'd at the Litigious Bar,
But Women Plaintiffs or Defendants are.

306 Adulterers *97*: Adulterer's *93*

They form the Process, all the Briefs they write.
The Topicks furnish, and the Pleas indite:
And teach the Toothless Lawyer how to Bite.   345
 They turn Virago's, too; the Wrastler's toyl
They try, and Smear their Naked Limbs with Oyl:
Against the Post, their wicker Shields they crush,
Flourish the Sword, and at the Plastron push.
Of every Exercise the Mannish Crew   350
Fulfils the Parts, and oft Excels us too:
Prepar'd not only in feign'd Fights t' engage,
But rout the Gladiators on the Stage.
What sence of shame in such a Breast can lye,
Inur'd to Arms, and her own Sex to fly?   355
Yet to be wholly Man she wou'd disclaim;
To quit her tenfold Pleasure at the Game,
For frothy Praises, and an Empty Name.
Oh what a decent Sight, 'tis to behold
All thy Wife's Magazine by Auction sold!   360
The Belt, the crested Plume, the several Suits
Of Armour, and the *Spanish* Leather Boots!
Yet these are they, that cannot bear the heat
Of figur'd Silks, and under Sarcenet sweat.
Behold the strutting *Amazonian* Whore,   365
She stands in Guard with her right Foot before:
Her Coats Tuck'd up; and all her Motions just,
She stamps, and then Cries hah at every thrust:
But laugh to see her tyr'd with many a bout,
Call for the Pot, and like a Man Piss out.   370
The Ghosts of Ancient *Romans*, shou'd they rise,
Wou'd grin to see their Daughters play a Prize.
 Besides, what endless Brawls by Wifes are bred:
The Curtain-Lecture makes a Mournful Bed.
Then, when she has thee sure within the Sheets,   375
Her Cry begins, and the whole Day repeats.
Conscious of Crimes her self, she teyzes first;
Thy Servants are accus'd; thy Whore is curst;
She Acts the jealous, and at Will she cries:
For Womens Tears are but the sweat of Eyes.   380
Poor Cuckold-Fool, thou think'st that Love sincere,

359 behold *97*: behold, *93*

And suck'st between her Lips, the falling Tear:
But search her Cabinet and thou shalt find
Each Tiller there, with Love Epistles lin'd.
Suppose her taken in a close embrace,   385
This you wou'd think so manifest a Case,
No Rhetorick cou'd defend, no Impudence outface:
And yet ev'n then she Cries the Marriage Vow,
A mental Reservation must allow;
And there's a silent bargain still imply'd,   390
The Parties shou'd be pleas'd on either side:
And both may for their private needs provide.
Tho Men your selves, and Women us you call,
Yet *Homo* is a Common Name for all.
There's nothing bolder than a Woman Caught;   395
Guilt gives 'em Courage to maintain their Fault.
    You ask from whence proceed these monstrous Crimes;
Once Poor, and therefore Chast in former times,
Our Matrons were: No Luxury found room
In low-rooft Houses, and bare Walls of Lome;   400
Their Hands with Labour hard'ned while 'twas Light,
And Frugal sleep supply'd the quiet Night.
While pinch't with want, their Hunger held 'em straight;
When [19] *Hannibal* was Hov'ring at the Gate:
But wanton now, and lolling at our Ease,   405
We suffer all th' invet'rate ills of Peace;
And wastful Riot, whose Destructive Charms
Revenge the vanquish'd World, of our Victorious Arms.
No Crime, no Lustful Postures are unknown;
Since Poverty, our Guardian-God, is gone: 410
Pride, Laziness, and all Luxurious Arts,
Pour like a Deluge in, from Foreign Parts:
Since Gold Obscene, and Silver found the way,
Strange Fashions with strange Bullion to convey,
And our plain simple Manners to betray.   415
    What care our Drunken Dames to whom they spread?
Wine, no distinction makes of Tail or Head.
Who lewdly Dancing at a Midnight-Ball,
For hot Eringoes, and Fat Oysters call:
Full Brimmers to their Fuddled Noses thrust;   420

388 ev'n 97: even 93   403 straight;] straight: 93 97

Brimmers the last Provocatives of Lust.
When Vapours to their swimming Brains advance,
And double Tapers on the Tables Dance.
    Now think what Bawdy Dialogues they have,
What *Tullia* talks to her confiding Slave;   425
At Modesty's old Statue: when by Night,
They make a stand, and from their Litters light;
The Good Man early to the Levee goes,
And treads the Nasty Paddle of his Spouse.
    The Secrets of the[20] Goddess nam'd the Good,   430
Are ev'n by Boys and Barbers understood:
Where the Rank Matrons, Dancing to the Pipe,
Gig with their Bums, and are for Action ripe;
With Musick rais'd, they spread abroad their Hair;
And toss their Heads like an enamour'd Mare: 435
Laufella lays her Garland by, and proves
The mimick Leachery of Manly Loves.
Rank'd with the Lady, the cheap Sinner lies;
For here not Blood, but Virtue gives the prize.
Nothing is feign'd, in this Venereal Strife;   440
'Tis downright Lust, and Acted to the Life.
So full, so fierce, so vigorous, and so strong;
That, looking on, wou'd make old [21]*Nestor* Young.
Impatient of delay, a general sound,
An universal Groan of Lust goes round;   445
For then, and only then, the Sex sincere is found.
Now is the time of Action; now begin,
They cry, and let the lusty Lovers in.
The Whoresons are asleep; Then bring the Slaves,
And Watermen, a Race of strong-back'd Knaves.   450
    I wish, at least, our Sacred Rights were free
From those Pollutions of Obscenity:
But 'tis well known [22]what Singer, how disguis'd
A lewd audacious Action enterpriz'd;
Into the Fair with Women mixt, he went,   455
Arm'd with a huge two-handed Instrument;
A grateful Present to those holy Quires,
Where the Mouse guilty of his Sex retires;
And ev'n Male-Pictures modestly are vaild;

431 ev'n 97: even 93   449 Slaves, 97: Slaves 93   459 ev'n 97: even 93

Yet no Profaneness on that Age prevail'd.   460
No Scoffers at Religious Rites were found;
Tho now, at every Altar they abound.

   I hear your cautious Counsel, you wou'd say,
Keep close your Women, under Lock and Key:
But, who shall keep those Keepers? Women, nurst   465
In Craft, begin with those, and Bribe 'em first.
The Sex is turn'd all Whore; they Love the Game;
And Mistresses, and Maids, are both the same.

   The poor *Ogulnia*, on the Poet's day,
Will borrow Cloaths, and Chair, to see the Play: 470
She, who before, had Mortgag'd her Estate;
And Pawn'd the last remaining piece of Plate.
Some, are reduc'd their utmost Shifts to try:
But Women have no shame of Poverty.
They live beyond their stint; as if their store   475
The more exhausted, wou'd increase the more:
Some Men, instructed by the Lab'ring Ant,
Provide against th' Extremities of want;
But Womankind, that never knows a mean,
Down to the Dregs their sinking Fortune drain: 480
Hourly they give, and spend, and wast, and wear;
And think no Pleasure can be bought too dear.

   There are, who in soft Eunuchs, place their Bliss;
To shun the scrubbing of a Bearded Kiss;
And scape Abortion; but their solid joy   485
Is[23] when the Page, already past a Boy,
Is Capon'd late; and to the Guelder shown,
With his two Pounders, to Perfection grown.
When all the Navel-string cou'd give, appears;
All but the Beard; and that's the Barber's loss, not theirs.   490
Seen from afar, and famous for his ware,
He struts into the Bath, among the Fair:
Th' admiring Crew to their Devotions fall;
And, kneeling, on their[24] new *Priapus* call.
Kerv'd for my Lady's use, with her he lies;   495
And let him drudge for her, if thou art wise;
Rather than trust him with thy Fav'rite Boy;
He proffers Death in proffering to enjoy.

     484 Kiss;] Kiss: *93 97*   495 my *97*: his *93*

If Songs they love, the Singer's Voice they force
Beyond his Compass, till his Quail-Pipe's hoarse: 500
His Lute and Lyre, with their embrace is worn;
With Knots they trim it, and with Gems adorn:
Run over all the Strings, and Kiss the Case;
And make Love to it, in the Master's place.

    A certain Lady once, of high Degree,   505
To *Janus* Vow'd, and *Vesta*'s Deity,
That [25]*Pollio* might, in Singing, win the Prize;
Pollio the Dear, the Darling of her Eyes:
She Pray'd, and Brib'd; what cou'd she more have done
For a Sick Husband, or an onely Son?   510
With her Face veil'd, and heaving up her hands,
The shameless Suppliant at the Altar stands:
The Forms of Prayer she solemnly pursues;
And, pale with Fear, the offer'd Entrails views.
Answer, ye Pow'rs: For, if you heard her Vow,   515
Your Godships, sure, had little else to do.

    This is not all; for[26] Actors, they implore:
An Impudence unknown to Heav'n before.
Th'[27] *Aruspex*, tir'd with this Religious Rout,
Is forc'd to stand so long, he gets the Gout.   520
But suffer not thy Wife abroad to roam:
If she love Singing, let her Sing at home;
Not strut in Streets, with *Amazonian* pace;
For that's to Cuckold thee, before thy Face.

    Their endless Itch of News, comes next in play;   525
They vent their own; and hear what others say.
Know what in *Thrace*, or what in *France* is done;
Th' Intrigues betwixt the Stepdam, and the Son.
Tell who Loves who, what Favours some partake;
And who is Jilted for another's sake.   530
What pregnant Widow, in what Month was made;
How oft she did, and doing, what she said.

    She, first, beholds the raging Comet rise:
Knows whom it threatens, and what Lands destroys.
Still, for the newest News, she lies in wait;   535
And takes Reports, just ent'ring at the Gate.
Wrecks, Floods, and Fires; what-ever she can meet,

    522 love] loves *97*

She spreads; and is the *Fame* of every Street.
  This is a Grievance; but the next is worse;
A very Judgment, and her Neighbours Curse.   540
For, if their barking-Dog, disturb her ease,
No Pray'r can bend her, no Excuse appease.
Th' unmanner'd Malefactor, is Arraign'd;
But first the Master, who the Curr Maintain'd,
Must feel the scourge: By Night she leaves her Bed;   545
By Night her Bathing Equipage is led,
That Marching Armies a less noise create;
She moves in Tumult, and she Sweats in State.
Mean while, her Guests their Appetites must keep;
Some gape for Hunger, and some gasp for Sleep.   550
At length she comes, all flush'd, but e're she sup,
Swallows a swinging Preparation-Cup;
And then, to clear her Stomach, spews it up.
The Deluge-Vomit, all the Floor o'reflows;
And the sour savour nauseates every Nose.   555
She Drinks again; again she spews a Lake;
Her wretched Husband sees, and dares not speak:
But mutters many a Curse, against his Wife;
And Damns himself, for chusing such a Life.
  But of all Plagues, the greatest is untold;   560
The Book-Learn'd Wife, in *Greek* and *Latin* bold.
The Critick-Dame, who at her Table sits;
Homer and *Virgil* quotes, and weighs their Wits;
And pities *Didoes* Agonizing Fits.
She has so far th' ascendant of the Board,   565
The Prating Pedant puts not in one Word:
The Man of Law is Non-plust, in his Sute;
Nay, every other Female Tongue is mute.
Hammers, and beating Anvils, you wou'd Swear,
And [28]*Vulcan* with his whole Militia there.   570
Tabours[29] and Trumpets cease; for she alone
Is able to Redeem the lab'ring Moon.
Ev'n Wit's a burthen, when it talks too long:
But she, who has no Continence of Tongue,
Should walk in Breeches, and shou'd wear a Beard;   575
And mix among the Philosophick Herd.

O what a midnight Curse has he, whose side
Is pester'd with a³⁰ Mood and Figure Bride!
Let mine, ye Gods, (if such must be my Fate)
No Logick Learn, nor History Translate: 580
But rather be a quiet, humble Fool:
I hate a Wife, to whom I go to School.
Who climbs the Grammar-Tree; distinctly knows
Where Noun, and Verb, and Participle grows;
Corrects her Country Neighbour; and, a Bed,   585
For breaking ³¹*Priscian*'s, breaks her Husband's Head.
    The Gawdy Gossip, when she's set agog,
In Jewels drest, and at each Ear a Bob,
Goes flaunting out, and in her trim of Pride,
Thinks all she says or does, is justifi'd.   590
When Poor, she's scarce a tollerable Evil;
But Rich, and Fine, a Wife's a very Devil.
    She duely, once a Month, renews her Face;
Mean time, it lies in Dawb, and hid in Grease;
Those are the Husband's Nights; she craves her due,   595
He takes fat Kisses, and is stuck in Glue.
But, to the Lov'd Adult'rer when she steers,
Fresh from the Bath, in brightness she appears:
For him the Rich *Arabia* sweats her Gum;
And precious Oyls from distant *Indies* come: } 600
How Haggardly so e're she looks at home.
Th' Eclipse then vanishes; and all her Face
Is open'd, and restor'd to ev'ry Grace.
The Crust remov'd, her Cheeks as smooth as Silk,
Are polish'd with a wash of Asses Milk;   605
And, shou'd she to the farthest *North* be sent,
A Train ³²of these attend her Banishment.
But, hadst thou seen her Plaistred up before,
'Twas so unlike a Face, it seem'd a Sore.
    'Tis worth our while, to know what all the day   610
They do; and how they pass their time away.
For, if o're-night, the Husband has been slack,
Or counterfeited Sleep, and turn'd his Back,   }
Next day, be sure, the Servants go to wrack.
The Chamber-Maid and Dresser, are call'd Whores;   615

600 come: *97*: come. *93*   604 Silk,] Silk; *93 97*

The Page is stript, and beaten out of Doors.
The whole House suffers for the Master's Crime;
And he himself, is warn'd, to wake another time.
   She hires Tormentors, by the Year; she Treats
Her Visitours, and talks; but still she beats.   620
Beats while she Paints her Face, surveys her Gown,
Casts up the days Account, and still beats on:
Tir'd out, at length, with an outrageous Tone,
She bids 'em, in the Devil's Name, begone.
Compar'd with such a Proud, Insulting Dame,   625
Sicilian[33] Tyrants may renounce their Name.
   For, if she hasts abroad, to take the Ayr,
Or goes to *Isis* Church, (the Bawdy, House of Pray'r,)
She hurries all her Handmaids to the Task;
Her Head, alone, will twenty Dressers ask.   630
Psecas, the chief, with Breast and Shoulders bare,
Trembling, considers every Sacred Hair;
If any Stragler from his Rank be found,
A pinch must, for the Mortal Sin, compound.
Psecas is not in Fault: But, in the Glass,   635
The Dame's Offended at her own ill Face.
That Maid is Banish'd; and another Girl
More dextrous, manages the Comb, and Curl:
The rest are summon'd, on a point so nice;
And first, the Grave Old Woman gives Advice.   640
The next is call'd, and so the turn goes round,
As each for Age, or Wisdom, is Renown'd:
Such Counsel, such delib'rate care they take,
As if her Life and Honour lay at stake.
With Curls, on Curls, they build[34] her Head before;   645
And mount it with a Formidable Tow'r.
A Gyantess she seems; but, look behind,
And then she dwindles to the Pigmy kind.
Duck-leg'd, short-wasted, such a Dwarf she is,
That she must rise on Tip-toes for a Kiss.   650
Mean while, her Husband's whole Estate is spent;
He may go bare while she receives his Rent.
She minds him not; she lives not as a Wife,
But like a Bawling Neighbour, full of Strife:

628 Pray'r *97*: Prayer *93*

Near him, in this alone, that she extends   655
Her Hate, to all his Servants, and his Friends.
  Bellona's Priests, an Eunuch at their Head,
About the Streets a mad Procession lead;
The[35] Venerable Guelding, large, and high,
O're-looks the Herd of his inferiour Fry.   660
His awkward Clergy-Men about him prance;
And beat the Timbrels to their Mystick Dance.
Guiltless of Testicles, they tear their Throats,
And squeak, in Treble, their Unmanly Notes.
Mean while, his Cheeks the Myter'd Prophet swells;   665
And Dire Presages of the Year foretels.
Unless with Eggs (his Priestly hire) they hast
To Expiate, and avert th' Autumnal blast.
And[36] add beside a murrey colour'd Vest,
Which, in their places, may receive the Pest: 670
And, thrown into the Flood, their Crimes may bear,
To purge th' unlucky Omens of the Year.
Th' Astonisht Matrons pay, before the rest;
That Sex is still obnoxious to the Priest.
  Through yce they beat, and plunge into the Stream,   675
If so the God has warn'd 'em in a Dream.
Weak in their Limbs, but in Devotion strong,
On their bare Hands and Feet they crawl along;
A whole Fields length, the Laughter of the Throng.
Shou'd *Io*, (*Io*'s Priest I mean) Command   680
A Pilgrimage to *Meroe*'s burning Sand,
Through Desarts they wou'd seek the secret Spring;
And Holy Water, for Lustration, bring.
How can they pay their Priests too much respect,
Who Trade with Heav'n and Earthly Gains neglect?   685
With him, Domestick Gods Discourse by Night;
By Day, attended by his Quire in white,
The Bald-pate Tribe runs madding through the Street,
And Smile to see with how much ease they Cheat.
The Ghostly Syre forgives the Wife's Delights,   690
Who Sins, through Frailty, on forbidden Nights:
And Tempts her Husband, in the Holy Time,
When Carnal Pleasure is a Mortal Crime.

675 yce] yee *93:* ye *97*   the] a *97*

The Sweating Image shakes its Head; but he
With Mumbled Prayers Attones the Deity.   695
The Pious Priesthood the Fat Goose receive,
And they once Brib'd, the Godhead must forgive.
   No sooner these remove, but full of Fear,
A Gypsie Jewess whispers in your Ear,
And begs an Alms: An High-Priest's Daughter she,   ⎫ 700
Vers'd in their *Talmud*, and Divinity;   ⎬
And Prophesies beneath a shady Tree.   ⎭
Her Goods a Basket, and old Hay her Bed,
She strouls, and Telling Fortunes, gains her Bread:
Farthings, and some small Monys, are her Fees;   705
Yet she Interprets all your Dreams for these.
Foretels th' Estate, when the Rich Unckle Dies,
And sees a Sweet-heart in the Sacrifice.
Such Toys, a Pidgeons Entrails can disclose;
Which yet th' *Armenian Augur* far outgoes: 710
In Dogs, a Victim more obscene, he rakes;
And Murder'd Infants, for Inspection, takes:
For Gain, his Impious Practice he pursues;
For Gain will his Accomplices Accuse.
   More Credit, yet, is to [37]*Chaldeans* giv'n;   715
What they foretell, is deem'd the Voice of Heav'n.
Their Answers, as from *Hammon*'s Altar, come;
Since now the *Delphian* Oracles are dumb.
And Mankind, ignorant of future Fate,
Believes what fond Astrologers relate.   720
   Of these the most in vogue is he, who sent
Beyond Seas, is return'd from Banishment.
His Art who to [38]Aspiring *Otho* sold;
And sure Succession to the Crown foretold.
For his Esteem, is in his Exile plac'd;   725
The more Believ'd, the more he was Disgrac'd.
No Astrologick Wizard Honour gains,
Who has not oft been Banisht, or in Chains.
He gets Renown, who, to the Halter near,
But narrowly escapes, and buys it dear.   730
   From him your Wife enquires the Planets Will;
When the black *Jaundies* shall her Mother Kill:

694 its] his *97*   700 she, *97*: she *93*

Her Sister's and her Unckle's end, wou'd know;
But, first, consults his Art, when you shall go.
And, what's the greatest Gift that Heav'n can give,   735
If, after her, th' Adulterer shall live.
She neither knows, nor cares to know the rest;
If ³⁹ *Mars* and *Saturn* shall the World infest;
Or *Jove* and *Venus*, with their Friendly Rays,
Will interpose, and bring us better days.   740
   Beware the Woman, too, and shun her Sight,
Who, in these Studies, does her self Delight.
By whom a greasie Almanack is born,
With often handling, like chaft Amber, worn:
Not now consulting, but consulted, she   745
Of the Twelve Houses, and their Lords, is free.
She, if the Scheme a fatal Journey show,
Stays safe at Home, but lets her Husband go.
If but a Mile she Travel out of Town,
The Planetary Hour must first be known;   750
And lucky moment: if her Eye but akes
Or itches, its Decumbiture she takes.
No Nourishment receives in her Disease,
But what the Stars, and ⁴⁰ *Ptolomy* shall please.
   The middle sort, who have not much to spare,   755
To Chiromancers cheaper Art repair,
Who clap the pretty Palm, to make the Lines more fair.
But the Rich Matron, who has more to give,
Her Answers from the ⁴¹ *Brachman* will receive:
Skill'd in the Globe and Sphere, he Gravely stands,   760
And, with his Compass, measures Seas and Lands.
   The Poorest of the Sex, have still an Itch
To know their Fortunes, equal to the Rich.
The Dairy-Maid enquires, if she shall take
The trusty Taylor, and the Cook forsake.   765
   Yet these, tho Poor, the Pain of Child-bed bear;
And, without Nurses, their own Infants rear:
You seldom hear of the Rich Mantle, spread
For the Babe, born in the great Lady's Bed.
Such is the Pow'r of Herbs; such Arts they use   770

736 th' Adulterer] th' Adult'rer *93:* the Adult'rer *97*   750 known; *97:*
known: *93*   751 moment:] moment; *93 97*

To make them Barren, or their Fruit to lose.
But thou, whatever Slops she will have bought,
Be thankful, and supply the deadly Draught:
Help her to make Manslaughter; let her bleed,
And never want for Savin at her need.   775
For, if she holds till her nine Months be run,
Thou may'st be Father to[42] an *Æthiop*'s Son:
A Boy, who ready gotten to thy hands,
By Law is to Inherit all thy Lands:
One of that hue, that shou'd he cross the way,   780
His[43] Omen wou'd discolour all the day.
    I pass the Foundling by, a Race unknown,
At Doors expos'd, whom Matrons make their own;
And into Noble Families advance,
A Nameless Issue, the blind work of Chance.   785
Indulgent Fortune does her Care employ,
And, smiling, broods upon the Naked Boy:
Her Garment spreads, and laps him in the Fold,
And covers, with her Wings, from nightly Cold:
Gives him her Blessing; puts him in a way;   790
Sets up the Farce, and laughs at her own Play.
Him she promotes; she favours him alone,
And makes Provision for him, as her own.
    The craving Wife, the force of Magick tries,
And Philters for th' unable Husband buys: 795
The Potion works not on the part design'd,
But turns his Brain, and stupifies his Mind.
The sotted Moon-Calf gapes, and staring on,
Sees his own Business by another done:
A long Oblivion, a benumming Frost,   800
Constrains his Head; and Yesterday is lost:
Some nimbler Juice wou'd make him foam, and rave,
Like that [44]*Cæsonia* to her *Caius* gave:
Who, plucking from the Forehead of the Fole
His Mother's Love, infus'd it in the Bowl: 805
The boiling Blood ran hissing in his Veins,
Till the mad Vapour mounted to his Brains.
The[45] Thund'rer was not half so much on Fire,
When *Juno*'s Girdle kindled his Desire.
What Woman will not use the Poys'ning Trade,   810

When *Cæsar*'s Wife the Precedent has made!
Let [46]*Agripina*'s Mushroom be forgot;
Giv'n to a Slav'ring, Old, unuseful Sot;
That only clos'd the driveling Dotard's Eyes;
And sent his Godhead downward to the Skies.   815
But this fierce Potion, calls for Fire and Sword;
Nor spares the Commons, when it strikes the Lord:
So many Mischiefs were in one combin'd;
So much one single Poys'ner cost Mankind.
　If Stepdames seek their Sons in Law to kill,   820
'Tis Venial Trespass; let them have their Will:
But let the Child, entrusted to the Care
Of his own Mother, of her Bread beware:
Beware the Food she reaches with her Hand;
The Morsel is intended for thy Land.   825
Thy Tutour be thy Taster, e're thou Eat;
There's Poyson in thy Drink, and in thy Meat.
　You think this feign'd; the Satyr in a Rage
Struts in the Buskins, of the Tragick Stage.
Forgets his Bus'ness is to Laugh and Bite;   830
And will, of Deaths, and dire Revenges Write.
Wou'd it were all a Fable, that you Read;
But[47] *Drymon*'s Wife pleads Guilty to the Deed.
I, (she confesses,) in the Fact was caught;
Two Sons dispatching, at one deadly Draught.   835
What Two, Two Sons, thou Viper, in one day?
Yes sev'n, she cries, if sev'n were in my way.
Medea's[48] Legend is no more a Lye;
Our Age adds Credit to Antiquity.
Great Ills, we grant, in former times did Reign: 840
And Murthers then were done: but not for Gain.
Less Admiration to great Crimes is due,
Which they through Wrath, or through Revenge pursue.
For, weak of Reason, impotent of Will,
The Sex is hurri'd headlong into Ill: 845
And, like a Cliff from its foundations torn,
By raging Earthquakes, into Seas is born.
But those are Fiends, who Crimes from thought begin;
And, cool in Mischief, meditate the Sin.

846 foundations] Foundation *97*

They Read th' Example of a Pious Wife,   850
Redeeming, with her own, her Husband's Life;
Yet, if the Laws did that Exchange afford,
Wou'd save their Lapdog sooner than their Lord
   Where e're you walk, the[49] *Belides* you meet;
And [50]*Clytemnestra*'s grow in every Street: 855
But here's the difference; *Agamemnon*'s Wife
Was a gross Butcher, with a bloody Knife:
But Murther, now, is to perfection grown:
And subtle Poysons are employ'd alone:
Unless some Antidote prevents their Arts,   860
And lines with Balsom all the Noble parts:
In such a case, reserv'd for such a need,
Rather than fail, the Dagger does the Deed.

EXPLANATORY NOTES

1 IN the Golden Age: when *Saturn* Reign'd.   2 *Fat with Acorns*: Acorns
were the Bread of Mankind, before Corn was found.   3 *Under Jove*:
When *Jove* had driven his Father into Banishment, the Silver Age began,
according to the Poets.   4 *Uneasie Justice*, &c. The Poet makes Justice
and Chastity Sisters; and says that they fled to Heaven together; and left 5
Earth for ever.   5 *Ceres Feast*. When the *Roman* Women were forbidden to bed with their Husbands.   6 *Jove* and *Mars*. Of whom more
Fornicating Stories are told, than any of the other Gods.   7 *Wondring
Pharos*. She fled to *Egypt*; which wonder'd at the Enormity of her Crime.
8 He tells the Famous Story of *Messalina*, Wife to the Emperor *Claudius*. 10
9 *Wealth has the Priviledge*, &c. His meaning is, that a Wife who brings a
large Dowry may do what she pleases, and has all the Priviledges of a
Widow.   10 *Berenice's Ring*. A Ring of great Price, which *Herod Agrippa*
gave to his Sister *Berenice*. He was King of the *Jews*, but Tributary to the
Romans.   11 *Cornelia*. Mother to the *Gracchi*, of the Family of the 15
Cornelii; from whence *Scipio* the *Affrican* was descended, who Triumph'd
over *Hannibal*.   12 *O Pæan*, &c. He alludes to the known Fable of
Niobe in *Ovid*. *Amphion* was her Husband: *Pæan* is *Apollo*, who with his
Arrows kill'd her Children, because she boasted that she was more fruit-
ful than *Latona*, *Apollo*'s Mother.   13 *The thirty Pigs*, &c. He alludes to 20
the white Sow in *Virgil*, who farrow'd thirty Pigs.   14 *The Grecian
Cant*. Women then learnt *Greek*, as ours speak *French*.   15 All the
Romans, even the most Inferiour, and most Infamous sort of them, had the
Power of making Wills.   16 *Go drag that Slave*, &c. These are the words
of the Wife.   17 *Your Reason why*, &c. The Answer of the Husband. 25

18 *Call'st thou that Slave a Man?* The Wife again.   19 *Hannibal.* A Famous *Carthaginian* Captain; who was upon the point of Conquering the *Romans.*   20 *The good Goddess.* At whose Feasts no Men were to be present.   21 *Nestor.* Who lived three hundred Years.   22 *What Singer,* &c. He alludes to the Story of *P. Clodius,* who, disguis'd in the Habit of a Singing Woman, went into the House of *Cæsar,* where the Feast of the Good Goddess was Celebrated; to find an opportunity with *Cæsar's* Wife *Pompeia.*   23 He taxes Women with their loving Eunuchs, who can get no Children; but adds that they only love such Eunuchs, as are guelded when they are already at the Age of Manhood.   24 *Priapus.* The God of Lust.   25 *Pollio.* A Famous Singing Boy.   26 That such an Actor whom they love might obtain the Prize.   27 *Th' Aruspex.* He who inspects the Entrails of the Sacrifice, and from thence, foretels the Successor.   28 *Vulcan.* The God of Smiths.   29 *Tabours and Trumpets,* &c. The Ancients thought that with such sounds, they cou'd bring the Moon out of her Eclipse.   30 *A Mood and Figure-Bride.* A Woman who has learn'd Logick.   31 A Woman-Grammarian, who corrects her Husband for speaking false Latin, which is call'd breaking *Priscian's* Head.   32 *A Train of these.* That is, of she Asses.   33 *Sicilian Tyrants.* Are grown to a Proverb in Latin, for their Cruelty.   34 This dressing up the Head so high, which we call a Tow'r, was an Ancient way amongst the *Romans.*   35 *Bellona's* Priests were a sort of Fortunetellers; and the High-Priest an Eunuch.   36 *And add beside,* &c. A Garment was given to the Priest, which he threw into the River; and that, they thought, bore all the Sins of the People, which were drown'd with it.   37 *Chaldæans* are thought to have been the first Astrologers.   38 *Otho* succeeded *Galba* in the Empire; which was foretold him by an Astrologer.   39 *Mars* and *Saturn* are the two Unfortunate Planets; *Jupiter* and *Venus,* the two Fortunate.   40 *Ptolomy.* A Famous Astrologer, an *Egyptian.*   41 The *Brachmans* are *Indian* Philosophers, who remain to this day; and hold, after *Pythagoras,* the Translation of Souls from one body to another.   42 *To an Æthiop's Son.* His meaning is, help her to any kind of Slops, which may cause her to miscarry; for fear she may be brought to Bed of a Blackmoor, which thou, being her Husband, art bound to Father; and that Bastard may by Law, Inherit thy Estate.   43 *His Omen,* &c. The *Romans* thought it ominous to see a Black-moor in the Morning, if he were the first Man they met.   44 *Cæsonia,* Wife to *Caius Caligula,* the great Tyrant: 'Tis said she gave him a Love-Potion, which flying up into his Head, distracted him; and was the occasion of his committing so many Acts of Cruelty.   45 *The Thunderer,* &c. The Story is in *Homer;* where *Juno* borrow'd the Girdle of *Venus,* call'd *Cestos;* to make *Jupiter* in love with her, while the *Grecians* and *Trojans* were fighting, that he might

not help the latter.   46 *Agrippina* was the Mother of the Tyrant *Nero*, who Poyson'd her Husband *Claudius*, that *Nero* might Succeed, who was her Son, and not *Britannicus*, who was the Son of *Claudius*, by a former 70 Wife.   47 The Widow of *Drymon* Poison'd her Sons, that she might Succeed to their Estate: This was done either in the Poet's time, or just before it.   48 *Medea*, out of Revenge to *Jason* who had forsaken her, kill'd the Children which she had by him.   49 *The Belides.* Who were fifty Sisters, Marry'd to fifty young Men, their Cousin-Germans; 75 and kill'd them all on their Wedding-Night, excepting *Hypermnestra*, who sav'd her Husband *Linus*.   50 *Clytemnestra.* The Wife of *Agamemnon*, who, in favour to her Adulterer *Egysthus*, was consenting to his Murther.

THE TENTH SATYR OF JUVENAL

ARGUMENT OF THE TENTH SATYR

The Poet's Design in this Divine Satyr, is to represent the various Wishes and Desires of Mankind; and to set out the Folly of 'em. He runs through all the several Heads of Riches, Honours, Eloquence, Fame for Martial Atchievements, Long-Life, and Beauty; and gives Instances in Each, how frequently they have prov'd the Ruin of Those that Own'd them. He concludes therefore, 5 *that since we generally chuse so ill for our selves; we shou'd do better to leave it to the Gods, to make the choice for us. All we can safely ask of Heaven, lies within a very small Compass. 'Tis but* Health of Body and Mind—*And if we have these, 'tis not much matter, what we want besides: For we have already enough to make us Happy.*   10

THE TENTH SATYR

Look round the Habitable World, how few
    Know their own Good; or knowing it, pursue.
How void of Reason are our Hopes and Fears!
What in the Conduct of our Life appears
So well design'd, so luckily begun,   5
But, when we have our wish, we wish undone?

76 *Hypermnestra 97: Hipermnestra 93*   78 *Egysthus 97: Estgyhus 93*

Whole Houses, of their whole Desires possest,
Are often Ruin'd, at their own Request.
In Wars, and Peace, things hurtful we require,
When made Obnoxious to our own Desire.   10

  With Laurels some have fatally been Crown'd;
Some who the depths of Eloquence have found,
In that unnavigable Stream were Drown'd.
The¹ Brawny Fool, who did his Vigour boast;
In that Presumeing Confidence was lost: 15
But more have been by Avarice opprest,
And Heaps of Money crouded in the Chest:
Unwieldy Sums of Wealth, which higher mount
Than Files of Marshall'd Figures can account.
To which the Stores of *Cræsus*, in the Scale,   20
Wou'd look like little Dolphins, when they sail
In the vast Shadow of the *British* Whale.

  For this, in *Nero*'s Arbitrary time,
When Virtue was a Guilt, and Wealth a Crime,
A Troop of Cut-Throat Guards were sent, to seize   25
The Rich Mens Goods, and gut their Palaces:
The Mob, Commission'd by the Government,
Are seldom to an Empty Garret, sent.
The Fearful Passenger, who Travels late,
Charg'd with the Carriage of a Paltry Plate,   30
Shakes at the Moonshine shadow of a Rush;
And sees a Red-Coat rise from every Bush:
The Beggar Sings, ev'n when he sees the place
Beset with Thieves, and never mends his pace.

  Of all the Vows, the first and chief Request   35
Of each, is to be Richer than the rest:
And yet no doubts the Poor Man's Draught controul;
He dreads no Poison in his homely Bowl.
Then fear the deadly Drug, when Gems Divine
Enchase the Cup, and sparkle in the Wine.   40

  Will you not now, the pair of Sages praise,
Who the same End pursu'd, by several Ways?
One pity'd, one contemn'd the Woful Times:
One laugh'd at Follies, one lamented Crimes:
Laughter is easie; but the Wonder lies   45
What stores of Brine supply'd the Weepers Eyes.

Democritus, cou'd feed his Spleen, and shake
His sides and shoulders till he felt 'em ake;
Tho in his Country Town, no Lictors were;
Nor Rods nor Ax nor Tribune did appear: 50
Nor all the Foppish Gravity of show
Which cunning Magistrates on Crowds bestow:
  What had he done, had he beheld, on high
Our *Prætor* seated, in Mock Majesty;
His Charriot rowling o're the Dusty place   55
While, with dumb Pride, and a set formal Face,
He moves, in the dull Ceremonial track,
With *Jove's* Embroyder'd Coat upon his back:
A Sute of Hangings had not more opprest
His Shoulders, than that long, Laborious Vest.   60
A heavy Gugaw, (call'd a Crown,) that spred
About his Temples, drown'd his narrow Head:
And wou'd have crush'd it, with the Massy Freight,
But that a sweating Slave sustain'd the weight:
A Slave in the same Chariot seen to ride,   65
To mortifie the mighty Madman's Pride.
Add now th' Imperial Eagle, rais'd on high,
With Golden Beak (the Mark of Majesty)
Trumpets before, and on the Left and Right,
A Cavalcade of Nobles, all in White: 70
In their own Natures false; and flatt'ring Tribes
But made his Friends, by Places and by Bribes.
  In his own Age *Democritus* cou'd find
Sufficient cause to laugh at Humane kind:
Learn from so great a Wit; a Land of Bogs   75
With Ditches fenc'd, a Heav'n Fat with Fogs,
May form a Spirit fit to sway the State;
And make the Neighb'ring Monarchs fear their Fate.
  He laughs at all the Vulgar Cares and Fears;
At their vain Triumphs, and their vainer Tears: 80
An equal Temper in his Mind he found,
When Fortune flatter'd him, and when she frown'd.
'Tis plain from hence that what our Vows request,
Are hurtful things, or Useless at the best.
  Some ask for Envy'd Pow'r; which publick Hate   85

71 false;] false, *93 97*   Tribes *97:* Tribes; *93*

Pursues, and hurries headlong to their Fate:
Down go the Titles; and the Statue Crown'd,
Is by base Hands in the next River Drown'd.
The Guiltless Horses, and the Chariot Wheel
The same Effects of Vulgar Fury feel: 90
The Smith prepares his Hammer for the Stroke,
While the Lung'd Bellows hissing Fire provoke;
Sejanus[2] almost first of *Roman* Names,
The great *Sejanus* crackles in the Flames:
Form'd in the Forge, the Pliant Brass is laid   ⎫   95
On Anvils; and of Head and Limbs are made,   ⎬
Pans, Cans, and Pispots, a whole Kitchin Trade.   ⎭

Adorn your Doors with Laurels; and a Bull
Milk white and large, lead to the Capitol;
Sejanus with a Rope, is drag'd along;   100
The Sport and Laughter of the giddy Throng!
Good Lord, they Cry, what Ethiop Lips he has,
How foul a Snout, and what a hanging Face:
By Heav'n I never cou'd endure his sight;
But say, how came his Monstrous Crimes to Light?   105
What is the Charge, and who the Evidence
(The Saviour of the Nation and the Prince?)
Nothing of this; but our Old *Cæsar* sent
A Noisie Letter to his Parliament:
Nay Sirs, if *Cæsar* writ, I ask no more: 110
He's Guilty; and the Question's out of Door.
How goes the Mob, (for that's a Mighty thing.)
When the King's Trump, the Mob are for the King:
They follow Fortune, and the Common Cry
Is still against the Rogue Condemn'd to Dye.   115

But the same very Mob; that Rascal crowd,
Had cry'd *Sejanus*, with a Shout as loud;
Had his Designs, (by Fortune's favour Blest)
Succeeded, and the Prince's Age opprest.
But long, long since, the Times have chang'd their Face,   120
The People grown Degenerate and base:
Not suffer'd now the Freedom of their choice,
To make their Magistrates, and sell their Voice.
Our Wise Fore-Fathers, Great by Sea and Land,

103 Face:] Face? *93 97*   110 more:] more *93 97*   116 crowd,] crowd *93 97*

Had once the Pow'r, and absolute Command;   125
All Offices of Trust, themselves dispos'd;
Rais'd whom they pleas'd, and whom they pleas'd, Depos'd.
But we who give our Native Rights away,
And our Inslav'd Posterity betray,
Are now reduc'd to beg an Alms, and go   130
On Holidays to see a Puppet show.
    There was a Damn'd Design, crys one, no doubt;
For Warrants are already Issued out:
I met *Brutidius* in a Mortal fright:
He's dipt for certain, and plays least in sight: 135
I fear the Rage of our offended Prince,
Who thinks the Senate slack in his defence!
Come let us haste, our Loyal Zeal to show,
And spurn the Wretched Corps of *Cæsar*'s Foe:
But let our Slaves be present there, lest they   140
Accuse their Masters, and for Gain betray.
    Such were the Whispers of those jealous Times,
About *Sejanus* Punishment, and Crimes.
    Now tell me truly, wou'dst thou change thy Fate
To be, like him, first Minister of State?   145
To have thy Levees Crowded with resort,
Of a depending, gaping, servile Court:
Dispose all Honours, of the Sword and Gown,
Grace with a Nod, and Ruin with a Frown;
To hold thy Prince in Pupill-Age and sway,   150
That Monarch, whom the Master'd World obey?
While he, intent on secret Lusts alone,
Lives to himself, abandoning the Throne;
Coopt³ in a narrow Isle, observing Dreams
With flatt'ring Wisards, and erecting Schemes!   155
    I well believe, thou wou'd'st be Great as he;
For every Man's a Fool to that Degree:
All wish the dire Prerogative to kill;
Ev'n they wou'd have the Pow'r, who want the Will:
But wou'dst thou have thy Wishes understood,   160
To take the Bad together with the Good?
Wou'dst thou not rather choose a small Renown,
To be the May'r of some poor Paltry Town,
Bigly to Look, and Barb'rously to speak;

To pound false Weights, and scanty Measures break?   165
Then, grant we that *Sejanus* went astray,
In ev'ry Wish, and knew not how to pray:
For he who grasp'd the World's exhausted Store
Yet never had enough, but wish'd for more,
Rais'd a Top-heavy Tow'r, of monst'rous height,   170
Which Mould'ring, crush'd him underneath the Weight.
    What did the mighty *Pompey*'s Fall beget?
And ruin'd ⁴him, who Greater than the Great,
The stubborn Pride of *Roman* Nobles broke;
And bent their Haughty Necks beneath his Yoke?   175
What else, but his immoderate Lust of Pow'r,
Pray'rs made, and granted in a Luckless Hour:
For few Usurpers to the Shades descend
By a dry Death, or with a quiet End.
    The Boy, who scarce has paid his Entrance down   180
To his proud Pedant, or declin'd a Noun,
(So small an Elf, that when the days are foul,
He and his Satchel must be born to School,)
Yet prays and hopes and aims at nothing less,
To⁵ prove a *Tully*, or *Demosthenes*:   185
But both those Orators, so much Renown'd,
In their own Depths of Eloquence were Drown'd:
The Hand and Head were never lost, of those
Who dealt in Dogrel, or who punn'd in Prose:
*Fortune*⁶ *foretun'd the Dying Notes of* Rome: 190
Till I, thy Consul sole, consol'd thy Doom.
His Fate had crept below the lifted Swords,
Had all his Malice been to Murther words.
I rather wou'd be *Mævius*, Thrash for Rhimes
Like his, the scorn and scandal of the Times,   195
Than ⁷that Philippique, fatally Divine,
Which is inscrib'd the Second, should be Mine.
    Nor he, the Wonder of the *Grecian* throng,
Who drove them with the Torrent of his Tongue,
Who shook the Theaters, and sway'd the State   200
Of *Athens*, found a more Propitious Fate.
Whom, born beneath a boding Horoscope,
His Sire, the Blear-Ey'd Vulcan of a Shop,

186 Orators, *97*: Orators; *93*

From *Mars* his Forge, sent to *Minerva*'s Schools,
To learn th' unlucky Art of wheedling Fools. 205
    With Itch of Honour, and Opinion, Vain,
All things beyond their Native worth we strain:
The[8] Spoils of War, brought to *Feretrian Jove*,
An empty Coat of Armour hung above
The Conquerours Chariot, and in Triumph born, 210
A Streamer from a boarded Gally torn,
A Chap-faln Beaver loosly hanging by
The cloven Helm, an Arch of Victory,
On whose high Convex sits a Captive Foe
And sighing casts a Mournful Look below; 215
Of ev'ry Nation, each Illustrious Name,
Such Toys as these have cheated into Fame:
Exchanging solid Quiet, to obtain
The Windy satisfaction of the Brain.
    So much the Thirst of Honour Fires the Blood; 220
So many wou'd be Great, so few be Good.
For who wou'd Virtue for her self regard,
Or Wed, without the Portion of Reward?
Yet this Mad Chace of Fame, by few pursu'd,
Has drawn Destruction on the Multitude: 225
This Avarice of Praise in Times to come,
Those long Inscriptions, crowded on the Tomb,
Shou'd some Wild Fig-Tree take her Native bent,
And heave below the gaudy Monument,
Wou'd crack the Marble Titles, and disperse 230
The Characters of all the lying Verse.
For Sepulchres themselves must crumbling fall
In times Abyss, the common Grave of all.
    Great *Hannibal* within the Ballance lay;
And tell how many Pounds his Ashes weigh; 235
Whom *Affrick* was not able to contain,
Whose length runs Level with th' Atlantick main,
And wearies fruitful *Nilus*, to convey
His Sun-beat Waters by so long a way;
Which *Ethiopia*'s double Clime divides, 240
And Elephants in other Mountains hides.
Spain first he won, the *Pyrenæans* past,

242 *Pyrenæans* 97: *Pyræneans* 93

And steepy *Alps*, the Mounds that Nature cast:
And with Corroding Juices, as he went,
A passage through the living Rocks he rent.   245
Then, like a Torrent, rowling from on high,
He pours his head-long Rage on *Italy*;
In three Victorious Battels overrun;
Yet still uneasie, Cries there's nothing done:
Till, level with the Ground, their Gates are laid;   250
And *Punick* Flags, on *Roman* Tow'rs displaid.

   Ask what a Face belong'd to this high Fame;
His Picture scarcely wou'd deserve a Frame:
A Sign-Post Dawber wou'd disdain to paint
The one Ey'd Heroe on his Elephant.   255
Now what's his End, O Charming Glory, say
What rare fifth Act, to Crown this huffing Play?
In one deciding Battel overcome,
He flies, is banisht from his Native home:
Begs refuge in a Foreign Court, and there   260
Attends his mean Petition to prefer:
Repuls'd by surly Grooms, who wait before
The sleeping Tyrant's interdicted Door.

   What wondrous sort of Death, has Heav'n design'd
Distinguish'd from the Herd of Humane Kind,   265
For so untam'd, so turbulent a Mind!
Nor Swords at hand, nor hissing Darts afar,
Are doom'd t' Avenge the tedious bloody War,
But Poyson, drawn through a Rings hollow plate,
Must finish him; a sucking Infant's Fate.   270
Go, climb the rugged *Alps*, Ambitious Fool,
To please the Boys, and be a Theme at School.

   One World suffis'd not *Alexander*'s Mind;
Coop't up, he seem'd in Earth and Seas confin'd:
And, strugling, stretch'd his restless Limbs about   275
The narrow Globe, to find a passage out.
Yet, enter'd in the⁹ Brick-built Town, he try'd
The Tomb, and found the strait dimensions wide:
"Death only this Mysterious Truth unfolds,
"The mighty Soul, how small a Body holds.   280

   Old¹⁰ *Greece* a Tale of *Athos* wou'd make out,
Cut from the Continent, and Sail'd about;

Seas hid with Navies, Chariots passing o're
The Channel, on a Bridge from shore to shore:
Rivers, whose depth no sharp beholder sees,   285
Drunk, at an Armies Dinner, to the Lees;
With a long Legend of Romantick things,
Which, in his Cups, the Bowsy Poet sings.
But how did he return, this haughty Brave
Who whipt the Winds, and made the Sea his Slave?   290
(Tho' *Neptune* took unkindly to be bound;
And *Eurus* never such hard usage found
In his *Eolian* Prisons under ground;)
What God so mean, ev'n ¹¹he who points the way,
So Merciless a Tyrant to Obey!   295
But how return'd he, let us ask again?
In a poor Skiff he pass'd the bloody Main,
Choak'd with the slaughter'd Bodies of his Train.
For Fame he pray'd, but let th' Event declare
He had no mighty penn'worth of his Pray'r.   300
    Jove grant me length of Life, and Years good store
Heap on my bending Back, I ask no more.
Both Sick and Healthful, Old and Young, conspire
In this one silly, mischievous desire.
Mistaken Blessing which Old Age they call,   305
'Tis a long, nasty, darksom Hospital.
A ropy Chain of Rhumes; a Visage rough,
Deform'd, Unfeatur'd, and a Skin of Buff.
A stitch-fal'n Cheek, that hangs below the Jaw;
Such Wrinckles, as a skillful Hand wou'd draw   310
For an old Grandam Ape, when, with a Grace,
She sits at squat, and scrubs her Leathern Face.
    In Youth, distinctions infinite abound;
No Shape, or Feature, just alike are found;
The Fair, the Black, the Feeble, and the Strong;   315
But the same foulness does to Age belong,
The self same Palsie, both in Limbs, and Tongue.
The Skull and Forehead one Bald Barren plain;
And Gums unarm'd to Mumble Meat in vain:
Besides th' Eternal Drivel, that supplies   320
The dropping Beard, from Nostrils, Mouth, and Eyes.

294 mean,] mean *93 97*   301 store *97:* store? *93*

His Wife and Children loath him, and, what's worse,
Himself does his offensive Carrion Curse!
Flatt'rers forsake him too; for who would kill
Himself, to be Remembred in a Will?   325
His taste, not only pall'd to Wine and Meat,
But to the Relish of a Nobler Treat.
The limber Nerve, in vain provok'd to rise,
Inglorious from the Field of Battel flies:
Poor Feeble Dotard, how cou'd he advance   330
With his Blew-head-piece, and his broken Lance?
Add, that endeavouring still without effect,
A Lust more sordid justly we suspect.
    Those Senses lost, behold a new defeat;
The Soul, dislodging from another seat.   335
What Musick, or Enchanting Voice, can chear
A Stupid, Old, Impenetrable Ear?
No matter in what Place, or what Degree
Of the full Theater he sits to see;
Cornets and Trumpets cannot reach his Ear: 340
Under an Actor's Nose, he's never near.
    His Boy must bawl, to make him understand
The Hour o'th' Day, or such a Lord's at hand:
The little Blood that creeps within his Veins,
Is but just warm'd in a hot Feaver's pains.   345
In fine, he wears no Limb about him sound:
With Sores and Sicknesses, beleaguer'd round:
Ask me their Names, I sooner cou'd relate
How many Drudges on Salt *Hippia* wait;
What Crowds of Patients the Town Doctor kills,   350
Or how, last fall, he rais'd the Weekly Bills.
What Provinces by *Basilus* were spoil'd,
What Herds of Heirs by Guardians are beguil'd:
How many bouts a Day that Bitch has try'd;
How many Boys that Pedagogue can ride!   355
What Lands and Lordships for their Owners know,
My Quondam Barber, but his Worship now.
    This Dotard of his broken Back complains,
One his Legs fail, and one his Shoulder pains:
Another is of both his Eyes bereft:

359 Shoulder pains] Shoulders pain *93 97*

And Envies who has one for Aiming left.
A Fifth with trembling Lips expecting stands;
As in his Child-hood, cram'd by others hands;
One, who at sight of Supper open'd wide
His Jaws before, and Whetted Grinders try'd;   365
Now only Yawns, and waits to be supply'd:
Like a young Swallow, when with weary Wings,
Expected Food, her fasting Mother brings.
   His loss of Members is a heavy Curse,
But all his Faculties decay'd, a worse!   370
His Servants Names he has forgotten quite:
Knows not his Friend who supp'd with him last Night:
Not ev'n the Children, he Begot and Bred;
Or his Will knows 'em not: For, in their stead,
In Form of Law, a common Hackney Jade,   375
Sole Heir, for secret Services, is made:
So lewd, and such a batter'd Brothel Whore,
That she defies all Commers, at her Door.
Well, yet suppose his Senses are his own,
He lives to be chief Mourner for his Son: 380
Before his Face his Wife and Brother burns;
He Numbers all his Kindred in their Urns.
These are the Fines he pays for living long;
And dragging tedious Age, in his own wrong:
Grief always Green, a House-hold still in Tears,   385
Sad Pomps: A Threshold throng'd with daily Biers;
And Liveries of Black for Length of Years.
   Next to the Raven's Age, the *Pylian*[12] King
Was longest liv'd of any two-leg'd thing;
Blest, to Defraud the Grave so long, to Mount   390
His[13] Numbred Years, and on his Right Hand Count;
Three Hundred Seasons, guzling Must of Wine:
But, hold a while, and hear himself Repine
At Fates Unequal Laws; and at the Clue
Which, [14]Merciless in length, the midmost Sister drew.   395
When his Brave Son upon the Fun'ral Pyre,
He saw extended, and his Beard on Fire;
He turn'd, and Weeping, ask'd his Friends, what Crime
Had Curs'd his Age to this unhappy Time?
   Thus Mourn'd Old *Peleus* for *Achilles* slain,   400

And thus *Ulysses* Father did complain.
  How Fortunate an End had *Priam* made,
Among his Ancestors a mighty shade,
While *Troy* yet stood: When *Hector* with the Race
Of Royal Bastards might his Funeral Grace: 405
Amidst the Tears of *Trojan* Dames inurn'd,
And by his Loyal Daughters, truly mourn'd.
Had Heaven so Blest him, he had Dy'd before
The fatal Fleet to *Sparta Paris* bore.
But mark what Age produc'd; he liv'd to see   410
His Town in Flames, his falling Monarchy:
In fine, the feeble Syre, reduc'd by Fate,
To change his Scepter for a Sword, too late,
His[15] last Effort before *Jove's* Altar tries;
A Souldier half, and half a Sacrifice: 415
Falls like an Oxe, that waits the coming blow;
Old and unprofitable to the Plough.
  At[16] least, he Dy'd a Man; his Queen surviv'd,
To Howl, and in a barking Body liv'd.
  I hasten to our own; Nor will relate   420
Great [17]*Mithridates*, and Rich [18]*Crœssus* Fate;
Whom *Solon* wisely Counsell'd to attend
The Name of Happy, till he knew his End.
  That *Marius* was an Exile, that he fled,
Was ta'ne, in Ruin'd *Carthage* beg'd his Bread,   425
All these were owing to a Life too long:
For whom had *Rome* beheld so Happy, Young!
High in his Chariot and with Lawrel Crown'd,
When he had led the *Cimbrian* Captives round
The *Roman* Streets; descending from his State,   430
In that Blest Hour he should have beg'd his Fate:
Then, then he might have dy'd of all admir'd,
And his Triumphant Soul with Shouts expir'd.
  Campania[19], Fortunes Malice to prevent,
To *Pompey* an indulgent Feavour sent: 435
But publick Pray'rs impos'd on Heav'n, to give
Their much Lov'd Leader an unkind Reprieve.

401 *Ulysses*] *Ulysses's* 93 97   411 Flames, 97: Flames 93   418 Man;] Man,
93 97   surviv'd, 97: surviv'd; 93   422 attend] attend, 93 97   424 fled,
97: fled 93   433 with] in 97   435 Feavour] Favour 93 97

The Cities Fate and his, conspir'd to save
The Head, reserv'd for an *Egyptian* Slave.

   Cethegus[20], tho a Traytor to the State,   440
And Tortur'd, scap'd this Ignominious Fate:
And *Sergius*[21], who a bad Cause bravely try'd,
All of a Piece, and undiminish'd Dy'd.

   To *Venus*, the fond Mother makes a Pray'r,
That all her Sons and Daughters may be Fair: 445
True, for the Boys a Mumbling Vow she sends;
But, for the Girls, the Vaulted Temple rends:
They must be finish'd Pieces: 'Tis allow'd
Diana's Beauty made *Latona* Proud;
And pleas'd, to see the Wond'ring People Pray   450
To the New-rising Sister of the Day.

   And yet *Lucretia*'s Fate wou'd bar that Vow:
And Fair [22]*Virginia* wou'd her Fate bestow
On *Rutila*; and change her Faultless Make
For the foul rumple of Her Camel back.   455

   But, for his Mother's Boy, the Beau, what frights
His Parents have by Day, what Anxious Nights!
Form join'd with Virtue is a sight too rare:
Chast is no Epithete to sute with Fair.
Suppose the same Traditionary strain   460
Of Rigid Manners, in the House remain;
Inveterate Truth, an Old plain *Sabine*'s Heart;
Suppose that Nature, too, has done her part;
Infus'd into his Soul a sober Grace,
And blusht a Modest Blood into his Face;   465
(For Nature is a better Guardian far,
Than Sawcy Pedants, or dull Tutors are:)
Yet still the Youth must ne're arrive at Man;
(So much Almighty Bribes, and Presents, can:)
Ev'n with a Parent, where Perswasions fail,   470
Mony is impudent, and will prevail.

   We never Read of such a Tyrant King,
Who guelt a Boy deform'd, to hear him Sing.
Nor *Nero*, in his more Luxurious Rage,
E're made a Mistress of an ugly Page: 475

Sporus, his Spouse, nor Crooked was, nor Lame
With Mountain Back, and Belly, from the Game
Cross-barr'd: But both his Sexes well became.
Go, boast your *Springal*, by his Beauty Curst
To Ills; nor think I have declar'd the worst: 480
His Form procures him Journey-Work; a strife
Betwixt Town-Madams, and the Merchant's Wife:
Guess, when he undertakes this publick War,
What furious Beasts offended Cuckolds are.

    Adult'rers are with Dangers round beset;   485
Born under *Mars*, they cannot scape the Net;
And from Revengeful Husbands oft have try'd
Worse handling, than severest Laws provide:
One stabs, one slashes, one, with Cruel Art,
Makes *Colon* suffer for the Peccant part.   490

    But your *Endymion*, your smooth, Smock-fac'd Boy,
Unrivall'd, shall a Beauteous Dame enjoy:
Not so: One more Salacious, Rich, and Old,
Out-bids, and buys her Pleasure for her Gold:
Now he must Moil, and Drudge, for one he loaths: 495
She keeps him High, in Equipage, and Cloaths:
She Pawns her Jewels, and her Rich Attire,
And thinks the Workman worthy of his Hire:
In all things else immoral, stingy, mean;
But, in her Lusts, a Conscionable Quean.   500

    She may be handsom, yet be Chast, you say:
Good Observator, not so fast away:
Did it not cost the[23] Modest Youth his Life,
Who shun'd th' Embraces of his Father's Wife?
And was not t'other[24] Stripling forc'd to fly,   505
Who, coldly, did his Patron's Queen deny;
And pleaded Laws of Hospitality?
The Ladies charg'd 'em home, and turn'd the Tail:
With shame they redn'd, and with spight grew Pale.
'Tis Dang'rous to deny the longing Dame;   510
She loses Pity, who has lost her Shame.

    Now[25] *Silius* wants thy Counsel, give Advice;
Wed *Cæsar*'s Wife, or Dye; the Choice is nice.
Her Comet-Eyes she darts on ev'ry Grace;
And takes a fatal liking to his Face.   515

Adorn'd with Bridal Pomp she sits in State;
The Publick Notaries and *Auspex* wait:
The Genial Bed is in the Garden drest;
The Portion paid, and ev'ry Rite express'd,
Which in a *Roman* Marriage is profest.   520
'Tis no stol'n Wedding, this; rejecting awe,
She scorns to Marry, but in Form of Law:
In this moot case, your Judgment: To refuse
Is present Death, besides the Night you lose.
If you consent, 'tis hardly worth your pain;   525
A Day or two of Anxious Life you gain:
Till lowd Reports through all the Town have past,
And reach the Prince: for Cuckolds hear the last.
Indulge thy Pleasure, Youth, and take thy swing:
For not to take, is but the self same thing: 530
Inevitable Death before thee lies;
But looks more kindly through a Ladies Eyes.
   What then remains? Are we depriv'd of Will?
Must we not Wish, for fear of wishing Ill?
Receive my Counsel, and securely move;   535
Intrust thy Fortune to the Pow'rs above.
Leave them to manage for thee, and to grant
What their unerring Wisdom sees thee want:
In Goodness as in Greatness they excel;
Ah that we lov'd our selves but half so well!   540
We, blindly by our headstrong Passions led,
Are hot for Action, and desire to Wed;
Then wish for Heirs: But to the Gods alone
Our future Offspring, and our Wives are known;
Th' audacious Strumpet, and ungracious Son.   545
   Yet, not to rob the Priests of pious Gain,
That Altars be not wholly built in vain;
Forgive the Gods the rest, and stand confin'd
To Health of Body, and Content of Mind:
A Soul, that can securely Death defie,   550
And count it Nature's Priviledge, to Dye;
Serene and Manly, harden'd to sustain
The load of Life, and Exercis'd in Pain;
Guiltless of Hate, and Proof against Desire;
That all things weighs, and nothing can admire: 555

That dares prefer the Toils of *Hercules*
To Dalliance, Banquets, and Ignoble ease.
  The Path to Peace is Virtue: What I show,
Thy Self may freely, on Thy Self bestow:
Fortune was never Worshipp'd by the Wise;   560
But, set aloft by Fools, Usurps the Skies.

EXPLANATORY NOTES

1 *MIlo*, of *Crotona*; who for a Tryal of his strength, going to rend an Oak, perish'd in the Attempt: For his Arms were caught in the Trunk of it; and he was devour'd by Wild Beasts.   2 *Sejanus* was *Tiberius*'s first Favourite; and while he continu'd so, had the highest Marks of Honour bestow'd on him; Statues and Triumphal Chariots were every where 5 erected to him. But as soon as he fell into Disgrace with the Emperor, these were all immediately dismounted; and the Senate and Common People insulted over him as meanly, as they had fawn'd on him before.   3 The Island of *Capreæ*, which lies about a League out at Sea from the *Campanian* Shore, was the Scene of *Tiberius*'s Pleasures in the latter part of his Reign. 10 There he liv'd for some Years with Diviners, Soothsayers, and worse Company—And from thence, dispatch'd all his Orders to the Senate. 4 *Julius Cæsar*, who got the better of *Pompey*, that was stil'd *the Great*. 5 *Demosthenes* and *Tully*, both dyed for their Oratory. *Demosthenes* gave himself Poyson, to avoid being carried to *Antipater*; one of *Alexander*'s Cap- 15 tains, who had then made himself Master of *Athens*. *Tully* was Murther'd by *M. Antony*'s Order, in Return, for those Invectives he had made against him.   6 The Latin of this Couplet is a Famous Verse of *Tully*'s, in which he sets out the Happiness of his own Consulship; Famous for the Vanity, and the ill Poetry of it. For *Tully* as he had a good deal of the one, 20 so he had no great share of the other.   7 The Orations of *Tully*, against *M. Antony*, were stil'd by him *Philippics*, in imitation of *Demosthenes*; who had given that Name before to those he made against *Philip* of *Macedon*. 8 This is a Mock-Account of a *Roman* Triumph.   9 *Babylon*, where *Alexander* dy'd.   10 *Xerxes*, is represented in History, after a very 25 Romantick Manner; affecting Fame beyond Measure, and doing the most Extravagant things, to compass it. Mount *Athos* made a Prodigious Promontory in the *Ægæan* Sea: He is said to have cut a Channel through it, and to have Sail'd round it. He made a Bridge of Boats over the *Hellespont*, where it was three Miles broad: And order'd a Whipping for the Winds 30 and Seas, because they had once crossed his Designs, as we have a very solemn account of it in *Herodotus*. But, after all these vain Boasts, he was shamefully beaten by *Themistocles* at *Salamis*; and return'd home, leaving most of his Fleet behind him.   11 *Mercury*, who was a God of the

lowest size, and employ'd always in Errands between Heaven and Hell. 35
And Mortals us'd him accordingly: For his Statues were anciently plac'd,
where Roads met; with Directions on the Fingers of 'em, pointing out the
several ways to Travellers.   12 *Nestor*, King of *Pylus*; who was 300
Years old, according to *Homer*'s account, at least, as he is understood by
his Expositors.   13 The Ancients counted by their Fingers. Their 40
Left Hands serv'd 'em till they came up to an Hundred. After that, they
us'd their *Right*, to express all greater Numbers.   14 The *Fates* were
three Sisters, which had all some peculiar Business assign'd 'em by the
Poets, in Relation to the Lives of Men. The First held the Distaff; the
Second Spun the Thread; and the Third cut it.   15 Whilst *Troy* was 45
Sacking by the *Greeks*, Old King *Priam* is said to have Buckled on his
Armour, to oppose 'em. Which he had no sooner done, but he was met by
Pyrrhus, and Slain before the Altar of *Jupiter*, in his own Palace, as we have
the Story finely told, in *Virgil*'s 2d *Æneid*.   16 *Hecuba*, his Queen,
escap'd the Swords of the *Grecians*, and outliv'd him. It seems, she be- 50
hav'd her self so fiercely, and uneasily to her Husband's Murtherers,
while she liv'd, that the Poets thought fit to turn her into a *Bitch*, when
she dy'd.   17 *Mithridates*, after he had disputed the Empire of the
World for 40 Years together, with the *Romans*, was at last depriv'd of
Life and Empire by *Pompey* the Great.   18 *Cræsus*, in the midst of his 55
Prosperity, making his Boast to *Solon*, how Happy he was, receiv'd this
Answer from the Wise Man, That no One could pronounce himself
Happy, till he saw what his End should be. The truth of this *Cræsus* found,
when he was put in Chains by *Cyrus*, and Condemned to die.   19 *Pom-*
pey, in the midst of his Glory, fell into a Dangerous Fit of Sickness, 60
at *Naples*. A great many Cities then made Publick Supplications for him.
He Recover'd, was beaten at *Pharsalia*, fled to *Ptolomy* King of *Ægypt*;
and, instead of receiving Protection at his Court, had his Head struck
off by his Order, to please *Cæsar*.   20 *Cethegus* was one that conspir'd with *Catiline*, and was put to Death by the Senate.   21 *Catiline* 65
dy'd Fighting.   22 *Virginia* was kill'd by her own Father, to prevent her being expos'd to the Lust of *Appius Claudius*, who had Ill
Designs upon her. The Story at large is in *Livy*'s Third Book; and 'tis
a remarkable one, as it gave occasion to the putting down the Power of
the *Decemviri*; of whom *Appius* was one.   23 *Hippolytus* the Son of 70
Theseus, was lov'd by his Mother in Law *Phædra*. But he not complying with her, she procur'd his Death.   24 *Bellerophon*, the Son of
King *Glaucus*, residing sometime at the Court of *Prætus* King of the
Argives, the Queen, *Sthenobœa*, fell in Love with him. But he refusing her,
she turn'd the Accusation upon Him; and he narrowly scap'd *Prætus*'s 75
Vengeance.   25 *Messalina*, Wife to the Emperor *Claudius*, Infamous for

her Lewdness. She set her Eyes upon *C. Silius*, a fine Youth; forc'd him to quit his own Wife, and Marry her with all the Formalities of a Wedding, whilst *Claudius Cæsar* was Sacrificing at *Hostia*. Upon his Return, he put both *Silius* and her to Death.　80

THE SIXTEENTH SATYR OF JUVENAL

ARGUMENT OF THE SIXTEENTH SATYR

The Poet in this Satyr, proves, that the Condition of a Souldier is much better than that of a Countryman. First, because a Countryman however Affronted, Provok'd, and Struck himself, dares not strike a Souldier: Who is only to be judg'd by a Court-Martial: And by the Law of Camillus, *which obliges him not to Quarrel without the Trenches, he is also assur'd to have a speedy hearing,* 5 *and quick dispatch: Whereas, the Townsman or Peasant, is delaid in his suit by frivolous Pretences, and not sure of Justice when he is heard in the Court. The Souldier is also Priviledg'd to make a Will; and to give away his Estate which he got in War, to whom he pleases, without Consideration of Parentage, or Relations; which is deny'd to all other* Romans. *This Satyr was written by* 10 Juvenal, *when he was a Commander in* Egypt: '*Tis certainly his, tho I think it not finish'd. And if it be well observ'd, you will find he intended an Invective against a standing Army.*

THE SIXTEENTH SATYR

WHAT vast Prerogatives, my *Gallus*, are
　　Accrewing to the mighty Man of War?
For, if into a lucky Camp I light,
Tho raw in Arms, and yet afraid to Fight,
Befriend me my good Stars, and all goes right.　　　5
One Happy Hour is to a Souldier better
Than Mother ¹*Juno*'s recommending Letter,
Or *Venus*, when to *Mars* she wou'd prefer
My Suit, and own the Kindness done to Her.
　　See what Our Common Priviledges are:　　　10
As first, no Sawcy Citizen shall dare

The Sixteenth Satyr. 11 first, 97: first 93

To strike a Souldier, nor when struck, resent
The wrong, for fear of farther Punishment:
Not tho his Teeth are beaten out, his Eyes
Hang by a String, in Bumps his Fore-head rise,   15
Shall He presume to mention his Disgrace,
Or Beg amends for his demolish'd Face.
A Booted Judge shall sit to try his Cause
Not by the Statute, but by Martial-Laws;
Which old ²*Camillus* order'd to confine   20
The Brawls of Souldiers to the Trench and Line:
A Wise Provision; and from thence 'tis clear
That Officers a Souldiers Cause shou'd hear:
And taking cognizance of Wrongs receiv'd,
An Honest Man may hope to be reliev'd.   25
So far 'tis well: But with a General cry
The Regiment will rise in Mutiny,
The Freedom of Their Fellow Rogue demand,
And, if refus'd, will threaten to Disband.
Withdraw thy Action, and depart in Peace;   30
The Remedy is worse than the Disease:
This Cause is worthy³ him who in the Hall
Wou'd for his Fee, and for his Client bawl:
But woud'st Thou Friend who hast two Legs alone,
(Which Heav'n be Prais'd, Thou yet may'st call Thy own,)   35
Woud'st Thou to run the Gantlet These expose
To a whole Company of ⁴Hob-nail'd Shoos?
Sure the good Breeding of Wise Citizens
Shou'd teach 'em more good Nature to their Shins.

    Besides, whom can'st Thou think so much thy Friend,   40
Who dares appear thy Business to defend?
Dry up thy Tears, and Pocket up th' Abuse,
Nor put thy Friend to make a bad excuse:
The Judge cries out, your Evidence produce.
Will He, who saw the Souldier's Mutton Fist,   45
And saw Thee maul'd, appear within the List;
To witness Truth? When I see one so Brave,
The Dead, think I, are risen from the Grave;
And with their long Spade Beards, and Matted Hair,
Our honest Ancestors, are come to take the Air.   50
Against a Clown, with more security,

A Witness may be brought to swear a Lye,
Than, tho his Evidence be Full and Fair,
To vouch a Truth against a Man of War.
 More Benefits remain, and claim'd as Rights,   55
Which are a standing Armies Perquisites.
If any Rogue vexatious Suits advance
Against me for my known Inheritance,
Enter by Violence my Fruitful Grounds,
Or take the Sacred Land-Mark from my Bounds,   60
Those Bounds, which with Procession and with Pray'r,
And [5]Offer'd Cakes, have been my Annual care:
Or if my Debtors do not keep their day,
Deny their Hands, and then refuse to pay;
I must with Patience all the Terms attend,   65
Among the common Causes that depend
Till mine is call'd; and that long look'd for day
Is still encumber'd with some new delay:
Perhaps[6] the Cloath of State is only spred,
Some of the *Quorum* may be Sick a Bed;   70
That Judge is Hot, and do'ffs his Gown, while This
O're Night was Bowsy, and goes out to Piss:
So many Rubs appear, the time is gone
For hearing, and the tedious Suit goes on:
But Buff, and Belt-Men, never know these Cares;   75
No Time, nor Trick of Law their Action Bars:
Their Cause They to an easier Issue put;
They will be heard, or They lug out, and cut.
Another Branch of their Revenue still
Remains beyond their boundless Right to kill,   80
Their[7] Father yet alive, impour'd to make a Will.
For, what their Prowess Gain'd, the Law declares
Is to themselves alone and to their Heirs:
No share of that goes back to the begettor;
But if the Son fights well, and Plunders better,   85
Like stout *Coranus*, his old shaking Sire
Does a Remembrance in his Will desire:
Inquisitive of Fights, and longs in vain
To find him in the Number of the Slain:
But still he lives, and rising by the War   90

75 Belt-Men, *97*: Belt-Men; *93* Cares;] Cares, *93 97*

Enjoyes his Gains, and has enough to spare:
For 'tis a Noble General's prudent part
To cherish Valour, and reward Desert:
Let him be dawb'd with Lace, live High, and Whore;
Sometimes be Lowzy, but be never Poor.   95

EXPLANATORY NOTES

1 *J*Uno was Mother to *Mars* the God of War: *Venus* was his Mistress.
2 *Camillus*; (who being first Banish'd, by his ungrateful Countrymen the
Romans, afterwards return'd, and freed them from the *Gaules*,) made a Law,
which prohibited the Souldiers from Quarrelling without the Camp, lest
upon that pretence, they might happen to be absent, when they ought to 5
be on Duty.   3 *This Cause is worthy him*, &c. The Poet Names a *Modenese*
Lawyer, whom he calls *Vagellius*; who was so Impudent that he wou'd
Plead any Cause, right or wrong, without Shame or Fear.   4 *Hob nail'd
Shoos*. The *Roman* Souldiers wore Plates of Iron under their Shoos, or stuck
them with Nails; as Countrymen do now.   5 Land-Marks were us'd 10
by the *Romans*, almost in the same manner, as now: And as we go once a
Year in Procession, about the Bounds of Parishes, and renew them, so they
offer'd Cakes upon the Stone, or Land-Mark.   6 The Courts of Judi-
cature were hung, and spread; as with us: But spread only before the
Hundred Judges were to sit, and judge Publick Causes, which were call'd 15
by *Lot*.   7 The *Roman* Souldiers had the Priviledge of making a Will,
in their Father's Life-time: Of what they had purchac'd in the Wars, as
being no part of their Patrimony. By this Will they had Power of excluding
their own Parents, and giving the Estate so gotten to whom they pleas'd.
Therefore, says the Poet, *Coranus*, (a Souldier Contemporary with *Juvenal*, 20
who had rais'd his Fortune by the Wars) was Courted by his own Father,
to make him his Heir.

THE SATIRES OF
AULUS PERSIUS FLACCUS

Sæpius in Libro memoratur Persius uno
Quam levis in tota Marsus Amazonide. Mart.

THE FIRST SATYR OF
AULUS PERSIUS FLACCUS

ARGUMENT OF THE PROLOGUE TO THE
FIRST SATYR

The Design of the Authour was to conceal his Name and Quality. He liv'd in the
dangerous Times of the Tyrant Nero; *and aims particularly at him, in most*
of his Satyrs. For which Reason, though he was a Roman *Knight, and of a*
plentiful Fortune, he wou'd appear in this Prologue, but a Beggarly Poet,
who Writes for Bread. After this, he breaks into the Business of the first Satyr: 5
which is, chiefly to decry the Poetry then in Fashion; and the Impudence of
those, who were endeavouring to pass their Stuff upon the World.

PROLOGUE

I NEVER did on cleft [1]*Pernassus* dream;
Nor taste the sacred *Heliconian* Stream:
Nor can remember when my Brain inspir'd,
Was, by the Muses, into madness fir'd.
My share in Pale [2]*Pyrene* I resign: 5
And claim no part in all the Mighty Nine.
Statues[3], with winding Ivy crown'd, belong
To nobler Poets, for a nobler Song:
Heedless of Verse, and hopeless of the Crown,
Scarce half a Wit, and more than half a Clown, 10
Before the[4] Shrine I lay my rugged Numbers down.
Who taught the Parrot Human Notes to try,
Or with a Voice endu'd the chatt'ring Pye?
'Twas witty Want, fierce Hunger to appease:
Want taught their Masters, and their Masters these. 15

Let Gain, that gilded Bait, be hung on high,
The hungry Witlings have it in their Eye:
Pies, Crows, and Daws, Poetick Presents bring:
You say they squeak; but they will swear they Sing.

ARGUMENT OF THE FIRST SATYR

I need not repeat, that the chief aim of the Authour is against bad Poets, in this
Satyr. But I must add, that he includes also bad Orators, who began at that
Time, (as Petronius *in the beginning of his Book tells us,) to enervate Manly*
Eloquence, by Tropes and Figures, ill plac'd, and worse apply'd. Amongst the
Poets, Persius *Covertly strikes at* Nero; *some of whose Verses he recites with*   5
Scorn and Indignation. He also takes notice of the Noblemen and their
abominable Poetry, who in the Luxury of their Fortune, set up for Wits, and
Judges. The Satyr is in Dialogue, betwixt the Authour and his Friend or
Monitor; who dissuades him from this dangerous attempt of exposing Great
Men. But Persius, *who is of a free Spirit, and has not forgotten that* Rome   10
was once a Commonwealth, breaks through all those difficulties, and boldly
Arraigns the false Judgment of the Age in which he Lives. The Reader may
observe that our Poet was a Stoick Philosopher; and that all his Moral
Sentences, both here, and in all the rest of his Satyrs, are drawn from the
Dogma's of that Sect.   15

THE FIRST SATYR

In Dialogue betwixt the Poet and his Friend, or Monitor

PERSIUS.

How anxious are our Cares; and yet how vain
The bent of our desires!

FRIEND.

        Thy Spleen contain:
For none will read thy Satyrs.

PERSIUS.

This to Me?

FRIEND.

None; or what's next to none; but two or three.   5
'Tis hard, I grant.

PERSIUS.

Tis nothing; I can bear
That paltry Scriblers have the Publick Ear:
That this vast universal Fool, the Town,
Shou'd cry up ¹*Labeo*'s Stuff, and cry me down.   10
They damn themselves; nor will my Muse descend
To clap with such, who Fools and Knaves commend:
Their Smiles and Censures are to me the same:
I care not what they praise, or what they blame.
In full Assemblies let the Crowd prevail: 15
I weigh no Merit by the common Scale.
The Conscience is the Test of ev'ry Mind;
Seek not thy self, without thy self, to find.
But where's that *Roman*?——Somewhat I wou'd say,
But Fear;——Let Fear, for once, to Truth give way.   20
Truth lends the Stoick Courage: when I look
On Humane Acts, and Read in Nature's Book,
From the first Pastimes of our Infant Age,
To elder Cares, and Man's severer Page;
When stern as Tutors, and as Uncles hard,   25
We lash the Pupil, and defraud the Ward:
Then, then I say——or wou'd say, if I durst—
But thus provok'd, I must speak out, or burst.

FRIEND.

Once more forbear.

PERSIUS.

I cannot rule my Spleen;   30
My scorn Rebels, and tickles me within.
    First, to begin at Home, our Authors write
In lonely Rooms, secur'd from publick sight;
Whether in Prose or Verse, 'tis all the same:
The Prose is Fustian, and the Numbers lame.   35
All Noise, and empty Pomp, a storm of words,
Lab'ring with sound, that little Sence affords.
They² Comb, and then they order ev'ry Hair: ⎫
A Gown, or White, or Scour'd to whiteness, wear: ⎬
A Birth-day Jewel bobbing at their Ear. ⎭   40
Next, gargle well their Throats; and thus prepar'd,
They mount, a God's Name, to be seen and heard
From their high Scaffold; with a Trumpet Cheek:

And Ogling all their Audience e're they speak.
The nauseous Nobles, ev'n the Chief of *Rome*,   45
With gaping Mouths to these Rehearsals come,
And pant with Pleasure, when some lusty line
The Marrow pierces, and invades the Chine.
At open fulsom Bawdry they rejoice;
And slimy Jests applaud with broken Voice.   50
Base Prostitute, thus dost thou gain thy Bread?
Thus dost thou feed their Ears, and thus art fed?
At his own filthy stuff he grins, and brays:
And gives the sign where he expects their praise.

   Why have I Learn'd, say'st thou, if thus confin'd,   55
I choak the Noble Vigour of my Mind?
Know, my wild³ Fig-Tree, which in Rocks is bred,
Will split the Quarry, and shoot out the Head.
Fine Fruits of Learning! Old Ambitious Fool,
Dar'st thou apply that Adage of the School;   60
As if 'tis nothing worth that lies conceal'd:
And *Science is not Science till Reveal'd?*
Oh, but 'tis Brave to be Admir'd, to see
The Crowd, with pointing Fingers, cry That's he:
That's he, whose wondrous Poem is become   65
A Lecture for the Noble Youth of *Rome*!
Who, by their Fathers, is at Feasts Renown'd:
And often quoted, when the Bowls go round.
Full gorg'd and flush'd, they wantonly Rehearse:
And add to Wine the Luxury of Verse.   70
One, clad in Purple, not to lose his time,
Eats, and recites some lamentable Rhime:
Some Senceless *Phyllis*, in a broken Note;
Snuffling at Nose, or croaking in his Throat:
Then, Graciously, the mellow Audience Nod: 75
Is not th' Immortal Authour made a God?
Are not his Manes blest, such Praise to have?
Lies not the Turf more lightly on his Grave?
And Roses (while his lowd Applause they Sing,)
Stand ready from his Sepulcher to spring?   80
   All these, you cry, but light Objections are;
Meer Malice, and you drive the Jest too far.
For does there Breath a Man, who can reject

A general Fame, and his own Lines neglect?
In[4] Cedar Tablets worthy to appear;   85
That need not Fish, or Franckincense to fear?
    Thou, whom I make the adverse part to bear,
Be answer'd thus: If I, by chance, succeed
In what I Write, (and that's a chance indeed;)
Know, I am not so stupid, or so hard,   90
Not to feel Praise, or Fames deserv'd Reward:
But this I cannot grant, that thy Applause
Is my Works ultimate, or only Cause.
Prudence can ne're propose so mean a prize:
For mark what Vanity within it lies.   95
Like *Labeo*'s Iliads; in whose Verse is found
Nothing but trifling care, and empty sound:
Such little Elegies as Nobles Write;
Who wou'd be Poets, in *Apollo*'s spight.
Them and their woful Works the Muse defies: 100
Products of[5] Citron Beds, and Golden Canopies.
To give thee all thy due, thou hast the Heart
To make a Supper, with a fine dessert;
And, to thy threed-bare Friend, a cast old Sute impart.
    Thus Brib'd, thou thus bespeak'st him, tell me Friend   105
(For I love Truth, nor can plain Speech offend,)
What says the World of me and of my Muse?
    The Poor dare nothing tell, but flatt'ring News:
But shall I speak? thy Verse is wretched Rhyme;
And all thy Labours are but loss of time.   110
Thy strutting Belly swells; thy Paunch is high;
Thou Writ'st not, but thou Pissest Poetry.
    All Authours, to their own defects, are blind;
Hadst thou but, [6]*Janus* like, a Face behind,
To see the People, what splay-Mouths they make;   115
To mark their Fingers, pointed at thy back;
Their Tongues loll'd out, a foot beyond the pitch,
When most a thirst, of an *Apulian* Bitch:
But Noble Scriblers are with Flatt'ry fed;
For none dare find their Faults, who Eat their Bread.   120
    To pass the Poets of Patrician Blood,
What is't the common Reader takes for good?
The Verse in fashion, is, when Numbers flow;

Soft without Sence, and without Spirit slow:
So smooth and equal, that no sight can find   125
The Rivet, where the polish'd piece was join'd.
So even all, with such a steady view,
As if he shut one Eye to level true.
Whether the Vulgar Vice his Satyr stings,
The Peoples Riots, or the Rage of Kings,   130
The gentle Poet is alike in all;
His Reader hopes no rise, and fears no fall.

    FRIEND.

Hourly we see, some Raw Pin-feather'd thing
Attempt to mount, and Fights, and Heroes sing;
Who, for false quantities, was whipt at School   135
But t'other day, and breaking Grammar Rule.
Whose trivial Art was never try'd, above
The bare description of a Native Grove:
Who knows not how to praise the Country store;
The Feasts, the Baskets, nor the fatted Bore;   140
Nor paint the flowry Fields, that paint themselves before:
Where *Romulus* was Bred, and ⁷*Quintius* Born,
Whose shining Plough-share was in Furrows worn,
Met by his trembling Wife, returning Home,
And Rustically Joy'd, as Chief of *Rome*:   145
She wip'd the Sweat, from the Dictator's Brow;
And, o're his Back, his Robe did rudely throw;
The Lictors bore, in State, their Lord's Triumphant Plough.
   Some, love to hear the Fustian Poet roar;
And some on Antiquated Authours pore: 150
Rummage for Sense; and think those only good
Who labour most, and least are understood.
When thou shalt see the Blear-Ey'd Fathers Teach
Their Sons, this harsh and mouldy sort of Speech;
Or others new affected ways to try,   155
Of wanton smoothness, Female Poetry;
One wou'd enquire, from whence this motley Stile
Did first our *Roman* Purity defile:
For our Old Dotards cannot keep their Seat;
But leap and catch at all that's obsolete.   160
   Others, by Foolish Ostentation led,

     The First Satyr. 141 before:] before. 93 97

When call'd before the Bar, to save their Head,
Bring trifling Tropes, instead of solid Sence:
And mind their Figures more than their Defence.
Are pleas'd to hear their thick-scull'd Judges cry   165
Well mov'd, oh finely said, and decently!
Theft, (says th' Accuser) to thy Charge I lay
O *Pedius*! What does gentle *Pedius* say?
Studious to please the Genius of the Times,
With Periods⁸, Points, and Tropes, he slurs his Crimes: 170
"He Robb'd not, but he Borrow'd from the Poor;
"And took but with intention to restore.
He lards with flourishes his long Harangue;
'Tis fine, say'st thou; what, to be Prais'd and Hang?
Effeminate *Roman*, shall such Stuff prevail   175
To tickle thee, and make thee wag thy Tail?
Say, shou'd a Shipwrack'd Saylor sing his woe,
Woud'st thou be mov'd to pity, or bestow
An Alms? What's more prepost'rous than to see
A Merry Beggar? Mirth in Misery?   180

    PERSIUS.
   He seems a Trap, for Charity, to lay:
And cons by Night, his Lesson for the day.

    FRIEND.
   But to raw Numbers, and unfinish'd Verse,
Sweet sound is added now, to make it Terse:
"'Tis tagg'd with Rhyme, like ⁹*Berecynthian Atys*,   185
"The mid part chimes with Art, which never flat is.
"The Dolphin brave, that cut the liquid Wave,
"Or He who in his line, can chine the long-rib'd *Apennine*.

    PERSIUS.
All this is Dogrel Stuff:

    FRIEND.
What if I bring   190
A Nobler Verse? ¹⁰*Arms and the Man I sing*.

    PERSIUS.
   Why name you *Virgil* with such Fops as these?
He's truly great; and must for ever please:
Not fierce, but awful is his Manly Page;
Bold is his Strength, but sober is his Rage.   195

174 what, 97: what 93

FRIEND.

What Poems think you soft? and to be read
With languishing regards, and bending Head?

PERSIUS.

"[11]Their crooked Horns the *Mimallonian* Crew
"With Blasts inspir'd: and *Bassaris* who slew
"The scornful Calf, with Sword advanc'd on high,   200
"Made from his Neck his haughty Head to fly.
"And *Mænas*, when with Ivy-bridles bound,
"She led the spotted Lynx, then *Evion* rung around;
"*Evion* from Woods and Floods repairing Ecchos sound.
Cou'd such rude Lines a *Roman* Mouth become,   205
Were any Manly Greatness left in *Rome*?
Mænas[12] and *Atys* in the Mouth were bred;
And never hatch'd within the lab'ring Head.
No Blood, from bitten Nails, those Poems drew:
But churn'd, like Spettle, from the Lips they flew.   210

FRIEND.

'Tis Fustian all; 'tis execrably bad:
But if they will be Fools, must you be mad?
Your Satyrs, let me tell you, are too fierce;
The Great will never bear so blunt a Verse.
Their Doors are barr'd against a bitter flout: 215
Snarl, if you please, but you shall snarl without.
Expect such Pay as railing Rhymes deserve,
Y'are in a very hopeful way to sterve.

PERSIUS.

Rather than so, uncensur'd let 'em be:
All, all is admirably well for me.   220
My harmless Rhyme shall scape the dire disgrace
Of Common-shores, and ev'ry pissing place.
Two[13] painted Serpents shall, on high, appear;
'Tis Holy Ground; you must not Urine here.
This shall be writ to fright the Fry away,   225
Who draw their little Bawbles, when they play.
[14]Yet old *Lucilius* never fear'd the times;
But lash'd the City, and dissected Crimes.
Mutius and *Lupus* both by Name he brought;
He mouth'd 'em, and betwixt his Grinders caught.   230
Unlike in method, with conceal'd design,

Did crafty *Horace* his low Numbers joyn:
And, with a sly insinuating Grace,
Laugh'd at his Friend, and look'd him in the Face:
Wou'd raise a Blush, where secret Vice he found;   235
And tickle, while he gently prob'd the Wound.
With seeming Innocence the Crowd beguil'd;
But made the desperate Passes, when he smil'd.

   Cou'd he do this, and is my Muse controll'd
By Servile Awe? Born free, and not be bold?   240
At least, I'll dig a hole within the Ground;
And to the trusty Earth commit the sound:
The Reeds shall tell you what the Poet fears,
King[15] Midas *has a Snout, and Asses Ears.*
This mean conceit, this darling Mystery,   245
Which thou think'st nothing, Friend thou shalt not buy:
Nor will I change, for all the flashy Wit,
That flatt'ring *Labeo* in his Iliads writ.

   [16]Thou, if there be a thou, in this base Town,
Who dares, with angry *Eupolis*, to frown;   250
He, who, with bold *Cratinus*, is inspir'd
With Zeal, and equal Indignation fir'd;
Who, at enormous Villany, turns pale,
And steers against it with a full-blown Sail,
Like *Aristophanes*; let him but smile   255
On this my honest Work, tho writ in homely Stile:
And if two Lines or three in all the Vein
Appear less drossy, read those Lines again.
May they perform their Author's just Intent;
Glow in thy Ears, and in thy Breast ferment.   260
But, from the reading of my Book and me,
Be far ye Foes of Virtuous Poverty:
Who[17] Fortune's fault upon the Poor can throw;
Point at the tatter'd Coat, and ragged Shooe;
Lay Nature's failings to their Charge; and jeer   265
The dim weak Eye-sight, when the Mind is clear.
When thou thy self, thus insolent in State,
Art but, perhaps, some Country Magistrate;
Whose Pow'r extends no farther than to speak
Big on the Bench, and scanty Weights to break.   270

   Him, also, for my Censor I disdain,

Who thinks all Science, as all Virtue vain:
Who counts Geometry, and Numbers, Toys:
And[18], with his Foot, the Sacred Dust destroys.
Whose Pleasure is to see a Strumpet tear   275
A Cynicks Beard, and lug him by the Hair.
Such, all the Morning, to the Pleadings run; ⎫
But, when the Bus'ness of the Day is done, ⎬
On Dice, and Drink, and Drabs, they spend their Afternoon. ⎭

EXPLANATORY NOTES ON THE PROLOGUE

1 *PErnassus*, and *Helicon*, were Hills Consecrated to the Muses; and the
suppos'd place of their abode. *Pernassus* was forked on the top; and from
Helicon ran a Stream; the Spring of which, was call'd the Muses Well.
2 *Pyrene*, a Fountain in *Corinth*; Consecrated also to the Muses.   3 Statues,
&c. The Statues of the Poets, were Crown'd with Ivy about their Brows.   5
4 Before the Shrine; that is, before the Shrine of *Apollo*, in his Temple at
Rome, call'd the *Palatine*.

EXPLANATORY NOTES ON THE FIRST SATYR

1 *LAbeo*'s Stuff. Nothing is remaining of *Atticus Labeo*, (so he is call'd by
the Learned *Casaubon*.) Nor is he mention'd by any other Poet, besides
Persius: *Casaubon*, from an old Commentator on *Persius*, says that he made 10
a very Foolish Translation of *Homer*'s *Iliads*.   2 *They Comb*, &c. He
describes a Poet preparing himself to Rehearse his Works in publick:
which was commonly perform'd in *August*. A Room was hir'd, or lent by
some Friend; a Scaffold was rais'd, and a Pulpit plac'd for him, who was
to hold forth; who borrow'd a new Gown, or scour'd his old one; and 15
Adorn'd his Ears with Jewels, *&c.*   3 *My wild Fig-Tree:* Trees of that
kind, grow wild in many parts of *Italy*; and make their way through
Rocks: Sometimes splitting the Tomb-stones.   4 The *Romans* wrote
on Cedar, and Cypress Tables, in regard of the duration of the Wood: Ill
Verses might justly be afraid of Franckincense; for the Papers in which 20
they were Written, were fit for nothing but to wrap it up.   5 *Products*
of Citron Beds, &c. Writings of Noblemen, whose Bedsteds were of the
Wood of *Citron*.   6 *Janus like*, &c. *Janus* was the first King of *Italy*; who
refug'd *Saturn*, when he was expell'd by his Son *Jupiter* from *Creet*; (or as
we now call it *Candia*.) From his Name, the first Month of the Year is call'd 25
January. He was Pictur'd with two Faces, one before, and one behind: As
regarding the past time, and the future. Some of the Mythologists, think

16 3] *Note om.* 97   18 4] *Notes 4, 5, 6 are disordered in 93 and 97*

he was *Noah*, for the Reason given above.   7 *Where* Romulus, *&c.* He
speaks of the Country in the foregoing Verses; the Praises of which, are
the most easie Theme for Poets; but which a bad Poet cannot Naturally 30
describe: Then he makes a digression, to *Romulus*, the first King of *Rome*,
who had a Rustical Education; and enlarges upon *Quintius Cincinnatus*, a
Roman Senator; who was call'd from the Plough, to be Dictator of *Rome*.
8 *In Periods*, &c. *Persius* here names Antitheses, or seeming Contradictions;
which in this place are meant for Rhetorical Flourishes, as I think, with 35
Casaubon.   9 *Berecynthian Atys*; or *Attin*, &c. Foolish Verses of *Nero*,
which the Poet repeats; and which cannot be Translated properly into
English.   10 *Arms and the Man*, &c. The first line of *Virgil's Æneids*.
11 *Their crooked Horns*, &c. Other Verses of *Nero*, that were meer bombast.
I only Note; that the Repetition of these and the former Verses of *Nero*, 40
might justly give the Poet a caution to conceal his Name.   12 *Mænas*
and *Atys*. Poems on the *Mænades*, who were Priestesses of *Bacchus*; and of
Atys, who made himself an Eunuch, to attend on the Sacrifices of *Cybele*,
call'd *Berecynthia* by the Poets; she was Mother of the Gods.   13 *Two
painted Serpents*, &c. Two Snakes twin'd with each other, were painted on 45
the Walls, by the Ancients, to shew the place was Holy.   14 *Yet old*
Lucilius, *&c. Lucilius* wrote long before *Horace*; who imitates his manner
of Satyr, but far excels him, in the design.   15 *King* Midas, *&c.* The
Story is vulgar, that *Midas* King of *Phrygia*, was made judge betwixt *Apollo*
and *Pan*, who was the best Musician; he gave the prize to *Pan*; and *Apollo* 50
in revenge gave him Asses Ears. He wore his Hair long to hide them: but
his Barber discovering them, and not daring to divulge the secret, dug
a hole in the ground, and whisper'd into it: the place was marshy; and
when the Reeds grew up, they repeated the words which were spoken by
the Barber. By *Midas*, the Poet meant *Nero*.   16 *Eupolis* and *Cratinus*, 55
as also *Aristophanes* mention'd afterwards, were all *Athenian* Poets; who
wrote that sort of Comedy, which was call'd the old Comedy, where the
People were Nam'd, who were Satyriz'd by those Authors.   17 *Who
Fortunes fault*, &c. The People of *Rome* in the time of *Persius*, were apt to
scorn the *Grecian* Philosophers, particularly the Cinicks and Stoicks, who 60
were the poorest of them.   18 *And with his foot*, &c. Arithmetick and
Geometry were Taught, on floors which were strew'd with dust, or sand;
in which the Numbers, and Diagrams were made and drawn, which they
might strike out again at Pleasure.

33 Dictator] Senator 97   35 for] *om.* 97

THE SECOND SATYR OF
AULUS PERSIUS FLACCUS

ARGUMENT OF THE SECOND SATYR

This Satyr, contains a most Grave, and Philosophical Argument, concerning
Prayers and Wishes. Undoubtedly, it gave occasion to Juvenal's *Tenth Satyr;*
And both of them had their Original from one of Plato's *Dialogues, call'd*
the second Alcibiades. *Our Author has induc'd it with great mastery of Art;*
by taking his rise, from the Birth-day of his Friend; on which occasions, 5
Prayers were made, and Sacrifices offer'd by the Native. Persius *commending*
first the Purity of his Friend's Vows, descends to the Impious and Immoral
Requests of others. The Satyr is divided into three parts. The first is the
Exordium to Macrinus, *which the Poet confines within the compass of four*
Verses. The second relates to the matter of the Prayers and Vows, and an 10
enumeration of those things, wherein Men commonly Sinn'd against right
Reason, and Offended in their Requests. The Third part consists, in shewing
the repugnancies of those Prayers and Wishes, to those of other Men, and
inconsistencies with themselves. He shews the Original of these Vows, and
sharply inveighs against them: And Lastly, not only corrects the false Opinion 15
of Mankind concerning them; but gives the True Doctrine of all Addresses
made to Heaven; and how they may be made acceptable to the Pow'rs above,
in excellent Precepts; and more worthy of a Christian than a Heathen.

THE SECOND SATYR

Dedicated to his Friend Plotius Macrinus *on his Birth-day*

L ET this auspicious Morning be exprest
   With a white[1] Stone, distinguish'd from the rest:
White as thy Fame, and as thy Honour clear;
And let new Joys attend, on thy new added year.
Indulge thy Genius, and o'reflow thy Soul,   5
Till thy Wit sparkle, like the chearful Bowl.
Pray; for thy Pray'rs the Test of Heav'n will bear;
Nor need'st thou take the Gods aside, to hear:
While others, ev'n the Mighty Men of *Rome*,

Argument. 10 *Verses. The 97: Verses, the 93*

Big swell'd with Mischief, to the Temples come;　　　10
And in low Murmurs, and with costly Smoak,
Heav'ns Help, to prosper their black Vows, invoke.
So boldly to the Gods Mankind reveal,
What from each other they, for shame, conceal.
　　Give me Good Fame, ye Pow'rs, and make me Just:　　15
Thus much the Rogue to Publick Ears will trust:
In private then:——When wilt thou, mighty *Jove*,
My Wealthy Uncle from this World remove?
Or——O thou Thund'rer's Son, great ²*Hercules*,
That once thy bounteous Deity wou'd please　　　20
To guide my Rake, upon the chinking sound
Of some vast Treasure, hidden under-ground!
　　Oh were my Pupil fairly knock'd o'th' head;
I shou'd possess th' Estate, if he were dead!
He's so far gone with Rickets, and with th' Evil,　　25
That one small Dose wou'd send him to the Devil.
　　This is my Neighbour *Nerius* his third Spouse,
Of whom in happy time he rids his House.
But my Eternal Wife!——Grant Heav'n I may
Survive to see the Fellow of this Day!　　　30
Thus, that thou may'st the better bring about
Thy Wishes, thou art wickedly devout:
In *Tiber* ducking thrice, by break of day,
To wash th' Obscenities of ³Night away.
But prithee tell me, ('tis a small Request)　　　35
With what ill thoughts of *Jove* art thou possest?
Wou'dst thou prefer him to some Man? Suppose
I dip'd among the worst, and *Staius* chose?
Which of the two wou'd thy wise Head declare
The trustier Tutor to an Orphan Heir?　　　40
Or, put it thus:——Unfold to *Staius*, straight,
What to *Jove*'s Ear thou didst impart of late:
He'll stare, and, O Good *Jupiter*! will cry;
Can'st thou indulge him in this Villany!
And think'st thou, *Jove* himself, with patience then,　　45
Can hear a Pray'r condemn'd by wicked men?
That, void of Care, he lolls supine in state,
And leaves his Bus'ness to be done by Fate?

Because his Thunder splits some burly Tree,
And is not darted at thy House and Thee?   50
Or that his Vengeance falls not at that time,
Just at the Perpetration of thy Crime;
And makes Thee a sad Object of our Eyes,
Fit for [4]*Ergenna*'s Pray'r, and Sacrifice?
What well-fed Off'ring to appease the God,   55
What pow'rful Present, to procure a Nod,
Hast thou in store? What Bribe hast thou prepar'd,
To pull him, thus unpunish'd, by the Beard?
    Our Superstitions with our life begin:
Th' Obscene old Grandam, or the next of Kin,   60
The New-born Infant from the Cradle takes,
And first of Spettle a [5]Lustration makes:
Then in the Spawl her Middle Finger dips,
Anoints the Temples, Forehead, and the Lips;
Pretending force of Magick to prevent,   65
By virtue of her nasty Excrement.
Then dandles him with many a mutter'd Pray'r;
That Heav'n wou'd make him some rich Miser's Heir;
Lucky to Ladies, and, in time, a King,
Which to insure, she adds a length of Navel-string.   70
But no fond Nurse is fit to make a Pray'r;
And *Jove*, if *Jove* be wise, will never hear;
Not tho' she prays in white, with lifted hands:
A Body made of Brass the Crone demands
For her lov'd Nurseling, strung with Nerves of Wire;   75
Tough to the last, and with no toil to tire:
Unconscionable Vows! which, when we use,
We teach the Gods, in Reason, to refuse.
Suppose They were indulgent to thy Wish;
Yet the fat Entrails, in the spatious Dish,   80
Wou'd stop the Grant: The very overcare,
And nauseous pomp, wou'd hinder half the Pray'r.
Thou hop'st with Sacrifice of Oxen slain,
To compass Wealth, and bribe the God of Gain,
To give thee Flocks and Herds, with large increase;   85
Fool! to expect 'em from a Bullock's Grease!
And think'st, that when the fatten'd Flames aspire,

51 at that *97*: at the *93*   65 Magick *97*: Witchcraft *93*

Thou see'st th' accomplishment of thy desire!
Now, now, my bearded Harvest gilds the plain,
The scanty Folds can scarce my Sheep contain,   } 90
And show'rs of Gold come pouring in amain!
Thus dreams the Wretch, and vainly thus dreams on,
Till his lank Purse declares his Money gone.

   Shou'd I present thee with rare figur'd Plate,
Or Gold as rich in Workmanship as Weight;   95
O how thy rising heart wou'd throb and beat,
And thy left side, with trembling pleasure, sweat!
Thou measur'st by thy self the Pow'rs Divine;
Thy Gods are burnish'd Gold, and Silver is their Shrine.
Thy puny Godlings of inferiour Race;   100
Whose humble Statues are content with Brass:
Shou'd some of These, in[6] Visions purg'd from fleam,
Foretel Events, or in a Morning Dream;
Ev'n those thou wou'dst in Veneration hold;
And, if not Faces, give 'em Beards of Gold.   105
The Priests, in Temples, now no longer care
For[7] *Saturn*'s Brass, or [8]*Numa*'s Earthen-ware;
Or Vestal Urns, in each Religious Rite:
This wicked Gold has put 'em all to flight.
O Souls, in whom no heav'nly Fire is found,   110
Fat Minds, and ever groveling on the ground!
We bring our Manners to the blest Abodes,
And think what pleases us, must please the Gods.
Of Oyl and *Casia* one th' Ingredients takes,
And, of the Mixture, a rich Ointment makes: 115
Another finds the way to dye in Grain:
And make[9] *Calabrian* Wool receive the *Tyrian* Stain:
Or from the Shells their Orient Treasure takes,
Or, for their golden Ore, in Rivers rakes;
Then melts the Mass: All these are Vanities!   120
Yet still some Profit from their Pains may rise:
But tell me, Priest, if I may be so bold,
What are the Gods the better for this Gold?
The Wretch that offers from his wealthy Store
These Presents, bribes the Pow'rs to give him more: 125
As[10] Maids to *Venus* offer Baby-Toys,

101 Brass:] Brass. *93 97*

To bless the Marriage-Bed with Girls and Boys.
But let us for the Gods a Gift prepare,
Which the Great Man's great Chargers cannot bear:
A Soul, where Laws both Humane and Divine,   130
In Practice more than Speculation shine:
A genuine Virtue, of a vigorous kind,
Pure in the last recesses of the Mind:
When with such Off'rings to the Gods I come;
A¹¹ Cake, thus giv'n, is worth a Hecatomb.   135

EXPLANATORY NOTES

1 *WHite Stone.* The *Romans* were us'd to mark their Fortunate Days, or any thing that luckily befell 'em, with a White Stone which they had from the Island *Creta*; and their Unfortunate with a Coal.   2 *Hercules* was thought to have the Key and Power of bestowing all hidden Treasure. 3 The Antients thought themselves tainted and polluted by Night it self, 5 as well as bad Dreams in the Night, and therefore purifi'd themselves by washing their Heads and Hands every Morning; which Custom the *Turks* observe to this day.   4 When any one was Thunderstruck, the Sooth-sayer (who is here call'd *Ergenna*) immediately repair'd to the place, to expiate the displeasure of the Gods, by sacrificing two Sheep.   5 The 10 Poet laughs at the superstitious Ceremonies which the Old Women made use of in their Lustration or Purification Days, when they nam'd their Children, which was done on the Eighth day to Females, and on the Ninth to Males.   6 *In Visions purg'd from Fleam,* &c. It was the Opinion both of *Grecians* and *Romans*, that the Gods, in Visions or Dreams, often reveal'd 15 to their Favourites a Cure for their Diseases, and sometimes those of others. Thus *Alexander* dreamt of an Herb which cur'd *Ptolomy.* These Gods were principally *Apollo* and *Esculapius*; but, in after times, the same Virtue and Good-will was attributed to *Isis* and *Osiris.* Which brings to my remembrance an odd passage in Sir *Tho. Brown's Religio Medici,* or in his 20 *Vulgar Errours*; the sense whereof is, *That we are beholding, for many of our Discoveries in Physick, to the courteous Revelation of Spirits.* By the Expression of *Visions purg'd from Phlegm,* our Author means such Dreams or Visions, as proceed not from Natural Causes, or Humours of the Body; but such as are sent from Heaven; and are, therefore, certain Remedies.   7 *For* 25 *Saturn's Brass,* &c. Brazen Vessels, in which the Publick Treasures of the *Romans* was kept: It may be the Poet means only old Vessels, which were all call'd Κρόνια; from the *Greek* Name of *Saturn.* Note also, that the *Roman* Treasury was in the Temple of *Saturn.*   8 *Numa's Earthen-ware.* Under

20 odd] old *97*   21 *Vulgar Errours 97*: vulgar Errours *93*   28 all] *om. 97*
28–29 Note . . . *Saturn.*] *om. 97*

Numa the second King of *Rome*, and for a long time after him, the Holy 30
Vessels for Sacrifice were of Earthen Ware; according to the Superstitious
Rites which were introduc'd by the same *Numa*: Tho afterwards, when
Memmius had taken *Corinth*, and *Paulus Emilius* had conquer'd *Macedonia*,
Luxury began amongst the *Romans*; and then their Utensils of Devotion
were of Gold and Silver, *&c*.   9 *And make* Calabrian *Wooll*, &c. The 35
Wooll of *Calabria* was of the finest sort in *Italy*; as *Juvenal* also tells us. The
Tyrian Stain, is the Purple Colour dy'd at *Tyrus*; and I suppose, but dare
not positively affirm, that the richest of that Dye was nearest our Crimson;
and not Scarlet, or that other Colour more approaching to the Blue. I have
not room to justifie my Conjecture.   10 *As Maids to* Venus, *&c*. Those 40
Baby-Toys were little Babies, or Poppets, as we call them; in Latin *Pupæ*;
which the Girls, when they came to the Age of puberty, or Child-bearing,
offer'd to *Venus*; as the Boys at Fourteen or Fifteen years of age offer'd their
Bullæ, or Bosses.   11 *A Cake thus given*, &c. A Cake of Barley, or course
Wheat-Meal, with the Bran in it: The meaning is, that God is pleas'd with 45
the pure and spotless heart of the Offerer; and not with the Riches of the
Offering. *Laberius* in the Fragments of his *Mimes*, has a Verse like this;
Puras, Deus, non plenas aspicit manus.—What I had forgotten before, in its
due place, I must here tell the Reader; That the first half of this Satyr was
translated by one of my Sons, now in *Italy*: But I thought so well of it, that 50
I let it pass without any Alteration.

THE THIRD SATYR OF
AULUS PERSIUS FLACCUS

ARGUMENT OF THE THIRD SATYR

Our Author has made two Satyrs concerning Study; the First and the Third:
The First related to Men; This to Young Students, whom he desir'd to be
Educated in the Stoick Philosophy: He himself sustains the Person of the
Master, or Præceptor, *in this admirable Satyr. Where he upbraids the*
Youth of Sloth, and Negligence in learning. Yet he begins with one Scholar 5
reproaching his Fellow Students with late rising to their Books. After which he
takes upon him the other part, of the Teacher. And addressing himself particu-
larly to Young Noblemen, tells them, That, by reason of their High Birth,
and the Great Possessions of their Fathers, they are careless of adorning their
Minds with Precepts of Moral Philosophy: And withall inculcates to them the 10
Miseries which will attend them in the whole Course of their Life, if they do

34 amongst] among 97

*not apply themselves betimes to the Knowledge of Virtue, and the End of their
Creation, which he pathetically insinuates to them.* The Title of this Satyr, in
some Ancient Manuscripts, was The Reproach of Idleness; *tho in others
of the Scholiasts, 'tis inscrib'd,* Against the Luxury and Vices of the Rich. 15
*In both of which the Intention of the Poet is pursu'd; but principally in the
former.*
I remember I translated this Satyr, when I was a *Kings-Scholar* at *West-
minster* School, for a *Thursday* Nights *Exercise*; and believe that it, and
many other of my *Exercises* of this nature, in *English Verse*, are still in 20
the Hands of my *Learned Master*, the Reverend Doctor *Busby*.

THE THIRD SATYR

I s this thy daily course? the glaring Sun
  Breaks in at ev'ry Chink: The Cattle run
To Shades, and Noon-tide Rays of Summer shun.
Yet plung'd in Sloth we lye; and snore supine,
As fill'd with Fumes of undigested Wine.   5
   This grave Advice some sober Student bears;
And loudly rings it in his Fellows Ears.
The yawning Youth, scarce half awake, essays
His lazy Limbs and dozy Head to raise:
Then rubs his gummy Eyes, and scrubs his Pate;   10
And cries I thought it had not been so late:
My Cloaths, make haste: why when! if none be near,
He mutters first, and then begins to swear:
And brays aloud, with a more clam'rous note,
Than an *Arcadian* Ass can stretch his throat.   15
   With much ado, his Book before him laid,
And[1] Parchment with the smoother side display'd;
He takes the Papers; lays 'em down agen;
And, with unwilling Fingers, tries the Pen:
Some peevish quarrel straight he strives to pick;   20
His Quill writes double, or his Ink's too thick;
Infuse more water; now 'tis grown so thin
It sinks, nor can the Character be seen.
   O Wretch, and still more wretched ev'ry day!
Are Mortals born to sleep their lives away!   25
Go back to what thy Infancy began,

Thou who wert never meant to be a Man:
Eat Pap and Spoon-meat; for thy Gugaws cry;
Be sullen, and refuse the Lullaby.
No more accuse thy Pen; but charge the Crime 30
On Native Sloth, and negligence of time.
Think'st thou thy Master, or thy Friends to cheat?
Fool, 'tis thy self, and that's a worse deceit.
Beware the publick Laughter of the Town;
Thou spring'st a Leak already in thy Crown. 35
A flaw is in thy ill-bak'd Vessel found;
'Tis hollow, and returns a jarring sound.

   Yet, thy moist Clay is pliant to Command;
Unwrought, and easie to the Potter's hand:
Now take the Mold; now bend thy Mind to feel 40
The first sharp Motions of the Forming Wheel.

   But thou hast Land; a Country Seat, secure
By a just Title; costly Furniture;
A² Fuming-Pan thy *Lares* to appease:
What need of Learning when a Man's at ease? 45
If this be not enough to swell thy Soul,
Then please thy Pride, and search the Herald's Roll:
Where thou shalt find thy famous Pedigree
Drawn³ from the Root of some old *Thuscan* Tree;
And thou, a Thousand, off, a Fool of long Degree. 50
Who, clad in⁴ Purple, canst thy Censor greet;
And, loudly, call him Cousin, in the Street.

   Such Pageantry be to the People shown:
There boast thy Horse's Trappings, and thy own:
I know thee to thy Bottom; from within 55
Thy shallow Centre, to thy outmost Skin:
Dost thou not blush to live so like a Beast;
So trim, so dissolute, so loosely drest?

   But, 'tis in vain: The Wretch is drench'd too deep;
His Soul is stupid, and his Heart asleep: 60
Fatten'd in Vice; so callous, and so gross;
He sins, and sees not; senseless of his Loss.
Down goes the Wretch at once; unskill'd to swim;
Hopeless to bubble up, and reach the Water's Brim.

   Great Father of the Gods, when, for our Crimes, 65
Thou send'st some heavy Judgment on the Times;

Some Tyrant-King, the Terrour of his Age,
The Type, and true Vicegerent of thy Rage;
Thus punish him: Set Virtue in his Sight,
With all her Charms adorn'd; with all her Graces bright: 70
But set her distant; make him pale to see
His Gains out-weigh'd by lost Felicity!
    Sicilian[5] Tortures, and the Brazen Bull,
Are Emblems, rather than express the Full
Of what he feels: Yet what he fears, is more: 75
The[6] Wretch, who sitting at his plenteous Board,
Look'd up, and view'd on high the pointed Sword
Hang o'er his Head, and hanging by a Twine,
Did with less Dread, and more securely Dine.
Ev'n in his Sleep he starts, and fears the Knife;   80
And, trembling, in his Arms, takes his Accomplice Wife:
Down, down he goes; and from his Darling-Friend
Conceals the Woes his guilty Dreams portend.
    When I was young, I, like a lazy Fool,
Wou'd blear my Eyes with Oyl, to stay from School: 85
Averse from Pains, and loath to learn the Part
Of *Cato*, dying with a dauntless Heart:
Though much, my Master, that stern Virtue prais'd,
Which, o'er the Vanquisher, the Vanquish'd rais'd:
And my pleas'd Father came, with Pride, to see   90
His Boy defend the *Roman* Liberty.
    But then my Study was to Cog the Dice
And dext'rously to throw the lucky Sice:
To shun Ames-Ace, that swept my Stakes away;
And watch the Box, for fear they shou'd convey   } 95
False Bones, and put upon me in the Play.
Careful, besides, the Whirling Top to whip;
And drive her giddy, till she fell asleep.
    Thy Years are ripe, nor art thou yet to learn
What's Good or Ill, and both their Ends discern: 100
Thou[7], in the Stoick Porch, severely bred,
Hast heard the *Dogma's* of great *Zeno* read:
Where on the Walls, by [8]*Polignotus* Hand,
The Conquer'd *Medians* in Trunk-Breeches stand.
Where the Shorn Youth, to Midnight-Lectures rise,   105

The Third Satyr. 72 out-weigh'd] out-vy'd 97

Rous'd from their Slumbers, to be early wise:
Where the coarse Cake, and homely Husks of Beans,
From pamp'ring Riot the young Stomach weans:
And⁹, where the *Samian* Y, directs thy Steps to run,
To Virtue's Narrow Steep, and Broad-way Vice to shun.   110
And yet thou snor'st; thou draw'st thy Drunken Breath,
Sour with Debauch; and sleep'st the Sleep of Death.
Thy Chaps are fallen, and thy Frame dis-joyn'd:
Thy Body as dissolv'd as is thy Mind.

    Hast thou not, yet, propos'd some certain End,   115
To which thy Life, thy ev'ry Act may tend?
Hast thou no Mark, at which to bend thy Bow;
Or like a Boy pursu'st the Carrion Crow
With Pellets, and with Stones from Tree to Tree;
A fruitless Toil; and liv'st *Extempore*?   120
Watch the Disease in time: For, when within
The Dropsy rages, and extends the Skin,
In vain for *Hellebore* the patient Cries;
And Fees the Doctor; but too late is wise:
Too late, for Cure, he proffers half his Wealth: 125
Conquest and *Guibbons* cannot give him Health.

    Learn Wretches; learn the Motions of the Mind:
Why you were made, for what you were design'd;
And the great Moral End of Humane Kind.
Study thy self: What Rank, or what degree   130
The wise Creator has ordain'd for thee:
And all the Offices of that Estate
Perform; and with thy Prudence guide thy Fate.

    Pray justly, to be heard: Nor more desire
Than what the Decencies of Life require.   135
Learn what thou ow'st thy Country, and thy Friend;
What's requisite to spare, and what to spend:
Learn this; and after, envy not the store
Of the Greaz'd Advocate, that Grinds the Poor:
Fat¹⁰ Fees from the defended *Umbrian* draws;   140
And only gains the wealthy Clients Cause.
To whom the *Marsians*¹¹ more Provision send,
Than he and all his Family can spend.
Gammons that give a relish to the taste;

119 Tree;] Tree: *93 97*   120 Toil;] Toil, *93 97*

And potted Fowl, and Fish come in so fast,   145
That, e're the first is out, the second stinks:
And mouldy Mother gathers on the brinks.
    But, here, some Captain of the Land, or Fleet,
Stout of his hands, but of a Souldiers Wit;
Cries, I have sense to serve my turn, in store;   150
And he's a Rascal who pretends to more.
Dammee, what-e're those Book-learn'd Blockheads say,
Solon's the veriest Fool in all the Play.
Top-heavy Drones, and always looking down,
(As over-Ballasted within the Crown!)   155
Mutt'ring, betwixt their Lips, some Mystick thing,
Which, well examin'd, is flat Conjuring.
Meer Madmen's Dreams: For, what the Schools have taught ⎫
Is only this, that nothing can be brought   ⎬
From nothing; and what is, can ne're be turn'd to nought. ⎭   160
Is it for this they study? to grow pale,
And miss the Pleasures of a Glorious Meal;
For this, in Rags accouter'd, they are seen,
And made the May-game of the publick spleen?
    Proceed, my Friend, and rail: But hear me tell   165
A story, which is just thy Parallel.
    A Spark, like thee, of the Man-killing Trade,
Fell sick; and thus to his Physician said;
Methinks I am not right in ev'ry part;
I feel a kind of trembling at my Heart: 170
My Pulse unequal, and my Breath is strong;
Besides, a filthy Fur upon my Tongue.
The Doctor heard him, exercis'd his skill;
And, after, bad him for four Days be still.
Three Days he took good Counsel, and began   175
To mend, and look like a recov'ring Man:
The fourth, he cou'd not hold from Drink; but sends
His Boy to one of his old trusty Friends:
Adjuring him, by all the Pow'rs Divine,   ⎫
To pity his Distress, who cou'd not Dine   ⎬ 180
Without a Flaggon of his healing Wine.   ⎭
He drinks a swilling Draught: And, lin'd within,
Will supple, in the Bath, his outward skin:
Whom shou'd he find, but his Physician there;

Who, wisely, bad him once again beware.   185
Sir, you look Wan, you hardly draw your Breath;
Drinking is Dangerous, and the Bath is Death:
'Tis Nothing, says the Fool; but, says the Friend,
This Nothing, Sir, will bring you to your end.
Do I not see your Dropsy-Belly swell?   190
Your yellow Skin?——No more of that; I'm well.
I have already Buried two or three
That stood betwixt a fair Estate and me,
And, Doctor, I may live to Bury thee.
Thou tell'st me, I look ill; and thou look'st worse: 195
I've done, says the Physician; take your Course.
The laughing Sot, like all unthinking Men,
Baths and gets Drunk; then Baths and Drinks again:
His Throat half throtled with Corrupted Fleam,
And breathing through his Jaws a belching steam: 200
Amidst his Cups with fainting shiv'ring seiz'd,
His Limbs dis-jointed, and all o're diseas'd,
His hand refuses to sustain the bowl:
And his Teeth chatter, and his Eye-balls rowl:
Till, with his Meat; he vomits out his Soul: 205
Then, Trumpets, Torches, and a tedious Crew
Of Hireling Mourners, for his Funeral due.
Our Dear departed Brother lies in State;
His Heels stretch'd out[12], and pointing to the Gate:
And Slaves, now manumis'd, on their dead Master wait.   210
They hoyst him on the Bier, and deal the Dole;
And there's an end of a Luxurious Fool.
    But, what's thy fulsom Parable to me?
My Body is from all Diseases free:
My temperate Pulse does regularly beat;   215
Feel, and be satisfi'd, my Hands and Feet:
These are not cold, nor those Opprest with heat.
Or lay thy hand upon my Naked Heart,
And thou shalt find me Hale in ev'ry part.
    I grant this true: But, still, the deadly wound   220
Is in thy Soul: 'Tis there thou art not sound:
Say, when thou seest a heap of tempting Gold,
Or a more tempting Harlot do'st behold;
Then, when she casts on thee a sidelong glance,

Then try thy Heart; and tell me if it Dance.   225
Some Course cold Salade is before thee set: ⎫
Bread, with the Bran perhaps, and broken Meat;   ⎬
Fall on, and try thy Appetite to eat.   ⎭
These are not Dishes for thy dainty Tooth:
What, hast thou got an Ulcer in thy Mouth?   230
Why stand'st thou picking? Is thy Pallat sore?
That Bete, and Radishes will make thee roar?
Such is th' unequal Temper of thy Mind;
Thy Passions, in extreams, and unconfin'd:
Thy Hair so bristles with unmanly Fears;   235
As Fields of Corn, that rise in bearded Ears.
And, when thy Cheeks with flushing Fury glow,   ⎫
The rage of boyling Caldrons is more slow;   ⎬
When fed with fuel and with flames below.   ⎭
With foam upon thy Lips, and sparkling Eyes,   240
Thou say'st, and do'st, in such outrageous wise;
That mad *Orestes*[13], if he saw the show,
Wou'd swear thou wert the Madder of the Two.

EXPLANATORY NOTES

1 *AND Parchment*, &c. The Students us'd to write their Notes on Parchments; the inside, on which they wrote, was white; the other side was Hairy: And commonly yellow. *Quintilian* reproves this Custom, and advises rather Table-books, lin'd with Wax, and a Stile, like that we use in our Vellum Table-books, as more easie.   2 *A Fumeing-Pan*, &c. Before 5 eating, it was Customary, to cut off some part of the Meat; which was first put into a Pan, or little Dish; then into the Fire; as an Offering to the Household Gods: This they called a *Libation*.   3 *Drawn from the Root*, &c. The *Thuscans* were accounted of most Ancient Nobility. *Horace* observes this, in most of his Compliments to *Mecenas*; who was deriv'd 10 from the Old Kings of *Tuscany*, now the Dominion of the Great Duke. 4 *Who Clad in Purple*, &c. The *Roman* Knights, attir'd in the Robe call'd *Trabea*, were Summon'd by the Censor, to appear before him; and to Salute him, in passing by, as their Names were call'd over. They led their Horses in their hand. See more of this, in *Pompey's* Life, written by 15 *Plutarch*.   5 *Sicilian Tortures*, &c. Some of the *Sicilian* Kings were so great Tyrants; that the Name is become Proverbial. The Brazen Bull is a known Story of *Phalaris*, one of those Tyrants; who when *Perillus*, a famous Artist, had presented him with a Bull of that Metal hollow'd

within, which when the Condemn'd Person was inclos'd in it, wou'd render 20
the sound of a Bull's roaring, caus'd the Workman to make the first Experiment. *Docuitq; suum mugire Juvencum.* 6 *The Wretch who sitting,* &c.
He alludes to the Story of *Damocles,* a Flatterer of one of those *Sicilian*
Tyrants, namely *Dionysius.* *Damocles* had infinitely extoll'd the Happiness
of *Kings. Dionysius* to convince him of the contrary, invited him to a Feast; 25
and Cloath'd him in Purple: But caus'd a Sword, with the point downward, to be hung over his Head, by a Silken Twine; which, when he perceiv'd, he cou'd Eat nothing of the Delicates that were set before him.
7 *Thou, in the Stoick Porch,* &c. The Stoicks taught their Philosophy, under
a *Porticus,* to secure their Scholars from the Weather. *Zeno* was the Chief 30
of that Sect. 8 *Polygnotus,* A Famous Painter; who drew the Pictures
of the *Medes* and *Persians,* Conquer'd by *Miltiades, Themistocles,* and other
Athenian Captains, on the Walls of the *Portico,* in their Natural Habits.
9 *And where the Samian Y,* &c. *Pithagoras* of *Samos,* made the allusion of the
Y, or Greek Upsilon, to Vice and Virtue. One side of the Letter being 35
broad, Characters Vice, to which the ascent is wide and easie. The other
side represents Virtue; to which the Passage is strait, and difficult: And
perhaps our Saviour might also allude to this, in those Noted words of the
Evangelist, *The way to Heaven,* &c. 10 *Fat Fees,* &c. *Casaubon* here
Notes, that among all the *Romans,* who were brought up to Learning, few 40
besides the Orators, or Lawyers, grew Rich. 11 The *Martians* and
Umbrians, were the most Plentiful, of all the Provinces in *Italy.* 12 *His*
Heels stretch'd out, &c. The *Romans* were Buried without the City; for which
Reason the Poet says, that the Dead man's heels were stretch'd out
towards the Gate. 13 *That Mad Orestes. Orestes* was Son to *Agamemnon* 45
and *Clitemnestra. Agamemnon,* at his return from the *Trojan* Wars, was slain
by *Ægysthus,* the Adulterer of *Clitemnestra. Orestes* to revenge his Fathers
Death, slew both *Ægysthus* and his Mother: For which he was punish'd
with Madness, by the *Eumenides,* or Furies, who continually haunted him.

THE FOURTH SATYR OF
AULUS PERSIUS FLACCUS

ARGUMENT OF THE FOURTH SATYR

Our Author, living in the time of Nero, *was Contemporary and Friend to the*
Noble Poet Lucan; *both of them, were sufficiently sensible, with all Good Men,*
how Unskilfully he manag'd the Commonwealth: And perhaps might guess at
his future Tyranny, by some Passages, during the latter part of his first five

years; tho he broke not out, into his greater Excesses, while he was restrain'd 5
by the Counsels and Authority of Seneca. Lucan *has not spar'd him in the*
Poem of his Pharsalia: *For his very Complement look'd asquint, as well as*
Nero. Persius *has been bolder, but with Caution likewise. For here, in the*
Person of Young Alcibiades, *he arraigns his Ambition of meddling with*
State Affairs, without Judgment or Experience. 'Tis probable that he makes 10
Seneca *in this Satyr, sustain the part of* Socrates, *under a borrow'd Name.*
And, withal, discovers some secret Vices of Nero, *concerning his Lust, his*
Drunkenness and his Effeminacy, which had not yet arriv'd to publick Notice.
He also reprehends the Flattery of his Courtiers, who endeavour'd to make all
his Vices pass for Virtues. Covetousness was undoubtedly none of his Faults; 15
but it is here describ'd as a Veyl cast over the True Meaning of the Poet, which
was to Satyrise his Prodigality, and Voluptuousness; to which he makes a transi-
tion. I find no Instance in History, of that Emperour's being a Pathique; *tho*
Persius *seems to brand him with it. From the two Dialogues of* Plato, *both*
call'd Alcibiades, *the Poet took the Arguments, of the Second and Third* 20
Satyr, but he inverted the order of them: For the third Satyr is taken from the
first of those Dialogues.

The Commentatours *before* Casaubon, *were ignorant of our Author's secret*
meaning; and thought he had only written against Young Noblemen in General,
who were too forward in aspiring to publick Magistracy: But this Excellent 25
Scholiast has unravell'd the whole Mystery: And made it apparent, that the
Sting of this Satyr, was particularly aim'd at Nero.

THE FOURTH SATYR

W HO-E'RE thou art, whose forward years are bent
    On State-Affairs, to guide the Government;
Hear, first, what [1]*Socrates*, of old, has said
To the lov'd Youth, whom he, at *Athens*, bred.
    Tell me, thou Pupil to great [2]*Pericles*,   5
Our second hope, my *Alcibiades*,
What are the grounds, from whence thou dost prepare
To undertake, so young, so vast a Care?
Perhaps thy Wit: (A Chance not often heard,
That Parts and Prudence, shou'd prevent the Beard:)   10

Argument. 5 greater] great 97   27 this 97: the 93
The Fourth Satyr. 5 Pupil 97: Pupil, 93

Tis seldom seen, that Senators so young,
Know when to speak, and when to hold their Tongue.
Sure thou art born to some peculiar Fate;
When the mad People rise against the State,
To look them into Duty: And command   15
An awful Silence with thy lifted hand.
Then to bespeak 'em thus: *Athenians*, know
Against right Reason all your Counsels go;
This is not Fair; nor Profitable that;
Nor t'other Question Proper for Debate.   20
But thou, no doubt, can'st set the business right;
And give each Argument its proper weight:
Know'st, with an equal hand, to hold the Scale:
See'st where the Reasons pinch, and where they fail:
And where Exceptions, o're the general Rule, prevail.   25
And, taught by Inspiration, in a trice,
Can'st³ punish Crimes, and brand offending Vice.

  Leave; leave to fathom such high points as these;
Nor be ambitious, e're thy time, to please:
Unseasonably Wise, till Age, and Cares,   30
Have form'd thy Soul, to manage Great Affairs.
Thy Face, thy Shape, thy Outside, are but vain:
Thou hast not strength such Labours to sustain:
Drink⁴ *Hellebore*, my Boy, drink deep, and purge thy brain.
  What aim'st thou at, and whither tends thy Care,   35
In what thy utmost Good? Delicious Fare;
And, then, to Sun thy self in open air.

  Hold, hold; are all thy empty Wishes such?
A good old Woman wou'd have said as much.
But thou art nobly born; 'tis true; go boast   40
Thy Pedigree, the thing thou valu'st most:
Besides thou art a Beau: What's that, my Child?
A Fop, well drest, extravagant, and wild:
She, that cries Herbs, has less impertinence;
And, in her Calling, more of common sense.   45

  None, none descends into himself; to find
The secret Imperfections of his Mind:
But ev'ry one is Eagle-ey'd, to see
Another's Faults, and his Deformity.

11 **seen,** that] seen that, *93*: seen that *97*   28 points] *Crimes 97*

Say, do'st thou know[5] *Vectidius*? Who, the Wretch   50
Whose Lands beyond the *Sabines* largely stretch;
Cover the Country; that a sailing Kite
Can scarce o'reflye 'em, in a day and night?
Him, do'st thou mean, who, spight of all his store,
Is ever Craving, and will still be Poor?   55
Who cheats for Half-pence, and who doffs his Coat,
To save a Farthing in a Ferry-Boat?
Ever a Glutton, at another's Cost,
But in whose Kitchin dwells perpetual Frost?
Who eats and drinks with his Domestick Slaves;   60
A verier Hind than any of his Knaves?
Born, with the Curse and Anger of the Gods,
And that indulgent Genius he defrauds?
At Harvest-home, and on the Sheering-Day,
When he shou'd[6] Thanks to *Pan* and *Pales* pay,   65
And better *Ceres*; trembling to approach
The little Barrel, which he fears to broach:
He 'says the Wimble, often draws it back,
And deals to thirsty Servants but a smack.
To a short Meal, he makes a tedious Grace,   70
Before the Barly Pudding comes in place:
Then, bids fall on; himself, for saving Charges,
A peel'd slic'd Onyon eats, and tipples Verjuice.
    Thus fares the Drudge: But thou, whose life's a Dream
Of lazy Pleasures, tak'st a worse Extream.   75
Tis all thy bus'ness, bus'ness how to shun;
To bask thy naked Body in the Sun;
Suppling thy stiffen'd Joints with fragrant Oyl:
Then, in thy spacious Garden, walk a while,
To suck the Moisture up, and soak it in: 80
And this, thou think'st, but vainly think'st, unseen.
But, know, thou art observ'd: And there are those
Who, if they durst, wou'd all thy secret sins expose.
The[7] depilation of thy modest part:
Thy *Catamite*, the Darling of thy Heart,   }   85
His Engine-hand, and ev'ry leuder Art.
When, prone to bear, and patient to receive,

---

76 how] now 97   77 bask 97: bas'k 93   naked Body in the] Body in the
naked 97

Thou tak'st the pleasure, which thou canst not give.
With odorous Oyl, thy head and hair are sleek:
And then thou kemb'st the Tuzzes on thy Cheek: 90
Of these thy Barbers take a costly care;
While thy salt Tail is overgrown with hair.
Not all thy Pincers, nor unmanly Arts,
Can smooth the roughness of thy shameful parts.
Not[8] five, the strongest that the *Circus* breeds,   95
From the rank Soil can root those wicked Weeds:
Tho, suppled first with Soap, to ease thy pain,
The stubborn Fern springs up, and sprouts again.
   Thus others we with Defamations wound,
While they stab us; and so the Jest goes round.   100
Vain are thy Hopes, to scape censorious Eyes;
Truth will appear, through all the thin Disguise:
Thou hast an Ulcer, which no Leach can heal;
Tho thy broad Shoulder-belt the Wound conceal.
Say thou art sound and hale in ev'ry part;   105
We know, we know thee rotten at thy heart.
We know thee sullen, impotent, and proud:
Nor canst thou cheat thy[9] Nerve, who cheat'st the Croud.
   But, when they praise me, in the Neighbourhood,
When the pleas'd People take me for a God,   110
Shall I refuse their Incense? Not receive
The loud Applauses which the Vulgar give?
   If thou do'st Wealth, with longing Eyes, behold;
And, greedily, art gaping after Gold;
If some alluring Girl, in gliding by,   115
Shall tip the wink, with a lascivious Eye,
And thou, with a consenting glance, reply;
If thou, thy own Sollicitor become,
And bid'st arise the lumpish *Pendulum*:
If thy lewd Lust provokes an empty storm,   120
And prompts to more than Nature can perform;
If, with thy[10] Guards, thou scour'st the Streets by night,
And do'st in Murthers, Rapes, and Spoils delight;
Please not thy self, the flatt'ring Crowd to hear;
Tis fulsom stuff, to feed thy itching Ear.   125
Reject the nauseous Praises of the Times:

            97 suppled] supple 97

Give thy base Poets back their cobbled Rhymes:
Survey thy[11] Soul, not what thou do'st appear,
But what thou art; and find the Beggar there.

EXPLANATORY NOTES

1 *SOcrates*, whom the Oracle of *Delphos* prais'd, as the wisest Man of his
Age, liv'd in the time of the *Peloponnesian* War. He, finding the Uncertainty
of Natural Philosophy, appli'd himself wholly to the Moral. He was
Master to *Xenophon* and *Plato*; and to many of the *Athenian* Young Noblemen; amongst the rest, to *Alcibiades*, the most lovely Youth then liv- 5
ing; Afterwards a Famous Captain; whose Life is written by *Plutarch*.
2 *Pericles* was Tutor, or rather Overseer of the Will of *Clinias*, Father to
Alcibiades. While *Pericles* liv'd, who was a wise Man, and an Excellent
Orator, as well as a Great General, the *Athenians* had the better of the War.
3 *Can'st punish Crimes*, &c. That is by Death. When the Judges wou'd Con- 10
demn a Malefactor, they cast their Votes into an Urn; as according to the
Modern Custom, a Ballotting-Box. If the Suffrages were mark'd with Θ
they signify'd the Sentence of Death to the Offendor; as, being the first
Letter of Θάνατος, which in English is Death.   4 *Drink Hellebore*, &c.
The Poet wou'd say; that such an ignorant Young Man, as he here 15
describes, is fitter to be govern'd himself, than to govern others. He
therefore advises him to drink *Hellebore*, which purges the Brain.   5 *Say,
dost thou know* Vectidius, *&c.* The Name of *Vectidius* is here us'd Appella-
tively to signifie any Rich Covetous Man; though perhaps there might
be a Man of that Name then living. I have Translated this passage Para- 20
phrastically, and loosely: And leave it for those to look on, who are not unlike the Picture.   6 *When He shou'd thanks*, &c. *Pan* the God of Shepherds,
and *Pales* the Goddess presiding over rural Affairs; whom *Virgil* invocates
in the beginning of his Second *Georgique*. I give the Epithete of *Better*, to
Ceres; because she first taught the Use of Corn for Bread, as the Poets tell 25
us. Men, in the first rude Ages, feeding only on Acorns, or Mast, instead
of Bread.   7 *The depilation of thy modest part*, &c. Our Author here taxes
Nero, covertly, with that effeminate Custom, now us'd in *Italy*, and
especially by *Harlots*, of smoothing their Bellies, and taking off the Hairs,
which grow about their Secrets. In *Nero's* time they were pull'd off with 30
Pincers; but now they use a Past, which apply'd to those Parts, when it
is remov'd, carries away with it those Excrescencies.   8 *Not five the
Strongest*, &c. The Learned *Holiday*, (who has made us amends for his bad
Poetry in this and the rest of these Satyrs, with his excellent Illustrations,)
here tells us, from good Authority, that the Number Five, does not allude 35

to the *Five Fingers* of one Man, who us'd them all, in taking off the Hairs
before mention'd; but to *Five Strong Men*, such as were skillful in the five
robust Exercises, then in Practice at *Rome*, and were perform'd in the
Circus, or publick place, ordain'd for them. These five he reckons up, in
this manner. 1. The *Cæstus*, or Whirlbatts, describ'd by *Virgil*, in his fifth 40
Eneid: And this was the most dangerous of all the rest. The 2d was the
Foot-race, The Third the *Discus*; like the throwing a weighty Ball; a sport
now us'd in *Cornwall*, and other parts of *England*: We may see it daily
practis'd in *Red-Lyon-Fields*. The Fourth was the *Saltus*, or Leaping: And
the Fifth *Wrastling Naked*, and besmear'd with Oyl. They who were Prac- 45
tis'd in these five Manly Exercises, were call'd Πένταθλοι.　　9 *Thy*
Nerve, &c. That is, thou can'st not deceive thy Obscene part, which is
weak, or Impotent, tho thou mak'st Ostentation of thy Performances with
Women.　　10 *If with thy Guards*, &c. *Persius* durst not have been so bold
with *Nero*, as I dare now; and therefore there is only an intimation of that 50
in him, which I publickly speak: I mean of *Nero's* walking the Streets by
Night, in disguise; and committing all sorts of Outrages: For which he was
sometimes well beaten.　　11 *Survey thy Soul*, &c. That is, look into thy
self; and examine thy own Conscience; there thou shalt find, that how
wealthy soever thou appear'st to the World, yet thou art but a Beggar; 55
because thou art destitute of all Virtues; which are the Riches of the Soul.
This also was a Paradox of the Stoick School.

THE FIFTH SATYR OF
AULUS PERSIUS FLACCUS

ARGUMENT OF THE FIFTH SATYR

The judicious Casaubon, *in his Proem to this Satyr tells us, that* Aristophanes
the Grammarian, being ask'd, what Poem of Archilochus *his Iambicks he*
preferr'd before the rest, answer'd, the longest. His answer may justly be
apply'd to this Fifth Satyr; which, being of a greater length than any of the
rest, is also, by far, the most instructive. For this Reason, I have selected it 5
from all the others; and inscrib'd it to my Learned Master Doctor Busby; *to*
whom I am not only oblig'd my self, for the best part of my own Education,
and that of my two Sons; but have also receiv'd from him the first and truest
Taste of Persius. *May he be pleas'd to find in this Translation, the Gratitude,*
or at least some small Acknowledgment of his unworthy Scholar, at the dis- 10
tance of 42 *Years, from the time when I departed from under his Tuition.*

45 were] om. 97　　54 Conscience; 97: Conscience, 93

This Satyr consists of two distinct Parts: The first contains the Praises of the
Stoick Philosopher Cornutus, *Master and Tutor to our* Persius. *It also*
declares the Love and Piety of Persius, *to his well-deserving Master: And the*
Mutual Friendship which continu'd betwixt them, after Persius *was now* 15
grown a Man. As also his Exhortation to Young Noblemen, that they wou'd
enter themselves into his Institution. From hence he makes an artful Transition
into the second Part of his Subject: Wherein he first complains of the Sloath of
Scholars; and afterwards perswades them to the pursuit of their true Liberty:
Here our Author excellently Treats that Paradox of the Stoicks, which 20
affirms, that the Wise or Virtuous Man is only Free; and that all Vicious
Men, are Naturally Slaves. And, in the Illustration of this Dogma, he takes
up the remaining part of this inimitable Satyr.

THE FIFTH SATYR

Inscrib'd to The Reverend Dr. *Busby*. *The Speakers* Persius, *and* Cornutus

PERS.

OF ancient use to Poets it belongs,
    To wish themselves an hundred Mouths and Tongues:
Whether to the well-lung'd Tragedians Rage,
They recommend their Labours of the Stage,
Or sing the *Parthian*, when transfix'd he lies,   5
Wrenching the *Roman* Javelin from his thighs.
    CORN.
And why wou'd'st thou these mighty Morsels chuse,
Of Words unchaw'd, and fit to choak the Muse?
Let Fustian Poets with their Stuff be gone,
And suck the Mists that hang o're *Helicon*;   10
When [1]*Progne*'s or [2]*Thyestes* Feast they write;
And, for the mouthing Actor, Verse indite.
Thou neither, like a Bellows, swell'st thy Face,
As if thou wert to blow the burning Mass
Of melting Ore; nor can'st thou strain thy Throat;   15
Or murmur in an undistinguish'd Note;
Like rowling Thunder till it breaks the Cloud,
And rattling Nonsense is discharg'd aloud.
Soft Elocution does thy Stile renown;

The Fifth Satyr. 11 Thyestes] Thyestes's 93 97

And the sweet Accents of the peaceful Gown: 20
Gentle or sharp, according to thy choice,
To laugh at Follies, or to lash at Vice.
Hence draw thy Theme; and to the Stage permit
Raw-head, and Bloody-Bones, and Hands and Feet,
Ragousts for *Tereus* or *Thyestes* drest; 25
Tis Task enough for thee t' expose a *Roman* Feast.
    PERS.
Tis not, indeed, my Talent to engage
In lofty Trifles, or to swell my Page
With Wind and Noise; but freely to impart,
As to a Friend, the Secrets of my heart: 30
And, in familiar Speech, to let thee know
How much I love thee; and how much I owe.
Knock on my Heart; for thou hast skill to find
If it sound solid, or be fill'd with Wind;
And, thro the veil of words, thou view'st the naked Mind. } 35
  For this a hundred Voices I desire;
To tell thee what an hundred Tongues wou'd tire;
Yet never cou'd be worthily exprest,
How deeply thou art seated in my Breast.
    When first my ³Childish Robe resign'd the charge; 40
And left me, unconfin'd, to live at large;
When now my golden *Bulla* (hung on high
To House-hold Gods) declar'd me past a Boy;
And my ⁴white Shield proclaim'd my Liberty:
When, with my wild Companions, I cou'd rowl 45
From Street to Street, and sin without controul;
Just at that Age, when Manhood set me free;
I then depos'd my self, and left the Reins to thee.
On thy wise Bosom I repos'd my Head;
And, by my better ⁵*Socrates*, was bred. 50
Then, thy streight Rule, set Virtue in my sight;
The crooked Line reforming by the right.
My Reason took the bent of thy Command;
Was form'd and polish'd by thy skilful hand:
Long Summer-days thy Precepts I reherse; 55
And Winter-nights were short in our converse:
One was our Labour, one was our Repose;

    24 Feet,] Feet. *93 97*

One frugal Supper did our Studies close.
  Sure on our Birth some friendly Planet shone:
And, as our[6] Souls, our Horoscope was one: 60
Whether the[7] mounting Twins did Heav'n adorn,
Or, with the rising[8] Ballance, we were born;
Both have the same Impressions from above;
And both have [9]*Saturn*'s rage, repell'd by *Jove*.
What Star I know not, but some Star I find,   65
Has giv'n Thee an Ascendant o're my Mind.
      CORN.
  Nature is ever various in her Frame:
Each has a different Will; and few the same:
The greedy Merchants, led by lucre, run
To the parch'd Indies, and the rising Sun;   70
From thence hot Pepper, and rich Drugs they bear,
Bart'ring for Spices, their *Italian* Ware.
The lazy Glutton safe at home will keep;
Indulge his Sloth, and batten with his Sleep:
One bribes for high Preferments in the State,   75
A second shakes the Box, and sits up late:
Another shakes the Bed; dissolving there,
Till Knots upon his Gouty Joints appear,
And Chalk is in his crippled Fingers found;
Rots like a Doddard Oke, and piecemeal falls to ground.   80
Then, his lewd Follies he wou'd late repent:
And his past years, that in a Mist were spent.
      PERS.
  But thou art pale, in nightly Studies, grown:
To make the [10]Stoick Institutes thy own:
Thou long with studious Care hast till'd our Youth;   85
And sown our well purg'd Ears with wholsom Truth:
From thee both old and young, with profit, learn
The bounds of Good and Evil to discern:
      CORN.
Unhappy he who does this Work adjourn;
And to To Morrow wou'd the search delay: 90
His lazy Morrow will be like to day.
      PERS.
But is one day of Ease too much to borrow?

CORN.

Yes sure: For Yesterday was once To Morrow.
That Yesterday is gone, and nothing gain'd;
And all thy fruitless days will thus be drain'd: 95
For thou hast more To Morrows yet to ask,
And wilt be ever to begin thy Task:
Who, like the hindmost Chariot Wheels, art curst;
Still to be near; but ne're to reach the first.
   O Freedom! first Delight of Humane Kind!   100
Not that which Bondmen from their Masters find,
The[11] Priviledge of Doles; nor yet t' inscribe
Their Names in[12] this or t'other *Roman* Tribe:
That false Enfranchisement, with ease is found:
Slaves are[13] made Citizens, by turning round.   105
How, replies one, can any be more free?
Here's *Dama*, once a Groom of low degree,
Not worth a Farthing, and a Sot beside;
So true a Rogue, for lying's sake he ly'd;
But, with a turn, a Freeman he became;   110
Now[14] *Marcus Dama* is his Worship's Name:
Good Gods! who wou'd refuse to lend a Sum,
If Wealthy *Marcus* Surety will become!
Marcus is made a Judge, and for a Proof
Of certain Truth, *He said it*, is enough.   115
A Will is to be prov'd; put in your Claim;
Tis clear, if[15] *Marcus* has subscrib'd his Name.
This is[16] true Liberty, as I believe;
What farther can we from our Caps receive, ⎫
Than as we please, without Control to live? ⎬   120
Not more to [17]Noble *Brutus* cou'd belong. ⎭
Hold, says the Stoick, your Assumption's wrong:
I grant true Freedom you have well defin'd: ⎫
But living as you list, and to your mind, ⎬
Are loosely tack'd; and must be left behind. ⎭   125
What, since the Prætor did my Fetters loose,
And left me freely at my own dispose,
May I not live without Control or Awe,
Excepting still the[18] Letter of the Law?
   Hear me with patience; while thy Mind I free   130
From those fond Notions of false Liberty:

Tis not the Prætor's Province to bestow
True Freedom; nor to teach Mankind to know
What to our selves, or to our Friends we owe.
He cou'd not set thee free from Cares and Strife;   135
Nor give the Reins to a lewd vicious life:
As well he for an Ass a Harp might string;
Which is against the Reason of the thing:
For Reason still is whisp'ring in your Ear,
Where you are sure to fail, th' Attempt forbear.   140
No need of Publick Sanctions, this to bind,
Which Nature has implanted in the Mind:
Not to pursue the Work, to which we're not design'd.

    Unskill'd in *Hellebore*, if thou shou'd'st try,
To mix it, and mistake the Quantity,   145
The Rules of Physick wou'd against thee cry.
The High-shoo'd Ploughman, shou'd he quit the Land,
To take the Pilot's Rudder in his hand,
Artless of Stars, and of the moving Sand,
The Gods wou'd leave him to the Waves and Wind: 150
And think all Shame was lost in Human-Kind.

    Tell me, my Friend, from whence hadst thou the skill,
So nicely to distinguish Good from Ill?
Or by the sound to judge of Gold and Brass;
What piece is Tinkers Metal, what will pass?   155
And what thou art to follow, what to flye,
This to condemn, and that to ratifie?
When to be Bountiful, and when to Spare,
But never Craving, or oppress'd with Care?
The Baits of Gifts, and Money to despise,   160
And look on Wealth with undesiring Eyes?
When thou can'st truly call these Virtues thine,
Be Wise and Free, by Heav'n's consent and mine.

    But thou, who lately of the common strain,
Wer't one of us, if still thou do'st retain   165
The same ill Habits, the same Follies too,
Gloss'd over only with a Saint-like show,
Then I resume the freedom which I gave,
Still thou art bound to Vice, and still a Slave.
Thou can'st not wag thy Finger, or begin   170

170 *Editor's italics*

The least light motion, but it tends to sin.

How's this? Not wag my Finger, he replies?
No, Friend; nor fuming Gums, nor Sacrifice,
Can ever make a Madman free, or wise.
"Virtue and[19] Vice are never in one Soul: 175
"A Man is wholly Wise, or wholly is a Fool.
A heavy Bumpkin, taught with daily care,
Can never dance three steps with a becoming air.

    PERS.

In spight of this my Freedom still remains.

    CORN.

Free, what, and fetter'd with so many Chains?   180
Can'st thou no other Master understand
Than [20]him that freed thee, by the Prætor's Wand?
Shou'd he, who was thy Lord, command thee now,
With a harsh Voice, and supercilious Brow,
To servile Duties, thou wou'd'st fear no more;   185
The Gallows and the Whip are out of door.
But if thy Passions lord it in thy Breast,
Art thou not still a Slave, and still opprest?

    Whether alone, or in thy Harlot's Lap,
When thou wou'd'st take a lazy Morning's Nap;   190
Up, up, says Avarice; thou snor'st again,
Stretchest thy Limbs, and yawn'st, but all in vain;
The Tyrant Lucre no denyal takes;
At his Command th' unwilling Sluggard wakes:
What must I do, he cries? What, says his Lord?   195
Why rise, make ready, and go streight aboord:
With Fish, from *Euxine* Seas, thy Vessel freight;
Flax, Castor, *Coan* Wines, the precious Weight
Of Pepper, and *Sabean* Incense, take
With thy own hands, from the tir'd Camel's back: 200
And with Post-haste thy running Markets make.
Be sure to turn the Penny; lye and swear,
Tis wholsom sin: But *Jove*, thou say'st, will hear:
Swear, Fool, or starve; for the Dilemma's even:
A Tradesman thou! and hope to go to Heav'n?   205

    Resolv'd for Sea, the Slaves thy Baggage pack;
Each saddled, with his Burden on his back:

Nothing retards thy Voyage, now; unless
Thy other Lord forbids, Voluptuousness:
And he may ask this civil Question; Friend,   210
What do'st thou make a Shipboord? to what end?
Art thou of *Bethlem*'s Noble College free?
Stark, staring mad; that thou wou'd'st tempt the Sea?
Cubb'd in a Cabbin, on a Mattress laid,
On a Brown *George*, with lowsie Swobbers fed,   215
Dead Wine that stinks of the *Boracchio*, sup
From a fowl Jack, or greasie Maple Cup?
Say, wou'd'st thou bear all this, to raise thy store
From Six i'th' Hundred, to Six Hundred more?
Indulge; and to thy Genius freely give: 220
For, not to live at ease, is not to live:
Death stalks behind thee, and each flying Hour
Does some loose Remnant of thy Life devour.
Live, while thou liv'st: For Death will make us all,
A Name, a nothing but an Old Wife's Tale.   225
    Speak; wilt thou Avarice, or Pleasure chuse
To be thy Lord: Take one, and one refuse.
But both, by turns, the Rule of thee will have:
And thou, betwixt 'em both, wilt be a Slave.
    Nor think when once thou hast resisted one,   230
That all thy Marks of Servitude are gone:
The strugling Greyhound gnaws his Leash in vain;
If, when 'tis broken, still he drags the Chain.
    Says[21] *Phædria* to his Man, Believe me, Friend,
To this uneasie Love I'le put an End: 235
Shall I run out of all? My Friends Disgrace,
And be the first lewd Unthrift of my Race?
Shall I the Neighbours Nightly rest invade
At her deaf Doors, with some vile Serenade?
Well hast thou freed thy self, his Man replies;   240
Go, thank the Gods; and offer Sacrifice.
Ah, says the Youth, if we unkindly part,
Will not the Poor fond Creature break her Heart?
Weak Soul! And blindly to Destruction led!
She break her Heart! She'll sooner break your Head.   245
She knows her Man, and when you Rant and Swear

    209 forbids, *97*: forbids; *93*   224 make *97*: makes *93*

Can draw you to her, *with a single Hair.*
But shall I not return? Now, when she Sues?
Shall I my own, and her Desires refuse?
Sir, take your Course: But my Advice is plain: 250
Once freed, 'tis Madness to resume your Chain.

    Ay; there's the Man, who loos'd from Lust and Pelf,
Less to the Prætor owes, than to himself.
But write him down a Slave, who, humbly proud,
With Presents begs Preferments from the Crowd;   255
That early [22]Suppliant who salutes the Tribes,
And sets the Mob to scramble for his Bribes:
That some old Dotard, sitting in the Sun,
On Holydays may tell, that such a Feat was done:
In future times this will be counted rare.   260

    Thy Superstition too may claim a share:
When Flow'rs are strew'd, and Lamps in order plac'd,
And Windows with Illuminations grac'd,
On [23]Herod's Day; when sparkling Bouls go round,
And *Tunny*'s Tails in savoury Sauce are drown'd,   265
Thou mutter'st Prayers obscene; nor do'st refuse
The Fasts and Sabbaths of the curtail'd *Jews.*
Then a crack'd[24] Eggshell thy sick Fancy frights:
Besides the Childish Fear of Walking Sprights.
Of o'regrown Guelding Priests thou art afraid;   270
The Timbrel, and the Squintifego Maid
Of *Isis*, awe thee; lest the Gods, for sin,
Shou'd, with a swelling Dropsie, stuff thy skin:
Unless three Garlick Heads the Curse avert,
Eaten each Morn, devoutly, next thy heart.   275

    Preach this among the brawny Guards, say'st thou,
And see if they thy Doctrine will allow:
The dull fat Captain, with a Hound's deep throat,
Wou'd bellow out a Laugh, in a Base Note:
And prize a hundred *Zeno's*, just as much   280
As a clipt Sixpence, or a Schilling *Dutch.*

EXPLANATORY NOTES

1 *PRogne* was Wife to *Tereus*, King of *Thracia*: *Tereus* fell in Love with *Philo-mela*, Sister to *Progne*; ravish'd her, and cut out her Tongue: In Revenge of

which *Progne* kill'd *Itys*, her own Son by *Tereus*; and serv'd him up at a Feast, to be eaten by his Father.   2 *Thyestes* and *Atreus* were Brothers, both Kings: *Atreus* to Revenge himself of his unnatural Brother, kill'd the 5 Sons of *Thyestes*; and invited him to eat them.   3 By the Childish Robe, is meant the *Prætexta*, or first Gowns which the *Roman* Children of Quality wore: These were Welted with Purple: And on those Welts were fasten'd the *Bullæ*; or little Bells; which when they came to the Age of *Puberty*, were hung up, and Consecrated to the *Lares*, or Household Gods. 10 4 The first Shields which the *Roman* Youths wore, were white, and without any Impress, or Device on them; to shew they had yet Atchiev'd nothing in the Wars.   5 *Socrates*, by the Oracle was declar'd to be the wisest of Man-kind: He instructed many of the *Athenian* Young Noblemen, in Morality; and amongst the rest, *Alcibiades*.   6 Astrologers divide the 15 Heaven into Twelve parts, according to the Number of the 12 Signs of the Zodiack: The Sign or Constellation which rises in the East, at the Birth of any Man, is call'd, the Ascendant: *Persius*, therefore, judges that *Cornutus* and he had the same, or a like Nativity.   7 The Sign of *Gemini*.   8 The Sign of *Libra*.   9 Astrologers have an Axiome, that 20 whatsoever *Saturn* ties, is loos'd by *Jupiter*: They account *Saturn* to be a Planet of a Malevolent Nature; and *Jupiter* of a Propitious Influence. 10 *Zeno* was the great Master of the Stoick Philosophy: And *Cleanthes* was second to him, in Reputation: *Cornutus*, who was Master or Tutor to *Persius*, was of the same School.   11 When a Slave was made free; he 25 had the Priviledge of a *Roman* Born; which was to have a share in the Donatives or Doles of Bread, *&c.* which were Distributed, by the Magistrates amongst the People.   12 The *Roman* People was Distributed into several Tribes: He who was made free was inroll'd into some one of them; and thereupon enjoy'd the common Priviledges of a *Roman* Citizen. 30 13 The Master, who intended to infranchise a Slave, carried him before the City Prætor, and turn'd him round, using these words; *I will that this Man be free.*   14 Slaves had only one Name before their Freedom: After it, they were admitted to a *Prænomen*, like our Christen'd Names: So *Dama*, is now call'd *Marcus Dama*.   15 At the Proof of a Testament, the 35 Magistrates were to subscribe their Names; as allowing the Legality of the Will.   16 Slaves, when they were set free, had a Cap given them, in Sign of their Liberty.   17 *Brutus* freed the *Roman* People from the Tyranny of the *Tarquins*; and chang'd the Form of the Government, into a glorious Common-wealth.   18 The Text of the *Roman* Laws, was 40 written in Red Letters; which was call'd the Rubrick; Translated here, in more general words, *The Letter of the Law.*   19 The Stoicks held this Paradox, That any one Vice, or Notorious Folly, which they call'd Madness, hinder'd a Man from being Virtuous: That a Man was of a piece, without a Mixture; either wholly Vicious, or Good; one Virtue or Vice, 45 according to them, including all the rest.   20 The Prætor held a Wand in his hand; with which he softly struck the Slave on the Head, when he declar'd him free.   21 This alludes to the Play of *Terence*, call'd the *Eunuch*; which was excellently imitated of late in English, by Sir *Charles Sedley*: In the first Scene of that Comedy, *Phædria* was introduc'd with his 50 Man *Pamphilus*, Discoursing, whether he shou'd leave his Mistress *Thais*, or return to her, now that she had invited him.   22 He who sued for any Office, amongst the *Romans* was call'd a Candidate; because he wore a white Gown: And sometimes Chalk'd it, to make it appear whiter. He rose early, and went to the *Levees* of those who headed the People: Saluted 55 also the Tribes severally, when they were gather'd together, to chuse their Magistrates; and Distributed a Largess amongst them, to engage them for their Voices: Much resembling our Elections of Parliament-Men. 23 The Commentators are divided, what *Herod* this was, whom our Author mentions: Whether *Herod* the Great, whose Birth-day might 60 possibly be Celebrated, after his Death, by the *Herodians*, a Sect amongst the *Jews*, who thought him their Messiah; or *Herod Agrippa*, living in the Author's time, and after it. The latter seems the more probable Opinion. 24 The Ancients had a Superstition, contrary to ours, concerning Egg-shells: They thought that if an Egg-shell were crack'd, or a Hole bor'd in 65 the bottom of it, they were Subject to the Power of Sorcery: We as vainly, break the bottom of an Egg-shell, and cross it, when we have eaten the Egg; lest some Hag shou'd make use of it, in bewitching us, or sailing over the Sea in it, if it were whole. The rest of the Priests of *Isis*, and her one-ey'd, or squinting Priestess, is more largely treated in the Sixth Satyr of 70 *Juvenal*, where the Superstitions of Women are related.

THE SIXTH SATYR OF
AULUS PERSIUS FLACCUS

ARGUMENT OF THE SIXTH SATYR

This Sixth Satyr Treats an admirable Common-place of Moral Philosophy; Of the true Use of Riches. They are certainly intended by the Power who bestows them, as Instruments and Helps of living Commodiously our selves; and of Administring to the Wants of others, who are Oppress'd by Fortune. There are two Extreams in the Opinions of Men concerning them. One Error, though on 5 the right hand, yet a great one, is, That they are no Helps to a Virtuous Life; The other places all our Happiness in the Acquisition and Possession of them: And this is, undoubtedly, the worse Extream. The Mean betwixt these, is the

Opinion of the Stoicks: Which is, That Riches may be Useful to the leading a
Virtuous Life; In case we rightly understand how to Give according to right 10
Reason; and how to receive what is given us by others. The Virtue of Giving
Well, is call'd Liberality: And 'tis of this Virtue, that Persius *writes in this*
Satyr: Wherein he not only shews the lawful Use of Riches, but also sharply
inveighs against the Vices which are oppos'd to it: And especially of those,
which consist in the Defects of Giving or Spending; or in the Abuse of Riches. 15
He writes to Cæsius Bassus *his Friend, and a Poet also. Enquires first of his*
Health and Studies; and afterwards informs him of his own; and where he is
now resident. He gives an account of himself, that he is endeavouring by little
and little to wear off his Vices; and particularly, that he is combating Ambi-
tion, and the Desire of Wealth. He dwells upon the latter Vice: And being 20
sensible, that few Men either Desire, or Use Riches as they ought, he en-
deavours to convince them of their Folly; which is the main Design of the
whole Satyr.

THE SIXTH SATYR

To Cæsius Bassus, *a Lyrick Poet*

HAS Winter caus'd thee, Friend, to change thy Seat,
   And seek, in [1]*Sabine* Air, a warm retreat?
Say, do'st thou yet the *Roman* Harp command?
Do the Strings Answer to thy Noble hand?
Great Master of the Muse, inspir'd to Sing   5
The Beauties of the first Created Spring;
The Pedigree of Nature to rehearse;
And sound the Maker's Work, in equal Verse.
Now[2], sporting on thy Lyre, the Loves of Youth,
Now Virtuous Age, and venerable Truth: 10
Expressing justly, *Sapho*'s wanton Art
Of Odes; and *Pindar*'s more Majestick part.
   For me, my warmer Constitution wants
More cold, than our *Ligurian* Winter grants;
And, therefore, to my Native Shores retir'd,   15
I view the Coast old *Ennius* once admir'd;
Where Clifts on either side their points display;
And, after, opening in an ampler way,
Afford the pleasing Prospect of the Bay.

'Tis worth your while, O *Romans*, to regard   20
The Port of *Luna*; says our Learned Bard:
Who, in³ a Drunken Dream, beheld his Soul
The Fifth within the Transmigrating roul:
Which first a Peacock, then *Euphorbus* was,
Then *Homer* next, and next *Pythagoras*;   } 25
And last of all the Line did into *Ennius* pass.

   Secure and free from Business of the State;
And more secure of what the vulgar Prate,
Here I enjoy my private Thoughts; nor care
What Rots for Sheep the *Southern* Winds prepare: 30
Survey the Neighb'ring Fields, and not repine,
When I behold a larger Crop than mine:
To see a Beggar's Brat in Riches flow,
Adds not a Wrinckle to my even Brow;
Nor, envious at the sight, will I forbear   35
My plentious Bowl, nor bate my bounteous Cheer.
Nor yet unseal the Dregs of Wine that stink
Of Cask; nor in a nasty Flaggon Drink;
Let others stuff their Guts with homely fare;
For Men of diff'rent Inclinations are;   } 40
Tho born, perhaps, beneath one common Star.
In minds and manners Twins oppos'd we see
In the same Sign, almost the same Degree:
One, Frugal, on his Birth-Day fears to dine:
Does at a Penny's cost in Herbs repine,   } 45
And hardly dares to dip his Fingers in the Brine.
Prepar'd as Priest of his own Rites, to stand,
He sprinkles Pepper with a sparing hand.
His Jolly Brother, opposite in sence,
Laughs at his Thrift; and lavish of Expence,   } 50
Quaffs, Crams, and Guttles, in his own defence.

   For me, I'le use my own; and take my share;
Yet will not Turbots for my Slaves prepare:
Nor be so nice in taste my self, to know
If what I swallow be a Thrush or no.   55
Live on thy Annual Income! Spend thy store;
And freely grind, from thy full Threshing-Floor;   }
Next Harvest promises as much or more.

Thus I wou'd live: But Friendship's holy Band,
And Offices of kindness hold my hand: } 60
My[4] Friend is Shipwreck'd on the *Brutian* Strand.
His Riches in th' *Ionian* Main are lost:
And he himself stands shiv'ring on the Coast;
Where, destitute of help, forlorn, and bare,
He wearies the Deaf Gods with Fruitless Pray'r.   65
Their Images, the Relicks of the Wrack,
Torn from the Naked Poop, are tided back,
By the wild Waves, and rudely thrown ashore,
Lye impotent: Nor can themselves restore.
The Vessel sticks and shews her open'd side,   70
And on her shatter'd Mast the Mews in Triumph ride.
From[5] thy new hope and from thy growing store,
Now lend Assistance, and relieve the Poor.
Come; do a Noble Act of Charity:
A Pittance of thy Land will set him free.   75
Let him not bear the Badges of a Wrack
Nor[6] beg with a blue Table on his back.
Nor tell me, that thy frowning Heir will say,
'Tis mine that Wealth thou squander'st thus away;
What is't to thee, if he neglect thy Urn;   80
Or[7] without Spices lets thy Body burn?
If Odours to thy Ashes he refuse,
Or buys Corrupted *Cassia* from the *Jews*?
All these, the wiser *Bestius* will reply,
Are empty Pomp, and Deadmen's Luxury: 85
We never knew this vain Expence, before
Th' effeminated *Grecians* brought it o're:
Now Toys and Trifles from their *Athens* come:
And Dates and Pepper have unsinnew'd *Rome*.
Our sweating Hinds their Sallads, now, defile;   90
Infecting homely Herbs with fragrant Oyl.
But, to thy Fortune be not thou a Slave;
For what hast thou to fear beyond the Grave?
And thou who gap'st for my Estate, draw near;
For I wou'd whisper somewhat in thy Ear.   95
Hear'st thou the News, my Friend? th' Express is come
With Laurell'd Letters from the Camp to *Rome*:
Cæsar[8] Salutes the Queen and Senate thus;

My Arms are, on the *Rhine*, Victorious.
From Mourning Altars sweep the Dust away: 100
Cease Fasting, and proclaim a Fat Thanksgiving Day.
The[9] goodly Empress, Jollily inclin'd,
Is, to the welcome Bearer, wond'rous kind:
And, setting her Goodhousewifry aside,
Prepares for all the Pageantry of Pride.   105
The[10] Captive *Germans*, of Gygantick size,
Are ranck'd in order, and are clad in frize:
The Spoils of Kings, and Conquer'd Camps we boast,
Their Arms in Trophies hang, on the Triumphal post.
    Now, for so many Glorious Actions done,   110
In Foreign parts, and mighty Battels won;
For Peace at Home, and for the publick Wealth
I mean to Crown a Bowl, to *Cæsar*'s Health:
Besides, in Gratitude for such high matters,
Know[11] I have vow'd two hundred Gladiators.   115
Say, woud'st thou hinder me from this Expence?
I Disinherit thee if thou dar'st take Offence.
Yet more a publick Largess I design
Of Oyl, and Pyes to make the People dine:
Controul me not for fear I change my Will.   120
    And yet methinks I hear thee grumbling still,
You give as if you were the *Persian* King;
Your Land does no such large Revenues bring.
Well; on my Terms thou wilt not be my Heir,
If thou car'st little, less shall be my care: 125
Were none of all my Father's Sisters left;
Nay were I of my Mother's Kin bereft;
None by an Uncle's, or a Grandam's side,
Yet I cou'd some adopted Heir provide.
I need but take my Journey half a day   130
From haughty *Rome*, and at *Aricea* stay;
Where Fortune throws poor *Manius* in my way.
Him will I chuse: What him, of humble Birth,
Obscure, a Foundling, and a Son of Earth?
Obscure! Why prithee what am I? I know   135
My Father, Grandsire, and great Grandsire too:
If farther I derive my Pedigree,

The Sixth Satyr. 120 Will. *97*: Will; *93*

I can but guess beyond the fourth degree.
The rest of my forgotten Ancestors,
Were Sons of Earth, like him, or Sons of Whores.   140
    Yet why shou'd'st thou, old covetous Wretch, aspire
To be my Heir, who might'st have been my Sire?
In Nature's Race, shou'd'st thou demand of me
My[12] Torch, when I in course run after thee?
Think I approach thee, like the God of Gain,   145
With Wings on Head, and Heels, as Poets feign:
Thy mod'rate Fortune from my Guift receive:
Now fairly take it, or as fairly leave.
But take it as it is, and ask no more.
What, when thou hast embezel'd all thy store?   150
Where's all thy Father left? 'Tis true, I grant,
Some I have mortgag'd, to supply my want:
The Legacies of *Tadius* too are flown:
All spent, and on the self same Errand gone.
How little then to my poor share will fall?   155
Little indeed, but yet that little's all.
    Nor tell me, in a dying Father's tone,
Be careful still of the main chance, my Son;
Put out the Principal, in trusty hands:
Live of the Use; and never dip thy Lands: 160
But yet what's left for me? What's left, my Friend,
Ask that again, and all the rest I spend.
Is not my Fortune at my own Command?
Pour Oyl; and pour it with a plenteous hand,
Upon my Sallads, Boy: Shall I be fed   165
With sodden Nettles, and a sing'd Sow's head?
Tis Holyday; provide me better Cheer:
Tis Holyday, and shall be round the Year.
Shall I my Houshold Gods, and Genius, cheat,
To make him rich, who grudges me my Meat?   170
That he may loll at ease; and pamper'd high,
When I am laid, may feed on Giblet Pye?
And when his throbbing Lust extends the Vein,
Have wherewithall his Whores to entertain?
Shall I in homespun Cloath be clad, that he   175
His Paunch in triumph may before him see?

176 see?] see. 93 97

Go Miser, go; for Lucre sell thy Soul;
Truck Wares for Wares, and trudge from Pole to Pole:
That Men may say, when thou art dead and gone,
See what a vast Estate he left his Son!   180
How large a Family of Brawny Knaves,
Well fed, and fat as [13]*Capadocian* Slaves!
Encrease thy Wealth, and double all thy Store;
Tis done: Now double that, and swell the score;
To ev'ry thousand add ten thousand more.   } 185
Then say[14], *Chrysippus*, thou who wou'd'st confine
Thy Heap, where I shall put an end to mine.

EXPLANATORY NOTES

1 *AND seek, in Sabine Air*, &c. All the Studious, and particularly the Poets,
about the end of *August*, began to set themselves on Work: Refraining
from Writing, during the Heats of the Summer. They wrote by Night;
and sate up the greatest part of it. For which Reason the Product of their
Studies, was call'd their *Elucubrations*; or Nightly Labours. They who had 5
Country Seats retir'd to them, while they Studied: As *Persius* did to his,
which was near the Port of the Moon in *Etruria*; and *Bassus* to his, which
was in the Country of the *Sabines*, nearer *Rome.*   2 *Now sporting on
thy Lyre*, &c. This proves *Cæsius Bassus* to have been a Lyrick Poet: 'Tis
said of him, that by an Eruption of the Flameing Mountain *Vesuvius*, 10
near which the greatest part of his Fortune lay, he was Burnt himself,
together with all his Writings.   3 *Who, in a Drunken Dream*, &c. I call
it a Drunken Dream of *Ennius*; not that my Author in this place gives me
any encouragement for the Epithete; but because *Horace*, and all who
mention *Ennius*, say he was an Excessive Drinker of Wine. In a Dream, or 15
Vision, call you it which you please, he thought it was reveal'd to him,
that the Soul of *Pithagoras* was Transmigrated into him: As *Pithagoras*,
before him believ'd, that himself had been *Euphorbus* in the Wars of *Troy.*
Commentators differ in placing the order of this Soul, and who had it first.
I have here given it to the Peacock; because it looks more according to the 20
Order of Nature, that it shou'd lodge, in a Creature of an Inferiour Species;
and so by Gradation rise to the informing of a Man. And *Persius* favours
me, by saying that *Ennius* was the Fifth from the *Pithagorean* Peacock.
4 *My Friend is Shipwreck'd on*, &c. Perhaps this is only a fine Transition of
the Poet, to introduce the business of the Satyr; and not, that any such 25
Accident had happen'd to one of the Friends of *Persius.* But, however, this
is the most Poetical Description of any in our Author: And since he and
Lucan were so great Friends, I know not but *Lucan* might help him, in two

or three of these Verses, which seem to be written in his stile; certain it is,
that besides this Description of a Shipwreck, and two Lines more, which 30
are at the End of the Second Satyr, our Poet has written nothing Elegantly.
I will therefore Transcribe both the passages, to justifie my Opinion. The
following are the last Verses saving one of the Second Satyr.

> *Compositum jus, fasque animo; sanctosque recessus*
> *Mentis, & incoctum generoso pectus honesto:*   35

The others are those in this present Satyr, which are subjoyn'd.

> — *trabe ruptâ, Bruttia Saxa*
> *Prendit Amicus inops: Remque omnem, surdaque vota*
> *Condidit Ionio: Jacet ipse in Littore; & unà*
> *Ingentes de puppe Dei: Jamque obvia Mergis*   40
> *Costa ratis laceræ* —

5 *From thy new hope*, &c. The Latin is, *Nunc & de Cespite vivo, frange aliquid.*
Casaubon only opposes the *Cespes vivus*, which word for word, is the living
Turf, to the Harvest or Annual Income; I suppose the Poet rather means,
sell a piece of Land already Sown; and give the Money of it to my Friend 45
who has lost all by Shipwreck: That is, do not stay till thou hast Reap'd;
but help him immediately, as his Wants require.   6 *Not Beg with a*
Blue Table, &c. *Holiday* Translates it a Green Table: The sence is the same;
for the Table was painted of the Sea Colour; which the Shipwreck'd
Person carried on his back, expressing his Losses thereby, to excite the 50
Charity of the Spectators.   7 *Or without Spices*, &c. The Bodies of the
Rich before they were burnt, were Imbalm'd with Spices; or rather Spices
were put into the Urn, with the Relicks of the Ashes. Our Author here
Names *Cinnamum* and *Cassia*, which *Cassia*, was sophisticated with *Cherry*
Gum: And probably enough by the *Jews*; who Adulterate all things which 55
they sell. But whether the Ancients were acquainted with the Spices of
the *Molucca* Islands, *Ceylon*, and other parts of the *Indies*; or whether their
Pepper and *Cinnamon*, &c. were the same with ours, is another Question.
As for *Nutmegs*, and *Mace*, 'tis plain, that the Latin Names of them are
Modern.   8 *Cæsar Salutes*, &c. The *Cæsar* here mention'd is *Caius* 60
Caligula; who affected to Triumph over the *Germans*, whom he never
Conquer'd; as he did over the *Britains*. And accordingly sent Letters wrapt
about with Laurels, to the Senate, and the Empress *Cæsonia*, whom I here
call Queen; though I know that name was not us'd amongst the *Romans*:
But the word Empress wou'd not stand in that Verse: For which Reason 65
I Adjourn'd it to another. The Dust which was to be swept away from the
Altars, was either the Ashes which were left there; after the last Sacrifice
for Victory; or might perhaps mean the Dust or Ashes, which were left
on the Altars, since some former Defeat of the *Romans*, by the *Germans*:

34 *animo*] *animi* 93 97

After which overthrow, the Altars had been neglected.   9 *Cæsonia* 70
Wife to *Caius Caligula*, who afterwards, in the Reign of *Claudius*, was propos'd, but ineffectually, to be Marry'd to him; after he had Executed
Messallina, for Adultery.   10 *The Captive Germans*, &c. He means only
such, as were to pass for *Germans*, in the Triumph: Large Body'd Men, as
they are still; whom the Empress Cloath'd New, with Course Garments; 75
for the greater Ostentation of the Victory.   11 *Know, I have vow'd Two
Hundred Gladiators.* A hundred pair of Gladiators, were beyond the Purse
of a private Man to give: Therefore this is only a threatning to his Heir,
that he cou'd do what he pleas'd with his Estate.   12 *Shou'd'st thou
demand of me, my Torch*, &c. Why shou'd'st thou, who art an Old Fellow, 80
hope to out-live me, and be my Heir, who am much Younger? He who
was first, in the Course, or Race, deliver'd the Torch, which he carried,
to him who was Second.   13 *Well Fed, and Fat as Cappadocian Slaves.* Who
were Famous, for their Lustiness; and being, as we call it, in good likeing.
They were set on a Stall when they were expos'd to Sale; to shew the good 85
Habit of their Body; and made to play Tricks before the Buyers, to shew
their Activity and Strength.   14 *Then say, Chrysippus*, &c. *Chrysippus* the
Stoick, invented a kind of Argument, consisting of more than three
Propositions; which is call'd *Sorites*; or a heap. But as *Chrysippus* cou'd never
bring his Propositions to a certain stint: So neither can a Covetous Man, 90
bring his Craving Desires to any certain Measure of Riches, beyond which,
he cou'd not wish for any more.

POEMS FROM
EXAMEN POETICUM

BEING THE THIRD PART OF Miscellany Poems.
Containing Variety of NEW TRANSLATIONS
OF THE *Ancient Poets.*
Together with many ORIGINAL COPIES,
BY THE *Most Eminent Hands.*

Hæc potior soboles: hinc Cæli tempore certo,
Dulcia mella premes.——Virgil. Geor. 4.
In medium quæsita reponunt. Ibid.

TO THE Right Honourable, MY
Lord *RADCLIFFE*

My Lord,

THESE Miscellany Poems, are by many Titles yours. The first they
claim from your acceptance of my Promise to present them to you;
before some of them were yet in being. The rest are deriv'd from your
own Merit, the exactness of your Judgment in Poetry, and the candour
of your Nature; easie to forgive some trivial faults when they come 5
accompanied, with countervailing Beauties. But after all, though these
are your equitable claims to a Dedication from other Poets, yet I must
acknowledge a Bribe in the case, which is your particular liking of my
Verses. 'Tis a vanity common to all Writers, to over-value their own
Productions; and 'tis better for me to own this failing in my self, than 10
the World to do it for me. For what other Reason have I spent my Life
in so unprofitable a Study? Why am I grown Old, in seeking so barren
a Reward as Fame? The same Parts and Application, which have made
me a Poet, might have rais'd me to any Honours of the Gown, which are
often given to Men of as little Learning and less Honesty than my self. 15
No Government has ever been, or ever can be, wherein Time-servers
and Blockheads will not be uppermost. The Persons are only chang'd,

Poems. Text from the first edition, 1693
To the Right Honourable, &c. 12 unprofitable] unprofitably 93

but the same juglings in State, the same Hypocrisie in Religion, the same Self-Interest, and Mis-mannagement, will remain for ever. Blood and Mony will be lavish'd in all Ages, only for the Preferment of new Faces, with old Consciences. There is too often a Jaundise in the Eyes of Great Men; they see not those they raise, in the same Colours with other Men. All whom they affect, look Golden to them; when the Gilding is only in their own distemper'd Sight. These Considerations, have given me a kind of Contempt for those who have risen by unworthy ways. I am not asham'd to be Little, when I see them so Infamously Great. Neither, do I know, why the Name of Poet should be Dishonourable to me; if I am truly one, as I hope I am; for I will never do any thing, that shall dishonour it: The Notions of Morality are known to all Men, none can pretend Ignorance of those Idea's which are In-born in Mankind; and if I see one thing, and practise the contrary, I must be Disingenuous, not to acknowledge a clear Truth, and Base to Act against the light of my own Conscience. For the Reputation of my Honesty, no Man can question it, who has any of his own: For that of my Poetry, it shall either stand by its own Merit; or fall for want of it. Ill Writers are usually the sharpest Censors: For they (as the best Poet, and the best Patron said), when in the full perfection of decay, turn Vinegar, and come again in Play. Thus the corruption of a Poet, is the Generation of a Critick: I mean of a Critick in the general acceptation of this Age: For formerly they were quite another Species of Men. They were Defendors of Poets, and Commentators on their Works: to Illustrate obscure Beauties; to place some passages in a better light, to redeem others from malicious Interpretations: to help out an Author's Modesty, who is not ostentatious of his Wit; and, in short, to shield him from the Ill-Nature of those Fellows, who were then call'd *Zoili*, and *Momi*, and now take upon themselves the Venerable Name of Censors. But neither *Zoilus*, nor he who endeavour'd to defame *Virgil*, were ever Adopted into the Name of Critick by the *Ancients*: what their Reputation was then, we know; and their Successours in this Age deserve no better. Are our Auxiliary Forces turn'd our Enemies? Are they, who, at best, are but Wits of the Second Order, and whose only Credit amongst Readers, is what they obtain'd by being subservient to the Fame of Writers, are these become Rebels of Slaves, and Usurpers of Subjects; or to speak in the most Honourable Terms of them, are they from our Seconds, become Principals against us? Does the Ivy undermine the Oke, which supports its weakness? What labour wou'd it cost them to put in a better Line, than the worst of those which they expunge in a True Poet? *Petronius*, the greatest Wit perhaps of all the *Romans*, yet when his Envy prevail'd upon his Judgment, to fall on *Lucan*, he fell himself in his attempt: He perform'd worse in his Essay 60 of the Civil War, than the Authour of the *Pharsalia*, and avoiding his Errours, has made greater of his own. *Julius Scaliger*, wou'd needs turn down *Homer*, and Abdicate him, after the possession of Three Thousand Years: Has he succeeded in his Attempt? He has indeed shown us some of those Imperfections in him, which are incident to Humane Kind: 65 But who had not rather be that *Homer* than this *Scaliger*? You see the same Hypercritick, when he endeavours to mend the beginning of *Claudian*, (a faulty Poet, and Living in a Barbarous Age;) yet how short he comes of him, and substitutes such Verses of his own, as deserves the *Ferula*. What a Censure has he made of *Lucan*, that he rather seems 70 to Bark than Sing? Wou'd any but a Dog, have made so snarling a Comparison? One wou'd have thought, he had Learn'd Latin, as late as they tell us he did Greek. Yet he came off, with a *pace tuâ*, by your good leave, *Lucan*; he call'd him not by those outrageous Names, of Fool, Booby, and Blockhead: He had somewhat more of good Manners, 75 than his Successours, as he had much more Knowledge. We have two sorts of those Gentlemen, in our Nation: Some of them proceeding with a seeming moderation and pretence of Respect, to the Dramatick Writers of this last Age, only scorn and vilifie the present Poets, to set up their Predecessours. But this is only in appearance; for their real 80 design is nothing less, than to do Honour to any Man, besides themselves. *Horace* took notice, of such Men in his Age: *Non Ingeniis favet ille, Sepultis; nostra sed impugnat; nos nostraque lividus odit.* 'Tis not with an ultimate intention to pay Reverence to the Manes of *Shakespear*, *Fletcher*, and *Ben Johnson*, that they commend their Writings, but to throw Dirt 85 on the Writers of this Age: Their *Declaration* is one thing, and their Practice is another. By a seeming veneration to our Fathers, they wou'd thrust out us their Lawful Issue, and Govern us themselves, under a specious pretence of Reformation. If they could compass their intent, what wou'd Wit and Learning get by such a change? If we are bad 90 Poets, they are worse, and when any of their woful pieces come abroad, the difference is so great betwixt them and good Writers, that there needs no Criticisms on our part to decide it. When they describe the Writers of this Age, they draw such monstrous figures of them, as resemble none of us: Our pretended Pictures are so unlike, that 'tis 95 evident we never sate to them: They are all Grotesque; the products

of their wild Imaginations, things out of Nature, so far from being
Copy'd from us, that they resemble nothing that ever was, or ever can
be. But there is another sort of Insects, more venomous than the former.
Those who manifestly aim at the destruction of our Poetical Church 100
and State. Who allow nothing to their Country-Men, either of this or
of the former Age. These attack the Living by raking up the Ashes of
the Dead. Well knowing that if they can subvert their Original Title
to the Stage, we who claim under them, must fall of course. Peace be
to the Venerable Shades of *Shakespear*, and *Ben Johnson*: None of the 105
Living will presume to have any competition with them: as they were
our Predecessours, so they were our Masters. We Trayl our Plays under
them: but, (as at the Funerals of a *Turkish* Emperour,) our Ensigns are
furl'd, or dragg'd upon the ground, in Honour to the Dead; so we may
lawfully advance our own, afterwards, to show that we succeed: If less 110
in Dignity, yet on the same Foot and Title, which we think too, we can
maintain, against the Insolence of our own Janizaries. If I am the Man,
as I have Reason to believe, who am seemingly Courted, and secretly
Undermin'd: I think I shall be able to defend my self, when I am openly
Attacqu'd. And to shew besides, that the *Greek* Writers only gave us the 115
Rudiments of a Stage, which they never finish'd. That many of the
Tragedies in the former Age amongst us, were without Comparison
beyond those of *Sophocles* and *Euripides*. But at present, I have neither the
leisure nor the means for such an Undertaking. 'Tis ill going to Law
for an Estate, with him who is in possession of it, and enjoys the present 120
Profits, to feed his Cause. But the *quantum mutatus* may be remember'd
in due time. In the mean while I leave the World to judge, who gave
the Provocation.

    This, my Lord, is, I confess, a long digression, from *Miscellany Poems*
to *Modern Tragedies*: But I have the ordinary Excuse of an Injur'd Man, 125
who will be telling his Tale unseasonably to his Betters. Though at the
same time, I am certain you are so good a Friend, as to take a Concern
in all things which belong to one who so truly Honours you. And
besides, being your self a Critick of the Genuine sort, who have Read
the best Authours, in their own Languages, who perfectly distinguish 130
of their several Merits, and in general prefer them to the Moderns, yet,
I know, you judge for the *English* Tragedies, against the *Greek* and *Latin*,
as well as against the *French*, *Italian* and *Spanish*, of these latter Ages.
Indeed there is a vast difference, betwixt arguing like *Perault*, in behalf
of the *French* Poets, against *Homer* and *Virgil*, and betwixt giving the 135
English Poets their undoubted due, of excelling *Æschylus*, *Euripides*, and

Sophocles. For if we or our greater Fathers, have not yet brought the *Drama* to an absolute Perfection, yet at least we have carried it much farther than those Ancient *Greeks*; who beginning from a *Chorus*, cou'd never totally exclude it, as we have done, who find it an unprofitable 140 incumbrance, without any necessity of Entertaining it amongst us; and without the possibility of establishing it here, unless it were supported by a Publick Charge. Neither can we accept of those Lay-Bishops, as some call them, who under pretence of reforming the Stage, wou'd intrude themselves upon us, as our Superiours, being indeed incom- 145 petent Judges of what is Manners, what Religion, and least of all, what is Poetry and Good Sense. I can tell them in behalf of all my Fellows, that when they come to Exercise a Jurisdiction over us, they shall have the Stage to themselves, as they have the Lawrel. As little can I grant, that the *French* Dramatick Writers, excel the *English*: Our Authours as 150 far surpass them in Genius, as our Souldiers Excel theirs in Courage: 'Tis true, in Conduct they surpass us either way: Yet that proceeds not so much from the greater Knowledge, as from the difference of Tasts in the two Nations. They content themselves with a thin Design, without Episodes, and manag'd by few Persons. Our Audience will not 155 be pleas'd, but with variety of Accidents, an Underplot, and many Actours. They follow the Ancients too servilely, in the Mechanick Rules, and we assume too much License to our selves, in keeping them only in view, at too great a distance. But if our Audience had their Tasts, our Poets could more easily comply with them, than the *French* 160 Writers cou'd come up to the Sublimity of our Thoughts, or to the difficult variety of our Designs. However it be, I dare establish it for a Rule of Practice on the Stage, that we are bound to please those, whom we pretend to Entertain: And that at any price, Religion and Good Manners only excepted. And I care not much, if I give this 165 handle, to our bad Illiterate Poetasters, for the defence of their *SCRIP-TIONS* as they call them. There is a sort of Merit in delighting the Spectatours; which is a Name more proper for them, than that of Auditours: Or else *Horace* is in the wrong, when he commends *Lucilius* for it. But these common places I mean to Treat at greater leisure: In 170 the mean time, submitting that little I have said, to your Lordship's Approbation, or your Censure, and chusing rather to Entertain you this way, as you are a Judge of Writing, than to oppress your Modesty, with other Commendations; which though they are your due, yet wou'd not be equally receiv'd, in this Satirical, and Censorious Age. 175 That which cannot without Injury be deny'd to you, is the easiness of your Conversation, far from Affectation or Pride: not denying even to Enemies, their just Praises. And this, if I wou'd dwell on any Theme of this Nature, is no vulgar Commendation to your Lordship. Without Flattery, my Lord, you have it in your Nature, to be a Patron and 180 Encourager of Good Poets, but your Fortune has not yet put into your Hands the opportunity of expressing it. What you will be hereafter, may be more than guess'd, by what you are at present. You maintain the Character of a Nobleman, without that Haughtiness which generally attends too many of the Nobility, and when you Converse with Gentle- 185 men, you forget not that you have been of their Order. You are Marryed to the Daughter of a King, who, amongst her other high Perfections, has deriv'd from him a Charming Behaviour, a winning Goodness, and a Majestick Person. The Muses and the Graces are the Ornaments of your Family. While the Muse Sings, the Grace accompanies her Voice: 190 even the Servants of the Muses have sometimes had the Happiness to hear her; and to receive their Inspirations from her.

I will not give my self the liberty of going farther; for 'tis so sweet to wander in a pleasing way, that I shou'd never arrive at my Journeys end. To keep my self from being belated in my Letter, and tiring your 195 Attention, I must return to the place where I was setting out. I humbly Dedicate to your Lordship, my own Labours in this Miscellany: At the same time, not arrogating to my self the Priviledge, of Inscribing to you, the Works of others who are join'd with me, in this undertaking; over which I can pretend no right. Your Lady and You have done me 200 the favour to hear me Read my Translations of *Ovid*: And you both seem'd not to be displeas'd with them. Whether it be the partiality of an Old Man to his Youngest Child, I know not: But they appear to me the best of all my Endeavours in this kind. Perhaps this Poet, is more easie to be Translated, than some others, whom I have lately attempted: 205 Perhaps too, he was more according to my Genius. He is certainly more palatable to the Reader, than any of the *Roman* Wits, though some of them are more lofty, some more Instructive, and others more Correct. He had Learning enough to make him equal to the best. But as his Verse came easily, he wanted the toyl of Application to amend it. He 210 is often luxuriant, both in his Fancy and Expressions; and as it has lately been observ'd, not always Natural. If Wit be pleasantry, he has it to excess: but if it be propriety, *Lucretius*, *Horace*, and above all *Virgil* are his Superiours. I have said so much of him already, in my Preface to his Heroical Epistles, that there remains little to be added in this 215 place. For my own part, I have endeavour'd to Copy his Character

what I cou'd in this Translation, even perhaps, farther than I shou'd
have done; to his very Faults. Mr. *Chapman* in his Translation of *Homer*,
professes to have done it somewhat paraphrastically; and that on set
purpose; his Opinion being, that a good Poet is to be Translated in that   220
manner. I remember not the Reason which he gives for it: But I suppose
it is, for fear of omitting any of his Excellencies: sure I am, that if it be
a Fault, 'tis much more pardonable, than that of those, who run into
the other extream, of a litteral, and close Translation, where the Poet
is confin'd so streightly to his Author's Words, that he wants elbow-   225
room, to express his Elegancies. He leaves him obscure; he leaves him
Prose, where he found him Verse. And no better than thus has *Ovid*
been serv'd by the so much admir'd *Sandys*. This is at least the Idea
which I have remaining of his Translation; for I never Read him since
I was a Boy. They who take him upon Content, from the Praises which   230
their Fathers gave him; may inform their Judgment by Reading him
again: And see, (if they understand the Original) what is become of
Ovid's Poetry, in his Version; whether it be not all, or the greatest part
of it evaporated. But this proceeded from the wrong Judgment of the
Age in which he Liv'd: They neither knew good Verse, nor lov'd it;   235
they were Scholars 'tis true, but they were Pedants. And for a just
Reward of their Pedantick pains, all their Translations want to be
Translated, into *English*.

   If I Flatter not my self, or if my Friends have not Flatter'd me, I have
given my Author's Sense, for the most part truly: For to mistake some-   240
times, is incident to all Men: And not to follow the *Dutch* Commentatours alwaies, may be forgiven to a Man, who thinks them, in the
general, heavy gross-witted Fellows; fit only to gloss on their own dull
Poets. But I leave a farther Satire on their Wit, till I have a better
opportunity, to shew how much I Love and Honour them. I have like-   245
wise attempted to restore *Ovid* to his Native sweetness, easiness, and
smoothness; and to give my Poetry a kind of Cadence, and, as we call
it, a run of Verse, as like the Original, as the *English* can come up to the
Latin. As he seldom uses any *Synalephas*, so I have endeavour'd to avoid
them, as often as I cou'd: I have likewise given him his own turns, both   250
on the Words and on the Thought: Which I cannot say are inimitable,
because I have Copyed them: and so may others, if they use the same
diligence: But certainly they are wonderfully Graceful in this Poet.
Since I have Nam'd the *Synalepha*, which is the cutting off one Vowel,
immediately before another, I will give an Example of it, from *Chapman*'s   255

251 Thought:] Thought *93*

Homer which lyes before me; for the benefit of those who understand
not the *Latine Prosodia*. 'Tis in the first Line of the Argument to the
First *Iliad*.

> Apollo's *Priest to th'* Argive *Fleet doth bring*, &c.

There we see he makes it not the *Argive*, but th' *Argive*, to shun the 260
shock of the two Vowels, immediately following each other. But in his
Second Argument, in the same Page, he gives a bad Example of the
quite contrary kind:

> Alpha *the Pray'r of* Chryses *Sings:*
> The *Army's Plague, the Strife of Kings.*   265

In these words *the Armies, the* ending with a Vowel, and *Armies* beginning with another Vowel, without cutting off the first, which by it had
been *th' Armies*, there remains a most horrible ill-sounding gap betwixt
those Words. I cannot say, that I have every way observ'd the Rule of
this *Synalepha*, in my Translation; but wheresoever I have not, 'tis a 270
fault in sound: The *French* and *Italians* have made it an inviolable Precept in their versification; therein following the severe Example of the
Latin Poets. Our Countrymen have not yet Reform'd their Poetry so
far; but content themselves with following the Licentious Practice of
the *Greeks*; who though they sometimes use *Synalepha's*, yet make no 275
difficulty very often, to sound one Vowel upon another; as *Homer* does,
in the very first line of *Alpha. Μῆνιν ἄειδε θεὰ Πηληιάδεω Ἀχιλῆος*. 'Tis
true, indeed, that in the second line, in these words *μυρὶ Ἀχαιοῖς*, and
ἀλγὲ ἔθηκεν, the *Synalepha* in revenge is twice observ'd. But it becomes
us, for the sake of *Euphony*, rather *Musas colere severiores*, with the *Romans*; 280
than to give into the looseness of the *Grecians*.

I have tir'd my self, and have been summon'd by the Press to send
away this Dedication; otherwise I had expos'd some other faults, which
are daily committed by our *English* Poets; which, with care and observation, might be amended. For after all, our Language is both Copious, 285
Significant, and Majestical; and might be reduc'd into a more harmonious sound. But for want of Publick Encouragement, in this *Iron
Age*, we are so far from making any progress in the improvement of our
Tongue, that in few years, we shall Speak and Write as Barbarously as
our Neighbours.   290

Notwithstanding my haste, I cannot forbear to tell your Lordship,
that there are two fragments of *Homer* Translated in this *Miscellany*;
one by Mr. *Congreve* (whom I cannot mention without the Honour
which is due to his Excellent Parts, and that entire Affection which I

bear him;) and the other by my self. Both the Subjects are pathetical; 295
and I am sure my Friend has added to the Tenderness which he found
in the Original; and, without Flattery, surpass'd his Author. Yet I
must needs say this in reference to *Homer*, that he is much more capable
of exciting the Manly Passions, than those of Grief and Pity. To cause
Admiration, is indeed the proper and adequate design of an Epick 300
Poem: And in that he has Excell'd even *Virgil*. Yet, without presuming
to Arraign our Master, I may venture to affirm, that he is somewhat
too Talkative, and more than somewhat too digressive. This is so
manifest, that it cannot be deny'd, in that little parcel which I have
Translated, perhaps too literally: There *Andromache* in the midst of her 305
Concernment, and Fright for *Hector*, runs off her Biass, to tell him a
Story of her Pedigree, and of the lamentable Death of her Father, her
Mother, and her Seven Brothers. The Devil was in *Hector*, if he knew
not all this matter, as well as she who told it him; for she had been his
Bed-fellow for many Years together: And if he knew it, then it must 310
be confess'd, that *Homer* in this long digression, has rather given us his
own Character, than that of the Fair Lady whom he Paints. His Dear
Friends the Commentators, who never fail him at a pinch, will needs
excuse him, by making the present Sorrow of *Andromache*, to occasion
the remembrance of all the past: But others think that she had enough 315
to do with that Grief which now oppress'd her, without running for
assistance to her Family. *Virgil*, I am confident, wou'd have omitted
such a work of supererrogation. But *Virgil* had the Gift of expressing
much in little, and sometimes in silence: For though he yielded much
to *Homer* in Invention, he more Excell'd him in his Admirable Judgment. 320
He drew the Passion of *Dido* for *Eneas*, in the most lively and most
natural Colours that are imaginable: *Homer* was ambitious enough of
moving pity; for he has attempted twice on the same subject of *Hector's*
death: First, when *Priam*, and *Hecuba* beheld his Corps, which was
drag'd after the Chariot of *Achilles*; and then in the Lamentation which 325
was made over him, when his Body was redeem'd by *Priam*; and the
same Persons again bewail his death with a Chorus of others to help the
cry. But if this last excite Compassion in you, as I doubt not but it will,
you are more oblig'd to the Translatour than the Poet. For *Homer*, as
I observ'd before, can move rage better than he can pity: He stirs up 330
the irascible appetite, as our Philosophers call it, he provokes to
Murther, and the destruction of God's Images; he forms and equips
those ungodly Man-killers, whom we Poets, when we flatter them, call
Heroes; a race of Men who can never enjoy quiet in themselves, 'till

they have taken it from all the World. This is *Homer*'s Commendation, 335 and such as it is, the Lovers of Peace, or at least of more moderate Heroism, will never Envy him. But let *Homer* and *Virgil* contend for the Prize of Honour, betwixt themselves, I am satisfied they will never have a third Concurrent. I wish Mr. *Congreve* had the leisure to Translate him, and the World the good Nature and Justice, to Encourage him 340 in that Noble Design, of which he is more capable than any Man I know. The Earl of *Mulgrave*, and Mr. *Waller*, two the best Judges of our Age, have assur'd me, that they cou'd never Read over the Translation of *Chapman*, without incredible Pleasure, and extreme Transport. This Admiration of theirs, must needs proceed from the Author himself: For 345 the Translator has thrown him down as low, as harsh Numbers, improper *English*, and a monstrous length of Verse cou'd carry him. What then wou'd he appear in the Harmonious Version, of one of the best Writers, Living in a much better Age than was the last? I mean for versification, and the Art of Numbers; for in the *Drama* we have not 350 arriv'd to the pitch of *Shakespear* and *Ben Johnson*. But here, my Lord, I am forc'd to break off abruptly, without endeavouring at a Compliment in the close. This *Miscellany*, is without dispute one of the best of the kind, which has hitherto been extant in our Tongue. At least, as Sir *Samuel Tuke* has said before me, a Modest Man may praise what's 355 not his own. My Fellows have no need of any Protection, but I humbly recommend my part of it, as much as it deserves, to your Patronage and Acceptance, and all the rest to your Forgiveness.

I am

My Lord,
Your Lordship's most
Obedient Servant,
John Dryden.

THE FIRST BOOK OF
OVID'S METAMORPHOSES

OF Bodies chang'd to various Forms I sing:
Ye Gods, from whom these Miracles did spring,
Inspire my Numbers with Cœlestial heat;
Till I, my long laborious Work compleat:
And add perpetual Tenour to my Rhimes,   5
Deduc'd from Nature's Birth, to *Cæsar*'s Times.

Before the Seas, and this Terrestrial Ball,
And Heav'ns high Canopy, that covers all,
One was the Face of Nature; if a Face,
Rather a rude and undigested Mass: 10
A lifeless Lump, unfashion'd, and unfram'd;
Of jarring Seeds; and justly Chaos nam'd.
No Sun was lighted up, the World to view;
No Moon did yet her blunted Horns renew:
Nor yet was Earth suspended in the Skye;   15
Nor pois'd, did on her own Foundations lye:
Nor Seas about the Shoars their Arms had thrown;
But Earth and Air and Water were in one.
Thus Air was void of light, and Earth unstable,
And Waters dark Abyss unnavigable.   20
No certain Form, on any was imprest;
All were confus'd, and each disturb'd the rest.
For hot and cold, were in one Body fixt;
And soft with hard, and light with heavy mixt.
  But God or Nature, while they thus contend,   25
To these intestine Discords put an end:
Then Earth from Air, and Seas from Earth were driv'n,
And grosser Air, sunk from Ætherial Heav'n.
Thus disembroil'd, they take their proper place;
The next of kin, contiguously embrace;   } 30
And Foes are sunder'd, by a larger space.
The force of Fire ascended first on high,
And took its dwelling in the vaulted Skie:
Then Air succeeds, in lightness next to Fire;
Whose Atoms from unactive Earth retire.   35
Earth sinks beneath, and draws a numerous throng
Of pondrous, thick, unweildy Seeds along.
About her Coasts, unruly Waters roar;
And, rising on a ridge, insult the Shoar.
Thus when the God, what ever God was he,   40
Had form'd the whole, and made the parts agree,
That no unequal portions might be found,
He moulded Earth into a spacious round:
Then with a breath, he gave the Winds to blow;
And bad the congregated Waters flow.   45
He adds the running Springs, and standing Lakes;

And bounding Banks for winding Rivers makes.
Some part, in Earth are swallow'd up; the most
In ample Oceans, disimbogu'd, are lost.
He shades the Woods, the Vallies he restrains　　　　50
With Rocky Mountains, and extends the Plains.
　And as five Zones th' Ætherial Regions bind,
Five Correspondent, are to Earth assign'd:
The Sun with Rays, directly darting down,
Fires all beneath, and fries the middle Zone:　　　　55
The two beneath the distant Poles, complain
Of endless Winter, and perpetual Rain.
Betwixt th' extreams, two happier Climates, hold
The Temper that partakes of Hot and Cold.
The Feilds of liquid Air, inclosing all,　　　　60
Surround the Compass of this Earthly Ball:
The lighter parts, lye next the Fires above;
The grosser near the watry Surface move:
Thick Clouds are spread, and Storms engender there, ⎫
And Thunders Voice, which wretched Mortals fear, ⎬ 65
And Winds that on their Wings, cold Winter bear. ⎭
Nor were those blustring Brethren left at large,
On Seas and Shoars, their fury to discharge:
Bound as they are, and circumscrib'd in place,
They rend the World, resistless, where they pass;　　　　70
And mighty marks of mischief leave behind;
Such is the Rage of their tempestuous kind.
First *Eurus* to the rising Morn is sent,
(The Regions of the balmy Continent;)
And *Eastern* Realms, where early *Persians* run,　　　　75
To greet the blest appearance of the Sun.
Westward, the wanton *Zephyr* wings his flight;
Pleas'd with the remnants of departing light:
Fierce *Boreas*, with his Off-spring, Issues forth
T' invade the frozen Waggon of the *North*.　　　　80
While frowning *Auster*, seeks the *Southern* Sphere;
And rots with endless Rain, th' unwholsom year.
　High o're the Clouds and empty Realms of wind,
The God a clearer space for Heav'n design'd;
Where Fields of Light, and liquid Æther flow;　　　　85

Purg'd from the pondrous dregs of Earth below.
　Scarce had the Pow'r distinguish'd these, when streight
The Stars, no longer overlaid with weight,
Exert their Heads, from underneath the Mass;
And upward shoot, and kindle as they pass,　　　　　　　}　90
And with diffusive Light, adorn their Heav'nly place.
Then, every void of Nature to supply,
With Forms of Gods he fills the vacant Skie:
New Herds of Beasts, he sends the plains to share:
New Colonies of Birds, to people Air:　　　　　　　}　95
And to their Oozy Beds, the finny Fish repair.
　A Creature of a more Exalted Kind
Was wanting yet, and then was Man design'd:
Conscious of Thought, of more capacious Breast,
For Empire form'd, and fit to rule the rest:　　　　　　100
Whether with particles of Heav'nly Fire
The God of Nature did his Soul Inspire,
Or Earth, but new divided from the Skie,
And, pliant, still, retain'd the Ætherial Energy:
Which Wise *Prometheus* temper'd into paste,　　　　　105
And mixt with living Streams, the Godlike Image cast.
Thus, while the mute Creation downward bend
Their Sight, and to their Earthy Mother tend,
Man looks aloft; and with erected Eyes
Beholds his own Hereditary Skies.　　　　　　　　　110
From such rude Principles our Form began;
And Earth was Metamorphos'd into Man.

The Golden Age

　The Golden Age was first; when Man yet New,　　　}
No Rule but uncorrupted Reason knew:
And, with a Native bent, did Good pursue.　　　　　}　115
Un-forc'd by Punishment, un-aw'd by fear,
His words were simple, and his Soul sincere:
Needless was written Law, where none opprest;
The Law of Man, was written in his Breast:
No suppliant Crowds, before the Judge appear'd,　　　}　120
No Court Erected yet, nor Cause was hear'd:
But all was safe, for Conscience was their Guard.　　　}

118 opprest;] opprest: *93*

The Mountain Trees in distant prospect please,
E're yet the Pine descended to the Seas:
E're Sails were spread, new Oceans to explore: 125
And happy Mortals, unconcern'd for more,
Confin'd their Wishes to their Native Shoar.
No walls, were yet; nor fence, nor mote nor mownd,
Nor Drum was heard, nor Trumpets angry sound:
Nor Swords were forg'd; but void of Care and Crime, 130
The soft Creation slept away their time.
The teeming Earth, yet guiltless of the Plough,
And unprovok'd, did fruitful Stores allow:
Content with Food, which Nature freely bred,
On Wildings, and on Strawberries they fed; 135
Cornels and Bramble-berries gave the rest,
And falling Acorns, furnisht out a Feast.
The Flow'rs un-sown, in Fields and Meadows reign'd:
And *Western* Winds, immortal Spring maintain'd.
In following years, the bearded Corn ensu'd, 140
From Earth unask'd, nor was that Earth renew'd.
From Veins of Vallies, Milk and Nectar broke;
And Honey sweating through the pores of Oak.

The Silver Age

But when Good *Saturne*, banish'd from above,
Was driv'n to Hell, the World was under *Jove*. 145
Succeeding times a Silver Age behold,
Excelling Brass, but more excell'd by Gold.
Then Summer, Autumn, Winter, did appear:
And Spring was but a Season of the Year.
The Sun his Annual course obliquely made, 150
Good days contracted, and enlarg'd the bad.
Then Air with sultry heats began to glow;
The wings of winds, were clogg'd with Ice and Snow;
And shivering Mortals, into Houses driv'n,
Sought shelter from th' inclemency of Heav'n. 155
Those Houses, then, were Caves, or homely Sheds;
With twining Oziers fenc'd; and Moss their Beds.
Then Ploughs, for Seed, the fruitful furrows broke,
And Oxen labour'd first, beneath the Yoke.

The Brazen Age

To this came next in course, the Brazen Age: 160
A Warlike Offspring, prompt to Bloody Rage,
Not Impious yet—

The Iron Age

————————Hard Steel succeeded then:
And stubborn as the Mettal, were the Men.
Truth, Modesty, and Shame, the World forsook,   165
Fraud, Avarice, and Force, their places took.
Then Sails were spread, to every Wind that blew.
Raw were the Sailors, and the Depths were new:
Trees rudely hollow'd, did the Waves sustain;
E're Ships in Triumph plough'd the watry Plain.   170
   Then Land-marks, limited to each his right:
For all before was common, as the light.
Nor was the Ground alone requir'd to bear
Her annual Income to the crooked share,
But greedy Mortals, rummaging her Store,   175
Digg'd from her Entrails first the precious Oar;
Which next to Hell, the prudent Gods had laid;
And that alluring ill, to sight displaid.
Thus cursed Steel, and more accursed Gold
Gave mischief birth, and made that mischief bold;   180
And double death, did wretched Man invade
By Steel assaulted, and by Gold betray'd.
Now, (brandish'd Weapons glittering in their hands,)
Mankind is broken loose from moral Bands;
No Rights of Hospitality remain: 185
The Guest by him who harbour'd him, is slain.
The Son in Law pursues the Father's life;
The Wife her Husband murders, he the Wife.
The Step-dame Poyson for the Son prepares;
The Son inquires into his Father's years.   190
Faith flies, and Piety in Exile mourns;
And Justice, here opprest, to Heav'n returns.

The Gyants War

   Nor were the Gods themselves more safe above;
Against beleaguer'd Heav'n, the Gyants move:

Hills pil'd on Hills, on Mountains, Mountains lie,   195
To make their mad approaches to the Skie.
Till *Jove*, no longer patient, took his time
T' avenge with Thunder their audacious Crime;
Red Light'ning plaid, along the Firmament,
And their demolish't Works to pieces rent.   200
Sing'd with the Flames, and with the Bolts transfixt,
With Native Earth, their Blood, the Monsters mixt:
The Blood, indu'd with animating heat,
Did in th' Impregnant Earth, new Sons beget:
They, like the Seed from which they sprung, accurst,   205
Against the Gods, Immortal Hatred nurst.
An Impious, Arrogant, and Cruel Brood:
Expressing their Original from Blood.
    Which, when the King of Gods beheld from high,
(Withal revolving in his memory,   210
What he himself had found on Earth of late,
Lycaon's Guilt, and his Inhuman Treate,)
He sigh'd; nor longer with his Pity strove;
But kindl'd to a Wrath becoming *Jove*:
    Then, call'd a General Council of the Gods;   215
Who Summon'd, Issue from their Blest Abodes,
And fill th' Assembly, with a shining Train.
A way there is, in Heavens expanded Plain,
Which when the Skies are clear, is seen below,
And Mortals, by the Name of Milky, know.   220
The Ground-work is of Stars; through which the Road
Lyes open to the Thunderer's Abode;
The Gods of greater Nations dwell around,
And on the Right and Left, the Palace bound;
The Commons where they can; the Nobler sort   225
With Winding-doors wide open, front the Court.
This Place, as far as Earth with Heav'n may vie,
I dare to call the *Loovre* of the Skie.
When all were plac'd, in Seats distinctly known,
And he, their Father, had assum'd the Throne,   230
Upon his Iv'ry Sceptre first he leant,
Then shook his Head, that shook the Firmament:
Air, Earth, and Seas, obey'd th' Almighty nod:

201 transfixt,] transfixt *93*   225 can;] can, *93*

And with a gen'ral fear, confess'd the God.
At length with Indignation, thus he broke   235
His awful silence, and the Pow'rs bespoke.
   I was not more concern'd in that debate
Of Empire, when our Universal State
Was put to hazard, and the Giant Race
Our Captive Skies, were ready to imbrace: 240
For tho' the Foe was fierce, the Seeds of all
Rebellion, sprung from one Original;
Now, wheresoever ambient waters glide,
All are corrupt, and all must be destroy'd.
Let me this Holy Protestation make,   245
By Hell, and Hell's inviolable Lake,
I try'd whatever in the God-Head lay:
But gangreen'd Members, must be lopt away,
Before the Nobler Parts, are tainted to decay.
There dwells below, a Race of Demi-Gods,   250
Of Nymphs in Waters, and of Fawns in Woods:
Who, tho not worthy yet, in Heav'n to live,
Let 'em, at least, enjoy that Earth we give.
Can these be thought securely lodg'd below,
When I my self, who no Superior know,   255
I, who have Heav'n and Earth at my command,
Have been attempted by *Lycaon*'s Hand?
   At this a murmur, thro' the Synod went,
And with one Voice they vote his Punishment.
Thus, when Conspiring Traytors dar'd to doom   260
The fall of *Cæsar*, and in him of *Rome*,
The Nations trembled, with a pious fear;
All anxious for their Earthly Thunderer:
Nor was their care, O *Cæsar*! less esteem'd
By thee, than that of Heav'n for *Jove* was deem'd.   265
Who with his Hand and Voice, did first restrain
Their Murmurs, then resum'd his Speech again.
The Gods to silence were compos'd, and sate
With Reverence, due to his Superior State.
   Cancel your pious Cares; already he   270
Has paid his Debt to Justice, and to me.
Yet what his Crimes, and what my Judgments were,
Remains for me, thus briefly to declare.

The Clamours of this vile degenerate Age,
The Cries of Orphans, and th' Oppressor's Rage 275
Had reach'd the Stars; I will descend, said I,
In hope to prove this loud Complaint a Lye.
Disguis'd in Humane Shape, I Travell'd round
The World, and more than what I hear'd, I found.
O're *Mænalus* I took my steepy way, 280
By Caverns infamous for Beasts of Prey:
Then cross'd *Cyllenè*, and the piny shade
More infamous, by Curst *Lycaon* made.
Dark Night had cover'd Heav'n and Earth, before
I enter'd his Unhospitable Door. 285
Just at my entrance, I display'd the Sign
That somewhat was approaching of Divine.
The prostrate People pray; the Tyrant grins;
And, adding Prophanation to his Sins,
I'll try, said he, and if a God appear, 290
To prove his Deity, shall cost him dear.
'Twas late; the Graceless Wretch, my Death prepares,
When I shou'd soundly Sleep, opprest with Cares:
This dire Experiment, he chose, to prove
If I were Mortal, or undoubted *Jove*: 295
But first he had resolv'd to taste my Pow'r;
Not long before, but in a luckless hour
Some Legates, sent from the *Molossian* State,
Were on a peaceful Errant come to Treat:
Of these he Murders one, he boils the Flesh; 300
And lays the mangl'd Morsels in a Dish:
Some part he Roasts; then serves it up, so drest,
And bids me welcome to this Humane Feast.
Mov'd with disdain, the Table I o're-turn'd;
And with avenging Flames, the Palace burn'd. 305
The Tyrant in a fright, for shelter, gains
The Neighb'ring Fields, and scours along the plains.
Howling he fled, and fain he wou'd have spoke;
But Humane Voice, his Brutal Tongue forsook.
About his lips, the gather'd foam he churns, 310
And, breathing slaughters, still with rage he burns,
But on the bleating Flock, his fury turns.

290 appear,] appear *93*

His Mantle, now his Hide, with rugged hairs
Cleaves to his back, a famish'd face he bears.
His arms descend, his shoulders sink away,　　　315
To multiply his legs for chace of Prey.
He grows a Wolf, his hoariness remains,
And the same rage in other Members reigns.
His eyes still sparkle in a narr'wer space:
His jaws retain the grin, and violence of face.　　　320
　　This was a single ruine, but not one
Deserves so just a punishment alone.
Mankind's a Monster, and th' Ungodly times
Confed'rate into guilt, are sworn to Crimes.
All are alike involv'd in ill, and all　　　325
Must by the same relentless Fury fall.
Thus ended he; the greater Gods assent;
By Clamours urging his severe intent;
The less fill up the cry for punishment.
Yet still with pity, they remember Man;　　　330
And mourn as much as Heav'nly Spirits can.
They ask, when those were lost of humane birth,
What he wou'd do with all this waste of Earth:
If his dispeopl'd World, he would resign
To Beasts, a mute, and more ignoble Line;　　　335
Neglected Altars must no longer smoke,
If none were left to worship and invoke.
To whom the Father of the Gods reply'd,
Lay that unnecessary fear aside.
Mine be the care, new People to provide.　　　340
I will from wondrous Principles ordain
A Race unlike the first, and try my skill again.
　　Already had he toss'd the flaming Brand;
And roll'd the Thunder in his spatious hand;
Preparing to discharge on Seas and Land:　　　345
But stopt, for fear thus violently driven,
The Sparks should catch his Axle-tree of Heav'n.
Remembring in the Fates, a time when Fire
Shou'd to the Battlements of Heav'n aspire.
And all his blazing Worlds above shou'd burn;　　　350
And all th' inferiour Globe, to Cinders turn.
His dire Artill'ry thus dismist, he bent

His thoughts to some securer Punishment.
Concludes to pour a Watry Deluge down;
And what he durst not burn, resolves to drown.   355
    The Northern breath, that freezes Floods, he binds;
With all the race of Cloud-dispelling Winds:
The South he loos'd, who Night and Horror brings;
And Foggs are shaken from his flaggy Wings.
From his divided Beard, two Streams he pours,   360
His head and rhumy eyes, distill in showers.
With Rain his Robe and heavy Mantle flow;
And lazy mists, are lowring on his brow:
Still as he swept along, with his clench't fist
He squeez'd the Clouds, th' imprison'd Clouds resist: 365
The Skies from Pole to Pole, with peals resound;
And show'rs inlarg'd, come pouring on the ground.
Then, clad in Colours of a various dye,
Junonian Iris, breeds a new supply;
To feed the Clouds: Impetuous Rain descends;   370
The bearded Corn, beneath the Burden bends:
Defrauded Clowns, deplore their perish'd grain;
And the long labours of the Year are vain.
    Nor from his Patrimonial Heav'n alone
Is *Jove* content to pour his Vengeance down.   375
Aid from his Brother of the Seas he craves;
To help him with Auxiliary Waves.
The watry Tyrant calls his Brooks and Floods,
Who rowl from mossie Caves (their moist abodes;)
And with perpetual Urns his Palace fill: 380
To whom in breif, he thus imparts his Will.
    Small Exhortation needs; your Pow'rs employ:
And this bad World, so *Jove* requires, destroy.
Let loose the Reins, to all your watry Store:
Bear down the Damms, and open every door.   385
    The Floods, by Nature Enemies to Land,
And proudly swelling with their new Command,
Remove the living Stones, that stopt their way,
And gushing from their Source, augment the Sea.

356 binds;] binds: *93*   362 flow;] flow: *93*   363 brow:] brow; *93*
375 down.] down, *93*

Then, with his Mace, their Monarch struck the Ground: } 390
With inward trembling, Earth receiv'd the wound;
And rising streams a ready passage found.
Th' expanded Waters gather on the Plain:
They flote the Fields, and over-top the Grain;
Then rushing onwards, with a sweepy sway,   395
Bear Flocks and Folds, and lab'ring Hinds away.
Nor safe their Dwellings were, for, sap'd by Floods,
Their Houses fell upon their Household Gods.
The solid Piles, too strongly built to fall,
High o're their Heads, behold a watry Wall: 400
Now Seas and Earth were in confusion lost;
A World of Waters, and without a Coast.
   One climbs a Cliff; one in his Boat is born;
And Ploughs above, where late he sow'd his Corn.
Others o're Chimney tops and Turrets row,   405
And drop their Anchors, on the Meads below:
Or downward driv'n, they bruise the tender Vine,
Or tost aloft, are knock't against a Pine.
And where of late, the Kids had cropt the Grass,
The Monsters of the deep, now take their place.   410
Insulting Nereids on the Cities ride,
And wondring Dolphins o're the Palace glide.
On leaves and masts of mighty Oaks they brouze;
And their broad Finns, entangle in the Boughs.
The frighted Wolf, now swims amongst the Sheep;   415
The yellow Lyon wanders in the deep:
His rapid force, no longer helps the Boar:
The Stag swims faster, than he ran before.
The Fowls, long beating on their Wings in vain,
Despair of Land, and drop into the Main.   420
Now Hills and Vales, no more distinction know;
And levell'd Nature, lies oppress'd below.
The most of Mortals perish in the Flood:
The small remainder dies for want of Food.
   A Mountain of stupendous height there stands   425
Betwixt th' *Athenian* and *Bœotian* Lands,
The bound of fruitful Fields, while Fields they were,
But then a Field of Waters did appear:
Parnassus is its name; whose forky rise

Mounts through the Clouds, and mates the lofty Skies. 430
High on the Summet of this dubious Cliff,
Deucalion wafting, moor'd his little Skiff.
He with his Wife were only left behind
Of perish'd Man; they two, were Humane Kind.
The Mountain Nymphs and *Themis* they adore, 435
And from her Oracles relief implore.
The most upright of Mortal Men was he;
The most sincere and holy Woman, she.
　When *Jupiter*, surveying Earth from high,
Beheld it in a Lake of Water lie, 440
That where so many Millions lately liv'd,
But two, the best of either Sex surviv'd;
He loos'd the Northern Wind; fierce *Boreas* flies
To puff away the Clouds and purge the Skies:
Serenely, while he blows, the Vapours, driven, 445
Discover Heav'n to Earth, and Earth to Heav'n.
The Billows fall, while *Neptune* lays his Mace
On the rough Sea, and smooths its furrow'd face.
Already *Triton*, at his call appears,
Above the Waves; a *Tyrian* Robe he wears; 　} 450
And in his hand a crooked Trumpet bears.
The Soveraign bids him peaceful sounds inspire;
And give the Waves the signal to retire.
His writhen Shell he takes; whose narrow vent
Grows by degrees into a large extent, 455
Then gives it breath; the blast, with doubling sound,
Runs the wide Circuit of the World around:
The Sun first heard it, in his early East,
And met the rattling Eccho's in the West.
The Waters, listning to the Trumpets roar, 460
Obey the Summons, and forsake the Shoar.
　A thin Circumference of Land appears;
And Earth, but not at once, her visage rears,
And peeps upon the Seas from upper Grounds;
The Streams, but just contain'd within their bounds, 465
By slow degrees into their Channels crawl:
And Earth increases, as the Waters fall.
In longer time the tops of Trees appear;

448 Sea] Seas *93*　　463 rears,] rears. *93*

Which Mud on their dishonour'd Branches bear.
   At length the World was all restor'd to view;   470
But desolate, and of a sickly hue:
Nature beheld her self, and stood aghast,
A dismal Desart, and a silent waste.
   Which when *Deucalion*, with a piteous look
Beheld, he wept, and thus to *Pyrrha* spoke: 475
Oh Wife, oh Sister, oh of all thy kind
The best and only Creature left behind,
By Kindred, Love, and now by Dangers joyn'd,
Of Multitudes, who breath'd the common Air,
We two remain; a Species in a pair: 480
The rest the Seas have swallow'd; nor have we
Ev'n of this wretched life a certainty.
The Clouds are still above; and, while I speak,
A second Deluge, o're our heads may break.
Shou'd I be snatch'd from hence, and thou remain,   485
Without relief, or Partner of thy pain,
How cou'd'st thou such a wretched Life sustain?
Shou'd I be left, and thou be lost, the Sea
That bury'd her I lov'd, shou'd bury me.
Oh cou'd our Father his old Arts inspire,   490
And make me Heir of his informing Fire,
That so I might abolisht Man retrieve,
And perisht People in new Souls might live.
But Heav'n is pleas'd, nor ought we to complain,
That we, th' Examples of Mankind, remain.   495
He said; the careful couple joyn their Tears;
And then invoke the Gods, with pious Prayers.
Thus, in Devotion having eas'd their grief,
From Sacred Oracles, they seek relief.
And to *Cephysus* Brook, their way pursue: 500
The Stream was troubl'd, but the Foord they knew;
With living Waters, in the Fountain bred,
They sprinkle first, their Garments, and their Head,
Then took the way, which to the Temple led.
The Roofs were all defil'd with Moss, and Mire,   505
The Desart Altars, void of Solemn Fire.
Before the Gradual, prostrate they ador'd;
The Pavement kiss'd, and thus the Saint implor'd.

O Righteous *Themis*, if the Pow'rs above
By Pray'rs are bent to pity, and to love, 510
If humane Miseries can move their mind;
If yet they can forgive, and yet be kind;
Tell, how we may restore, by second birth,
Mankind, and People desolated Earth.
Then thus the gracious Goddess, nodding, said; 515
Depart, and with your Vestments veil your head:
And stooping lowly down, with loosn'd Zones,
Throw each behind your backs, your mighty Mother's bones.
Amaz'd the pair, and mute with wonder stand,
Till *Pyrrha* first refus'd the dire command. 520
Forbid it Heav'n, said she, that I shou'd tear
Those Holy Reliques from the Sepulchre:
They ponder'd the mysterious words again,
For some new sence; and long they sought in vain:
At length *Deucalion* clear'd his cloudy brow, 525
And said, the dark *Ænigma* will allow
A meaning, which if well I understand,
From Sacriledge will free the Gods Command:
This Earth our mighty Mother is, the Stones
In her capacious Body, are her Bones. 530
These we must cast behind: with hope and fear
The Woman did the new solution hear:
The Man diffides in his own Augury,
And doubts the Gods; yet both resolve to try.
Descending from the Mount, they first unbind 535
Their Vests, and veil'd, they cast the Stones behind:
The Stones (a Miracle to Mortal View,
But long Tradition makes it pass for true)
Did first the Rigour of their Kind expell,
And, suppl'd into softness, as they fell, 540
Then swell'd, and swelling, by degrees grew warm;
And took the Rudiments of Humane Form.
Imperfect shapes: in Marble such are seen
When the rude Chizzel does the Man begin;
While yet the roughness of the Stone remains, 545
Without the rising Muscles, and the Veins.
The sappy parts, and next resembling juice,

512 forgive,] forgive; *93*   kind;] kind, *93*

Were turn'd to moisture, for the Bodies use:
Supplying humours, blood, and nourishment;
The rest, (too solid to receive a bent;)   550
Converts to bones; and what was once a vein
Its former Name, and Nature did retain.
By help of Pow'r Divine, in little space
What the Man threw, assum'd a Manly face;
And what the Wife, renew'd the Female Race.   } 555
Hence we derive our Nature; born to bear
Laborious life; and harden'd into care.

   The rest of Animals, from teeming Earth
Produc'd, in various forms receiv'd their birth.
The native moisture, in its close retreat,   560
Digested by the Sun's Ætherial heat,
As in a kindly Womb, began to breed:
Then swell'd, and quicken'd by the vital seed.
And some in less, and some in longer space,
Were ripen'd into form, and took a several face.   565
Thus when the *Nile* from *Pharian* Fields is fled,
And seeks with Ebbing Tides, his ancient Bed,
The fat Manure, with Heav'nly Fire is warm'd;
And crusted Creatures, as in Wombs are form'd;
These, when they turn the Glebe, the Peasants find;   570
Some rude; and yet unfinish'd in their Kind:
Short of their Limbs, a lame imperfect Birth;
One half alive; and one of lifeless Earth.

   For heat and moisture, when in Bodies joyn'd,
The temper that results from either Kind   575
Conception makes; and fighting till they mix,
Their mingl'd Atoms in each other fix.
Thus Nature's hand, the Genial Bed prepares,
With Friendly Discord, and with fruitful Wars.

   From hence the surface of the Ground, with Mud   580
And Slime besmear'd, (the fæces of the Flood)
Receiv'd the Rays of Heav'n; and sucking in
The Seeds of Heat, new Creatures did begin:
Some were of sev'ral sorts produc'd before,
But of new Monsters, Earth created more.   585

Unwillingly, but yet she brought to light
Thee, *Python* too, the wondring World to fright,
And the new Nations, with so dire a sight:
So monstrous was his bulk, so large a space
Did his vast Body, and long Train embrace.   590
Whom *Phœbus* basking on a Bank espy'd;
E're now the God his Arrows had not try'd
But on the trembling Deer, or Mountain Goat;
At this new Quarry, he prepares to shoot.
Though every Shaft took place, he spent the Store   595
Of his full Quiver; and 'twas long before
Th' expiring Serpent wallow'd in his Gore.
Then, to preserve the Fame of such a deed,
For *Python* slain, he *Pythian* Games decreed.
Where Noble Youths for Mastership shou'd strive,   600
To Quoit, to Run, and Steeds and Chariots drive;
The Prize was Fame: In witness of Renown
An Oaken Garland did the Victor crown.
The Lawrel was not yet for Triumphs born;
But every Green, alike by *Phœbus* worn,   605
Did with promiscuous Grace, his flowing Locks adorn.

The Transformation of Daphne *into a Lawrel*

The first and fairest of his Loves, was she
Whom not blind Fortune, but the dire decree
Of angry *Cupid* forc'd him to desire:
Daphne her name, and *Peneus* was her Sire.   610
Swell'd with the Pride, that new Success attends,
He sees the Stripling, while his Bow he bends
And thus insults him; thou lascivious Boy,
Are Arms like these, for Children to employ?
Know such atchivements are my proper claim;   615
Due to my vigour, and unerring aim:
Resistless are my Shafts, and *Python* late
In such a feather'd Death, has found his fate.
Take up thy Torch, (and lay my Weapons by,)
With that the feeble Souls of Lovers fry.   620

594 Quarry,] Quarry; 93   611 attends,] attends 93   619 by,] by 93

To whom the Son of *Venus* thus reply'd,
Phœbus thy Shafts are sure on all beside,
But mine on *Phœbus*, mine the Fame shall be
Of all thy Conquests, when I conquer thee.
 He said, and soaring, swiftly wing'd his flight: 625
Nor stopt but on *Parnassus* airy height.
Two diff'rent Shafts, he from his Quiver draws;
One to repel desire, and one to cause.
One Shaft is pointed with refulgent Gold;
To bribe the Love, and make the Lover bold: 630
One blunt, and tipt with Lead, whose base allay
Provokes disdain, and drives desire away.
The blunted bolt, against the Nymph he drest:
But with the sharp, transfixt *Apollo*'s Breast.
 Th' enamour'd Deity, pursues the Chace; 635
The scornful Damsel shuns his loath'd Embrace:
In hunting Beasts of Prey, her Youth employs;
And *Phœbe* Rivals in her rural Joys.
With naked Neck she goes, and Shoulders bare;
And with a Fillet binds her flowing Hair. 640
By many Suitors sought, she mocks their pains,
And still her vow'd Virginity maintains.
Impatient of a Yoke, the name of Bride
She shuns, and hates the Joys she never try'd.
On Wilds and Woods she fixes her desire: 645
Nor knows what Youth and kindly Love inspire.
Her Father chides her oft; thou ow'st, says he,
A Husband to thy self, a Son to me.
She, like a Crime, abhors the Nuptial Bed:
She glows with blushes, and she hangs her head. 650
Then casting round his Neck her tender Arms,
Sooths him with blandishments, and filial Charms:
Give me, my Lord, she said, to live and die
A spotless Maid, without the Marriage Tye.
'Tis but a small request; I beg no more 655
Than what *Diana*'s Father gave before.
The good old Sire, was softn'd to consent;
But said her Wish wou'd prove her Punishment:
For so much Youth, and so much Beauty joyn'd
Oppos'd the State, which her desires design'd. 660

The God of light, aspiring to her Bed
Hopes what he seeks, with flattering fancies fed;
And is, by his own Oracles mis-led.
And as in empty Fields, the Stubble burns,   665
Or nightly Travellers, when day returns,
Their useless Torches, on dry Hedges throw,
That catch the Flames, and kindle all the row;
So burns the God, consuming in desire,
And feeding in his Breast a fruitless Fire:
Her well-turn'd Neck he view'd (her Neck was bare)   670
And on her Shoulders her dishevel'd Hair;
Oh were it comb'd, said he, with what a grace
Wou'd every waving Curl, become her Face!
He view'd her Eyes, like Heavenly Lamps that shone,
He view'd her Lips, too sweet to view alone,   675
Her taper Fingers, and her panting Breast;
He praises all he sees, and for the rest
Believes the Beauties yet unseen are best:
Swift as the Wind, the Damsel fled away,
Nor did for these alluring Speeches stay: 680
Stay Nymph, he cry'd, I follow not a Foe:
Thus from the Lyon, trips the trembling Doe;
Thus from the Wolf the frightn'd Lamb removes,
And, from pursuing Faulcons, fearful Doves,
Thou shunn'st a God, and shunn'st a God that loves.   685
Ah, lest some thorn shou'd pierce thy tender foot,
Or thou shou'd'st fall in flying my pursuit!
To sharp uneven ways thy steps decline;
Abate thy speed, and I will bate of mine.
Yet think from whom thou dost so rashly fly;   690
Nor basely born, nor Shepherd's Swain am I.
Perhaps thou know'st not my Superior State;
And, from that ignorance, proceeds thy hate.
Me *Claros*, *Delphos*, *Tenedos* obey,
These Hands the *Patareian* Scepter sway.   695
The King of Gods begot me: What shall be,
Or is, or ever was, in Fate, I see.
Mine is th' invention of the charming Lyre;
Sweet notes, and Heav'nly numbers I inspire.

Sure is my Bow, unerring is my Dart;   700
But ah more deadly his, who pierc'd my Heart.
Med'cine is mine; what Herbs and Simples grow
In Fields and Forrests, all their pow'rs I know;
And am the great Physician call'd, below.
Alas that Fields and Forrests can afford   705
No Remedies to heal their Love-sick Lord!
To cure the pains of Love, no Plant avails:
And his own Physick; the Physician fails.
   She heard not half; so furiously she flies;
And on her Ear, th' imperfect accent dies.   710
Fear gave her Wings; and as she fled, the wind
Increasing, spread her flowing Hair behind:
And left her Legs and Thighs expos'd to view;
Which made the God more eager to pursue.
The God was young, and was too hotly bent   715
To lose his time in empty Compliment.
But led by Love, and fir'd with such a sight,
Impetuously pursu'd his near delight.
   As when th' impatient Greyhound slipt from far,
Bounds o're the Glebe to course the fearful Hare,   720
She in her speed, does all her safety lay;
And he with double speed pursues the Prey;
O're-runs her at the sitting turn, and licks
His Chaps in vain, and blows upon the Flix;
She scapes, and for the neighb'ring Covert strives,   725
And gaining shelter, doubts if yet she lives:
If little things with great we may compare,
Such was the God, and such the flying Fair.
She urg'd by fear, her feet did swiftly move;
But he more swiftly, who was urg'd by Love.   730
He gathers ground upon her in the chace:
Now breaths upon her Hair, with nearer pace;
And just is fast'ning on the wish'd Embrace.
The Nymph grew pale, and in a mortal fright,
Spent with the labour of so long a flight: 735
And now despairing, cast a mournful look
Upon the Streams of her Paternal Brook:
Oh help, she cry'd, in this extreamest need.

          724 Flix;] Flix, *93*

If Water Gods are Deities indeed:
Gape Earth, and this unhappy Wretch intomb;   740
Or change my form, whence all my sorrows come.
Scarce had she finish'd, when her Feet she found
Benumm'd with cold, and fasten'd to the Ground:
A filmy rind about her Body grows;
Her Hair to Leaves, her Arms extend to Boughs: 745
The Nymph is all into a Lawrel gone:
The smoothness of her Skin, remains alone.

　　Yet *Phœbus* loves her still, and casting round
Her Bole, his Arms, some little warmth he found.
The Tree still panted in th' unfinish'd part,   750
Not wholly vegetive, and heav'd her Heart.
He fixt his Lips upon the trembling Rind;
It swerv'd aside, and his Embrace declin'd.
To whom the God, because thou can'st not be
My Mistress, I espouse thee for my Tree: 755
Be thou the prize of Honour and Renown;
The deathless Poet, and the Poem crown.
Thou shalt the *Roman* Festivals adorn,
And, after Poets, be by Victors worn.
Thou shalt returning *Cæsar*'s Triumph grace;   760
When Pomps shall in a long Procession pass.
Wreath'd on the Posts before his Palace wait;
And be the sacred Guardian of the Gate.
Secure from Thunder, and unharm'd by *Jove*,
Unfading as th' immortal Pow'rs above: 765
And as the locks of *Phœbus* are unshorn,
So shall perpetual green thy Boughs adorn.
The grateful Tree was pleas'd with what he sed;
And shook the shady Honours of her Head.

The Transformation of Io into a Heyfar

　　An ancient Forrest in *Thessalia* grows;   770
Which *Tempe*'s pleasing Valley does inclose:
Through this the rapid *Peneus* takes his course;
From *Pindus* rowling with impetuous force:
Mists from the Rivers mighty fall arise;
And deadly damps inclose the cloudy Skies: 775

750 part,] part: *93*

Perpetual Fogs are hanging o're the Wood;
And sounds of Waters deaf the Neighbourhood.
Deep, in a Rocky Cave, he makes abode:
(A Mansion proper for a mourning God.)
Here he gives Audience; issuing out Decrees   780
To Rivers, his dependant Deities.
On this occasion hither they resort;
To pay their homage and to make their Court.
All doubtful, whether to congratulate
His Daughter's Honour, or lament her Fate.   785
Sperchæus, crown'd with Poplar, first appears;
Then old *Apidanus* came crown'd with years:
Enipeus turbulent, *Amphrisos* tame;
And *Æas*, last with lagging Waters came.
Then, of his Kindred Brooks, a numerous throng,   790
Condole his loss; and bring their Urns along.
Not one was wanting of the watry Train,
That fill'd his Flood, or mingl'd with the Main:
But *Inachus*, who in his Cave, alone,
Wept not anothers losses, but his own.   795
For his dear *Io*, whether stray'd, or dead,
To him uncertain, doubtful tears he shed.
He sought her through the World; but sought in vain;
And no where finding, rather fear'd her slain.
    Her, just returning from her Father's Brook,   800
Jove had beheld, with a desiring look:
And oh fair Daughter of the Flood, he sed,
Worthy alone of *Jove*'s Imperial Bed;
Happy whoever shall those Charms possess;
The King of Gods, nor is thy Lover less,   805
Invites thee to yon cooler Shades; to shun
The scorching Rays of the Meridian Sun.
Nor shalt thou tempt the dangers of the Grove
Alone, without a Guide; thy Guide is *Jove*.
No puny Pow'r, but he whose high Command   810
Is unconfin'd, who rules the Seas and Land;
And tempers Thunder in his awful hand.
Oh fly not; (for she fled from his Embrace,)
O're *Lerna*'s Pastures, he pursu'd the Chace;

814 Chace;] Chace: *93*

Along the Shades of the *Lyrcæan* Plain;   815
At length the God, who never asks in vain,
Involv'd with Vapours, imitating Night,
Both Air and Earth; and then suppress'd her flight,
And mingling force with Love enjoy'd the full delight.

   Mean time the jealous *Juno*, from on high,   820
Survey'd the fruitful Fields of *Arcady*:
And wonder'd that the mist shou'd over-run
The face of Day-light, and obscure the Sun.
No Nat'ral cause she found, from Brooks, or Bogs,
Or marshy Lowlands, to produce the Fogs: 825
Then round the Skies she sought for *Jupiter*;
Her faithless Husband; but no *Jove* was there:
Suspecting now the worst, or I, she said,
Am much mistaken, or am much betray'd.
With fury she precipitates her flight: 830
Dispels the shadows of dissembled Night;
And to the day restores his native light.
Th' Almighty *Leacher*, careful to prevent
The consequence, foreseeing her descent,
Transforms his Mistress in a trice; and now   835
In *Io*'s place appears a lovely Cow.
So slick her skin, so faultless was her make,
Ev'n *Juno* did unwilling pleasure take
To see so fair a Rival of her Love;
And what she was, and whence, enquir'd of *Jove*:   840
Of what fair Herd, and from what Pedigree?
The God, half caught, was forc'd upon a lye:
And said she sprung from Earth; she took the word,
And begg'd the beauteous Heyfar of her Lord.
What should he do, 'twas equal shame to *Jove*   845
Or to relinquish, or betray his Love:
Yet to refuse so slight a Gift, wou'd be
But more t' increase his Consort's Jealousie:
Thus fear and love, by turns his heart assail'd;
And stronger love had sure, at length prevail'd: 850
But some faint hope remain'd, his jealous Queen
Had not the Mistress through the Heyfar seen.
The cautious Goddess, of her Gift possest,

815 Lyrcæan] Lyrnæan 93   818 flight,] flight 93.

Yet harbour'd anxious thoughts within her breast;
As she who knew the falshood of her *Jove*;　　　　855
And justly fear'd some new relapse of Love.
Which to prevent, and to secure her care,
To trusty *Argus*, she commits the Fair.
　　The head of *Argus* (as with Stars the Skies)
Was compass'd round, and wore an hundred eyes.　　860
But two by turns their lids in slumber steep;
The rest on duty still their station keep;
Nor cou'd the total Constellation sleep.
Thus, ever present, to his eyes and mind,
His Charge was still before him, tho' behind.　　865
In Fields he suffer'd her to feed by Day,
But when the setting Sun, to Night gave way,
The Captive Cow he summon'd with a call;
And drove her back, and ty'd her to the Stall.
On Leaves of Trees, and bitter Herbs she fed,　　870
Heav'n was her Canopy, bare Earth her Bed:
So hardly lodg'd: and to digest her Food,
She drank from troubl'd Streams, defil'd with Mud.
Her woeful Story, fain she wou'd have told
With hands upheld, but had no hands to hold.　　875
Her head to her ungentle Keeper bow'd,
She strove to speak, she spoke not, but she low'd:
Affrighted with the noise, she look'd around,
And seem'd t' inquire the Author of the sound.
　　Once on the Banks where often she had play'd,　　880
(Her Father's Banks) she came, and there survey'd
Her alter'd visage, and her branching head;
And starting, from her self she wou'd have fled.
Her fellow Nymphs, familiar to her eyes,
Beheld, but knew her not in this disguise.　　885
Ev'n *Inachus* himself was ignorant;
And in his Daughter, did his Daughter want.
She follow'd where her Fellows went, as she
Were still a Partner of the Company:
They stroke her Neck, the gentle Heyfar stands,　　890
And her Neck offers to their stroaking Hands.

872 lodg'd:] lodg'd, *93*　　　　873 Mud.] Mud, *93*

Her Father gave her Grass; the Grass she took;
And lick'd his Palms, and cast a piteous look;
And in the language of her eyes, she spoke.
She wou'd have told her name, and ask't relief,   895
But wanting words, in tears she tells her grief.
Which, with her foot she makes him understand;
And prints the name of *Io* in the Sand.

   Ah wretched me, her mournful Father cry'd,
She, with a sigh, to wretched me reply'd;   900
About her Milk-white neck, his arms he threw;
And wept, and then these tender words ensue.
And art thou she, whom I have sought around
The World, and have at length so sadly found?
So found is worse than lost: with mutual words   905
Thou answer'st not, no voice thy tongue affords:
But sighs are deeply drawn from out thy breast;
And speech deny'd, by lowing is express'd.
Unknowing I, prepar'd thy Bridal Bed;
With empty hopes of happy Issue fed.   910
But now the Husband of a Herd must be
Thy Mate, and bell'wing Sons thy Progeny.
Oh, were I mortal, Death might bring relief;
But now my God-head, but extends my grief:
Prolongs my woes, of which no end I see,   915
And makes me curse my Immortality!
More had he said, but, fearful of her stay,
The Starry Guardian drove his Charge away,
To some fresh Pasture; on a hilly height
He sate himself, and kept her still in sight.   920

   The Eyes of Argus *Transform'd into a Peacock's Train*
   Now *Jove* no longer cou'd her suff'rings bear;
But call'd in haste his airy Messenger,
The Son of *Maya*, with severe decree
To kill the Keeper, and to set her free.
With all his Harness soon the God was sped,   925
His flying Hat was fastned on his Head,
Wings on his Heels were hung, and in his Hand,
He holds the Virtue of the Snaky Wand.
The liquid Air, his moving Pinions wound,

And, in a moment, shoot him on the ground.   930
Before he came in sight, the crafty God
His Wings dismiss'd, but still retain'd his Rod:
That Sleep procuring Wand, wise *Hermes* took,
But made it seem to sight, a Shepherd's Hook.
With this, he did a Herd of Goats controul;   935
Which by the way he met, and slily stole.
Clad like a Country Swain, he Pip'd and Sung;
And playing drove his jolly Troop along.
   With pleasure, *Argus* the Musician heeds;
But wonders much at those new vocal Reeds.   940
And whosoe're thou art, my Friend, said he,
Up hither drive thy Goats, and play by me:
This Hill has browz for them, and shade for thee.
The God, who was with ease induc'd to climb,
Began Discourse to pass away the time;   945
And still betwixt, his Tuneful Pipe he plyes;
And watch'd his Hour, to close the Keeper's Eyes.
With much ado, he partly kept awake;
Not suff'ring all his Eyes repose to take:
And ask'd the Stranger, who did Reeds invent,   950
And whence began so rare an Instrument?

The Transformation of Syrinx *into Reeds*

   Then *Hermes* thus; a Nymph of late there was,
Whose Heav'nly Form, her Fellows did surpass.
The Pride and Joy of Fair *Arcadia*'s plains,
Belov'd by Deities, Ador'd by Swains: 955
Syrinx her Name, by *Sylvans* oft pursu'd,
As oft she did the Lustful Gods delude:
The Rural, and the Woodland Pow'rs disdain'd;
With *Cynthia* Hunted, and her Rites maintain'd:
Like *Phœbe* clad, even *Phœbe*'s self she seems,   960
So Tall, so Streight, such well proportion'd Limbs:
The nicest Eye did no distinction know,
But that the Goddess bore a Golden Bow,
Distinguish'd thus, the sight she cheated too.
Descending from *Lycæus*, *Pan* admires   965
The Matchless Nymph, and burns with new Desires.

930 ground.] ground, *93*   943 thee.] thee; *93*

A Crown of Pine, upon his Head he wore;
And thus began her pity to implore.
But e're he thus began, she took her flight
So swift, she was already out of sight.   970
Nor stay'd to hear the Courtship of the God;
But bent her course to *Ladon*'s gentle Flood:
There by the River stopt, and tyr'd before;
Relief from water Nymphs her Pray'rs implore.

  Now while the Lustful God, with speedy pace,   975
Just thought to strain her in a strict Embrace,
He fill'd his Arms with Reeds, new rising on the place.
And while he sighs, his ill-success to find,
The tender Canes were shaken by the wind:
And breath'd a mournful Air, unhear'd before;   980
That much surprizing *Pan*, yet pleas'd him more.
Admiring this new Musick, thou, he sed,
Who can'st not be the Partner of my Bed,
At least shalt be the Consort of my Mind:
And often, often to my Lips be joyn'd.   985
He form'd the Reeds, proportion'd as they are,
Unequal in their length, and wax'd with Care,
They still retain the Name of his Ungrateful Fair.

  While *Hermes* pip'd and sung, and told his tale,
The Keeper's winking Eyes began to fail;   990
And drowsie slumber, on the lids to creep,
'Till all the Watchman was, at length, asleep.
Then soon the God, his Voice and Song supprest;
And with his pow'rful Rod, confirm'd his rest:
Without delay his crooked Faulchion, drew,   995
And at one fatal stroak, the Keeper slew.
Down from the Rock, fell the dissever'd head,
Opening its Eyes in Death; and falling bled:
And mark'd the passage with a crimson trail;
Thus *Argus* lies in pieces cold and pale: 1000
And all his hundred Eyes, with all their light,
Are clos'd at once, in one perpetual night.
These *Juno* takes, that they no more may fail,
And spreads them in her Peacock's gaudy tail.
  Impatient to revenge her injur'd Bed   1005

982 sed,] sed 93

She wreaks her anger, on her Rival's head;
With furies frights her, from her Native Home;
And drives her gadding, round the World to roam.
Nor ceas'd her madness and her flight, before
She touch'd the limits of the *Pharian* Shore.   1010
At length, arriving on the Banks of *Nile*,
Weary'd with length of ways, and worn with toil,
She laid her down; and leaning on her Knees,
Invok'd the Cause of all her Miseries:
And cast her languishing regards above   1015
For help from Heav'n and her ungrateful *Jove*.
She sigh'd, she wept, she low'd, 'twas all she cou'd;
And with unkindness seem'd to tax the God.
Last, with an humble Pray'r, she begg'd Repose,
Or Death at least, to finish all her Woes.   1020
Jove heard her Vows, and with a flatt'ring look,
In her behalf, to jealous *Juno* spoke.
He cast his Arms about her Neck, and sed,
Dame rest secure; no more thy Nuptial Bed
This Nymph shall violate; by *Styx* I swear,   1025
And every Oath that binds the Thunderer.
The Goddess was appeas'd; and at the word
Was *Io* to her former shape restor'd.
The rugged Hair began to fall away;
The sweetness of her Eyes did only stay;   1030
Tho' not so large; her crooked Horns decrease;
The wideness of her Jaws and Nostrils cease:
Her Hoofs to Hands return, in little space:
The five long taper Fingers take their place.
And nothing of the Heyfar now is seen,   1035
Beside the native whiteness of the Skin.
Erected on her Feet she walks again;
And Two the duty of the Four sustain.
She tries her Tongue; her silence softly breaks,
And fears her former lowings when she speaks: 1040
A Goddess now, through all th' *Egyptian* State:
And serv'd by Priests, who in white Linnen wait.
    Her Son was *Epaphus*, at length believ'd
The Son of *Jove*, and as a God receiv'd:
With Sacrifice ador'd, and publick Pray'rs,   1045

He common Temples with his Mother shares.
Equal in years and Rival in Renown
With *Epaphus*, the youthful *Phaeton*
Like Honour claims; and boasts his Sire the Sun.
His haughty Looks, and his assuming Air   1050
The Son of *Isis* cou'd no longer bear:
Thou tak'st thy Mother's word, too far, said he,
And hast usurp'd thy boasted Pedigree.
Go base Pretender to a borrow'd Name.
Thus tax'd, he blush'd with anger, and with shame;   1055
But shame repress'd his Rage: the daunted Youth
Soon seeks his Mother, and enquires the truth:
Mother, said he, this Infamy was thrown
By *Epaphus* on you, and me your Son.
He spoke in publick, told it to my face;   1060
Nor durst I vindicate the dire disgrace:
Even I, the bold, the sensible of wrong,
Restrain'd by shame, was forc'd to hold my Tongue.
To hear an open Slander is a Curse;
But not to find an Answer, is a worse.   1065
If I am Heav'n-begot, assert your Son
By some sure Sign: and make my Father known,
To right my Honour, and redeem your own.
He said, and saying cast his arms about
Her Neck, and begg'd her to resolve the Doubt.   1070
  'Tis hard to judge if *Climenè* were mov'd
More by his Pray'r, whom she so dearly lov'd,
Or more with fury fir'd, to find her Name
Traduc'd, and made the sport of common Fame.
She stretch'd her Arms to Heav'n, and fix'd her Eyes   1075
On that fair Planet, that adorns the Skies;
Now by those Beams, said she, whose holy Fires
Consume my Breast, and kindle my desires;
By him, who sees us both, and chears our sight,
By him the publick Minister of light,   1080
I swear that *Sun* begot thee; if I lye
Let him his chearful Influence deny:
Let him no more this perjur'd Creature see;
And shine on all the World, but only me:
If still you doubt your Mother's Innocence,   1085

His Eastern Mansion is not far from hence,
With little pains, you to his *Levè* go,
And from himself, your Parentage may know.
With joy, th' ambitious Youth, his Mother heard,
And eager, for the Journey soon prepar'd.   1090
He longs the World beneath him to survey;
To guide the Chariot; and to give the day.
From *Meroe*'s burning Sands, he bends his course,
Nor less in *India*, feels his Father's force:
His Travel urging, till he came in sight;   1095
And saw the Palace by the Purple light.

THE FABLE OF *IPHIS* and *IANTHE*

From the Ninth Book of the Metamorphoses

THE Fame of this, perhaps, through *Crete* had flown:
   But *Crete* had newer Wonders of her own,
In *Iphis* chang'd: For, near the *Gnossian* bounds,
(As loud Report the Miracle resounds)
At *Phæstus* dwelt a man of honest blood: 5
But meanly born, and not so rich as good;
Esteem'd and lov'd by all the Neighbourhood.
Who to his Wife, before the time assign'd
For Child-birth came; thus bluntly spoke his mind.
If Heav'n, said *Lygdus*, will vouchsafe to hear;   10
I have but two Petitions to prefer:
Short pains for thee; for me a Son and Heir.
Girls cost as many throws, in bringing forth:
Besides when born, the Titts are little worth.
Weak puling things, unable to sustain   15
Their share of Labour, and their Bread to gain.
If, therefore, thou a Creature shalt produce
Of so great Charges, and so little Use,
(Bear witness Heav'n, with what reluctancy,)
Her hapless Innocence I doom to dye.   20
He said, and tears the common grief display
Of him who bade, and her who must obey.

Yet *Telethusa* still persists to find
Fit Arguments to move a Father's mind:
T' extend his Wishes to a larger scope;   25
And in one Vessel not confine his hope.
Lygdus continues hard: her time drew near,
And she her heavy load cou'd scarcely bear:
When slumb'ring, in the latter shades of Night,
Before th' approaches of returning light,   30
She saw, or thought she saw, before her Bed
A glorious Train, and *Isis* at their head:
Her Moony Horns were on her Forehead plac'd,
And yellow Sheaves her shining Temples grac'd:
A Mitre, for a Crown, she wore on high: 35
The Dog and dappl'd Bull were waiting by;
Osyris, sought along the Banks of *Nile*;
The silent God; the sacred Crocodile:
And, last, a long procession moving on,
With Timbrels, that assist the lab'ring Moon.   40
Her slumbers seem'd dispell'd, and, broad awake,
She heard a Voice, that thus distinctly spake.
My Votary, thy Babe from Death defend;
Nor fear to save whate're the Gods will send.
Delude with Art, thy Husband's dire Decree;   45
When danger calls, repose thy trust on me:
And know thou hast not serv'd a thankless Deity.
This Promise made; with Night the Goddess fled:
With joy the Woman wakes, and leaves her Bed:
Devoutly lifts her spotless hands on high;   50
And prays the Pow'rs, their Gift to ratifie.
    Now grinding pains proceed to bearing throws,
Till its own weight the burden did disclose.
'Twas of the beauteous Kind: and brought to light
With secresie, to shun the Father's sight.   55
Th' indulgent Mother did her Care employ;
And pass'd it on her Husband for a Boy.
The Nurse was conscious of the Fact alone:
The Father paid his Vows, as for a Son;
And call'd him *Iphis*, by a common Name   60
Which either Sex, with equal right may claim.

The Fable of Iphis. 23 find] find, *93*   59 Son;] Son. *93*

Iphis, his Grandsire was; the Wife was pleas'd,
Of half the fraud, by Fortune's favour eas'd:
The doubtful Name was us'd without deceit,
And Truth was cover'd with a pious Cheat.   65
The Habit shew'd a Boy, the beauteous Face
With manly fierceness mingl'd Female grace.

Now thirteen years of Age were swiftly run,
When the fond Father thought the time drew on
Of settling in the World, his only Son.   70
Ianthe was his choice; so wondrous fair
Her Form alone with *Iphis* cou'd compare;
A Neighbour's Daughter of his own Degree;
And not more blest with Fortunes Goods than he.

They soon espous'd; for they with ease were joyn'd,   75
Who were before Contracted in the Mind.
Their Age the same; their Inclinations too:
And bred together, in one School they grew.
Thus, fatally dispos'd to mutual fires,
They felt, before they knew, the same desires.   80
Equal their flame, unequal was their care;
One lov'd with Hope, one languish'd in Despair.
The Maid accus'd the ling'ring days alone:
For whom she thought a man, she thought her own.
But *Iphis* bends beneath a greater grief;   85
As fiercely burns, but hopes for no relief.
Ev'n her Despair, adds fuel to her fire;
A Maid with madness does a Maid desire.

And, scarce refraining tears, alas, said she,
What issue of my love remains for me!   90
How wild a Passion works within my Breast,
With what prodigious Flames am I possest!
Cou'd I the Care of Providence deserve,
Heav'n must destroy me, if it wou'd preserve.
And that's my Fate; or sure it wou'd have sent   95
Some usual Evil for my punishment:
Not this unkindly Curse; to rage and burn
Where Nature shews no prospect of return.
Nor Cows for Cows consume with fruitless fire,
Nor Mares when hot, their fellow Mares desire: 100

70 Son.] Son, 93

The Father of the Fold supplies his Ewes; ⎫
The Stag through secret Woods his Hind pursues: ⎬
And Birds for Mates, the Males of their own Species chuse. ⎭
Her Females Nature guards from Female flame, ⎫
And joyns two Sexes to preserve the Game: 105
Wou'd I were nothing, or not what I am! ⎭
Crete fam'd for Monsters wanted of her Store;
Till my new Love produc'd one Monster more.
The Daughter of the Sun a Bull desir'd,
And yet ev'n then, a Male, a Female fir'd: 110
Her passion was extravagantly new;
But mine is much the madder of the two.
To things impossible she was not bent;
But found the Means to compass her Intent.
To cheat his Eyes, she took a different shape: 115
Yet still she gain'd a Lover, and a leap.
Shou'd all the Wit of all the World conspire,
Shou'd *Dædalus* assist my wild desire,
What Art can make me able to enjoy,
Or what can change *Ianthe* to a Boy?   120
Extinguish then thy passion, hopeless Maid,
And recollect thy Reason for thy aid.
Know what thou art, and love as Maidens ought;
And drive these Golden Wishes from thy thought.
Thou canst not hope thy fond desires to gain;   125
Where Hope is wanting, Wishes are in vain.
    And yet no Guards, against our Joys conspire;
No jealous Husband, hinders our desire:
My Parents are propitious to my Wish
And she her self consenting to the bliss.   130
All things concur, to prosper our Design:
All things to prosper any Love but mine.
And yet I never can enjoy the Fair:
'Tis past the Pow'r of Heav'n to grant my Pray'r.
Heav'n has been kind, as far as Heav'n can be;   135
Our Parents with our own desires agree,
But Nature, stronger than the Gods above,
Refuses her assistance to my love.
She sets the Bar, that causes all my pain:
One Gift refus'd, makes all their Bounty vain.   140

And now the happy day is just at hand,
To bind our Hearts in *Hymen*'s Holy Band:
Our Hearts, but not our Bodies: thus, accurs'd,
In midst of water, I complain of thirst.
Why com'st thou, *Juno*, to these barren Rites,   145
To bless a Bed, defrauded of delights?
Or why shou'd *Hymen* lift his Torch on high,
To see two Brides in cold Embraces lye?
   Thus love-sick *Iphis* her vain Passion mourns:
With equal ardour fair *Ianthe* burns: 150
Invoking *Hymen*'s Name and *Juno*'s Pow'r
To speed the work, and haste the happy hour.
   She hopes, while *Telethusa* fears the day;
And strives to interpose some new delay:
Now feigns a sickness, now is in a fright   155
For this bad Omen, or that boding sight.
But having done whate're she cou'd devise,
And empty'd all her Magazine of lies,
The time approach'd: the next ensuing day
The Fatal Secret must to light betray.   160
Then *Telethusa* had recourse to Pray'r,
She and her Daughter with dishevell'd hair:
Trembling with fear, great *Isis* they ador'd;
Embrac'd her Altar, and her aid implor'd.
   Fair Queen, who dost on fruitful *Egypt* smile,   ⎫ 165
Who sway'st the Sceptre of the *Pharian* Isle,   ⎬
And sev'n-fold falls of disimbogueing *Nile*;   ⎭
Relieve, in this our last distress, she said,
A suppliant Mother, and a mournful Maid.
Thou Goddess, thou wert present to my sight;   170
Reveal'd I saw thee, by thy own fair light:
I saw thee in my Dream, as now I see
With all thy marks of awful Majesty:
The Glorious Train, that compass'd thee around;
And heard the hollow Timbrels holy sound.   175
Thy Words I noted, which I still retain;
Let not thy Sacred Oracles be vain.
That *Iphis* lives, that I my self am free
From shame and punishment, I owe to thee.
On thy Protection, all our hopes depend: 180

Thy Counsel sav'd us, let thy Pow'r defend.
   Her tears pursu'd her words; and while she spoke
The Goddess nodded, and her Altar shook:
The Temple doors, as with a blast of wind,
Were heard to clap; the Lunar Horns that bind 185
The brows of *Isis*, cast a blaze around;
The trembling Timbrel, made a murm'ring sound.
   Some hopes these happy Omens did impart;
Forth went the Mother with a beating Heart:
Not much in fear, nor fully satisfi'd; 190
But *Iphis* follow'd with a larger stride:
The whiteness of her Skin forsook her Face;
Her looks emboldn'd, with an awful Grace;
Her Features and her Strength together grew;
And her long Hair, to curling Locks withdrew. 195
Her sparkling Eyes, with Manly Vigour shone,
Big was her Voice, Audacious was her Tone.
The latent Parts, at length reveal'd, began
To shoot, and spread, and burnish into Man.
The Maid becomes a Youth; no more delay 200
Your Vows, but look, and confidently pay.
Their Gifts, the Parents to the Temple bear:
The Votive Tables, this Inscription wear;
Iphis the Man, has to the Goddess paid,
The Vows that *Iphis* offer'd, when a Maid. 205
   Now, when the Star of Day had shewn his face,
Venus and *Juno* with their Presence grace
The Nuptial Rites, and *Hymen* from above
Descending to compleat their happy Love:
The Gods of Marriage, lend their mutual aid; 210
And the warm Youth enjoys the lovely Maid.

THE FABLE OF ACIS, POLYPHEMUS, AND GALATEA

From the Thirteenth Book of the Metamorphoses

GALATEA *relates the Story*

*A*CIS, the Lovely Youth, whose loss I mourn,
From *Faunus* and the Nymph *Symethis* born,
Was both his Parents pleasure: but, to me
Was all that Love cou'd make a Lover be.
The Gods our Minds in mutual Bands did joyn;   5
I was his only Joy, as he was mine.
Now sixteen Summers the sweet Youth had seen;
And doubtful Down, began to shade his Chin:
When *Polyphemus* first disturb'd our Joy;
And lov'd me fiercely, as I lov'd the Boy.   10
Ask not which passion in my Soul was high'r,
My last Aversion, or my first Desire:
Nor this the greater was, nor that the less:
Both were alike; for both were in excess.
Thee, *Venus*, thee, both Heav'n and Earth obey;   15
Immense thy Pow'r, and boundless is thy Sway.
The *Cyclops*, who defi'd th' Ætherial Throne,
And thought no Thunder louder than his own,
The terrour of the Woods, and wilder far
Than Wolves in Plains, or Bears in Forrests are,   20
Th' Inhumane Host, who made his bloody Feasts
On mangl'd Members, of his butcher'd Guests,
Yet felt the force of Love, and fierce Desire,
And burnt for me, with unrelenting Fire.
Forgot his Caverns, and his woolly care,   ⎫
Assum'd the softness of a Lover's Air;   ⎬ 25
And comb'd, with Teeth of Rakes, his rugged hair.   ⎭
Now with a crooked Sythe his Beard he sleeks;
And mows the stubborn Stubble of his Cheeks:
Now, in the Crystal Stream he looks, to try   30
His Simagres, and rowls his glaring eye.
His Cruelty and thirst of Blood are lost;
And Ships securely sail along the Coast.

The Prophet *Telemus* (arriv'd by chance
Where *Ætna*'s Summets to the Seas advance,   35
Who mark'd the Tracts of every Bird that flew,
And sure Presages from their flying drew,)
Foretold the *Cyclops*, that *Ulysses* hand
In his broad eye, shou'd thrust a flaming Brand.
The Giant, with a scornful grin reply'd,   40
Vain Augur, thou hast falsely prophesi'd;
Already Love, his flaming Brand has tost;
Looking on two fair Eyes, my sight I lost.
Thus, warn'd in vain, with stalking pace he strode,
And stamp'd the Margine of the briny Flood,   45
With heavy steps: and weary, sought agen,
The cool Retirement of his gloomy Den.
    A Promontory sharp'ning by degrees,
Ends in a Wedge, and over-looks the Seas:
On either side, below, the water flows;   50
This airy walk, the Giant Lover chose.
Here, on the midst he sate: his Flocks, unled,
Their Shepherd follow'd, and securely fed.
A Pine so burly, and of length so vast,
That sailing Ships requir'd it for a Mast,   55
He weilded for a Staff; his steps to guide:
But laid it by, his Whistle while he try'd.
A hundred Reeds, of a prodigious growth,
Scarce made a Pipe, proportion'd to his mouth:
Which, when he gave it wind, the Rocks around,   60
And watry Plains, the dreadful hiss resound.
I heard the Ruffian-Shepherd rudely blow
Where, in a hollow Cave, I sat below;
On *Acis* bosom I my head reclin'd:
And still preserve the Poem in my mind.   65
    Oh lovely *Galatea*, whiter far
Than falling Snows, and rising Lillies are;
More flowry than the Meads, as Crystal bright,
Erect as Alders, and of equal height:
More wanton than a Kid, more sleek thy Skin   70
Than Orient Shells, that on the Shores are seen.
Than Apples fairer, when the boughs they lade,
Pleasing as Winter Suns or Summer Shade:

More grateful to the sight, than goodly Planes;
And softer to the touch, than down of Swans;   75
Or Curds new turn'd: and sweeter to the taste
Than swelling Grapes, that to the Vintage haste:
More clear than Ice, or running Streams, that stray
Through Garden Plots, but ah more swift than they.
    Yet, *Galatea*, harder to be broke,   80
Than Bullocks, unreclaim'd to bear the Yoke,
And far more stubborn, than the knotted Oak:
Like sliding Streams, impossible to hold;
Like them fallacious, like their Fountains cold.
More warping than the Willow, to decline   85
My warm Embrace, more brittle than the Vine;
Immoveable and fixt in thy disdain;
Rough as these Rocks, and of a harder grain.
More violent than is the rising Flood;
And the prais'd Peacock is not half so proud.   90
Fierce as the Fire, and sharp as Thistles are,
And more outragious than a Mother-Bear:
Deaf as the billows to the Vows I make;
And more revengeful, than a trodden Snake.
In swiftness fleeter, than the flying Hind;   95
Or driven Tempests, or the driving Wind.
All other faults, with patience I can bear;
But swiftness is the Vice I only fear.
    Yet if you knew me well, you wou'd not shun
My Love, but to my wish'd Embraces run: 100
Wou'd languish in your turn, and court my stay;
And much repent of your unwise delay.
    My Palace, in the living Rock, is made
By Nature's hand; a spacious pleasing Shade:
Which neither heat can pierce, nor cold invade.   105
My Garden fill'd with Fruits you may behold,
And Grapes in clusters, imitating Gold;
Some blushing Bunches of a purple hue:
And these and those, are all reserv'd for you.
Red Strawberries, in shades, expecting stand,   110
Proud to be gather'd by so white a hand.
Autumnal Cornels, latter Fruit provide;
And Plumbs to tempt you, turn their glossy side:

Not those of common kinds; but such alone
As in *Phæacian* Orchards might have grown: 115
Nor Chestnuts shall be wanting to your Food,
Nor Garden-fruits, nor Wildings of the Wood;
The laden Boughs for you alone shall bear;
And yours shall be the product of the Year.

The Flocks you see, are all my own; beside   120
The rest that Woods, and winding Vallies hide;
And those that folded in the Caves abide.
Ask not the numbers of my growing Store;
Who knows how many, knows he has no more.
Nor will I praise my Cattel, trust not me;   125
But judge your self, and pass your own decree:
Behold their swelling Dugs; the sweepy weight
Of Ews that sink beneath the Milky fraight;
In the warm Folds, their tender Lambkins lye;
Apart from Kids, that call with humane cry.   130
New Milk in Nut-brown Bowls, is duely serv'd
For daily Drink; the rest for Cheese reserv'd.
Nor are these House-hold Dainties all my Store:
The Fields and Forrests will afford us more;
The Deer, the Hare, the Goat, the Salvage Boar,   135
All sorts of Ven'son; and of Birds the best;
A pair of Turtles taken from the Nest.
I walk'd the Mountains, and two Cubs I found,
(Whose Dam had left 'em on the naked ground,)
So like, that no distinction cou'd be seen: 140
So pretty, they were Presents for a Queen;
And so they shall; I took 'em both away;
And keep, to be Companions of your Play.

Oh raise, fair Nymph, your Beauteous Face above
The Waves; nor scorn my Presents, and my Love.   145
Come, *Galatea*, come, and view my face;
I late beheld it, in the watry Glass;
And found it lovelier than I fear'd it was.
Survey my towring Stature, and my Size:
Not *Jove*, the *Jove* you dream that rules the Skies,   150
Bears such a bulk, or is so largely spread:
My Locks, (the plenteous Harvest of my head)

The Fable of Acis. 135 Boar,] Boar. *93*   150 Skies,] Skies *93*

Hang o're my Manly Face; and dangling down
As with a shady Grove, my shoulders crown.
Nor think, because my limbs and body bear   155
A thick set underwood of bristling hair,
My shape deform'd; what fouler sight can be
Than the bald Branches of a leafless Tree?
Foul is the Steed, without a flowing Main:
And Birds without their Feathers and their Train.   160
Wool decks the Sheep; and Man receives a Grace
From bushy Limbs, and from a bearded Face.
My forehead, with a single eye is fill'd,
Round as a Ball, and ample as a Shield.
The Glorious Lamp of Heav'n, the Radiant Sun   165
Is Nature's eye; and she's content with one.
Add, that my Father sways your Seas, and I
Like you am of the watry Family.
I make you his, in making you my own;
You I adore; and kneel to you alone: 170
Jove, with his Fabled Thunder I despise,
And only fear the lightning of your eyes.
Frown not, fair Nymph; yet I cou'd bear to be
Disdain'd, if others were disdain'd with me.
But to repulse the *Cyclops*, and prefer   175
The Love of *Acis*, (Heav'ns) I cannot bear.
But let the Stripling please himself; nay more,
Please you, tho' that's the thing I most abhor;
The Boy shall find, if e're we cope in Fight,
These Giant Limbs, endu'd with Giant Might.   180
His living Bowels, from his Belly torn,
And scatter'd Limbs, shall on the Flood be born:
Thy Flood, ungrateful Nymph, and fate shall find
That way for thee, and *Acis* to be joyn'd.
For oh I burn with Love, and thy Disdain   185
Augments at once my Passion, and my pain.
Translated *Ætna* flames within my Heart,
And thou, Inhumane, wilt not ease my smart.
     Lamenting thus in vain, he rose, and strode
With furious paces to the Neighb'ring Wood: 190
Restless his feet, distracted was his walk;

        166 she's] is *93*   178 abhor;] abhor, *93*

Mad were his motions, and confus'd his talk.
Mad as the vanquish'd Bull, when forc'd to yield
His lovely Mistress, and forsake the Field.
   Thus far unseen I saw: when fatal chance   195
His looks directing, with a sudden glance,
Acis and I, were to his sight betray'd;
Where nought suspecting we securely play'd.
From his wide mouth, a bellowing cry he cast,
I see, I see; but this shall be your last: 200
A roar so loud made *Ætna* to rebound;
And all the *Cyclops* labour'd in the sound.
Affrighted with his monstrous Voice, I fled,
And in the Neighb'ring Ocean, plung'd my head.
Poor *Acis* turn'd his back, and help, he cry'd;   205
Help, *Galatea*, help, my Parent Gods,
And take me dying, to your deep Abodes.
The *Cyclops* follow'd: but he sent before
A Rib, which from the living Rock he tore:
Though but an Angle reach'd him of the Stone,   210
The mighty Fragment was enough alone
To crush all *Acis*; 'twas too late to save,
But what the Fates allow'd to give, I gave:
That *Acis* to his Lineage should return;
And rowl, among the River Gods, his Urn.   215
Straight issu'd from the Stone, a Stream of blood;
Which lost the Purple, mingling with the Flood.
Then, like a troubl'd Torrent, it appear'd:
The Torrent too, in little space was clear'd.
The Stone was cleft, and through the yawning chink,   220
New Reeds arose on the new River's brink.
The Rock, from out its hollow Womb, disclos'd
A sound like Water in its course oppos'd.
When, (wondrous to behold,) full in the Flood,
Up starts a Youth, and Navel high he stood.   225
Horns from his Temples rise; and either Horn
Thick Wreaths of Reeds, (his Native growth) adorn.
Were not his Stature taller than before,
His bulk augmented, and his beauty more,
His colour blue, for *Acis* he might pass: 230

199 cast,] cast *93*   209 tore:] tore, *93*   229 more,] more: *93*

And *Acis* chang'd into a Stream he was.
But mine no more; he rowls along the Plains
With rapid motion, and his Name retains.

SONG TO A Fair, Young LADY,
Going out of the TOWN In the SPRING

1

ASK not the Cause, why sullen *Spring*
    So long delays her Flow'rs to bear;
Why warbling Birds forget to sing,
    And Winter Storms invert the Year?
Chloris is gone; and Fate provides   5
To make it *Spring*, where she resides.

2

Chloris is gone, the Cruel Fair;
    She cast not back a pitying Eye:
But left her Lover in Despair;
    To sigh, to languish, and to die: 10
Ah, how can those fair Eyes endure
To give the Wounds they will not cure!

3

Great God of Love, why hast thou made
    A Face that can all Hearts command,
That all Religions can invade,   15
    And change the Laws of ev'ry Land?
Where thou hadst plac'd such Pow'r before,
Thou shou'dst have made her Mercy more.

4

When *Chloris* to the Temple comes,
    Adoring Crowds before her fall;   20
She can restore the Dead from Tombs,
    And ev'ry Life but mine recall.
I only am by Love design'd
To be the Victim for Mankind.

PROLOGUE TO THE UNIVERSITY
OF *OXFORD*, 1681

T HE fam'd *Italian* Muse, whose Rhymes advance
   Orlando, and the *Paladins* of *France*,
Records, that when our Wit and Sense is flown,
'Tis lodg'd within the Circle of the Moon
In Earthen Jars, which one, who thither soar'd,   5
Set to his Nose, snufft up, and was restor'd.
What e're the Story be, the Moral's true,
The Wit we lost in Town, we find in you.
Our Poets their fled Parts may draw from hence,
And fill their windy Heads with sober Sense.   10
When *London* Votes with *Southwark*'s disagree,
Here they may find their long lost Loyalty.
Here busie Senates, to th' old Cause inclin'd,
May snuff the Votes their Fellows left behind:
Your Country Neighbours, when their Grain grows dear,   15
May come and find their *last Provision* here:
Whereas we cannot much lament our loss,
Who neither carry'd back, nor brought one Cross;
We look'd what Representatives wou'd bring,
But they help'd us, just as they did the King.   20
Yet we despair not, for we now lay forth
The *Sybill*'s Books, to those who know their worth:
And tho the first was Sacrific'd before,
These Volumes doubly will the price restore.
Our Poet bade us hope this Grace to find,   25
To whom by long Prescription you are kind.
He, whose undaunted Muse, with Loyal Rage,
Has never spar'd the Vices of the Age,
Here finding nothing that his Spleen can raise,
Is forc'd to turn his Satire into Praise.   30

PROLOGUE

G ALLANTS, a bashful Poet bids me say
  He's come to lose his Maidenhead to day.
Be not too fierce, for he's but green of *Age*;

And ne're, till now, debauch'd upon the Stage.
He wants the suff'ring part of Resolution;   5
And comes with blushes to his Execution.
E're you deflow'r his Muse, he hopes the Pit
Will make some Settlement upon his Wit.
Promise him well, before the Play begin;
For he wou'd fain be cozen'd into Sin.   10
'Tis not but that he knows you mean to fail;
But, if you leave him after being frail,
He'll have, at least, a fair pretence to rail;
To call you base, and swear you us'd him ill,
And put you in the new Deserters Bill: 15
Lord, what a Troop of perjur'd Men we see;
Enow to fill another Mercury!
But this the Ladies may with patience brook:
Their's are not the first Colours you forsook!
He wou'd be loath the *Beauties* to offend;   20
But, if he shou'd, he's not too old to mend.
He's a young Plant, in his first Year of bearing,
But his Friend swears, he will be worth the reering.
His gloss is still upon him: tho 'tis true
He's yet unripe, yet take him for the blue.   25
You think an *Apricot* half green is best;
There's sweet and sour: and one side good at least.
Mango's and Limes, whose nourishment is little,
Tho' not for Food, are yet preserv'd for Pickle.
So this green Writer, may pretend, at least,   30
To whet your Stomachs for a better Feast.
He makes this difference in the Sexes too,
He sells to Men, he gives himself to you.
To both, he wou'd contribute some delight;
A mere Poetical Hermaphrodite.   35
Thus he's equipped, both to be woo'd, and woo;
With *Arms* offensive, and defensive too;
'Tis hard, he thinks, if neither part will do.

Veni Creator Spiritus,
Translated in PARAPHRASE

CREATOR Spirit, by whose aid
The World's Foundations first were laid,
Come visit ev'ry pious Mind;
Come pour thy Joys on Human Kind:
From Sin, and Sorrow set us free;   5
And make thy Temples worthy Thee.

O, Source of uncreated Light,
The Father's promis'd *Paraclite*!
Thrice Holy Fount, thrice Holy Fire,
Our Hearts with Heav'nly Love inspire;   10
Come, and thy Sacred Unction bring
To Sanctifie us, while we sing!

Plenteous of Grace, descend from high,
Rich in thy sev'n-fold Energy!
Thou strength of his Almighty Hand,   15
Whose Pow'r does Heav'n and Earth command:
Proceeding Spirit, our Defence,
Who do'st the Gift of Tongues dispence,
And crown'st thy Gift, with Eloquence!

Refine and purge our Earthy Parts;   20
But, oh, inflame and fire our Hearts!
Our Frailties help, our Vice controul;
Submit the Senses to the Soul;
And when Rebellious they are grown,
Then, lay thy hand, and hold 'em down.   25

Chace from our Minds th' Infernal Foe;
And Peace, the fruit of Love, bestow:
And, lest our Feet shou'd step astray,
Protect, and guide us in the way.

Make us Eternal Truths receive,   30
And practise, all that we believe:
Give us thy self, that we may see
The Father and the Son, by thee.

Immortal Honour, endless Fame
Attend th' Almighty Father's Name: 35
The Saviour Son, be glorify'd,
Who for lost Man's Redemption dy'd:
And equal Adoration be
Eternal *Paraclete*, to thee.

RONDELAY

I

CHLOE found *Amyntas* lying
    All in Tears, upon the Plain;
Sighing to himself, and crying,
    Wretched I, to love in vain!
Kiss me, Dear, before my dying;   5
    Kiss me once, and ease my pain!

2

Sighing to himself, and crying
    Wretched I, to love in vain:
Ever scorning and denying
    To reward your faithful Swain: 10
Kiss me, Dear, before my dying;
    Kiss me once, and ease my pain!

3

Ever scorning, and denying
    To reward your faithful Swain;
Chloe, laughing at his crying,   15
    Told him that he lov'd in vain:
Kiss me, Dear, before my dying;
    Kiss me once, and ease my pain!

4

Chloe, laughing at his crying,
    Told him that he lov'd in vain: 20
But repenting, and complying,
    When he kiss'd, she kiss'd again:
Kiss'd him up, before his dying;
    Kiss'd him up, and eas'd his pain.

An EPITAPH ON THE Lady *WHITMORE*

FAIR, Kind, and True, a Treasure each alone;
A Wife, a Mistress, and a Friend in one;
Rest in this Tomb, rais'd at thy Husband's cost,
Here sadly summing, what he had, and lost.
Come Virgins, e're in equal Bands you join,   5
Come first and offer at her Sacred Shrine;
Pray but for half the Vertues of this Wife,
Compound for all the rest, with longer Life,
And wish your Vows like hers may be return'd,
So Lov'd when Living, and when Dead so Mourn'd.   10

AN EPITAPH, ON Sir *Palmes Fairborne*'s TOMB
IN *Westminster*-Abby

Sacred
To the Immortal Memory of Sir Palmes Fairborne, *Knight, Governor of*
Tangier; *in execution of which Command he was mortally wounded by a Shot*
from the Moors, *then Besieging the Town, in the 46th. year of his Age.*
October 24th. *1680.*

YE Sacred Relicks which your Marble keep,
Here undisturb'd by Wars in quiet sleep:
Discharge the trust which when it was below
Fairborne's undaunted Soul did undergo,
And be the Towns Palladium from the Foe.   5
Alive and dead these Walls he will defend,
Great Actions great Examples must attend.
The *Candian* Siege his early Valour knew,
Where *Turkish* Blood did his young hands imbrew.
From thence returning with deserv'd Applause,   10
Against the *Moors* his well-flesh'd Sword he draws;
The same the Courage, and the same the Cause.

An Epitaph, on Sir Palmes Fairborne's Tomb. Text collated with Poetical Recreations...
Part II. By several Gentlemen of the Universities, and Others, *1688, and the inscrip-*
tion on the tomb (I)   Heading in 88: *An Epitaph to the Memory (and fix't on the*
Tomb) of Sir Palme Fairborn, *Governour of* Tangier, *who, in Execution of his Command, was*
Mortally Wounded by a Shot from the Moors, *that then besieged the Town*, Octob. 24. 1680
1 your] this 88   3 it] he I   4 undaunted] disdaunted I   6 these
Walls he will] he will these Walls 88

His Youth and Age, his Life and Death combine,
As in some great and regular design,
All of a Piece throughout, and all Divine. } 15
Still nearer Heaven his Vertues shone more bright,
Like rising flames expanding in their height,
The *Martyr*'s Glory Crown'd the Soldiers Fight. }
More bravely *Brittish* General never fell,
Nor General's Death was e're reveng'd so well, 20
Which his pleas'd Eyes beheld before their close,
Follow'd by thousand Victims of his Foes.
To his lamented loss for time to come,
His pious Widow Consecrates this Tomb.

THE Last parting OF *Hector* and *Andromache*.
FROM THE SIXTH BOOK OF *Homer*'s Iliads

ARGUMENT

Hector, *returning from the Field of Battel, to visit* Helen *his Sister-in-Law, and his Brother* Paris, *who had fought unsuccessfully hand to hand, with* Menelaus, *from thence goes to his own Palace to see his Wife* Andromache, *and his Infant Son* Astyanax. *The description of that Interview, is the Subject of this Translation.*

THUS having said, brave *Hector* went to see
His Virtuous Wife, the fair *Andromache*.
He found her not at home; for she was gone
(Attended by her Maid and Infant Son,)
To climb the steepy Tow'r of *Ilion*: } 5
From whence with heavy Heart she might survey
The bloody business of the dreadful Day.
Her mournful Eyes she cast around the Plain,
And sought the Lord of her Desires in vain.
But he, who thought his peopled Palace bare, 10
When she, his only Comfort, was not there;
Stood in the Gate, and ask'd of ev'ry one,

16 Vertues] Vertue *I*   17 their] the *88*   23–24 *om. 88*   23 time]
Times *I*
   The Last Parting of Hector and Andromache. 5 Ilion:] Ilion. *93*.

Which way she took, and whither she was gone:
If to the Court, or with his Mother's Train,
In long Procession to *Minerva*'s Fane?   15
The Servants answer'd, neither to the Court
Where *Priam*'s Sons and Daughters did resort,
Nor to the Temple was she gone, to move
With Prayers the blew-ey'd Progeny of *Jove*;
But, more solicitous for him alone,   20
Than all their safety, to the Tow'r was gone,
There to survey the Labours of the Field;
Where the *Greeks* conquer, and the *Trojans* yield.
Swiftly she pass'd, with Fear and Fury wild,
The Nurse went lagging after with the Child.   25

    This heard, the Noble *Hector* made no stay;
Th' admiring Throng divide, to give him way:
He pass'd through every Street, by which he came,
And at the Gate he met the mournful Dame.
    His Wife beheld him, and with eager pace,   30
Flew to his *Arms*, to meet a dear Embrace:
His Wife, who brought in Dow'r *Cilicia*'s Crown;
And, in her self, a greater Dow'r alone:
Aëtion's Heyr, who on the Woody Plain
Of *Hippoplacus* did in *Thebe* reign.   35
Breathless she flew, with Joy and Passion wild,
The Nurse came lagging after with her Child.
    The *Royal Babe* upon her *Breast* was laid;
Who, like the Morning Star, his beams display'd.
Scamandrius was his Name which *Hector* gave,   40
From that fair Flood which *Ilion*'s Wall did lave:
But him *Astyanax* the *Trojans* call,
From his great Father who defends the Wall.
    Hector beheld him with a silent Smile,
His tender Wife stood weeping by, the while: 45
Prest in her own, his Warlike hand she took,
Then sigh'd, and thus Prophetically spoke.
    Thy dauntless Heart (which I foresee too late,)
Too daring Man, will urge thee to thy Fate:
Nor dost thou pity, with a Parent's mind,   50
This helpless Orphan whom thou leav'st behind;
Nor me, th' unhappy Partner of thy *Bed*;

Who must in Triumph by the *Greeks* be led:
They seek thy Life; and in unequal Fight,
With many will oppress thy single Might: 55
Better it were for miserable me
To die before the Fate which I foresee.
For ah what comfort can the World bequeath
To *Hector*'s Widow, after *Hector*'s death!

   Eternal Sorrow and perpetual Tears   60
Began my Youth, and will conclude my Years:
I have no Parents, Friends, nor Brothers left;
By stern *Achilles* all of Life bereft.
Then when the Walls of *Thebes* he o'rethrew,
His fatal Hand my Royal Father slew;   65
He slew *Aëtion*, but despoil'd him not;
Nor in his hate the Funeral Rites forgot;
Arm'd as he was he sent him whole below;
And reverenc'd thus the Manes of his Foe:
A Tomb he rais'd; the Mountain Nymphs around,   70
Enclos'd with planted Elms the Holy Ground.

   My sev'n brave *Brothers* in one fatal Day
To Death's dark Mansions took the mournful way:
Slain by the same *Achilles*, while they keep
The bellowing Oxen and the bleating Sheep.   75
My Mother, who the Royal Scepter sway'd,
Was Captive to the cruel Victor made:
And hither led: but hence redeem'd with Gold,
Her Native Country did again behold.
And but beheld: for soon *Diana*'s Dart   80
In an unhappy Chace transfix'd her Heart.

   But thou, my *Hector*, art thy self alone,
My Parents, Brothers, and my Lord in one:
O kill not all my Kindred o're again,
Nor tempt the Dangers of the dusty Plain;   85
But in this Tow'r, for our Defence, remain.
Thy Wife and Son are in thy Ruin lost:
This is a Husband's and a Father's Post.
The *Scæan* Gate commands the Plains below;
Here marshal all thy Souldiers as they go;   90
And hence, with other Hands, repel the Foe.
By yon wild Fig-tree lies their chief ascent,

And thither all their Pow'rs are daily bent:
The two *Ajaces* have I often seen,
And the wrong'd Husband of the *Spartan* Queen: 95
With him his greater *Brother*; and with these
Fierce *Diomede* and bold *Meriones*:
Uncertain if by *Augury*, or chance,
But by this easie rise they all advance;
Guard well that Pass, secure of all beside.   100
To whom the Noble *Hector* thus reply'd.

   That and the rest are in my daily care;
But shou'd I shun the Dangers of the War,
With scorn the *Trojans* wou'd reward my pains,
And their proud Ladies with their sweeping Trains.   105
The *Grecian* Swords and Lances I can bear:
But loss of Honour is my only Fear.
Shall *Hector*, born to War, his *Birth-right* yield,
Belie his Courage and forsake the Field?
Early in rugged *Arms* I took delight;   110
And still have been the foremost in the Fight:
With dangers dearly have I bought Renown,
And am the Champion of my Father's Crown.

   And yet my mind forebodes, with sure presage,
That *Troy* shall perish by the *Grecian* Rage.   115
The fatal Day draws on, when I must fall;
And Universal Ruine cover all.
Not *Troy* it self, tho' built by Hands Divine,
Nor *Priam*, nor his People, nor his Line,
My Mother, nor my *Brothers* of Renown,   120
Whose Valour yet defends th' unhappy Town,
Not these, nor all their Fates which I foresee,
Are half of that concern I have for thee.
I see, I see thee in that fatal Hour,
Subjected to the Victor's cruel Pow'r: 125
Led hence a Slave to some insulting Sword:
Forlorn and trembling at a Foreign Lord.
A spectacle in *Argos*, at the Loom,
Gracing with *Trojan* Fights, a *Grecian* Room;
Or from deep Wells, the living Stream to take,   130
And on thy weary Shoulders bring it back.
While, groaning under this laborious Life,

They insolently call thee *Hector*'s Wife;
Upbraid thy *Bondage* with thy Husband's name;
And from my Glory propagate thy Shame.   135
This when they say, thy Sorrows will encrease
With anxious thoughts of former Happiness;
That he is dead who cou'd thy wrongs redress.
But I opprest with Iron Sleep before,
Shall hear thy unavailing Cries no more.   140
    He said.
Then, holding forth his *Arms*, he took his *Boy*,
(The Pledge of Love, and other hope of *Troy*;)
The fearful Infant turn'd his Head away;
And on his Nurse's Neck reclining lay,   145
His unknown Father shunning with affright,
And looking back on so uncouth a sight.
Daunted to see a Face with Steel o're-spread,
And his high Plume, that nodded o're his Head.
His Sire and Mother smil'd with silent Joy;   150
And *Hector* hasten'd to relieve his *Boy*;
Dismiss'd his burnish'd Helm, that shone afar,
(The Pride of Warriours, and the Pomp of War:)
Th' *Illustrious Babe*, thus reconcil'd, he took:
Hugg'd in his *Arms*, and kiss'd, and thus he spoke.   155
    Parent of Gods, and Men, propitious *Jove*,
And you bright Synod of the Pow'rs above;
On this my Son your Gracious Gifts bestow;
Grant him to live, and great in *Arms* to grow:
To Reign in *Troy*; to Govern with Renown: 160
To shield the People, and assert the Crown:
That, when hereafter he from War shall come,
And bring his *Trojans* Peace and Triumph home,
Some aged Man, who lives this act to see,
And who in former times remember'd me,   165
May say the Son in Fortitude and Fame
Out-goes the Mark; and drowns his Father's Name:
That at these words his Mother may rejoice:
And add her Suffrage to the publick Voice.
    Thus having said,   170
He first with suppliant Hands the Gods ador'd:

133 Wife;] Wife. *93*

Then to the Mother's *Arms* the Child restor'd:
With Tears and Smiles she took her Son, and press'd
Th' Illustrious Infant to her fragrant *Breast*.
He wiping her fair Eyes, indulg'd her Grief,   175
And eas'd her Sorrows with this last Relief.
  My Wife and Mistress, drive thy fears away;
Nor give so bad an Omen to the Day:
Think not it lies in any *Grecian*'s Pow'r,
To take my Life before the fatal Hour.   180
When that arrives, nor good nor bad can fly
Th' irrevocable Doom of Destiny.
Return, and to divert thy thoughts at home,
There task thy Maids, and exercise the Loom,
Employ'd in Works that Womankind become.   185
The Toils of War, and Feats of Chivalry
Belong to Men, and most of all to me.
At this, for new Replies he did not stay,
But lac'd his Crested Helm, and strode away:
  His lovely Consort to her House return'd: 190
And looking often back in silence mourn'd:
Home when she came, her secret Woe she vents,
And fills the Palace with her loud Laments:
Those loud Laments her ecchoing Maids restore,
And *Hector*, yet alive, as dead deplore.   195

To my Dear Friend Mr. Congreve,
On His COMEDY, call'd The Double-Dealer

WELL then; the promis'd hour is come at last;
   The present Age of Wit obscures the past:
Strong were our Syres; and as they Fought they Writ,
Conqu'ring with force of Arms, and dint of Wit;
Theirs was the Gyant Race, before the Flood;   5
And thus, when *Charles* Return'd, our Empire stood.
Like *Janus* he the stubborn Soil manur'd,
With Rules of Husbandry the rankness cur'd:
Tam'd us to manners, when the Stage was rude;
And boistrous *English* Wit, with Art indu'd.   10
Our Age was cultivated thus at length;
But what we gain'd in skill we lost in strength.
Our Builders were, with want of Genius, curst;
The second Temple was not like the first:
Till You, the best *Vitruvius*, come at length;   15
Our Beauties equal; but excel our strength.
Firm *Dorique* Pillars found Your solid Base: ⎫
The Fair *Corinthian* Crowns the higher Space;   ⎬
Thus all below is Strength, and all above is Grace. ⎭
In easie Dialogue is *Fletcher*'s Praise: 20
He mov'd the mind, but had not power to raise.
Great *Johnson* did by strength of Judgment please:
Yet doubling *Fletcher*'s Force, he wants his Ease.
In differing Tallents both adorn'd their Age;
One for the Study, t'other for the Stage.   25
But both to *Congreve* justly shall submit,
One match'd in Judgment, both o'er-match'd in Wit.
In Him all Beauties of this Age we see;   ⎫
Etherege his Courtship, *Southern*'s Purity;   ⎬
The Satire, Wit, and Strength of Manly *Witcherly*. ⎭ 30
All this in blooming Youth you have Atchiev'd;
Nor are your foil'd Contemporaries griev'd;
So much the sweetness of your manners move,
We cannot envy you because we Love.

To . . . Mr. Congreve. Text from The Double-Dealer, A Comedy, *1694*
32 Nor] Now *94*

Fabius might joy in *Scipio*, when he saw　　　　　35
A Beardless Consul made against the Law,
And joyn his Suffrage to the Votes of *Rome*;
Though He with *Hannibal* was overcome.
Thus old *Romano* bow'd to *Raphel's* Fame;
And Scholar to the Youth he taught, became.　　40
　　Oh that your Brows my Lawrel had sustain'd,
Well had I been Depos'd, if You had reign'd!
The Father had descended for the Son;
For only You are lineal to the Throne.
Thus when the State one *Edward* did depose;　45
A Greater *Edward* in his room arose.
But now, not I, but Poetry is curs'd;
For *Tom* the Second reigns like *Tom* the first.
But let 'em not mistake my Patron's part;
Nor call his Charity their own desert.　　　　50
Yet this I Prophesy; Thou shalt be seen,
(Tho' with some short Parenthesis between:)
High on the Throne of Wit; and seated there,
Not mine (that's little) but thy Lawrel wear.
Thy first attempt an early promise made;　　　55
That early promise this has more than paid.
So bold, yet so judiciously you dare,
That Your least Praise, is to be Regular.
Time, Place, and Action, may with pains be wrought,
But Genius must be born; and never can be taught.　60
This is Your Portion; this Your Native Store;
Heav'n that but once was Prodigal before,
To *Shakespeare* gave as much; she cou'd not give him more.
　　Maintain Your Post: That's all the Fame You need;
For 'tis impossible you shou'd proceed.　　　　65
Already I am worn with Cares and Age;
And just abandoning th' Ungrateful Stage:
Unprofitably kept at Heav'ns expence,
I live a Rent-charge on his Providence:
But You, whom ev'ry Muse and Grace adorn,　　70
Whom I foresee to better Fortune born,
Be kind to my Remains; and oh defend,
Against Your Judgment, Your departed Friend!

73 Judgment,] Judgment *94*

Let not the Insulting Foe my Fame pursue;
But shade those Lawrels which descend to You: 75
And take for Tribute what these Lines express:
You merit more; nor cou'd my Love do less.

PROLOGUE, EPILOGUE and SONGS
from *LOVE TRIUMPHANT*

PROLOGUE

Spoken by Mr. *Betterton*

As when some Treasurer lays down the Stick;
 Warrants are Sign'd for ready Mony thick:
And many desperate Debentures paid;
Which never had been, had his Lordship staid:
So now, this Poet, who forsakes the Stage, 5
Intends to gratifie the present Age.
One Warrant shall be Sign'd for every Man;
All shall be Wits that will; and *Beaux* that can:
Provided still, this Warrant be not shown,
And you be Wits, but to your selves alone. 10
Provided too; you rail at one another:
For there's no one Wit, will allow a Brother.
Provided also; that you spare this Story,
Damn all the Plays that e're shall come before ye.
If one by chance prove good in half a score, 15
Let that one pay for all; and Damn it more.
For if a good one scape among the Crew,
And you continue Judging as you do;
Every bad Play will hope for Damning too.
You might Damn this, if it were worth your pains, 20
Here's nothing you will like; no fustian Scenes,
And nothing too of——you know what he means.
No double *Entendrès*, which you Sparks allow;
To make the Ladies look they know not how;

Prologue, Epilogue and Songs. Text from Love Triumphant; or, Nature will Prevail. A Tragi-Comedy, *1694*

Simply as 'twere; and knowing both together,   25
Seeming to fan their Faces in cold Weather.
But here's a Story which no Books relate;
Coin'd from our own Old Poet's Addle-pate.
The Fable has a Moral too, if sought:
But let that go; for upon second Thought,   } 30
He fears but few come hither to be Taught.
Yet if you will be profited, you may;
And he would Bribe you too, to like his Play.
He Dies, at least to us, and to the Stage,
And what he has, he leaves this Noble Age.   35
He leaves you first, all Plays of his Inditing,
The whole Estate, which he has got by Writing.
The Beaux may think this nothing but vain Praise,
They'l find it something; the Testator says:
For half their Love, is made from scraps of Plays.   } 40
To his worst Foes, he leaves his Honesty;
That they may thrive upon't as much as he.
He leaves his Manners to the Roaring Boys,
Who come in Drunk, and fill the House with noise.
He leaves to the dire Critiques of his Wit,   45
His Silence and Contempt of all they Writ.
To *Shakespear*'s Critique, he bequeaths the Curse,
To find his faults; and yet himself make worse:
A precious Reader in Poetique Schools,
Who by his own Examples damns his Rules.   50
Last for the Fair, he wishes you may be,
From your dull Critiques, the Lampooners free.
Tho' he pretends no Legacy to leave you,
An Old Man may at least good wishes give you.
Your Beauty names the Play; and may it prove,   55
To each, an Omen of Triumphant Love.

EPILOGUE

Now, in Good Manners, nothing shou'd be sed
   Against this Play, because the Poet's dead.
The Prologue told us of a Moral here:
Wou'd I cou'd find it, but the Devil knows where.

Prologue. 48 worse:] worse. *94*

If in my Part it lyes, I fear he means   5
To warn us of the Sparks behind our Scenes:
For if you'l take it on *Dalinda*'s Word,
'Tis a hard Chapter to refuse a Lord.
The Poet might pretend this Moral too,
That when a Wit and Fool together woo;   10
The Damsel (not to break an Ancient Rule,)
Shou'd leave the Wit, and take the Wealthy Fool.
This he might mean, but there's a Truth behind,
And since it touches none of all our Kind,
But Masks and Misses; faith, I'le speak my Mind.   15
What, if he Taught our Sex more cautious Carriage,
And not to be too Coming before Marriage:
For fear of my Misfortune in the Play,
A Kid brought home upon the Wedding day:
I fear there are few *Sancho's* in the Pit,   20
So good as to forgive, and to forget;
That will, like him, restore us into Favour,
And take us after on our good Behaviour.
Few, when they find the Mony Bag is rent,
Will take it for good Payment on content.   25
But in the Telling, there the difference is,
Sometimes they find it more than they cou'd wish.
Therefore be warn'd, you Misses and you Masks,
Look to your hits, nor give the first that asks.
Tears, Sighs, and Oaths, no truth of Passion prove,   30
True Settlement alone, declares true Love.
For him that Weds a Puss, who kept her first,
I say but little, but I doubt the worst:
The Wife that was a Cat may mind her house,
And prove an Honest, and a Careful Spouse;   35
But faith I wou'd not trust her with a Mouse.

Song of *Jealousie*

I

WHAT State of Life can be so blest
       As Love, that warms a Lover's Breast?
Two Souls in one, the same desire

To grant the Bliss, and to require!
But if in Heav'n a Hell we find,   5
'Tis all from thee,
O Jealousie!
'Tis all from thee,
O Jealousie!
Thou Tyrant, Tyrant Jealousie,   10
Thou Tyrant of the Mind!

2

All other ills, tho sharp they prove,
Serve to refine, and perfect Love:
In absence, or unkind disdain,
Sweet Hope relieves the Lover's pain: 15
But ah, no Cure but Death we find,
To set us free
From Jealousie:
O Jealousie!
Thou Tyrant, Tyrant Jealousie,   20
Thou Tyrant of the Mind.

3

False, in thy Glass all Objects are,
Some set too near, and some too far:
Thou art the Fire of endless Night,
The Fire that burns, and gives no Light.   25
All Torments of the Damn'd we find
In only thee
O Jealousie!
Thou Tyrant, Tyrant Jealousie,
Thou Tyrant of the Mind!   30

Song for a GIRL

1

YOUNG I am, and yet unskill'd
How to make a Lover yield:
How to keep, or how to gain,
When to Love; and when to feign:

2

Take me, take me, some of you,   5
While I yet am Young and True;
E're I can my Soul disguise;
Heave my Breasts, and roul my Eyes.

3

Stay not till I learn the way,
How to Lye, and to Betray: 10
He that has me first, is blest,
For I may deceive the rest.

4

Cou'd I find a blooming Youth;
Full of Love, and full of Truth,
Brisk, and of a janty meen,   15
I shou'd long to be Fifteen.

To Sir *Godfrey Kneller*

ONCE I beheld the fairest of her Kind;
(And still the sweet Idea charms my Mind:)
True she was dumb; for Nature gaz'd so long,
Pleas'd with her work, that she forgot her Tongue:
But, smiling, said, She still shall gain the Prize;   5
I only have transferr'd it to her Eyes.
Such are thy Pictures, *Kneller*. Such thy Skill,
That Nature seems obedient to thy Will:
Comes out, and meets thy Pencil in the draught:
Lives there, and wants but words to speak her thought.   10
At least thy Pictures look a Voice; and we
Imagine sounds, deceiv'd to that degree,
We think 'tis somewhat more than just to see.
   Shadows are but privations of the Light,
Yet when we walk, they shoot before the Sight;   15
With us approach, retire, arise and fall;
Nothing themselves, and yet expressing all.

To Sir Godfrey Kneller. Text from The Annual Miscellany, *1694, collated with* Poems on Various Occasions, *1701, where it is headed* To Sir Godfrey Kneller, Principal Painter to His Majesty

Such are thy Pieces; imitating Life
So near, they almost conquer'd in the strife;
And from their animated Canvass came,   20
Demanding Souls; and loosen'd from the Frame.
    Prometheus, were he here, wou'd cast away
His *Adam*, and refuse a Soul to Clay:
And either wou'd thy Noble Work Inspire;
Or think it warm enough, without his Fire.   25
    But vulgar Hands, may vulgar Likeness raise,
This is the least Attendant on thy Praise:
From hence the Rudiments of Art began;
A Coal, or Chalk, first imitated Man:
Perhaps, the Shadow taken on a Wall,   30
Gave out-lines to the rude Original:
E're Canvass yet was strain'd: before the Grace
Of blended Colours found their use and place:
Or Cypress Tablets, first receiv'd a Face.
    By slow degrees, the Godlike Art advanc'd;   35
As Man grew polish'd, Picture was inhanc'd;
Greece added posture, shade, and perspective;
And then the Mimick Piece began to Live.
Yet perspective was lame; no distance true;
But all came forward in one common view: 40
No point of Light was known, no bounds of Art;
When Light was there, it knew not to depart:
But glaring on remoter Objects play'd;
Not languish'd, and insensibly decay'd.
    Rome rais'd not Art, but barely kept alive;   45
And with Old *Greece*, unequally did strive:
Till *Goths* and *Vandals*, a rude *Northern* Race,
Did all the matchless Monuments deface.
Then all the Muses in one ruine lye;
And Rhyme began t' enervate Poetry.   50
Thus in a stupid Military State,
The Pen and Pencil find an equal Fate.
Flat Faces, such as wou'd disgrace a Skreen,
Such as in *Bantam*'s Embassy were seen,
Unrais'd, unrounded, were the rude delight   55
Of Brutal Nations, only born to Fight.
    Long time the Sister Arts, in Iron sleep,

A heavy Sabbath did supinely keep;
At length, in *Raphael*'s Age, at once they rise;
Stretch all their Limbs, and open all their Eyes.   60
   Thence rose the *Roman*, and the *Lombard* Line:
One colour'd best, and one did best design.
Raphael's like *Homer*'s, was the Nobler part;
But *Titian*'s Painting, look'd like *Virgil*'s Art.
   Thy Genius gives thee both; where true design,   65
Postures unforc'd, and lively Colours joyn.
Likeness is ever there; but still the best,
Like proper Thoughts in lofty Language drest.
Where Light to Shades descending, plays, not strives;
Dyes by degrees, and by degrees revives.   70
Of various parts a perfect whole is wrought:
Thy Pictures think, and we Divine their Thought.

* Shake-
spear's Picture
drawn by Sir
Godfrey Knel-
ler, and given
to the Author.

   *Shakespear thy Gift, I place before my sight;
With awe, I ask his Blessing e're I write;
With Reverence look on his Majestick Face;   75
Proud to be less; but of his Godlike Race.
His Soul Inspires me, while thy Praise I write,
And I like *Teucer*, under *Ajax* Fight;
Bids thee through me, be bold; with dauntless breast
Contemn the bad, and Emulate the best.   80
Like his, thy Criticks in th' attempt are lost;
When most they rail, know then, they envy most.
In vain they snarl a-loof; a noisy Crow'd,
Like Womens Anger, impotent and loud.
While they their barren Industry deplore,   85
Pass on secure; and mind the Goal before:
Old as she is, my Muse shall march behind;
Bear off the blast, and intercept the wind.
Our Arts are Sisters; though not Twins in Birth:
For Hymns were sung in *Edens* happy Earth,   90
By the first Pair; while *Eve* was yet a Saint;
Before she fell with Pride, and learn'd to paint.
Forgive th' allusion; 'twas not meant to bite;
But Satire will have room, where e're I write.
For oh, the Painter Muse; though last in place,   95
Has seiz'd the Blessing first, like *Jacob*'s Race.

   73 note *given*] *presented 1701*   *91–94 om. 1701*   95 For] But *1701*

Apelles Art, an *Alexander* found;
And *Raphael* did with *Leo*'s Gold abound;
But *Homer*, was with barren Lawrel Crown'd.
Thou hadst thy *Charles* a while, and so had I;   100
But pass we that unpleasing Image by.
Rich in thy self; and of thy self Divine,
All Pilgrims come and offer at thy Shrine.
A graceful truth thy Pencil can Command;
The fair themselves go mended from thy hand: 105
Likeness appears in every Lineament;
But Likeness in thy Work is Eloquent:
Though Nature, there, her true resemblance bears,
A nobler Beauty in thy Piece appears.
So warm thy Work, so glows the gen'rous frame,   110
Flesh looks less living in the Lovely Dame.
    Thou paint'st as we describe, improving still,
When on wild Nature we ingraft our skill:
But not creating Beauties at our Will.
    Some other Hand perhaps may reach a Face;   115
But none like thee, a finish'd Figure place:
None of this Age; for that's enough for thee,
The first of these Inferiour Times to be:
Not to contend with Heroes Memory.
    Due Honours to those mighty Names we grant,   120
But Shrubs may live beneath the lofty Plant:
Sons may succeed their greater Parents gone;
Such is thy Lott; and such I wish my own.
    But Poets are confin'd in Narr'wer space;
To speak the Language of their Native Place: 125
The Painter widely stretches his command:
Thy Pencil speaks the Tongue of ev'ry Land.
From hence, my Friend, all Climates are your own;
Nor can you forfeit, for you hold of none.
All Nations all Immunities will give   130
To make you theirs; where e're you please to live;
And not seven Cities; but the World wou'd strive.
    Sure some propitious Planet then did Smile,
When first you were conducted to this Isle:
(Our Genius brought you here, t' inlarge our Fame)   135

115-23 *om.* 1701

(For your good Stars are ev'ry where the same)
Thy matchless hand, of ev'ry Region free,
Adopts our Climate; not our Climate thee.

He travel'd very young into Italy. *Great *Rome* and *Venice* early did impart
To thee th' Examples of their wondrous Art.   140
Those Masters then but seen, not understood,
With generous Emulation fir'd thy Blood:
For what in Nature's Dawn the Child admir'd,
The Youth endeavour'd, and the Man acquir'd.

That yet thou hast not reach'd their high Degree   145
Seems only wanting to this Age, not thee:
Thy Genius bounded by the Times like mine,
Drudges on petty Draughts, nor dare design
A more Exalted Work, and more Divine.
For what a Song, or senceless Opera   150
Is to the Living Labour of a Play;
Or, what a Play to *Virgil*'s Work wou'd be,
Such is a single Piece to History.

But we who Life bestow, our selves must live;
Kings cannot Reign, unless their Subjects give.   155
And they who pay the Taxes, bear the Rule:
Thus thou sometimes art forc'd to draw a Fool:
But so his Follies in thy Posture sink,
The senceless Ideot seems at least to think.

Good Heav'n! that Sots and Knaves shou'd be so vain,   160
To wish their vile Resemblance may remain!
And stand recorded, at their own request,
To future Days, a Libel or a Jeast.
Mean time, while just Incouragement you want,
You only Paint to Live, not Live to Paint.   165
Else shou'd we see, your Noble Pencil trace
Our Unities of Action, Time, and Place.
A whole compos'd of parts; and those the best;
With ev'ry various Character exprest.
Heroes at large; and at a nearer view;   170
Less, and at distance, an Ignobler Crew.
While all the Figures in one Action joyn,
As tending to Compleat the main Design.

145 That] If *1701*   146 Seems] 'Tis *1701*   160–3 Good . . . Jeast.
(Good . . . Jeast.) *1701*   164–5 om. *1701*

More cannot be by Mortal Art exprest;
But venerable Age shall add the rest.   175
For Time shall with his ready Pencil stand;
Retouch your Figures, with his ripening hand.
Mellow your Colours, and imbrown the Teint;
Add every Grace, which Time alone can grant:
To future Ages shall your Fame convey;   180
And give more Beauties, than he takes away.

AN ODE,

ON THE DEATH OF Mr. Henry Purcell;

Late Servant to his Majesty,
and Organist of the Chapel Royal,
and of St. *Peter*'s *Westminster*

The ODE

I

M ARK how the Lark and Linnet Sing,
  With rival Notes
They strain their warbling Throats,
   To welcome in the Spring.
   But in the close of Night,   5
When *Philomel* begins her Heav'nly lay,
  They cease their mutual spight,
  Drink in her Musick with delight,
And list'ning and silent, and silent and list'ning,
   and list'ning and silent obey.

II

So ceas'd the rival Crew when *Purcell* came,   10
They Sung no more, or only Sung his Fame.
Struck dumb they all admir'd the God-like Man,
   The God-like Man,
   Alas, too soon retir'd,
   As He too late began.   15

An Ode. Text from the first edition, 1696. The text accompanying the music has 12, 13 the
matchless Man   21 turn'd the jarring Spheres

We beg not Hell, our *Orpheus* to restore,
Had He been there,
Their Sovereigns fear
Had sent Him back before.
The pow'r of Harmony too well they know,   20
He long e'er this had Tun'd their jarring Sphere,
And left no Hell below.

III

The Heav'nly Quire, who heard his Notes from high,
Let down the Scale of Musick from the Sky:
They handed him along,   25
And all the way He taught, and all the way they Sung.
Ye Brethren of the *Lyre*, and tunefull Voice,
Lament his lott: but at your own rejoyce.
Now live secure and linger out your days,
The Gods are pleas'd alone with *Purcell's Layes*,   30
Nor know to mend their Choice.

EPILOGUE to *The Husband His own Cuckold*

THE PREFACE OF
Mr. *Dryden*, to his Son's Play

. . . *For what remains, both my Son and I are extreamly oblig'd to my dear Friend Mr.* Congreve, *whose Excellent Prologue was one of the greatest Ornaments of the Play. Neither is my Epilogue the worst which I have written; though it seems at the first sight to expose our young Clergy with too much freedom. It was on that Consideration that I had once begun it otherwise, and deliver'd the Copy of it to be spoken, in case the first part of it had given offence. This I will give you partly in my own justification, and partly too, because I think it not unworthy of your sight. Only remembring you that the last line connects the sense to the ensuing part of it. Farewell, Reader, if you are a Father you will forgive me, if not, you will when you are a Father.*

TIME was when none cou'd Preach without Degrees,
And seven years toil at Universities:
But when the Canting Saints came once in play,
The Spirit did their bus'ness in a day:

Epilogue. Text from The Husband His own Cuckold. A Comedy, *1696*

A Zealous Cobler with the gift of Tongue,   5
If he cou'd Pray six hours, might Preach as long:
Thus, in the Primitive Times of Poetry,
The Stage to none but Men of sense was free.
But thanks to your judicious tast, my Masters,
It lies in common now to Poetasters.   10
You set them up, and 'till you dare Condemn,
The Satire lies on you, and not on them.
When Mountebanks their Drugs at Market cry,
Is it their fault to sell, or yours to buye?
'Tis true, they write with ease, and well they may,   ⎫ 15
Fly-blows are gotten every Summers day,   ⎬
The Poet does but buz, and there's a Play.   ⎭

Wit's not his business, *&c.*

EPILOGUE

Spoken by Mrs. *Bracegirdle*

LIKE some raw Sophister that mounts the Pulpit,
So trembles a young Poet at a full Pit.
Unus'd to Crowds, the Parson quakes for fear,
And wonders how the Devil he durst come there;
Wanting three Talents needful for the Place,   5
Some Beard, some Learning, and some little Grace:
Nor is the Puny Poet void of Care;   ⎫
For Authors, such as our new Authors are,   ⎬
Have not much Learning, nor much Wit to spare: ⎭
And as for Grace, to tell the truth, there's scarce one, 10
But has as little as the very Parson:
Both say, they Preach and Write for your Instruction:
But 'tis for a Third Day, and for Induction.
The difference is, that tho' you like the Play,
The Poet's gain is ne'er beyond his Day.   15
But with the Parson 'tis another Case,
He, without Holiness, may rise to Grace;
The Poet has one disadvantage more,   ⎫
That if his Play be dull, he's Damn'd all o'er,   ⎬
Not only a damn'd Blockhead, but damn'd Poor.   ⎭ 20

But Dullness well becomes the Sable Garment;
I warrant that ne'er spoil'd a Priest's Preferment:
Wit's not his Business, and as Wit now goes,
Sirs, 'tis not so much yours as you suppose,
For you like nothing now but nauseous Beaux.   25
You laugh not, Gallants, as by proof appears,
At what his Beauship says, but what he wears;
So 'tis your Eyes are tickled, not your Ears:
The Taylor and the Furrier find the Stuff,
The Wit lies in the Dress, and monstrous Muff.   30
The Truth on't is, the Payment of the Pit
Is like for like, Clipt Money for Clipt Wit.
You cannot from our absent Author hope
He should equip the Stage with such a Fop:
Fools Change in *England*, and new Fools arise,   35
For tho' th' Immortal Species never dies,
Yet ev'ry Year new Maggots make new Flies.
But where he lives abroad, he scarce can find
One Fool, for Million that he left behind.

THE WORKS OF VIRGIL:

Containing His PASTORALS, GEORGICS, AND ÆNEIS.

Translated into English Verse

Sequiturque Patrem non passibus Æquis. Virg. Æn. 2.

The Works of Virgil. Text from the first edition, 1697, collated with the second edition, 1698, and Tonson's Miscellanies. See Commentary

TO THE RIGHT HONOURABLE
Hugh Lord Clifford, BARON of Chudleigh

My Lord,

I HAVE *found it not more difficult to Translate* Virgil, *than to find such Patrons as I desire for my Translation. For though* England *is not wanting in a Learned Nobility, yet such are my unhappy Circumstances, that they have confin'd me to a narrow choice. To the greater part, I have not the Honour to be known; and to some of them I cannot shew at present, by any publick Act, that* 5 *grateful Respect which I shall ever bear them in my heart. Yet I have no reason to complain of Fortune, since in the midst of that abundance I could not possibly have chosen better, than the Worthy Son of so Illustrious a Father. He was the Patron of my Manhood, when I Flourish'd in the opinion of the World; though with small advantage to my Fortune, 'till he awaken'd the remembrance of my* 10 *Royal Master. He was that* Pollio, *or that* Varus, *who introduc'd me to* Augustus: *And tho' he soon dismiss'd himself from State-Affairs, yet in the short time of his Administration he shone so powerfully upon me, that like the heat of a* Russian-*Summer, he ripen'd the Fruits of Poetry in a cold Clymate; and gave me wherewithal to subsist at least, in the long Winter which succeeded.* 15 *What I now offer to your Lordship, is the wretched remainder of a sickly Age, worn out with Study, and oppress'd by Fortune: without other support than the Constancy and Patience of a Christian. You, my Lord, are yet in the flower of your Youth, and may live to enjoy the benefits of the Peace which is promis'd* Europe: *I can only hear of that Blessing: for Years, and, above all things, want* 20 *of health, have shut me out from sharing in the happiness. The Poets, who condemn their* Tantalus *to Hell, had added to his Torments, if they had plac'd him in* Elysium, *which is the proper Emblem of my Condition. The Fruit and the Water may reach my Lips, but cannot enter: And if they cou'd, yet I want a Palate as well as a Digestion. But it is some kind of pleasure to me, to please those* 25 *whom I respect. And I am not altogether out of hope, that these* Pastorals *of* Virgil *may give your Lordship some delight, though made English by one, who scarce remembers that Passion which inspir'd my Author when he wrote them. These were his first Essay in Poetry, (if the* Ceiris *was not his:) And it was more excusable in him to describe Love when he was young, than for me to Translate* 30 *him when I am Old. He died at the Age of fifty two, and I began this Work in my great* Clymacterique. *But having perhaps a better constitution than my Author, I have wrong'd him less, considering my Circumstances, than those who have attempted him before, either in our own, or any Modern Language. And though this Version is not void of Errours, yet it comforts me that the faults of* 35 *others are not worth finding. Mine are neither gross nor frequent, in those* Eclogues, *wherein my Master has rais'd himself above that humble Stile in which* Pastoral *delights, and which I must confess is proper to the Education and Converse of* Shepherds: *for he found the strength of his Genius betimes, and was even in his youth preluding to his* Georgics, *and his* Æneis. *He cou'd not forbear* 40 *to try his Wings, though his Pinions were not harden'd to maintain a long laborious flight. Yet sometimes they bore him to a pitch as lofty, as ever he was able to reach afterwards. But when he was admonish'd by his subject to descend, he came down gently circling in the air, and singing to the ground. Like a Lark, melodious in her mounting, and continuing her Song 'till she alights: still pre-* 45 *paring for a higher flight at her next sally, and tuning her voice to better musick.* The Fourth, *the* Sixth, *and the* Eighth Pastorals, *are clear Evidences of this truth. In the three first he contains himself within his bounds; but Addressing to* Pollio, *his great Patron, and himself no vulgar Poet, he no longer cou'd restrain the freedom of his Spirit, but began to assert his Native Character, which is* 50 *sublimity. Putting himself under the conduct of the same* Cumæan Sybil, *whom afterwards he gave for a Guide to his* Æneas. *'Tis true he was sensible of his own boldness; and we know it by the* Paulo Majora, *which begins his* Fourth Eclogue. *He remember'd, like young* Manlius, *that he was forbidden to Engage; but what avails an express Command to a youthful Courage, which presages* 55 *Victory in the attempt? Encourag'd with Success, he proceeds farther in the* Sixth, *and invades the Province of Philosophy. And notwithstanding that* Phœbus *had forewarn'd him of Singing Wars, as he there confesses, yet he pre-sum'd that the search of Nature was as free to him as to* Lucretius, *who at his Age explain'd it according to the Principles of* Epicurus. *In his* Eighth 60 Eclogue, *he has innovated nothing; the former part of it being the Complaint and Despair of a forsaken Lover: the latter, a Charm of an Enchantress, to renew a lost Affection. But the Complaint perhaps contains some Topicks which are above the Condition of his Persons; and our Author seems to have made his Herdsmen somewhat too Learn'd for their Profession: The Charms are also of the* 65 *same nature, but both were Copied from* Theocritus, *and had receiv'd the applause of former Ages in their Original. There is a kind of Rusticity in all those pompous Verses; somewhat of a Holiday Shepherd strutting in his Country Buskins. The like may be observ'd, both in the* Pollio, *and the* Silenus; *where the Similitudes are drawn from the Woods and Meadows. They seem to me to repre-* 70 *sent our Poet betwixt a Farmer, and a Courtier, when he left* Mantua *for* Rome, *and drest himself in his best Habit to appear before his Patron: Somewhat too fine for the place from whence he came, and yet retaining part of its simplicity. In the* Ninth Pastoral *he Collects some Beautiful passages which were scatter'd in* Theocritus, *which he cou'd not insert into any of his former* Eclogues, *and yet* 75 *was unwilling they shou'd be lost. In all the rest he is equal to his* Sicilian *Master, and observes like him a just decorum, both of the Subject, and the Persons. As particularly in the Third* Pastoral; *where one of his Shepherds describes a Bowl, or Mazer, curiously Carv'd.*

In Medio duo signa: Conon, & quis fuit alter,   80
Descripsit radio, totum qui Gentibus orbem.

He remembers only the name of Conon, *and forgets the other on set purpose: (whether he means* Anaximander *or* Eudoxus *I dispute not,) but he was certainly forgotten, to shew his Country Swain was no great Scholar.*

After all, I must confess that the Boorish Dialect of Theocritus *has a secret* 85 *charm in it, which the* Roman *Language cannot imitate, though* Virgil *has drawn it down as low as possibly he cou'd; as in the* Cujum pecus, *and some other words, for which he was so unjustly blam'd by the bad Criticks of his Age, who cou'd not see the Beauties of that* merum Rus, *which the Poet describ'd in those expressions. But* Theocritus *may justly be preferr'd as the Original, with-* 90 *out injury to* Virgil, *who modestly contents himself with the second place, and glories only in being the first who transplanted* Pastoral *into his own Country; and brought it there to bear as happily as the Cherry-trees which* Lucullus *brought from* Pontus.

Our own Nation has produc'd a third Poet in this kind, not inferiour to the 95 *two former. For the Shepherd's Kalendar of* Spencer, *is not to be match'd in any Modern Language. Not even by* Tasso's Amynta, *which infinitely transcends* Guarini's *Pastor-Fido, as having more of Nature in it, and being almost wholly clear from the wretched affectation of Learning. I will say nothing of the Piscatory Eclogues, because no modern* Latin *can bear Criticism. 'Tis no* 100 *wonder that rolling down through so many barbarous Ages, from the Spring of* Virgil, *it bears along with it the filth and ordures of the* Goths *and* Vandals. *Neither will I mention Monsieur* Fontinelle, *the living Glory of the* French. *'Tis enough for him to have excell'd his Master* Lucian, *without attempting to compare our miserable Age with that of* Virgil, *or* Theocritus. *Let me only* 105 *add, for his reputation,*

——Si Pergama dextrâ
Defendi possint, etiam hâc defensa fuissent.

But Spencer *being Master of our Northern Dialect, and skill'd in* Chaucer's *English, has so exactly imitated the* Doric *of* Theocritus, *that his Love is a* 110 *perfect Image of that Passion which God infus'd into both Sexes, before it was corrupted with the Knowledge of Arts, and the Ceremonies of what we call good Manners.*

My Lord, I know to whom I dedicate: And cou'd not have been induc'd by any motive to put this part of Virgil, *or any other, into unlearned Hands. You* 115 *have read him with pleasure, and I dare say, with admiration in the* Latine, *of which you are a Master. You have added to your Natural Endowments, which without flattery are Eminent, the superstructures of Study, and the knowledge of good Authors. Courage, Probity, and Humanity are inherent in you. These Vertues have ever been habitual to the Ancient House of* Cumberland, *from* 120 *whence you are descended, and of which our Chronicles make so honourable mention in the long Wars betwixt the Rival Families of* York *and* Lancaster. *Your Forefathers have asserted the Party which they chose 'till death, and dy'd for its defence in the Fields of Battel. You have besides the fresh remembrance of your Noble Father; from whom you never can degenerate.*   125

———Nec imbellem, feroces
Progenerant Aquilæ Columbam.

It being almost morally impossible for you to be other than you are by kind; I need neither praise nor incite your Vertue. You are acquainted with the Roman *History, and know without my information that Patronage and Clientship always* 130 *descended from the Fathers to the Sons; and that the same* Plebeian Houses, *had recourse to the same* Patrician Line, *which had formerly protected them: and follow'd their Principles and Fortunes to the last. So that I am your Lordship's by descent, and part of your Inheritance. And the natural inclination, which I have to serve you, adds to your paternal right, for I was wholly yours from the* 135 *first moment, when I had the happiness and honour of being known to you. Be pleas'd therefore to accept the Rudiments of* Virgil's *Poetry: Coursely Translated I confess, but which yet retains some Beauties of the Author, which neither the barbarity of our Language, nor my unskilfulness cou'd so much sully, but that they appear sometimes in the dim mirrour which I hold before you. The Subject* 140 *is not unsuitable to your Youth, which allows you yet to Love, and is proper to your present Scene of Life. Rural Recreations abroad, and Books at home, are the innocent Pleasures of a Man who is early Wise; and gives Fortune no more hold of him, than of necessity he must. 'Tis good, on some occasions to think beforehand as little as we can; to enjoy as much of the present as will not endanger* 145 *our futurity; and to provide our selves of the* Vertuoso's *Saddle, which will be sure to amble, when the World is upon the hardest trott. What I humbly offer to your Lordship, is of this nature. I wish it pleasant, and am sure 'tis innocent.*

127 Aquilæ Columbam 98: Aquilam Columbæ 97

May you ever continue your esteem for Virgil; *and not lessen it, for the faults of his Translatour; who is with all manner of Respect, and sense of Gratitude,* 150
My Lord,
Your Lordship's most Humble,
and most Obedient Servant,
JOHN DRYDEN.

VIRGIL'S PASTORALS

THE FIRST PASTORAL.
OR, Tityrus *and* Melibœus

THE ARGUMENT

The Occasion of the First Pastoral was this. When Augustus *had setled himself in the* Roman *Empire, that he might reward his* Veteran *Troops for their past Service, he distributed among 'em all the Lands that lay about* Cremona *and* Mantua: *turning out the right Owners for having sided with his Enemies.* Virgil *was a Sufferer among the rest; who afterwards recover'd his* 5 *Estate by* Mecænas's *Intercession, and as an Instance of his Gratitude compos'd the following Pastoral; where he sets out his own Good Fortune in the Person of* Tityrus, *and the Calamities of his* Mantuan *Neighbours in the Character of* Melibœus.

MELIBŒUS

BENEATH the Shade which Beechen Boughs diffuse,
You *Tity'rus* entertain your Silvan Muse:
Round the wide World in Banishment we rome,
Forc'd from our pleasing Fields and Native Home:
While stretch'd at Ease you sing your happy loves: 5
And *Amarillis* fills the shady Groves.

TITYRUS

These blessings, Friend, a Deity bestow'd:
For never can I deem him less than God.
The tender Firstlings of my Woolly breed
Shall on his holy Altar often bleed. 10

He gave my Kine to graze the Flowry Plain:
And to my Pipe renew'd the Rural Strain.

MELIBŒUS

  I envy not your Fortune, but admire,
That while the raging Sword and wastful Fire
Destroy the wretched Neighbourhood around,   15
No Hostile Arms approach your happy ground.
Far diff'rent is my Fate: my feeble Goats
With pains I drive from their forsaken Cotes.
And this you see I scarcely drag along,
Who yeaning on the Rocks has left her Young;   20
(The Hope and Promise of my failing Fold:)
My loss by dire Portents the Gods foretold:
For had I not been blind I might have seen
Yon riven Oak, the fairest of the Green,
And the hoarse Raven, on the blasted Bough,   25
By croaking from the left presag'd the coming Blow.
But tell me, *Tityrus*, what Heav'nly Power
Preserv'd your Fortunes in that fatal Hour?

TITYRUS

  Fool that I was, I thought Imperial *Rome*
Like *Mantua*, where on Market-days we come,   30
And thether drive our tender Lambs from home.
So Kids and Whelps their Syres and Dams express:
And so the Great I measur'd by the Less.
But Country Towns, compar'd with her, appear
Like Shrubs, when lofty Cypresses are near.   35

MELIBŒUS

What great Occasion call'd you hence to *Rome*?

TITYRUS

  Freedom, which came at length, tho' slow to come:
Nor did my Search of Liberty begin,
Till my black Hairs were chang'd upon my Chin.
Nor *Amarillis* wou'd vouchsafe a look,   40
Till *Galatea*'s meaner bonds I broke.

The First Pastoral. 26 by croaking from the left 98: With frequent Crokes 97.
See Commentary   41 *Galatea*'s 98: *Galeatea*'s 97

Till then a helpless, hopeless, homely Swain,
I sought not freedom, nor aspir'd to Gain:
Tho' many a Victim from my Folds was bought,
And many a Cheese to Country Markets brought,   45
Yet all the little that I got, I spent,
And still return'd as empty as I went.

MELIBŒUS

We stood amaz'd to see your Mistress mourn;
Unknowing that she pin'd for your return:
We wonder'd why she kept her Fruit, so long,   50
For whom so late th' ungather'd Apples hung.
But now the Wonder ceases, since I see
She kept them only, *Tityrus*, for thee.
For thee the bubling Springs appear'd to mourn,
And whisp'ring Pines made vows for thy return.   55

TITYRUS

What shou'd I do! while here I was enchain'd,
No glimpse of Godlike Liberty remain'd:
Nor cou'd I hope in any place, but there,
To find a God so present to my Pray'r.
There first the Youth of Heav'nly Birth I view'd;   60
For whom our Monthly Victims are renew'd.
He heard my Vows, and graciously decreed
My Grounds to be restor'd, my former Flocks to feed.

MELIBŒUS

O Fortunate Old Man! whose Farm remains
For you sufficient, and requites your pains,   } 65
Tho' Rushes overspread the Neighb'ring Plains.
Tho' here the Marshy Grounds approach your Fields,
And there the Soyl a stony Harvest yields.
Your teeming Ewes shall no strange Meadows try,
Nor fear a Rott from tainted Company.   70
Behold yon bord'ring Fence of Sallow Trees
Is fraught with Flow'rs, the Flow'rs are fraught with Bees:
The buisie Bees with a soft murm'ring Strain
Invite to gentle sleep the lab'ring Swain.

57 remain'd:] remain'd? *97 98*

While from the Neighb'ring Rock, with Rural Songs, 75
The Pruner's Voice the pleasing Dream prolongs;
Stock-Doves and Turtles tell their Am'rous pain,
And from the lofty Elms of Love complain.

TITYRUS

Th' Inhabitants of Seas and Skies shall change,
And Fish on shoar and Stags in Air shall range, 80
The banish'd *Parthian* dwell on *Arar*'s brink,
And the blue *German* shall the *Tigris* drink:
E're I, forsaking Gratitude and Truth,
Forget the Figure of that Godlike Youth.

MELIBŒUS

But we must beg our Bread in Climes unknown, 85
Beneath the scorching or the freezing Zone.
And some to far *Oaxis* shall be sold;
Or try the *Lybian* Heat, or *Scythian* Cold.
The rest among the *Britans* be confin'd;
A Race of Men from all the World dis-join'd. 90
O must the wretched Exiles ever mourn,
Nor after length of rowl'ing Years return?
Are we condemn'd by Fates unjust Decree,
No more our Houses and our Homes to see?
Or shall we mount again the Rural Throne, 95
And rule the Country Kingdoms, once our own!
Did we for these Barbarians plant and sow,
On these, on these, our happy Fields bestow?
Good Heav'n, what dire Effects from Civil Discord flow!
Now let me graff my Pears, and prune the Vine; 100
The Fruit is theirs, the Labour only mine.
Farewel my Pastures, my Paternal Stock,
My fruitful Fields, and my more fruitful Flock!
No more, my Goats, shall I behold you climb
The steepy Cliffs, or crop the flow'ry Thyme! 105
No more, extended in the Grot below,
Shall see you browzing on the Mountain's brow
The prickly Shrubs; and after on the bare,
Lean down the Deep Abyss, and hang in Air.

89 *Britans*] *Britains* 98

No more my Sheep shall sip the Morning Dew; ⟩ 110
No more my Song shall please the Rural Crue:
Adieu, my tuneful Pipe! and all the World adieu!

TITYRUS

This Night, at least, with me forget your Care;
Chesnuts and Curds and Cream shall be your fare:
The Carpet-ground shall be with Leaves o'respread; 115
And Boughs shall weave a Cov'ring for your Head.
For see yon sunny Hill the Shade extends;
And curling Smoke from Cottages ascends.

THE SECOND PASTORAL. OR, ALEXIS

THE ARGUMENT

*The Commentators can by no means agree on the Person of Alexis, but are all of
opinion that some Beautiful Youth is meant by him, to whom Virgil here makes
Love; in Corydon's Language and Simplicity. His way of Courtship is wholly
Pastoral: He complains of the Boys Coyness, recommends himself for his Beauty
and Skill in Piping; invites the Youth into the Country, where he promises him 5
the Diversions of the Place; with a suitable Present of Nuts and Apples: But
when he finds nothing will prevail, he resolves to quit his troublesome Amour,
and betake himself again to his former Business.*

YOUNG *Corydon,* th' unhappy Shepherd Swain,
    The fair *Alexis* lov'd, but lov'd in vain:
And underneath the Beechen Shade, alone,
Thus to the Woods and Mountains made his moan.
Is this, unkind *Alexis,* my reward, 5
And must I die unpitied, and unheard?
Now the green Lizard in the Grove is laid,
The Sheep enjoy the coolness of the Shade;
And *Thestilis* wild Thime and Garlike beats
For Harvest Hinds, o'respent with Toyl and Heats: 10
While in the scorching Sun I trace in vain
Thy flying footsteps o're the burning Plain.
The creaking Locusts with my Voice conspire,
They fry'd with Heat, and I with fierce Desire.

How much more easie was it to sustain   15
Proud *Amarillis*, and her haughty Reign,
The Scorns of Young *Menalcas*, once my care,
Tho' he was black, and thou art Heav'nly fair.
Trust not too much to that enchanting Face;
Beauty's a Charm, but soon the Charm will pass: 20
White Lillies lie neglected on the Plain,
While dusky Hyacinths for use remain.
My Passion is thy Scorn; nor wilt thou know
What Wealth I have, what Gifts I can bestow:
What Stores my Dairies and my Folds contain;   25
A thousand Lambs that wander on the Plain:
New Milk that all the Winter never fails,
And all the Summer overflows the Pails:
Amphion sung not sweeter to his Herd,
When summon'd Stones the *Theban* Turrets rear'd.   30
Nor am I so deform'd; for late I stood
Upon the Margin of the briny Flood:
The Winds were still, and if the Glass be true,
With *Daphnis* I may vie, tho' judg'd by you.
O leave the noisie Town, O come and see   35
Our Country Cotts, and live content with me!
To wound the Flying Deer, and from their Cotes
With me to drive a-Field, the browzing Goats:
To pipe and sing, and in our Country Strain
To Copy, or perhaps contend with *Pan*.   40
Pan taught to joyn with Wax unequal Reeds,
Pan loves the Shepherds, and their Flocks he feeds:
Nor scorn the Pipe; *Amyntas*, to be taught,
With all his Kisses would my Skill have bought.
Of seven smooth joints a mellow Pipe I have,   45
Which with his dying Breath *Damætas* gave:
And said, This, *Corydon*, I leave to thee;
For only thou deserv'st it after me.
His Eyes *Amyntas* durst not upward lift,
For much he grudg'd the Praise, but more the Gift.   50
Besides two Kids that in the Valley stray'd,
I found by chance, and to my fold convey'd:
They drein two bagging Udders every day;

The Second Pastoral. 43 scorn 97 (*errata*): scorns 97 (*text*)

And these shall be Companions of thy Play.
Both fleck'd with white, the true *Arcadian* Strain,   55
Which *Thestilis* had often beg'd in vain:
And she shall have them, if again she sues,
Since you the Giver and the Gift refuse.
Come to my longing Arms, my lovely care,
And take the Presents which the Nymphs prepare.   60
White Lillies in full Canisters they bring,
With all the Glories of the Purple Spring:
The Daughters of the Flood have search'd the Mead
For Violets pale, and cropt the Poppy's Head:
The Short *Narcissus* and fair Daffodil,   65
Pancies to please the Sight, and Cassia sweet to smell:
And set soft Hyacinths with Iron blue,
To shade marsh Marigolds of shining Hue.
Some bound in Order, others loosely strow'd,
To dress thy Bow'r, and trim thy new Abode.   70
My self will search our planted Grounds at home,
For downy Peaches and the glossie Plum:
And thrash the Chesnuts in the Neighb'ring Grove,
Such as my *Amarillis* us'd to love.
The Laurel and the Myrtle sweets agree;   75
And both in Nosegays shall be bound for thee.
Ah, *Corydon*, ah poor unhappy Swain,
Alexis will thy homely Gifts disdain:
Nor, should'st thou offer all thy little Store,
Will rich *Iolas* yield, but offer more.   80
What have I done, to name that wealthy Swain,
So powerful are his Presents, mine so mean!
The Boar amidst my Crystal Streams I bring;
And Southern Winds to blast my flow'ry Spring.
Ah, cruel Creature, whom dost thou despise?   85
The Gods to live in Woods have left the Skies.
And Godlike *Paris* in th' *Idean* Grove,
To *Priam*'s Wealth prefer'd *Oenone*'s Love.
In Cities which she built, let *Pallas* Reign;
Tow'rs are for Gods, but Forrests for the Swain.   90
The greedy Lyoness the Wolf pursues,
The Wolf the Kid, the wanton Kid the Browze:

62 Spring:] Spring, *97 98*

Alexis thou art chas'd by *Corydon*;
All follow sev'ral Games, and each his own.
See from afar the Fields no longer smoke,   95
The sweating Steers unharnass'd from the Yoke,
Bring, as in Triumph, back the crooked Plough;
The Shadows lengthen as the Sun goes Low.
Cool Breezes now the raging Heats remove;
Ah, cruel Heaven! that made no Cure for Love!   100
I wish for balmy Sleep, but wish in vain:
Love has no bounds in Pleasure, or in Pain.
What frenzy, Shepherd, has thy Soul possess'd,
Thy Vinyard lies half prun'd, and half undress'd.
Quench, *Corydon*, thy long unanswer'd fire: 105
Mind what the common wants of Life require.
On willow Twigs employ thy weaving care:
And find an easier Love, tho' not so fair.

THE THIRD PASTORAL. OR, PALÆMON

Menalcas, Damætas, Palæmon

THE ARGUMENT

Damætas *and* Menalcas, *after some smart strokes of Country Railery, resolve to try who has the most Skill at a Song; and accordingly make their Neighbour* Palæmon *Judge of their Performances: Who, after a full hearing of both Parties, declares himself unfit for the Decision of so weighty a Controversie, and leaves the Victory undetermin'd.*

MENALCAS

HO, Swain, what Shepherd owns those ragged Sheep?

DAMÆTAS

Ægon's they are, he gave 'em me to keep.

MENALCAS

Unhappy Sheep of an Unhappy Swain.
While he *Neæra* courts, but courts in vain,
And fears that I the Damsel shall obtain;   5

The Third Pastoral. 1 Swain *98*: Groom *97*   3 Swain.] Swain, *97 98*

Thou, Varlet, dost thy Master's gains devour:
Thou milk'st his Ewes, and often twice an hour;
Of Grass and Fodder thou defraud'st the Dams:
And of their Mothers Duggs the starving Lambs.

DAMÆTAS

Good words, young Catamite, at least to Men: 10
We know who did your Business, how, and when.
And in what Chappel too you plaid your prize;
And what the Goats observ'd with leering Eyes:
The Nymphs were kind, and laught, and there your safety lies.

MENALCAS

Yes, when I crept the Hedges of the Leys; 15
Cut *Micon*'s tender Vines, and stole the Stays.

DAMÆTAS

Or rather, when beneath yon ancient Oak,
The Bow of *Daphnis* and the Shafts you broke:
When the fair Boy receiv'd the Gift of right;
And but for Mischief, you had dy'd for spight. 20

MENALCAS

What Nonsense wou'd the Fool thy Master prate,
When thou, his Knave, can'st talk at such a rate!
Did I not see you, Rascal, did I not!
When you lay snug to snap young *Damon*'s Goat?
His Mungril bark'd, I ran to his relief, 25
And cry'd, There, there he goes; stop, stop the Thief.
Discover'd and defeated of your Prey,
You sculk'd behind the Fence, and sneak'd away.

DAMÆTAS

An honest Man may freely take his own;
The Goat was mine, by singing fairly won. 30
A solemn match was made; He lost the Prize,
Ask *Damon*, ask if he the Debt denies;
I think he dares not, if he does, he lyes.

MENALCAS

Thou sing with him, thou Booby; never Pipe
Was so profan'd to touch that blubber'd Lip: 35
Dunce at the best; in Streets but scarce allow'd
To tickle, on thy Straw, the stupid Crowd.

DAMÆTAS

To bring it to the Trial, will you dare
Our Pipes, our Skill, our Voices to compare?
My Brinded Heifar to the Stake I lay;   40
Two Thriving Calves she suckles twice a day:
And twice besides her Beestings never fail
To store the Dairy, with a brimming Pail.
Now back your singing with an equal Stake.

MENALCAS

That shou'd be seen, if I had one to make.   45
You know too well I feed my Father's Flock:
What can I wager from the common Stock?
A Stepdame too I have, a cursed she,
Who rules my Hen-peck'd Sire, and orders me.
Both number twice a day the Milky Dams;   50
And once she takes the tale of all the Lambs.
But since you will be mad, and since you may
Suspect my Courage, if I should not lay;
The Pawn I proffer shall be full as good:
Two Bowls I have, well turn'd of Beechen Wood;   55
Both by divine *Alcimedon* were made;
To neither of them yet the Lip is laid.
The Lids are Ivy, Grapes in clusters lurk,
Beneath the Carving of the curious Work.
Two Figures on the sides emboss'd appear;   60
Conon, and what's his Name who made the Sphere,
And shew'd the Seasons of the sliding Year,
Instructed in his Trade the Lab'ring Swain,
And when to reap, and when to sowe the Grain?

DAMÆTAS

And I have two, to match your pair, at home;   65
The Wood the same, from the same Hand they come:

The kimbo Handles seem with Bears-foot carv'd;
And never yet to Table have been serv'd:
Where *Orpheus* on his Lyre laments his Love,
With Beasts encompass'd, and a dancing Grove: 70
But these, nor all the Proffers you can make,
Are worth the Heifar which I set to stake.

MENALCAS

No more delays, vain Boaster, but begin:
I prophecy before-hand I shall win.
Palæmon shall be Judge how ill you rhime,   75
I'll teach you how to brag another time.

DAMÆTAS

Rhymer come on, and do the worst you can:
I fear not you, nor yet a better Man.
With Silence, Neighbour, and Attention wait:
For 'tis a business of a high Debate.   80

PALÆMON

Sing then; the Shade affords a proper place;
The Trees are cloath'd with Leaves, the Fields with Grass;
The Blossoms blow; the Birds on bushes sing;
And Nature has accomplish'd all the Spring.
The Challenge to *Damætas* shall belong,   85
Menalcas shall sustain his under Song:
Each in his turn your tuneful numbers bring;
By turns the tuneful Muses love to sing.

DAMÆTAS

From the great Father of the Gods above
My Muse begins; for all is full of *Jove*;   90
To *Jove* the care of Heav'n and Earth belongs;
My Flocks he blesses, and he loves my Songs.

MENALCAS

Me *Phœbus* loves; for He my Muse inspires;
And in her Songs, the warmth he gave, requires.

88 By *98*: In *97*

For him, the God of Shepherds and their Sheep,   95
My blushing Hyacinths, and my Bays I keep.

DAMÆTAS

My *Phyllis* Me with pelted Apples plyes,
Then tripping to the Woods the Wanton hies:
And wishes to be seen, before she flies.

MENALCAS

But fair *Amyntas* comes unask'd to me;   100
And offers Love; and sits upon my knee:
Not *Delia* to my Dogs is known so well as he.

DAMÆTAS

To the dear Mistress of my Love-sick Mind,
Her Swain a pretty Present has design'd:
I saw two Stock-doves billing, and e're long   105
Will take the Nest, and Hers shall be the Young.

MENALCAS

Ten ruddy Wildings in the Wood I found,
And stood on tip-toes, reaching from the ground;
I sent *Amyntas* all my present Store;
And will, to Morrow, send as many more.   110

DAMÆTAS

The lovely Maid lay panting in my arms;
And all she said and did was full of Charms.
Winds on your Wings to Heav'n her Accents bear;
Such words as Heav'n alone is fit to hear.

MENALCAS

Ah! what avails it me, my Love's delight,   115
To call you mine, when absent from my sight!
I hold the Nets, while you pursue the Prey;
And must not share the Dangers of the Day.

DAMÆTAS

I keep my Birth-day: send my *Phillis* home;
At Sheering-time, *Iolas*, you may come.   120

97 My . . . plyes, 98: With pelted Fruit, me *Galatea* plyes; 97. *See* **Commentary**

MENALCAS

With *Phillis* I am more in grace than you:
Her Sorrow did my parting-steps pursue:
Adieu my Dear, she said, a long Adieu.

DAMÆTAS

The Nightly Wolf is baneful to the Fold,
Storms to the Wheat, to Budds the bitter Cold;   125
But from my frowning Fair, more Ills I find,
Than from the Wolves, and Storms, and Winter-wind.

MENALCAS

The Kids with pleasure browze the bushy Plain,
The Show'rs are grateful to the swelling Grain:
To teeming Ewes the Sallow's tender tree;   130
But more than all the World my Love to me.

DAMÆTAS

Pollio my Rural Verse vouchsafes to read:
A Heyfar, Muses, for your Patron breed.

MENALCAS

My *Pollio* writes himself; a Bull be bred,
With spurning Heels, and with a butting Head.   135

DAMÆTAS

Who *Pollio* loves, and who his Muse admires,
Let *Pollio*'s fortune crown his full desires.
Let Myrrh instead of Thorn his Fences fill:
And Show'rs of Hony from his Oaks distil.

MENALCAS

Who hates not living *Bavius*, let him be   140
(Dead *Mævius*) damn'd to love thy Works and thee:
The same ill taste of Sense wou'd serve to join
Dog Foxes in the Yoak, and sheer the Swine.

134 himself;] himself, 97 98

DAMÆTAS

Ye Boys, who pluck the Flow'rs, and spoil the Spring,
Beware the secret Snake, that shoots a sting.   145

MENALCAS

Graze not too near the Banks, my jolly Sheep,
The Ground is false, the running Streams are deep:
See, they have caught the Father of the Flock;
Who drys his Fleece upon the neighb'ring Rock.

DAMÆTAS

From Rivers drive the Kids, and sling your Hook;   150
Anon I'll wash 'em in the shallow Brook.

MENALCAS

To fold, my Flock; when Milk is dry'd with heat,
In vain the Milk-maid tugs an empty Teat.

DAMÆTAS

How lank my Bulls from plenteous pasture come!
But Love that drains the Herd, destroys the Groom.   155

MENALCAS

My Flocks are free from Love; yet look so thin,
Their bones are barely cover'd with their Skin.
What magick has bewitch'd the woolly Dams,
And what ill Eyes beheld the tender Lambs?

DAMÆTAS

Say, where the round of Heav'n, which all contains,   160
To three short Ells on Earth our sight restrains:
Tell that, and rise a *Phœbus* for thy pains.

MENALCAS

Nay tell me first, in what new Region springs
A Flow'r, that bears inscrib'd the names of Kings:
And thou shalt gain a Present as Divine   165
As *Phœbus* self; for *Phillis* shall be thine.

PALÆMON

So nice a diff'rence in your Singing lyes,
That both have won, or both deserv'd the Prize.
Rest equal happy both; and all who prove
The bitter Sweets, and pleasing Pains of Love.   170
Now dam the Ditches, and the Floods restrain:
Their moisture has already drench'd the Plain.

THE FOURTH PASTORAL. OR, POLLIO

THE ARGUMENT

The Poet celebrates the Birth-day of Saloninus, *the Son of* Pollio, *born in the
Consulship of his Father, after the taking of* Salonæ, *a City in* Dalmatia.
*Many of the Verses are translated from one of the Sybils, who prophesie of our
Saviour's Birth.*

*S*ICILIAN Muse begin a loftier strain!
Though lowly Shrubs and Trees that shade the Plain,
Delight not all; *Sicilian* Muse, prepare
To make the vocal Woods deserve a Consul's care.
The last great Age, foretold by sacred Rhymes,   5
Renews its finish'd Course, *Saturnian* times
Rowl round again, and mighty years, begun
From their first Orb, in radiant Circles run.
The base degenerate Iron-off-spring ends;
A golden Progeny from Heav'n descends;   10
O chast *Lucina* speed the Mothers pains,
And haste the glorious Birth; thy own *Apollo* reigns!
The lovely Boy, with his auspicious Face,
Shall *Pollio*'s Consulship and Triumph grace;
Majestick Months set out with him to their appointed Race.   } 15
The Father banish'd Virtue shall restore,
And Crimes shall threat the guilty world no more.
The Son shall lead the life of Gods, and be
By Gods and Heroes seen, and Gods and Heroes see.

The Fourth Pastoral. Argument. Saloninus *84 97*: Salonius *92 98*
3–4 Delight not all; . . . care. *97 98*: *84 and 92 have*
        Delight not all, if thither I repair,
        My Song shall make 'em worth a Consul's care.

5 Age, *97 98*: Age *84 92*

The jarring Nations he in peace shall bind,   20
And with paternal Virtues rule mankind.
Unbidden Earth shall wreathing Ivy bring,   ⎫
And fragrant Herbs (the promises of Spring)   ⎬
As her first Off'rings to her Infant King.   ⎭
The Goats with strutting Duggs shall homeward speed,   25
And lowing Herds, secure from Lyons feed.
His Cradle shall with rising flow'rs be crown'd;
The Serpents Brood shall die: the sacred ground
Shall Weeds and pois'nous Plants refuse to bear,
Each common Bush shall *Syrian* Roses wear.   30
But when Heroick Verse his Youth shall raise,
And form it to Hereditary Praise;
Unlabour'd Harvests shall the Fields adorn,
And cluster'd Grapes shall blush on every Thorn.
The knotted Oaks shall show'rs of Honey weep,   35
And through the matted Grass the liquid Gold shall creep.
Yet, of old Fraud some footsteps shall remain,
The Merchant still shall plough the deep for gain:
Great Cities shall with Walls be compass'd round;
And sharpen'd Shares shall vex the fruitful ground.   40
Another *Tiphys* shall new Seas explore,
Another *Argos* land the Chiefs, upon th' *Iberian* Shore.
Another *Helen* other Wars create,
And great *Achilles* urge the *Trojan* Fate:
But when to ripen'd Man-hood he shall grow,   45
The greedy Sailer shall the Seas forego;
No Keel shall cut the Waves for foreign Ware;
For every Soil shall every Product bear.
The labouring Hind his Oxen shall disjoyn,   ⎫
No Plow shall hurt the Glebe, no Pruning-hook the Vine: ⎬ 50
Nor wooll shall in dissembled colours shine.   ⎭
But the luxurious Father of the Fold,
With native Purple, or unborrow'd Gold,
Beneath his pompous Fleece shall proudly sweat:
And under *Tyrian* Robes the Lamb shall bleat.   55

36 Gold *97 (errata)*: Cold *97 (text)*   42 Another . . . Shore. *97 98*: *84 and
92 have*

Another *Argos* on th' *Iberian* Shore
Shall land the chosen Chiefs:

44 And . . . Fate: *97 98*: And great *Achilles* shall be sent to urge the *Trojan* Fate: *84 92*

The Fates, when they this happy Web have spun,
Shall bless the sacred Clue, and bid it smoothly run.
Mature in years, to ready Honours move,
O of Cœlestial Seed! O foster Son of *Jove*!
See, labouring Nature calls thee to sustain   60
The nodding frame of Heav'n, and Earth, and Main;
See to their Base restor'd, Earth, Seas, and Air,
And joyful Ages from behind, in crowding Ranks appear.
To sing thy Praise, wou'd Heav'n my breath prolong
Infusing Spirits worthy such a Song;   65
Not *Thracian Orpheus* should transcend my Layes,
Nor *Linus* crown'd with never-fading Bayes:
Though each his Heav'nly Parent shou'd inspire;
The Muse instruct the Voice, and *Phœbus* tune the Lyre.
Shou'd *Pan* contend in Verse, and thou my Theme,   70
Arcadian Judges should their God condemn.
Begin, auspicious Boy, to cast about
Thy Infant Eyes, and with a smile, thy Mother single out;
Thy Mother well deserves that short delight,
The nauseous Qualms of ten long Months and Travail to requite. 75
Then smile; the frowning Infants Doom is read,
No God shall crown the Board, nor Goddess bless the Bed.

THE FIFTH PASTORAL. OR, DAPHNIS

THE ARGUMENT

Mopsus *and* Menalcas, *two very expert Shepherds at a Song, begin one by consent to the Memory of* Daphnis; *who is suppos'd by the best Criticks to represent* Julius Cæsar. Mopsus *laments his Death,* Menalcas *proclaims his Divinity. The whole Eclogue consisting of an Elegie and an Apotheosis.*

MENALCAS

SINCE on the Downs our Flocks together feed,
And since my Voice can match your tuneful Reed,
Why sit we not beneath the grateful Shade,
Which Hazles, intermix'd with Elms, have made?

---

58 ready *97 98*: awful *84 92*   59 Seed *97 98*: Stem *84 92*   63 in crowding
Ranks *97 98*: stand crowding to *84 92*   70 in Verse *97 98*: with me *84 92*

MOPSUS

Whether you please that Silvan Scene to take,   5
Where whistling Winds uncertain Shadows make:
Or will you to the cooler Cave succeed,
Whose Mouth the curling Vines have overspread?

MENALCAS

Your Merit and your Years command the Choice:
Amyntas only rivals you in Voice.   10

MOPSUS

What will not that presuming Shepherd dare,
Who thinks his Voice with *Phœbus* may compare?

MENALCAS

Begin you first; if either *Alcon*'s Praise,
Or dying *Phillis* have inspir'd your Lays:
If her you mourn, or *Codrus* you commend,   15
Begin, and *Tityrus* your Flock shall tend.

MOPSUS

Or shall I rather the sad Verse repeat,
Which on the Beeches bark I lately writ:
I writ, and sung betwixt; now bring the Swain
Whose Voice you boast, and let him try the Strain.   20

MENALCAS

Such as the Shrub to the tall Olive shows,
Or the pale Sallow to the blushing Rose;
Such is his Voice, if I can judge aright,
Compar'd to thine, in sweetness and in height.

MOPSUS

No more, but sit and hear the promis'd Lay,   25
The gloomy Grotto makes a doubtful day.
The Nymphs about the breathless Body wait
Of *Daphnis*, and lament his cruel Fate.

The Trees and Floods were witness to their Tears:
At length the rumour reach'd his Mother's Ears.   30
The wretched Parent, with a pious haste,
Came running, and his lifeless Limbs embrac'd.
She sigh'd, she sob'd, and, furious with despair,
She rent her Garments, and she tore her Hair:
Accusing all the Gods and every Star.   35
The Swains forgot their Sheep, nor near the brink
Of running Waters brought their Herds to drink.
The thirsty Cattle, of themselves, abstain'd
From Water, and their grassy Fare disdain'd.
The death of *Daphnis* Woods and Hills deplore,   40
They cast the sound to *Lybia*'s desart Shore;
The *Lybian* Lyons hear, and hearing roar.
Fierce Tygers *Daphnis* taught the Yoke to bear;
And first with curling Ivy dress'd the Spear:
Daphnis did Rites to *Bacchus* first ordain;   45
And holy Revels for his reeling Train.
As Vines the Trees, as Grapes the Vines adorn,
As Bulls the Herds, and Fields the Yellow Corn;
So bright a Splendor, so divine a Grace,
The glorious *Daphnis* cast on his illustrious Race.   50
When envious Fate the Godlike *Daphnis* took,
Our guardian Gods the Fields and Plains forsook:
Pales no longer swell'd the teeming Grain,
Nor *Phœbus* fed his Oxen on the Plain:
No fruitful Crop the sickly Fields return;   55
But Oats and Darnel choak the rising Corn.
And where the Vales with Violets once were crown'd,
Now knotty Burrs and Thorns disgrace the Ground.
Come, Shepherds, come, and strow with Leaves the Plain;
Such Funeral Rites your *Daphnis* did ordain.   60
With Cypress Boughs the Crystal Fountains hide,
And softly let the running Waters glide;
A lasting Monument to *Daphnis* raise;
With this Inscription to record his Praise,
Daphnis, the Fields Delight, the Shepherd's Love,   65
Renown'd on Earth, and deify'd above.
Whose Flock excell'd the fairest on the Plains,
But less than he himself surpass'd the Swains.

MENALCAS

Oh Heavenly Poet! such thy Verse appears,
So sweet, so charming to my ravish'd Ears, 70
As to the weary Swain, with cares opprest,
Beneath the Silvan Shade, refreshing Rest:
As to the feavorish Travellor, when first
He finds a Crystal Stream to quench his thirst.
In singing, as in piping, you excell; 75
And scarce your Master could perform so well.
O fortunate young Man, at least your Lays
Are next to his, and claim the second Praise.
Such as they are my rural Songs I join,
To raise our *Daphnis* to the Pow'rs Divine; 80
For *Daphnis* was so good, to love what-e're was mine.

MOPSUS

How is my Soul with such a Promise rais'd!
For both the Boy was worthy to be prais'd,
And *Stimichon* has often made me long,
To hear, like him, so soft so sweet a Song. 85

MENALCAS

Daphnis, the Guest of Heav'n, with wondring Eyes,
Views in the Milky Way, the starry Skyes:
And far beneath him, from the shining Sphere,
Beholds the moving Clouds, and rolling Year.
For this, with chearful Cries the Woods resound; 90
The Purple Spring arrays the various ground:
The Nymphs and Shepherds dance; and *Pan* himself is Crown'd.
The Wolf no longer prowls for nightly Spoils,
Nor Birds the Sprindges fear, nor Stags the Toils:
For *Daphnis* reigns above; and deals from thence 95
His Mothers milder Beams, and peaceful Influence.
The Mountain tops unshorn, the Rocks rejoice;
The lowly Shrubs partake of Humane Voice.
Assenting Nature, with a gracious nod,
Proclaims him, and salutes the new-admitted God. 100
Be still propitious, ever good to thine:
Behold four hallow'd Altars we design;

And two to thee, and two to *Phœbus* rise;
On both are offer'd Annual Sacrifice.
The holy Priests, at each returning year,   105
Two Bowls of Milk, and two of Oil shall bear;
And I my self the Guests with friendly Bowls will chear.
Two Goblets will I crown with sparkling Wine,
The gen'rous Vintage of the *Chian* Vine;
These will I pour to thee, and make the Nectar thine.   110
In Winter shall the Genial Feast be made
Before the fire; by Summer in the shade.
Damætas shall perform the Rites Divine;
And *Lictian Ægon* in the Song shall join.
Alphesibœus, tripping, shall advance;   115
And mimick Satyrs in his antick Dance.
When to the Nymphs our annual Rites we pay,
And when our Fields with Victims we survey:
While savage Boars delight in shady Woods,
And finny Fish inhabit in the Floods;   120
While Bees on Thime, and Locusts feed on Dew,
Thy grateful Swains these Honours shall renew.
Such Honours as we pay to Pow'rs Divine,
To *Bacchus* and to *Ceres*, shall be thine.
Such annual Honours shall be giv'n, and thou   125
Shalt hear, and shalt condemn thy Suppliants to their Vow.

MOPSUS

What Present worth thy Verse can *Mopsus* find!
Not the soft Whispers of the Southern Wind,
That play through trembling Trees, delight me more;
Nor murm'ring Billows on the sounding Shore;   130
Nor winding Streams that through the Valley glide;
And the scarce cover'd Pebbles gently chide.

MENALCAS

Receive you first this tuneful Pipe; the same
That play'd my *Coridon*'s unhappy Flame.
The same that sung *Neæra*'s conqu'ring Eyes;   135
And, had the Judge been just, had won the Prize.

The Fifth Pastoral. 104 both are *98*: each is *97*

MOPSUS

Accept from me this Sheephook in exchange,
The Handle Brass; the Knobs in equal range.
Antigenes, with Kisses, often try'd
To beg this Present, in his Beauty's Pride;   } 140
When Youth and Love are hard to be deny'd.
But what I cou'd refuse, to his Request,
Is yours unask'd, for you deserve it best.

THE SIXTH PASTORAL. OR, SILENUS

THE ARGUMENT

Two young Shepherds Chromis *and* Mnasylus, *having been often promis'd a
Song by* Silenus, *chance to catch him asleep in this Pastoral; where they bind
him hand and foot, and then claim his Promise.* Silenus *finding they wou'd be
put off no longer, begins his Song; in which he describes the Formation of the
Universe, and the Original of Animals, according to the* Epicurean *Philo-* 5
*sophy; and then runs through the most surprising Transformations which have
happen'd in Nature since her Birth. This Pastoral was design'd as a Complement to* Syro *the* Epicurean, *who instructed* Virgil *and* Varus *in the
Principles of that Philosophy.* Silenus *acts as Tutor,* Chromis *and* Mnasylus
as the two Pupils.

I FIRST transferr'd to *Rome Sicilian* Strains:
Nor blush'd the *Dorick* Muse to dwell on *Mantuan* Plains.
But when I try'd her tender Voice, too young;
And fighting Kings, and bloody Battels sung,
Apollo check'd my Pride; and bade me feed   5
My fatning Flocks, nor dare beyond the Reed.
Admonish'd thus, while every Pen prepares
To write thy Praises, *Varus*, and thy Wars,
My Past'ral Muse her humble Tribute brings;
And yet not wholly uninspir'd she sings.   10
For all who read, and reading, not disdain
These rural Poems, and their lowly Strain,
The name of *Varus* oft inscrib'd shall see,
In every Grove, and every vocal Tree;   }
And all the Silvan reign shall sing of thee: } 15

Thy name, to *Phœbus* and the Muses known,

Shall in the front of every Page be shown;

For he who sings thy Praise, secures his own.

Proceed, my Muse: Two Satyrs, on the ground,

Stretch'd at his Ease, their Syre *Silenus* found.   20

Dos'd with his fumes, and heavy with his Load,

They found him snoring in his dark abode;

And seis'd with Youthful Arms the drunken God.

His rosie Wreath was dropt not long before,

Born by the tide of Wine, and floating on the floor.   25

His empty Can, with Ears half worn away,

Was hung on high, to boast the triumph of the day.

Invaded thus, for want of better bands,

His Garland they unstring, and bind his hands:

For by the fraudful God deluded long,   30

They now resolve to have their promis'd Song.

Ægle came in, to make their Party good;

The fairest *Nais* of the neighbouring Flood:

And, while he stares around, with stupid Eyes,

His Brows with Berries, and his Temples dyes.   35

He finds the Fraud, and, with a Smile, demands

On what design the Boys had bound his hands.

Loose me, he cry'd; 'twas Impudence to find

A sleeping God, 'tis Sacriledge to bind.

To you the promis'd Poem I will pay;   40

The Nymph shall be rewarded in her way.

He rais'd his voice; and soon a num'rous throng

Of tripping Satyrs crowded to the Song.

And Sylvan Fauns, and Savage Beasts advanc'd,

And nodding Forests to the Numbers danc'd.   45

Not by *Hæmonian* Hills the *Thracian* Bard,

Nor awful *Phœbus* was on *Pindus* heard,

With deeper silence, or with more regard.

He sung the secret Seeds of Nature's Frame;

How Seas, and Earth, and Air, and active Flame,   50

Fell through the mighty Void; and in their fall

Were blindly gather'd in this goodly Ball.

The tender Soil then stiffning by degrees,

Shut from the bounded Earth, the bounding Seas.

The Sixth Pastoral. 20 *Silenus* 98: *Sylenus* 97   33 Flood:] Flood, *97 98*

Then Earth and Ocean various Forms disclose;　　　　　55
And a new Sun to the new World arose.
And Mists condens'd to Clouds obscure the Skie;
And Clouds dissolv'd, the thirsty Ground supply.
The rising Trees the lofty Mountains grace:　　　　　⎫
The lofty Mountains feed the Savage Race,　　　　　⎬ 60
Yet few, and Strangers, in th' unpeopl'd Place.　　　⎭
From thence the birth of Man the Song pursu'd,
And how the World was lost, and how renew'd.
The Reign of *Saturn*, and the Golden Age;
Prometheus Theft, and *Jove*'s avenging Rage.　　　65
The Cries of *Argonauts* for *Hylas* drown'd;
With whose repeated Name the Shoars resound.
Then mourns the madness of the *Cretan* Queen;
Happy for her if Herds had never been.
What fury, wretched Woman, seiz'd thy Breast!　　　70
The Maids of *Argos* (tho with rage possess'd,
Their imitated lowings fill'd the Grove)
Yet shun'd the guilt of thy prepost'rous Love.
Nor sought the Youthful Husband of the Herd,　　　⎫
Though lab'ring Yokes on their own Necks they fear'd;　⎬ 75
And felt for budding Horns on their smooth forheads rear'd.⎭
Ah, wretched Queen! you range the pathless Wood;
While on a flowry Bank he chaws the Cud:
Or sleeps in Shades, or thro' the Forest roves;
And roars with anguish for his absent Loves.　　　　80
Ye Nymphs, with toils, his Forest-walk surround;
And trace his wandring Footsteps on the ground.
But, ah! perhaps my Passion he disdains;
And courts the milky Mothers of the Plains.
We search th' ungrateful Fugitive abroad;　　　　　85
While they at home sustain his happy load.
He sung the Lover's fraud; the longing Maid,
With golden Fruit, like all the Sex, betray'd.
The Sisters mourning for their Brother's loss;

---

60 Race, *98*: Race. *97*　　　　61 *added in 98*　　　73 thy *97* (*errata*): this *97* (*text*)
74 Herd, *98*: Herd; *97*　　　75–76] *98*: *97 has*
　　　　　　Tho tender and untry'd the Yoke he fear'd.
　　　　　　Tho soft and white as flakes of falling Snow;
　　　　　　And scarce his budding Horns had arm'd his brow.

See Commentary

Their Bodies hid in Barks, and furr'd with Moss. 90
How each a rising Alder now appears;
And o're the *Po* distils her Gummy Tears.
Then sung, how *Gallus* by a Muses hand,
Was led and welcom'd to the sacred Strand.
The Senate rising to salute their Guest; 95
And *Linus* thus their gratitude express'd.
Receive this Present, by the Muses made;
The Pipe on which th' *Ascræan* Pastor play'd:
With which of old he charm'd the Savage Train:
And call'd the Mountain Ashes to the Plain. 100
Sing thou on this, thy *Phœbus*; and the Wood
Where once his Fane of *Parian* Marble stood.
On this his ancient Oracles rehearse;
And with new Numbers grace the God of Verse.
Why shou'd I sing the double *Scylla's* Fate, 105
The first by Love transform'd, the last by Hate;
A beauteous Maid above, but Magick Arts,
With barking Dogs deform'd her neather parts;
What Vengeance on the passing Fleet she pour'd,
The Master frighted, and the Mates devour'd. 110
Then ravish'd *Philomel* the Song exprest;
The Crime reveal'd; the Sisters cruel Feast;
And how in Fields the Lapwing *Tereus* reigns;
The warbling Nightingale in Woods complains.
While *Progne* makes on Chymney tops her moan; 115
And hovers o're the Palace once her own.
Whatever Songs besides, the *Delphian* God
Had taught the Laurels, and the *Spartan* Flood,
Silenus sung: the Vales his Voice rebound;
And carry to the Skies the sacred Sound. 120
And now the setting Sun had warn'd the Swain
To call his counted Cattle from the Plain:
Yet still th' unweary'd Syre pursues the tuneful Strain.
Till unperceiv'd the Heav'ns with Stars were hung:
And sudden Night surpriz'd the yet unfinish'd Song. 125

106 Hate;] Hate. *97 98*   108 parts;] parts. *97 98*

THE SEVENTH PASTORAL. OR, MELIBŒUS

THE ARGUMENT

Melibœus *here gives us the Relation of a sharp Poetical Contest between* Thyrsis *and* Corydon*; at which he himself and* Daphnis *were present; who both declar'd for* Corydon.

BENEATH a Holm, repair'd two jolly Swains;
Their Sheep and Goats together graz'd the Plains.
Both young *Arcadians*, both alike inspir'd
To sing, and answer as the Song requir'd.
Daphnis, as Umpire, took the middle Seat;   5
And Fortune thether led my weary Feet.
For while I fenc'd my Myrtles from the Cold,
The Father of my Flock had wander'd from the Fold.
Of *Daphnis* I enquir'd; he, smiling, said,
Dismiss your Fear, and pointed where he fed.   10
And, if no greater Cares disturb your Mind,
Sit here with us, in covert of the Wind.
Your lowing Heyfars, of their own accord,
At wat'ring time will seek the neighb'ring Ford.
Here wanton *Mincius* windes along the Meads,   15
And shades his happy Banks with bending Reeds:
And see from yon old Oak, that mates the Skies,
How black the Clouds of swarming Bees arise.
What shou'd I do! nor was *Alcippe* nigh,
Nor absent *Phillis* cou'd my care supply,   20
To house, and feed by hand my weaning Lambs,
And drain the strutting Udders of their Dams?
Great was the strife betwixt the Singing Swains:
And I preferr'd my Pleasure to my Gains.
Alternate Rhime the ready Champions chose: 25
These *Corydon* rehears'd, and *Thyrsis* those.

CORYDON

Yee Muses, ever fair, and ever young,
Assist my Numbers, and inspire my Song.
With all my *Codrus* O inspire my Breast,
For *Codrus* after *Phœbus* sings the best.   30

Or if my Wishes have presum'd too high,
And stretch'd their bounds beyond Mortality,
The praise of artful Numbers I resign:
And hang my Pipe upon the Sacred Pine.

THYRSIS

Arcadian Swains, your Youthful Poet crown   35
With Ivy Wreaths; tho surly *Codrus*, frown.
Or if he blast my Muse with envious Praise,
Then fence my Brows with *Amuletts* of Bays.
Lest his ill Arts or his malicious Tongue
Shou'd poyson, or bewitch my growing Song.   40

CORYDON

These Branches of a Stag, this tusky Boar
(The first essay of Arms untry'd before)
Young *Mycon* offers, *Delia*, to thy Shrine;
But speed his hunting with thy Pow'r divine,
Thy Statue then of *Parian* Stone shall stand;   45
Thy Legs in Buskins with a Purple Band.

THYRSIS

This Bowl of Milk, these Cakes, (our Country Fare,)
For thee, *Priapus*, yearly we prepare,
Because a little Garden is thy care.
But if the falling Lambs increase my Fold,   50
Thy Marble Statue shall be turn'd to Gold.

CORYDON

Fair *Galathea*, with thy silver Feet,
O, whiter than the Swan, and more than *Hybla* sweet;
Tall as a Poplar, taper as the Bole,
Come charm thy Shepherd, and restore my Soul.   55
Come when my lated Sheep, at night return;
And crown the silent Hours, and stop the rosy Morn.

THYRSIS

May I become as abject in thy sight,
As Sea-weed on the Shore, and black as Night:

The Seventh Pastoral. 48 prepare,] prepare. 97 98

Rough as a Bur, deform'd like him who chaws　　　　60
Sardinian Herbage to contract his Jaws;
Such and so monstrous let thy Swain appear,
If one day's Absence looks not like a Year.
Hence from the Field, for Shame: the Flock deserves
No better Feeding, while the Shepherd starves.　　　65

CORYDON

Ye mossy Springs, inviting easie Sleep,
Ye Trees, whose leafy Shades those mossy Fountains keep,
Defend my Flock, the Summer heats are near,
And Blossoms on the swelling Vines appear.

THYRSIS

With heapy Fires our chearful Hearth is crown'd;　　70
And Firs for Torches in the Woods abound:
We fear not more the Winds, and wintry Cold,
Than Streams the Banks, or Wolves the bleating Fold.

CORYDON

Our Woods, with Juniper and Chesnuts crown'd,
With falling Fruits and Berries paint the Ground;　　} 75
And lavish Nature laughs, and strows her Stores around.
But if *Alexis* from our Mountains fly,
Ev'n running Rivers leave their Channels dry.

THYRSIS

Parch'd are the Plains, and frying is the Field,
Nor with'ring Vines their juicy Vintage yield.　　　80
But if returning *Phillis* bless the Plain,
The Grass revives; the Woods are green again;　　　}
And *Jove* descends in Show'rs of kindly Rain.

CORYDON

The Poplar is by great *Alcides* worn:
The Brows of *Phœbus* his own Bays adorn.　　　　85
The branching Vine the jolly *Bacchus* loves;
The *Cyprian* Queen delights in Mirtle Groves.

With Hazle, *Phillis* crowns her flowing Hair;
And while she loves that common Wreath to wear,
Nor Bays, nor Myrtle Bows, with Hazle shall compare. } 90

THYRSIS

The towring Ash is fairest in the Woods;
In Gardens Pines, and Poplars by the Floods:
But if my *Lycidas* will ease my Pains,
And often visit our forsaken Plains;
To him the tow'ring Ash shall yield in Woods; 95
In Gardens Pines, and Poplars by the Floods.

MELIBŒUS

These Rhymes I did to Memory commend,
When Vanquish'd *Thyrsis* did in vain contend;
Since when, tis *Corydon* among the Swains,
Young *Corydon* without a Rival Reigns. 100

THE EIGHTH PASTORAL.
OR, PHARMACEUTRIA

THE ARGUMENT

This Pastoral contains the Songs of Damon *and* Alphesibœus. *The first of 'em bewails the loss of his Mistress, and repines at the Success of his Rival* Mopsus. *The other repeats the Charms of some Enchantress, who endeavour'd by her Spells and Magic to make* Daphnis *in Love with her.*

THE mournful Muse of two despairing Swains,
The Love rejected, and the Lovers' pains,
To which the salvage *Linxes* listning stood;
The Rivers stood on heaps, and stop'd the running Flood,
The hungry Herd their needful Food refuse; 5
Of two despairing Swains, I sing the mournful Muse.
Great *Pollio*, thou for whom thy *Rome* prepares

88 Hair;] Hair, *97 98*   89 wear,] wear; *97 98*   97–100] *98: 97 has*
I've heard: and, *Thyrsis*, you contend in vain: }
For *Corydon*, young *Corydon* shall reign, }
The Prince of Poets, on the *Mantuan* Plain. }
See Commentary
The Eighth Pastoral. 2 pains,] pains; *97 98*   3 stood;] stood, *97*: stood. *98*

The ready Triumph of thy finish'd Wars,
Whither *Timavus* or th' *Illirian* Coast,
Whatever Land or Sea thy presence boast;⠀⠀⠀⠀⠀⠀10
Is there an hour in Fate reserv'd for me,
To Sing thy Deeds in Numbers worthy thee?
In numbers like to thine, cou'd I rehearse
Thy lofty Tragick Scenes, thy labour'd Verse;
The World another *Sophocles* in thee,⠀⠀⠀⠀⠀⠀15
Another *Homer* shou'd behold in me:
Amidst thy Laurels let this Ivy twine,
Thine was my earlyest Muse; my latest shall be thine.
⠀⠀Scarce from the World the Shades of Night withdrew;
Scarce were the Flocks refresh'd with Morning Dew,⠀⠀20
When *Damon* stretch'd beneath an Olive Shade,
And wildly staring upwards, thus inveigh'd
Against the conscious Gods, and curs'd the cruel Maid.
Star of the Morning, why dost thou delay?
Come, *Lucifer*, drive on the lagging Day.⠀⠀⠀⠀⠀25
While I my *Nisa*'s perjur'd Faith deplore;
Witness ye Pow'rs, by whom she falsly swore!
The Gods, alas, are Witnesses in vain;
Yet shall my dying Breath to Heav'n complain.
Begin with me, my Flute, the sweet *Mænalian* Strain.⠀⠀30
⠀⠀The Pines of *Mænalus*, the vocal Grove,
Are ever full of Verse, and full of Love:
They hear the Hinds, they hear their God complain;
Who suffer'd not the Reeds to rise in vain:
Begin with me, my Flute, the sweet *Mænalian* Strain.⠀⠀35
Mopsus triumphs; he weds the willing Fair:
When such is *Nisa*'s choice, what Lover can despair!
Now Griffons join with Mares; another Age
Shall see the Hound and Hind their Thirst asswage,
Promiscuous at the Spring: Prepare the Lights,⠀⠀⠀⠀40
O *Mopsus*! and perform the bridal Rites.
Scatter thy Nuts among the scrambling Boys:
Thine is the Night; and thine the Nuptial Joys.
For thee the Sun declines: O happy Swain!
Begin with me, my Flute, the sweet *Mænalian* Strain.⠀⠀45
⠀⠀O, *Nisa*! Justly to thy Choice condemn'd,

19 the World the Shades of Night 97 (*errata*): our upper World the Shades 97 (*text*)

Whom hast thou taken, whom hast thou contemn'd!
For him, thou hast refus'd my browzing Herd,
Scorn'd my thick Eye-brows, and my shaggy Beard.
Unhappy *Damon* sighs, and sings in vain: 50
While *Nisa* thinks no God regards a Lover's pain.
Begin with me, my Flute, the sweet *Mænalian* Strain.
 I view'd thee first; how fatal was the View!
And led thee where the ruddy Wildings grew,
High on the planted hedge, and wet with Morning Dew. 55
Then scarce the bending Branches I cou'd win;
The callow Down began to cloath my Chin;
I saw, I perish'd; yet indulg'd my Pain:
Begin with me, my Flute, the sweet *Mænalian* Strain.
 I know thee, Love; in Desarts thou wert bred; 60
And at the Dugs of Salvage Tygers fed:
Alien of Birth, Usurper of the Plains:
Begin with me, my Flute, the sweet *Mænalian* Strains.
 Relentless Love the cruel Mother led,
The Blood of her unhappy Babes to shed: 65
Love lent the Sword; the Mother struck the blow;
Inhuman she; but more inhuman thou.
Alien of Birth, Usurper of the Plains:
Begin with me, my Flute, the sweet *Mænalian* Strains.
 Old doting Nature change thy Course anew: 70
And let the trembling Lamb the Wolf pursue:
Let Oaks now glitter with *Hesperian* Fruit,
And purple Daffodils from Alder shoot.
Fat Amber let the Tamarisk distil:
And hooting Owls contend with Swans in Skill. 75
Hoarse *Tity'rus* strive with *Orpheus* in the Woods:
And challenge fam'd *Arion* on the Floods.
Or, oh! let Nature cease; and *Chaos* reign:
Begin with me, my Flute, the sweet *Mænalian* Strain.
 Let Earth be Sea; and let the whelming Tide, 80
The lifeless Limbs of luckless *Damon* hide:
Farewel, ye secret Woods, and shady Groves,
Haunts of my Youth, and conscious of my Loves!
From yon high Cliff I plunge into the Main;
Take the last Present of thy dying Swain: 85
And cease, my silent Flute, the sweet *Mænalian* Strain.

Now take your Turns, ye Muses, to rehearse
His Friend's Complaints; and mighty Magick Verse.
Bring running Water; bind those Altars round
With Fillets; and with Vervain strow the Ground: 90
Make fat with Frankincense the sacred Fires;
To re-inflame my *Daphnis* with Desires.
'Tis done, we want but Verse. Restore, my Charms,
My lingring *Daphnis* to my longing Arms.

    Pale *Phœbe*, drawn by Verse from Heav'n descends: 95
And *Circe* chang'd with Charms *Ulysses* Friends.
Verse breaks the Ground, and penetrates the Brake;
And in the winding Cavern splits the Snake.
Verse fires the frozen Veins: Restore, my Charms,
My lingring *Daphnis* to my longing Arms.   100

    Around his waxen Image, first I wind
Three woollen Fillets, of three Colours join'd:
Thrice bind about his thrice devoted head,
Which round the sacred Altar thrice is led.
Unequal Numbers please the Gods: my Charms,   105
Restore my *Daphnis* to my longing Arms.

    Knit with three knots, the Fillets, knit 'em streight;
And say, These Knots to Love I consecrate.
Haste, *Amaryllis*, haste; restore, my Charms,
My lovely *Daphnis* to my longing Arms.   110

    As Fire this Figure hardens, made of Clay;
And this of Wax with Fire consumes away;
Such let the Soul of cruel *Daphnis* be;
Hard to the rest of Women; soft to me.
Crumble the sacred Mole of Salt and Corn,   115
Next in the Fire the Bays with Brimstone burn.
And while it crackles in the Sulphur, say,
This, I for *Daphnis* burn; thus *Daphnis* burn away.
This Laurel is his Fate: Restore, my Charms,
My lovely *Daphnis* to my longing Arms.   120

    As when the raging Heyfar, through the Grove,
Stung with Desire, pursues her wand'ring Love;
Faint at the last, she seeks the weedy Pools,
To quench her thirst, and on the Rushes rowls,
Careless of Night, unmindful to return;   125

88 Complaints 98: Complaint 97   124 rowls,] rowls: 97 98   125 return;] return, 97 98

Such fruitless Fires perfidious *Daphnis* burn,
While I so scorn his Love; Restore, my Charms,
My lingring *Daphnis* to my longing Arms.

These Garments once were his; and left to me;
The Pledges of his promis'd Loyalty: 130
Which underneath my Threshold I bestow;
These Pawns, O sacred Earth! to me my *Daphnis* owe.
As these were his, so mine is he; my Charms,
Restore their lingring Lord to my deluded Arms.

These poys'nous Plants, for Magick use design'd,   135
(The noblest and the best of all the baneful Kind,)
Old *Mæris* brought me from the *Pontick* Strand:
And cull'd the Mischief of a bounteous Land.
Smear'd with these pow'rful Juices, on the Plain,
He howls a Wolf among the hungry Train: 140
And oft the mighty Negromancer boasts,
With these, to call from Tombs the stalking Ghosts:
And from the roots to tear the standing Corn;
Which, whirld aloft, to distant Fields is born.
Such is the strength of Spells; restore, my Charms,   145
My lingring *Daphnis* to my longing Arms.

Bear out these Ashes; cast 'em in the Brook;
Cast backwards o're your head, nor turn your look:
Since neither Gods, nor Godlike Verse can move,
Break out ye smother'd Fires, and kindle smother'd Love.   150
Exert your utmost pow'r, my lingring Charms,
And force my *Daphnis* to my longing Arms.

See, while my last endeavours I delay,
The waking Ashes rise, and round our Altars play!
Run to the Threshold, *Amaryllis*, hark,   155
Our *Hylas* opens, and begins to bark.
Good Heav'n! may Lovers what they wish believe;
Or dream their wishes, and those dreams deceive!
No more, my *Daphnis* comes; no more, my Charms;
He comes, he runs, he leaps to my desiring Arms.   160

126 burn,] burn. 97 98

THE NINTH PASTORAL.
OR, LYCIDAS, *and* MŒRIS

THE ARGUMENT

When Virgil *by the Favour of* Augustus *had recover'd his Patrimony near*
Mantua, *and went in hope to take possession, he was in danger to be slain by*
Arius *the* Centurion, *to whom those Lands were assign'd by the Emperour*
in reward of his Service against Brutus *and* Cassius. *This Pastoral therefore*
is fill'd with complaints of his hard Usage; and the persons introduc'd, are the 5
Bayliff of Virgil, Mœris, *and his Friend* Lycidas.

LYCIDAS

H O *Mœris*! whither on thy way so fast?
This leads to Town.

MŒRIS

O *Lycidas* at last
The time is come, I never thought to see,
(Strange revolution for my Farm and me)   5
When the grim Captain in a surly tone
Cries out, pack up ye Rascals and be gone.
Kick'd out, we set the best face on't we cou'd,
And these two Kids, t' appease his angry Mood
I bear, of which the Furies give him good.   10

LYCIDAS

Your Country Friends were told another Tale;
That from the sloaping Mountain to the Vale,
And dodder'd Oak, and all the Banks along,
Menalcas sav'd his Fortune with a Song.

MŒRIS

Such was the News, indeed, but Songs and Rhimes   15
Prevail, as much in these hard iron times,

The Ninth Pastoral. Argument. 4 *Pastoral 97 98: Eclogue 84 92*   6 Virgil, Mœris,
and his Friend Lycidas *97 98:* Virgil, *and his Friend 84 92*
10 Furies *97 98:* Devil *84 92*   11 Your . . . another *97 98:* Good Gods, I heard
a quite contrary *84 92*

As would a plump of trembling Fowl, that rise
Against an Eagle sousing from the Skies.
And had not *Phœbus* warn'd me by the croak
Of an old Raven from a hollow Oak,   20
To shun debate, *Menalcas* had been slain,
And *Mœris* not surviv'd him to complain.

LYCIDAS

Now Heaven defend! could barbarous rage induce
The Brutal Son of *Mars*, t' insult the sacred Muse!
Who then shou'd sing the Nymphs, or who rehearse   25
The waters gliding in a smoother Verse!
Or *Amaryllis* praise, that heavenly lay,
That shorten'd as we went, our tedious way;
O *Tityrus*, tend my herd and see them fed;
To Morning pastures, Evening waters led: }30
And 'ware the *Lybian* Ridgils butting head.

MŒRIS

Or what unfinish'd He to *Varus* read;
Thy name, O *Varus* (if the kinder pow'rs
Preserve our plains, and shield the *Mantuan* Tow'rs
Obnoxious by *Cremonas* neighb'ring Crime,)   35
The wings of Swans, and stronger pinion'd Rhyme,
Shall raise aloft, and soaring bear above
Th' immortal Gift of gratitude to *Jove*.

LYCIDAS

Sing on, sing on, for I can ne're be cloy'd,
So may thy Swarms the baleful Eugh avoid: 40
So may thy Cows their burden'd Bags distend
And Trees to Goats their willing branches bend.
Mean as I am, yet have the Muses made
Me free, a Member of the tuneful Trade:
At least the Shepherds seem to like my lays,   45
But I discern their flattery from their praise:
I nor to *Cinna*'s Ears, nor *Varus* dare aspire;
But gabble like a Goose, amidst the Swan-like quire.

17 plump] plume *92*   23 induce *97 98*: prevail *84 92*   24 The Brutal . . .
Muse! *97 98*: So far, the sacred Muses to assail? *84 92*   27 praise, *97 98*:
praise *84 92*   30 pastures, *97 98*: pastures *84 92*   42 bend. *97 98*: bend; *84 92*

MŒRIS

'Tis what I have been conning in my mind:
Nor are they Verses of a Vulgar kind.   50
Come *Galatea*, come, the Seas forsake,
What pleasures can the Tides with their hoarse murmurs make?
See on the Shore inhabits purple spring;
Where Nightingales their Love-sick ditty sing;
See Meads with purling Streams, with Flow'rs the ground,   ⎫ 55
The Grottoes cool, with shady Poplars crown'd,   ⎬
And creeping Vines on Arbours weav'd around.   ⎭
Come then and leave the Waves tumultuous roar,
Let the wild surges vainly beat the shore.

LYCIDAS

Or that sweet Song I heard with such delight;   60
The same you sung alone one starry night;
The tune I still retain, but not the words.

MŒRIS

Why, *Daphnis*, dost thou search in old Records,
To know the seasons when the stars arise?
See *Cæsars* Lamp is lighted in the Skies: 65
The star, whose rays the blushing grapes adorn,
And swell the kindly ripening ears of Corn.
Under this influence, graft the tender shoot;
Thy Childrens Children shall enjoy the fruit.
The rest I have forgot, for Cares and Time   70
Change all things, and untune my soul to rhime:
I cou'd have once sung down a Summers Sun,
But now the Chime of Poetry is done.
My voice grows hoarse; I feel the Notes decay,
As if the Wolves had seen me first to day.   75
But these, and more then I to mind can bring,
Menalcas has not yet forgot to sing.

LYCIDAS

Thy faint Excuses but inflame me more;
And now the Waves roul silent to the shore.

57 on *97 98*: to *84 92*

Husht winds the topmost branches scarcely bend   80
As if thy tuneful Song they did attend:
Already we have half our way o'recome;
Far off I can discern *Bianors* Tomb;
Here, where the Labourers hands have form'd a Bow'r
Of wreathing trees, in singing waste an hour.   85
Rest here thy weary Limbs, thy Kids lay down,
We've day before us yet, to reach the Town:
Or if e're night the gathering Clouds we fear,
A Song will help the beating storm to bear.
And that thou maist not be too late abroad,   90
Sing, and I'le ease thy shoulders of thy Load.

MŒRIS

Cease to request me, let us mind our way;
Another Song requires another day.
When good *Menalcas* comes, if he rejoyce,
And find a friend at Court, I'le find a voice.   95

THE TENTH PASTORAL. OR, GALLUS

THE ARGUMENT

Gallus *a great Patron of* Virgil, *and an excellent Poet, was very deeply in Love with one* Citheris, *whom he calls* Lycoris; *and who had forsaken him for the Company of a Souldier. The Poet therefore supposes his Friend* Gallus *retir'd in his heighth of Melancholy into the Solitudes of* Arcadia, (*the celebrated Scene of Pastorals;*) *where he represents him in a very languishing Condition,* 5 *with all the Rural Deities about him, pitying his hard Usage, and condoling his Misfortune.*

THY sacred Succour, *Arethusa*, bring,
    To crown my Labour: 'tis the last I sing.
Which proud *Lycoris* may with Pity view;
The Muse is mournful, tho' the Numbers few.
Refuse me not a Verse, to Grief and *Gallus* due.   5
So may thy Silver Streams beneath the Tide,
Unmix'd with briny Seas, securely glide.
Sing then, my *Gallus*, and his hopeless Vows;
Sing, while my Cattle crop the tender Browze.

87 us yet, *97 98*: us, yet *84 92*   92 request *97 98*: entreat *84 92*

The vocal Grove shall answer to the Sound,   10
And Echo, from the Vales, the tuneful Voice rebound.
What Lawns or Woods withheld you from his Aid,
Ye Nymphs, when *Gallus* was to Love betray'd;
To Love, unpity'd by the cruel Maid?
Not steepy *Pindus* cou'd retard your Course,   15
Nor cleft *Parnassus*, nor th' *Aonian* Source:
Nothing that owns the Muses cou'd suspend
Your Aid to *Gallus*, *Gallus* is their Friend.
For him the lofty Laurel stands in Tears;
And hung with humid Pearls the lowly Shrub appears.   20
Mænalian Pines the Godlike Swain bemoan;
When spread beneath a Rock he sigh'd alone;
And cold *Lycæus* wept from every dropping Stone.
The Sheep surround their Shepherd, as he lyes:
Blush not, sweet Poet, nor the name despise: 25
Along the Streams his Flock *Adonis* fed;
And yet the Queen of Beauty blest his Bed.
The Swains and tardy Neat-herds came, and last
Menalcas, wet with beating Winter Mast.
Wond'ring, they ask'd from whence arose thy Flame;   30
Yet, more amaz'd, thy own *Apollo* came.
Flush'd were his Cheeks, and glowing were his Eyes:
Is she thy Care, is she thy Care, he cries?
Thy false *Lycoris* flies thy Love and thee;
And for thy Rival tempts the raging Sea,   35
The Forms of horrid War, and Heav'ns Inclemency.
Sylvanus came: his Brows a Country Crown
Of Fennel, and of nodding Lillies, drown.
Great *Pan* arriv'd; and we beheld him too,
His Cheeks and Temples of Vermilion Hue.   40
Why, *Gallus*, this immod'rate Grief, he cry'd:
Think'st thou that Love with Tears is satisfi'd?
The Meads are sooner drunk with Morning Dews;
The Bees with flow'ry Shrubs, the Goats with Brouze.
Unmov'd, and with dejected Eyes, he mourn'd: 45
He paus'd, and then these broken Words return'd.
'Tis past; and Pity gives me no Relief:
But you, *Arcadian* Swains, shall sing my Grief:
And on your Hills, my last Complaints renew;

So sad a Song is onely worthy you.   50
How light wou'd lye the Turf upon my Breast,
If you my Suff'rings in your Songs exprest?
Ah! that your Birth and Bus'ness had been mine;
To penn the Sheep, and press the swelling Vine!
Had *Phyllis* or *Amyntas* caus'd my Pain,   55
Or any Nymph, or Shepherd on the Plain,
Tho *Phyllis* brown, tho black *Amyntas* were,
Are Violets not sweet, because not fair?
Beneath the Sallows, and the shady Vine,
My Loves had mix'd their pliant Limbs with mine;   60
Phyllis with Myrtle Wreaths had crown'd my Hair,
And soft *Amyntas* sung away my Care.
Come, see what Pleasures in our Plains abound;
The Woods, the Fountains, and the flow'ry ground.
As you are beauteous, were you half so true,   65
Here cou'd I live, and love, and dye with only you.
Now I to fighting Fields am sent afar,
And strive in Winter Camps with toils of War;
While you, (alas, that I shou'd find it so!)
To shun my sight, your Native Soil forgo,   70
And climb the frozen *Alps*, and tread th' eternal Snow.
Ye Frosts and Snows her tender Body spare,
Those are not Limbs for Ysicles to tear.
For me, the Wilds and Desarts are my Choice;
The Muses, once my Care; my once harmonious Voice.   75
There will I sing, forsaken and alone,
The Rocks and hollow Caves shall echo to my Moan.
The Rind of ev'ry Plant her Name shall know;
And as the Rind extends, the Love shall grow.
Then on *Arcadian* Mountains will I chase   80
(Mix'd with the Woodland Nymphs) the Salvage Race.
Nor Cold shall hinder me, with Horns and Hounds,
To thrid the Thickets, or to leap the Mounds.
And now methinks o're steepy Rocks I go;
And rush through sounding Woods, and bend the *Parthian* Bow: 85
As if with Sports my Sufferings I could ease,
Or by my Pains the God of Love appease.
My Frenzy changes, I delight no more
On Mountain tops, to chace the tusky Boar;

No Game but hopeless Love my thoughts pursue: 90
Once more ye Nymphs, and Songs, and sounding Woods adieu.
Love alters not for us, his hard Decrees,
Not tho beneath the *Thracian* Clime we freeze;
Or *Italy*'s indulgent Heav'n forgo;
And in mid-Winter tread *Sithonian* Snow.   95
Or when the Barks of Elms are scorch'd, we keep
On *Meroes* burning Plains the *Lybian* Sheep.
In Hell, and Earth, and Seas, and Heav'n above,
Love conquers all; and we must yield to Love.
My Muses, here your sacred Raptures end: 100
The Verse was what I ow'd my suff'ring Friend.
This while I sung, my Sorrows I deceiv'd,
And bending Osiers into Baskets weav'd.
The Song, because inspir'd by you, shall shine:
And *Gallus* will approve, because 'tis mine.   105
Gallus, for whom my holy Flames renew,
Each hour, and ev'ry moment rise in view:
As Alders, in the Spring, their Boles extend;
And heave so fiercely, that the Bark they rend.
Now let us rise, for hoarseness oft invades   110
The Singer's Voice, who sings beneath the Shades.
From Juniper, unwholsom Dews distill,
That blast the sooty Corn; the with'ring Herbage kill;
Away, my Goats, away: for you have browz'd your fill.

TO THE RIGHT HONOURABLE *PHILIP*
Earl of *Chesterfield*, &c.

My Lord,

I CANNOT *begin my Address to your Lordship, better than in the words of* Virgil,

> ——Quod optanti, Divum promittere Nemo
> Auderet, volvenda Dies, en, attulit ultrò.

Seven Years together I have conceal'd the longing which I had to appear before 5
you: A time as tedious as Æneas *pass'd in his wandring Voyage, before he*
reach'd the promis'd Italy. But I consider'd, that nothing which my meanness
cou'd produce, was worthy of your Patronage. At last this happy Occasion

The Tenth Pastoral. 95 Sithonian 98: Scythonian 97

offer'd, of Presenting to you the best Poem of the best Poet. If I balk'd this *opportunity, I was in despair of finding such another; and if I took it, I was still* 10 *uncertain whether you wou'd vouchsafe to accept it from my hands. 'Twas a bold* *venture which I made, in desiring your permission to lay my unworthy Labours* *at your feet. But my rashness has succeeded beyond my hopes: And you have been* *pleas'd not to suffer an Old Man to go discontented out of the World, for want of* *that protection, of which he had been so long Ambitious. I have known a Gentle-* 15 *man in disgrace, and not daring to appear before King* Charles *the Second,* *though he much desir'd it: At length he took the confidence to attend a fair Lady* *to the Court, and told His Majesty, that under her protection he had presum'd to* *wait on him. With the same humble confidence I present my self before your* *Lordship, and attending on* Virgil *hope a gracious reception. The Gentleman* 20 *succeeded, because the powerful Lady was his Friend; but I have too much injur'd* *my great Author, to expect he should intercede for me. I wou'd have Translated* *him, but according to the litteral* French *and* Italian *Phrases, I fear I have* *traduc'd him. 'Tis the fault of many a well-meaning Man, to be officious in a* *wrong place, and do a prejudice, where he had endeavour'd to do a service.* Virgil 25 *wrote his* Georgics *in the full strength and vigour of his Age, when his Judg-* *ment was at the height, and before his Fancy was declining. He had, (according* *to our homely Saying) his full swing at this Poem, beginning it about the Age* *of Thirty Five; and scarce concluding it before he arriv'd at Forty. 'Tis* *observ'd both of him, and* Horace, *and I believe it will hold in all great Poets;* 30 *that though they wrote before with a certain heat of Genius which inspir'd them,* *yet that heat was not perfectly digested. There is requir'd a continuance of* *warmth to ripen the best and Noblest Fruits. Thus* Horace *in his First and* *Second Book of* Odes, *was still rising, but came not to his* Meridian *'till the* *Third. After which his Judgment was an overpoize to his Imagination: He* 35 *grew too cautious to be bold enough, for he descended in his Fourth by slow* *degrees, and in his* Satires *and* Epistles, *was more a Philosopher and a Critick* *than a Poet. In the beginning of Summer the days are almost at a stand, with* *little variation of length or shortness, because at that time the Diurnal Motion* *of the Sun partakes more of a Right Line, than of a Spiral. The same is the method* 40 *of Nature in the frame of Man. He seems at Forty to be fully in his Summer* *Tropick; somewhat before, and somewhat after, he finds in his Soul but small* *increases or decays. From Fifty to Threescore the Ballance generally holds even,* *in our colder Clymates: For he loses not much in Fancy; and Judgment, which* *is the effect of Observation, still increases: His succeeding years afford him little* 45 *more than the stubble of his own Harvest: Yet if his Constitution be healthful, his* *Mind may still retain a decent vigour; and the Gleanings of that* Ephraim, *in* *Comparison with others, will surpass the Vintage of* Abiezer. *I have call'd this*

somewhere by a bold Metaphor, a green Old Age; but Virgil *has given me his*
Authority for the Figure.   50

    Jam Senior; sed Cruda Deo, viridisq; Senectus.

    Amongst those few who enjoy the advantage of a latter Spring, your Lordship
is a rare Example: Who being now arriv'd at your great Clymacterique, *yet*
give no proof of the least decay in your Excellent Judgment, and comprehension
of all things, which are within the compass of Humane Understanding. Your 55
Conversation is as easie as it is instructive, and I cou'd never observe the least
vanity or the least assuming in any thing you said: but a natural unaffected
Modesty, full of good sense, and well digested. A clearness of Notion, express'd
in ready and unstudied words. No Man has complain'd, or ever can, that you have
discours'd too long on any Subject: for you leave us in an eagerness of Learning 60
more; pleas'd with what we hear, but not satisfy'd, because you will not speak
so much as we cou'd wish. I dare not excuse your Lordship from this fault; for
though 'tis none in you, 'tis one to all who have the happiness of being known to
you. I must confess the Criticks make it one of Virgil's *Beauties, that having said*
what he thought convenient, he always left somewhat for the imagination of his 65
Readers to supply: That they might gratifie their fancies, by finding more, in
what he had written, than at first they cou'd; and think they had added to his
thought, when it was all there before-hand, and he only sav'd himself the expence
of words. However it was, I never went from your Lordship, but with a longing
to return, or without a hearty Curse to him who invented Ceremonies in the World, 70
and put me on the necessity of withdrawing, when it was my interest as well as
my desire, to have given you a much longer trouble. I cannot imagine (if your
Lordship will give me leave to speak my thoughts) but you have had a more than
ordinary vigour in your Youth. For too much of heat is requir'd at first, that
there may not too little be left at last. A Prodigal Fire is only capable of large 75
remains: And yours, my Lord, still burns the clearer in declining. The Blaze is
not so fierce as at the first, but the Smoak is wholly vanish'd; and your Friends
who stand about you, are not only sensible of a chearful warmth, but are kept at an
awful distance by its force. In my small Observations of Mankind, I have ever
found, that such as are not rather too full of Spirit when they are young, 80
degenerate to dullness in their Age. Sobriety in our riper years is the effect of a
well-concocted warmth; but where the Principles are only Phlegm, what can be
expected from the waterish Matter, but an insipid Manhood, and a stupid old
Infancy; Discretion in Leading-strings, and a confirm'd ignorance on Crutches?
Virgil *in his Third* Georgic, *when he describes a Colt, who promises a Courser* 85
for the Race, or for the Field of Battel, shews him the first to pass the Bridge,
which trembles under him, and to stem the torrent of the flood. His beginnings

must be in rashness; a Noble Fault: But Time and Experience will correct that Errour, and tame it into a deliberate and well-weigh'd Courage; which knows both to be cautious and to dare, as occasion offers. Your Lordship is a Man of Honour, 90 *not only so unstain'd, but so unquestion'd, that you are the living Standard of that Heroick Vertue; so truly such, that if I wou'd flatter you, I cou'd not. It takes not from you, that you were born with Principles of Generosity and Probity: But it adds to you, that you have cultivated Nature, and made those Principles, the Rule and Measure of all your Actions. The World knows this, without my telling:* 95 *Yet Poets have a right of Recording it to all Posterity.*

Dignum Laude Virum, Musa vetat Mori.

Epaminondas, Lucullus, *and the two first* Cæsars, *were not esteem'd the worse Commanders, for having made Philosophy, and the Liberal Arts their Study.* Cicero *might have been their Equal, but that he wanted Courage. To* 100 *have both these Vertues, and to have improv'd them both, with a softness of Manners, and a sweetness of Conversation, few of our Nobility can fill that Character: One there is, and so conspicuous by his own light, that he needs not*

Digito monstrari, & dicier Hic est.

To be Nobly Born, and of an Ancient Family, is in the extreams of Fortune, 105 *either good or bad; for Virtue and Descent are no Inheritance. A long Series of Ancestours shews the Native with great advantage at the first; but if he any way degenerate from his Line, the least Spot is visible on Ermine. But to preserve this whiteness in its Original Purity, you, my Lord, have, like that Ermine, forsaken the common Track of Business, which is not always clean: You have chosen for* 110 *your self a private Greatness, and will not be polluted with Ambition. It has been observ'd in former times, that none have been so greedy of Employments, and of managing the Publick, as they who have least deserv'd their Stations. But such only merit to be call'd Patriots, under whom we see their Country Flourish. I have laugh'd sometimes (for who wou'd always be a* Heraclitus?*) when* 115 *I have reflected on those Men, who from time to time have shot themselves into the World. I have seen many Successions of them; some bolting out upon the Stage with vast applause, and others hiss'd off, and quitting it with disgrace. But while they were in action, I have constantly observ'd, that they seem'd desirous to retreat from Business: Greatness they said was nauseous, and a* 120 *Crowd was troublesome; a quiet privacy was their Ambition. Some few of them I believe said this in earnest, and were making a provision against future want, that they might enjoy their Age with ease: They saw the happiness of a private Life, and promis'd to themselves a Blessing, which every day it was in their power to possess. But they deferr'd it, and linger'd still at Court, because they thought* 125 *they had not yet enough to make them happy: They wou'd have more, and laid in*

G g

to make their Solitude Luxurious. A wretched Philosophy, which Epicurus
never taught them in his Garden: They lov'd the prospect of this quiet in reversion,
but were not willing to have it in possession; they wou'd first be Old, and made as
sure of Health and Life, as if both of them were at their dispose. But put them 130
to the necessity of a present choice, and they preferr'd continuance in Power: Like
the Wretch who call'd Death to his assistance, but refus'd it when he came. The
Great Scipio *was not of their Opinion, who indeed sought Honours in his Youth,*
and indur'd the Fatigues with which he purchas'd them. He serv'd his Country
when it was in need of his Courage and his Conduct, 'till he thought it was time 135
to serve himself: But dismounted from the Saddle, when he found the Beast which
bore him, began to grow restiff and ungovernable. But your Lordship has given
us a better Example of Moderation. You saw betimes that Ingratitude is not con-
fin'd to Commonwealths; and therefore though you were form'd alike, for the
greatest of Civil Employments, and Military Commands, yet you push'd not your 140
Fortune to rise in either; but contented your self with being capable, as much as
any whosoever, of defending your Country with your Sword, or assisting it with
your Counsel, when you were call'd. For the rest, the respect and love which was
paid you, not only in the Province where you live, but generally by all who had
the happiness to know you, was a wise Exchange for the Honours of the Court: A 145
place of forgetfulness, at the best, for well deservers. 'Tis necessary for the
polishing of Manners, to have breath'd that Air, but 'tis infectious even to the
best Morals to live always in it. 'Tis a dangerous Commerce, where an honest
Man is sure at the first of being Cheated; and he recovers not his Losses, but by
learning to Cheat others. The undermining Smile becomes at length habitual; and 150
the drift of his plausible Conversation, is only to flatter one, that he may betray
another. Yet 'tis good to have been a looker on, without venturing to play; that
a Man may know false Dice another time, though he never means to use them. I
commend not him who never knew a Court, but him who forsakes it because he
knows it. A young Man deserves no praise, who out of melancholy Zeal leaves the 155
World before he has well try'd it, and runs headlong into Religion. He who
carries a Maidenhead into a Cloyster, is sometimes apt to lose it there, and to
repent of his Repentance. He only is like to endure Austerities, who has already
found the inconvenience of Pleasures. For almost every Man will be making
Experiments in one part or another of his Life: And the danger is the less when 160
we are young: For having try'd it early, we shall not be apt to repeat it after-
wards. Your Lordship therefore may properly be said to have chosen a Retreat;
and not to have chosen it 'till you had maturely weigh'd the advantages of rising
higher with the hazards of the fall. Res non parta labore, sed relicta, *was*
thought by a Poet, to be one of the requisites to a happy Life. Why shou'd a 165
reasonable Man put it into the power of Fortune to make him miserable, when his

Ancestours have taken care to release him from her? Let him venture, says Horace, Qui Zonam perdidit. *He who has nothing, plays securely, for he may win, and cannot be poorer if he loses. But he who is born to a plentiful Estate, and is Ambitious of Offices at Court, sets a stake to Fortune, which she can seldom* 170 *answer: If he gains nothing, he loses all, or part of what was once his own; and if he gets, he cannot be certain but he may refund.*

In short, however he succeeds, 'tis Covetousness that induc'd him first to play, and Covetousness is the undoubted sign of ill sense at bottom. The Odds are against him that he loses, and one loss may be of more consequence to him, than all his 175 *former winnings. 'Tis like the present War of the* Christians *against the* Turk; *every year they gain a Victory, and by that a Town; but if they are once defeated, they lose a Province at a blow, and endanger the safety of the whole Empire. You, my Lord, enjoy your quiet in a Garden, where you have not only the leisure of thinking, but the pleasure to think of nothing which can discompose your* 180 *Mind. A good Conscience is a Port which is Land-lock'd on every side, and where no Winds can possibly invade, no Tempests can arise. There a Man may stand upon the Shore, and not only see his own Image, but that of his Maker, clearly reflected from the undisturb'd and silent waters. Reason was intended for a Blessing, and such it is to Men of Honour and Integrity; who desire no more,* 185 *than what they are able to give themselves; like the happy Old* Corycian, *whom my Author describes in his Fourth* Georgic; *whose Fruits and Salads on which he liv'd contented, were all of his own growth, and his own Plantation.* Virgil *seems to think that the Blessings of a Country Life are not compleat, without an improvement of Knowledge by Contemplation and Reading.* 190

> O Fortunatos nimiùm, bona si sua norint
> Agricolas!

'Tis but half possession not to understand that happiness which we possess: A foundation of good Sense, and a cultivation of Learning, are requir'd to give a seasoning to Retirement, and make us taste the blessing. God has bestow'd on your 195 *Lordship the first of these, and you have bestow'd on your self the second.* Eden *was not made for Beasts, though they were suffer'd to live in it, but for their Master, who studied God in the Works of his Creation. Neither cou'd the Devil have been happy there with all his Knowledge, for he wanted Innocence to make him so. He brought Envy, Malice, and Ambition into Paradise, which sour'd* 200 *to him the sweetness of the Place. Wherever inordinate Affections are, 'tis Hell. Such only can enjoy the Country, who are capable of thinking when they are there, and have left their Passions behind them in the Town. Then they are prepar'd for Solitude; and in that Solitude is prepar'd for them*

> Et secura quies, & nescia fallere vita. 205

As I began this Dedication with a Verse of Virgil, *so I conclude it with another. The continuance of your Health, to enjoy that Happiness which you so well deserve, and which you have provided for your self, is the sincere and earnest Wish of*

Your Lordship's most Devoted,
and most Obedient Servant,
JOHN DRYDEN.

VIRGIL'S GEORGICS

THE FIRST BOOK OF THE GEORGICS

THE ARGUMENT

The Poet, in the beginning of this Book, propounds the general Design of each Georgic: And after a solemn Invocation of all the Gods who are any way related to his Subject, he addresses himself in particular to Augustus, *whom he complements with Divinity; and after strikes into his Business. He shews the different kinds of Tillage proper to different Soils, traces out the Original 5 of Agriculture, gives a Catalogue of the Husbandman's Tools, specifies the Employments peculiar to each Season, describes the changes of the Weather, with the Signs in Heaven and Earth that fore-bode them. Instances many of the Prodigies that happen'd near the time of* Julius Cæsar's *Death. And shuts up all with a Supplication to the Gods for the Safety of* Augustus, *and the 10 Preservation of* Rome.

WHAT makes a plenteous Harvest, when to turn
　　The fruitful Soil, and when to sowe the Corn;
The Care of Sheep, of Oxen, and of Kine;
And how to raise on Elms the teeming Vine:
The Birth and Genius of the frugal Bee, 　　　　　　5
I sing, *Mecænas,* and I sing to thee.
　　Ye Deities! who Fields and Plains protect,
Who rule the Seasons, and the Year direct;
Bacchus and fost'ring *Ceres,* Pow'rs Divine,
Who gave us Corn for Mast, for Water Wine; 　　　10

The First Book. 10 Wine;] Wine. *97 98*

Ye Fawns, propitious to the Rural Swains,
Ye Nymphs that haunt the Mountains and the Plains,
Join in my Work, and to my Numbers bring
Your needful Succour, for your Gifts I sing.
And thou, whose Trident struck the teeming Earth,   15
And made a Passage for the Coursers Birth.
And thou, for whom the *Cæan* Shore sustains
Thy Milky Herds, that graze the Flow'ry Plains.
And thou, the Shepherds tutelary God,
Leave, for a while, O *Pan*! thy lov'd Abode: 20
And, if *Arcadian* Fleeces be thy Care,
From Fields and Mountains to my Song repair.
Inventor, *Pallas*, of the fat'ning Oyl;
Thou Founder of the Plough and Plough-man's Toyl;
And thou, whose Hands the Shrowd-like Cypress rear; } 25
Come all ye Gods and Goddesses, that wear
The rural Honours, and increase the Year.
You, who supply the Ground with Seeds of Grain;
And you, who swell those Seeds with kindly Rain:
And chiefly thou, whose undetermin'd State   30
Is yet the Business of the Gods Debate:
Whether in after Times to be declar'd
The Patron of the World, and *Rome*'s peculiar Guard,
Or o're the Fruits and Seasons to preside,
And the round Circuit of the Year to guide,   35
Pow'rful of Blessings, which thou strew'st around,
And with thy Goddess Mother's Myrtle crown'd.
Or wilt thou, *Cæsar*, chuse the watry Reign,
To smooth the Surges, and correct the Main?
Then Mariners, in Storms, to thee shall pray, } 40
Ev'n utmost *Thule* shall thy Pow'r obey;
And *Neptune* shall resign the Fasces of the Sea.
The wat'ry Virgins for thy Bed shall strive,
And *Tethys* all her Waves in Dowry give.
Or wilt thou bless our Summers with thy Rays,   45
And seated near the Ballance, poise the Days:
Where in the Void of Heav'n a Space is free,
Betwixt the *Scorpion* and the *Maid* for thee.
The *Scorpion* ready to receive thy Laws,

23 Oyl;] Oyl, *97 98*   35 guide,] guide. *97 98*

Yields half his Region, and contracts his Claws.   50
Whatever part of Heav'n thou shalt obtain,
(For let not Hell presume of such a Reign;
Nor let so dire a Thirst of Empire move
Thy Mind, to leave thy Kindred Gods above;)
Tho' *Greece* admires *Elysium*'s blest Retreat,   55
Tho' *Proserpine* affects her silent Seat,
And importun'd by *Ceres* to remove,
Prefers the Fields below to those above:
But thou, propitious *Cæsar*, guide my Course,
And to my bold Endeavours add thy Force.   60
Pity the Poet's and the Ploughman's Cares,
Int'rest thy Greatness in our mean Affairs,
And use thy self betimes to hear and grant our Pray'rs.

   While yet the Spring is young, while Earth unbinds
Her frozen Bosom to the Western Winds;   65
While Mountain Snows dissolve against the Sun,
And Streams, yet new, from Precipices run:
Ev'n in this early Dawning of the Year,
Produce the Plough, and yoke the sturdy Steer,
And goad him till he groans beneath his Toil,   70
'Till the bright Share is bury'd in the Soil.
That Crop rewards the greedy Peasant's Pains,
Which twice the Sun, and twice the Cold sustains,
And bursts the crowded Barns, with more than promis'd Gains.
But e're we stir the yet unbroken Ground,   75
The various Course of Seasons must be found;
The Weather, and the setting of the Winds,
The Culture suiting to the sev'ral Kinds
Of Seeds and Plants; and what will thrive and rise,
And what the Genius of the Soil denies.   80
This Ground with *Bacchus*, that with *Ceres* suits:
That other loads the Trees with happy Fruits.
A fourth with Grass, unbidden, decks the Ground:
Thus *Tmolus* is with yellow Saffron crown'd:
India, black Ebon and white Ivory bears: 85
And soft *Idume* weeps her od'rous Tears.
Thus *Pontus* sends her Beaver Stones from far;

52–54 (For . . . above;)] For . . . above. *97 98. See Commentary*   58 above:]
above, *97 98*   63 hear and grant our *98*: hear our *97*   67 run:] run. *97 98*

And naked *Spanyards* temper Steel for War.
Epirus for th' *Elean* Chariot breeds,
(In hopes of Palms,) a Race of running Steeds.   90
This is the Orig'nal Contract; these the Laws
Impos'd by Nature, and by Nature's Cause,
On sundry Places, when *Deucalion* hurl'd
His Mother's Entrails on the desart World:
Whence Men, a hard laborious Kind, were born.   95
Then borrow part of Winter for thy Corn;
And early with thy Team the Gleeb in Furrows turn.
That while the Turf lies open, and unbound,
Succeeding Suns may bake the Mellow Ground.
But if the Soil be barren, only scar   100
The Surface, and but lightly print the Share,
When cold *Arcturus* rises with the Sun:
Lest wicked Weeds the Corn shou'd over-run
In watry Soils; or lest the barren Sand
Shou'd suck the Moisture from the thirsty Land.   105
Both these unhappy Soils the Swain forbears,
And keeps a Sabbath of alternate Years:
That the spent Earth may gather heart again;
And, better'd by Cessation, bear the Grain.
At least where Vetches, Pulse, and Tares have stood,   110
And Stalks of Lupines grew (a stubborn Wood:)
Th' ensuing Season, in return, may bear
The bearded product of the Golden Year.
For Flax and Oats will burn the tender Field,
And sleepy Poppies harmful Harvests yield.   115
But sweet Vicissitudes of Rest and Toyl
Make easy Labour, and renew the Soil.
Yet sprinkle sordid Ashes all around,
And load with fat'ning Dung thy fallow Ground.
Thus change of Seeds for meagre Soils is best;   120
And Earth manur'd, not idle, though at rest.
    Long Practice has a sure Improvement found,
With kindled Fires to burn the barren Ground;
When the light Stubble, to the Flames resign'd,
Is driv'n along, and crackles in the Wind.   125
Whether from hence the hollow Womb of Earth
Is warm'd with secret Strength for better Birth,

Or when the latent Vice is cur'd by Fire,
Redundant Humours thro' the Pores expire;
Or that the Warmth distends the Chinks, and makes   130
New Breathings, whence new Nourishment she takes;
Or that the Heat the gaping Ground constrains,
New Knits the Surface, and new Strings the Veins;
Lest soaking Show'rs shou'd pierce her secret Seat,
Or freezing *Boreas* chill her genial Heat;   135
Or scorching Suns too violently beat.

   Nor is the Profit small, the Peasant makes;
Who smooths with Harrows, or who pounds with Rakes
The crumbling Clods: Nor *Ceres* from on high
Regards his Labours with a grudging Eye;   140
Nor his, who plows across the furrow'd Grounds,
And on the Back of Earth inflicts new Wounds:
For he with frequent Exercise Commands
Th' unwilling Soil, and tames the stubborn Lands.

   Ye Swains, invoke the Pow'rs who rule the Sky,   145
For a moist Summer, and a Winter dry:
For Winter drout rewards the Peasant's Pain,
And broods indulgent on the bury'd Grain.
Hence *Mysia* boasts her Harvests, and the tops
Of *Gargarus* admire their happy Crops.   150
When first the Soil receives the fruitful Seed,
Make no delay, but cover it with speed:
So fenc'd from Cold; the plyant Furrows break,
Before the surly Clod resists the Rake.
And call the Floods from high, to rush amain   155
With pregnant Streams, to swell the teeming Grain.
Then when the fiery Suns too fiercely play,
And shrivell'd Herbs on with'ring Stems decay,
The wary Ploughman, on the Mountain's Brow,
Undams his watry Stores, huge Torrents flow;   160
And, ratling down the Rocks, large moisture yield,
Temp'ring the thirsty Fever of the Field:
And lest the Stem, too feeble for the freight,
Shou'd scarce sustain the head's unweildy weight,
Sends in his feeding Flocks betimes t' invade   165
The rising bulk of the luxuriant Blade;

162 Field:] Field. *97 98*

E're yet th' aspiring Off-spring of the Grain
O'retops the ridges of the furrow'd Plain:
And drains the standing Waters, when they yield
Too large a Bev'rage to the drunken Field.   170
But most in Autumn, and the show'ry Spring,
When dubious Months uncertain weather bring;
When Fountains open, when impetuous Rain
Swells hasty Brooks, and pours upon the Plain;
When Earth with Slime and Mud is cover'd o're,   175
Or hollow places spue their wat'ry Store.
Nor yet the Ploughman, nor the lab'ring Steer,
Sustain alone the hazards of the Year:
But glutton Geese, and the *Strymonian* Crane,
With foreign Troops, invade the tender Grain: 180
And tow'ring Weeds malignant Shadows yield;
And spreading *Succ'ry* choaks the rising Field.
The Sire of Gods and Men, with hard Decrees,
Forbids our Plenty to be bought with Ease:
And wills that Mortal Men, inur'd to toil,   185
Shou'd exercise, with pains, the grudging Soil.
Himself invented first the shining Share,
And whetted Humane Industry by Care:
Himself did Handy-Crafts and Arts ordain;
Nor suffer'd Sloath to rust his active Reign.   190
E're this, no Peasant vex'd the peaceful Ground;
Which only Turfs and Greens for Altars found:
No Fences parted Fields, nor Marks nor Bounds
Distinguish'd Acres of litigious Grounds:
But all was common, and the fruitful Earth   195
Was free to give her unexacted Birth.
Jove added Venom to the Viper's Brood,
And swell'd, with raging Storms, the peaceful Flood:
Commission'd hungry Wolves t' infest the Fold,
And shook from Oaken Leaves the liquid Gold: 200
Remov'd from Humane reach the chearful Fire,
And from the Rivers bade the Wine retire:
That studious Need might useful Arts explore;
From furrow'd Fields to reap the foodful Store:
And force the Veins of clashing Flints t' expire   205

200 Gold:] Gold. *97 98*

The lurking Seeds of their Cœlestial Fire.
Then first on Seas the hollow'd Alder swam;
Then Sailers quarter'd Heav'n, and found a Name
For ev'ry fix'd and ev'ry wandring Star:
The *Pleiads, Hyads,* and the Northern Car.   210
Then Toils for Beasts, and Lime for Birds were found,
And deep-mouth Dogs did Forrest Walks surround:
And casting Nets were spread in shallow Brooks,
Drags in the Deep, and Baits were hung on Hooks.
Then Saws were tooth'd, and sounding Axes made;   215
(For Wedges first did yielding Wood invade.)
And various Arts in order did succeed,
(What cannot endless Labour urg'd by need?)
   First *Ceres* taught, the Ground with Grain to sow,
And arm'd with Iron Shares the crooked Plough;   220
When now *Dodonian* Oaks no more supply'd
Their Mast, and Trees their Forrest-fruit deny'd.
Soon was his Labour doubl'd to the Swain,
And blasting Mildews blackned all his Grain.
Tough Thistles choak'd the Fields, and kill'd the Corn,   225
And an unthrifty Crop of Weeds was born.
Then Burrs and Brambles, an unbidden Crew
Of graceless Guests, th' unhappy Field subdue:
And Oats unblest, and Darnel domineers,
And shoots its head above the shining Ears.   230
So that unless the Land with daily Care
Is exercis'd, and with an Iron War,
Of Rakes and Harrows, the proud Foes expell'd,
And Birds with clamours frighted from the Field;
Unless the Boughs are lopp'd that shade the Plain,   235
And Heav'n invok'd with Vows for fruitful Rain:
On other Crops you may with envy look,
And shake for Food the long abandon'd Oak.
Nor must we pass untold what Arms they wield,
Who labour Tillage and the furrow'd Field: 240
Without whose aid the Ground her Corn denys,
And nothing can be sown, and nothing rise.
The crooked Plough, the Share, the tow'ring height
Of Waggons, and the Cart's unweildy weight;

236 Rain:] Rain, *97 98*

The Sled, the Tumbril, Hurdles and the Flail,   245
The Fan of *Bacchus*, with the flying Sail:
These all must be prepar'd, if Plowmen hope
The promis'd Blessing of a Bounteous Crop.
Young Elms with early force in Copses bow,
Fit for the Figure of the crooked Plough.   250
Of eight Foot long a fastned Beam prepare,
On either side the Head produce an Ear,
And sink a Socket for the shining Share.
Of Beech the Plough-tail, and the bending Yoke;
Or softer Linden harden'd in the Smoke.   255
I cou'd be long in Precepts, but I fear
So mean a Subject might offend your Ear.
Delve of convenient Depth your thrashing Floor;
With temper'd Clay, then fill and face it o're:
And let the weighty Rowler run the round,   260
To smooth the Surface of th' unequal Ground;
Lest crack'd with Summer Heats the flooring flies,
Or sinks, and thro' the Crannies Weeds arise.
For sundry Foes the Rural Realm surround:
The Field Mouse builds her Garner under ground;   265
For gather'd Grain the blind laborious Mole,
In winding Mazes works her hidden Hole.
In hollow Caverns Vermine make abode,
The hissing Serpent, and the swelling Toad:
The Corn devouring Weevel here abides,   270
And the wise Ant her wintry Store provides.
   Mark well the flowring Almonds in the Wood;
If od'rous Blooms the bearing Branches load,
The Glebe will answer to the Sylvan Reign,
Great Heats will follow, and large Crops of Grain.   275
But if a Wood of Leaves o're-shade the Tree,
Such and so barren will thy Harvest be:
In vain the Hind shall vex the thrashing Floor,
For empty Chaff and Straw will be thy Store.
Some steep their Seed, and some in Cauldrons boil   280
With vigorous Nitre, and with Lees of Oyl,
O're gentle Fires; th' exuberant Juice to drain,

---

246 Sail:] Sail. *97 98*   265 ground;] ground, *97 98*   270 Weevel] Weezel
97 98. See Commentary

And swell the flatt'ring Husks with fruitful Grain.
Yet is not the Success for Years assur'd,
Tho chosen is the Seed, and fully cur'd;   285
Unless the Peasant, with his Annual Pain,
Renews his Choice, and culls the largest Grain.
Thus all below, whether by Nature's Curse,
Or Fates Decree, degen'rate still to worse.
So the Boats brawny Crew the Current stem,   290
And, slow advancing, struggle with the Stream:
But if they slack their hands, or cease to strive,
Then down the Flood with headlong haste they drive.
      Nor must the Ploughman less observe the Skies,
When the *Kidds*, *Dragon*, and *Arcturus* rise,   295
Than Saylors homeward bent, who cut their Way
Thro' *Helle*'s stormy Streights, and Oyster-breeding Sea.
But when *Astrea*'s Ballance, hung on high,
Betwixt the Nights and Days divides the Sky,
Then Yoke your Oxen, sow your Winter Grain;   300
'Till cold *December* comes with driving Rain.
Lineseed and fruitful Poppy bury warm,
In a dry Season, and prevent the Storm.
Sow Beans and Clover in a rotten Soyl,
And Millet rising from your Annual Toyl;   305
When with his Golden Horns, in full Cariere,
The Bull beats down the Barriers of the Year;
And *Argo* and the Dog forsake the Northern Sphere.
      But if your Care to Wheat alone extend,
Let *Maja* with her Sisters first descend,   310
And the bright *Gnosian* Diadem downward bend;
Before you trust in Earth your future Hope:
Or else expect a listless lazy Crop.
Some Swains have sown before, but most have found
A husky Harvest, from the grudging Ground.   315
Vile Vetches wou'd you sow, or Lentils lean,
The Growth of *Egypt*, or the Kidney-bean?
Begin when the slow Waggoner descends,
Nor cease your sowing till Mid-winter ends:
For this, thro' twelve bright Signs *Apollo* guides   320
The Year, and Earth in sev'ral Climes divides.

308 *Argo*] *Argos* 97 98. *See Commentary*   311 bend;] bend: 97 98   312 Hope:] Hope; 97 98

Five Girdles bind the Skies, the torrid Zone
Glows with the passing and repassing Sun.
Far on the right and left, th' extreams of Heav'n,
To Frosts and Snows, and bitter Blasts are giv'n.   325
Betwixt the midst and these, the Gods assign'd
Two habitable Seats for Humane Kind:
And cross their limits cut a sloping way,
Which the twelve Signs in beauteous order sway.
Two Poles turn round the Globe; one seen to rise   330
O're *Scythian* Hills, and one in *Lybian* Skies.
The first sublime in Heav'n, the last is whirl'd
Below the Regions of the nether World.
Around our Pole the spiry Dragon glides,
And like a winding Stream the Bears divides;   335
The less and greater, who by Fates Decree
Abhor to dive beneath the Southern Sea:
There, as they say, perpetual Night is found
In silence brooding on th' unhappy ground:
Or when *Aurora* leaves our Northern Sphere,   340
She lights the downward Heav'n, and rises there.
And when on us she breaths the living Light,
Red *Vesper* kindles there the Tapers of the Night.
From hence uncertain Seasons we may know;
And when to reap the Grain, and when to sow: 345
Or when to fell the Furzes, when 'tis meet
To spread the flying Canvass for the Fleet.
Observe what Stars arise or disappear;
And the four Quarters of the rolling Year.
But when cold Weather and continu'd Rain,   350
The lab'ring Husband in his House restrain:
Let him forecast his Work with timely care,
Which else is huddl'd, when the Skies are fair:
Then let him mark the Sheep, or whet the shining Share.
Or hollow Trees for Boats, or number o're   355
His Sacks, or measure his increasing Store:
Or sharpen Stakes, or head the Forks, or twine
The Sallow Twigs to tye the stragling Vine:
Or wicker Baskets weave, or aire the Corn,
Or grinded Grain betwixt two Marbles turn.   360
No Laws, Divine or Human, can restrain

From necessary Works, the lab'ring Swain.
Ev'n Holy-days and Feasts permission yield,
To float the Meadows, or to fence the Field,
To Fire the Brambles, snare the Birds, and steep   365
In wholsom Water-falls the woolly Sheep.
And oft the drudging Ass is driv'n, with Toyl,
To neighb'ring Towns with Apples and with Oyl:
Returning late, and loaden home with Gain
Of barter'd Pitch, and Hand-mills for the Grain.   370
   The lucky Days, in each revolving Moon,
For Labour chuse: The Fifth be sure to shun;
That gave the Furies and pale *Pluto* Birth,
And arm'd, against the Skies, the Sons of Earth.
With Mountains pil'd on Mountains, thrice they strove   375
To scale the steepy Battlements of *Jove*:
And thrice his Lightning and red Thunder play'd,
And their demolish'd Works in Ruin laid.
The Sev'nth is, next the Tenth, the best to joyn
Young Oxen to the Yoke, and plant the Vine.   380
Then Weavers stretch your Stays upon the Weft:
The Ninth is good for Travel, bad for Theft.
Some Works in dead of Night are better done;
Or when the Morning Dew prevents the Sun.
Parch'd Meads and Stubble mow, by *Phœbe*'s Light;   385
Which both require the Coolness of the Night:
For Moisture then abounds, and Pearly Rains
Descend in Silence to refresh the Plains.
The Wife and Husband equally conspire,
To work by Night, and rake the Winter Fire: 390
He sharpens Torches in the glim'ring Room,
She shoots the flying Shuttle through the Loom:
Or boils in Kettles Must of Wine, and skims
With Leaves, the Dregs that overflow the Brims.
And till the watchful Cock awakes the Day,   395
She sings to drive the tedious hours away.
But in warm Weather, when the Skies are clear,
By Daylight reap the Product of the Year:
And in the Sun your golden Grain display,

364 To float the Meadows, or *98*: The Meads to water, and *97*   393 skims] *97*
(*errata*): Skins *97* (*text*)

And thrash it out, and winnow it by Day.   400
Plough naked, Swain, and naked sow the Land,
For lazy Winter numbs the lab'ring Hand.
In Genial Winter, Swains enjoy their Store,
Forget their Hardships, and recruit for more.
The Farmer to full Bowls invites his Friends,   405
And what he got with Pains, with Pleasure spends.
So Saylors, when escap'd from stormy Seas,
First crown their Vessels, then indulge their Ease.
Yet that's the proper Time to thrash the Wood
For Mast of Oak, your Fathers homely Food.   410
To gather Laurel-berries, and the Spoil
Of bloody Myrtles, and to press your Oyl.
For stalking Cranes to set the guileful Snare,
T' inclose the Stags in Toyls, and hunt the Hare.
With *Balearick* Slings, or *Gnossian* Bow,   415
To persecute from far the flying Doe;
Then, when the Fleecy Skies new cloath the Wood,
And cakes of rustling Ice come rolling down the Flood.
   Now sing we stormy Stars, when Autumn weighs
The Year, and adds to Nights, and shortens Days;   420
And Suns declining shine with feeble Rays:
What Cares must then attend the toiling Swain;
Or when the low'ring Spring, with lavish Rain,
Beats down the slender Stem and bearded Grain:
While yet the Head is green, or lightly swell'd   425
With Milky-moisture, over-looks the Field.
Ev'n when the Farmer, now secure of Fear,
Sends in the Swains to spoil the finish'd Year:
Ev'n while the Reaper fills his greedy hands,
And binds the golden Sheafs in brittle bands: 430
Oft have I seen a sudden Storm arise,
From all the warring Winds that sweep the Skies:
The heavy Harvest from the Root is torn,
And whirl'd aloft the lighter Stubble born;
With such a force the flying rack is driv'n;   435
And such a Winter wears the face of Heav'n:
And oft whole sheets descend of slucy Rain,
Suck'd by the spongy Clouds from off the Main:

The lofty Skies at once come pouring down,
The promis'd Crop and golden Labours drown.   440
The Dykes are fill'd, and with a roaring sound
The rising Rivers float the nether ground;
And Rocks the bellowing Voice of boiling Seas rebound.
The Father of the Gods his Glory shrouds,
Involv'd in Tempests, and a Night of Clouds.   445
And from the middle Darkness flashing out,
By fits he deals his fiery Bolts about.
Earth feels the Motions of her angry God,
Her Entrails tremble, and her Mountains nod;
And flying Beasts in Forests seek abode: 450
Deep horrour seizes ev'ry Humane Breast,
Their Pride is humbled, and their Fear confess'd:
While he from high his rowling Thunder throws,
And fires the Mountains with repeated blows:
The Rocks are from their old Foundations rent;   455
The Winds redouble, and the Rains augment:
The Waves on heaps are dash'd against the Shoar,
And now the Woods, and now the Billows roar.
   In fear of this, observe the starry Signs,
Where *Saturn* houses, and where *Hermes* joins.   460
But first to Heav'n thy due Devotions pay,
And Annual Gifts on *Ceres* Altars lay.
When Winter's rage abates, when chearful Hours
Awake the Spring, and Spring awakes the Flow'rs,
On the green Turf thy careless Limbs display,   465
And celebrate the mighty Mother's day.
For then the Hills with pleasing Shades are crown'd,
And Sleeps are sweeter on the silken Ground:
With milder Beams the Sun securely shines;
Fat are the Lambs, and luscious are the Wines.   470
Let ev'ry Swain adore her Pow'r Divine,
And Milk and Honey mix with sparkling Wine:
Let all the Quire of Clowns attend the Show,
In long Procession, shouting as they go;
Invoking her to bless their yearly Stores,   475
Inviting Plenty to their crowded Floors.
Thus in the Spring, and thus in Summer's Heat,
Before the Sickles touch the ripening Wheat,

On *Ceres* call; and let the lab'ring Hind
With Oaken Wreaths his hollow Temples bind:　480
On *Ceres* let him call, and *Ceres* praise,
With uncouth Dances, and with Country Lays.
　And that by certain signs we may presage
Of Heats and Rains, and Wind's impetuous rage,
The Sov'reign of the Heav'ns has set on high　485
The Moon, to mark the Changes of the Skye:
When Southern blasts shou'd cease, and when the Swain
Shou'd near their Folds his feeding Flocks restrain.
For e're the rising Winds begin to roar,
The working Seas advance to wash the Shoar:　490
Soft whispers run along the leavy Woods,
And Mountains whistle to the murm'ring Floods:
Ev'n then the doubtful Billows scarce abstain
From the toss'd Vessel on the troubled Main:
When crying Cormorants forsake the Sea,　495
And stretching to the Covert wing their way:
When sportful Coots run skimming o're the Strand;
When watchful Herons leave their watry Stand,
And mounting upward, with erected flight,
Gain on the Skyes, and soar above the sight.　500
And oft before tempest'ous Winds arise,
The seeming Stars fall headlong from the Skies;
And, shooting through the darkness, guild the Night
With sweeping Glories, and long trails of Light:
And Chaff with eddy Winds is whirl'd around,　505
And dancing Leaves are lifted from the Ground;
And floating Feathers on the Waters play.
But when the winged Thunder takes his way
From the cold North, and East and West ingage,
And at their Frontiers meet with equal rage,　510
The Clouds are crush'd, a glut of gather'd Rain
The hollow Ditches fills, and floats the Plain,
And Sailors furl their dropping Sheets amain.
Wet weather seldom hurts the most unwise,
So plain the Signs, such Prophets are the Skies:　515
The wary Crane foresees it first, and sails
Above the Storm, and leaves the lowly Vales:
The Cow looks up, and from afar can find

The change of Heav'n, and snuffs it in the Wind.
The Swallow skims the River's watry Face,   520
The Frogs renew the Croaks of their loquacious Race.
The careful Ant her secret Cell forsakes,
And drags her Egs along the narrow Tracks.
At either Horn the Rainbow drinks the Flood,
Huge Flocks of rising Rooks forsake their Food,   525
And, crying, seek the Shelter of the Wood.
Besides, the sev'ral sorts of watry Fowls,
That swim the Seas, or haunt the standing Pools:
The Swans that sail along the Silver Flood,
And dive with stretching Necks to search their Food;   530
Then lave their Backs with sprinkling Dews in vain,
And stem the Stream to meet the promis'd Rain.
The Crow with clam'rous Cries the Show'r demands,
And single stalks along the Desart Sands.
The nightly Virgin, while her Wheel she plies,   535
Foresees the Storm impending in the Skies,
When sparkling Lamps their sputt'ring Light advance,
And in the Sockets Oyly Bubbles dance.
    Then after Show'rs, 'tis easie to descry
Returning Suns, and a serener Sky: 540
The Stars shine smarter, and the Moon adorns,
As with unborrow'd Beams, her sharpen'd Horns.
The filmy *Gossamer* now flitts no more,
Nor *Halcyons* bask on the short Sunny Shoar:
Their Litter is not toss'd by Sows unclean,   545
But a blue droughty Mist descends upon the Plain.
And Owls, that mark the setting Sun, declare
A Star-light Evening, and a Morning fair.
Tow'ring aloft, avenging *Nisus* flies,
While dar'd below the guilty *Scylla* lies.   550
Where-ever frighted *Scylla* flies away,
Swift *Nisus* follows, and pursues his Prey.
Where injur'd *Nisus* takes his Airy Course,
Thence trembling *Scylla* flies and shuns his Force.
This punishment pursues th' unhappy Maid,   555
And thus the purple Hair is dearly paid.
Then, thrice the Ravens rend the liquid Air,

And croaking Notes proclaim the settled fair.
Then, round their Airy Palaces they fly,
To greet the Sun; and seis'd with secret Joy, 560
When Storms are over-blown, with Food repair
To their forsaken Nests, and callow Care.
Not that I think their Breasts with Heav'nly Souls
Inspir'd, as Man, who Destiny controls.
But with the changeful Temper of the Skies, 565
As Rains condense, and Sun-shine rarifies;
So turn the Species in their alter'd Minds,
Compos'd by Calms, and discompos'd by Winds.
From hence proceeds the Birds harmonious Voice:
From hence the Crows exult, and frisking Lambs rejoice. 570
Observe the daily Circle of the Sun,
And the short Year of each revolving Moon:
By them thou shalt foresee the following day;
Nor shall a starry Night thy Hopes betray.
When first the Moon appears, if then she shrouds 575
Her silver Crescent, tip'd with sable Clouds;
Conclude she bodes a Tempest on the Main,
And brews for Fields impetuous Floods of Rain.
Or if her Face with fiery Flushing glow,
Expect the ratling Winds aloft to blow. 580
But four Nights old, (for that's the surest Sign,)
With sharpen'd Horns if glorious then she shine:
Next Day, nor only that, but all the Moon,
Till her revolving Race be wholly run;
Are void of Tempests, both by Land and Sea, 585
And Saylors in the Port their promis'd Vow shall pay.
Above the rest, the Sun, who never lies,
Foretels the change of Weather in the Skies:
For if he rise, unwilling to his Race,
Clouds on his Brows, and Spots upon his Face; 590
Or if thro' Mists he shoots his sullen Beams,
Frugal of Light, in loose and stragling Streams:
Suspect a drisling Day, with Southern Rain,
Fatal to Fruits, and Flocks, and promis'd Grain.
Or if *Aurora*, with half open'd Eyes, 595
And a pale sickly Cheek, salute the Skies;

570 Crows] Cows *97 98. See Commentary* 587 lies,] lies; *97 98*

How shall the Vine, with tender Leaves, defend
Her teeming Clusters, when the Storms descend?
When ridgy Roofs and Tiles can scarce avail,
To barr the Ruin of the ratling Hail.   600
But more than all, the setting Sun survey,
When down the Steep of Heav'n he drives the Day.
For oft we find him finishing his Race,
With various Colours erring on his Face;
If fiery red his glowing Globe descends,   605
High Winds and furious Tempests he portends.
But if his Cheeks are swoln with livid blue,
He bodes wet Weather by his watry Hue.
If dusky Spots are vary'd on his Brow,
And, streak'd with red, a troubl'd Colour show;   610
That sullen Mixture shall at once declare
Winds, Rain, and Storms, and Elemental War:
What desp'rate Madman then wou'd venture o're
The *Frith*, or haul his Cables from the Shoar?
But if with Purple Rays he brings the Light,   615
And a pure Heav'n resigns to quiet Night:
No rising Winds, or falling Storms, are nigh:
But Northern Breezes through the Forrest fly:
And drive the rack, and purge the ruffl'd Sky.
Th' unerring Sun by certain Signs declares,   620
What the late Ev'n, or early Morn prepares:
And when the South projects a stormy Day,
And when the clearing North will puff the Clouds away.
    The Sun reveals the Secrets of the Sky;
And who dares give the Source of Light the Lye?   625
The change of Empires often he declares,
Fierce Tumults, hidden Treasons, open Wars.
He first the Fate of *Cæsar* did foretel,
And pity'd *Rome*, when *Rome* in *Cæsar* fell.
In Iron Clouds conceal'd the Publick Light: 630
And Impious Mortals fear'd Eternal Night.
    Nor was the Fact foretold by him alone:
Nature her self stood forth, and seconded the Sun.
Earth, Air, and Seas, with Prodigies were sign'd,
And Birds obscene, and howling Dogs divin'd.   635
What Rocks did *Ætna*'s bellowing Mouth expire

From her torn Entrails! and what Floods of Fire!
What Clanks were heard, in *German* Skies afar,
Of Arms and Armies, rushing to the War!
Dire Earthquakes rent the solid *Alps* below,   640
And from their Summets shook th' Eternal Snow.
Pale Specters in the close of Night were seen;
And Voices heard of more than Mortal Men.
In silent Groves, dumb Sheep and Oxen spoke;
And Streams ran backward, and their Beds forsook: 645
The yawning Earth disclos'd th' Abyss of Hell:
The weeping Statues did the Wars foretel;
And Holy Sweat from Brazen Idols fell.
Then rising in his Might, the King of Floods,
Rusht thro' the Forrests, tore the lofty Woods;   650
And rolling onward, with a sweepy Sway,
Bore Houses, Herds, and lab'ring Hinds away.
Blood sprang from Wells, Wolfs howl'd in Towns by Night,
And boding Victims did the Priests affright.
Such Peals of Thunder never pour'd from high;   655
Nor forky Light'nings flash'd from such a sullen Sky.
Red Meteors ran a-cross th' Etherial Space;
Stars disappear'd, and Comets took their place.
For this, th' *Emathian* Plains once more were strow'd
With *Roman* Bodies, and just Heav'n thought good   660
To fatten twice those Fields with *Roman* Blood.
Then, after length of Time, the lab'ring Swains,
Who turn the Turfs of those unhappy Plains,
Shall rusty Piles from the plough'd Furrows take,
And over empty Helmets pass the Rake.   665
Amaz'd at Antick Titles on the Stones,
And mighty Relicks of Gygantick Bones.
   Ye home-born Deities, of Mortal Birth!
Thou Father *Romulus*, and Mother Earth,
Goddess unmov'd! whose Guardian Arms extend   670
O're *Thuscan Tiber*'s Course, and *Roman* Tow'rs defend;
With youthful *Cæsar* your joint Pow'rs ingage,
Nor hinder him to save the sinking Age.
O! let the Blood, already spilt, atone

656 Nor forky Light'nings . . . such a sullen *98*: Nor Light'ning . . . so serene a *97*
657 a-cross *98*: along *97*

For the past Crimes of curst *Laomedon*! 675
Heav'n wants thee there, and long the Gods, we know,
Have grudg'd thee, *Cæsar*, to the World below.
Where Fraud and Rapine, Right and Wrong confound;
Where impious Arms from ev'ry part resound,
And monstrous Crimes in ev'ry Shape are crown'd; 680
The peaceful Peasant to the Wars is prest;
The Fields lye fallow in inglorious Rest.
The Plain no Pasture to the Flock affords,
The crooked Scythes are streightned into Swords:
And there *Euphrates* her soft Off-spring Arms, 685
And here the *Rhine* rebellows with Alarms:
The neighb'ring Cities range on sev'ral sides,
Perfidious *Mars* long plighted Leagues divides,
And o're the wasted World in Triumph rides.
So four fierce Coursers starting to the Race, 690
Scow'r thro' the Plain, and lengthen ev'ry Pace:
Nor Reins, nor Curbs, nor threat'ning Cries they fear,
But force along the trembling Charioteer.

THE SECOND BOOK OF THE GEORGICS

THE ARGUMENT

*The Subject of the following Book is Planting. In handling of which Argument,
the Poet shews all the different Methods of raising Trees: Describes their
Variety; and gives Rules for the management of each in particular. He then
points out the Soils in which the several Plants thrive best: And thence takes
occasion to run out into the Praises of* Italy. *After which he gives some* 5
*Directions for discovering the Nature of every Soil; prescribes Rules for the
Dressing of Vines, Olives, &c. And concludes the Georgic with a Panegyric
on a Country Life.*

THUS far of Tillage, and of Heav'nly Signs;
Now sing my Muse the growth of gen'rous Vines:
The shady Groves, the Woodland Progeny,
And the slow Product of *Minerva*'s Tree.
Great Father *Bacchus*! to my Song repair; 5

690 Reins 98: Reigns 97

For clustring Grapes are thy peculiar Care:
For thee large Bunches load the bending Vine,
And the last Blessings of the Year are thine.
To thee his Joys the jolly Autumn owes,
When the fermenting Juice the Vat o'reflows. 10
Come strip with me, my God, come drench all o're
Thy Limbs in Must of Wine, and drink at ev'ry Pore.
　Some Trees their birth to bounteous Nature owe:
For some without the pains of Planting grow.
With Osiers thus the Banks of Brooks abound, 15
Sprung from the watry Genius of the Ground:
From the same Principles grey Willows come;
Herculean Poplar, and the tender Broom.
But some from Seeds inclos'd in Earth arise:
For thus the mastful Chesnut mates the Skies. 20
Hence rise the branching Beech and vocal Oke,
Where *Jove* of old Oraculously spoke.
Some from the Root a rising Wood disclose;
Thus Elms, and thus the salvage Cherry grows.
Thus the green Bays, that binds the Poet's Brows, 25
Shoots and is shelter'd by the Mother's Boughs.
　These ways of Planting, Nature did ordain,
For Trees and Shrubs, and all the Sylvan Reign.
Others there are, by late Experience found:
Some cut the Shoots, and plant in furrow'd ground: 30
Some cover rooted Stalks in deeper Mold:
Some cloven Stakes; and (wond'rous to behold,)
Their sharpen'd ends in Earth their footing place,
And the dry Poles produce a living Race.
Some bowe their Vines, which bury'd in the Plain, 35
Their tops in distant Arches rise again.
Others no Root require, the Lab'rer cuts
Young Slips, and in the Soil securely puts.
Ev'n Stumps of Olives, bar'd of Leaves, and dead,
Revive, and oft redeem their wither'd head. 40
'Tis usual now, an Inmate Graff to see,
With Insolence invade a Foreign Tree:
Thus Pears and Quinces from the Crabtree come;
And thus the ruddy Cornel bears the Plum.

Then let the Learned Gard'ner mark with care   45
The Kinds of Stocks, and what those Kinds will bear:
Explore the Nature of each sev'ral Tree;
And known, improve with artful Industry:
And let no spot of idle Earth be found,
But cultivate the Genius of the Ground.   50
For open *Ismarus* will *Bacchus* please;
Taburnus loves the shade of Olive Trees.
  The Virtues of the sev'ral Soils I sing,
Mecænas, now thy needful Succour bring!
O thou! the better part of my Renown,   55
Inspire thy Poet, and thy Poem crown:
Embarque with me, while I new Tracts explore,
With flying sails and breezes from the shore:
Not that my song, in such a scanty space,
So large a Subject fully can embrace: 60
Not tho I were supply'd with Iron Lungs,
A hundred Mouths, fill'd with as many Tongues:
But steer my Vessel with a steady hand,
And coast along the Shore in sight of Land.
Nor will I tire thy Patience with a train   65
Of Preface, or what ancient Poets feign.
The Trees, which of themselves advance in Air,
Are barren kinds, but strongly built and fair:
Because the vigour of the Native Earth
Maintains the Plant, and makes a Manly Birth.   70
Yet these, receiving Graffs of other Kind,
Or thence transplanted, change their salvage Mind:
Their Wildness lose, and quitting Nature's part,
Obey the Rules and Discipline of Art.
The same do Trees, that, sprung from barren Roots   75
In open fields, transplanted bear their Fruits.
For where they grow the Native Energy
Turns all into the Substance of the Tree,
Starves and destroys the Fruit, is only made
For brawny bulk, and for a barren shade.   80
The Plant that shoots from Seed, a sullen Tree
At leisure grows, for late Posterity;
The gen'rous flavour lost, the Fruits decay,
And salvage Grapes are made the Birds ignoble prey.

Much labour is requir'd in Trees, to tame 85
Their wild disorder, and in ranks reclaim.
Well must the ground be dig'd, and better dress'd,
New Soil to make, and meliorate the rest.
Old Stakes of Olive Trees in Plants revive;
By the same Methods *Paphian* Myrtles live: 90
But nobler Vines by Propagation thrive.
From Roots hard Hazles, and from Cyens rise
Tall Ash, and taller Oak that mates the Skies:
Palm, Poplar, Firr, descending from the Steep
Of Hills, to try the dangers of the Deep. 95
The thin-leav'd *Arbute*, Hazle graffs receives,
And Planes huge Apples bear, that bore but Leaves.
Thus Mastful Beech the bristly Chesnut bears,
And the wild Ash is white with blooming Pears.
And greedy Swine from grafted Elms are fed, 100
With falling Acorns, that on Oaks are bred.
   But various are the ways to change the state
Of Plants, to Bud, to Graff, t' Inoculate.
For where the tender Rinds of Trees disclose
Their shooting Gems, a swelling Knot there grows; 105
Just in that space a narrow Slit we make,
Then other Buds from bearing Trees we take:
Inserted thus, the wounded Rind we close,
In whose moist Womb th' admitted Infant grows.
But when the smoother Bole from Knots is free, 110
We make a deep Incision in the Tree;
And in the solid Wood the Slip inclose.
The bat'ning Bastard shoots again and grows:
And in short space the laden Boughs arise,
With happy Fruit advancing to the Skies. 115
The Mother Plant admires the Leaves unknown,
Of Alien Trees, and Apples not her own.
   Of vegetable Woods are various Kinds,
And the same Species are of sev'ral Minds.
Lotes, Willows, Elms, have diff'rent Forms allow'd, 120
So fun'ral Cypress rising like a Shrowd.
Fat Olive Trees of sundry Sorts appear:
Of sundry Shapes their unctuous Berries bear.

96 *Arbute,* Hazle 97 *(errata)*: *Arbute* Hazle, 97 *(text)*   112 inclose.] inclose, 97 98

Radij long Olives, *Orchit's* round produce,
And bitter *Pausia*, pounded for the Juice.   125
Alcinous Orchard various Apples bears:
Unlike are Bergamotes and pounder Pears.
Nor our *Italian* Vines produce the Shape,
Or Tast, or Flavour of the *Lesbian* Grape.
The *Thasian* Vines in richer Soils abound,   130
The *Mareotique* grow in barren Ground.
The *Psythian* Grape we dry: *Lagæan* Juice,
Will stamm'ring Tongues, and stagg'ring Feet produce.
Rathe ripe are some, and some of later kind,
Of Golden some, and some of Purple Rind.   135
How shall I praise the *Ræthean* Grape divine,
Which yet contends not with *Falernian* Wine!
Th' *Aminean* many a Consulship survives,
And longer than the *Lydian* Vintage lives,
Or high *Phanæus* King of *Chian* growth: 140
But for large quantities, and lasting both,
The less *Argitis* bears the Prize away.
The *Rhodian*, sacred to the Solemn Day,
In second Services is pour'd to *Jove*;
And best accepted by the Gods above.   145
Nor must *Bumastus* his old Honours lose,
In length and largeness like the Dugs of Cows.
I pass the rest, whose ev'ry Race and Name,
And Kinds, are less material to my Theme.
Which who wou'd learn, as soon may tell the Sands,   150
Driv'n by the Western Wind on *Lybian* Lands.
Or number, when the blust'ring *Eurus* roars,
The Billows beating on *Ionian* Shoars.
    Nor ev'ry Plant on ev'ry Soil will grow;
The Sallow loves the watry Ground, and low.   155
The Marshes, Alders; Nature seems t' ordain
The rocky Cliff for the wild Ashe's reign:
The baleful Yeugh to Northern Blasts assigns;
To Shores the Myrtles, and to Mounts the Vines.
    Regard th' extremest cultivated Coast,   160
From hot *Arabia* to the *Scythian* Frost:

---

139 lives, *98*: lives? *97* (*text*): lives. *97* (*errata*)

All sort of Trees their sev'ral Countries know;
Black Ebon only will in *India* grow:
And od'rous Frankincense on the *Sabæan* Bough.
Balm slowly trickles through the bleeding Veins   165
Of happy Shrubs, in *Idumæan* Plains.
The green *Egyptian* Thorn, for Med'cine good;
With *Ethiops* hoary Trees and woolly Wood,
Let others tell: and how the *Seres* spin
Their fleecy Forests in a slender Twine.   170
With mighty Trunks of Trees on *Indian* shoars,
Whose height above the feather'd Arrow soars,
Shot from the toughest Bow; and by the Brawn
Of expert Archers, with vast Vigour drawn.
Sharp tasted Citrons *Median* Climes produce: 175
Bitter the Rind, but gen'rous is the Juice:
A cordial Fruit, a present Antidote
Against the direful Stepdam's deadly Draught;
Who mixing wicked Weeds with Words impure,
The Fate of envy'd Orphans wou'd procure.   180
Large is the Plant, and like a Laurel grows,
And did it not a diff'rent Scent disclose,
A Laurel were: the fragrant Flow'rs contemn
The stormy Winds, tenacious of their Stem.
With this the *Medes*, to lab'ring Age, bequeath   185
New Lungs, and cure the sourness of the Breath.
   But neither *Median* Woods, (a plenteous Land,)
Fair *Ganges*, *Hermus* rolling Golden Sand,
Nor *Bactria*, nor the richer *Indian* Fields,
Nor all the Gummy Stores *Arabia* yields;   190
Nor any foreign Earth of greater Name,
Can with sweet *Italy* contend in Fame.
No Bulls, whose Nostrils breath a living Flame,
Have turn'd our Turf, no Teeth of Serpents here
Were sown, an armed Host, and Iron Crop to bear.   195
But fruitful Vines, and the fat Olives fraight,
And Harvests heavy with their fruitful weight,
Adorn our Fields; and on the chearful Green,
The grazing Flocks and lowing Herds are seen.
The Warrior Horse, here bred, is taught to train,   200

178 Draught;] Draught: 97 98

There flows *Clitumnus* thro' the flow'ry Plain;
Whose Waves, for Triumphs after prosp'rous War,
The Victim Ox, and snowy Sheep prepare.
Perpetual Spring our happy Climate sees,
Twice breed the Cattle, and twice bear the Trees;   205
And Summer Suns recede by slow degrees.
   Our Land is from the Rage of Tygers freed,
Nor nourishes the Lyon's angry Seed;
Nor pois'nous Aconite is here produc'd,
Or grows unknown, or is, when known, refus'd.   210
Nor in so vast a length our Serpents glide,
Or rais'd on such a spiry Volume ride.
   Next add our Cities of Illustrious Name,
Their costly Labour and stupend'ous Frame:
Our Forts on steepy Hills, that far below   215
See wanton Streams, in winding Valleys flow.
Our twofold Seas, that washing either side,
A rich Recruit of Foreign Stores provide.
Our spacious Lakes; thee, *Larius*, first; and next
Benacus, with tempest'ous Billows vext.   220
Or shall I praise thy Ports, or mention make
Of the vast Mound, that binds the *Lucrine* Lake.
Or the disdainful Sea, that, shut from thence,
Roars round the Structure, and invades the Fence;
There, where secure the *Julian* Waters glide,   225
Or where *Avernus* Jaws admit the *Tyrrhene* Tide.
Our Quarries deep in Earth, were fam'd of old,
For Veins of Silver, and for Ore of Gold.
Th' Inhabitants themselves, their Country grace;
Hence rose the *Marsian* and *Sabellian* Race: 230
Strong limb'd and stout, and to the Wars inclin'd,
And hard *Ligurians*, a laborious Kind,
And *Volscians* arm'd with Iron-headed Darts.
Besides, an Off-spring of undaunted Hearts,
The *Decij, Marij*, great *Camillus* came   235
From hence, and greater *Scipio*'s double Name:
And mighty *Cæsar*, whose victorious Arms,

202–3 War, . . . prepare. *97 (errata)*: Wars, . . . prepares. *97 (text)*   207 Rage]
Land *98*   224 Fence;] Fence. *97 98*   232 Kind,] Kind. *97 98*   234
Besides,] Besides *97 98*

To farthest *Asia*, carry fierce Alarms:
Avert unwarlike *Indians* from his *Rome*;
Triumph abroad, secure our Peace at home. 240
   Hail, sweet *Saturnian* Soil! of fruitful Grain
Great Parent, greater of Illustrious Men.
For thee my tuneful Accents will I raise,
And treat of Arts disclos'd in Ancient Days:
Once more unlock for thee the sacred Spring, 245
And old *Ascræan* Verse in *Roman* Cities sing.
   The Nature of their sev'ral Soils now see,
Their Strength, their Colour, their Fertility:
And first for Heath, and barren hilly Ground,
Where meagre Clay and flinty Stones abound; 250
Where the poor Soil all Succour seems to want,
Yet this suffices the *Palladian* Plant.
Undoubted Signs of such a Soil are found,
For here wild Olive-shoots o'respread the ground,
And heaps of Berries strew the Fields around. 255
But where the Soil, with fat'ning Moisture fill'd,
Is cloath'd with Grass, and fruitful to be till'd:
Such as in chearful Vales we view from high;
Which dripping Rocks with rowling Streams supply,
And feed with Ooze; where rising Hillocks run 260
In length, and open to the Southern Sun;
Where Fern succeeds, ungrateful to the Plough:
That gentle ground to gen'rous Grapes allow.
Strong Stocks of Vines it will in time produce,
And overflow the Vats with friendly Juice. 265
Such as our Priests in golden Goblets pour
To Gods, the Givers of the chearful hour.
Then when the bloated *Thuscan* blows his Horn,
And reeking Entrails are in Chargers born.
   If Herds or fleecy Flocks be more thy Care, 270
Or Goats that graze the Field, and burn it bare:
Then seek *Tarentum*'s Lawns, and farthest Coast,
Or such a Field as hapless *Mantua* lost:
Where Silver Swans sail down the wat'ry Rode,
And graze the floating Herbage of the Flood. 275
There Crystal Streams perpetual tenour keep,

262 Plough:] Plough, *97 98*

Nor Food nor Springs are wanting to thy Sheep.
For what the Day devours, the nightly Dew
Shall to the Morn in Perly Drops renew.
Fat crumbling Earth is fitter for the Plough,   280
Putrid and loose above, and black below:
For Ploughing is an imitative Toil,
Resembling Nature in an easie Soil.
No Land for Seed like this, no Fields afford
So large an Income to the Village Lord: 285
No toiling Teams from Harvest-labour come
So late at Night, so heavy laden home.
The like of Forest Land is understood,
From whence the surly Ploughman grubs the Wood,
Which had for length of Ages idle stood.   290
Then Birds forsake the Ruines of their Seat,
And flying from their Nests their Callow Young forget.
The course lean Gravel, on the Mountain sides,
Scarce dewy Bev'rage for the Bees provides:
Nor Chalk nor crumbling Stones, the food of Snakes, 295
That work in hollow Earth their winding Tracks.
The Soil exhaling Clouds of subtile Dews,
Imbibing moisture which with ease she spews;
Which rusts not Iron, and whose Mold is clean,
Well cloath'd with chearful Grass, and ever green, 300
Is good for Olives and aspiring Vines,
Embracing Husband Elms in am'rous twines;
Is fit for feeding Cattle, fit to sowe,
And equal to the Pasture and the Plough.
Such is the Soil of fat *Campanian* Fields,   305
Such large increase the Land that joins *Vesuvius* yields:
And such a Country cou'd *Acerra* boast,
Till *Clanius* overflow'd th' unhappy Coast.
  I teach thee next the diff'ring Soils to know;
The light for Vines, the heavyer for the Plough. 310
Chuse first a place for such a purpose fit,
There dig the solid Earth, and sink a Pit:
Next fill the hole with its own Earth agen,

289 surly *98*: spleenful *97* 296 Tracks *97 (errata)*: Tracts *97 (text)* 301
Vines,] Vines; *97 98* 302 twines;] twines, *97 98* 306 the Land that
joins *Vesuvius 98*: *Vesuvian Nola 97*

And trample with thy Feet, and tread it in:
Then if it rise not to the former height   315
Of superfice, conclude that Soil is light;
A proper Ground for Pasturage and Vines.
But if the sullen Earth, so press'd, repines
Within its native Mansion to retire,
And stays without, a heap of heavy Mire;   320
'Tis good for Arable, a Glebe that asks
Tough Teams of Oxen, and laborious Tasks.
   Salt Earth and bitter are not fit to sow,
Nor will be tam'd or mended with the Plough.
Sweet Grapes degen'rate there, and Fruits declin'd   325
From their first flav'rous Taste, renounce their Kind.
This Truth by sure Experiment is try'd;
For first an Osier Colendar provide
Of Twigs thick wrought, (such toiling Peasants twine,
When thro' streight Passages they strein their Wine;)   330
In this close Vessel place that Earth accurs'd,
But fill'd brimful with wholsom Water first;
Then run it through, the Drops will rope around,
And by the bitter Taste disclose the Ground.
The fatter Earth by handling we may find,   335
With Ease distinguish'd from the meagre Kind:
Poor Soil will crumble into Dust, the Rich
Will to the Fingers cleave like clammy Pitch:
Moist Earth produces Corn and Grass, but both
Too rank and too luxuriant in their Growth.   340
Let not my Land so large a Promise boast,
Lest the lank Ears in length of Stem be lost.
The heavier Earth is by her Weight betray'd,
The lighter in the poising Hand is weigh'd:
'Tis easy to distinguish by the Sight   345
The Colour of the Soil, and black from white.
But the cold Ground is difficult to know,
Yet this the Plants that prosper there, will show;
Black Ivy, Pitch Trees, and the baleful Yeugh.
These Rules consider'd well, with early Care,   350
The Vineyard destin'd for thy Vines prepare:
But, long before the Planting, dig the Ground,
With Furrows deep that cast a rising Mound:

The Clods, expos'd to Winter Winds, will bake:
For putrid Earth will best in Vineyards take,   355
And hoary Frosts, after the painful Toyl
Of delving Hinds, will rot the Mellow Soil.

Some Peasants, not t' omit the nicest Care,
Of the same Soil their Nursery prepare,
With that of their Plantation; lest the Tree   360
Translated, should not with the Soil agree.
Beside, to plant it as it was, they mark
The Heav'ns four Quarters on the tender Bark;
And to the North or South restore the Side,
Which at their Birth did Heat or Cold abide.   365
So strong is Custom; such Effects can Use
In tender Souls of pliant Plants produce.

Chuse next a Province, for thy Vineyards Reign,
On Hills above, or in the lowly Plain:
If fertile Fields or Valleys be thy Choice,   370
Plant thick, for bounteous *Bacchus* will rejoice
In close Plantations there: But if the Vine
On rising Ground be plac'd, or Hills supine,
Extend thy loose Battalions largely wide,
Opening thy Ranks and Files on either Side: 375
But marshall'd all in order as they Stand,
And let no Souldier straggle from his Band.
As Legions in the Field their Front display,
To try the Fortune of some doubtful Day,
And move to meet their Foes with sober Pace,   380
Strict to their Figure, tho' in wider Space;
Before the Battel joins, while from afar
The Field yet glitters with the Pomp of War,
And equal *Mars*, like an impartial Lord,
Leaves all to Fortune, and the dint of Sword;   385
So let thy Vines in Intervals be set,
But not their Rural Discipline forget:
Indulge their Width, and add a roomy Space,
That their extreamest Lines may scarce embrace:
Nor this alone t' indulge a vain Delight,   390
And make a pleasing Prospect for the Sight:

But, for the Ground it self this only Way,
Can equal Vigour to the Plants convey;
Which crowded, want the room, their Branches to display.
  How deep they must be planted, woud'st thou know? 395
In shallow Furrows Vines securely grow.
Not so the rest of Plants; for *Joves* own Tree,
That holds the Woods in awful Sov'raignty,
Requires a depth of Lodging in the Ground;
And, next the lower Skies, a Bed profound: 400
High as his topmost Boughs to Heav'n ascend,
So low his Roots to Hell's Dominion tend.
Therefore, nor Winds, nor Winters Rage o'rethrows
His bulky Body, but unmov'd he grows.
For length of Ages lasts his happy Reign, 405
And Lives of Mortal Man contend in vain.
Full in the midst of his own Strength he stands,
Stretching his brawny Arms, and leafy Hands;
His Shade protects the Plains, his Head the Hills commands.
  The hurtful Hazle in thy Vineyard shun; 410
Nor plant it to receive the setting Sun:
Nor break the topmost Branches from the Tree;
Nor prune, with blunted Knife, the Progeny.
Root up wild Olives from thy labour'd Lands:
For sparkling Fire, from Hinds unwary Hands, 415
Is often scatter'd o're their unctuous rinds,
And after spread abroad by raging Winds.
For first the smouldring Flame the Trunk receives,
Ascending thence, it crackles in the Leaves:
At length victorious to the Top aspires, 420
Involving all the Wood in smoky Fires;
But most, when driv'n by Winds, the flaming Storm,
Of the long Files destroys the beauteous Form.
In Ashes then th' unhappy Vineyard lies,
Nor will the blasted Plants from Ruin rise: 425
Nor will the wither'd Stock be green again,
But the wild Olive shoots, and shades th' ungrateful Plain.
Be not seduc'd with Wisdom's empty Shows,
To stir the peaceful Ground when *Boreas* blows.
When Winter Frosts constrain the Field with Cold, 430

421 in *98*: with *97*   Fires;] Fires, *97 98*

The fainty Root can take no steady hold.
But when the Golden Spring reveals the Year,
And the white Bird returns, whom Serpents fear:
That Season deem the best to plant thy Vines.
Next that, is when Autumnal Warmth declines: 435
E're Heat is quite decay'd, or Cold begun,
Or *Capricorn* admits the Winter Sun.
   The Spring adorns the Woods, renews the Leaves;
The Womb of Earth the genial Seed receives.
For then Almighty *Jove* descends, and pours   440
Into his buxom Bride his fruitful Show'rs.
And mixing his large Limbs with hers, he feeds
Her Births with kindly Juice, and fosters teeming Seeds.
Then joyous Birds frequent the lonely Grove,
And Beasts, by Nature stung, renew their Love.   445
Then Fields the Blades of bury'd Corn disclose,   ⎫
And while the balmy Western Spirit blows,   ⎬
Earth to the Breath her Bosom dares expose.   ⎭
With kindly Moisture then the Plants abound,
The Grass securely springs above the Ground;   450
The tender Twig shoots upward to the Skies,
And on the Faith of the new Sun relies.
The swerving Vines on the tall Elms prevail,
Unhurt by Southern Show'rs or Northern Hail.
They spread their Gems the genial Warmth to share: 455
And boldly trust their Buds in open Air.
In this soft Season (Let me dare to sing,)   ⎫
The World was hatch'd by Heav'ns Imperial King: ⎬
In prime of all the Year, and Holydays of Spring.   ⎭
Then did the new Creation first appear;   460
Nor other was the Tenour of the Year:
When laughing Heav'n did the great Birth attend,
And Eastern Winds their Wintry Breath suspend:

457 (Let me dare to sing,) 98: (so sweet Poets sing) 97. *See Commentary*   460–7
Then . . . rise. 98: 97 *has*
           Earth knew no Season then, but Spring alone:
           On the moist Ground the Sun serenely shone:
           Then Winter Winds their blustring Rage forbear,
           And in a silent Pomp proceeds the mighty Year.
           Sheep soon were sent to people flow'ry Fields,
           And salvage Beasts were banish'd into Wilds.
           Then Heav'n was lighted up with Stars; and Man,
           A hard relentless Race, from Stones began.

Then Sheep first saw the Sun in open Fields;
And salvage Beasts were sent to Stock the Wilds: 465
And Golden Stars flew up to Light the Skies,
And Man's relentless Race, from Stony Quarries rise.
Nor cou'd the tender, new Creation, bear
Th' excessive Heats or Coldness of the Year:
But chill'd by Winter, or by Summer fir'd,   470
The middle Temper of the Spring requir'd.
When Warmth and Moisture did at once abound,
And Heav'ns Indulgence brooded on the Ground.
    For what remains, in depth of Earth secure
Thy cover'd Plants, and dung with hot Manure;   475
And Shells and Gravel in the Ground inclose;
For thro' their hollow Chinks the Water flows:
Which, thus imbib'd, returns in misty Dews,
And steeming up, the rising Plant renews.
Some Husbandmen, of late, have found the Way,   ⎱ 480
A hilly Heap of Stones above to lay,   ⎰
And press the Plants with Sherds of Potters Clay.
This Fence against immod'rate Rain they found:
Or when the Dog-star cleaves the thirsty Ground.
Be mindful when thou hast intomb'd the Shoot,   485
With Store of Earth around to feed the Root;
With Iron Teeth of Rakes and Prongs, to move
The crusted Earth, and loosen it above.
Then exercise thy sturdy Steers to plough
Betwixt thy Vines, and teach thy feeble Row   490
To mount on Reeds, and Wands, and, upward led,
On Ashen Poles to raise their forky Head.
On these new Crutches let them learn to walk,
Till swerving upwards, with a stronger Stalk,
They brave the Winds, and, clinging to their Guide,   495
On tops of Elms at length triumphant ride.
But in their tender Nonage, while they spread
Their Springing Leafs, and lift their Infant Head,
And upward while they shoot in open Air,
Indulge their Child-hood, and the Nurseling spare.   500
Nor exercise thy Rage on new-born Life,

472 When . . . abound, *98*: When Infant Nature was with **Quiet crown'd**, *97*
489 sturdy *98*: strugling *97*

But let thy Hand supply the Pruning-knife;
And crop luxuriant Straglers, nor be loath
To strip the Branches of their leafy Growth:
But when the rooted Vines, with steady Hold,   505
Can clasp their Elms, then Husbandman be bold
To lop the disobedient Boughs, that stray'd
Beyond their Ranks: let crooked Steel invade
The lawless Troops, which Discipline disclaim,
And their superfluous Growth with Rigour tame.   510
Next, fenc'd with Hedges and deep Ditches round,
Exclude th' incroaching Cattle from thy Ground,
While yet the tender Gems but just appear,
Unable to sustain th' uncertain Year;
Whose Leaves are not alone foul Winter's Prey,   515
But oft by Summer Suns are scorch'd away;
And worse than both, become th' unworthy Browze
Of Buffalo's, salt Goats, and hungry Cows.
For not *December*'s Frost that burns the Boughs,
Nor Dog-days parching Heat that splits the Rocks,   520
Are half so harmful as the greedy Flocks:
Their venom'd Bite, and Scars indented on the Stocks.
For this the Malefactor Goat was laid
On *Bacchus* Altar, and his forfeit paid.
At *Athens* thus old Comedy began,   525
When round the Streets the reeling Actors ran;
In Country Villages, and crossing ways,
Contending for the Prizes of their Plays:
And glad, with *Bacchus*, on the grassie soil,
Leapt o're the Skins of Goats besmear'd with Oyl.   530
Thus *Roman* Youth deriv'd from ruin'd *Troy*,
In rude *Saturnian* Rhymes express their Joy:
With Taunts, and Laughter loud, their Audience please,
Deform'd with Vizards, cut from Barks of Trees:
In jolly Hymns they praise the God of Wine,   535
Whose Earthen Images adorn the Pine;
And there are hung on high, in honour of the Vine:
A madness so devout the Vineyard fills.
In hollow Valleys and on rising Hills;
On what e're side he turns his honest face,   540

524 *Bacchus*] *Bacchus*'s 97 98   538 Vineyard 98: Vineyards 97

And dances in the Wind, those Fields are in his grace.
To *Bacchus* therefore let us tune our Lays,
And in our Mother Tongue resound his Praise.
Thin Cakes in Chargers, and a Guilty Goat,
Dragg'd by the Horns, be to his Altars brought;   545
Whose offer'd Entrails shall his Crime reproach,
And drip their Fatness from the Hazle Broach.
To dress thy Vines new labour is requir'd,
Nor must the painful Husbandman be tir'd:
For thrice, at least, in Compass of the Year,   550
Thy Vineyard must employ the sturdy Steer,
To turn the Glebe; besides thy daily pain
To break the Clods, and make the Surface plain:
T' unload the Branches or the Leaves to thin,
That suck the Vital Moisture of the Vine.   555
Thus in a Circle runs the Peasant's Pain,
And the Year rowls within it self again.
Ev'n in the lowest Months, when Storms have shed
From Vines the hairy Honours of their Head;
Not then the drudging Hind his Labour ends;   560
But to the coming Year his Care extends:
Ev'n then the naked Vine he persecutes;
His Pruning Knife at once Reforms and Cuts.
Be first to dig the Ground, be first to burn
The Branches lopt, and first the Props return   565
Into thy House, that bore the burden'd Vines;
But last to reap the Vintage of thy Wines.
Twice in the Year luxuriant Leaves o'reshade
The incumber'd Vine; rough Brambles twice invade:
Hard Labour both! commend the large excess   570
Of spacious Vineyards; cultivate the less.
Besides, in Woods the Shrubs of prickly Thorn,
Sallows and Reeds, on Banks of Rivers born,
Remain to cut; for Vineyards useful found,
To stay thy Vines, and fence thy fruitful Ground.   575
Nor when thy tender Trees at length are bound;
When peaceful Vines from Pruning Hooks are free,
When Husbands have survey'd the last degree,
And utmost Files of Plants, and order'd ev'ry Tree;
Ev'n when they sing at ease in full Content,   580

Insulting o're the Toils they underwent;
Yet still they find a future Task remain;
To turn the Soil, and break the Clods again:
And after all, their Joys are unsincere,
While falling Rains on ripening Grapes they fear.   585
Quite opposite to these are Olives found,
No dressing they require, and dread no wound;
Nor Rakes nor Harrows need, but fix'd below,
Rejoyce in open Air, and unconcerndly grow.
The Soil it self due Nourishment supplies: 590
Plough but the Furrows, and the Fruits arise:
Content with small Endeavours, 'till they spring.
Soft Peace they figure, and sweet Plenty bring:
Then Olives plant, and Hymns to *Pallas* sing.
   Thus Apple Trees, whose Trunks are strong to bear   595
Their spreading Boughs, exert themselves in Air:
Want no supply, but stand secure alone,
Not trusting foreign Forces, but their own:
'Till with the ruddy freight the bending Branches groan.
Thus Trees of Nature, and each common Bush,   600
Uncultivated thrive, and with red Berries blush.
Vile Shrubs are shorn for Browze: the tow'ring hight
Of unctuous Trees, are Torches for the Night.
And shall we doubt, (indulging easie Sloath,)
To sow, to set, and to reform their growth?   605
To leave the lofty Plants; the lowly kind,
Are for the Shepherd, or the Sheep design'd.
Ev'n humble Broom and Osiers have their use,
And Shade for Sleep, and Food for Flocks produce;
Hedges for Corn, and Honey for the Bees: 610
Besides the pleasing Prospect of the Trees.
How goodly looks *Cytorus*, ever green
With Boxen Groves, with what delight are seen
Narycian Woods of Pitch, whose gloomy shade,
Seems for retreat of heav'nly Muses made!   615
But much more pleasing are those Fields to see,
That need not Ploughs, nor Human Industry.
Ev'n cold *Caucasean* Rocks with Trees are spread,
And wear green Forests on their hilly Head.

615 heav'nly *98*: thoughtful *97*

Tho' bending from the blast of Eastern Storms,   620
Tho' shent their Leaves, and shatter'd are their Arms;
Yet Heav'n their various Plants for use designs:
For Houses Cedars, and for Shipping Pines.
Cypress provides for Spokes, and Wheels of Wains:
And all for Keels of Ships, that scour the watry Plains.   625
Willows in Twigs are fruitful, Elms in Leaves,
The War, from stubborn Myrtle Shafts receives:
From Cornels Jav'lins, and the tougher Yeugh
Receives the bending Figure of a Bow.
Nor Box, nor Limes, without their use are made,   630
Smooth-grain'd, and proper for the Turner's Trade:
Which curious Hands may kerve, and Steel with Ease invade.
Light Alder stems the *Po*'s impetuous Tide,
And Bees in hollow Oaks their Hony hide.
Now ballance, with these Gifts, the fumy Joys   635
Of Wine, attended with eternal Noise.
Wine urg'd to lawless Lust the *Centaurs* Train,
Thro' Wine they quarrell'd, and thro' Wine were slain.
     Oh happy, if he knew his happy State!
The Swain, who, free from Business and Debate,   640
Receives his easy Food from Nature's Hand,
And just Returns of cultivated Land!
No Palace, with a lofty Gate, he wants,
T' admit the Tydes of early Visitants.
With eager Eyes devouring, as they pass,   645
The breathing Figures of *Corinthian* Brass.
No Statues threaten, from high Pedestals;
No *Persian* Arras hides his homely Walls,
With Antick Vests; which thro' their shady fold,
Betray the Streaks of ill dissembl'd Gold.   650
He boasts no Wool, whose native white is dy'd
With Purple Poyson of *Assyrian* Pride.
No costly Drugs of *Araby* defile,
With foreign Scents, the Sweetness of his Oyl.
But easie Quiet, a secure Retreat,   655
A harmless Life that knows not how to cheat,
With homebred Plenty the rich Owner bless,
And rural Pleasures crown his Happiness.

640 Debate,] Debate; *97 98*

Unvex'd with Quarrels, undisturb'd with Noise,
The Country King his peaceful Realm enjoys: 660
Cool Grots, and living Lakes, the Flow'ry Pride
Of Meads, and Streams that thro' the Valley glide;
And shady Groves that easie Sleep invite,
And after toilsome Days, a soft repose at Night.
Wild Beasts of Nature in his Woods abound;   665
And Youth, of Labour patient, plow the Ground,
Inur'd to Hardship, and to homely Fare.
Nor venerable Age is wanting there,
In great Examples to the Youthful Train:
Nor are the Gods ador'd with Rites prophane.   670
From hence *Astrea* took her Flight, and here
The Prints of her departing Steps appear.
   Ye sacred Muses, with whose Beauty fir'd,
My Soul is ravish'd, and my Brain inspir'd:
Whose Priest I am, whose holy Fillets wear;   675
Wou'd you your Poet's first Petition hear,
Give me the Ways of wandring Stars to know:
The Depths of Heav'n above, and Earth below.
Teach me the various Labours of the Moon,
And whence proceed th' Eclipses of the Sun.   680
Why flowing Tides prevail upon the Main,
And in what dark Recess they shrink again.
What shakes the solid Earth, what Cause delays
The Summer Nights, and shortens Winter Days.
But if my heavy Blood restrain the Flight   685
Of my free Soul, aspiring to the Height
Of Nature, and unclouded Fields of Light:
My next Desire is, void of Care and Strife,
To lead a soft, secure, inglorious Life.
A Country Cottage near a Crystal Flood,   690
A winding Vally, and a lofty Wood.
Some God conduct me to the sacred Shades,
Where Bacchanals are sung by *Spartan* Maids.
Or lift me high to *Hemus* hilly Crown;
Or in the Plains of *Tempe* lay me down: 695
Or lead me to some solitary Place,
And cover my Retreat from Human Race.

664 soft *98*: sweet *97*   676 Poet's *98*: *Virgil's 97*

Happy the Man, who, studying Nature's Laws,
Thro' known Effects can trace the secret Cause.
His Mind possessing, in a quiet state,   700
Fearless of Fortune, and resign'd to Fate.
And happy too is he, who decks the Bow'rs
Of Sylvans, and adores the Rural Pow'rs:
Whose Mind, unmov'd, the Bribes of Courts can see;
Their glitt'ring Baits, and Purple Slavery.   705
Nor hopes the People's Praise, nor fears their Frown,
Nor, when contending Kindred tear the Crown,
Will set up one, or pull another down.
   Without Concern he hears, but hears from far,
Of Tumults and Descents, and distant War: 710
Nor with a Superstitious Fear is aw'd,
For what befals at home, or what abroad.
Nor envies he the Rich their heapy Store,
Nor his own Peace disturbs, with Pity for the Poor.
He feeds on Fruits, which, of their own accord,   715
The willing Ground, and laden Trees afford.
From his lov'd Home no Lucre him can draw;
The Senates mad Decrees he never saw;
Nor heard, at bawling Bars, corrupted Law.
Some to the Seas, and some to Camps resort,   720
And some with Impudence invade the Court.
In foreign Countries others seek Renown,
With Wars and Taxes others waste their own.
And Houses burn, and houshold Gods deface,
To drink in Bowls which glitt'ring Gems enchase: 725
To loll on Couches, rich with *Cytron* Steds,
And lay their guilty Limbs in *Tyrian* Beds.
This Wretch in Earth intombs his Golden Ore,
Hov'ring and brooding on his bury'd Store.
Some Patriot Fools to pop'lar Praise aspire,   730
Or Publick Speeches, which worse Fools admire.
While from both Benches, with redoubl'd Sounds,
Th' Applause of Lords and Commoners abounds.
Some through Ambition, or thro' Thirst of Gold;
Have slain their Brothers, or their Country sold: 735
And leaving their sweet Homes, in Exile run

714 Nor . . . for *98*: Nor with a helpless Hand condoles *97*   731 Or *98*: By *97*

To Lands that lye beneath another Sun.
 The Peasant, innocent of all these Ills,
With crooked Ploughs the fertile Fallows tills;
And the round Year with daily Labour fills.   740
From hence the Country Markets are supply'd:
Enough remains for houshold Charge beside;
His Wife, and tender Children to sustain,
And gratefully to feed his dumb deserving Train.
Nor cease his Labours, till the Yellow Field   745
A full return of bearded Harvest yield:
A Crop so plenteous, as the Land to load,
O'recome the crowded Barns, and lodge on Ricks abroad.
Thus ev'ry sev'ral Season is employ'd:
Some spent in Toyl, and some in Ease enjoy'd.   750
The yeaning Ewes prevent the springing Year;
The laded Boughs their Fruits in Autumn bear.
'Tis then the Vine her liquid Harvest yields,
Bak'd in the Sun-shine of ascending Fields.
The Winter comes, and then the falling Mast,   755
For greedy Swine, provides a full repast.
Then Olives, ground in Mills, their fatness boast,
And Winter Fruits are mellow'd by the Frost.
His Cares are eas'd with Intervals of bliss,
His little Children climbing for a Kiss,   760
Welcome their Father's late return at Night;
His faithful Bed is crown'd with chast delight.
His Kine with swelling Udders ready stand,
And, lowing for the Pail, invite the Milker's hand.
His wanton Kids, with budding Horns prepar'd,   765
Fight harmless Battels in his homely Yard:
Himself in Rustick Pomp, on Holy-days,
To Rural Pow'rs a just Oblation pays;
And on the Green his careless Limbs displays.
The Hearth is in the midst; the Herdsmen round   770
The chearful Fire, provoke his health in Goblets crown'd.
He calls on *Bacchus*, and propounds the Prize;
The Groom his Fellow Groom at Buts defies;
And bends his Bow, and levels with his Eyes.
Or stript for Wrestling, smears his Limbs with Oyl,   775
And watches with a trip his Foe to foil.

Such was the life the frugal *Sabines* led;
So *Remus* and his Brother God were bred:
From whom th' austere *Etrurian* Virtue rose,
And this rude life our homely Fathers chose.   780
Old *Rome* from such a Race deriv'd her birth,
(The Seat of Empire, and the conquer'd Earth:)
Which now on sev'n high Hills triumphant reigns,
And in that compass all the World contains.
E're *Saturn*'s Rebel Son usurp'd the Skies,   785
When Beasts were only slain for Sacrifice:
While peaceful *Crete* enjoy'd her ancient Lord,
E're sounding Hammers forg'd th' inhumane Sword:
E're hollow Drums were beat, before the Breath
Of brazen Trumpets rung the Peals of Death;   790
The good old God his Hunger did asswage
With Roots and Herbs, and gave the Golden Age.
But over labour'd with so long a Course,
Tis time to set at ease the smoking Horse.

THE THIRD BOOK OF THE GEORGICS

THE ARGUMENT

*This Book begins with an Invocation of some Rural Deities, and a Compliment
to Augustus: After which Virgil directs himself to* Mecænas, *and enters on
his Subject. He lays down Rules for the Breeding and Management of Horses,
Oxen, Sheep, Goats, and Dogs: And interweaves several pleasant Descriptions
of a Chariot-Race, of the Battel of the Bulls, of the Force of Love, and of the* 5
Scythian *Winter. In the latter part of the Book he relates the Diseases incident
to Cattel; and ends with the Description of a fatal Murrain that formerly
rag'd among the* Alps.

THY Fields, propitious *Pales*, I reherse;
   And sing thy Pastures in no vulgar Verse,
Amphrysian Shepherd; the *Lycæan* Woods;
Arcadia's flowry Plains, and pleasing Floods.
   All other Themes, that careless Minds invite,   5

The Third Book. The Argument *not in* 94

Are worn with use; unworthy me to write.
Busiris Altars, and the dire Decrees
Of hard *Euristheus*, ev'ry Reader sees:
Hylas the Boy, *Latona's* erring Isle,
And *Pelops* Iv'ry Shoulder, and his Toyl   10
For fair *Hippodamé*, with all the rest
Of *Grecian* Tales, by Poets are exprest:
New ways I must attempt, my groveling Name
To raise aloft, and wing my flight to Fame.
    I, first of *Romans*, shall in Triumph come   15
From conquer'd *Greece*, and bring her Trophies home:
With Foreign Spoils adorn my native place;
And with *Idume's* Palms, my *Mantua* grace.
Of *Parian* Stone a Temple will I raise,
Where the slow *Mincius* through the Vally strays: 20
Where cooling Streams invite the Flocks to drink:
And Reeds defend the winding water's brink.
Full in the midst shall mighty *Cæsar* stand:
Hold the chief Honours; and the Dome command.
Then I, conspicuous in my *Tyrian* Gown,   25
(Submitting to his Godhead my Renown)
A hundred Coursers from the Goal will drive:
The Rival Chariots in the Race shall strive.
All *Greece* shall flock from far, my Games to see;
The Whorlbat, and the rapid Race, shall be   30
Reserv'd for *Cæsar*, and ordain'd by me.
My self, with Olive crown'd, the Guifts will bear:
Ev'n now methinks the publick shouts I hear;
The passing Pageants, and the Pomps appear.
I, to the Temple, will conduct the Crew: 35
The Sacrifice and Sacrificers view;
From thence return, attended with my Train,
Where the proud Theatres disclose the Scene:
Which interwoven *Britains* seem to raise,
And shew the *Triumph* which their *Shame* displays.   40
High o're the Gate, in Elephant and Gold,
The Crowd shall *Cæsar's Indian* War behold;
The *Nile* shall flow beneath; and on the side,
His shatter'd Ships on Brazen Pillars ride.

7 *Busiris*] Busiri's *94 97 98*   10 *Pelops*] Pelop's *94 97 98*

Next him *Niphates* with inverted Urn,   45
And dropping Sedge, shall his *Armenia* mourn;
And *Asian* Cities in our Triumph born.
With backward Bows the *Parthians* shall be there;
And, spurring from the Fight, confess their fear.
A double Wreath shall crown our *Cæsar*'s Brows;   50
Two differing Trophies, from two different Foes.
Europe with *Africk* in his Fame shall join;
But neither Shore his Conquest shall confine.
The *Parian* Marble, there, shall seem to move,
In breathing Statues, not unworthy *Jove*.   55
Resembling Heroes, whose Etherial Root
Is *Jove* himself, and *Cæsar* is the Fruit.
Tros and his Race the Sculptor shall employ;
And He the God who built the Walls of *Troy*.
Envy her self at last, grown pale and dumb;   60
(By *Cæsar* combated and overcome)
Shall give her Hands; and fear the curling Snakes
Of lashing Furies, and the burning Lakes:
The pains of Famisht *Tantalus* shall feel;
And *Sisyphus* that labours up the Hill   65
The rowling Rock in vain; and curst *Ixion*'s Wheel.

   Mean time we must pursue the *Silvan* Lands;
(Th' abode of Nymphs,) untouch'd by former Hands:
For such, *Mæcenas*, are thy hard Commands.
Without thee nothing lofty can I sing;   70
Come then, and with thy self thy Genius bring:
With which Inspir'd, I brook no dull delay.
Cytheron loudly calls me to my way;
Thy Hounds, *Taygetus*, open and pursue their prey.
High *Epidaurus* urges on my speed,   75
Fam'd for his Hills, and for his Horses breed:
From Hills and Dales the chearful Cries rebound:
For Eccho hunts along; and propagates the sound.

   A time will come, when my maturer Muse,
In *Cæsar*'s Wars, a Nobler Theme shall chuse.   80
And through more Ages bear my Soveraign's Praise;
Than have from *Tithon* past to *Cæsar*'s Days.

   The Generous Youth, who studious of the Prize,
The Race of running Coursers multiplies;

Or to the Plough the sturdy Bullock breeds,   85
May know that from the Dam the worth of each proceeds:
The Mother Cow must wear a lowring look,
Sour headed, strongly neck'd, to bear the yoke.
Her double Dew-lap from her Chin descends:
And at her Thighs the pond'rous burthen ends.   90
Long are her sides and large, her Limbs are great;
Rough are her Ears, and broad her horny Feet.
Her Colour shining black, but fleak'd with white;
She tosses from the Yoke; provokes the Fight:
She rises in her gate, is free from fears;   95
And in her Face a Bull's Resemblance bears:
Her ample Forehead with a Star is Crown'd;
And with her length of Tail she sweeps the ground.
The Bull's Insult at Four she may sustain;
But, after Ten, from Nuptial Rites refrain.   100
Six Seasons use; but then release the Cow,
Unfit for Love, and for the lab'ring Plough.
　　Now while their Youth is fill'd with kindly Fire,
Submit thy Females to the lusty Sire:
Watch the quick motions of the frisking Tail,   105
Then serve their fury with the rushing Male,
Indulging Pleasure lest the Breed shou'd fail.
　　In Youth alone, Unhappy Mortals Live;
But, ah! the mighty Bliss is fugitive;
Discolour'd Sickness, anxious Labours come,   110
And Age, and Death's inexorable Doom.
　　Yearly thy Herds in vigour will impair;
Recruit and mend 'em with thy Yearly care:
Still propagate, for still they fall away,
'Tis prudence to prevent th' entire decay.   115
　　Like Diligence requires the Courser's Race;
In early choice; and for a longer space.
The Colt, that for a Stallion is design'd,
By sure presages shows his Generous Kind,
Of able Body, sound of Limb and Wind.   120
Upright he walks, on Pasterns firm and straight;
His motions easy; prancing in his Gate.
The first to lead the way, to tempt the flood;
To pass the Bridge unknown, nor fear the trembling wood.

Dauntless at empty noises; lofty neck'd; 125
Sharp headed, Barrel belly'd, broadly back'd.
Brawny his Chest, and deep, his Colour gray;
For Beauty dappled, or the brightest Bay:
Faint White and Dun will scarce the Rearing pay.

    The fiery Courser, when he hears from far, 130
The sprightly Trumpets, and the shouts of War,
Pricks up his Ears; and trembling with delight,
Shifts place, and paws; and hopes the promis'd Fight.
On his right shoulder his thick Mane reclin'd,
Ruffles at speed; and dances in the wind. 135
His horny Hoofs are jetty-black, and round;
His Chine is double; starting, with a bound
He turns the Turf, and shakes the solid ground.
Fire from his Eyes, Clouds from his Nostrils flow:
He bears his Rider headlong on the Foe. 140

    Such was the Steed in *Græcian* Poets fam'd,
Proud *Cyllarus*, by *Spartan Pollux* tam'd:
Such Coursers bore to Fight the God of *Thrace*;
And such, *Achilles*, was thy Warlick Race.
In such a Shape, grim *Saturn* did restrain 145
His Heav'nly Limbs, and flow'd with such a Mane.
When, half surpriz'd, and fearing to be seen,
The Leatcher gallop'd from his Jealous Queen:
Ran up the ridges of the Rocks amain;
And with shrill Neighings fill'd the Neighbouring Plain. 150

    But worn with Years, when dire Diseases come,
Then hide his not Ignoble Age, at Home:
In peace t' enjoy his former Palms and Pains;
And gratefully be kind to his Remains.
For when his Blood no Youthful Spirits move, 155
He languishes and labours in his Love.
And when the sprightly Seed shou'd swiftly come,
Dribling he drudges, and defrauds the Womb.
In vain he burns, like hasty stubble fires;
And in himself his former self requires. 160

    His Age and Courage weigh: nor those alone,

130 Courser, *97 98*: Courser *94*   131 Trumpets *94 98*: Trumpet *97*   137
starting, *97 98*: starting *94*   142 *Pollux 94 98*: *Castor 97*   145 grim *94*
98: old *97*   150 Neighbouring *94 98*: Neigb'ring *97*   159 hasty *94 98*:
fainty *97*

But note his Father's Virtues and his own;
Observe if he disdains to yield the Prize;
Of Loss impatient, proud of Victories.

   Hast thou beheld, when from the Goal they start,   165
The Youthful Charioteers with heaving Heart,
Rush to the Race; and panting, scarcely bear
Th' extreams of feaverish hope, and chilling fear;
Stoop to the Reins, and lash with all their force;
The flying Chariot kindles in the course: 170
And now a-low; and now aloft they fly,
As born through Air, and seem to touch the Sky.
No stop, no stay, but clouds of sand arise;
Spurn'd, and cast backward on the follower's Eyes.
The hindmost blows the foam upon the first: 175
Such is the love of Praise: an Honourable Thirst.

   Bold *Ericthonius* was the first, who joyn'd
Four Horses for the rapid Race design'd;
And o're the dusty wheels presiding sat;
The *Lapythæ* to Chariots, add the State   180
Of Bits and Bridles; taught the Steed to bound;
To run the Ring, and trace the mazy round.
To stop, to fly, the Rules of War to know:
T' obey the Rider; and to dare the Foe.

   To choose a Youthful Steed, with Courage fir'd;   185
To breed him, break him, back him, are requir'd
Experienc'd Masters; and in sundry ways:
Their Labours equal, and alike their Praise.
But once again the batter'd Horse beware,
The weak old Stallion will deceive thy care.   190
Though Famous in his Youth for force and speed,
Or was of *Argos* or *Epirian* breed,
Or did from *Neptune*'s Race, or from himself proceed.

   These things premis'd, when now the Nuptial time
Approaches for the stately Steed to climb;   195
With Food inable him, to make his Court;
Distend his Chine, and pamper him for sport.
Feed him with Herbs, whatever thou can'st find,

---

162 and *94 98*: with *97*   166 heaving *98*: beating *94 97*   171 a-low; and
now aloft *94 98*: aloft; and now alow *97*   172 As . . . seem *94 98*: Now seem
to sink in Earth, and now *97. See Commentary*   180 add the *94 98*: added *97*

Of generous warmth; and of salacious kind.
Then water him, and (drinking what he can)   200
Encourage him to thirst again, with Bran.
Instructed thus, produce him to the Faire;
And joyn in Wedlock to the longing Mare.
For if the Sire be faint, or out of case,
He will be copied in his famish'd Race: 205
And sink beneath the pleasing Task assign'd;
(For all's too little for the craving Kind.)
    As for the Females, with industrious care
Take down their Mettle, keep 'em lean and bare;
When conscious of their past delight, and keen   210
To take the leap, and prove the sport again:
With scanty measure then supply their food;
And, when athirst, restrain 'em from the flood:
Their Bodies harrass, sink 'em when they run;
And fry their melting Marrow in the Sun.   215
Starve 'em, when Barns beneath their burthen groan,
And winnow'd Chaff, by western winds is blown.
For fear the ranckness of the swelling Womb
Shou'd scant the passage, and confine the room.
Lest the fat Furrows shou'd the sense destroy   220
Of Genial Lust; and dull the Seat of Joy.
But let 'em suck the Seed with greedy force;
And close involve the Vigour of the Horse.
    The Male has done; thy Care must now proceed   *Here the*
To teeming Females; and the promis'd breed.   *Poet returns*
                                                to Cows.   225
First let 'em run at large; and never know
The taming Yoak, or draw the crooked Plough.
Let 'em not leap the Ditch, or swim the Flood;
Or lumber o're the Meads; or cross the Wood.
But range the Forest, by the silver side   230
Of some cool Stream, where Nature shall provide
Green Grass and fatning Clover for their fare;
And Mossy Caverns for their Noontide lare:
With Rocks above, to shield the sharp Nocturnal air.

203 the longing *97 98*: th' expecting *94*   223 close involve *98*: there enclose *94*
97   224 *marginal note, 94 only*   224-5 The Male . . . breed. *94 98: 97 has*
                No more of Coursers yet: We now proceed
                To teeming Kine; and their laborious breed.

233 Noontide *94 98*: Evening *97*

About th' *Alburnian* Groves, with Holly green,   235
Of winged Insects mighty swarms are seen:
This flying Plague (to mark its quality;)
Oestros the *Grecians* call: *Asylus*, we:
A fierce loud buzzing Breez; their stings draw blood;
And drive the Cattel gadding through the Wood.   240
Seiz'd with unusual pains, they loudly cry,
Tanagrus hastens thence; and leaves his Channel dry.
This Curse the jealous *Juno* did invent;
And first employ'd for *Io*'s Punishment.
To shun this Ill, the cunning Leach ordains   245
In Summer's Sultry Heats (for then it reigns)
To feed the Females, e're the Sun arise,
Or late at Night, when Stars adorn the Skies.

     When she has calv'd, then set the Dam aside;
And for the tender Progeny provide.   250
Distinguish all betimes, with branding Fire;
To note the Tribe, the Lineage, and the Sire.
Whom to reserve for Husband of the Herd;
Or who shall be to Sacrifice preferr'd;
Or whom thou shalt to turn thy Glebe allow;   255
To smooth the Furrows, and sustain the Plough:
The rest, for whom no Lot is yet decreed,
May run in Pastures, and at pleasure feed.
The Calf, by Nature and by Genius made
To turn the Glebe, breed to the Rural trade.   260
Set him betimes to School; and let him be
Instructed there in Rules of Husbandry:
While yet his Youth is flexible and green;
Nor bad Examples of the World has seen.
Early begin the stubborn Child to break;   265
For his soft Neck, a supple Collar make
Of bending Osiers; and (with time and care
Enur'd that easie Servitude to bear)
Thy flattering Method on the Youth pursue:
Join'd with his School-Fellows, by two and two,   270
Perswade 'em first to lead an empty Wheel,
That scarce the dust can raise; or they can feel:
In length of Time produce the lab'ring Yoke

235, 249 *Editor's paragraphs*   256 smooth the *98*: harrow *94 97*

And shining Shares, that make the Furrow smoak.
E're the licentious Youth be thus restrain'd,   275
Or Moral Precepts on their Minds have gain'd;
Their wanton Appetites not only feed
With delicates of Leaves, and marshy Weed,
But with thy Sickle reap the rankest land:
And minister the blade, with bounteous hand.   280
Nor be with harmful parsimony won
To follow what our homely Sires have done;
Who fill'd the Pail with Beestings of the Cow:
But all her Udder to the Calf allow.

   If to the Warlike Steed thy Studies bend,   285
Or for the Prize in Chariots to contend;
Near *Pisa's* Flood the rapid Wheels to guide,
Or in *Olympian* Groves aloft to ride;
The generous labours of the Courser, first
Must be with sight of Arms and sounds of Trumpets nurst: 290
Inur'd the groaning Axle-tree to bear;
And let him clashing Whips in Stables hear.
Sooth him with praise; and make him understand
The loud Applauses of his Master's hand:
This from his weaning, let him well be taught;   295
And then betimes in a soft Snaffle wrought:
Before his tender Joints with Nerves are knit;
Untry'd in Arms, and trembling at the Bit.
But when to four full Springs his years advance,
Teach him to run the round, with pride to prance;   300
And (rightly manag'd) equal time to beat;
To turn, to bound in measure; and Curvet.
Let him, to this, with easie pains be brought:
And seem to labour, when he labours not.
Thus, form'd for speed, he challenges the wind;   305
And leaves the *Scythian* Arrow far behind:
He scours along the Field, with loosen'd Reins;
And treads so light, he scarcely prints the plains.
Like *Boreas* in his race, when rushing forth,
He sweeps the Skies, and clears the cloudy North: 310
The waving Harvest bends beneath his blast;
The Forest shakes, the Groves their Honours cast;

298 Untry'd in *98*: Guiltless of *94 97*

He flies aloft, and with impetuous roar
Pursues the foaming Surges to the shoar.
Thus o're th' *Elean* Plains, thy well-breath'd Horse   315
Impels the flying Carr, and wins the Course.
Or, bred to *Belgian* Waggons, leads the way;
Untir'd at night, and chearful all the Day.
    When once he's broken, feed him full and high:
Indulge his growth, and his gaunt sides supply.   320
Before his training, keep him poor and low;
For his stout stomach with his food will grow;
The pamper'd Colt will Discipline disdain,
Impatient of the Lash, and restiff to the Rein.
    Wou'dst thou their Courage and their Strength improve,   325
Too soon they must not feel the stings of Love.
Whether the Bull or Courser be thy Care,
Let him not leap the Cow, nor mount the Mare.
The youthful Bull must wander in the Wood;
Behind the Mountain, or beyond the Flood: 330
Or, in the Stall at home his Fodder find;
Far from the Charms of that alluring Kind.
With two fair Eyes his Mistress burns his breast;
He looks, and languishes, and leaves his rest;
Forsakes his Food, and pining for the Lass,   335
Is joyless of the Grove, and spurns the growing grass.
The soft Seducer, with enticing Looks,
The bellowing Rivals to the Fight provokes.
    A beauteous Heifer in the Woods is bred;
The stooping Warriours, aiming head to head,   340
Engage their clashing Horns; with dreadful sound
The Forrest rattles, and the Rocks rebound.
They fence, they push, and pushing loudly roar;
Their Dewlaps and their sides are bath'd in goar.
Nor when the War is over, is it Peace;   345
Nor will the vanquish'd Bull his Claim release:
But feeding in his Breast his ancient Fires,
And cursing Fate, from his proud Foe retires.
Driv'n from his Native Land, to foreign Grounds,
He with a gen'rous rage resents his Wounds;   350
His ignominious flight, the Victor's boast,

316 Impels the flying Carr *98*: Sustains the goring Spurs *94 97*

And more than both, the Loves, which unreveng'd he lost.
Often he turns his Eyes, and, with a groan,
Surveys the pleasing Kingdoms, once his own.
And therefore to repair his strength he tries: 355
Hardning his Limbs with painful Exercise,
And rough upon the flinty Rock he lies.
On prickly Leaves, and on sharp Herbs he feeds,
Then to the Prelude of a War proceeds.
His Horns, yet sore, he tries against a Tree: 360
And meditates his absent Enemy.
He snuffs the Wind, his heels the Sand excite;
But, when he stands collected in his might,
He roars, and promises a more successful fight.
Then, to redeem his Honour at a blow,   365
He moves his Camp, to meet his careless Foe.
Not with more madness, rolling from afar,
The spumy Waves proclaim the watry War:
And mounting upwards, with a mighty roar,
March onwards, and insult the rocky shoar.   370
They mate the middle Region with their height;
And fall no less, than with a Mountain's weight;
The Waters boil, and belching from below
Black Sands, as from a forceful Engine throw.

    Thus every Creature, and of every Kind,   375
The secret Joys of sweet Coition find:
Not only Man's Imperial Race; but they
That wing the liquid Air, or swim the Sea,
Or haunt the Desart, rush into the flame:
For Love is Lord of all; and is in all the same.   380
    'Tis with this rage, the Mother Lion stung,
Scours o're the Plain; regardless of her young:
Demanding Rites of Love, she sternly stalks;
And hunts her Lover in his lonely Walks.
Tis then the shapeless Bear his Den forsakes;   385
In Woods and Fields a wild destruction makes.
Boars whet their Tusks; to battel Tygers move;
Enrag'd with hunger, more enrag'd with love.
Then wo to him, that in the desart Land

Of *Lybia* travels, o're the burning Sand.   390
The Stallion snuffs the well-known Scent afar;
And snorts and trembles for the distant Mare:
Nor Bitts nor Bridles, can his rage restrain;
And rugged Rocks are interpos'd in vain:
He makes his way o're Mountains, and contemns   395
Unruly Torrents, and unfoorded Streams.
The bristled Boar, who feels the pleasing wound,
New grinds his arming Tusks, and digs the ground.
The sleepy Leacher shuts his little Eyes;
About his churning Chaps the frothy bubbles rise: 400
He rubs his sides against a Tree; prepares
And hardens both his Shoulders for the Wars.
   What did the *Youth*, when Love's unerring Dart   *Leander.*
Transfixt his Liver; and inflam'd his heart?
Alone, by night, his watry way he took;   405
About him, and above, the Billows broke:
The Sluces of the Skies were open spread;
And rowling Thunder rattl'd o're his head.
The raging Tempest call'd him back in vain;
And every boding Omen of the Main.   410
Nor cou'd his Kindred; nor the kindly force
Of weeping Parents, change his fatal Course.
No, not the dying Maid, who must deplore
His floating Carcass on the *Sestian* shore.
   I pass the Wars that spotted *Linx's* make   415
With their fierce Rivals, for the Females sake:
The howling Wolves, the Mastiffs amorous rage;
When ev'n the fearful Stag dares for his Hind engage.
But far above the rest, the furious Mare,
Barr'd from the Male, is frantick with despair.   420
For when her pouting Vent declares her pain,
She tears the Harness, and she rends the Rein;
For this; (when *Venus* gave them rage and pow'r)
Their Masters mangl'd Members they devour;
Of Love defrauded in their longing Hour.   425
For Love they force through Thickets of the Wood,
They climb the steepy Hills, and stem the Flood.
   When at the Spring's approach their Marrow burns,

(For with the Spring their Genial Warmth returns)
The Mares to Cliffs of rugged Rocks repair, 430
And with wide Nostrils snuff the Western Air:
When (wondrous to relate) the Parent Wind,
Without the Stallion, propagates the Kind.
Then fir'd with amorous rage, they take their flight
Through Plains, and mount the Hills unequal height; 435
Nor to the North, nor to the Rising Sun,
Nor Southward to the Rainy Regions run,
But boring to the West, and hov'ring there
With gaping Mouths, they draw prolifick air:
With which impregnate, from their Groins they shed 440
A slimy Juice, by false Conception bred.
The Shepherd knows it well; and calls by Name
Hippomanes, to note the Mothers Flame.
This, gather'd in the Planetary Hour,
With noxious Weeds, and spell'd with words of pow'r, 445
Dire Stepdames in the Magick Bowl infuse;
And mix, for deadly draughts, the poys'nous juice.
But time is lost, which never will renew,
While we too far the pleasing Path pursue;
Surveying Nature, with too nice a view. 450

 Let this suffice for Herds: our following Care
Shall woolly Flocks, and shaggy Goats declare.
Nor can I doubt what Oyl I must bestow,
To raise my Subject from a Ground so low:
And the mean Matter which my Theme affords, 455
T' embellish with magnificence of Words.
But the commanding Muse my Chariot guides;
Which o're the dubious Cliff securely rides:
And pleas'd I am, no beaten Road to take:
But first the way to new Discov'ries make. 460
 Now, Sacred *Pales*, in a lofty strain,
I sing the Rural Honours of thy Reign.
First with assiduous care, from Winter keep
Well fodder'd in the Stalls, thy tender Sheep.
Then spread with Straw, the bedding of thy fold; 465
With Fern beneath, to fend the bitter cold.
That free from Gouts thou may'st preserve thy Care:
And clear from Scabs, produc'd by freezing Air.

Next let thy Goats officiously be nurst;
And led to living Streams; to quench their thirst.   470
Feed 'em with Winter-brouze, and for their lare
A Cot that opens to the South prepare:
Where basking in the Sun-shine they may lye,
And the short Remnants of his heat enjoy.
This during Winter's drizly Reign be done: 475
Till the new Ram receives th' exalted Sun:
For hairy Goats of equal profit are
With woolly Sheep, and ask an equal care.
Tis true, the Fleece, when drunk with *Tyrian* Juice,
Is dearly sold; but not for needful use: 480
For the sallacious Goat encreases more;
And twice as largely yields her milky store.
The still distended Udders never fail;
But when they seem exhausted, swell the Pail.
Mean time the Pastor shears their hoary Beards;   485
And eases of their Hair, the loaden Herds.
Their Camelots warm in Tents, the Souldier hold;
And shield the shiv'ring Mariner from cold.
   On Shrubs they brouze, and on the bleaky top
Of rugged Hills, the thorny Bramble crop.   490
Attended with their bleating Kids they come
At Night unask'd, and mindful of their home;
And scarce their swelling Bags the threshold overcome.
So much the more thy diligence bestow
In depth of Winter, to defend the Snow: 495
By how much less the tender helpless Kind,
For their own ills, can fit Provision find.
Then minister the browze, with bounteous hand;
And open let thy Stacks all Winter stand.
But when the Western Winds with vital pow'r   500
Call forth the tender Grass, and budding Flower;
Then, at the last, produce in open Air
Both Flocks; and send 'em to their Summer fare.
Before the Sun, while *Hesperus* appears;
First let 'em sip from Herbs the pearly tears   505

469 nurst] nurs'd *97 98*   488 shiv'ring *98*: wretched *94 97*   490 rugged
97 98: barren *94*   491 bleating Kids *98*: Family *94 97*   495 Snow: *97 98*:
Snow. *94*

Of Morning Dews: And after break their Fast
On Green-sword Ground; (a cool and grateful tast:)
But when the day's fourth hour has drawn the Dews,
And the Sun's sultry heat their thirst renews;
When creaking Grashoppers on Shrubs complain, 510
Then lead 'em to their wat'ring Troughs again.
In Summer's heat, some bending Valley find,
Clos'd from the Sun, but open to the Wind:
Or seek some ancient Oak, whose Arms extend
In ample breadth, thy Cattle to defend: 515
Or solitary Grove, or gloomy Glade;
To shield 'em with its venerable Shade.
Once more to wat'ring lead; and feed again
When the low Sun is sinking to the Main.
When rising *Cynthia* sheds her silver Dews; 520
And the cool Evening-breeze the Meads renews:
When Linnets fill the Woods with tuneful sound,
And hollow shoars the *Halcyons* Voice rebound.
  Why shou'd my Muse enlarge on *Lybian* Swains;
Their scatter'd Cottages, and ample Plains? 525
Where oft the Flocks, without a Leader stray;
Or through continu'd Desarts take their way;
And, feeding, add the length of night to day.
Whole Months they wander, grazing as they go;
Nor Folds, nor hospitable Harbour know. 530
Such an extent of Plains, so vast a space
Of Wilds unknown, and of untasted Grass
Allures their Eyes: The Shepherd last appears,
And with him all his Patrimony bears:
His House and household Gods! his trade of War, 535
His Bow and Quiver; and his trusty Cur.
Thus, under heavy Arms, the Youth of *Rome*
Their long laborious Marches overcome;
Chearly their tedious Travels undergo:
And pitch their sudden Camp before the Foe. 540
  Not so the *Scythian* Shepherd tends his Fold;
Nor he who bears in *Thrace* the bitter cold:
Nor he, who treads the bleak *Meotian* Strand;

Or where proud *Ister* rouls his yellow Sand.
Early they stall their Flocks and Herds; for there   545
No Grass the Fields, no Leaves the Forests wear.
The frozen Earth, lies buried there, below
A hilly heap, sev'n Cubits deep in Snow:
And all the *West* Allies of stormy *Boreas* blow.

   The Sun from far, peeps with a sickly face;   550
Too weak the Clouds, and mighty Fogs to chace;
When up the Skies, he shoots his rosie Head;
Or in the ruddy Ocean seeks his Bed.
Swift Rivers, are with sudden Ice constrain'd;
And studded Wheels are on its back sustain'd.   555
An Hostry now for Waggons; which before
Tall Ships of burthen, on its Bosom bore.
The brazen Cauldrons, with the Frost are flaw'd;
The Garment, stiff with Ice, at Hearths is thaw'd.
With Axes first they cleave the Wine, and thence   560
By weight, the solid portions they dispence.
From Locks uncomb'd, and from the frozen Beard,
Long Icicles depend; and crackling sounds are heard.
Mean time perpetual Sleet, and driving Snow,
Obscure the Skies, and hang on Herds below.   565
The starving Cattle perish in their stalls;
Huge Oxen stand enclos'd in wintry walls
Of Snow congeal'd; whole Herds are bury'd there
Of mighty Stags, and scarce their Horns appear.
The dextrous Huntsman wounds not these afar,   570
With Shafts or Darts; or makes a distant War,
With Dogs; or pitches Toyls to stop their flight;
But close engages in unequal fight.
And while they strive in vain to make their way
Through hills of Snow, and pitifully bray;   575
Assaults with dint of Sword, or pointed Spears,
And homeward, on his back, the joyful burthen bears.
The Men to subterranean Caves retire;
Secure from cold; and crowd the chearful fire:
With Trunks of Elms and Oaks, the Hearth they load,   580
Nor tempt th' inclemency of Heav'n abroad.
Their jovial Nights, in frollicks and in play

They pass, to drive the tedious Hours away.
And their cold Stomachs with crown'd Goblets cheer,
Of windy Cyder, and of barmy Beer. 585
Such are the cold *Ryphæan* Race; and such
The savage *Scythian*, and unwarlick *Dutch*.
Where Skins of Beasts, the rude *Barbarians* wear;
The spoils of Foxes, and the furry Bear.
   Is wool thy care? Let not thy Cattle go 590
Where Bushes are, where Burs and Thistles grow;
Nor in too rank a pasture let 'em feed:
Then of the purest white select thy Breed.
Ev'n though a snowy Ram thou shalt behold,
Prefer him not in haste, for Husband to thy Fold. 595
But search his Mouth; and if a swarthy Tongue
Is underneath his humid Pallat hung;
Reject him, lest he darken all the Flock;
And substitute another from thy Stock.
Twas thus with Fleeces milky white (if we 600
May trust report,) *Pan* God of *Arcady*
Did bribe thee *Cynthia*; nor didst thou disdain
When call'd in woody shades, to cure a Lover's pain.
   If Milk be thy design, with plenteous hand
Bring Clover-Grass; and from the marshy Land 605
Salt Herbage for the fodd'ring Rack provide;
To fill their Bags, and swell the milky Tide:
These raise their Thirst, and to the Taste restore
The savour of the Salt, on which they fed before.
   Some, when the Kids their Dams too deeply drain, 610
With gags and muzzles their soft mouths restrain.
Their Morning Milk, the *Peasants* press at Night:
Their Evening Meal, before the rising Light
To Market bear, or sparingly they steep
With seas'ning Salt, and stor'd, for Winter keep. 615
   Nor last, forget thy faithful Dogs: but feed
With fatning Whey the Mastiff's Generous breed;
And *Spartan* Race; who for the Folds relief
Will prosecute with Cries the Nightly Thief:
Repulse the prouling Woolf, and hold at Bay 620
The Mountain Robbers, rushing to the Prey.

   617 breed; *97 98*: breed: *94*   620 Bay] Bay, *94 97 98*

With cries of Hounds, thou may'st pursue the fear
Of flying Hares, and chace the fallow Deer;
Rouze from their desart Dens, the brisl'd rage
Of Boars, and beamy Stags in toyls engage.   625
   With smoak of burning Cedar scent thy walls:
And fume with stinking *Galbanum* thy Stalls:
With that rank Odour from thy dwelling place
To drive the Viper's brood, and all the venom'd Race.
For often under Stalls unmov'd, they lye,   630
Obscure in shades, and shunning Heav'ns broad Eye.
And Snakes, familiar, to the Hearth succeed,
Disclose their Eggs, and near the Chimny breed.
Whether, to Roofy Houses they repair,
Or Sun themselves abroad in open Air,   635
In all abodes of pestilential Kind,
To Sheep and Oxen, and the painful Hind.
Take, Shepherd take, a plant of stubborn Oak;
And labour him with many a sturdy stroke:
Or with hard Stones, demolish from a far   640
His haughty Crest, the seat of all the War.
Invade his hissing Throat, and winding spires;
Till stretcht in length, th' unfolded Foe retires.
He drags his Tail; and for his Head provides:
And in some secret cranny slowly glides;   } 645
But leaves expos'd to blows, his back and batter'd sides.
   In fair *Calabria's* woods, a Snake is bred,
With curling Crest, and with advancing Head:
Waving he rolls, and makes a winding track;
His Belly spotted, burnisht is his back: 650
While Springs are broken, while the *Southern* Air
And dropping Heav'ns, the moysten'd Earth repair,
He lives on standing Lakes, and trembling Bogs,
And fills his Maw with Fish, or with loquacious Frogs.
But when, in muddy Pools, the water sinks;   655
And the chapt Earth is furrow'd o're with chinks;
He leaves the Fens, and leaps upon the ground;
And hissing, rowls his glaring Eyes around.
With Thirst inflam'd, impatient of the heats,
He rages in the Fields, and wide destruction threats.   660

637 painful *97 98*: sweating *94*

Oh let not Sleep, my closing Eyes invade,
In open Plains, or in the secret Shade,
When he, renew'd in all the speckl'd pride
Of pompous Youth, has cast his slough aside:
And in his Summer Liv'ry rowls along: 665
Erect, and brandishing his forky Tongue,
Leaving his Nest, and his imperfect Young;
And thoughtless of his Eggs, forgets to rear
The hopes of Poyson, for the following Year.
    The Causes and the Signs shall next be told,   670
Of ev'ry Sickness that infects the Fold.
A scabby Tetter on their pelts will stick,
When the raw Rain, has pierc'd 'em to the quick:
Or searching Frosts, have eaten through the skin,
Or burning Icicles are lodg'd within: 675
Or when the Fleece is shorn, if sweat remains
Unwash'd, and soaks into their empty veins:
When their defenseless Limbs, the Brambles tear;
Short of their Wool, and naked from the Sheer.
Good Shepherds after sheering, drench their Sheep,   680
And their Flocks Father (forc'd from high to leap)
Swims down the stream, and plunges in the deep.
They noint their naked Limbs, with mother'd Oyl;
Or from the founts, where living Sulphurs boyl,
They mix a Med'cine to foment their Limbs;   685
With Scum, that on the molten Silver swims.
Fat Pitch, and black Bitumen, add to these;
Besides the waxen labour of the Bees;
And *Hellebore*, and *Squills* deep rooted in the Seas.
Receits abound; but searching all thy Store,   690
The best is still at hand, to launch the Sore:
And cut the Head; for till the Core be found,
The secret Vice is fed, and gathers ground.
While making *fruitless moan*, the *Shepherd* stands,
And when the *launching Knife* requires his hands,   695
Vain help, with idle Prayers from Heav'n demands.
Deep in their Bones, when Feavers fix their seat,
And rack their Limbs; and lick the vital heat;
The ready Cure to cool the raging pain,

683 noint] oint 97 98

Is underneath the Foot to breathe a Vein.   700
This Remedy the *Scythian* Shepherds found;
Th' Inhabitants of *Thracia*'s hilly ground
And *Gelons* use it; when for Drink and Food
They mix their cruddl'd Milk with Horses Blood.
    But where thou seest a single Sheep remain   705
In shades aloof, or couch'd upon the Plain;
Or listlesly to crop the tender Grass;
Or late to lag behind, with truant pace:
Revenge the Crime; and take the Traytor's head,
E're in the faultless Flock the dire Contagion spread.   710
    On Winter Seas we fewer Storms behold,
Than foul Diseases that infect the Fold.
Nor do those Ills, on single Bodies prey;
But oft'ner bring the Nation to decay;
And sweep the present Stock, and future Hope away.   715
    A Dire Example of this Truth appears;
When, after such a Length of rowling Years,
We see the Naked *Alps*, and Thin Remains
Of scatter'd Cotts, and yet Unpeopl'd Plains:
Once fill'd with Grazing Flocks, the Shepherds Happy Reigns. 720
    Here from the vicious Air, and sickly Skies,
A Plague did on the dumb Creation rise:
During th' Autumnal Heats, th' Infection grew,
Tame Cattle, and the Beasts of Nature slew.
Poys'ning the Standing Lakes; and Pools Impure;   725
Nor was the foodful Grass in Fields secure.
Strange Death! For when the thirsty Fire had drunk
Their vital Blood, and the dry Nerves were shrunk;
When the contracted Limbs were cramp'd, ev'n then
A watrish Humour swell'd and ooz'd again: 730
Converting into Bane the kindly Juice,
Ordain'd by Nature for a better use.
The Victim Ox, that was for Altars prest,
Trim'd with white Ribbons, and with Garlands drest,
Sunk of himself, without the Gods Command: 735
Preventing the slow Sacrificer's Hand.
Or, by the holy Butcher, if he fell,
Th' Inspected Entrails, cou'd no Fates Foretel.

708 pace:] pace; *94 97 98*

Nor, laid on Altars, did pure Flames arise;
But Clouds of smouldring Smoke, forbad the Sacrifice.   740
Scarcely the Knife was redden'd with his Gore,
Or the Black Poyson stain'd the sandy floor.
The thriven Calves in Meads their Food forsake,
And render their sweet Souls before the plenteous Rack.
The fawning Dog runs mad; the wheasing Swine   745
With Coughs is choak'd; and labours from the Chine:
The Victor Horse, forgetful of his Food,
The Palm renounces, and abhors the Flood.
He paws the Ground, and on his hanging ears
A doubtful Sweat in clammy drops appears: 750
Parch'd is his Hide, and rugged are his Hairs.
Such are the Symptoms of the young Disease;
But in Time's process, when his pains encrease,
He rouls his mournful Eyes, he deeply groans
With patient sobbing, and with manly Moans.   755
He heaves for Breath: which, from his Lungs supply'd,
And fetch'd from far, distends his lab'ring side.
To his rough Palat, his dry Tongue succeeds;
And roapy Gore, he from his Nostrils bleeds.
A Drench of Wine has with success been us'd;   760
And through a Horn, the generous Juice infus'd:
Which timely taken op'd his closing Jaws;
But, if too late, the Patient's death did cause.
For the too vig'rous Dose, too fiercely wrought;
And added Fury to the Strength it brought.   765
Recruited into Rage, he grinds his Teeth
In his own Flesh, and feeds approaching Death.
Ye Gods, to better Fate, good Men dispose;
And turn that Impious Errour on our Foes!
  The Steer, who to the Yoke was bred to bow,   770
(Studious of Tillage; and the crooked Plough)
Falls down and dies; and dying spews a Flood
Of foamy Madness, mix'd with clotted Blood.
The Clown, who cursing Providence repines,
His Mournful Fellow from the Team disjoyns: 775
With many a groan, forsakes his fruitless care;
And in th' unfinish'd Furrow, leaves the Share.
The pineing Steer, no Shades of lofty Woods,

Nor floury Meads can ease; nor Crystal floods
Roul'd from the Rock: His flabby Flanks decrease;   780
His Eyes are settled in a stupid peace.
His bulk too weighty for his Thighs is grown;
And his unweildy Neck, hangs drooping down.
Now what avails his well-deserving Toyl
To turn the Glebe; or smooth the rugged Soyl!   785
And yet he never supt in solemn State,
Nor undigested Feasts did urge his Fate;
Nor Day, to Night, luxuriously did joyn;
Nor surfeited on rich *Campanian* Wine.
Simple his Beverage; homely was his Food,   790
The wholesom Herbage, and the running Flood;
No dreadful Dreams awak'd him with affright;
His Pains by Day, secur'd his Rest by Night.
   'Twas then that *Buffalo's* ill pair'd, were seen
To draw the Carr of *Jove's* Imperial Queen   795
For want of Oxen; and the lab'ring Swain
Scratch'd with a Rake, a Furrow for his Grain:
And cover'd with his hand, the shallow Seed again.
He Yokes himself, and up the Hilly height,
With his own Shoulders, draws the Waggon's weight.   800
   The nightly Woolf, that round th' Enclosure proul'd
To leap the Fence; now plots not on the Fold,
Tam'd with a sharper Pain. The fearful Doe
And flying Stag, amidst the Grey-Hounds go:
And round the Dwellings roam of Man, their fiercer Foe.   805
The scaly Nations of the Sea profound,
Like Shipwreck'd Carcasses are driv'n aground:
And mighty *Phocæ*, never seen before
In shallow Streams, are stranded on the shore.
The Viper dead, within her Hole is found: 810
Defenceless was the shelter of the ground.
The water-Snake, whom Fish and Paddocks fed,
With staring Scales lies poyson'd in his Bed:
To Birds their Native Heav'ns contagious prove,
From Clouds they fall, and leave their Souls above.   815
   Besides, to change their Pasture 'tis in vain:
Or trust to Physick; Physick is their Bane.

802 Fold,] Fold. *94 97 98*   808 *Phocæ 97 98*: Sea-Calves *94*

The Learned Leaches in despair depart:
And shake their Heads, desponding of their Art.
   Tisiphone, let loose from under ground,   820
Majestically pale, now treads the round:
Before her drives Diseases, and affright;
And every moment rises to the sight:
Aspiring to the Skies; encroaching on the light.
The Rivers and their Banks, and Hills around,   825
With lowings, and with dying bleats resound.
At length, she strikes an Universal blow;
To Death at once, whole Herds of Cattle go:
Sheep, Oxen, Horses fall; and, heap'd on high,
The diff'ring Species in Confusion lie.   830
Till, warn'd by frequent ills, the way they found,
To lodge their loathsom Carrion, underground.
For, useless to the Currier were their Hides:
Nor cou'd their tainted Flesh, with Ocean Tides
Be freed from filth; nor cou'd *Vulcanian* flame   835
The Stench abolish; or the Savour tame.
Nor safely cou'd they shear their fleecy store;
(Made drunk with poysonous Juice, and stiff with gore:)
Or touch the Web: But if the Vest they wear,
Red Blisters rising on their Paps appear: 840
And flaming Carbuncles; and noisom Sweat,
And clammy Dews, that loathsom Lice beget:
Till the slow creeping Evil eats his way,
Consumes the parching Limbs; and makes the Life his prey.

THE FOURTH BOOK OF THE GEORGICS

THE ARGUMENT

*Virgil has taken care to raise the Subject of each Georgic: In the First he has
only dead Matter on which to work. In the second he just steps on the World
of Life, and describes that degree of it which is to be found in Vegetables. In
the third he advances to Animals. And in the last, singles out the Bee, which
may be reckon'd the most sagacious of 'em, for his Subject.*   5
*In this Georgic he shews us what Station is most proper for the Bees, and when
they begin to gather Honey: how to call 'em home when they swarm; and how*

831 Till,] Till *94 97 98*

to part 'em when they are engag'd in Battel. From hence he takes occasion to
discover their different Kinds; and, after an Excursion, relates their prudent
and politick Administration of Affairs, and the several Diseases that often rage 10
in their Hives, with the proper Symptoms and Remedies of each Disease. In the
last place he lays down a method of repairing their Kind, supposing their whole
Breed lost; and gives at large the History of its Invention.

THE Gifts of Heav'n my foll'wing Song pursues,
   Aerial Honey, and Ambrosial Dews.
Mæcenas, read this other part, that sings
Embattel'd Squadrons and advent'rous Kings:
A mighty Pomp, tho' made of little Things.   5
Their Arms, their Arts, their Manners I disclose,
And how they War, and whence the People rose:
Slight is the Subject, but the Praise not small,
If Heav'n assist, and *Phœbus* hear my Call.

  First, for thy Bees a quiet Station find,   10
And lodge 'em under Covert of the Wind:
For Winds, when homeward they return, will drive
The loaded Carriers from their Ev'ning Hive.
Far from the Cows and Goats insulting Crew,
That trample down the Flow'rs, and brush the Dew: 15
The painted Lizard, and the Birds of Prey,
Foes of the frugal Kind, be far away:
The Titmouse, and the Peckers hungry Brood,
And *Progne,* with her Bosom stain'd in Blood:
These rob the trading Citizens, and bear   20
The trembling Captives thro' the liquid Air;
And for their callow young a cruel Feast prepare.
But near a living Stream their Mansion place,
Edg'd round with Moss, and tufts of matted Grass:
And plant (the Winds impetuous rage to stop,)   25
Wild Olive Trees, or Palms, before the buisy Shop:
That when the youthful Prince, with proud allarm,
Calls out the vent'rous Colony to swarm;
When first their way thro' yielding Air they wing,
New to the Pleasures of their native Spring;   30
The Banks of Brooks may make a cool retreat
For the raw Souldiers from the scalding Heat:

The Fourth Book. 17 away:] away. *97 98*   27 proud *98:* loud *97*

And neighb'ring Trees, with friendly Shade invite
The Troops unus'd to long laborious Flight.
Then o're the running Stream, or standing Lake,   35
A Passage for thy weary People make;
With Osier Floats the standing Water strow;
Of massy Stones make Bridges, if it flow:
That basking in the Sun thy Bees may lye,
And resting there, their flaggy Pinions dry: 40
When late returning home, the laden Host,
By raging Winds is wreck'd upon the Coast.
Wild Thyme and Sav'ry set around their Cell,
Sweet to the Taste, and fragrant to the Smell:
Set rows of Rosemary with flow'ring Stem,   45
And let the purple Vi'lets drink the Stream.
   Whether thou build the Palace of thy Bees
With twisted Osiers, or with Barks of Trees;
Make but a narrow Mouth: for as the Cold
Congeals into a Lump the liquid Gold;   50
So 'tis again dissolv'd by Summer's heat,
And the sweet Labours both Extreams defeat.
And therefore, not in vain, th' industrious Kind
With dawby Wax and Flow'rs the Chinks have lin'd.
And, with their Stores of gather'd Glue, contrive   55
To stop the Vents, and Crannies of their Hive.
Not Birdlime, or *Idean* Pitch produce
A more tenacious Mass of clammy Juice.
   Nor Bees are lodg'd in Hives alone, but found
In Chambers of their own, beneath the Ground: 60
Their vaulted Roofs are hung in Pumices,
And in the rotten Trunks of hollow Trees.
   But plaister thou the chinky Hives with Clay,
And leafy Branches o're their Lodgings lay.
Nor place them where too deep a Water flows,   65
Or where the Yeugh their pois'nous Neighbour grows:
Nor rost red Crabs t' offend the niceness of their Nose.
Nor near the steaming Stench of muddy Ground;
Nor hollow Rocks that render back the Sound,
And doubled Images of Voice rebound.   70
   For what remains, when Golden Suns appear,
And under Earth have driv'n the Winter Year:

The winged Nation wanders thro' the Skies,
And o're the Plains, and shady Forrest flies:
Then stooping on the Meads and leafy Bow'rs;   75
They skim the Floods, and sip the purple Flow'rs.
Exalted hence, and drunk with secret Joy,
Their young Succession all their Cares employ:
They breed, they brood, instruct and educate,
And make Provision for the future State: 80
They work their waxen Lodgings in their Hives,
And labour Honey to sustain their Lives.
But when thou seest a swarming Cloud arise,
That sweeps aloft, and darkens all the Skies:
The Motions of their hasty Flight attend;   85
And know to Floods, or Woods, their airy march they bend.
Then Melfoil beat, and Honey-suckles pound,
With these alluring Savours strew the Ground;
And mix with tinkling Brass, the Cymbals droning Sound.
Streight to their ancient Cells, recall'd from Air,   90
The reconcil'd Deserters will repair.
But if intestine Broils allarm the Hive,
(For two Pretenders oft for Empire strive)
The Vulgar in divided Factions jar;
And murm'ring Sounds proclaim the Civil War.   95
Inflam'd with Ire, and trembling with Disdain,
Scarce can their Limbs, their mighty Souls contain.
With Shouts, the Cowards Courage they excite,
And martial Clangors call 'em out to fight:
With hoarse Allarms the hollow Camp rebounds,   100
That imitates the Trumpets angry Sounds:
Then to their common Standard they repair;
The nimble Horsemen scour the Fields of Air.
In form of Battel drawn, they issue forth,
And ev'ry Knight is proud to prove his Worth.   105
Prest for their Country's Honour, and their King's,
On their sharp Beaks they whet their pointed Stings;
And exercise their Arms, and tremble with their Wings.
Full in the midst, the haughty Monarchs ride,
The trusty Guards come up, and close the Side;   110
With Shouts the daring Foe to Battel is defy'd.
Thus in the Season of unclouded Spring,

To War they follow their undaunted King:
Crowd thro' their Gates, and in the Fields of Light,
The shocking Squadrons meet in mortal Fight: 115
Headlong they fall from high, and wounded wound,
And heaps of slaughter'd Souldiers bite the Ground.
Hard Hailstones lye not thicker on the Plain;
Nor shaken Oaks such Show'rs of Acorns rain.
With gorgeous Wings the Marks of Sov'raign Sway,   120
The two contending Princes make their way;
Intrepid thro' the midst of danger go;
Their friends encourage, and amaze the Foe.
With mighty Souls in narrow Bodies prest,
They challenge, and encounter Breast to Breast;   125
So fix'd on Fame, unknowing how to fly,
And obstinately bent to win or dye;
That long the doubtful Combat they maintain,
Till one prevails (for one can only Reign.)
Yet all those dreadful deeds, this deadly fray,   ⎫   130
A cast of scatter'd Dust will soon alay,   ⎬
And undecided leave the Fortune of the day.   ⎭
When both the Chiefs are sund'red from the Fight,
Then to the lawful King restore his Right.
And let the wastful Prodigal be slain,   135
That he, who best deserves, alone may reign.
With ease distinguish'd is the Regal Race,
One Monarch wears an honest open Face;
Shap'd to his Size, and Godlike to behold,
His Royal Body shines with specks of Gold,   140
And ruddy Skales; for Empire he design'd,
Is better born, and of a Nobler Kind.
That other looks like Nature in disgrace,   ⎫
Gaunt are his sides, and sullen is his face: ⎬
And like their grizly Prince appears his gloomy Race: ⎭   145
Grim, ghastly, rugged, like a thirsty train   ⎫
That long have travel'd through a desart plain,   ⎬
And spet from their dry Chaps the gather'd dust again.   ⎭
The better Brood, unlike the Bastard Crew,
Are mark'd with Royal streaks of shining hue;   150
Glitt'ring and ardent, though in Body less:

139 Shap'd to his Size *98*: Large are his Limbs *97*

From these at pointed Seasons hope to press
Huge heavy Honey-Combs, of Golden Juice,
Not only sweet, but pure, and fit for use:
T' allay the Strength and Hardness of the Wine,   155
And with old *Bacchus*, new Metheglin join.

   But when the Swarms are eager of their play,
And loath their empty Hives, and idly stray,
Restrain the wanton Fugitives, and take
A timely Care to bring the Truants back.   160
The Task is easy: but to clip the Wings
Of their high-flying Arbitrary Kings:
At their Command, the People swarm away;
Confine the Tyrant, and the Slaves will stay.

   Sweet Gardens, full of Saffron Flow'rs, invite   165
The wandring Gluttons, and retard their Flight.
Besides, the God obscene, who frights away,
With his Lath Sword, the Thiefs and Birds of Prey.
With his own hand, the Guardian of the Bees,
For Slips of Pines, may search the Mountain Trees: 170
And with wild Thyme and Sav'ry, plant the Plain,
'Till his hard horny Fingers ake with Pain:
And deck with fruitful Trees the Fields around,
And with refreshing Waters drench the Ground.

   Now, did I not so near my Labours end,   ⎫ 175
Strike Sail, and hast'ning to the Harbour tend;   ⎬
My Song to Flow'ry Gardens might extend.   ⎭
To teach the vegetable Arts, to sing
The *Pæstan* Roses, and their double Spring:
How Succ'ry drinks the running Streams, and how   180
Green Beds of Parsley near the River grow;
How Cucumers along the Surface creep,
With crooked Bodies, and with Bellies deep:
The late *Narcissus*, and the winding Trail
Of Bears-foot, Myrtles green, and Ivy pale.   185
For where with stately Tow'rs *Tarentum* stands,
And deep *Galesus* soaks the yellow Sands,
I chanc'd an Old *Corycian* Swain to know,   ⎫
Lord of few Acres, and those barren too;   ⎬
Unfit for Sheep or Vines, and more unfit to sow: ⎭ 190

Yet lab'ring well his little Spot of Ground,
Some scatt'ring Potherbs here and there he found:
Which cultivated with his daily Care,
And bruis'd with Vervain, were his frugal Fare.
Sometimes white Lyllies did their Leaves afford, 195
With wholsom Poppy-flow'rs, to mend his homely Board:
For late returning home he sup'd at ease,
And wisely deem'd the Wealth of Monarchs less:
The little of his own, because his own, did please.
To quit his Care, he gather'd first of all 200
In Spring the Roses, Apples in the Fall:
And when cold Winter split the Rocks in twain,
And Ice the running Rivers did restrain,
He strip'd the Bears-foot of its leafy growth;
And, calling Western Winds, accus'd the Spring of sloath. 205
He therefore first among the Swains was found,
To reap the Product of his labour'd Ground,
And squeese the Combs with Golden Liquor Crown'd.
His Limes were first in Flow'rs, his lofty Pines,
With friendly Shade, secur'd his tender Vines. 210
For ev'ry Bloom his Trees in Spring afford,
An Autumn Apple was by tale restor'd.
He knew to rank his Elms in even rows;
For Fruit the grafted Peartree to dispose:
And tame to Plums, the sourness of the Sloes. 215
With spreading Planes he made a cool retreat,
To shade good Fellows from the Summer's heat.
But streighten'd in my space, I must forsake
This Task; for others afterwards to take.
    Describe we next the Nature of the Bees, 220
Bestow'd by *Jove* for secret Services:
When by the tinkling Sound of Timbrels led,
The King of Heav'n in *Cretan* Caves they fed.
Of all the Race of Animals, alone
The Bees have common Cities of their own: 225
And common Sons, beneath one Law they live,
And with one common Stock their Traffick drive.
Each has a certain home, a sev'ral Stall:
All is the States, the State provides for all.
Mindful of coming Cold, they share the Pain: 230

And hoard, for Winter's use, the Summer's gain.
Some o're the Publick Magazines preside,
And some are sent new Forrage to provide:
These drudge in Fields abroad, and those at home
Lay deep Foundations for the labour'd Comb,   235
With dew, *Narcissus* Leaves, and clammy Gum.
To pitch the waxen Flooring some contrive:
Some nurse the future Nation of the Hive:
Sweet Honey some condense, some purge the Grout;
The rest, in Cells apart, the liquid *Nectar* shut.   240
All, with united Force, combine to drive
The lazy Drones from the laborious Hive.
With Envy stung, they view each others Deeds:
With Diligence the fragrant Work proceeds.
As when the *Cyclops*, at th' Almighty Nod,   245
New Thunder hasten for their angry God:
Subdu'd in Fire the Stubborn Mettal lyes,
One brawny Smith the puffing Bellows plyes;
And draws, and blows reciprocating Air:
Others to quench the hissing Mass prepare: 250
With lifted Arms they order ev'ry Blow,
And chime their sounding Hammers in a Row;
With labour'd Anvils *Ætna* groans below.
Strongly they strike, huge Flakes of Flames expire,
With Tongs they turn the Steel, and vex it in the Fire.   255
If little things with great we may compare,
Such are the Bees, and such their busie Care:
Studious of Honey, each in his Degree,
The youthful Swain, the grave experienc'd Bee:
That in the Field; this in Affairs of State,   260
Employ'd at home, abides within the Gate:
To fortify the Combs, to build the Wall,
To prop the Ruins lest the Fabrick fall:
But late at Night, with weary Pinions come
The lab'ring Youth, and heavy laden home.   265
Plains, Meads, and Orchards all the day he plies,
The gleans of yellow Thime distend his Thighs:
He spoils the Saffron Flow'rs, he sips the blues
Of Vi'lets, wilding Blooms, and Willow Dews.

253 labour'd *98*: strokes of *97*   257 busie *98*: native *97*

Their Toyl is common, common is their Sleep;   270
They shake their Wings when Morn begins to peep;
Rush through the City Gates without delay,
Nor ends their Work, but with declining Day:
Then having spent the last remains of Light,
They give thir Bodies due repose at Night: 275
When hollow Murmurs of their Ev'ning Bells,
Dismiss the sleepy Swains, and toll 'em to their Cells.
When once in Beds their weary Limbs they steep,
No buzzing Sounds disturb thir Golden Sleep.
'Tis sacred Silence all. Nor dare they stray,   280
When Rain is promis'd, or a stormy Day:
But near the City Walls their Watring take,
Nor Forrage far, but short Excursions make.
    And as when empty Barks on Billows float,
With sandy Ballast Sailors trim the Boat;   285
So Bees bear Gravel Stones, whose poising Weight
Steers thro' the whistling Winds their steddy Flight.
    But what's more strange, their modest Appetites,
Averse from *Venus*, fly the nuptial Rites.
No lust enervates their Heroic Mind,   290
Nor wasts their Strength on wanton Woman-Kind.
But in their Mouths reside their Genial Pow'rs,
They gather Children from the Leaves and Flow'rs.
Thus make they Kings to fill the Regal Seat;
And thus their little Citizens create: 295
And waxen Cities build, and Palaces of State.
And oft on Rocks their tender Wings they tear,
And sink beneath the Burthens which they bear.
Such Rage of Honey in their Bosom beats:
And such a Zeal they have for flow'ry Sweets.   300
    Thus tho' the race of Life they quickly run,
Which in the space of sev'n short Years is done;
Th' immortal Line in sure Succession reigns,
The Fortune of the Family remains:
And Grandsires, Grandsons the long List contains.   305
    Besides, not *Egypt*, *India*, *Media* more
With servile Awe, their Idol King adore:

301-2 run, . . . done;] run; . . . done, 97 98   302 sev'n 98: seven 97
305 Grandsires,] Grandsires 97 98. See *Commentary*

While he survives, in Concord and Content
The Commons live, by no Divisions rent;
But the great Monarch's Death dissolves the Government.   310
All goes to Ruin, they themselves contrive
To rob the Honey, and subvert the Hive.
The King presides, his Subjects Toil surveys;
The servile Rout their careful *Cæsar* praise:
Him they extol, they worship him alone,   315
They crowd his Levees, and support his Throne:
They raise him on their shoulders with a Shout:
And when their Sov'raigns Quarrel calls 'em out,
His Foes to mortal Combat they defy,
And think it honour at his feet to die.   320
    Induc'd by such Examples, some have taught
That Bees have Portions of Etherial Thought:
Endu'd with Particles of Heavenly Fires:
For God the whole created Mass inspires;
Thro' Heav'n, and Earth, and Oceans depth he throws   325
His Influence round, and kindles as he goes.
Hence Flocks, and Herds, and Men, and Beasts, and Fowls
With Breath are quicken'd; and attract their Souls.
Hence take the Forms his Prescience did ordain,
And into him at length resolve again.   330
No room is left for Death, they mount the Sky,
And to their own congenial Planets fly.
    Now when thou hast decreed to seize their Stores,
And by Prerogative to break their Doors:
With sprinkl'd Water first the City choak,   335
And then pursue the Citizens with Smoak.
Two Honey Harvests fall in ev'ry Year:
First, when the pleasing *Pleiades* appear,
And springing upward spurn the briny Seas:
Again, when their affrighted Quire surveys   340
The watry *Scorpion* mend his Pace behind,
With a black Train of Storms, and winter Wind;
They plunge into the Deep, and safe Protection find.
Prone to Revenge, the Bees, a wrathful Race,
When once provok'd assault th' Agressor's Face: 345
And through the purple Veins a passage find;

318 Quarrel] Quarrels *98*

There fix their Stings, and leave their Souls behind.
  But if a pinching Winter thou foresee,
And woud'st preserve thy famish'd Family;
With fragrant Thyme the City fumigate,   350
And break the waxen Walls to save the State.
For lurking Lizards often lodge, by Stealth,
Within the Suburbs, and purloyn their Wealth.
And Lizards shunning Light, a dark Retreat
Have found in Combs, and undermin'd the Seat.   355
Or lazy Drones, without their Share of Pain;
In Winter Quarters free, devour the Gain:
Or Wasps infest the Camp with loud Alarms,
And mix in Battel with unequal Arms:
Or secret Moaths are there in Silence fed;   360
Or Spiders in the Vault, their snary Webs have spred.
  The more oppress'd by Foes, or Famine pin'd;
The more increase thy Care to save the sinking Kind.
With Greens and Flow'rs recruit their empty Hives,
And seek fresh Forrage to sustain their Lives.   365
  But since they share with Man one common Fate,
In Health and Sickness, and in Turns of State;
Observe the Symptoms when they fall away,
And languish with insensible Decay.
They change their Hue, with hagger'd Eyes they stare,   370
Lean are their Looks, and shagged is their Hair:
And Crowds of dead, that never must return ⎫
To their lov'd Hives, in decent Pomp are born: ⎬
Their Friends attend the Herse, the next Relations Mourn. ⎭
The sick, for Air before the Portal gasp,   375
Their feeble Legs within each other clasp.
Or idle in their empty Hives remain,
Benum'd with Cold, and listless of their Gain.
Soft Whispers then, and broken Sounds are heard,
As when the Woods by gentle Winds are stir'd.   380
Such stifled noise as the close Furnace hides,
Or dying Murmurs of departing Tides.
This when thou seest, *Galbanean* Odours use,
And Honey in the sickly Hive infuse.

354 Lizards shunning 97 (*errata*): Worms that shun the 97 (*text*). See **Commentary**
366 Man *98*: us *97*

Thro' reeden Pipes convey the Golden Flood,   385
T' invite the People to their wonted Food.
Mix it with thicken'd Juice of sodden Wines,
And Raisins from the Grapes of *Psythian* Vines:
To these add pounded Galls, and Roses dry,
And with *Cecropian* Thyme, strong scented Centaury.   390
  A Flow'r there is that grows in Meadow Ground,
Amellus call'd, and easy to be found;
For from one Root the rising Stem bestows
A Wood of Leaves, and vi'let-purple Boughs:
The Flow'r it self is glorious to behold,   395
And shines on Altars like refulgent Gold:
Sharp to the Taste, by Shepherds near the Stream
Of *Mella* found, and thence they gave the Name.
Boyl this restoring Root in gen'rous Wine,
And set beside the Door, the sickly Stock to dine.   400
But if the lab'ring Kind be wholly lost,
And not to be retriev'd with Care or Cost;
'Tis time to touch the Precepts of an Art,
Th' *Arcadian* Master did of old impart:
And how he stock'd his empty Hives again;   405
Renew'd with putrid Gore of Oxen slain.
An ancient Legend I prepare to sing,
And upward follow Fame's immortal Spring.
  For where with sev'n-fold Horns mysterious *Nile*
Surrounds the Skirts of *Egypt*'s fruitful Isle,   410
And where in Pomp the Sun-burnt People ride
On painted Barges, o're the teeming Tide,
Which pouring down from *Ethiopian* Lands,
Makes green the Soyl with Slime, and black prolific Sands;
That length of Region, and large Tract of Ground,   415
In this one Art a sure relief have found.
First, in a place, by Nature closs, they build
A narrow Flooring, gutter'd, wall'd, and til'd.
In this, four Windows are contriv'd, that strike
To the four Winds oppos'd, their Beams oblique.   420
A Steer of two Years old they take, whose Head
Now first with burnish'd Horns begins to spread:
They stop his Nostrils, while he strives in vain
To breath free Air, and struggles with his Pain.

Knock'd down, he dyes: his Bowels bruis'd within,   425
Betray no Wound on his unbroken Skin.
Extended thus, in this obscene Abode,
They leave the Beast; but first sweet Flow'rs are strow'd
Beneath his Body, broken Boughs and Thyme,
And pleasing Cassia just renew'd in prime.   430
This must be done, e're Spring makes equal Day,
When *Western* Winds on curling Waters play:
E're painted Meads produce their Flow'ry Crops,
Or Swallows twitter on the Chimney Tops.
The tainted Blood, in this close Prison pent,   435
Begins to boyl and through the Bones ferment.
Then, wondrous to behold, new Creatures rise,
A moving Mass at first, and short of Thighs;
'Till shooting out with Legs, and imp'd with Wings,
The Grubs proceed to Bees with pointed Stings: 440
And more and more affecting Air, they try
Their tender Pinions, and begin to fly:
At length, like Summer Storms from spreading Clouds,
That burst at once, and pour impetuous Floods;
Or Flights of Arrows from the *Parthian* Bows,   445
When from afar they gaul embattel'd Foes;
With such a Tempest thro' the Skies they Steer;
And such a form the winged Squadrons bear.
     What God, O Muse! this useful Science taught?
Or by what Man's Experience was it brought?   450
     Sad *Aristæus* from fair *Tempe* fled,
His Bees with Famine, or Diseases dead:
On *Peneus* Banks he stood, and near his holy Head.
And while his falling Tears the Stream supply'd,
Thus mourning, to his Mother Goddess cry'd.   455
Mother *Cyrene*, Mother, whose abode
Is in the depth of this immortal Flood:
What boots it, that from *Phœbus* Loyns I spring,
The third by him and thee, from Heav'ns high King?
O! Where is all thy boasted Pity gone,   460
And Promise of the Skies to thy deluded Son?
Why didst thou me, unhappy me, create?
Odious to Gods, and born to bitter Fate.

453 *Peneus*] *Peneus*'s *97 98*   458 *Phœbus*] *Phœbus*'s *97 98*

Whom, scarce my Sheep, and scarce my painful Plough,
The needful Aids of Human Life allow;   465
So wretched is thy Son, so hard a Mother thou.
Proceed, inhuman Parent in thy Scorn;
Root up my Trees, with Blites destroy my Corn;
My Vineyards Ruin, and my Sheepfolds burn.
Let loose thy Rage, let all thy Spite be shown,   470
Since thus thy hate persues the Praises of thy Son.
But from her Mossy Bow'r below the Ground,
His careful Mother heard the Plaintive sound;
Encompass'd with her Sea-green Sisters round.
One common Work they ply'd: their Distaffs full   475
With carded Locks of blue *Milesian* Wool.
Spio with *Drymo* brown, and *Xanthe* fair,
And sweet *Phyllodoce* with long dishevel'd Hair:
Cydippe with *Licorias*, one a Maid,
And one that once had call'd *Lucina's* Aid.   480
Clio and *Beroe*, from one Father both,
Both girt with Gold, and clad in particolour'd Cloth.
Opis the meek, and *Deiopeia* proud;
Nisæa softly, with *Ligæa* loud;
Thalia joyous, *Ephyre* the sad,   485
And *Arethusa* once *Diana's* Maid,
But now, her Quiver left, to Love betray'd.
To these, *Climene* the sweet Theft declares,
Of *Mars*; and *Vulcans* unavailing Cares:
And all the Rapes of Gods, and ev'ry Love,   490
From antient *Chaos* down to youthful *Jove.*
    Thus while she sings, the Sisters turn the Wheel,
Empty the wooly Rock, and fill the Reel.
A mournful Sound, agen the Mother hears;
Agen the mournful Sound invades the Sisters' Ears: 495
Starting at once from their green Seats, they rise;
Fear in their Heart, Amazement in their Eyes.
But *Arethusa* leaping from her Bed,
First lifts above the Waves her beauteous Head;
And, crying from afar, thus to *Cyrene* said.   500
O Sister! not with causeless Fear possest,

471 thy hate persues 98: thou hat'st 97   489 *Mars*; 98: *Mars* 97
495 Sisters'] Sister's 97 98

No Stranger Voice disturbs thy tender Breast.
'Tis *Aristeus*, 'tis thy darling Son,
Who to his careless Mother makes his Moan.
Near his Paternal Stream he sadly stands,   505
With down-cast Eyes, wet Cheeks, and folded Hands:
Upbraiding Heav'n from whence his Lineage came,
And cruel calls the Gods, and cruel thee, by Name.
    Cyrene mov'd with Love, and seiz'd with Fear,
Cries out, conduct my Son, conduct him here: 510
'Tis lawful for the Youth, deriv'd from Gods,
To view the Secrets of our deep Abodes.
At once she wav'd her Hand on either side,
At once the Ranks of swelling Streams divide.
Two rising Heaps of liquid Crystal stand,   515
And leave a Space betwixt, of empty Sand.
Thus safe receiv'd, the downward track he treads,
Which to his Mother's watry Palace leads.
With wond'ring Eyes he views the secret Store
Of Lakes, that pent in hollow Caverns, roar.   520
He hears the crackling Sound of Coral Woods,
And sees the secret Source of subterranean Floods.
And where, distinguish'd in their sev'ral Cells,
The Fount of *Phasis*, and of *Lycus* dwells;
Where swift *Enipeus* in his Bed appears,   525
And *Tiber* his Majestick Forehead rears.
Whence *Anio* flows, and *Hypanis*, profound,
Breaks through th' opposing Rocks with raging Sound.
Where *Po* first issues from his dark abodes,
And, awful in his Cradle, rules the Floods.   530
Two Golden Horns on his large Front he wears,
And his grim Face a Bull's Resemblance bears.
With rapid Course he seeks the sacred Main,
And fattens, as he runs, the fruitful Plain.
    Now to the Court arriv'd, th' admiring Son   535
Beholds the vaulted Roofs of *Pory* Stone;
Now to his Mother Goddess tells his Grief,
Which she with Pity hears, and promises Relief.
Th' officious Nymphs, attending in a Ring,
With Waters drawn from their perpetual Spring,   540
From earthly dregs his Body purify,

And rub his Temples, with fine Towels, dry:
Then load the Tables with a lib'ral Feast,
And honour with full Bowls their friendly Guest.
The sacred Altars are involv'd in Smoak,   545
And the bright Quire their kindred Gods invoke.
Two Bowls the Mother fills with *Lydian* Wine;
Then thus, Let these be pour'd, with Rites divine,
To the great Authors of our wat'ry Line.
To Father Ocean, this; and this, she said,   550
Be to the Nymphs his sacred Sisters paid,
Who rule the wat'ry Plains, and hold the woodland Shade.
She sprinkl'd thrice, with Wine, the Vestal Fire,
Thrice to the vaulted Roof the Flames aspire.
Rais'd with so blest an Omen, she begun,   555
With Words like these, to chear her drooping Son.
In the *Carpathian* Bottom makes abode
The Shepherd of the Seas, a Prophet and a God;
High o're the Main in wat'ry Pomp he rides,
His azure Carr and finny Coursers guides: 560
Proteus his Name: to his *Pallenian* Port,
I see from far the weary God resort.
Him, not alone, we River Gods adore,
But aged *Nereus* hearkens to his Lore.
With sure foresight, and with unerring Doom,   565
He sees what is, and was, and is to come.
This *Neptune* gave him, when he gave to keep
His scaly Flocks, that graze the wat'ry deep.
Implore his Aid, for *Proteus* onely knows
The secret Cause, and Cure of all thy Woes.   570
But first the wily Wizard must be caught,
For unconstrain'd he nothing tells for naught;
Nor is with Pray'rs, or Bribes, or Flatt'ry bought.
Surprise him first, and with hard Fetters bind;
Then all his Frauds will vanish into Wind.   575
I will my self conduct thee on thy Way,
When next the Southing Sun inflames the Day:
When the dry Herbage thirsts for Dews in vain,
And Sheep, in Shades, avoid the parching Plain.

Then will I lead thee to his secret Seat; ⎫ 580
When weary with his Toyl, and scorch'd with Heat, ⎬
The wayward Sire frequents his cool Retreat. ⎭
His Eyes with heavy Slumber overcast;
With Force invade his Limbs, and bind him fast:
Thus surely bound, yet be not over bold, 585
The slipp'ry God will try to loose his hold:
And various Forms assume, to cheat thy sight;
And with vain Images of Beasts affright.
With foamy Tusks will seem a bristly Boar,
Or imitate the Lion's angry Roar; 590
Break out in crackling Flames to shun thy Snare,
Or Hiss a Dragon, or a Tyger stare:
Or with a Wile, thy Caution to betray,
In fleeting Streams attempt to slide away.
But thou, the more he varies Forms, beware 595
To strain his Fetters with a stricter Care:
'Till tiring all his Arts, he turns agen
To his true Shape, in which he first was seen.
   This said, with *Nectar* she her Son anoints;
Infusing Vigour through his mortal Joynts: 600
Down from his Head the liquid Odours ran;
He breath'd of Heav'n, and look'd above a Man.
   Within a Mountain's hollow Womb, there lies
A large Recess, conceal'd from Human Eyes;
Where heaps of Billows, driv'n by Wind and Tide, ⎫ 605
In Form of War, their wat'ry Ranks divide; ⎬
And there, like Centries set, without the Mouth abide: ⎭
A Station safe for Ships, when Tempests roar,
A silent Harbour, and a cover'd Shoar.
Secure within resides the various God, 610
And draws a Rock upon his dark Abode.
Hether with silent Steps, secure from Sight, ⎫
The Goddess guides her Son, and turns him from the Light: ⎬
Her self, involv'd in Clouds, precipitates her Flight. ⎭
   'Twas Noon; the sultry Dog-star from the Sky 615
Scorch'd *Indian* Swains, the rivell'd Grass was dry;

589 will seem *98*: he seems *97*   590 imitate *98*: imitates *97*   591 Break *98*:
Breaks *97*   591–2 Snare . . . stare] Snares . . . stares *97 98. See Commentary*
592 Or Hiss a Dragon *98*: A Dragon hisses *97*   594 attempt *98*: attempts *97*

The Sun with flaming Arrows pierc'd the Flood,
And, darting to the bottom, bak'd the Mud:
When weary *Proteus*, from the briny Waves,
Retir'd for Shelter to his wonted Caves: 620
His finny Flocks about their Shepherd play,
And rowling round him, spirt the bitter Sea.
Unweildily they wallow first in Ooze,
Then in the shady Covert seek Repose.
Himself their Herdsman, on the middle Mount,   625
Takes of his muster'd Flocks a just Account.
So, seated on a Rock, a Shepherd's Groom
Surveys his Ev'ning Flocks returning Home:
When lowing Calves, and bleating Lambs, from far,
Provoke the prouling Wolf to nightly War.   630
Th' Occasion offers, and the Youth complies:
For scarce the weary God had clos'd his Eyes;
When rushing on, with shouts, he binds in Chains
The drowzy Prophet, and his Limbs constrains.
He, not unmindful of his usual Art,   635
First in dissembled Fire attempts to part:
Then roaring Beasts, and running Streams he tryes,
And wearies all his Miracles of Lies:
But having shifted ev'ry Form to scape,
Convinc'd of Conquest, he resum'd his shape: 640
And thus, at length, in human Accent spoke.
Audacious Youth, what madness cou'd provoke
A Mortal Man t' invade a sleeping God?
What Buis'ness brought thee to my dark abode?
  To this, th' audacious Youth; Thou know'st full well   645
My Name, and Buis'ness, God, nor need I tell:
No Man can *Proteus* cheat; but *Proteus* leave
Thy fraudful Arts, and do not thou deceive.
Foll'wing the Gods Command, I come t' implore
Thy Help, my perish'd People to restore.   650
  The Seer, who could not yet his Wrath asswage,
Rowl'd his green Eyes, that sparkl'd with his Rage;
And gnash'd his Teeth, and cry'd, No vulgar God
Pursues thy Crimes, nor with a Common Rod.
Thy great Misdeeds have met a due Reward,   655

And *Orpheus* dying Pray'rs at length are heard.
For Crimes, not his, the Lover lost his Life,
And at thy Hands requires his murther'd Wife:
Nor (if the Fates assist not) canst thou scape
The just Revenge of that intended Rape.   660
To shun thy lawless Lust, the dying Bride,
Unwary, took along the River's side:
Nor, at her Heels perceiv'd the deadly Snake,
That kept the Bank, in Covert of the Brake.
But all her fellow Nymphs the Mountains tear   665
With loud Laments, and break the yielding Air:
The Realms of *Mars* remurmur'd all around,
And Echoes to th' *Athenian* Shoars rebound.
Th' unhappy Husband, Husband now no more,
Did on his tuneful Harp his Loss deplore,   670
And sought, his mournful Mind with Musick to restore.
On thee, dear Wife, in Desarts all alone,
He call'd, sigh'd, sung, his Griefs with Day begun,
Nor were they finish'd with the setting Sun.
Ev'n to the dark Dominions of the Night,   675
He took his way, thro' Forrests void of Light:
And dar'd amidst the trembling Ghosts to sing,
And stood before th' inexorable King.
Th' Infernal Troops like passing Shadows glide,
And, list'ning, crowd the sweet Musician's side.   680
Not flocks of Birds when driv'n by Storms, or Night,
Stretch to the Forest with so thick a flight.
Men, Matrons, Children, and th' unmarry'd Maid,
*The mighty Heroes more Majestic shade;
And Youths on Fun'ral Piles before their Parents laid.   685
All these *Cocytus* bounds with squalid Reeds,
With Muddy Ditches, and with deadly Weeds:
And baleful *Styx* encompasses around,
With Nine slow circling Streams, th' unhappy ground.
Ev'n from the depths of Hell the Damn'd advance,   690
Th' Infernal Mansions nodding seem to dance;
The gaping three-mouth'd Dog forgets to snarl,

---

* *This whole Line is taken from the Marquess of* Normanby's *Translation.*

---

656 Orpheus] Orpheus's 97 98

The Furies harken, and their Snakes uncurl:
Ixion seems no more his Pains to feel,
But leans attentive on his standing Wheel.   695
    All Dangers past, at length the lovely Bride,
In safety goes, with her Melodious Guide;
Longing the common Light again to share,
And draw the vital breath of upper Air:
He first, and close behind him follow'd she,   700
For such was *Proserpine*'s severe Decree.
When strong Desires th' impatient Youth invade;
By little Caution and much Love betray'd:
A fault which easy Pardon might receive,
Were Lovers Judges, or cou'd Hell forgive.   705
For near the Confines of Etherial Light,
And longing for the glimm'ring of a sight,
Th' unwary Lover cast his Eyes behind,
Forgetful of the Law, nor Master of his Mind.
Straight all his Hopes exhal'd in empty Smoke;   710
And his long Toils were forfeit for a Look.
Three flashes of blue Light'ning gave the sign
Of Cov'nants broke, three peals of Thunder joyn.
Then thus the Bride; What fury seiz'd on thee,
Unhappy Man! to lose thy self and Me?   715
Dragg'd back again by cruel Destinies,
An Iron Slumber shuts my swimming Eyes.
And now farewel, involv'd in Shades of Night,
For ever I am ravish'd from thy sight.
In vain I reach my feeble hands, to joyn   720
In sweet Embraces; ah! no longer thine!
She said, and from his Eyes the fleeting Fair
Retir'd like subtile Smoke dissolv'd in Air;
And left her hopeless Lover in despair.
In vain, with folding Arms, the Youth assay'd   725
To stop her flight, and strain the flying Shade:
He prays, he raves, all Means in vain he tries,
With rage inflam'd, astonish'd with surprise;
But she return'd no more, to bless his longing Eyes.
Nor wou'd th' Infernal Ferry-Man once more   730
Be brib'd, to waft him to the farther shore.
What shou'd He do, who twice had lost his Love?

What Notes invent, what new Petitions move?
Her Soul already was consign'd to Fate,
And shiv'ring in the leaky Sculler sate.   735
For sev'n continu'd Months, if Fame say true,
The wretched Swain his Sorrows did renew;
By *Strymon*'s freezing Streams he sate alone,
The Rocks were mov'd to pity with his moan:
Trees bent their heads to hear him sing his Wrongs,   740
Fierce Tygers couch'd around, and loll'd their fawning Tongues.
    So, close in Poplar Shades, her Children gone,
The Mother Nightingale laments alone:
Whose Nest some prying Churl had found, and thence,
By Stealth, convey'd th' unfeather'd Innocence.   745
But she supplies the Night with mournful Strains,
And melancholy Musick fills the Plains.
    Sad *Orpheus* thus his tedious Hours employs,
Averse from *Venus*, and from nuptial Joys.
Alone he tempts the frozen Floods, alone   750
Th' unhappy Climes, where Spring was never known:
He mourn'd his wretched Wife, in vain restor'd,
And *Pluto*'s unavailing Boon deplor'd.
    The *Thracian* Matrons, who the Youth accus'd,
Of Love disdain'd, and Marriage Rites refus'd: 755
With Furies, and Nocturnal *Orgies* fir'd,
At length, against his sacred Life conspir'd.
Whom ev'n the salvage Beasts had spar'd, they kill'd,
And strew'd his mangl'd Limbs about the Field.
Then, when his Head, from his fair Shoulders torn,   760
Wash'd by the Waters, was on *Hebrus* born;
Ev'n then his trembling Tongue invok'd his Bride;
With his last Voice, *Eurydice*, he cry'd,
Eurydice, the Rocks and River-banks reply'd.
This answer *Proteus* gave, nor more he said,   755
But in the Billows plung'd his hoary Head;
And where he leap'd, the Waves in Circles widely spread.
    The Nymph return'd, her drooping Son to chear,
And bade him banish his superfluous fear:

736 sev'n *98:* seven *97*
747 And . . . Plains. *98: 97 has*
                With one continu'd Tenor still complains;
                Which fills the Forrest, and the neighb'ring Plains.

For now, said she, the Cause is known, from whence　770
Thy Woe succeeded, and for what Offence:
The Nymphs, Companions of th' unhappy Maid,
This punishment upon thy Crimes have laid;
And sent a Plague among thy thriving Bees.
With Vows and suppliant Pray'rs their Pow'rs appease:　775
The soft *Napæan* Race will soon repent
Their Anger, and remit the Punishment.
The secret in an easy Method lies;
Select four Brawny Bulls for Sacrifice,
Which on *Lycæus* graze, without a Guide;　780
Add four fair Heifars yet in Yoke untry'd:
For these, four Altars in their Temple rear,
And then adore the Woodland Pow'rs with Pray'r.
From the slain Victims pour the streaming Blood,
And leave their Bodies in the shady Wood:　785
Nine Mornings thence, *Lethean* Poppy bring,
T' appease the *Manes* of the Poets King:
And to propitiate his offended Bride,
A fatted Calf, and a black Ewe provide:
This finish'd, to the former Woods repair.　790
His Mother's Precepts he performs with care;
The Temple visits, and adores with Pray'r.
Four Altars raises, from his Herd he culls,
For Slaughter, four the fairest of his Bulls;
Four Heifars from his Female Store he took,　795
All fair, and all unknowing of the Yoke.
Nine Mornings thence, with Sacrifice and Pray'rs,
The Pow'rs aton'd, he to the Grove repairs.
Behold a Prodigy! for from within
The broken Bowels, and the bloated Skin,　800
A buzzing noise of Bees his Ears alarms,
Straight issue through the Sides assembling Swarms:
Dark as a Cloud they make a wheeling Flight,
Then on a neighb'ring Tree, descending, light:
Like a large Cluster of black Grapes they show,　805
And make a large dependance from the Bough.
　　Thus have I sung of Fields, and Flocks, and Trees,
And of the waxen Work of lab'ring Bees;

801 his *98*: their *97*

While mighty *Cæsar*, thund'ring from afar,
Seeks on *Euphrates* Banks the Spoils of War: 810
With conq'ring Arms asserts his Country's Cause,
With Arts of Peace the willing People draws:
On the glad Earth the Golden Age renews,
And his great Father's Path to Heav'n pursues.
While I at *Naples* pass my peaceful Days,   815
Affecting Studies of less noisy Praise;
And bold, through Youth, beneath the Beechen Shade,
The Lays of Shepherds, and their Loves have plaid.

811 Arms] Arts 98